Contemporary
Linguistic Analysis

An Introduction

Contemporary Linguistic Analysis

An Introduction

Ninth Edition

Edited by

William O'Grady

UNIVERSITY OF HAWAII AT MANOA
UNIVERSITY OF PRINCE EDWARD ISLAND

and

John Archibald

UNIVERSITY OF VICTORIA

 Pearson

Pearson Canada Inc., 26 Prince Andrew Place, North York, Ontario M3C 2H4.

9780134652306

1 2019

Library and Archives Canada Cataloguing in Publication

Title: Contemporary linguistic analysis : an introduction / edited by William O'Grady, University of Hawaii at Manoa, University of Prince Edward Island and John Archibald, University of Victoria.

Names: O'Grady, William, editor. | Archibald, John, editor.

Description: Ninth edition.

Identifiers: Canadiana 20190169273 | ISBN 9780134652306 (softcover)

Subjects: LCSH: Linguistic analysis (Linguistics)—Textbooks. | LCSH: Linguistics—Canada—Textbooks. | LCGFT: Textbooks.

Classification: LCC P126 .C66 2019 | DDC 410—dc23

To the memory of Michael Dobrovolsky,
founding co-editor of
Contemporary Linguistic Analysis

Convinced at once that, in order to break loose from the beaten paths of opinions and systems, it was necessary to proceed in my study of man and society by scientific methods, and in a rigorous manner, I devoted one year to philology and grammar; linguistics, or the natural history of speech, being, of all the sciences, that which best suited the researches which I was about to commence.

PIERRE-JOSEPH PROUDHON, *WHAT IS PROPERTY?* (1840)

Brief Contents

Contents

Preface

From its inception, the basic goal of *Contemporary Linguistic Analysis* has been to provide a cutting-edge introduction to the discipline of linguistics while at the same time covering phenomena that are of special interest and relevance to the linguistic situation in Canada. Indeed, *Contemporary Linguistic Analysis* was the first textbook to offer such a focus.

These dual objectives have grown increasingly challenging in recent years, as work in the various subdisciplines of linguistics becomes more technical and far-reaching. As the size of the textbook increased in response to these trends, it became necessary to search for new solutions to the problem of just how much an introductory textbook can and should cover. It has often been difficult to decide where to draw the line between essential and advanced material, of course, and we have gained some appreciation for what it feels like to be the Minister of Finance in tough economic times. The pressing need to reduce and restructure is constantly challenged by cries of "Don't cut there." After much experimentation and compromise (a Canadian virtue if ever there was one), we have arrived at a division of labour that we all—editors, referees, and publisher—feel reasonably comfortable with. We hope that this will still allow instructors the flexibility to create the kind of introductory course that they want for their students.

New to this Edition

The ninth edition has been modified to reflect changes in the discipline as well as comments from faculty and students who used the eighth edition. These modifications include

- An entirely new and updated chapter on semantics.
- A first-ever chapter on bilingualism, with special focus on the situation in Canada.
- Access to an alternate version of the syntax chapter – on the companion website – which focuses on the techniques of basic syntactic description that can be used independently of generative grammar.
- Revision of individual chapters to update and clarify their content, in addition to revised end-of-chapter exercises that allow students to work through some of the concepts discussed in the chapter.
- A revised Study Guide offering practice exercises covering all 16 chapters of the textbook, accompanied by an instructor answer key.

Acknowledgments

As has been the case from its inception in the early 1980s, *Contemporary Linguistic Analysis* has benefited from the comments, advice, and assistance of many people. Over the years, we have consistently received extraordinary support from our publisher's executive team, first at Copp Clark, later at Addison Wesley Longman, and now at Pearson Canada. We would particularly like to acknowledge the pioneering efforts of Les Petriw, Brian Henderson, Jeff Miller, and the late Linda Scott and Steve Mills.

Heartfelt thanks are also due to the many people who have taken the time to offer their suggestions and corrections: (in alphabetical order) Jennifer Abel, Victoria Anderson, Mark Aronoff, Howard Aronson, Peter Avery, Henry Bain, Keira Ballantyne, Byron Bender, Derek Bickerton, Chad Blecke, Marina Blekher, Didier Bloch, Vaiana Bloch, Robert Blust, Vit Bubenik, Patrick Burke, Ed Burstynsky, Gary Byma, Amber Camp, Lyle Campbell, Steven Carey, Andrew Carnie, Jack Chambers, Harold Chester, Kevin Cheung, Shuji Chiba, Miho Choo, Michael Clauss, Richard Compton, Vanna Condax, Eung-Do Cook, Lynda Costello, John Davison, Kamil Deen, John DeFrancis, Denise Devenuto, Michael Dobrovolsky, Annette Dominik, Nicole Domingue, Katie Drager, Elan Dresher, Matthew Dryer, Karine Dupuis, Amitabh Dwivedi, Carrie Dyck, Sheila Embleton, Evile Feleti, Pamela Erlichman, Robert Fisher, Darin Flynn, Michael Forman, Donald Frantz, Ali Al Ghail, Inge Genee, Donna Gerdts, Kevin Gregg, John Haiman, Alice Harris, Margaret Hayes, John Hewson, Joyce Hildebrand, Robert Hsu, David Ingram, Ricky Jacobs, Marcela Jonas, Kazue Kanno, Brian King, James Kirchner, Sandra Kirkham, Emily Korth, Marta Kutas, Dawn Lee, Jinhwa Lee, Hsiu-chuan Liao, Gary Libben, Heidi Lorimor, Mats Lundälv (Blissymbolics Communication International), Anatole Lyovin, Mary C. Marino, Martha McGinnis, Barry Meislin, Yves-Charles Morin, Anna Moro, Woody Mott, Robert Murray, Chandan Narayan, Jon Nissenbaum, Judith Nylvek, Michael O'Grady, George Patterson, David Pentland, Mary Pepper, Julia Peters, David Peterson, Marilyn Philips, Laura Pratt, Terry Pratt and the students in his linguistics course at the University of Prince Edward Island, R. Radhakrishnan, Jonathan Rahn, Lawrence Reid, Keren Rice, Elizabeth Ritter, Lorna Rowsell, Yutaka Sato, Coral Sayce, Nicole Schauder, Albert Schütz, Carson Schütze, Peter Seyffert, Patricia Shaw, Ronald Southerland, Lois Stanford, Stanley Starosta, Magda Stroinska, Leone Sveinson, Nozomi Tanaka, Allison Teasdale, Alain Thomas, Rory Turnbull, Charles Ulrich, Tim Vance, Theo Venneman, Douglas Walker, Avivah Wargon, Lydia White, James Woodward, Norio Yamada, Youri Zabbal and Nava Zvaig.

Joanne Sutherland got our ninth edition underway and supervised its development from start to finish; her assistance and wisdom were much appreciated. Judith Nylvek served as both technical reviewer and proof reader, along with Jennifer Abel. Their work was crucial to the finished product that you now hold in your hands. We also thank the team at Pearson (present and past) for their assistance and support: Keriann McGoogan, Madhu Ranadive, Ainsley Somerville, and others working behind the scenes.

As the demands of producing a wide-ranging, state-of-the-art textbook increase with each edition, it has become necessary to coordinate the tasks of copy editing, technical fact checking, critical reading, and strategic rewriting, by placing them in the hands of a single person. There was only one person to whom we could turn—the extraordinary Joyce Hildebrand of Speargrass Communications. Joyce is at once a trained linguist, a published writer, and a professional copy editor. No one in the world has been able to combine those three gifts in the way that she has. She is among the elite editors in her profession, and we are forever in her debt for the guidance and assistance that she provided on this project and on its predecessor. Words—even words that she edited for us—would not suffice to express our gratitude.

About this book

Linguistics provides students with an ideal introduction to the kind of thinking we call "scientific." Such thinking proceeds from the identification of problems and puzzles, to hypotheses about how they can be solved, to the careful testing and extension of these hypotheses. But science is more than a formal activity. One of the great pleasures offered students of linguistics is the discovery of the impressive body of subconscious knowledge that underlies language use. This book attempts to emphasize the importance of this knowledge as well as to introduce the scientific methodology used to uncover and understand.

Although *Contemporary Linguistic Analysis* has the distinction of being the first linguistics textbook designed primarily for a Canadian readership, it seeks to do much more than simply provide coverage of linguistic phenomena peculiar to Canada. As the title suggests, we have attempted an introduction to linguistic analysis as it is practised at this stage in the development of our discipline. While we do not ignore or reject other fruitful approaches to linguistics, we have taken the generative paradigm as basic for two reasons. First, generative linguistics provides a relatively coherent and integrated approach to basic linguistic phenomena. Phonetics, phonology, morphology, syntax, and semantics are viewed within this framework, as perhaps in no other, as fully integrated and interrelated. Second, the generative approach has been widely influential in its application to a broad range of other linguistic phenomena over the past several decades, including the study of first and second language learning, historical linguistics, typology, psycholinguistics, and neurolinguistics.

The extent of our "contemporariness" has been limited by the inevitable compromise between the need to present basic concepts in a pedagogically sound manner, and the demands of sophisticated and competing recent approaches. In some cases, early versions of our chapters were judged "too contemporary" by instructors who were not specialists in the subfields in question. This led to substantial revisions and a somewhat more traditional approach to certain issues than was originally intended. Nonetheless, we have made every effort to provide what is promised by the title—an introductory text that provides a solid grounding in basic linguistic concepts—as well as a text that prepares the student for work in the discipline as it is currently practiced.

No textbook can be all things to all users. We hope that this book will provide students with not only a broad introduction to linguistic analysis, but also a greater appreciation of the wonder of human language.

List of technical abbreviations

*	(in front of words or sentences) unacceptable
#	word boundary
1	first person
1	primary stress
2	second person
2	secondary stress
3	third person
A	adjective
Abl	ablative case
Abs	absolutive case
Acc	accusative case
Adv	adverb
AdvP	adverb phrase
Af	affix
ag	agent
AP	adjective phrase
Aux	auxiliary verb
B	bound root
C	complementizer
C	consonant
caus	cause
CG	constricted glottis
cmpl	completed action
C_0	any number of consonants
Co	coda
Com	comitative
CP	complementizer phrase
CT	computerized axial tomography
DA	derivational affix
Dat	dative case
Deg	degree word
DR	delayed release
EEG	electroencephalogram
Erg	ergative case
ERP	event-related potentials
ESL	English as a second language
FN	first name
Fut	future tense
Gen	genitive case
go	goal
H	high tone
IA	inflectional affix
indic	indicative
IP	inflectional phrase (= S)
IPA	International Phonetic Alphabet
L	low tone
L1	first language
L2	second language
LN	last name
Loc	locative case
Loc	location
M	mid tone
N	noun
N	nucleus
Nom	nominative case
NP	noun phrase
O	(direct) object
O	onset
Obl	oblique
OE	Old English
P	preposition, postposition
Pass	passive
PET	positron emission tomography
PIE	Proto-Indo-European
pl	plural
PP	prepositional phrase
PR	phonetic representation
Prs	present tense
Pst	past tense
R	rhyme
R	rounded
RC	relative cause
REA	right ear advantage
recip	recipient
S	sentence
S	subject
σ	syllable
SES	socioeconomic status
SG	spread glottis
sg	singular
SLA	second language acquisition
th	theme
T	title alone
TLN	title + last name
Top	topic
UG	Universal Grammar
UR	underlying representation
UR	unrounded
V	verb
V	vowel
VP	verb phrase
W	woman
Wd	word

Language: a preview

Language is the lifeblood of humanity.
ANONYMOUS

LANGUAGE is at the heart of all things human. We use it when we're talking, listening, reading, writing—and thinking. It underpins social relationships and communities; it forges the emotional bond between parent and child; it's the vehicle for literature and poetry. Language is not just a part of us; language *defines* us. All normal human beings have at least one language, and it is impossible to imagine the sorts of achievement that we see in civilization and science without the opportunities for communication offered by language.

Linguistics is the study of how language works—how it is used, how it is acquired, how it changes over time, how it is represented in the brain, and so on. It is concerned not only with the properties of the world's more than 7000 living languages but also with the abilities and adaptations that have made it possible for our species to create and use language in the first place.

1.1 Specialization for language

Our species, *Homo sapiens*, made its appearance 100 000 to 200 000 years ago, by many estimates. Early humans were anatomically like us—they had not only large brains but also vocal

---

Language Matters How Many Languages Are There in the World Today?

That's not an easy question, since little is known about the linguistic situation in many parts of the world. The most complete compilation to date can be found in the twenty-first edition of *Ethnologue: Languages of the World*, edited by Gary Simons and Charles Fennig (Dallas: SIL International, 2018), which lists 7097 living languages.

But this is not the whole story. Many languages have only two or three hundred speakers (or fewer), and many others are in grave danger of demise as Indigenous peoples throughout the world lose their traditional cultures and homelands. You can find out more by reading *The Last Speakers: The Quest to Save the World's Most Endangered Languages*, by K. David Harrison (Washington, DC: National Geographic Society, 2010) or *The Oxford Handbook of Endangered Languages*, edited by Kenneth L. Rehg and Lyle Campbell (Oxford, UK: Oxford University Press, 2018). Up-to-date information is also available at the websites of the Endangered Languages Project (www.endangeredlanguages.com) and Terralingua (www.terralingua.org), among others.

tracts capable of producing speech. Archaeological evidence (such as tools, carvings, and cave paintings) suggests that they also had the type of intellect that could accompany language.

Hundreds of thousands of years of evolution created a special capacity for language in humans that is not found in any other species. The evidence is literally inside us. Our speech organs (the lungs, larynx, tongue, teeth, lips, soft palate, and nasal passages) were—and still are—primarily concerned with breathing and eating. However, they have also all become highly specialized for use in language. Their structure and shape is unique to our species, as is the highly developed network of neural pathways that controls them during speech production (see table 1.1). Indeed, the bundle of nerves controlling the vocal cords is among the densest in the entire body.

TABLE 1.1	The dual functions of the speech organs	
Organ	**Survival function**	**Speech function**
Lungs	to exchange carbon dioxide and oxygen	to supply air for speech
Vocal cords	to create a seal over the passage to the lungs	to produce vibrations for speech sounds
Tongue	to move food to the teeth and back into the throat	to articulate vowels and consonants
Teeth	to break up food	to provide a place of articulation for consonants
Lips	to seal the oral cavity	to articulate vowels and consonants
Nose	to assist in breathing and smelling	to provide nasal resonance during speech

Human beings are also specially equipped for the perception of speech. Newborns respond differently to human voices than to other types of sounds, and six-month-old infants are able to perceive subtle differences among sounds in languages that they have never heard before.

Of course, language is much more than just speech sounds and does not even have to be oral. In sign languages, meaning is conveyed via gestures, body posture, and facial expressions rather than through sounds. Moreover, much of what makes language special can be neither heard nor seen because it involves the way in which the human mind goes about forming words, building sentences, and interpreting the speech of others.

Language Matters **Sign Language**

There are many misconceptions about sign languages, the most prevalent being that they are just a way to 'spell out' an oral language. Although 'finger spelling' of words from an oral language is sometimes used (to indicate names or technical terms, for instance), sign languages are independent systems of communication, with their own vocabulary and grammatical rules. That's why British Sign Language and American Sign Language (ASL) are mutually unintelligible. And it's why Québec Sign Language (Langue des signes québécoise) is similar in many respects to American Sign Language (the variety of sign language used in other parts of Canada as well as in the U.S.), despite major differences between French and English. You can find out more about ASL on the U.S. National Institutes of Health website at www.nidcd.nih.gov.

1.2 A creative system

What, precisely, is language? What does it mean to know a language? To answer these questions, it is first necessary to understand the resources that a language makes available to its **native speakers**, those who have acquired it as children in a natural setting (say, a home rather than a classroom).

The breadth and diversity of human thought and experience place great demands on language. Because there are always new things to say, new experiences to report, and new challenges to confront, language has to allow for **creativity**, giving us the freedom to produce and understand new words and sentences as the need arises.

The creativity of language goes hand in hand with a second defining characteristic—the presence of systematic constraints that establish the boundaries within which innovation can occur. We can be innovative in our use of language, but there are rules to the game—and those rules are an integral part of our knowledge of language. As a preliminary illustration of this, consider the process that we use to create verbs from nouns in English, as shown in table 1.2. (For now, you can think of verbs as words that name actions and nouns as words that name things.)

TABLE 1.2 Nouns used as verbs	
Noun use	**Verb use**
pull the boat onto the *beach*	*beach* the boat
keep the airplane on the *ground*	*ground* the airplane
tie a *knot* in the string	*knot* the string
put the wine in *bottles*	*bottle* the wine
catch the fish with a *spear*	*spear* the fish
clean the floor with a *mop*	*mop* the floor

As the sentences in (1) show, we have a great deal of freedom to innovate in the formation of such verbs.

(1) *a.* I *wristed* the ball over the net.
   b. He would try to *stiff-upper-lip* it through.
   c. She *Houdini'd* her way out of the locked closet.

However, this freedom also has limits. For instance, a new verb is rarely coined if a word with the intended meaning already exists. Although we say *jail the robber* to mean 'put the robber in jail', we do not say *prison the robber* to mean 'put the robber in prison'. This is because the well-established verb *imprison* already has the meaning that the new form would have.

There are also constraints on the meaning and use of particular subclasses of these verbs. One such constraint involves verbs that are created from time expressions such as *summer*, *holiday*, and so on.

(2) *a.* Julia *summered* in Paris.
   b. Harry *wintered* in Mexico.
   c. Bob *holidayed* in France.
   d. Harry and Julia *honeymooned* in Hawaii.

Language Matters **Disagreeing about Language Use**

People sometimes object to innovation in language. The following "letter to the editor" is a case in point:

"I was shocked and appalled to read in yesterday's newspaper the following phrase: *Nash's knee injury impacted his ability to score.* As anyone with a modicum of education or who owns a dictionary will tell you, *impact* is a noun. You have used it as a verb. This is clearly nonsensical and provides further evidence of the crumbling of our public education system and the decline of language in general. If your editorial offices are not in the possession of a suitable dictionary, I would be happy to provide one for you." Languages change, and so do dictionaries—the second edition of the *Canadian Oxford Dictionary* (Oxford University Press, 2004) lists *impact* as a verb.

Although the sentences in (2) all sound natural, not all time expressions can be used in this way. (Throughout this book, an asterisk is used to indicate that an utterance is unacceptable.)

> **(3)** *a.* *Jerome *midnighted* in the streets.
>   *b.* *Andrea *nooned* at the restaurant.
>   *c.* *Philip *one o'clocked* at the airport.

These examples show that when a verb is created from a time expression, it must be given a very specific interpretation—roughly paraphrasable as 'to be somewhere for the period of time X'. Thus, *to summer in London* is 'to be in London for the summer', *to holiday in France* is 'to be in France for the holidays', and so on. Since *noon* and *midnight* express *points* in time rather than extended *periods* of time, they cannot be used to create new verbs of this type.[1]

Moreover, there are constraints on what verbs that are derived from nouns can mean. For instance, *winter in Hawaii* can only mean 'spend the winter in Hawaii', not 'make it snow in Hawaii' or 'stay in Hawaii until winter begins'. Without such constraints, creativity would run amok, undermining rather than enhancing communication.

Systematic rule-governed creativity is the hallmark of all aspects of language. Consider how sounds are combined to form words. Certain patterns of sounds, like the novel forms in (4), look and sound like English words—all they lack is a meaning.

> **(4)** *a.* prasp
>   *b.* flib
>   *c.* traf

In contrast, the forms in (5) contain combinations of sounds that English does not permit; they simply do not have the shape of English words.

> **(5)** *a.* *psapr
>   *b.* *bfli
>   *c.* *ftra

Still other constraints determine how suffixes can be used to create words from other words. Imagine, for example, that the word *soleme* entered the English language (used perhaps for a newly discovered atomic particle). As a speaker of English, you would then automatically know that something with the properties of a soleme could be called *solemic.* You would also know that to make something solemic is to *solemicize* it, and you would call this process *solemicization.* Further, you would know that the *c* is pronounced as *s* in *solemicize* but as *k* in *solemic,* and that both words are pronounced with the stress on the second syllable. (You would say *soLEmic,* not *SOlemic* or *soleMIC.*)

Nowhere is the ability to deal with novel utterances more obvious than in the production and comprehension of sentences. Apart from a few fixed expressions and greetings (*What's up?, How're things?, No way!*), much of what you say, hear, and read in the course of a day consists of sentences that are new to you. In conversations, lectures, newscasts, and textbooks, you are regularly exposed to novel combinations of words, unfamiliar ideas, and new information. Consider, for instance, the paragraph that you are currently reading. It's unlikely that you've ever seen any of these sentences before, yet you were able to understand them without difficulty.

Not all new sentences are acceptable, however. The words in (6) are all familiar, but they are simply not arranged in the right way to make a sentence of English.

(6) *Frightened dog this cat the that chased mouse a.
   (cf. This dog frightened the cat that chased a mouse.)

As with other aspects of language, the ability to form and interpret sentences is subject to systematic limitations.

1.3   Grammar and linguistic competence

As we have just seen, speakers of a language are able to produce and understand an unlimited number of utterances, including many that are novel and unfamiliar. At the same time, they are able to recognize that certain utterances are not acceptable and do not belong in their language. Knowledge of this type, which is often called **linguistic competence**, constitutes the central subject matter of linguistics and of this book.

In investigating linguistic competence, linguists focus on the mental system that allows human beings to form and interpret the sounds, words, and sentences of their language. Linguists often call this system a **grammar** and break it down into the components in table 1.3.

TABLE 1.3   The components of a grammar

Component	Domain
Phonetics	the articulation and perception of speech sounds
Phonology	the patterning of speech sounds
Morphology	word formation
Syntax	sentence formation
Semantics	the interpretation of words and sentences

As you can see, the term *grammar* is used in a special way within linguistics. To a linguist, a grammar is not a book, nor is it concerned with just the form of words and sentences. Rather, it is the intricate network of knowledge that underlies our ability to use language.

The study of grammar lies at the core of our attempts to understand what language is and what it means to know a language. Five simple points should help clarify why the investigation of grammatical systems is so important to contemporary linguistic analysis.

1.3.1 Generality: all languages have a grammar

One of the most fundamental claims of modern linguistic analysis is that all languages have a grammar. It could not be any other way. If a language is spoken, it must have a phonetic and phonological system; since it has words and sentences, it must also have a morphology and a syntax; and since these words and sentences have systematic meanings, there must be semantic principles as well.

It is not unusual to hear the remark that some language—say, Acadian French, Cree, or Swahili—has no grammar. (This is especially common in the case of languages that are not written or are not taught in schools and universities.) Unfamiliar languages sometimes appear to an untrained observer to have no grammar, perhaps because their grammatical systems are different from those of more frequently studied languages. In Warlpiri (an indigenous language of Australia, also spelled Walbiri), for example, the relative ordering of words is so free that the English sentence *The two dogs see several kangaroos* could be translated by the equivalent of any of the following sentences. (The word 'now' is used informally to help express present tense.)

(7) *a.* Dogs two now see kangaroos several.
    b. See now dogs two kangaroos several.
    c. See now kangaroos several dogs two.
    d. Kangaroos several now dogs two see.
    e. Kangaroos several now see dogs two.

Although Warlpiri does not restrict the order of words in the way English does, its grammar imposes other types of requirements. For example, in the sentence above, Warlpiri speakers must place the ending *lu* on the word for 'dogs' to indicate that it names the animals that do the seeing rather than the animals that are seen. In English, by contrast, this information is conveyed by placing *two dogs* in front of the verb *see* and *several kangaroos* after it.

Rather than showing that Warlpiri has no grammar, such differences simply demonstrate that it has a grammar that is unlike the grammar of English in certain respects. This point holds across the board: although no two languages have exactly the same grammar, every language has a grammar.

A similar point can be made about different varieties of the same language. Newfoundland English, Jamaican English, and Hawaiian English each have pronunciations, vocabulary items, and sentence patterns that may appear unusual to outsiders. But this does not mean that they have no grammar; it just means that their grammars differ in particular ways from those of more familiar varieties of English.

Language Matters **Regularization**

Why and how does the English spoken in one area end up being different from the English spoken in other places? One powerful force is *regularization*—the tendency to drive out exceptions by replacing them with a form that fits with a more general pattern.

With one exception, English verbs all have a single past tense form—*I just arrived, you just arrived, s/he just arrived*; *I left, you left, s/he left*; and so on. The exception is the verb *be*, which has two forms—*was* and *were*: *I was there, you were there, s/he was there.*

Regularization has taken care of this anomaly in at least two varieties of English. In Yorkshire English (northern England), only *were* is used: *I were there, you were there, s/he were there.* In Appalachian English (West Virginia and parts of nearby states), things have gone the other way— only *was* has been retained: *I was there, you was there, s/he was there.*

1.3.2 Parity: all grammars are equal

Contrary to popular belief, there is no such thing as a 'primitive' language, even in places untouched by modern science and technology. Indeed, some of the most complex linguistic phenomena we know about are found in societies that have neither writing nor electricity.

Moreover, there is no such thing as a 'good grammar' or a 'bad grammar'. In fact, all grammars do essentially the same thing: they tell speakers how to form and interpret the words and sentences of their language. The form and meaning of those words and sentences vary from language to language and even from community to community, of course, but each language works for its speakers.

Linguists sometimes clash over this point with people who are upset about the use of 'nonstandard' varieties of English that permit sentences such as *I seen that, They was there, He didn't do nothing, She ain't here,* and so forth. Depending on where you live and who you talk to, speaking in this way can have negative consequences: it may be harder to win a scholarship, to get a job, or to be accepted in certain social circles. This is an undeniable fact about the social side of language. From a purely linguistic point of view, however, there is absolutely nothing wrong with grammars that permit such structures. They work for their speakers, and they deserve to be studied in the same objective fashion as the varieties of English spoken by the rich and educated.

The bottom line for linguists is that the analysis of language must reflect the way it is actually used, not someone's idealized vision of how it should be used. The psychologist Steven Pinker offers the following illustration to make the same point.

Imagine that you are watching a nature documentary. The video shows the usual gorgeous footage of animals in their natural habitats. But the voiceover reports some troubling facts. Dolphins do not execute their swimming strokes properly. White-crowned sparrows carelessly debase their calls. Chickadees' nests are incorrectly constructed, pandas hold bamboo in the wrong paw, the song of the humpback whale contains several well-known errors, and the monkey's cries have been in a state of chaos and degeneration for hundreds of years. Your reaction would probably be, What on earth could it mean for the song of the humpback whale to contain an "error"? Isn't the song of the humpback whale whatever the humpback whale decides to sing?

As Pinker goes on to observe, language is like the song of the humpback whale. The way to determine whether a particular sentence is permissible is to find people who speak the language and observe how they use it.

In sum, linguists don't even think of trying to rate languages as good or bad, simple or complex. Rather, they investigate language in much the same way that other scientists study snails or stars—with the goal of figuring out how it works. This same point is sometimes made by noting that linguistics is **descriptive**, not **prescriptive**. Its goal is to describe and explain the facts of languages, not to change them.

1.3.3 Universality: all grammars are alike in basic ways

In considering how grammars can differ from each other, it is easy to lose sight of something even more intriguing and important—the existence of principles and properties shared by all human languages.

For example, all languages use a small set of contrastive sounds that help distinguish words from each other (like the *t* and *d* sounds that allow us to recognize *to* and *do* as different words). There are differences in precisely which sounds particular languages use, but there are also fundamental similarities. For instance, all languages have more consonant sounds (*p*, *t*, *d*, etc.) than vowel sounds (*a*, *e*, *i*); any language that has a *d* sound almost certainly has a *t* sound as well; and all languages have a vowel that sounds like the 'ah' in *far*.

There are also universal constraints on how words can be put together to form sentences. For example, in describing a situation in which Ned lost his own wallet, many languages can use the equivalent of the first sentence below, with *his* coming after *Ned*, but no language can use the second sentence to describe this situation, with *he* coming before *Ned*.

(8) *a.* Ned lost his wallet.
    b. He lost Ned's wallet.

Moreover, even when languages do differ from each other, the amount of variation is restricted in certain ways. For example, some languages (like English) place question words at the beginning of the sentence. In (9), for example, the word *what* originates after *donate* and is moved to the beginning of the sentence to create the question.

Language Matters Don't End That Sentence with a Preposition

One of the better-known prescriptive rules of English is 'Don't end a sentence with a preposition.' (In other words, say 'To whom were you talking?', not 'Who were you talking to?'.) The problem with this rule is that people don't speak that way. Prepositions often occur at the end of a sentence in English, and trying to prevent this from happening leads to all sorts of unnatural-sounding constructions, as Winston Churchill illustrated (in a famous but possibly apocryphal story) when he said, tongue in cheek, "This is the kind of tedious nonsense up with which I will not put."

Here's an extreme case of prepositions ending a sentence. A young girl, unhappy with the book that her father had brought upstairs for her bedtime story, was heard to say: "What did you bring the book I didn't want to be read to out of up for?" This sentence ends with five prepositions—an extreme case, admittedly, but it's still English!

    (9) What did Mary donate to the library?

Other languages, like Mandarin, make no such changes.

    (10) Mali juan shenme gei tushuguan?
           Mary donate what to library

But no language uniformly places question words at the *end* of the sentence.

In other cases, variation is constrained by strong tendencies rather than absolute prohibitions. Take three-word sentences such as *Canadians like hockey*, for instance. Such sentences have six logically possible orders.

    (11) *a.* Canadians like hockey.
          b. Canadians hockey like.
          c. Like Canadians hockey.
          d. Like hockey Canadians.
          e. Hockey like Canadians.
          f. Hockey Canadians like.

All other things being equal, we would expect to find each order employed in about one-sixth of the world's languages. In fact, more than 95 percent of the world's languages adopt one of the first three orders for basic statements (and the vast majority of those use one or the other of the first two orders). Only a small handful of languages use any of the last three orders as basic.

These are not isolated examples. As you'll see as you continue your study of linguistics, languages are fundamentally alike in important ways.

1.3.4 Mutability: all grammars change over time

The features of language that are not universal and fixed are subject to change over time. Indeed, the grammars of all languages are constantly changing. Some of these changes are relatively minor and occur very quickly (for example, the addition of new words such as *bitcoin*, *twerk*, *selfie*, *unfriend*, and *carbon footprint* to the vocabulary of English). Other changes have a more dramatic effect on the overall form of the language and typically take place over a long period of time. One such change involves the manner in which we negate sentences in English. Prior to 1200, English formed negative constructions by placing *ne* before the verb and a variant of *not* after it.

    (12) *a.* Ic *ne* seye *not*. ('I don't say.')
          b. He *ne* speketh *nawt*. ('He does not speak.')

By 1400 or thereabouts, the use of *ne* had decreased dramatically, and *not* (or *nawt*) typically occurred by itself after the verb.

    (13) *a.* I seye *not* the wordes. ('I don't say the words.')
          b. We saw *nawt* the knyghtes. ('We didn't see the knights.')

It was not until several centuries later that English adopted its current practice of allowing *not* to occur after only certain types of verbs (*do*, *have*, *will*, and so on).

Language Matters **Verbs Again**

A thousand years ago, more than three hundred English verbs formed their past tense by making an internal change (*drive/drove*, *eat/ate*, etc.) rather than by adding a suffix (e.g., *walk/walked*, *dance/danced*). Today, about half as many verbs do this. The past tense of *heave* used to be *hove*; now it is *heaved*. The past tense of *thrive* used to be *throve*; now it is *thrived*. The past tense of *chide* ('scold') used to be *chid*; now it is *chided*. And so on. These past tense forms have all changed to the more regular *-ed* pattern.

Then why aren't all verbs regular? One factor involves frequency: more frequent forms tend to resist regularization. That's why the most enduring irregular past tense forms in English (*was* and *were* for *be*, *had* for *have*, *went* for *go*, *came* for *come*, and so on) involve high-frequency verbs. To find out more, read *Words and Rules* by Steven Pinker (New York: Basic Books, 1999).

---

(14) *a.* I will *not* say the words. (versus *I will say not the words.)

b. He did *not* see the knights. (versus *He saw not the knights.)

These changes illustrate the effect of language change over time. The structures exemplified in (13) are archaic by today's standards, and those in (12) sound completely foreign to speakers of modern English.

Through the centuries, those who believed that certain varieties of language are better than others frequently expressed concern over what they perceived to be the deterioration of English. In 1710, for example, the writer Jonathan Swift (author of *Gulliver's Travels*) lamented "the continual Corruption of our English Tongue." Among the corruptions to which he objected were contractions such as *he's* for *he is*, although he had no objection to *'tis* for *it is*!

Similar concerns have been expressed about the state of English spoken in Canada. In 1857, members of the Canadian Institute in Toronto heard a speech describing Canadian English as "a corrupt dialect growing up amongst our population." The speaker objected to the use of words such as *lot* (for 'a division of land'), *boss* (for 'master'), *store* (for 'shop'), *fix* (for 'mend'), and *guess* (for 'think', as in *I guess I'll go*). Judging by current usage, he objected in vain.

Linguists reject the view that languages attain a state of perfection at some point in their history and that subsequent changes lead to deterioration and corruption. Change is a natural part of the history of every language. The job of linguists is to describe it and explain it, not to stop it.

1.3.5 Inaccessibility: grammatical knowledge is subconscious

Knowledge of a grammar differs in important ways from knowledge of arithmetic, traffic rules, and other subjects that are taught at home or in school: it is largely subconscious and not accessible to introspection—you can't figure out how it works just by thinking about it. As an example of this, consider your pronunciation of the past tense suffix, written as *ed*, in the following words.

(15) *a.* hunted

b. slipped

c. buzzed

You probably didn't notice it before, but the *ed* ending has three different pronunciations in these words. Whereas you say *id* in *hunted*, you say *t* in *slipped* and *d* in *buzzed*. Moreover, if you heard the new verb *flib*, you would form the past tense as *flibbed* and pronounce the ending as *d*. If you are a native speaker of English, you acquired the grammatical subsystem regulating this aspect of speech when you were a child, and it now exists subconsciously in your mind, allowing you to automatically make the relevant contrasts.

The same is true for virtually everything else about language. Once we go beyond the most obvious things (such as whether words like *the* and *a* come before or after a noun), the average person can't say much about how language works. For example, try explaining to someone who is not a native speaker of English why we can say *I went to school* but not **I went to supermarket*. Or try to figure out for yourself how the word *or* works. Matters are seemingly straightforward in a sentence such as the following, which means something like 'Either Aisha drank tea, or she drank coffee—I don't know which.'

(16) Aisha drank tea or coffee.

But *or* has a different interpretation in the next sentence.

(17) Aisha didn't drink tea or coffee.

Now it seems to mean 'and'—'Aisha didn't drink tea and she didn't drink coffee,' not 'Aisha didn't drink tea or she didn't drink coffee—I don't know which.'

As you can see, being able to interpret these sentences is not the same thing as knowing *why* they have the particular meanings that they do. Speakers of a language know what sounds right and what doesn't sound right, but they are almost never able to say how they know.

Because most of what we know about our language is subconscious, the analysis of human linguistic systems requires considerable effort and ingenuity. As is the case in all scientific endeavours, observable facts (about the pronunciation of words, the interpretation of sentences, and so on) must be used to draw inferences about the sometimes invisible mechanisms (atoms, cells, or grammars, as the case may be) that are ultimately responsible for these phenomena.

Summing up

Human language is characterized by **creativity**. Speakers of a language have access to a **grammar**, a mental system that allows them to form and interpret both familiar and novel utterances. The grammar governs the articulation, perception, and patterning of speech sounds; the formation of words and sentences; and the interpretation of utterances. All languages have grammars that are equal in their expressive capacity, and all speakers of a language have (subconscious) knowledge of its grammar. The existence of such linguistic systems in humans is the product of unique anatomical and cognitive specialization not found in other species.

Notes

[1] Not all nouns naming periods of time can be converted into verbs, however. Thus, for reasons that are not yet understood, the nouns *autumn* and *week* do not make very good verbs.

*They autumned/weeked in the Maritimes.

Recommended reading

Bickerton, Derek. 1990. *Language and Species*. Chicago: University of Chicago Press.

Crystal, David. 2018. *The Cambridge Encyclopedia of the English Language*. 3rd ed. New York: Cambridge University Press.

Pinker, Steven. 1994. *The Language Instinct: How the Human Mind Creates Language*. New York: William Morrow.

Exercises

1. The following sentences contain verbs created from nouns in accordance with the process described in section 1.2 of this chapter. Describe the meaning of each of these new verbs.
   a) We hip hopped the night away.
   b) He dog-teamed his way across the Arctic.
   c) We unicycled to Oregon.
   d) Gino solar-panelled his roof.
   e) He hula hooped his way across the park.
   f) We Tesla'd to Toronto.
   g) We'll have to Ajax the sink.
   h) She Windexed the windows.
   i) You should dreadlock your hair.
   j) Let's carton the eggs.

2. Using the examples in the preceding exercise as a model, create five new verbs from nouns. Build a sentence around each of these new verbs to show its meaning.

3. Which of the following forms are possible words of English? Show the words to an acquaintance and see if you agree on your judgments.
   a) mbood   e) sproke
   b) frall   f) flube
   c) coofp   g) wordms
   d) ktleem   h) bsarn

4. Imagine that you are an advertising executive and that your job involves inventing new names for products. Create four new forms that are possible words of English and four that are not.

5. Part of linguistic competence involves the ability to recognize whether novel utterances are acceptable. Consider the following sentences and determine which are possible

sentences in English. For each unacceptable sentence, change the sentence (as little as possible) to make it acceptable, and compare the two.
a) Binh's mother left himself with nothing to eat.
b) Miriam is eager to talk to.
c) This is the man who I took a picture of.
d) Colin made Rhiannon a sandwich.
e) Is the dog sleeping the bone again?
f) Adisa prepared Zena a cake.
g) Ahmed cleaned the garden up.
h) Ahmed cleaned up the garden.
i) Ahmed cleaned up it.
j) I hope you to leave.
k) That you likes liver surprises me.

6. Consider the following sentences, each of which is acceptable to some speakers of English. Try to identify the prescriptive rules that are violated in each case.
a) He don't know about the race.
b) You was out when I called.
c) There is twenty horses registered in the show.
d) That window's broke, so be careful.
e) Jim and me are gonna go campin' this weekend.
f) Who did you come with?
g) I seen the parade last week.
h) He been lost in the woods for ten days.
i) My car needs cleaned 'cause of all the rain.
j) Julie ain't got none.
k) Somebody left their book on the train.
l) Murray hurt hisself in the game.

What is the reaction of linguists to the claim that sentences of this sort are 'wrong'?

7. An interesting feature of the variety of English spoken in Hawaii involves the form of the possessive pronoun that shows up in the following context.

That belongs to me. It's *mines*.

Make a list of other possessive pronoun forms in standard English by filling in the spaces below.

That belongs to you. It's _____.
That belongs to him. It's _____.
That belongs to her. It's _____.
That belongs to us. It's _____.
That belongs to them. It's _____.

What process in language change appears to be responsible for the form *mines*?

To learn more about the topics discussed in this chapter, visit the Companion Website for Contemporary Linguistic Analysis.

MICHAEL DOBROVOLSKY

Phonetics: the sounds of language

I shall whisper
Heavenly labials in a world of gutturals.

WALLACE STEVENS, "THE PLOT AGAINST THE GIANT" (1917)

WE DO NOT need to speak in order to use language. Language can be written, manually signed, mechanically reproduced, and even synthesized by computers. Nevertheless, speech remains the primary way in which humans express themselves through language. Our species spoke long before we began to write, and this long history of spoken language is reflected in our anatomical specialization for speech. Humans also appear to have specialized neural mechanisms for the perception of speech sounds. Because language and speech are so closely linked, we begin our study of language by examining the inventory and structure of the sounds of speech. This branch of linguistics is called **phonetics**.

Human languages display a wide variety of sounds, called **phones** (from Greek *phōnē* 'sound, voice') or **speech sounds**. The class of possible speech sounds is finite, and a portion of the total set will be found in the inventory of any human language. Humans can also make sounds with the vocal tract that do not occur in speech, such as the sound made by inhaling through one corner of the mouth or the 'raspberry' produced by sticking out the tongue and blowing hard across it. (**To hear this sound, go to the Companion Website.**) Nonetheless, a very wide range of sounds is found in human language (600 consonants and 200 vowels, according to one estimate), including the click made by drawing the tongue hard away from the upper molars on one side of the mouth (imagine making a sound to get a horse to move) or the sound made by constricting the upper part of the throat while breathing out. Any human, whether child or adult, can learn to produce any human speech sound.

Linguists undertake the study of phonetics in two ways. One approach involves analyzing the physiological mechanisms of speech production. This is known as **articulatory phonetics**. The other approach, **acoustic phonetics**, is concerned with measuring and analyzing the physical properties of the sound waves we produce when we speak. Both approaches are indispensable to an understanding of speech. This chapter focuses on articulatory phonetics but also makes some reference to the acoustic properties of sounds and to acoustic analysis.

2.1 Phonetic transcription

Since the sixteenth century, efforts have been made to devise a universal system for transcribing the sounds of speech. The best-known system, the **International Phonetic Alphabet (IPA)**, has been evolving since 1888. This system of transcription attempts to represent each sound of human speech with a single symbol. These symbols are enclosed in brackets [ ] to indicate that the transcription is phonetic and does not represent simple spelling. For example, the sound spelled *th* in English <u>*this*</u> is transcribed as [ð] (the symbol is called *eth*, as in w<u>*eath*</u>er). The IPA uses this symbol to represent that sound in whichever language it is heard, whether it is English, Spanish, or Turkmen (a Turkic language spoken in Central Asia and written in the Cyrillic alphabet), as shown in table 2.1.

TABLE 2.1   Use of [ð] in transcribing speech phonetically

Language	Spelling	IPA	Meaning
English	<u>th</u>is	[ðɪs]	'this'
Spanish	bo<u>d</u>a	[boða]	'wedding'
Turkmen	a<u>д</u>ak	[aðak]	'foot'

Language Matters Sounds and Spelling

Although the relationship between sound and symbol in IPA is one to one, things are very different in the writing system of English—as a quick look at the words *rough, through, bough, though,* and *cough* illustrates. All these words contain *ough,* but the letters represent different sounds in each word—and sometimes even a different number of sounds. In the word *rough,* they represent two sounds, while in *through,* they represent only one. The absence of a one-to-one correspondence between a symbol and a sound in English spelling is also evident when we look at the letter 'o', which is pronounced differently in *go, hot, women, more,* and *mutton.*

George Bernard Shaw, the famous playwright who described a character in his play *Pygmalion* as an "energetic phonetic enthusiast" (a description that could just as easily be applied to Shaw himself), illustrated the problem in the following anecdote. Imagine a new word coming into the English language that is spelled *ghoti.* How would this word be pronounced? In an attempt to demonstrate what he felt were the inadequacies of the English spelling system, Shaw argued that the word could be pronounced as 'fish'. How so? Note the pronunciations of the italicized segments in the following words:

enou*gh* → f
w*o*men → i
na*ti*on → sh

Shaw felt that any writing system that could represent 'fish' with the string of letters *ghoti* was in desperate need of reform.

The use of a standardized phonetic alphabet with a one-to-one correspondence between sound and symbol enables linguists to transcribe languages consistently and accurately. In North American usage, though, some phonetic symbols differ from those employed by IPA transcription. For example, the sound heard at the beginning of the English word _shark_ is transcribed as [ʃ] in IPA, but often as [š] in North America. In this book, we employ IPA transcription, but we note common North American symbols where relevant.

If you wish to start practising the phonetic transcription of English, turn to tables 2.16 and 2.17 for examples.

2.11 Units of representation

Anyone who hears a language spoken for the first time finds it hard to break up the flow of speech into individual units. Even when hearing our native language spoken, we do not focus attention on individual sounds as much as we do on the meanings of words, phrases, and sentences.

The IPA represents speech in the form of **segments**—individual phones like [p], [s], or [m]. Segments are produced by coordinating a number of individual articulatory gestures including jaw movement, lip shape, and tongue placement.

2.12 Segments

We have defined the segment as an individual speech sound (phone). The analysis of speech in terms of sound segments, or phones, is supported by several kinds of evidence.

Errors in speech production provide one kind of evidence for the existence of segments. Slips of the tongue such as _renumeration_ for _remuneration_ and _melcome wat_ for _welcome mat_ show segments shifting and reversing position within and across words. This suggests that segments are individual units of linguistic structure that should be represented individually in a system of transcription.

The relative invariance of speech sounds in human language also suggests that segmental phonetic transcription is a well-motivated way of transcribing speech. The sounds of speech remain invariant enough from language to language for us to transcribe them consistently. A _p_ sound is much the same in English, Russian, or Uzbek. The fact that when producing a _p_ sound, English speakers press their lips together while Russian speakers draw theirs slightly inward does not make the sounds different enough to warrant separate symbols. But the sounds _p_ and _t_ are distinct enough from each other in languages the world over to be consistently transcribed with separate symbols.

Language Matters The Muscles of Speech

The bundle of nerves controlling the vocal folds is among the densest in the entire body. There are about forty different muscles in the vocal tract. Although they aren't all used for all sounds, coordinating those that are used at any particular moment requires exquisite timing to activate all the necessary muscles at precisely the right instant.

Source: Peter F. MacNeilage, _The Origin of Speech_ (New York: Oxford University Press, 2008), p. 4.

2.2 The sound-producing system

Sound is produced when air is set in motion. Think of the speech production mechanism as consisting of an air supply, a sound source that sets the air in motion in ways specifically relevant to speech production, and a set of filters that modify the sound in various ways (see figure 2.1). The air supply is provided by the lungs. The sound source is in the larynx, where a set of muscles called the **vocal folds** (or **vocal cords**—not *chords*) is located. The filters are the passages above the larynx, collectively known as the **vocal tract**: the tube of the throat between the larynx and the oral cavity, which is called the **pharynx**; the oral cavity; and the nasal cavity.

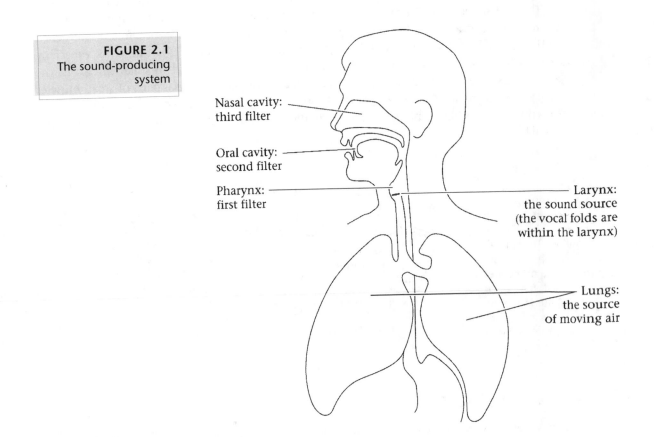

FIGURE 2.1
The sound-producing system

Nasal cavity: third filter

Oral cavity: second filter

Pharynx: first filter

Larynx: the sound source (the vocal folds are within the larynx)

Lungs: the source of moving air

2.2.1 The lungs

In order to produce the majority of sounds in the world's languages, we take air into the lungs and expel it during speech. (A small number of phones are made with air as it flows *into* the vocal tract. **Samples of these and other sounds can be heard on the Companion Website.**)

A certain level of air pressure is needed to keep the speech mechanism functioning steadily. The pressure is maintained by the action of various sets of muscles coming into play during the course of an utterance. The primary muscles are the **intercostals** (the muscles between the ribs) and the **diaphragm** (the large sheet of muscle separating the chest cavity from the abdomen). The intercostals raise the ribcage to allow air to flow into the lungs during inhalation, while the diaphragm helps to control the release of air during exhalation for speech so that we can speak for a reasonable period of time between breaths.

The larynx

As air flows out of the lungs up the **trachea** (windpipe), it passes through a box-like structure made of cartilage and muscle; this is the **larynx** (commonly known as the voice box or Adam's apple), as shown in figure 2.2. The main portion of the larynx is formed by the **thyroid cartilage**, which spreads outward at its front like the head of a plow. The thyroid cartilage rests on the ring-shaped **cricoid cartilage**. Fine sheets of muscle flare from the inner sides of the thyroid cartilage, forming the paired vocal folds. The inner edges of the vocal folds are attached to the vocal ligaments. The vocal folds can be pulled apart or drawn closer together, especially at their back (or posterior) ends, where each is attached to one of two small cartilages, the **arytenoids**. The arytenoids are opened, closed, and rotated by several pairs of small muscles (not shown in figure 2.2). As air passes through the space between the vocal folds, which is called the **glottis**, different glottal states are produced, depending on the positioning of the vocal folds.

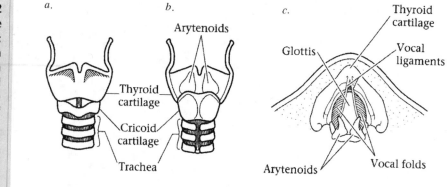

FIGURE 2.2
The larynx: *a.* from the front; *b.* from the back; *c.* from above, with the vocal folds in open position. The striated lines in *c.* indicate muscles, a number of which have been eliminated from the drawings in order to show the cartilages more clearly.

2.2.3 Glottal states

The vocal folds may be positioned in a number of ways to produce different glottal states. The first two glottal states presented in figure 2.3 are commonly encountered in most of the world's languages. The third diagram describes the glottal state that underlies a common speech phenomenon, and the fourth illustrates one of a number of glottal states not encountered in English.

Voiceless

When the vocal folds are pulled apart as illustrated in the first drawing in figure 2.3, air passes directly through the glottis without much interference. Any sound made with the vocal folds

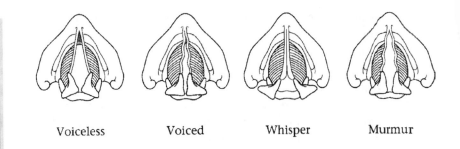

FIGURE 2.3 Four glottal states: the drawings represent the vocal folds and glottis from above; the anterior (front) portion of the larynx is at the top. The small triangles represent the arytenoid cartilages, which help spread or close the vocal folds.

| Voiceless | Voiced | Whisper | Murmur |

in this position is said to be **voiceless**. The initial sounds of *fish*, *sing*, and *house* are all voiceless. You can confirm a sound's voicelessness by touching your fingers to your larynx as you produce it. You will not feel any vibration from the vocal folds being transmitted to your fingertips. Voicelessness is a true speech state distinct from breathing; the vocal folds are not as far apart during speech voicelessness as they are in silent breathing.

Voiced

When the vocal folds are brought close together but not tightly closed, air passing between them causes them to vibrate, producing sounds that are said to be **voiced**. (See the second illustration in figure 2.3.) You can determine whether a sound is voiced in the same way you determined voicelessness. By lightly touching your fingers to your larynx as you produce an extended version of the initial sounds of the words *zip* or *vow*, or any vowel, you can sense the vibration of the vocal folds within the larynx. It can be helpful to contrast voiced versus voiceless sounds while resting your hand on your throat. Produce the following pairs of sounds and decide which are voiced and which are voiceless.

> [ffffffffffffffffffffffff] versus [vvvvvvvvvvvvvvvvvvvvvv]
> [ssssssssssssssssssssssss] versus [zzzzzzzzzzzzzzzzzzzzzzzz]

On which sounds did you feel vibration? Some people find it easier to hear this distinction in another way. Perform the same exercise as given above but this time with your fingers in your ears. You will feel much greater resonance with the sounds that are voiced. These techniques can be helpful as you try to hear which phones are voiced and which are voiceless.

Whisper

Another glottal state produces a **whisper**. Whispering is voiceless, but, as shown in figure 2.3, the vocal folds are adjusted so that the anterior (front) portions are pulled close together, while the posterior (back) portions are apart.

Murmur

Yet another glottal state produces a **murmur**, also known as **breathy voice**. Sounds produced with this glottal configuration are voiced, but the vocal folds are relaxed to allow enough air to escape to produce a simultaneous breathy effect. There are languages in the world that use breathy voice as an integral part of the sound system. Although it is difficult to generalize, sometimes when you see words or place names that have been borrowed into English with spellings such as 'bh' as in *Bhagavad-Gita*, 'dh' as in *dharma* or *dhal*, or 'gh' as in *ghee*, they can represent murmured sounds. **To hear these sounds, go to the Companion Website.**

These four glottal states represent only some of the possibilities of sound production at the glottis. The total number of glottal states is still undecided, but there are more than a dozen. Combined with various articulations made above the larynx, they produce a wide range of phones. Before examining phones in more detail, we will consider the three major classes of speech sound.

2.3 Sound classes

The sounds of language can be grouped into **natural classes** based on the phonetic properties that they share. You have already seen what some of these properties can be. All voiced sounds, for example, form a class, as do all voiceless sounds. The most basic division among sounds is into two major classes, **vowels** and **consonants**. Another class of sounds, the **glides**, shares properties of both vowels and consonants. Each class of sounds has a number of distinguishing features.

2.3.1 Vowels and consonants

Vowels and consonants can be distinguished on the basis of differences in articulation or by their acoustic properties. We can also distinguish among these elements with respect to whether they function as syllabic or non-syllabic elements.

The articulatory difference

Consonantal sounds, which may be voiced ([v]) or voiceless ([f]), are made with either a complete closure ([p]) or a narrowing ([f]) of the vocal tract. The airflow is either blocked momentarily or restricted so much that noise is produced as air flows past the constriction. In contrast, vowels are produced with little obstruction in the vocal tract (you will note that for all vowels, the tip of your tongue stays down by your lower front teeth) and are usually voiced.

The acoustic difference

As a result of the difference in articulation, consonants and vowels differ in the way they sound. Vowels are more sonorous (acoustically powerful) than consonants, and so we perceive them as louder and longer lasting.

Syllabic and non-syllabic sounds

The greater sonority of vowels allows them to form the basis of **syllables**. A syllable can be defined as a peak of sonority surrounded by less sonorous segments. The peak of sonority is usually a vowel; in fact, a vowel can be a syllable by itself. For example, the words *a* and *go* each contain one syllable, the word *laughing* two syllables, and the word *telephone* three syllables. In counting the syllables in these words, we are in effect counting the vowels. A vowel is thus said to form the **nucleus** of a syllable. In section 2.5.7, we will see that certain types of consonants can form syllabic nuclei as well.

In (1), the initial sounds of the words in the left column are all consonants; those on the right are all vowels.

(1) <u>t</u>ake   <u>a</u>bove
     <u>c</u>art   <u>a</u>t
     <u>f</u>eel   <u>ee</u>l
     <u>j</u>ump   <u>i</u>t
     <u>th</u>ink   <u>u</u>gly
     <u>b</u>ell   <u>o</u>pen

Table 2.2 sums up the differences between consonants and vowels.

TABLE 2.2 Major differences between syllabic and non-syllabic elements	
Vowels (and other syllabic elements)	**Consonants (non-syllabic elements)**
■ are produced with relatively little obstruction in the vocal tract ■ are more sonorous	■ are produced with a complete closure or narrowing of the vocal tract ■ are less sonorous

2.3.2 Glides

A type of sound that shows properties of both consonants and vowels is called a glide. Glides may be thought of as rapidly articulated vowels—this is the auditory impression they produce. Glides are produced with an articulation like that of a vowel. However, they either move quickly to another articulation, as do the initial glides in <u>y</u>et or <u>w</u>et, or quickly terminate, as do the word-final glides in *boy* and *no<u>w</u>*. You can feel how little movement is necessary to move from a vowel articulation to a glide articulation when you pronounce the following phrases:

> s<u>ee y</u>ou later
> wh<u>o w</u>ould do that

Make the vowel sound in the word *see* ([i]) and then make the glide in the word *you* ([j]). Now go back and forth from [i] to [j] and note that the small articulatory movement can cause us to perceive one sound as a vowel and the other as a glide. The same pattern emerges when you produce the vowel in *who* ([u]) and the glide in *would* ([w]).

Even though they are vowel-like in articulation, glides pattern as consonants. For example, glides can never form the nucleus of a syllable. Since glides show properties of both consonants and vowels, the terms *semivowel* and *semiconsonant* may be used interchangeably with the term *glide*.

Consonant articulation

Airflow is modified in the vocal tract by the placement of the tongue and the positioning of the lips. These modifications occur at specific **places** (or **points**) **of articulation**. The major places of articulation used in speech production are outlined in this section. Figure 2.4 provides a midsagittal section, or cutaway view, of the vocal tract on which each place of articulation has been indicated.

The tongue

The primary articulating organ is the tongue. It can be raised, lowered, thrust forward or retracted, and even rolled back. The sides of the tongue can also be raised or lowered.

Phonetic description refers to five areas of the tongue. The **tip** is the narrow area at the front. Just behind the tip lies the **blade**. The main mass of the tongue is called the **body**, and the hindmost part of the tongue that lies in the mouth (versus the throat) is called the **back**. The body and back of the tongue can also be referred to jointly as the **dorsum**. The **root** of the tongue is contained in the upper part of the throat (pharynx).

FIGURE 2.4
The vocal tract and places of articulation

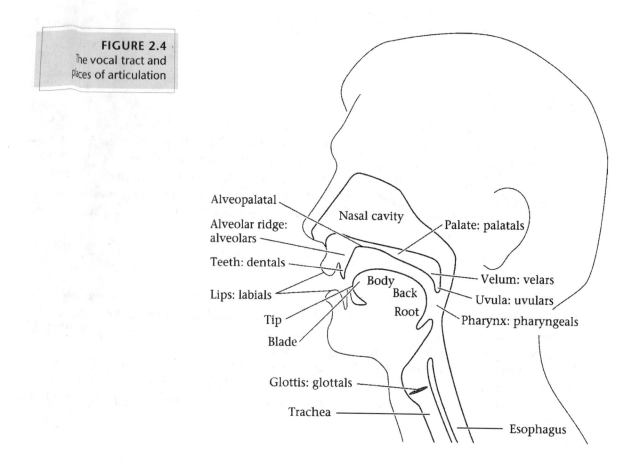

2.4.2 Places of articulation

Each point at which the airstream can be modified to produce a different sound is called a place of articulation. Places of articulation are found at the lips, within the oral cavity, in the pharynx, and at the glottis (see figure 2.5 *a–e*).

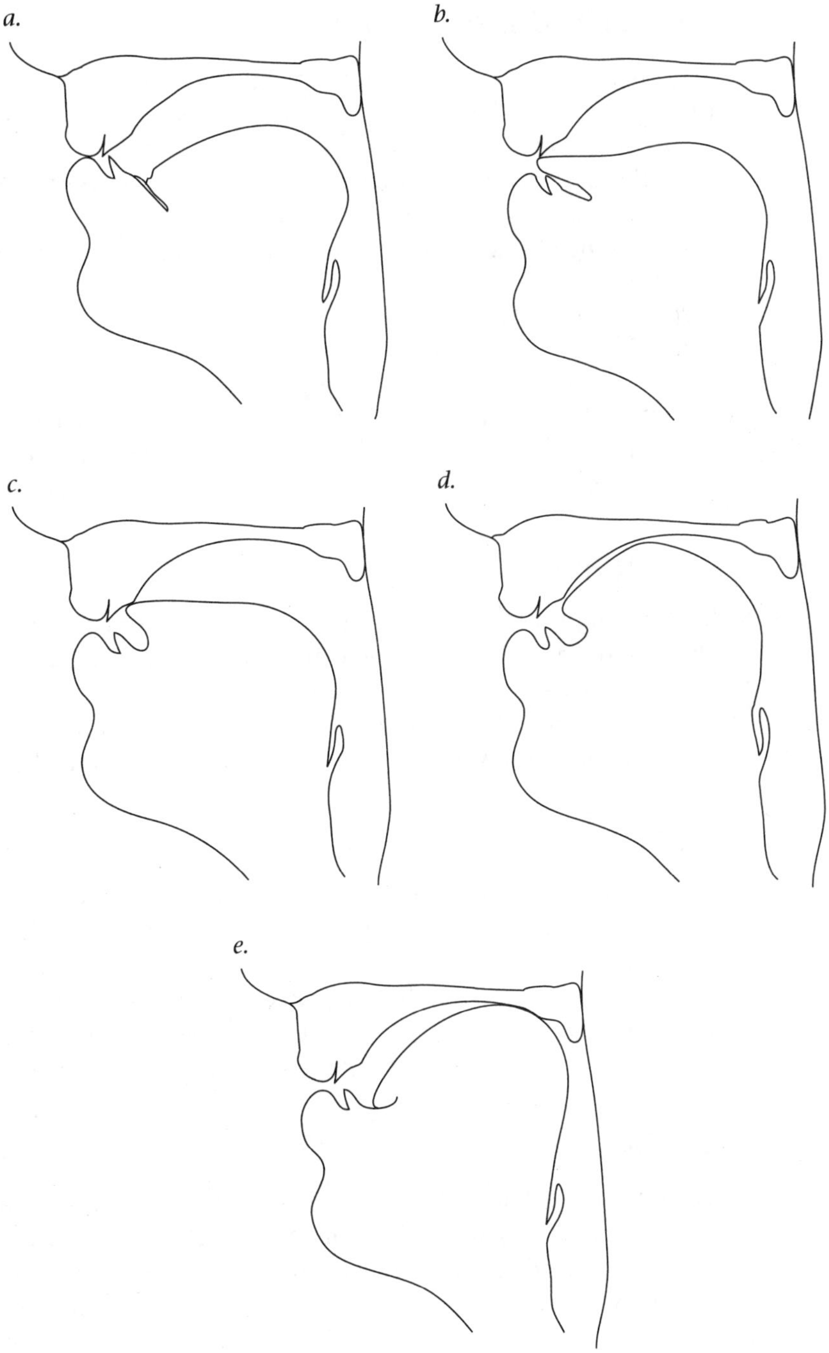

FIGURE 2.5
Places of articulation:
a. the labial sound at the beginning of *peer*;
b. the interdental sound at the beginning of *this*;
c. the alveolar sound at the beginning of *top*;
d. the alveopalatal sound at the beginning of *show*;
e. the velar sound at the beginning of *call*.

Labial

Any sounds made with closure or near-closure of the lips are said to be **labials**. Sounds involving both lips are termed **bilabials**; sounds involving the lower lip and upper teeth are called **labiodentals**. English includes the bilabials heard word-initially in *peer*, *bin*, and *month* and the labiodentals heard initially in *fire* and *vow*.

Dental and interdental

Some phones are produced with the tongue placed against or near the teeth. Sounds made in this way are called **dentals**. European French has dental sounds at the beginning of the words *temps* 'time', *dire* 'say', *sept* 'seven', and *zéro*.

If the tongue is placed between the teeth, the sound is said to be **interdental**. English has two interdentals, corresponding to the initial consonants of the words *this* and *thing*. (If you have difficulty distinguishing these two sounds, try the voicing test described in section 2.2.3 above.)

Alveolar

Within the oral cavity, a small ridge protrudes from just behind the upper front teeth. This is called the **alveolar ridge**. The tongue may touch or be brought near this ridge. Alveolar sounds are heard at the beginning of the English words *top*, *deer*, *soap*, *zip*, *lip*, and *neck*. Some languages, such as Spanish, have an *r* that is made by touching the tongue to the alveolar ridge.

Alveopalatal and palatal

Just behind the alveolar ridge, the roof of the mouth rises sharply. This area is known as the **alveopalatal** area (**palatoalveolar** in some books). Alveopalatal consonants are heard in the English words *show*, *measure*, *chip*, and *judge*.

The highest part of the roof of the mouth is called the **palate**, and sounds produced with the tongue on or near this area are called **palatals**. The word-initial phone in *yes* is a palatal glide.

Velar

The soft area toward the rear of the roof of the mouth is called the **velum**. Sounds made with the tongue touching or near this position are called **velars**. Velars are heard in English at the beginning of the words *call* and *guy*, and at the end of the word *hang*. The glide heard word-initially in *wet* is called a **labiovelar**, since the tongue body is raised near the velum and the lips are rounded at the same time. We refer to the velar aspect of the sound as its *primary* place of articulation while the labial aspect is a *secondary* place of articulation.

Uvular

The small fleshy flap of tissue known as the **uvula** hangs down from the velum. Sounds made with the tongue near or touching this area are called **uvulars**. English has no uvulars, but the *r* sound of standard European French is uvular. The Inuktitut language has a voiceless uvular stop [q] as found in the name of the city Iqaluit. (**To hear these sounds, go to the Companion Website.**)

Pharyngeal

The area of the throat between the uvula and the larynx is known as the pharynx. Sounds made through the modification of airflow in this region by retracting the tongue or constricting the pharynx are called **pharyngeals**. Pharyngeals can be found in many dialects of Arabic, but not in English. (**To hear these sounds, go to the Companion Website.**)

Glottal

Sounds produced using the vocal folds as primary articulators are called **glottals**. The sound at the beginning of the English words _heave_ and _hog_ is made at the glottis. You can also hear a glottal sound in the Cockney English pronunciation of the 'tt' in words like _better_ or _bottle_.

2.5 Manners of articulation

The lips, tongue, velum, and glottis can be positioned in different ways to produce different sound types. These various configurations are called **manners of articulation**.

2.5.1 Oral versus nasal phones

A basic distinction in manner of articulation is between **oral** and **nasal** phones. When the velum is raised, blocking the airflow through the nasal cavity, oral sounds are produced. The velum can also be lowered to allow air to pass through the nasal cavity, producing a sound that is nasal. Both consonants and vowels can be nasal, in which case they are generally voiced. (All nasals represented in this chapter are voiced.) The consonants at the end of the English words _sun_, _sum_, and _sung_ are nasal. For many speakers of English, the vowels of words such as _bank_ and _wink_ are also slightly nasal because of their proximity to nasal consonants.

2.5.2 Stops

Stops are made with a complete closure either in the oral cavity or at the glottis. In the world's languages, stops are found at bilabial, dental, alveolar, alveopalatal, palatal, velar, uvular, and glottal places of articulation.

In English, bilabial, alveolar, and velar oral and nasal stops occur in the words shown in table 2.3. Note that [ŋ] does not occur word-initially in English, though it can in other languages.

The glottal stop is commonly heard in English in the expression _uh-uh_ [ʔʌʔʌ], meaning 'no'. The two vowels in this utterance are each preceded by a momentary closing of the airstream at the glottis. In some British dialects, the glottal stop is commonly heard in place of the [t] in a word like _bottle_. You may see this glottal stop spelled with an apostrophe (_bo'l_).

TABLE 2.3   English stops and their transcription

Bilabial		Transcription
Voiceless	s<u>p</u>an	[p]
Voiced	<u>b</u>an	[b]
Nasal (Voiced)	<u>m</u>an	[m]
Alveolar		
Voiceless	s<u>t</u>un	[t]
Voiced	<u>d</u>ot	[d]
Nasal (Voiced)	<u>n</u>ot	[n]
Velar		
Voiceless	s<u>c</u>ar	[k]
Voiced	<u>g</u>ap	[g]
Nasal (Voiced)	wi<u>ng</u>	[ŋ] (the symbol is called *eng or engma*)
Glottal		
Voiceless		[ʔ]

A grid for stops

Table 2.4 presents a grid on which the stop consonants of English are arranged according to place of articulation. As you can see, each oral stop, with one exception, has voiced and voiceless counterparts. The glottal stop is always voiceless. It is produced with the vocal folds drawn firmly together and the arytenoids drawn forward; since no air can pass through the glottis, the vocal folds cannot be set in motion.

TABLE 2.4   English stop consonants

	Bilabial	Alveolar	Velar	Glottal
Voiceless	[p]	[t]	[k]	[ʔ]
Voiced	[b]	[d]	[g]	
Nasal	[m]	[n]	[ŋ]	

2.5.3 Fricatives

Fricatives are consonants produced with a continuous airflow through the mouth. They belong to a large class of sounds called **continuants** (a class that also includes vowels and glides), all of which share this property. The fricatives form a special class of continuants; during their production, they are accompanied by a continuous audible noise because the air passes through a very narrow opening either at the glottis or at some point higher in the vocal tract.

English fricatives

English has voiceless and voiced labiodental fricatives at the beginning of the words *fat* and *vat*, voiceless and voiced interdental fricatives word-initially in the words *thin* and *those*, voiceless and voiced alveolar fricatives word-initially in *sing* and *zip*, and a voiceless alveopalatal fricative word-initially in *ship*. The voiced alveopalatal fricative is rare in English. It is the first consonant in the word *azure* and is also heard in the words *pleasure* and *rouge*. The voiceless glottal fricative of English is heard in *hotel* and *hat*. See the transcription of English fricatives in table 2.5.

Special note must be taken of the alveolar fricatives [s] and [z]. English speakers commonly produce these sounds in one of two ways. Some speakers raise the tongue tip to the alveolar ridge (or to just behind the upper front teeth) and allow the air to pass through a grooved channel in the tongue. Other speakers form this same channel using the blade of the tongue; the tip is placed behind the lower front teeth.

TABLE 2.5 The transcription of English fricatives

Glottal state	Place of articulation	Transcription
	Labiodental	
Voiceless	fan	[f]
Voiced	van	[v]
	Interdental	
Voiceless	thin	[θ]
Voiced	then	[ð]
	Alveolar	
Voiceless	sun	[s]
Voiced	zip	[z]
	Alveopalatal	
Voiceless	ship	[ʃ]
Voiced	azure	[ʒ]
	Glottal	
Voiceless	hat	[h]

A grid for fricatives

Table 2.6 presents a grid on which the fricative consonants of English are arranged according to place of articulation. As in table 2.5, dentals are not distinguished from alveolars, since most languages have sounds with either one place of articulation or the other, but not both. Note that IPA [ʃ] and [ʒ] correspond to North American [š] and [ž], respectively.

TABLE 2.6	English fricatives				
	Labiodental	**Interdental**	**Alveolar**	**Alveopalatal**	**Glottal**
Voiceless	[f]	[θ]	[s]	[ʃ]	[h]
Voiced	[v]	[ð]	[z]	[ʒ]	

2.5.4 Affricates

When a stop articulation is released, the tongue moves rapidly away from the place of articulation. However, some non-continuant consonants show a slow release of the closure; these sounds are called **affricates**. English has only two affricates, both of which are alveopalatal. They are heard word-initially in *church* and *jump* and are transcribed as [tʃ] and [dʒ], respectively.

A grid for affricates

Table 2.7 presents a grid showing the two English affricates. Note that IPA [tʃ] and [dʒ] correspond to North American [č] and [ǰ], respectively.

TABLE 2.7	English affricates
	Alveopalatal (= Palatoalveolar)
Voiceless	[tʃ]
Voiced	[dʒ]

Stridents and sibilants

At the beginning of this chapter, it was noted that acoustic as well as articulatory criteria are sometimes used in describing speech sounds. An acoustic criterion comes into play to describe fricatives and affricates, which are subdivided into two types based on their relative loudness. The noisier fricatives and affricates are called **stridents** (see table 2.8). Their quieter counterparts, such as [θ] or [ð], are considered non-strident. Stridents are also known as **sibilants**.

TABLE 2.8	Strident fricatives and affricates in English	
Place of articulation	**Strident**	
	Voiceless	*Voiced*
Alveolar	[s]	[z]
Alveopalatal	[ʃ]	[ʒ]
Alveopalatal	[tʃ]	[dʒ]

2.5.5 Voice lag and aspiration

After the release of certain voiceless stops in English, you can hear a brief delay before the voicing of a following vowel. Since the delay in the onset of vocalic voicing is accompanied by the release of air, the traditional term for this phenomenon is **aspiration**. It is transcribed with a small raised [ʰ] after the aspirated consonant. Table 2.9 provides some examples of aspirated and unaspirated consonants in English (some vowel symbols are introduced here as well). Notice that the sounds that have both aspirated and unaspirated varieties are all voiceless stops. In other languages, voiceless fricatives and affricates may also be aspirated or unaspirated.

TABLE 2.9	Aspirated and unaspirated consonants in English		
Aspirated		**Unaspirated**	
[pʰæt]	pat	[spæt]	spat
[tʰʌb]	tub	[stʌb]	stub
[kʰowp]	cope	[skowp]	scope

Figure 2.6 shows how aspiration of a voiceless consonant takes place, using the aspirated consonant [pʰ] as an example. Though the sequence of articulations takes place continuously, the figure illustrates only certain moments.

FIGURE 2.6 Aspirated consonant production (English *pill*)

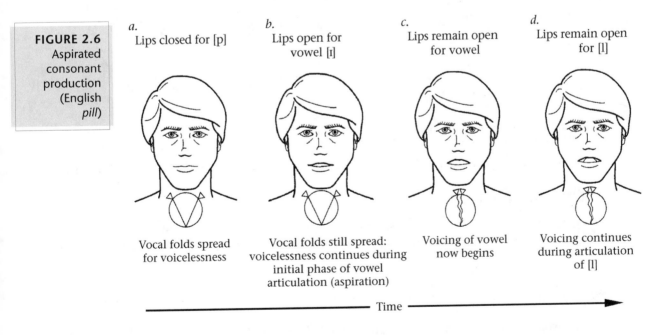

a. Lips closed for [p]

b. Lips open for vowel [ɪ]

c. Lips remain open for vowel

d. Lips remain open for [l]

Vocal folds spread for voicelessness

Vocal folds still spread: voicelessness continues during initial phase of vowel articulation (aspiration)

Voicing of vowel now begins

Voicing continues during articulation of [l]

⟶ Time ⟶

Figures 2.7 and 2.8 show the relation between articulation and voicing for unaspirated and voiced consonants. The unaspirated consonant, such as the [p] of English *spill*, shows voicing of the vowel very soon after release of the consonant closure. The voiced initial [b] of

English *bill* shows voicing just before the release of the bilabial closure. In figure 2.8, note how voicing precedes the release of the labial articulators.

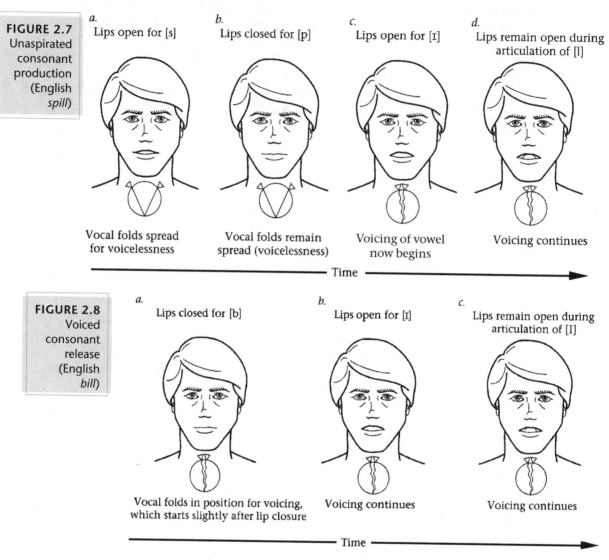

FIGURE 2.7
Unaspirated consonant production (English *spill*)

a.
Lips open for [s]

b.
Lips closed for [p]

c.
Lips open for [ɪ]

d.
Lips remain open during articulation of [l]

Vocal folds spread for voicelessness

Vocal folds remain spread (voicelessness)

Voicing of vowel now begins

Voicing continues

Time

FIGURE 2.8
Voiced consonant release (English *bill*)

a.
Lips closed for [b]

b.
Lips open for [ɪ]

c.
Lips remain open during articulation of [l]

Vocal folds in position for voicing, which starts slightly after lip closure

Voicing continues

Voicing continues

Time

Unreleased stops

Up to now we have described how stops may be either aspirated or unaspirated. Here we introduce a third variant: the *unreleased* stop. Pronounce the words in the following lists:

pave   cap
Tom   pot
king   back

The words in the first column have the stops ([pʰ], [tʰ], and [kʰ]) released into the following vowel. However, in the second column, it is quite common not to release the word-final stops at all. When you pronounce the word *cap* you may well end with your lips closed, and in *pot* and *back* your tongue can stay on the roof of your mouth. The phonetic symbol for this is a raised [̚] as in [p˺]. In some languages, a word-final stop is always unreleased. This is the case in Korean, where *pap* 'rice' is always pronounced [pap˺]. (Since transcribing all phonetic details can become cumbersome, the symbols indicating aspiration or an unreleased stop are sometimes omitted in the remainder of this chapter when they are not relevant to the point being discussed.)

2.5.6 Liquids

Among the sounds commonly found in the world's languages are *l* and *r* and their numerous variants. They form a special class of consonants known as **liquids**. Although there is a great deal of variation in the production of *l*s and *r*s in the languages of the world, they are nonetheless similar enough to be grouped together in a single category: they are all oral sonorous consonants.

English laterals

Varieties of *l* are called **laterals**. The most commonly used lateral liquid in English, transcribed as [l], is articulated with the tip of the tongue touching the alveolar ridge while air escapes through the mouth along the lowered sides of the tongue.

Because laterals are generally voiced, the term *lateral* is usually used to mean 'voiced lateral'. Still, there are instances of voiceless laterals in speech. The voiceless dental or alveolar lateral is written with an additional phonetic symbol, called a **diacritic**. In this case, the diacritic is a circle beneath the symbol: [l̥]. The first sound in the name Lloyd, as it is pronounced in Welsh, is a voiceless lateral. This sound can also be heard in the English words *please* and *clear*. You will hear this more clearly if you try lengthening the *l* as you pronounce these words aloud. **To learn how to pronounce the Welsh version of the sound, go to the Companion Website.**

English *r*s

Numerous varieties of *r* are also heard in the world's languages. This section describes the types found in English. The *r* of English as it is spoken in Canada and the United States is made by curling the tongue tip back and bunching the tongue upward and back in the mouth, as shown in figure 2.9. This *r*, which is known as a **retroflex** *r*, is heard in *ride* and *car*. IPA transcription favours [ɻ] for this sound, though it also offers the symbol [r], which we use in this book.

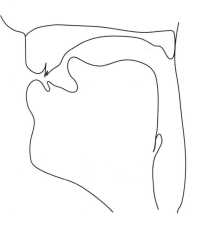

FIGURE 2.9
The retroflex sound at the beginning of *red*.

Another sound commonly identified with *r* is the **flap**. The flap is produced when the tongue tip strikes the alveolar ridge as it quickly passes across it. It is heard in the North American English pronunciation of *bitter* and *butter*, and in some British pronunciations of *very*. It is commonly transcribed as [ɾ] and is generally voiced. Table 2.10 presents the liquids *r*, *l*, and the flap of North American English, including Canadian English.

TABLE 2.10   English liquids

		Alveolar	
Laterals		voiced	[l]
		voiceless	[l̥]
*r*s	retroflex	voiced	[r]
		voiceless	[r̥]
	flap		[ɾ]

Language Matters **Another Kind of *l***

Pronounce the words in the following two lists:

leaf	fall
lie	milk
lawn	steal

Notice that the *l* sounds are not pronounced in the same way. In the first column, the *l* is made with the tongue tip touching the alveolar ridge (as described in section 2.5.6). This type of *l* is commonly referred to as a *clear l*. In the second column, however, the *l* sound is made with additional constriction further back in the mouth (at the velum). This type of *l* is known technically as a *velarized l* and more casually as a *dark l*. It is represented by the phonetic symbol [ɫ] (see figure 2.10).

FIGURE 2.10 Variants of English l: a. clear *l* as in *lean*; b. dark *l* as in *bail*.

a.

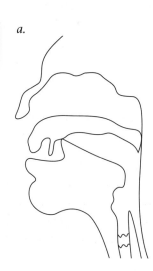

b.

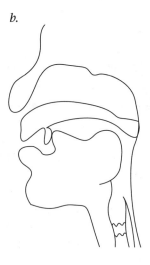

2.5.7 Syllabic liquids and nasals

Liquids and nasals are more sonorous than other consonants and in this respect are more like vowels than are the other consonants. In fact, they are so sonorous that they may function as syllabic nuclei. When they do so, they are called **syllabic liquids** and **syllabic nasals** (see table 2.11). Syllabic liquids and nasals are found in many of the world's languages, including English. In transcription, they are usually marked with a short vertical diacritic line underneath.

TABLE 2.11	Syllabic liquids and nasals in English		
	Syllabic		**Non-syllabic**
bottle	[bɑɾl̩]	lift	[lɪft]
funnel	[fʌnl̩]	pill	[pʰɪl]
bird	[bərd], [bɚd], or [br̩d]	rat	[ræt]
her	[hər], [hɚ], or [hr̩]	car	[kʰar]
hidden	[hɪdn̩]	now	[naw]
'm-m'	[ʔm̩ʔm̩] (meaning 'no')	mat	[mæt]

To be clear, then, the [n] in a word like *no* is not syllabic because it does not form the nucleus of the syllable. *No* is a one-syllable word and has one vowel. However, the [n] in some two-syllable words is syllabic. The second syllable in *hidden*, for example, has [n] as its nucleus. Therefore, whether a segment is syllabic or not is directly related to how it functions in the syllable.

Unfortunately for beginning linguistics students, North American transcription is not always consistent here. The syllabic *r* sound heard in words like *bird* and *her* is often transcribed in North America as a vowel-*r* sequence: [ər]. (The vowel symbol is presented in section 2.6.3.) The IPA symbol for this sound is [ɚ]. For many linguists, the following transcriptions would be taken as notationally equivalent variants:

[hɪdən]	and	[hɪdn̩]
[bʌɾər]	and	[bʌɾr̩] or [bʌɾɚ]

2.5.8 Glides

Recall that a glide is a very rapidly articulated non-syllabic segment. The two glides of Canadian English are [j] of *yes* and *boy* and [w] of *wet* and *now*. The IPA symbol [j] (called yod) corresponds to the [y] of North American transcription.

The [j] is a palatal glide (sometimes described as alveopalatal as well) whose articulation is virtually identical to that of the vowel [i] of *see*. You can verify this by pronouncing a [j] in an extended manner; it will sound very close to an [i].

The glide [w] is made with the tongue raised and pulled back near the velum and with the lips protruding, or **rounded**. For this reason, it is sometimes called a labiovelar. The [w] corresponds closely in articulation to the vowel [u] of *who*. This can be verified by extending the pronunciation of [w]. We will consider [w] a rounded velar glide for purposes of description. Some speakers of English also have a voiceless (labio)velar glide, transcribed [ʍ], in the words *when*, *where*, and *which* (but not in *witch*).

Table 2.12 provides a summary of the places and manners of articulation of English consonants.

TABLE 2.12	English consonants: places and manners of articulation								
Manner of articulation		**Place of articulation**							
		Labial	Labiodental	Interdental	Alveolar	Alveopalatal Palatal		Velar	Glottal
Stop	voiceless	p			t			k	ʔ
	voiced	b			d			g	
Fricative	voiceless		f	θ	s	ʃ			h
	voiced		v	ð	z	ʒ			
Affricate	voiceless					tʃ			
	voiced					dʒ			
Nasal	voiced	m			n			ŋ	
Liquid	voiced								
	lateral voiced				l				
	retroflex				r				
Glide	voiceless							ʍ	
	voiced						j	w	

Language Matters **Which Witch Is Which?**

Do you make a distinction in your pronunciation of the following pairs of words?

weather	whether
witch	which
wither	whither

Ask some of your friends (of different ages and geographical origins) to pronounce these words. Do they make a distinction?

Language Matters **What's the World's Most Unusual Speech Sound?**

Pirahã, a language with only a couple of hundred speakers in Brazil, has a sound that is produced as follows: the tongue tip first touches the alveolar ridge and then comes out of the mouth, almost touching the upper chin as the underblade of the tongue makes contact with the lower lip. Technically speaking, this is known as a 'voiced lateralized apical-alveolar/sublaminal-labial double flap with egressive lung air'. (Fortunately, for all concerned, the sound is only used in "certain special types of speech performance.")

Sources: Peter Ladefoged and Ian Maddieson, *The Sounds of the World's Languages* (Malden, MA: Blackwell, 1996); Daniel Everett, "Phonetic Rarities in Pirahã," *Journal of the International Phonetic Association* 12, 2 (1982): 94–96.

2.6 Vowels

Vowels are sonorous, syllabic sounds made with the vocal tract more open than it is for consonant and glide articulations. Different vowel sounds (also called vowel *qualities*) are produced by varying the placement of the body of the tongue (remember that for vowels your tongue tip is behind your lower front teeth) and shaping the lips. The shape of the vocal tract can be further altered by protruding the lips to produce rounded vowels or by lowering the velum to produce a nasal vowel. Finally, vowels may be tense or lax, depending on the degree of vocal tract constriction during their articulation. This section on vowels introduces most of the basic vowels of English.

2.6.1 Simple vowels and diphthongs

English vowels are divided into two major types, **simple vowels** and **diphthongs**. Simple vowels do not show a noticeable change in quality during their articulation. The vowels of *pit*, *set*, *cat*, *dog*, *but*, *put*, and the first vowel of *suppose* are all simple vowels.

Diphthongs are vowels that exhibit a change in quality within a single syllable. English diphthongs show changes in quality that are due to tongue movement away from the initial vowel articulation toward a glide position. In the vowels classified as *major* diphthongs, the change in articulation is quite extreme and hence easy to hear. Listen to the change in articulation in the following words: *buy* ([aj]), *boy* ([oj]), and *now* ([aw]). Each of these diphthongs starts in one position (e.g., [a]) and ends up in another position (e.g., [w]). In *minor* diphthongs, the change in position of the articulators is less dramatic. If you listen carefully and note the change in your tongue position as you say *play* ([ej]) and your lip position as you say *go* ([ow]), you will realize that in each of these diphthongs, too, the starting position is different from the ending position. In the vowels of words like *heed* and *lose*, the change is more difficult to hear and in fact is not made by all English speakers, so we will not transcribe these as diphthongs. Some instructors, however, may ask that you transcribe them in the diphthongized form.[1]

Language Matters Cross-Dialectal Variation

One of the best ways to learn to appreciate some of the fine differences in vowel articulation is to think of some cross-dialectal variation in English. Let us first consider the question of the minor diphthongs in [ej] and [ow]. In Canadian English, these sounds are diphthongs (as reflected in our transcription), but this is not the case in *all* dialects of English. In Jamaican English, words like *go* and *say* have simple vowels and would be transcribed as [go] and [se]. **To listen to these sounds and note the difference, please go to the Companion Website.**

Comparison across dialects can also help us to understand why we have used the [a] symbol in the major diphthongs. In articulatory terms, the [a] sound is made at the front of the mouth with the tongue a bit lower than [æ]. You can hear this sound in many Romance languages (like French or Spanish) in words like *la* or *gato*. However, you can also hear [a] in Canadian English in words that have an [r] following the vowel. Say the following words as naturally as you can: *car*, *farm*, *heart*. Now try to say the same words, but stop before you pronounce the [r] sound. You will notice that the vowel in *car* ([a]) is not the same as the vowel in *saw* ([ɑ]). This [a] vowel is, in fact, where we start articulating our diphthongs. If you try to say words like *ride* and *round* with an [ɑ] sound rather than an [a], you will find yourself speaking with one variety of a British accent. **To hear these sounds, go to the Companion Website.**

Table 2.13 presents the simple vowels and diphthongs of English. The diphthongs are transcribed as vowel-glide sequences. Although diphthongs are complex in an articulatory sense (and are therefore transcribed as a vowel plus a glide), they still act as a single vowel in some respects. For example, our judgments tell us that both *pin* (simple vowel) and *pint* (diphthong) are single syllable words. Having a diphthong doesn't add a syllable to a word. Compare the pronunciation of the single syllable 'line' [lajn] and the disyllabic 'lion' [lajən]. Even when you stretch out the pronunciation of a diphthong, it does not become two syllables.

TABLE 2.13 Some simple vowels and diphthongs of Canadian English					
Simple vowels		**Minor diphthongs**		**Major diphthongs**	
p<u>i</u>t	[ɪ]	s<u>ay</u>	[ej]	m<u>y</u>	[aj]
s<u>e</u>t	[ɛ]	gr<u>ow</u>	[ow]	n<u>ow</u>	[aw]
p<u>u</u>t	[ʊ]			b<u>oy</u>	[oj]
c<u>u</u>t	[ʌ]				
m<u>a</u>t	[æ]				
d<u>o</u>g	[ɑ]				
h<u>ea</u>t	[i]				
l<u>o</u>se	[u]				

2.6.2 Basic parameters for describing vowels

Vowel articulations are not as easy to feel at first as consonant articulations because the vocal tract is not narrowed as much. To become acquainted with vowel articulation, alternately pronounce the vowels of *he* and *awe*. You will feel the tongue move from a **high** front to a **low** back position. Once you feel this tongue movement, alternate between the vowels of *awe* and *at*. You will feel the tongue moving from the low **back** to low **front** position. Finally, alternate between the vowels of *he* and *who*. You will notice that in addition to a tongue movement between the high front and high back positions, you are also rounding your lips for the [u]. Figure 2.11 shows a midsagittal view of the tongue position for the vowels [i], [ɑ], and [u] based on X-ray studies of speech.

FIGURE 2.11 Tongue position and transcription for three English vowels

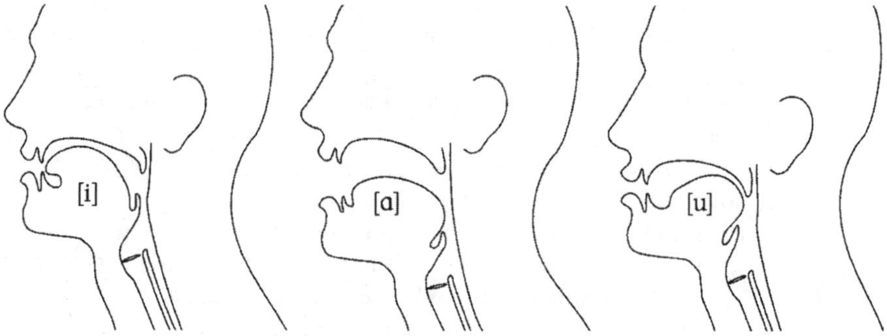

Vowels for which the tongue is neither raised nor lowered are called **mid vowels**. The front vowel of English *m<u>a</u>de* and *f<u>a</u>me* is mid, front, and unrounded. The vowel of *c<u>o</u>de* and *s<u>oa</u>k* is mid, back, and rounded. In the case of diphthongs, the articulatory descriptions refer to the tongue position of the vowel nucleus, not the following glide. The vowels presented so far in this section are summed up in table 2.14. Note that in describing the vowels, the articulatory parameters are presented in the order *height, backness, rounding*.

TABLE 2.14	Basic phonetic parameters for describing Canadian English vowels	
h<u>ea</u>t	[i]	high front unrounded
f<u>a</u>te	[ej]	mid front unrounded
m<u>a</u>d	[æ]	low front unrounded
S<u>ue</u>	[u]	high back rounded
b<u>oa</u>t	[ow]	mid back rounded
s<u>u</u>n	[ʌ]	mid central unrounded
c<u>o</u>t, c<u>au</u>ght	[ɑ]	low back unrounded

Language Matters More Cross-Dialectal Variation

In some dialects of English, you will hear the mid back rounded lax vowel [ɔ]. If you know what speakers of certain New York dialects sound like when they say words like *coffee* or how speakers of certain British dialects say words like *saw*, you will know what this vowel sounds like. Even in Canadian English, though, you will find the [ɔ] in some words. Say the word *more* as naturally as you can. Now say the same word but stop before you get to the [r]. You will find that you have said something like [mɔ] and not [mow]. While this is often transcribed as [o], note that you do not make a diphthong here. As we saw with the [a] sound discussed above, there is something special about vowels that occur before [r]. **To listen to these sounds, please go to the Companion Website.**

As shown in table 2.14, in standard Canadian English, there is no difference between the vowels of a pair of words like *cot* and *caught*, both of which contain the vowel [ɑ]. In some dialects of North American English, as well as in many other dialects of English worldwide, the vowel of *caught* (and certain other words such as *law*) is the mid back rounded lax vowel [ɔ].

Tongue positions for some English vowels are illustrated in figure 2.12. The trapezoid corresponds roughly to the space within which the tongue moves, which is wider at the top of the oral cavity and more restricted at the bottom. Non-front vowels are traditionally divided into central and back vowels (see figures 2.12 and 2.13); often the term *back* alone is used for all non-front vowels. **To hear these sounds, go to the Companion Website.**[2]

FIGURE 2.12 Basic tongue positions for English vowels

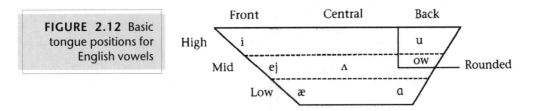

2.6.3 **Tense and lax vowels**

All the vowels illustrated in figure 2.12 except [æ] and [ʌ] are **tense**. Tense vowels are produced with greater vocal tract constriction than non-tense vowels and are longer in duration than non-tense vowels. Some vowels of English are made with roughly the same tongue position as the tense vowels but with a less constricted articulation; they are called **lax**. The representation of vowels and their articulatory positions (figure 2.12) is expanded in figure 2.13 to include both tense and lax vowels, as well as the major diphthongs.

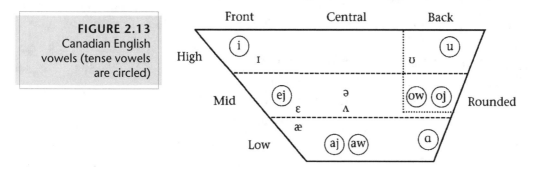

FIGURE 2.13
Canadian English vowels (tense vowels are circled)

Table 2.15 provides examples from English comparing tense and lax vowels. Note that not all the vowels come in tense/lax pairs. The difference between two of the vowels illustrated in table 2.15 is often not easy to hear at first. Both the vowel [ʌ] in *cut*, *dud*, *pluck*, and *Hun*, and the vowel [ə] of *Canada*, *about*, *tomahawk*, and *sofa* are mid, central, unrounded, and lax. The vowel of the second set of examples, called **schwa**, is referred to as a **reduced vowel**. In addition to being lax, its duration is briefer than that of any of the other vowels.

TABLE 2.15 Tense and lax vowels in Canadian English

Tense		Lax	
heat	[i]	hit	[ɪ]
mate	[ej]	met	[ɛ]
—	—	mat	[æ]
shoot	[u]	should	[ʊ]
coat	[ow]	—	—
—	—	cut	[ʌ]
—	—	Canada	[ə]
lock	[ɑ]	—	—
lies	[aj]		
loud	[aw]		
boy	[oj]		

A simple test can help determine whether vowels are tense or lax. In English, monosyllabic words spoken in isolation do not end in lax vowels. We find *see* [si], *say* [sej], *Sue* [su], *so* [sow], and *saw* [sɑ] in English, but not *[sɪ], *[sɛ], *[sæ], *[sʊ], or *[sʌ]. Schwa, however, frequently appears in unstressed syllables (syllables perceived as less prominent) in polysyllabic words like *sof*[ə] and *Can*[ə]*d*[ə]. (See section 2.8.3 for a discussion of stress.) It should be pointed out—especially for those who think their ears are deceiving them—that many speakers produce the final vowel in the last two examples as [ʌ], not as [ə].

This rather formidable crowd of vowels should not intimidate you. If you are a native speaker of English, you have been using these vowels most of your life. Learning to hear them consciously and transcribe them is not a difficult task. If you are a non-native speaker of English, **you may wish to access the sound files on the Companion Website** to practise listening to these sounds. The next section provides more examples of the transcription of English consonants and vowels.

2.7 Phonetic transcription of Canadian English consonants and vowels

Tables 2.16 and 2.17 present the phonetic symbols for consonants and vowels commonly used to transcribe Canadian English. To illustrate how each symbol is used, one word is transcribed completely, and then some other words in which the same sound is found are given. You will notice that in the example words, the spelling of the sound may vary. Be careful of this when you transcribe words phonetically—the sound of a word, not its spelling, is what is transcribed!

TABLE 2.16   Transcribing English consonants

Symbol	Word	Transcription	More examples
[pʰ]	pit	[pʰɪt]	pain, upon, apart
[p]	spit	[spɪt]	spar, crispy, upper, Yuppie, culprit, bumper
[tʰ]	tick	[tʰɪk]	tell, attire, terror, Tutu
[t]	stuck	[stʌk]	stem, hunter, nasty, mostly
[kʰ]	keep	[kʰip]	cow, kernel, recur
[k]	skip	[skɪp]	scatter, uncle, blacklist, likely
[tʃ]	chip	[tʃɪp]	lunch, lecher, ditch, belch
[dʒ]	judge	[dʒʌdʒ]	germ, journal, budgie, wedge
[b]	bib	[bɪb]	boat, liberate, rob, blast
[d]	dip	[dɪp]	dust, sled, draft
[ɾ]	butter	[bʌɾər]	madder, matter, hitting, writer, rider
[g]	get	[gɛt]	gape, mugger, twig, gleam
[f]	fit	[fɪt]	flash, coughing, proof, phlegmatic, gopher
[v]	vat	[væt]	vote, oven, prove
[θ]	thick	[θɪk]	thought, ether, teeth, three, bathroom
[ð]	though	[ðow]	then, bother, teethe, bathe
[s]	sip	[sɪp]	psychology, fasten, lunacy, bass, curse, science
[z]	zap	[zæp]	Xerox, scissors, desire, zipper, fuzzy

(Continued)

TABLE 2.16   Transcribing English consonants (Continued)

Symbol	Word	Transcription	More examples
[ʃ]	ship	[ʃɪp]	shock, nation, mission, glacier, wish
[ʒ]	azure	[æʒər]	measure, rouge, visual, garage (for some speakers), Taj Mahal
[h]	hat	[hæt]	who, ahoy, forehead, behind
[j]	yet	[jɛt]	use (before the *u*), yes, cute (between the *c* and the *u*)
[w]	witch	[wɪtʃ]	wait, weird, now, queen (between the *q* and the *ee*)
[ʍ]	which	[ʍɪtʃ]	what, where, when (only for some speakers)
[l]	leaf	[lif]	loose, lock, alive, hail
[l̩]	huddle	[hʌdl̩]	bottle, needle
[r]	reef	[rif]	rod, arrive, tear
[ɾ]	bird	[bɾd]	early, hurt, stir, purr, doctor
[m]	moat	[mowt]	mind, humour, shimmer, sum, thumb
[m̩]	'm-m'	[ʔm̩ʔm̩]	bottom, random
[n]	note	[nowt]	now, winner, angel, sign, wind
[n̩]	sadden	[sædn̩]	Jordan, mitten
[ŋ]	sing	[sɪŋ]	singer, longer, bank, twinkle

TABLE 2.17   Transcribing English vowels

Symbol	Word	Transcription	More examples
[i]	fee	[fi]	she, cream, believe, receive, serene, amoeba, creepy
[ɪ]	fit	[fɪt]	hit, income, definition, been (for some speakers)
[ej]	fate	[fejt]	they, clay, grain, gauge, engage, great, sleigh
[ɛ]	let	[lɛt]	led, head, says, said, sever, guest
[æ]	bat	[bæt]	panic, racket, laugh, Vancouver
[u]	boot	[but]	to, two, loose, brew, Louise, Lucy, through
[ʊ]	book	[bʊk]	should, put, hood
[ow]	note	[nowt]	no, throat, though, slow, toe, oaf, O'Conner
[oj]	boy	[boj]	voice, boil, toy
[ɑ]	saw	[sɑ]	cot, caught, father, bought, across, Toronto
[ʌ]	shut	[ʃʌt]	other, udder, tough, lucky, was, flood
[ə]	roses	[rowzəz]	collide, hinted, telegraph, (to) suspect
[aw]	crowd	[krawd]	(to) house, plow, bough
[aj]	lies	[lajz]	my, tide, thigh, buy

2.8 Suprasegmentals

All phones have certain inherent **suprasegmental** or **prosodic properties** that form part of their makeup no matter what their place or manner of articulation. These properties are **pitch**, **loudness**, and **length**.

All sounds give us a subjective impression of being relatively higher or lower in pitch. Pitch is the auditory property of a sound that enables us to place it on a scale that ranges from low to high. Pitch is especially noticeable in sonorous sounds: vowels, glides, liquids, and nasals. Even stop and fricative consonants convey different pitches. This is particularly apparent among the fricatives, as you can hear by extending the pronunciation of [s] and then of [ʃ]; the [s] is clearly higher pitched. All sounds have some degree of intrinsic loudness as well, or they could not be heard. Moreover, all sounds occupy a certain stretch of time—they give the subjective impression of length.

2.8.1 Pitch: tone and intonation

Speakers of any language have the ability to control the level of pitch in their speech. This is accomplished by controlling the tension of the vocal folds and the amount of air that passes through the glottis. The combination of tensed vocal folds and greater air pressure results in higher pitch on vowels and sonorant consonants, whereas less tense vocal folds and lower air pressure result in lower pitch. Two kinds of controlled pitch movement found in human language are called **tone** and **intonation**.

Tone

A language is said to have tone or to be a **tone language** when differences in word meaning are signalled by differences in pitch. Pitch on forms in tone languages functions very differently from the movement of pitch in a non-tone language. When a speaker of English says *a car?* with a rising pitch, the word *car* refers to the same type of object as when it is pronounced on a different pitch level or with a different pitch contour. In contrast, when a speaker of the tone language Mandarin pronounces the form *ma* with a falling pitch ([mà]), it means 'scold', but when the same form (*ma*) is pronounced with a rising pitch, as [má], the meaning is 'hemp' (see figure 2.16). **To hear a four-way contrast involving tone in Mandarin, go to the Companion Website.** There is no parallel to anything like this in non-tone languages such as English and French.

Unlike Mandarin, which has falling and rising tones, some languages show only what are known as level tones. Tsúut'ína (or Sarcee), an Athabaskan language spoken in Alberta, has high-, mid-, and low-pitch level tones. In figure 2.14, the uppercase letters H, M, and L stand for high, mid, and low tones, respectively. An **association line** drawn from the letters to the vowels links the segments with their respective tones.

FIGURE 2.14 Tsúut'ína level tones ([ɬ] is a voiceless lateral fricative)	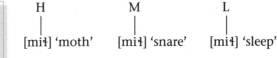

Level tones that signal meaning differences are called **register tones**: two or three register tones are the norm in most of the world's register tone languages, though four have been reported for Mazatec, a language spoken in Mexico.

A single tone may be associated with more than one syllabic element. In Mende, spoken in West Africa, certain polysyllabic forms show the same tone on each syllable. (In table 2.18, the diacritic [´] indicates a high tone and the diacritic [`] indicates a low tone.)

TABLE 2.18	High-tone and low-tone words in Mende
pélé	'banana'
háwámá	'waistline'
kpàkàlì	'tripod chair'

The notation in figure 2.15 allows us to represent the tone as characteristic of an entire form. The single underlying tone unit is associated with all vowels.

FIGURE 2.15
Tone as a word feature in Mende

In some languages, tones can change pitch within a single syllabic element. Moving pitches that signal meaning differences are called **contour tones**. In Mandarin, both register and contour tones are heard. Contour tones are shown by pitch level notation lines that converge above the vowel. Figure 2.16 shows one (high) register tone and three different contour tones.

FIGURE 2.16
Register and contour tones in Mandarin

H			MLH		
[ma]	'mother'	high tone	[ma]	'horse'	fall rise
MH			HL		
[ma]	'hemp'	mid rise	[ma]	'scold'	high fall

Tone can sometimes have a grammatical function. In Bini, a language spoken in Nigeria, tone can signal differences in the tense of a verb (such as past versus present), as figure 2.17 shows.

FIGURE 2.17
Tense and tone in Bini

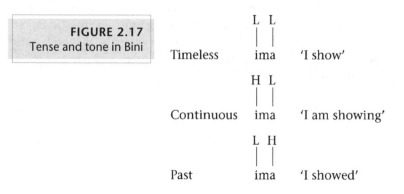

Timeless	ima	'I show'
Continuous	ima	'I am showing'
Past	ima	'I showed'

Although tones may seem exotic to native speakers of European languages, they are very widespread. Tone languages are found throughout North and South America, sub-Saharan Africa, and the Far East.

Intonation

Pitch movement in spoken utterances that is not related to differences in word meaning is called **intonation**. It makes no difference to the meaning of the word *seven*, for example, whether it is pronounced with a rising pitch or a falling pitch.

Intonation often does serve to convey information of a broadly meaningful nature, however. For example, the falling pitch we hear at the end of a statement in English such as *Fred parked the car* signals that the utterance is complete. For this reason, falling intonation at the end of an utterance is called a **terminal (intonation) contour**. Conversely, a rising or level intonation, called a **non-terminal (intonation) contour**, often signals incompleteness. Non-terminal contours are often heard on the non-final forms in lists and telephone numbers.

In questions, final rising intonations also signal a kind of incompleteness in that they indicate that a conversational exchange is not finished: *Are you hungry?* However, English interrogatives that contain question words like *who*, *what*, *when*, and *how* (for example, *What did you buy?*) ordinarily do not have rising intonation. It is as if the question word itself is enough to indicate that an answer is expected.

Language Matters **Intonation and Punctuation**

Punctuation marks in English often serve to indicate intonation patterns. If you just read an unpunctuated sequence such as

> *John said William is brilliant*

you might not recognize the ambiguity of the utterance, as shown below:

> *John said, "William is brilliant."*
> *"John," said William, "is brilliant."*

Repeat each of the above sentences and note how your intonation helps to convey the right meaning.

Although intonation can be represented graphically as in figures 2.18 and 2.19, a more formal way of representing intonation is shown in figure 2.20. Here, as in tonal representation, L and H are relative terms for differences in pitch. The letters H and L are placed above the syllabic elements on which the pitch change occurs. The dotted lines indicate that the lowering pitch spreads across the remaining pitch-bearing elements. (A richer notational scheme is known as ToBi [Tones and Break indices]. A free online course on this system is available; for more information, go to the Companion Website.)

| **FIGURE 2.18** Rising non-terminal intonations in a list and a telephone number |

Sally   Fred   Helen   andJoe

two   eight   four   two   five   one   three

FIGURE 2.19
Non-terminal intonation in a question

Did you have a nice $tim_{e?}$

FIGURE 2.20
A terminal contour

L   H L

There's an elephant in here.

Rising intonation on names or requests is commonly heard in addressing people. Its use indicates that the speaker is opening a conversation or that some further action is expected from the addressee, as shown in figure 2.21.

FIGURE 2.21
Two non-terminal contours

L H   H   L H

Margo? Is that you?

The complex use of intonation has just been touched on here. For example, rising intonation is often used to express politeness, as in *Please sit down*. Some linguists think that this is an extension of the 'open-ended mode' of intonation and that since a rising intonation indicates that a further response is expected (but not demanded) of the addressee, a sentence uttered with a rising intonation sounds less like an order and so is more polite.

Intonation and tone

Tone and intonation are not mutually exclusive. Tone languages show intonation of all types. This is possible since tones are not absolute but relative pitches. For example, a tone is perceived as high if it is high relative to the pitches around it. As long as this relative difference is maintained, the pitch distinctions will also be maintained. This is shown graphically in figure 2.22, which represents the overall pitch of a declarative sentence in Igbo, a West African language with register tones. Note how an Igbo speaker clearly maintains the distinction among the pitch registers even as the overall pitch of the utterance falls. Each high tone is always lower than the preceding high tone but higher than the low tone that immediately precedes it. This phenomenon is known as **downdrift**.

FIGURE 2.22
Tone and intonation: downdrift in Igbo

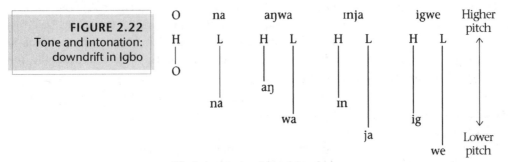

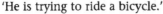

'He is trying to ride a bicycle.'

2.8.2 Length

Many languages have vowels and consonants whose articulation takes longer relative to that of other vowels and consonants. This phenomenon, known as **length**, is widespread in the world's languages. Length is indicated in phonetic transcription by the use of an IPA-style colon [ː] (or simply a colon [:] in North American transcription) placed after the segment in question.

Hungarian, German, Cree, and Finnish are a few of the many languages that have long and short vowels. Yapese, a language spoken on the island of Yap in the Western Pacific, shows short and long vowels in pairs of words such as those in table 2.19.

TABLE 2.19	Short and long vowels in Yapese			
[θis]	'to topple'		[θiːs]	'(a) post'
[pul]	'to gather'		[puːl]	'moon'
[ʔer]	'near you'		[ʔeːr]	'part of a lagoon'

Italian has short and long consonants in pairs of words such as those shown in table 2.20. Long and short consonants are also found in many other languages, including Finnish, Turkish, and Hungarian.

TABLE 2.20	Short and long consonants in Italian				
fato	[fatɔ]	'fate'	fatto	[fatːɔ]	'fact'
fano	[fanɔ]	'grove'	fanno	[fanːɔ]	'they do'
casa	[kasa]	'house'	cassa	[kasːa]	'box'

2.8.3 Stress

In any utterance, some vowels are perceived as more prominent than others. In a word such as *banana,* the second vowel is more prominent than the other two. In a word such as *telegraphic* [tɛ̀ləgrǽfɪk], the two vowel nuclei that are more prominent than the others are [ɛ] and [æ]. A syllabic nucleus that is perceived to be more prominent than other nuclei in the word is said to be stressed.

Stress is a cover term for the combined effects of pitch, loudness, and length—the result of which is perceived prominence. In each language, the effect of these prosodic features varies. In general, English stressed vowels are higher in pitch, longer, and louder than unstressed ones. In some languages, the impression of vowel prominence results from a different interaction of the prosodic parameters than is found in English. In Modern Greek, for example, syllables tend to be of equal length. Stress, therefore, is manifested by a change only in pitch and loudness and not in syllable length. Tone languages do not change the pitch level or contour of tones to mark stress. In many of these languages, relative prominence is marked by exaggerating the vowel length or pitch contour.

There are various ways to mark stress in phonetic transcription. North American transcription commonly uses an acute accent [´] placed over the vowel nucleus in question to mark the most prominent or **primary stress** and a grave accent [ˋ] to mark the second most prominent or **secondary stress** or stresses. (This should not be confused with the use of the same diacritics to mark tone in tone languages.) Stress can also be marked by placing numbers above the stressed vowels, usually [1] for a primary stress and [2] for a secondary stress. The word *telegraphic* can therefore be transcribed in either of the following ways:

(2)   2   1
        [tèləgrǽfɪk]   or   [tɛləgrǽfɪk]

The examples in table 2.21 illustrate some differences in English stress placement.

TABLE 2.21	Differing stress placement in English		
(an) áddress	[ǽdrɛs]	(to) addréss	[ədrés]
(a) présent	[p r ɛ́ z ə n t]	(to) presént	[prəzɛ́nt]
télegràph	[t ɛ́ l ə gr ǽ f]		
télegraphỳ	[t əlɛ́ gr əf ì]		
tèlegráphic	[t ɛ̀ l ə gr ǽf ɪ k]		

In these examples, you can also see that the quality of certain vowels varies depending on whether they are stressed or unstressed. This phenomenon is common in English, Russian, Palauan, and many other languages, but is not universal.

2.9 Speech production

Up to this point we have, for the most part, been describing phonetic segments as if they existed in isolation and did not affect one another. However, speech production is not a series of isolated events. The articulatory organs interact with each other (as we saw in section 2.5.5) and many fine adjustments are carried out very rapidly as we speak. As a consequence, speech production often results in the articulation of one sound affecting that of another sound.

2.9.1 Coarticulation

In order to articulate a sequence of phonetic segments, we have to plan a complex series of muscular movements. Due to the rapidity of speech (we can produce many segments per second) and the design of the vocal tract, if our goal is to produce a [pl] sequence, we cannot produce the two sounds independently of each other. Indeed, early speech synthesizers that produced speech in this way were practically unintelligible. Rather, as the sequence [pl] is produced, the tongue tip will start to move toward the alveolar ridge *before* the lips separate. The term **coarticulation** is used for situations such as this in which more than one articulator (here the lips and the tongue tip) is active.

2.9.2 Processes

Articulatory adjustments that occur during the production of connected speech are called **processes**. Processes change the nature of the individual segment. Their cumulative effect often results in making words easier to articulate, and in this sense, they are said to make speech more efficient. For example, when speakers of English say the word *bank*, they do not delay lowering the velum until the exact moment the nasal consonant articulation is reached. Instead, most English speakers begin lowering the velum for a nasal consonant almost as soon as they begin to articulate the vowel that precedes it.

In a parallel manner, when speakers use a palatal [k̟] in a word such as *key* (the [̟] indicates a palatal articulation), they are speaking more efficiently since they are making a less drastic adjustment in moving from the articulation of a more palatal [k̟] to that of a high front vowel than they would make in moving from a velar [k] to a high front vowel. Even more drastically, a speaker of English who says [pɾejd] for *parade* is making a major adjustment that results in a more efficient articulation: the two syllables of a careful pronunciation of *parade* are reduced to one by dropping the unstressed vowel of the first syllable; the tongue position for [r] is anticipated during pronunciation of the [p]; and the voicelessness of the initial stop is carried on through the [ɾ̥] (the [̥] signals voicelessness).

Some processes appear to make articulation less, not more, efficient. For example, English speakers often lengthen consonants and vowels when they are asked to repeat a word that someone has not heard clearly. The following kind of exchange is typical.

(3) "It's Fred."
"Did you say, 'It's red'?"
"No, I said, 'Fffreeed!'"

Lengthening segments results in a greater articulatory effort, but the process results in a more distinct form that is easier to perceive.

Another process that results in more easily perceivable speech adds a segment under certain conditions. When speaking slowly and carefully in a noisy environment, for example, English speakers often insert a vowel inside a group of consonants. This breaks up the sequence of consonants into separate syllables. To judge from the use people often make of this process when they wish to be clearly understood, it may well make words easier to perceive.

(4) "Stop screaming!"
"What? Stop dreaming?"
"I said, 'Stop sc[ə]reaming!'"

These examples show that there are two basic reasons for the existence of articulatory processes. Some processes result in a *more efficient articulation* of a series of sounds in that the precise timing and coordination of speech is relaxed to various degrees. Other processes result in a *more distinct output*, which is easier to perceive than fluent or rapid everyday speech. Although these two types of processes might at first appear to be contradictory, each serves a particular end in speech production.

2.9.3 Some common articulatory processes

Only a finite number of processes operate in language, though their end result is a great deal of linguistic variability. In this section, we survey some of the most common of these processes.

Assimilation

A number of different processes, collectively known as **assimilation**, result from the influence of one segment on another. Assimilation always results in a sound becoming more like another nearby sound in terms of one or more of its phonetic characteristics.

Nasalization of a vowel before a nasal consonant (nasal assimilation) is caused by speakers anticipating the lowering of the velum in advance of a nasal segment. The result is that the preceding segment takes on the nasality of the following consonant, as in [kæ̃nt] 'can't'. (Nasality is marked with a tilde [~].) This type of assimilation is known as **regressive assimilation**, since the nasalization is, in effect, moving *backwards* to a preceding segment.

The nasalization of vowels following nasal consonants in Scots Gaelic is an example of **progressive assimilation**, since the nasality moves *forward* from the nasal consonant onto the vowel (see table 2.22). It results from not immediately raising the velum after the production of a nasal stop.

TABLE 2.22	Progressive nasalization of vowels in Scots Gaelic
[mõːr]	'big'
[nĩ]	'cattle'
[mũ]	'about'
[nẽːl]	'cloud'

Voicing assimilation is also widespread. For many speakers of English, voiceless liquids and glides occur after voiceless stops in words such as *please* [pl̥iz], *try* [tr̥aj], and *cure* [kj̥ur]. These sounds are said to be devoiced in this environment. **Devoicing** is a kind of assimilation since the vocal folds are not set in motion immediately after the release of the voiceless consonant closure.

The opposite of devoicing is **voicing**. In Dutch, voiceless fricatives assimilate to the voicing of the stops that follow them, in anticipation of the voiced consonant. For example, the word *af* [ɑf] 'off, over' is pronounced with a [v] in the words *afbellen* 'to cancel' and *afdekken* 'to cover'.

Assimilation for place of articulation is also widespread in the world's languages. Nasal consonants are very likely to undergo this type of assimilation, as shown in table 2.23.

TABLE 2.23	Assimilation for place of articulation in English
possible	impossible
potent	impotent
tolerable	intolerable
tangible	intangible

The negative form of each of the words on the left is made with either *im-* or *in-*. In both cases, the form shows a nasal consonant that has the same place of articulation as the stop consonant that follows it: labial in the case of *possible* and *potent*, and alveolar in the case of *tolerable* and *tangible*. In informal speech, many English speakers pronounce words like *inconsequential* and *inconsiderate* with an [ŋ], assimilating the nasal to the place of articulation of the [k] that follows it, even though the spelling remains *n*. Assimilation can also be heard in pronunciations such as *Va*[ŋ]*couver*. Assimilation may even cross the boundary between words. In rapid speech, it is not uncommon to hear people pronounce phrases such as *in code* as [ɪŋkʰowd].

The preceding English examples show regressive assimilation for place of articulation. An example from German shows progressive assimilation that again affects nasal consonants (see table 2.24). In careful speech, certain German verb forms are pronounced with a final [ən], as in *laden* 'to invite', *loben* 'to praise', and *backen* 'to bake'. In informal speech, the final [ən] is reduced to a syllabic nasal, which takes on the place of articulation of the preceding consonant. (Recall that the diacritic line under the phonetically transcribed nasals indicates that they are syllabic.)

TABLE 2.24 Progressive assimilation in German

	Careful speech	Informal speech	
laden	[laːdən]	[laːdn̩]	'to invite'
loben	[loːbən]	[loːbm̩]	'to praise'
backen	[bakən]	[bakŋ̩]	'to bake'

Flapping is a process in which a dental or alveolar stop articulation changes to a flap [ɾ] articulation. In English, this process applies to [t] and [d] when they occur between vowels, the first of which is generally stressed. Flaps are heard in the casual speech pronunciation of words such as *butter, writer, fodder,* and *wading,* and even in phrases such as *I bought it* [ajbáɾɪt]. The alveolar flap is always voiced. Flapping is considered a type of assimilation because it involves a stop consonant being weakened and becoming less stop-like when it occurs between vowels, which involve no closure at all in the vocal tract.

Dissimilation

Dissimilation, the opposite of assimilation, results in two sounds becoming less alike in articulatory or acoustic terms. The resulting sequence of sounds is easier to articulate and distinguish. It is a much rarer process than assimilation. One commonly heard example of dissimilation in English occurs in words ending with three consecutive fricatives, such as *fifths*. Many speakers dissimilate the final [fθs] sequence to [fts], apparently to break up the sequence of three fricatives with a stop.

Deletion

Deletion is a process that removes a segment from certain phonetic contexts. Deletion occurs in everyday rapid speech in many languages. In English, a schwa [ə] is often deleted when the next vowel in the word is stressed, as shown in table 2.25. (Notice that in the first two words, the deletion of the schwa creates the environment for the [r] to become devoiced.)

TABLE 2.25 Deletion of [ə] in English		
Slow speech	**Rapid speech**	
[pəréjd]	[pr̥éjd]	parade
[kərówd]	[kr̥ówd]	corrode
[səpówz]	[spówz]	suppose

Deletion also occurs as an alternative to dissimilation in words such as *fifths*. Many speakers delete the [θ] of the final consonant cluster and say [fɪfs]. In very rapid speech, both the second [f] and the [θ] are sometimes deleted, resulting in [fɪs].

Epenthesis

Epenthesis is a process that inserts a syllabic or a non-syllabic segment within an existing string of segments. For example, in careful speech, the words *warmth* and *something* are pronounced [wormθ] and [sʌ̃mθɪ̃ŋ] (see table 2.26). It is common in casual speech for speakers to insert a [p] between the [m] and the [θ] and pronounce the words [wormpθ] and [sʌ̃mpθɪ̃ŋ]. Consonant epenthesis of this type is another example of a coarticulation phenomenon. In English, the articulatory transition from a sonorant consonant to a non-sonorant appears to be eased by the insertion of a consonant that shares properties of both segments. Notice that the epenthesized consonants are all non-sonorant, have the same place of articulation as the sonorant consonant to their left, and have the same voicing as the non-sonorant consonant to their right (see figure 2.23).

Vowels may also be inserted epenthetically. In Turkish, a word never begins with two consonants. When words are borrowed into Turkish, an epenthetic vowel is inserted between certain sequences of two initial consonants, creating a new and permissible sequence (see table 2.27). (While the reason for the differences among the inserted vowels need not concern us here, note that they are always high; see section 2.10 for more of these and other unfamiliar symbols.)

TABLE 2.26 Some examples of English consonant epenthesis		
Word	**Non-epenthesized pronunciation**	**Epenthesized pronunciation**
something	[sʌ̃mθɪ̃ŋ]	[sʌ̃mpθɪ̃ŋ]
warmth	[wormθ]	[wormpθ]
length	[lɛ̃ŋθ]	[lɛ̃ŋkθ]
prince	[prɪ̃ns]	[prɪ̃nts]
tenth	[tɛ̃nθ]	[tɛ̃ntθ]

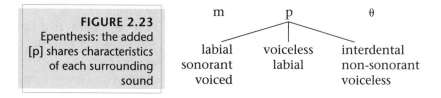

FIGURE 2.23
Epenthesis: the added [p] shares characteristics of each surrounding sound

TABLE 2.27	Vowel epenthesis in Turkish
Source word	**Turkish form**
train	[tɪren]
club	[kylʏp]
sport	[sɯpor]

Metathesis

Metathesis is a process that reorders a sequence of segments. This often results in a sequence of phones that is easier to articulate. It is common to hear metathesis in the speech of children, who often cannot pronounce all the consonant sequences that adults can. For example, some English-speaking children pronounce *spaghetti* as *pesghetti* [pəskɛɾi]. In this form, the initial sequence [spə], which is often difficult for children to pronounce, is metathesized to [pəs].

The pronunciations of *prescribe* and *prescription* as *perscribe* and *perscription* are often-cited examples of metathesis in adult speech. In these cases, metathesis appears to facilitate the pronunciation of a successive consonant-*r* sequence at the beginning of a word.

Vowel reduction

In many languages, the articulation of vowels may move to a more central position when the vowels are unstressed. This process is known as **vowel reduction**. Typically, the outcome of vowel reduction is a schwa [ə]; this can be observed in pairs of related words that show different stress placement, such as *Canada* [kʰǽnədə] versus *Canadian* [kʰənéjdiən]. If you listen carefully to these words, you'll notice that the first vowel is [æ] when stressed (in *Canada*) but schwa when unstressed (in *Canadian*). And the second vowel is [ej] when stressed (in *Canadian*) but schwa when unstressed (in *Canada*).

2.10 Other vowels and consonants

So far, this chapter has focused on the vowels and consonants of English. Many but not all of these sounds are found in other languages. Moreover, many of the sounds found in other languages do not occur in English. Tables 2.28 and 2.29 introduce a number of non-English vowels and consonants that are relevant to the discussion and problems throughout this book. Once the basic articulatory parameters have been understood, it's not a big jump to describe and to pronounce new and unfamiliar sounds.

Remember that phonetic descriptions are universal—they apply to the sounds of any human language. If you encounter the description 'voiced velar fricative', you know that the sound is a voiced continuant consonant made at the velum (i.e., the same place as the stop [g]). If you want to make this sound, the articulatory description can guide you: make a near closure at the velum, draw your vocal cords together, and allow airflow to pass through. If you come across the description 'high front rounded vowel' and want to produce this sound, make the high front unrounded vowel [i] and then round the lips to produce the high front rounded vowel [y].

For detailed descriptions and examples of the sounds presented in table 2.28, go to the Companion Website.

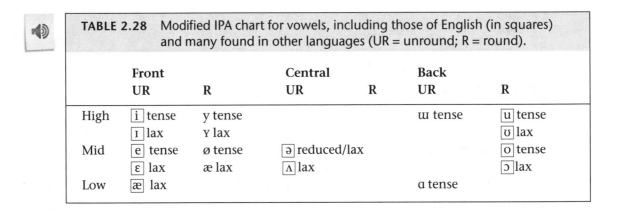

TABLE 2.28 Modified IPA chart for vowels, including those of English (in squares) and many found in other languages (UR = unround; R = round).

	Front		Central		Back	
	UR	R	UR	R	UR	R
High	$\boxed{i}$ tense	y tense			ɯ tense	$\boxed{u}$ tense
	$\boxed{ɪ}$ lax	ʏ lax				$\boxed{ʊ}$ lax
Mid	$\boxed{e}$ tense	ø tense	ə reduced/lax			$\boxed{o}$ tense
	$\boxed{ɛ}$ lax	æ lax	$\boxed{ʌ}$ lax			$\boxed{ɔ}$ lax
Low	$\boxed{æ}$ lax				ɑ tense	

TABLE 2.29 Modified IPA chart for consonants, including some of the sounds of English (in squares) and many sounds found in other languages. Voiceless phones are always on the left of pairs with the same place of articulation.

	Bilabial	Labiodental	Dental	Alveolar	Alveopalatal	Retroflex	Palatal	Velar	Uvular	Pharyngeal	Glottal
Stop	$\boxed{p}\boxed{b}$			$\boxed{t}\,\boxed{d}$		ʈ ɖ	c ɟ	$\boxed{k}\boxed{g}$	q ɢ		$\boxed{ʔ}$
Fricative	ɸ β	$\boxed{f}\boxed{v}$	$\boxed{θ\,ð}$	$\boxed{s}\,\boxed{z}$	$\boxed{ʃ}\boxed{ʒ}$	ʂ ʐ	ç ʝ	x ɣ	χ	ħ ʕ	$\boxed{h}$ ɦ
Nasal	$\boxed{m}$	ɱ		$\boxed{n}$		ɳ	ɲ	$\boxed{ŋ}$			
Trill				r̃					R		
Flap				$\boxed{ɾ}$							
Other *rs*				$\boxed{r}$							
Glide							ɥ $\boxed{j}$	ʍ $\boxed{w}$			
Lateral											
Liquid				$\boxed{l̩}\,\boxed{l}$			ʎ̥ ʎ				
Fricative				ɬ ɮ							

Summing up

The study of the sounds of human language is called **phonetics**. These sounds are widely transcribed by means of the **International Phonetic Alphabet.**

The sounds of language are commonly described in **articulatory** and **acoustic** terms and fall into two major types: syllabic sounds (**vowels, syllabic liquids,** and **syllabic nasals**) and non-syllabic sounds (**consonants** and **glides**). Sounds may be **voiced** or **voiceless,** and **oral** or **nasal.**

Consonants and glides are produced at various **places of articulation: labial, dental, alveolar, alveopalatal, palatal, velar, uvular, glottal,** and **pharyngeal.** At the places of articulation, the airstream is modified by different **manners of articulation** and the resulting sounds are **stops, fricatives, affricates, liquids,** or **glides.**

Vowels are produced with less drastic closure and are described with reference to tongue position (**high, mid, low, back,** and **front**), tension (**tense** or **lax**), and lip rounding (**rounded** or **unrounded**). Language also exhibits **suprasegmental** phenomena such as **tone, intonation,** and **stress.**

Notes

[1.] There is still a great deal of discussion among linguists on the subject of diphthongs. English vowels that show a change in quality are considered diphthongs as long as the change in quality *follows* the vowel nucleus. Words such as *yes* and *wet* are considered to begin with a glide that is not an integral part of the vocalic nucleus. However, in transcribing other languages (Finnish, for example), sounds like [jɛ] and [wo] are considered to be diphthongs. For now, treat the diphthongs presented in table 2.13 as single vowel segments and the initial two sounds of words like *yes* and *wet* as distinct segments.

[2.] The symbol [ʌ] is widely used by North American linguists to represent a mid central vowel (our practice here), even though standard IPA employs it as a symbol for a mid, fully back vowel. See Peter Ladefoged and Keith Johnson, *A Course in Phonetics*, 7th ed. (Stamford, CT: Cengage Learning, 2015), 95–96.

Recommended reading

Catford, J.C. 2001. *A Practical Introduction to Phonetics*. 2nd ed. New York, NY: Oxford University Press.

Kent, Ray D., and Charles Read. 2002. *The Acoustic Analysis of Speech*. 2nd ed. San Diego, CA: Singular Publishing Group.

Ladefoged, Peter, and Keith Johnson. 2015. *A Course in Phonetics*. 7th ed. Stamford, CT: Cengage Learning.

Ladefoged, Peter, and Ian Maddieson. 1995. *The Sounds of the World's Languages.* Cambridge, MA: Blackwell.

Pullum, Geoffrey K., and William A. Ladusaw. 1996. *Phonetic Symbol Guide*. 2nd ed. Chicago: University of Chicago Press.

Rogers, Henry. 1991. *Theoretical and Practical Phonetics*. Toronto: Copp Clark Pitman.
Shearer, William M. 1968. *Illustrated Speech Anatomy*. Springfield, IL: Charles C. Thomas.
Walker, Douglas C. 1984. *The Pronunciation of Canadian French*. Ottawa: University of Ottawa Press.

Exercises

1. In order to become more aware of the difference between English spelling and pronunciation, do the following:
   a) Give as many examples as you can of different ways to pronounce the letter 'u'.
   b) Give two examples of words where the 'gh' in the spelling is pronounced (e.g., 'cough') and two examples of words where the 'gh' in the spelling is not pronounced (e.g., 'taught').
   c) Give examples of different letter combinations that can represent the [ej] sound in English spelling.

2. How many segments are there in the following words?
   a) up
   b) think
   c) pour
   d) walked
   e) pterodactyl
   f) exhibit
   g) attack
   h) offending

3. Is the first sound in each of the following words voiced or voiceless?
   a) thus
   b) moth
   c) xylophone
   d) chasm
   e) Victoria
   f) Honolulu
   g) post
   h) thumb
   i) sure
   j) lumpy
   k) doll
   l) unite
   m) wing
   n) ghoul
   o) knee
   p) juice

4. Using the words in question 3, state whether the last sound of each word is voiced or voiceless.

5. For each of the following pairs of sounds, state whether they have the same or different places of articulation. Then identify the place of articulation for each sound.
   a) [g] : [ŋ] velar
   b) [p] : [k] bilabial, velar
   c) [t] : [d] alveolar
   d) [w] : [j] glides but labialvelar or velar
   e) [m] : [n] labial alveolar
   f) [ð] : [s] dental, alveolar
   g) [θ] : [ð] dental v/voiced
   h) [s] : [t]
   i) [t] : [tʃ]
   j) [f] : [v]
   k) [l] : [r]
   l) [h] : [ʃ]

6. For each of the following pairs of sounds, state whether they have the same or different manners of articulation. Then identify the manner of articulation for each sound.
   a) [b] : [t]
   b) [d] : [z]
   c) [v] : [h]
   d) [tʃ] : [dʒ]
   e) [v] : [θ]
   f) [l] : [r]
   g) [w] : [j]
   h) [m] : [ŋ]
   i) [tʃ] : [ʃ]
   j) [l] : [j]
   k) [b] : [g]
   l) [p] : [f]

7. For each of the following articulatory descriptions, write the symbol for the sound described.

a) voiced velar stop g
b) voiced palatal glide j
c) voiceless labiodental fricative f
d) voiced bilabial nasal m

e) voiceless alveolar fricative s
f) high back rounded tense vowel u
g) voiced interdental fricative ð
h) low front unrounded vowel

8. Which of the following pairs of words have the same vowel? Mark each pair as *same* or *different*. Then transcribe the vowel in each word.

a) ban   hand *same* æ
b) push ʊ   food u *different*
c) cot   bought *same* ɑ
d) ghost   lock
e) mush   what
f) seem   sit
g) catch   watch

h) nail   whale
i) line   take
j) cloud   run
k) plan   hat
l) lunch   whoosh
m) bid   key
n) get   frame

9. Find a generalization that applies to the members of the following groups of sounds. *Example:* [b d g u m j] are all *voiced*. Avoid overly general answers such as 'consonant' or 'vowel'.

a) [p t k g]
b) [u ʊ o]
c) [ɪ ɛ æ ʊ] *Unrounded, lax p.78 vowels*
d) [aj aw oj]

e) [f v θ z h]
f) [t d n l r]
g) [p t k s f θ tʃ]
h) [v ð ʒ æ] *voiced fricatives?*
?

10. Transcribe the following words.

a) rich
b) goes
c) things
d) debt
e) could
f) jug
g) ridge
h) ghost

i) myth
j) shock
k) top
l) gem
m) guess
n) vex
o) wrong
p) Butch

q) crows
r) Scotch
s) yes
t) should
u) cup
v) lathe
w) buff
x) sham

11. Transcribe the following words paying particular attention to whether the voiceless stops are aspirated.

a) tog
b) kid
c) attain
d) despise
e) elbow
f) haul
g) juice dʒus
h) thimble

i) peas
j) stun
k) Oscar
l) cooler
m) sigh
n) hulk
o) explode
p) tube

q) spell
r) cord
s) accord
t) astound
u) pool
v) wheeze
w) remove
x) clinical

12. Using H, L, and association lines, transcribe the intonation of the following English phrases. Compare your results with the transcriptions of some classmates. Are they the same? If they aren't, what factors (e.g., emotion or context) might account for the differences?
    a) Are you leaving?
    b) What are you doing over there?
    c) Take a seat, please.

13. Mark primary and (where necessary) secondary stresses on the following words. It is not necessary to transcribe them.   *primary /*
                                                                                                                           secondary
    a) Cánada   f) (the) récord   k) Canádianìze
    b) bóokcàse   →compound g) (to) recórd   l) góvernment
    c) retùrn   →word 2 stress h) cínema   m) governméntal
    d) greenhouse   i) attáin   n) contról
    e) anecdote   j) aróma   o) Vancouver Canucks

14. Find a fluent speaker of a language other than English and transcribe phonetically ten words of that language. If you encounter any sounds for which symbols are not found in this chapter, attempt to describe them in phonetic terms and then invent diacritics to help you transcribe them.

15. Compare the careful speech and rapid speech pronunciations of the following English words and phrases. Then name the process or processes that make the rapid speech pronunciation different from the careful speech. (Stress is omitted here.)

	Careful speech	Rapid speech
a) in my room	[ɪn maj rum]	[ɪm maj rum] *regressive assimilation to the sound after*
b) I see them	[aj si ðɛm]	[aj siəm]
c) I see him	[aj si hɪm]	[aj siəm]
d) within	[wɪθɪn]	[wɪðɪn] *two vowels/voicing?*
e) balloons	[bəlunz]	[blunz]
f) popsicle	[pʰapsɪkʰəl]	[pʰapskəl] *vowel deletion*
g) sit down	[sɪt dawn]	[sɪɾawn]
h) sandwich	[sændwɪtʃ]	[sæmwɪtʃ]
i) Scotch tape	[skatʃ tʰejp]	[kʰatʃ stejp]
j) protection	[pɹowtʰɛkʃən]	[pətʰɛkʃən]
k) Toronto	[təɹanow]	[tɹanə]
l) Pam will seat you	[pʰæm wɪl sit ju]	[pʰæml̩sitʃju]

To learn more about the topics discussed in this chapter and listen to the audio exercises, visit the Companion Website for *Contemporary Linguistic Analysis*.

WILLIAM O'GRADY | CARRIE DYCK | YVAN ROSE |
EWA CZAYKOWSKA-HIGGINS | MICHAEL DOBROVOLSKY

3

Phonology: contrasts and patterns

A person's tongue is a twisty thing, there are plenty of words there of every kind, and the range of words is wide, and their variation.

HOMER, *THE ILIAD*

AS THE study of phonetics shows, human beings can produce and perceive a very large number of speech sounds. Of course, no human language exploits *all* of these possibilities. Instead, every language makes its own particular selection from the range of possible speech sounds and organizes them into a system of contrasts and patterns. This system makes up a language's **phonology.**

Phonological analysis takes place at three levels. First, and most obviously, it is concerned with the relationships among individual speech sounds, or segments. But there is also a need for analysis at both a higher level and a lower level.

At a higher level, it is necessary to think about how sounds are organized into syllables, units of phonological organization that are crucial to the patterning of sounds, as we will soon see. And at a lower level, we must consider features—the articulatory and acoustic building blocks of sounds that are also crucial to understanding why sound systems have the particular contrasts and patterns that they do. Let's begin by looking at segments and how they are used to make the contrasts that allow us to distinguish words from each other.

3.1 Segments

Speakers make dozens, perhaps hundreds, of phonetic distinctions as they use their language. One such distinction, which is easy to notice for speakers of English, is the difference between [n] and [ŋ] in words like *win* [wɪn] and *wing* [wɪŋ].

Another distinction, which is much less obvious, involves the difference between the [n] in *one time*, which is alveolar (the tip of the tongue makes contact with the alveolar ridge), and the [n̪] in *one thing*, which is dental (the tip of the tongue touches the back of the upper front teeth).

[wʌn] *one time*   [wʌn̪] *one thing*

This is a real difference, but you'll notice it only if you pay deliberate attention to exactly where the tip of your tongue touches as you say *one* in each of these phrases.

What is happening here is that 'n' has a dental pronunciation in front of another dental consonant (the [θ] of *thing*) but retains its usual alveolar place of articulation elsewhere. This is an automatic adjustment, of which speakers are typically not even conscious since it doesn't affect the meaning of the word *one*. But the choice of the final consonant in *win* and *wing* is deliberate and creates a contrast between two different words. Herein lies a key insight of phonological analysis.

3.1.1 Phonemes and allophones

A major objective of phonology is to organize a language's sounds into **contrastive segments** called **phonemes**, based on whether the sounds can be used to distinguish between words. For example, the sounds [n] and [ŋ] are assigned to separate phonemes in English, since the difference between them can be used to distinguish one word from another—as in *win* versus *wing* or *sun* versus *sung*. On the other hand, [n] and [n̪] are analyzed as **allophones**, or variants, of the same phoneme, since the difference between them is not used to distinguish between words in English.

When representing a phoneme and its allophones, we co-opt the symbol for the most widely used allophone (if there is more than one) to represent the phoneme, which we write between slashes. The phonological status of the sounds [n], [n̪], and [ŋ] can be represented as follows:

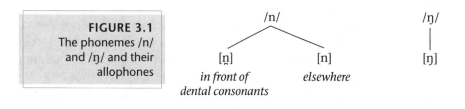

FIGURE 3.1
The phonemes /n/ and /ŋ/ and their allophones

As depicted here, the sounds [n] and [n̪] are allophones of the same phoneme because they don't contrast with each other. On the other hand, /n/ and /ŋ/ are separate phonemes because of the contrasts into which they enter (*win – wing*, etc.).

The same sort of analysis applies to vowels. If you're a native speaker of English, it's easy to hear the difference between [i] and [ɪ] in words like *beat* [bit] and *bit* [bɪt]. So we know that there's a phoneme /i/ and a phoneme /ɪ/. But notice that the /i/ in *beat* is shorter than the /i/ in *bead*.

      [bit] *beat*   [biːd] *bead*

What is happening here, roughly speaking, is that English vowels of all types are automatically lengthened in front of voiced **obstruents** (oral stops, fricatives, and affricates) like [d] but not in other positions. Although this difference is a natural part of speech in English, it is not used to distinguish between words—even if you deliberately lengthen the vowel in *beat*, it's still the same word. This tells us that [iː] and [i] should be assigned to the same phoneme, as illustrated in figure 3.2.

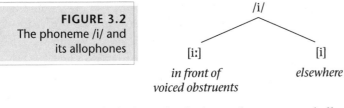

FIGURE 3.2
The phoneme /i/ and its allophones

It might help to think about phonemes and allophones as follows. Phonemes are mental categories—they exist in your mind for the purpose of creating contrasts among words. Allophones are physical sounds that occur in particular positions when words are spoken—they are produced in your vocal tract as you speak.

Organizing a language's sounds into phonemes requires special attention to two factors—minimal pairs and complementary distribution.

3.1.2 Minimal pairs

A **minimal pair** consists of two words that differ by only one segment in the same position. Thus, *win* and *wing* make up a minimal pair since they differ only in terms of their final consonant. And *beat* and *bit* constitute a minimal pair since they too differ by just one segment (the vowel in the middle of the word). Here are some additional examples.

(1) Some other minimal pairs:

    a. contrast in initial position:

        [**s**ɪp] *sip* — [**z**ɪp] *zip*

    b. contrast in medial position:

        [i**θ**ɚ] *ether* — [i**ð**ɚ] *either*

    c. contrast in final position:

        [sʌ**m**] *sum* — [sʌ**n**] *sun*

When two sounds can create a minimal pair, we know that they belong to separate phonemes. So /s/ and /z/ are separate phonemes, as are /θ/ and /ð/, and /m/ and /n/.

Table 3.1 presents some minimal pairs that illustrate various consonant contrasts in English. It is important to remember that minimal pairs are established on the basis of sound and not spelling, so *cheap* and *jeep* make up a minimal pair despite the multiple differences in the way they are spelled.

TABLE 3.1	Some consonant contrasts in English						
feel	/f/	*thigh*	/θ/	*sip*	/s/	*cheap*	/tʃ/
veal	/v/	*thy*	/ð/	*zip*	/z/	*jeep*	/dʒ/
sum	/m/	*leaf*	/l/	*yet*	/j/		
sun	/n/	*reef*	/ɾ/	*wet*	/w/		
sung	/ŋ/						

As the examples in Table 3.2 show, vowel contrasts in English can also be established with the help of minimal pairs. (For now, we will treat diphthongs as single segments.)

TABLE 3.2   Some vowel contrasts in English

beet	/i/		*bait*	/ej/
bit	/ɪ/		*bet*	/ɛ/
bat	/æ/			
cooed	/u/		*coat*	/ow/
could	/ʊ/		*cot*	/ɑ/[1]
			cut	/ʌ/
loud	/aw/			
lied	/aj/			
Lloyd	/oj/			

3.1.3 Complementary distribution

How do we go about identifying allophones of the same phoneme—such as [n] and [n̪] or [i] and [iː] in English? Non-contrastive differences like these typically arise when a segment's articulation is affected by its neighbours: that is, it has one pronunciation in one position or **environment** and another pronunciation in other environments. When two sounds occur in non-overlapping, (i.e., mutually exclusive) environments, they are said to be in **complementary distribution.**

As we have seen, English [n̪] and [n] work this way: we find dental [n̪] in front of other dental sounds (like [θ] and [ð]), and we find [n] elsewhere.

(2) An example of complementary distribution:

    a. [n̪] occurs in front of dental consonants such as [θ] and [ð]:

       one thing, on them, in there

    b. [n] occurs elsewhere:

       one ship, one egg, one cent, one dollar

And of course English [iː] and [i] are in complementary distribution too: [iː] occurs in front of voiced obstruents, and [i] occurs elsewhere—in front of voiceless obstruents like [t] in *heat* and [s] in *cease*, in front of the nasal consonant in *lean*, and so on.

(3) Another example of complementary distribution:

    a. [iː] occurs in front of voiced obstruents:

       heed, seize, leave

    b. [i] occurs elsewhere:

       heat, cease, leaf, lean, sea

In sum, phonetic distinctions may or may not create contrasts that distinguish between words. When they do, the sounds in question belong to separate phonemes; when they don't, the sounds in question are allophones of the same phoneme. An appendix at the end of the chapter lays out a detailed procedure for identifying a language's phonemes and allophones.

Canadian Raising

An example of complementary distribution that is strongly associated with Canadian English involves the diphthongs /aj/ and /aw/. In the speech of most Canadian English speakers, the vowel portion of these diphthongs raises to /ʌ/ in certain positions. This phenomenon has been dubbed **Canadian Raising** (although it is also heard in some varieties of American speech).

TABLE 3.3	Some examples of Canadian Raising		
Raising		**No raising**	
[ʌjs]	ice	[ajz]	eyes
[lʌjs]	lice	[lajz]	lies
[trʌjt]	trite	[trajd]	tried
[trʌjp]	tripe	[trajb]	tribe
[flʌjt]	flight	[flaj]	fly
[hʌws]	house (noun)	[hawz]	(to) house (verb)
[lʌwt]	lout	[lawd]	loud
[skʌwt]	scout	[kaw]	cow

As you can see, the diphthongs [ʌj] and [aj] are in complementary distribution: [ʌj] occurs before the class of voiceless consonants ([s, t, p], etc.) and [aj] occurs elsewhere. A parallel relationship holds between the vowels [aw] and [ʌw] (see figure 3.3).

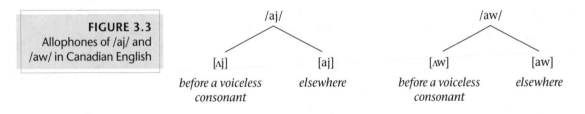

FIGURE 3.3
Allophones of /aj/ and /aw/ in Canadian English

3.1.4 Differences in phonemes across languages

Sounds that contrast with each other in one language might not do so in another. For example, the difference between the vowels [ɛ] and [æ] is crucial to English, as we can see from minimal pairs like *Ben* [bɛn] and *ban* [bæn]. But in Turkish, this difference is not contrastive. A Turkish speaker may pronounce the word for 'I' as [bɛn] or [bæn], with no difference in meaning.

TABLE 3.4	Language-specific vowel contrasts: Canadian English versus Turkish		
Canadian English		**Turkish**	
[bɛn]	'Ben'	[bɛn]	'I'
[bæn]	'ban'	[bæn]	'I'

Conversely, sounds that do not contrast in English, such as long and short vowels, may contrast in another language. There are no minimal pairs of the type [si]/[siː] in English. But in Japanese and many other languages, short and long vowels contrast, as the examples in table 3.5 show.

TABLE 3.5	Short/long vowel contrasts in Japanese		
[tori]	'bird'	[odzisan]	'uncle'
[toriː]	'shrine gate'	[odziːsan]	'grandfather'

So whereas the sounds [iː] and [i] belong to the same phoneme in English, they belong to different phonemes in Japanese.

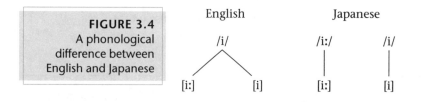

FIGURE 3.4
A phonological difference between English and Japanese

An analysis of voiceless stops in English and Khmer (Cambodian) illustrates the same point.

TABLE 3.6	Voiceless stops in English and Khmer		
English		**Khmer**	
[p]	[pʰ]	[p]	[pʰ]
[t]	[tʰ]	[t]	[tʰ]
[k]	[kʰ]	[k]	[kʰ]

As can be seen in table 3.6, both languages have aspirated and unaspirated voiceless stops. In English, the difference between the two types of stop is not contrastive: there are no minimal pairs like [pɪk] and [pʰɪk]. In Khmer, though, unaspirated and aspirated voiceless stops contrast with each other, as the minimal pairs in table 3.7 show.

TABLE 3.7	Some Khmer minimal pairs				
[pɔːŋ]	'to wish'	[tɔp]	'to support'	[kat]	'to cut'
[pʰɔːŋ]	'also'	[tʰɔp]	'be suffocated'	[kʰat]	'to polish'

So although English and Khmer have phonetically similar sounds, they are very different phonologically, as figure 3.5 shows.

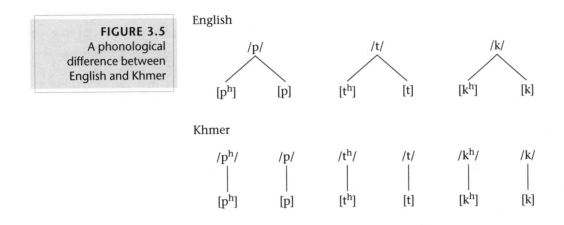

FIGURE 3.5
A phonological difference between English and Khmer

Language Matters What about Dental and Alveolar *n*?

The distinction between dental [n̪] and alveolar [n] is not contrastive in English. That seems natural to us, since the difference seems so hard to hear. But in some languages, that very difference is used to distinguish between words, and there are minimal pairs to prove it. One such language is Malayalam (a Dravidian language of south India); another is Arrernte (a language of Australia), from which the following minimal pair is taken.

[n̪əmə] 'fall (rain)'   [nəmə] 'sit'

You know what that means—/n̪/ and /n/ are separate phonemes in Arrernte and Malayalam.

Source: Based on V. Anderson, *The Perception of Coronals in Western Arrernte*, Proceedings of the Fifth European Conference on Speech Communication and Technology 1 (1997): 389–92.

3.1.5 Two things to watch for

As we've already seen, the simplest and best way to show that two sounds contrast with each other (that is, that they belong to separate phonemes) is to find a minimal pair. Occasionally, though, gaps in a language's vocabulary make it difficult to find minimal pairs for contrasting sounds. Under these circumstances, it is sometimes possible to rely on **near-minimal pairs** that contain differences other than the one involving the key contrast, as long as the extra differences don't involve sounds right next to the contrast. One such example in English is [mɪʃən] and [vɪʒən], *mission and vision*. Although not a perfect minimal pair, these words can help establish that [ʃ] and [ʒ] contrast with each other if actual minimal pairs are not available. (In fact, there are a few minimal pairs for the [ʃ]/[ʒ] distinction, such as *mesher* and *measure*, but they are few and far between, and could easily be missed.)

Sometimes, even near-minimal pairs are not available to establish that two sounds contrast with each other. A notorious example of this involves [h] and [ŋ] in English. Because [h] occurs only at the beginning of syllables and [ŋ] occurs only at the end of syllables, we don't find the usual minimal or near-minimal pairs. There are lots of words like *hope* and *ham*, with [h] in initial position, but no words like *ngope* and *ngam* to contrast with them. And there are lots of words like *long* and *king*, with [ŋ] in final position, but no words like *loh* and *kih*. This does not mean that [h] and [ŋ] are allophones of the same phoneme, though. As our earlier definition makes clear, the allophones of a phoneme must be phonetically similar to each other. Because [h] and [ŋ] are so different phonetically, we can be confident in assigning them to separate phonemes even in the absence of minimal and near-minimal pairs.

Special cases like these occur infrequently and, for the most part, they can be ignored in beginning work on phonology—unless of course your instructor decides otherwise.

3.1.6 Differences in the distribution of allophones across languages

Just as the phonemic contrasts found in each language are specific to that language, so the distribution of individual allophones can vary from language to language. The phenomenon of vowel nasalization illustrates this.

It is common to have nasal allophones for vowels when there is a nasal consonant nearby. In English, for example, vowels are nasal in front of nasal consonants but not after them. By placing a finger on the side of your nose, you may be able to feel the nasal vibrations in the vowel of *on* and *bunk*, especially if you pronounce these words slowly. In contrast, you'll feel few, if any, nasal vibrations for the vowel in *no* or *neat*.

TABLE 3.8 Nasalization in English	
In front of a nasal consonant (nasalization)	**After a nasal consonant (little or no nasalization)**
on [ãn]	*no* [now]
bunk [bᴀ̃ŋk]	*neat* [nit]

As a first approximation, we can summarize this pattern as follows.

(4) In English, nasal allophones of vowels are found right before a nasal consonant.

In Scots Gaelic, however, vowels are nasalized on both sides of a nasal consonant.

TABLE 3.9 Nasalization in Scots Gaelic			
Before a nasal consonant		**After a nasal consonant**	
[rũːn]	'secret'	[mõːr]	'big'
		[nĩ]	'cattle'
		[nẽːl]	'cloud'

The generalization governing the distribution of nasal vowels in Scots Gaelic can be stated as follows.

(5) Nasal allophones of vowels in Scots Gaelic are found right before or right after a nasal consonant.

3.1.7 Phonetic and phonological representations

So far, we have seen that each language has a set of contrastive phonemes (which can be established largely by means of the minimal pair test) and that phonemes can have predictable phonetic variants or allophones (which are in complementary distribution with each other). A word can be represented either phonemically or phonetically (allophonically), depending on the amount and type of information that is relevant.

Whereas a word's **phonological representation** consists only of its component phonemes, its **phonetic representation** carries additional information about phonetic details—including aspiration, devoicing of liquids, vowel lengthening, nasalization, and so on. These details are predictable in English: simplifying just a bit, a voiceless stop is aspirated in front of a vowel, a liquid that occurs after a voiceless stop is voiceless, a vowel that occurs right before a nasal consonant is nasalized, and so on.

Because these phonetic characteristics have nothing to do with contrasts between words, they don't belong in the phonological representation; the place for non-contrastive details of this sort is in the phonetic representation, as illustrated in table 3.10. (Since phonetic representations become very complex if every fine point of speech is included, it is common to omit phonetic details that are not directly relevant to the point under discussion. We follow that practice here.)

TABLE 3.10	Sample phonemic and phonetic representations in English		
Word	Phonemic representation	Phonetic representation	Extra information in the phonetic representation
tied	/tajd/	[tʰajd]	aspiration
creep	/krip/	[kr̥ip]	voicelessness of the liquid
bead	/bid/	[biːd]	vowel lengthening
on	/ɑn/	[ɑ̃n]	nasalization of the vowel

Remember that the phonemic representation corresponds to what is in your head, while the phonetic representation corresponds to what comes out of your mouth. Because phonetic details are added as we speak, the phonetic representation ends up being much more specific than the phonemic representation, which includes only contrasts that distinguish between words.

Mid vowels and glides in English

Sometimes it is possible to predict not only the choice of allophones in the phonetic representation, but also the appearance of entirely new segments. One example of this concerns the mid tense vowels [e] and [o], which are diphthongized in most dialects of English: [e] occurs with [j], as in [dej] *day*, and [o] occurs with [w], as in [dow] *dough*. The choice of glide is not arbitrary: [w] is back and rounded, just like [o], and [j] is non-back and unrounded, like [e].

[dej] *day*	[dow] *dough*
[e] + [j]	[o] + [w]
(both non-back and unrounded)	(both back and rounded)

The following generalization states the distribution of the two glides.

(6) A mid tense vowel in English is predictably followed by a glide that has the same backness and roundness.[2]

Thus, although the phonetic representations of English mid tense vowels include the glides, the corresponding phonemic representations do not (see table 3.11).

TABLE 3.11   Phonemic and phonetic representations for English mid tense vowels

Word	Phonemic representation	Phonetic representation	Extra segment in the phonetic representation
day	/de/	[dej]	the glide [j]
dough	/do/	[dow]	the glide [w]

Once again, we see that the phonemic representation contains only information that is not predictable. Phonetic details—whether they are about vowel nasalization or which glide follows a mid vowel—are added later. We'll return to this point in section 3.4, where we discuss the operations that add these details.

3.2 Syllables

The syllable is a highly perceptible phonological unit. Speakers of a language are generally aware of syllables, and they typically have no trouble counting them. (A dot is used to mark the boundary between two syllables.)

TABLE 3.12   Some examples of English syllables

/ə.plɑd/	*applaud*
/di.klajn/	*decline*
/ɛk.sɪt/	*exit*
/ɪm.prə.vajz/	*improvise*

What most speakers don't consciously know, however, is just how important syllables are to the phonology of their language.

> ### Language Matters **That's Not the Right Word**
>
> Syllables also matter for how words are organized in our mental dictionary. We can see this in *malapropisms*—mischosen words such as *equivocal* for *equivalent*, *emanate* for *emulate*, or *participate* for *precipitate*. Malapropisms tend to be phonologically similar to the intended word, and in the vast majority of cases, they have the same number of syllables, too.
>
> Source: Based on D. Faye and A. Cutler, "Malapropisms and the Structure of the Mental Lexicon," *Linguistic Inquiry* 8 (1977): 505–20.

3.2.1 Types of syllable patterns

Languages vary from each other in terms of the complexity of the syllables that they allow. In some languages, a (C)V template is strictly followed—all syllables consist of either a vowel by itself or a consonant followed by a vowel. Hawaiian works this way. The Hawaiian greeting *aloha* illustrates both types of syllables within a single word:

/a.lo.ha/
V.CV.CV

When a word with a different type of syllable structure is borrowed into Hawaiian from another language, adjustments have to be made. That's why the borrowed English word *cloak* /klok/ is pronounced /ko.lo.ka/ in Hawaiian, with each syllable consisting of a consonant and a vowel.

Korean has the somewhat more complex syllable template (C)V(C)—it allows the syllable types exemplified in table 3.13.

TABLE 3.13	Syllable types in Korean	
V only:	/i/	'teeth'
CV:	/pʰa/	'onion'
VC:	/il/	'work'
CVC:	/son/	'hand'

French is one step more complex in that it allows up to two consonants at the beginning and end of its syllables.

TABLE 3.14	Some syllable types in French	
V only:	/o/	*eau* 'water'
CV:	/fu/	*fou* 'fool'
CVC:	/mas/	*masse* 'mass'
CCV:	/pri/	*prix* 'prize'
VCC:	/ɛst/	*est* 'east'

Still more complex is the syllable template for English, which allows up to three consonants at the beginning of a syllable, as in *stream* /strim/, and up to four at the end, as in *sixths*

/sɪksθs/. Very few words have this sort of complexity in their syllable structure, however, and special constraints are in play in such cases. For instance, three-consonant sequences are possible at the beginning of a syllable only if the first consonant is /s/, the second a voiceless stop, and the third a liquid or glide, as happens in *stream, spring, squeak,* and so forth. The term **phonotactics** is used for the branch of phonology that is concerned with permissible combinations of phonemes.

Although English allows many different types of syllables, not all phonotactic possibilities are permitted, of course. That is why English-speaking students learning Russian often react to the consonant cluster at the beginning of a word like *vprog* (/fprɔk/ 'value, good') by either adding a vowel (/fəprɔk/) or deleting the initial consonant (/prɔk/).

Some phonotactic constraints are quite language-specific (like the prohibition against having more than one consonant at the beginning of a syllable). Others are much more general: very few languages allow a syllable to begin with a liquid followed by a stop (compare /lbu/ to /blu/ *blue,* with the reverse order). In section 3.2.3, we will consider two principles that help explain why some phonotactic sequences are more likely than others in the world's languages.

3.2.2 Syllable structure

Syllables comply with the following basic design in all languages.

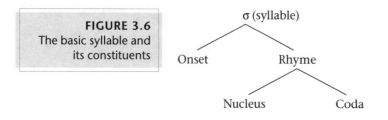

FIGURE 3.6
The basic syllable and its constituents

In the vast majority of languages, nuclei have to be vowels or diphthongs. However, some languages are more permissive. For example, English allows sonorant consonants to function as syllabic nuclei in words such as *rhythm* /rɪ.ðm̩/ or *pickle* /pɪ.kl̩/. (A consonant that functions as a syllabic nucleus is marked by the diacritic [̩] and is often called a 'syllabic consonant'.)

All languages appear to allow an **onset** consisting of at least one consonant to the left of the nucleus, and some even require that every syllable have an onset (e.g., Senufo, Klamath). As we have already seen, there are differences among languages in terms of how many consonants appear in onsets—Korean allows just one, French permits two, English allows up to three, and so on.

Many languages permit a **coda** consisting of one or more consonants to the right of the nucleus, but many ban codas altogether (e.g., Hua, Cayuvava, and Sesotho, in addition to Hawaiian), and no language requires that every syllable have a coda. In addition, we often find a larger number of consonant types in onsets than in codas. For example, German allows both voiced and voiceless obstruents in onsets, but any obstruent in a coda must be voiceless. That's why the German word for 'dog', *Hund,* is pronounced [hʊnt].

> ### Language Matters Why Rhymes Are Called Rhymes
>
> It's no coincidence that the word *rhyme* is used for the portion of the syllable consisting of the nucleus and the coda (if there is a coda). As you can see by considering the following excerpt from a poem by Bliss Carman, that is the part of a syllable that creates rhyming in poetry. Pay special attention to the ends of the first and third lines, and to the ends of the second and fourth lines.
>
>> Where are the ships I used to know,
>> That came to port on the Fundy tide
>> Half a century ago,
>> In beauty and stately pride?
>
> Excerpted from "The Ships of Saint John" by Bliss Carman (1861–1929)

Building syllable structure

A simple three-step procedure governs the construction of syllables.

Step a *Nucleus formation:* Since the syllable nucleus is the only obligatory constituent of a syllable, it is constructed first. Each vowel segment in a word makes up a syllabic **nucleus**. To represent this, link a vowel to an N (for nucleus) symbol above it by drawing an association line. Above each N, place an R symbol (for **rhyme**), and above that, place a σ symbol (for syllable).

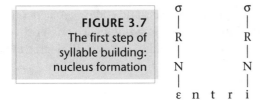

FIGURE 3.7
The first step of syllable building: nucleus formation

Step b *Onset formation:* The longest permissible sequence of consonants to the left of each nucleus is the onset of the syllable. Link these consonants to an O(nset) symbol and join it to the σ symbol above the vowel to the right (see figure 3.8). In the word *entry*, the first syllable has no onset. The second nucleus is preceded by three consonants, but the longest permissible sequence is just /tr/—recall that English allows three consonants in a row at the beginning of a syllable only if the first one is /s/.

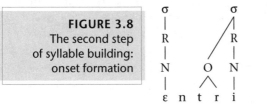

FIGURE 3.8
The second step of syllable building: onset formation

Step c *Coda formation:* Any remaining unassociated consonants to the right of each nucleus form the coda and are linked to a C(oda) symbol above them. This coda is then associated with the syllable nucleus, making up the rhyme. A syllable with a coda is called a **closed syllable**, while a syllable without a coda is called **open**. As can be seen in figure 3.9, the first syllable in *entry* is closed and the second one is open.

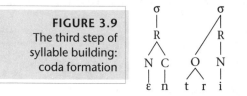

FIGURE 3.9
The third step of syllable building: coda formation

Language Matters Speaking Pig Latin

One version of the English language game known as Pig Latin is played by displacing the onset of the first syllable of a word to the end of the word and then tacking on the vowel *ay* [ej]: thus, *long* becomes *ong-l-ay*, and *sweet* becomes *eet-sw-ay*.

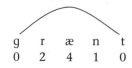

This provides evidence that syllable onsets are a real part of speakers' linguistic knowledge.

3.2.3 Basic syllables

In languages that allow more than one consonant to appear in onsets and codas, two general principles apply; syllables that follow these principles are called **basic syllables**. The first principle, the **Sonority Requirement**, makes reference to sonority (roughly, a sound's degree of resonance).

(7) *The Sonority Requirement*
    In basic syllables, sonority rises before the nucleus and declines after the nucleus.

A sonority scale is provided in figure 3.10, with the numbers from 0 to 4 indicating relative sonority levels. (Remember that an obstruent is an oral stop, a fricative, or an affricate.)

FIGURE 3.10
The sonority scale

0	1	2	3	4
Obstruent	Nasal	Liquid	Glide	Vowel

The sonority profile of basic syllables can be seen in a monosyllabic word like *grant* /grænt/. There is rising sonority within the onset, peak sonority at the nucleus, and falling sonority within the coda. The nucleus represents the peak of sonority in the syllable.

FIGURE 3.11
The sonority profile of *grant*

g   r   æ   n   t
0   2   4   1   0

In contrast, there are no words such as */rgænt/, with falling sonority in the onset.

```
r    g    æ    n    t
2    0    4
↑    ↑
```

falling sonority in the onset

And there are no words such as *gratn*, with rising sonority in the coda.

```
g    r    æ    t    n
0    2    4    0    1
               ↑    ↑
```

rising sonority in the coda

Don't be fooled by words such as *button* /bʌtn̩/. It consists of two syllables: /bʌ.tn̩/, with /t/ in the onset of the second syllable and /n̩/ functioning as the nucleus.

TABLE 3.15   Some onsets in English that comply with the Sonority Requirement

Labial + sonorant		Alveolar + sonorant		Velar + sonorant	
/pl/	please	/tr/	trade	/kl/	clean
/pr/	proud	/tw/	twin	/kr/	cream
/pj/	pure	/sr/	Sri Lanka	/kw/	queen
/br/	bring	/sl/	slow	/kj/	cute
/bl/	blight	/dr/	dry	/gr/	grow
/fr/	free			/gl/	glow

The second major principle with which basic syllables must comply is the **Binarity Requirement,** which can be stated as follows.

(8) *The Binarity Requirement*
    Within basic syllables, each constituent can be at most binary (i.e., branching into two).

This means that an onset or coda can't contain more than two consonants. Thus, a word such as *grant*, with two consonants in its onset and two in its coda, represents the most complex basic syllable permitted in English.

FIGURE 3.12
The syllable structure
of *grant*

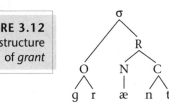

3.2.4 Syllables with a more complex structure

In fact, of course, English permits syllables whose structure is more complex than that of *grant*—for example, *stream* has three consonants in its onset, and *ranks* has three in its coda. Not only do these syllables have too many consonants in their onsets and codas (remember the Binary Requirement), but they also violate the Sonority Requirement. In *stream*, the initial /st/ has a flat rather than rising sonority profile—both segments are voiceless obstruents. And in *ranks*, the final /ks/ is also flat, rather than falling.

```
s   t   r   i   m          r   æ   ŋ   k   s
0   0   2                      1   0   0
↑   ↑                              ↑   ↑
```
flat sonority in the onset   *flat sonority in the coda*

Interestingly, such complex syllables are rare in the world's language and are subject to special restrictions in languages in which they occur.

- ■ 'Extra' consonants tend to occur at word edges—either at the beginning or the end, as in the case of the /s/ in *stream* and *ranks*, rather than in the middle.
- ■ In English, only /s/ can serve as an 'extra' consonant in onsets, which is why all CCC onsets begin with /s/ (*stream*, *split*, *scream*, etc.). In coda position, the 'extra' consonant is always voiceless and made with the tip of the tongue, such as the /s/ in *ranks* /ræŋks/, the /t/ in *clamped* /klæmpt/, and the /θ/ in *twelfth* /twɛlfθ/. It's also worth noting that the extra coda consonant in these and many other cases is not an inherent part of the word—it's added as a grammatical ending (suffix) to mark past tense, plurality, or some other contrast.

When drawing the structure of these more complex syllables, some linguists indicate the marginal status of consonants that violate the Sonority and/or Binarity Requirements by placing them in an **appendix** position, outside the onset or coda of the syllable with which they are associated.

FIGURE 3.13
Appendix consonants

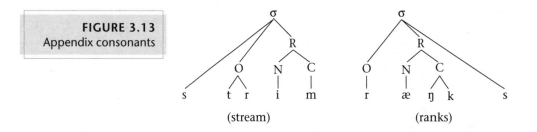

(stream)   (ranks)

Violations of the Sonority and Binarity Requirements are also common in Russian (to take just one example), which permits the onset sequences illustrated in table 3.16, among others.

TABLE 3.16   Some onset sequences in Russian

[psa] 'dog's'
[fslux] 'aloud'
[mgla] 'fog'

3.2.5 Stress and syllables

A basic feature of English pronunciation is the use of stress to increase the acoustic prominence of particular syllables: the stress falls on the first syllable in *Canada*, the second syllable in *agenda*, and so on. Because English vocabulary is so varied, with mixed Germanic and Latinate origins, the location of stress is sometimes unpredictable. Nonetheless, we know that syllable structure affects stress placement in a large number of cases.

Stress placement in English is sensitive to syllable 'weight', which is determined by the composition of its rhyme.

> **Heavy syllable:** The rhyme consists of a vowel plus either a glide or a consonant.
> (A vowel plus glide combination is treated as a complex nucleus.)
> **Light syllable:** The rhyme consists of just a vowel or of a syllabic consonant.

Thus the syllables *bad* (vowel plus consonant) and *by* (vowel plus glide) are heavy, while the syllable *bee* is light, as is the second syllable in words such as *button* or *cancel*, whose rhyme consists of a syllabic consonant.

The basic stress rule for English verbs (ignoring suffixes, which have effects of their own) can be stated as follows.

(9) Basic stress rule for English verbs with more than one syllable:
Stress falls on the final syllable if it is heavy;
otherwise, it falls on the second-to-last (penultimate) syllable.

Table 3.17 presents some examples illustrating the effect of this rule. (Stress in transcriptions is marked by the symbol ' at the beginning of the syllable.)

TABLE 3.17 Stress in English verbs

Final syllable is heavy (stress falls on that syllable)	Final syllable is light (stress falls on the penultimate syllable)
arrive /əˈrajv/	hurry /ˈhʌ.ri/
destroy /dəˈstroj/	button /ˈbʌ.tn̩/
advise /ədˈvajz/	cancel /ˈkæn.sl̩/
insist /ɪnˈsɪst/	study /ˈstʌ.di/
consult /kənˈsʌlt/	carry /ˈkæ.ri/ or /ˈkɛ.ri/
allow /əˈlaw/	belittle /biˈlɪ.tl̩/
interrupt /ɪn.təˈrʌpt/	recover /riˈkʌ.vɚ/

Exceptions include *edit, promise, astonish,* and *embarrass*, all with stress on the second-to-last syllable despite the presence of an apparently strong final syllable.

The basic rule for nouns (once again ignoring suffixes) can be stated as follows.

(10) Basic stress rule for English nouns with more than one syllable:
Stress falls on the second-to-last (penultimate) syllable.

The effect of this rule can be seen in the pronunciation of words such as *English, city, kidney, elbow,* and *effort*, all of which have stress on the penultimate syllable. Its effects can also be seen in the contrasts between noun-verb pairs in table 3.18, with stress on the second-to-last syllable in the case of nouns and on the final syllable in the case of verbs.

TABLE 3.18 Stress in English noun and verb pairs	
Nouns	**Verbs**
a convert	to convert someone
a convict	to convict someone
a discount	to discount something
an increase	to increase something
a refill	to refill something
a permit	to permit something
a suspect	to suspect someone

A further effect of syllable structure can be seen in nouns that are longer than two syllables. In such cases, we generally find stress on the second-to-last syllable if that syllable is heavy; otherwise, the stress falls on the third-to-last (antepenultimate) syllable. (Even the predictable glides are represented here to make it easier to see which syllables are heavy.)

TABLE 3.19 Stress in English nouns longer than two syllables	
Penultimate syllable is heavy (stress on penultimate syllable)	**Penultimate syllable is light (stress on antepenultimate syllable)**
horizon /hə.ˈraj.zn̩/	Canada /ˈkæ.nə.də/
vacation /və.ˈkej.ʃn̩/	citizen /ˈsɪ.tə.zn̩/
aroma /ə.ˈrow.mə/	cinema /ˈsɪ.nə.mə/
potato /pə.ˈtej.to/	America /ə.ˈmɛ.rə.kə/
veranda /və.ˈræn.də/	analysis /ə.ˈnæ.lə.səs/
agenda /ə.ˈdʒɛn.də/	arithmetic /ə.ˈrɪθ.mə.tɪk/

Exceptions to these generalizations include *result, giraffe, sardine, ballet, and Tennessee,* all of which have stress on the final syllable, as well as *banana, Alabama, and committee,* with stress on a light second-to-last syllable.

Language Matters **Syllabification in Writing**

It is important not to confuse phonological syllable structure with the breaks that are used when a word won't fit at the end of a line in writing. These breaks, marked by hyphens, often align with phonological syllable boundaries—as in *re-write, un-der,* and *da-ta.* But one case in particular creates serious divergences: in writing, a consonant that occurs between vowels goes with the first vowel if that vowel is lax. Check the words *digit* and *method* in your dictionary, and you'll see that they're syllabified as *dig-it* and *meth-od,* in contrast to /dɪ.dʒɪt/ and /mɛ.θəd/ in phonology. Which of these syllabifications better corresponds to the pronunciation?

3.2.6 Syllable-based phonology

Syllables play a major role in the operation of phonological processes, including some that are vital to English.

Aspiration in English

We have already seen that the English voiceless stops /p, t, k/ can be aspirated, as in *pan* [pʰæn], *tan* [tʰæn], and *kin* [kʰɪn]. But what are the precise conditions under which the aspirated allophone is used? Table 3.20 provides some relevant data.

TABLE 3.20	English aspiration				
A (aspiration)		**B (no aspiration)**		**C (no aspiration)**	
[pʰæn]	*pan*	[spæn]	*span*	[slæp]	*slap*
[tʰæn]	*tan*	[stæn]	*Stan*	[slɑt]	*slot*
[kʰɪn]	*kin*	[skɪn]	*skin*	[sɪk]	*sick*
[pʰl̥æn]	*plan*	[splɪt]	*split*		
[tʰɹ̥aj]	*try*	[strɑŋ]	*strong*		
[kʰl̥in]	*clean*	[skrim]	*scream*		

A preliminary generalization can be stated very simply with reference to syllable structure.

(11) English voiceless stops are aspirated syllable-initially.

The voiceless consonants in the words in Column A are all syllable-initial and they undergo aspiration. In contrast, no aspiration is found in the words in columns B and C since the voiceless stops appear either as the second segment in a syllable onset (in *span, skin*, etc.), or in a coda, as in *slap* and *slot*.

So far, so good. But when we look *inside* words, aspiration is more puzzling—the syllable-initial voiceless stops in column A of table 3.21 are aspirated but those in column B are not.

TABLE 3.21	Syllables and English aspiration		
A (aspiration)		**B (little or no aspiration)**	
upon	[ə.ˈpʰɑn]	*upper*	[ˈʌ.pɚ]
atomic	[ə.ˈtʰɑ.mɪk]	*atom*	[ˈæ.təm] or [ˈæ.ɾəm]
attack	[ə.ˈtʰæk]	*attic*	[ˈæ.tɪk] or [ˈæ.ɾɪk]
akin	[ə.ˈkʰɪn]	*aching*	[ˈej.kɪŋ]

We can make sense of this if we take into account the fact that syllables can be stressed or unstressed. (Recall that a stressed syllable is perceived to be more prominent than its neighbours—compare *phoneme*, with stress on the first syllable, with *phonemic*, which has stress on the second syllable.)

Notice that the aspirated stops in table 3.21 all occur at the beginning of a stressed syllable. Stress seems not to matter when the voiceless stop is at the beginning of a word—the /p/ of *police* [pʰə.'lis] and *parade* [pʰə.'rejd] is aspirated even though the initial syllable is unstressed. But it does matter when the syllable occurs inside the word. The right generalization seems to be something like this:

(12) English voiceless stops are aspirated when they occur at the beginning of a syllable that is word-initial or that is stressed.

Vowel length in English

Vowel length in English offers yet another example of the phonological relevance of syllables. We have already seen that, as a first approximation, vowels are lengthened in front of a voiced obstruent in English, but not elsewhere.

TABLE 3.22 Phonetic vowel length in English			
A (vowel lengthening)		**B (no vowel lengthening)**	
bad	[bæːd]	*bat*	[bæt]
Abe	[eːjb]	*ape*	[ejp]
phase	[feːjz]	*face*	[fejs]
leave	[liːv]	*leaf*	[lif]
tag	[tʰæːg]	*tack*	[tʰæk]
brogue	[broːwg]	*broke*	[browk]
		say	[sej]
		meal	[mil]
		soar	[sor]
		show	[ʃow]

It turns out, though, that this is not quite right: lengthening takes place only if the voiced obstruent is in the coda position of *the same syllable* as the vowel. As the next examples show, if the consonant is in the onset of the next syllable, the vowel is not lengthened.

TABLE 3.23 Short vowels before a voiced onset obstruent in the next syllable		
obey	[ow.bej]	(compare to *lobe* [loːwb])
redo	[ri.du]	(compare to *read* [riːd])
crazy	[krej.zi]	(compare to *craze* [krejːz])
ogre	[ow.gɚ]	(compare to *brogue* [broːwg])
Odin	[ow.dɪn]	(compare to *ode* [oːwd])

Once again, syllable structure is crucial.

(13) English vowels are lengthened when followed by a voiced obstruent in the coda position of the same syllable.

Uvular consonants in Quechua

Yet another syllable-based phenomenon occurs in Quechua (spoken in Peru), where the voiceless uvular stop /q/ has two allophones. The fricative allophone [χ] is found in coda positions—that is, at the end of syllables.

[tʃeχ.niŋ] 'he hates'   [soχ.ta] 'six'   [al.qoχ] 'dog'
    ↑   ↑   ↑

The stop allophone [q] is found elsewhere (i.e., at the beginning of syllables).

[qaŋ] 'you'   [no.qa] 'I'   [al.qoχ] 'dog'
   ↑   ↑   ↑

The generalization can be stated as follows:

(14) The [χ] allophone of /q/ is used in the coda position in Quechua.

As these and other examples show, the use of syllabic representations in phonology permits us to make more accurate statements about allophonic patterns in language than would otherwise be possible.

3.3 Features

As noted at the beginning of the chapter, linguists consider features to be the most basic units of phonology. **Features** are like atoms; they are the basic building blocks of speech sounds.

3.3.1 Features as phonetically grounded elements

The study of phonetics shows that speech is produced by a number of independent but coordinated articulatory adjustments such as voicing, tongue position, lip rounding, and so on. For example, when we produce the voiceless bilabial stop [p], the vocal cords in the larynx are open and not vibrating; hence, the sound is voiceless. At the same time, the lips are pressed together to block the flow of air through the vocal tract, thereby creating a labial stop. Features such as [± voice], [LABIAL], and the like allow us to identify the building blocks of phonemes. This has advantages for various aspects of phonological analysis.

Features and natural classes

A first advantage of features is that they give us an economical way of characterizing natural classes. **Natural classes** are groups of sounds with similar properties. Consider, for example, the set of English sounds in figure 3.14.

All these sounds belong to the class of obstruents, which share the feature [–sonorant]; this feature distinguishes them from nasals (/m, n, ŋ/) and liquids (/l, r/). The feature [voice] distinguishes two subclasses of obstruents: the voiceless segments /p, t, k, f, s, ʃ/ (all [–voice]) and the voiced segments /b, d, g, v, z, ʒ/ (all [+voice]). A third feature, [continuant], which has to do with whether a sound is produced with continuous airflow through the oral cavity, distinguishes the stops /p, t, k, b, d, g/ (all [–continuant]) from the fricatives /f, s, ʃ, v, z, ʒ/ (all [+continuant]). By using just three features, we are able to capture the nine different natural classes of sounds summarized in table 3.24.

FIGURE 3.14
Natural classes:
obstruents in English

	[− sonorant]	
[− voice]		[+ voice]
p		b
t		d	[− continuant]
k		g
f		v
s		z	[+ continuant]
ʃ		ʒ

TABLE 3.24   Nine natural classes: obstruents in English

[−sonorant]	[−sonorant −continuant]	[−sonorant +continuant]	[−sonorant −voice]	[−sonorant +voice]	[−sonorant −continuant −voice]	[−sonorant −continuant +voice]	[−sonorant +continuant −voice]	[−sonorant +continuant +voice]
p t k	p t k	f s ʃ	p t k	b d g	p t k	b d g	f s ʃ	v z ʒ
b d g	b d g	v z ʒ	f s ʃ	v z ʒ				
f s ʃ								
v z ʒ								

A natural class requires fewer features to define it than to define any one of its members. In table 3.24, the largest class, that of the obstruents, is defined by only one feature, [−sonorant], while the four classes containing three segments each are defined by three features each.

The importance of natural classes in phonology stems from the fact that the members of a natural class tend to behave alike with respect to patterns and processes. In English, for instance, the class of voiceless stops /p, t, k/, defined by the features [−sonorant, −continuant, −voice], are the only segments that can be aspirated. The consonants before which vowels can lengthen also make up a natural class—they are all voiced obstruents ([−sonorant, +voice]). And so on. Having the right system of features is essential for grouping sounds together in an insightful way.

Table 3.25 provides an additional illustration of the use of features to distinguish natural classes—in this case, the class of front and back vowels in English.

TABLE 3.25   Using features to capture natural classes

[−back]	[+back]	[+tense]
Front vowels	*Back vowels*	*Tense vowels*
/i/	/u/	/i/
/ɪ/	/ʊ/	/e/
/e/	/o/	/u/
/ɛ/	/ʌ/	/o/
/æ/	/ɑ/	/ɑ/

Features and contrasts

A second advantage of features is that they provide insights into a language's system of phonemic contrasts. We are missing something important about English if we simply say that that /p/ contrasts with /b/, /t/ with /d/, /f/ with /v/, /θ/ with /ð/, /s/ with /z/, and so on. The key point is that voiced obstruents contrast with voiceless obstruents. Put another way, [voice] is a **distinctive feature** in English—which is why voiced phonemes contrast with their voiceless counterparts.

In contrast, [aspirated] is not a distinctive feature in English. That's why we don't find contrasts between [p] and [pʰ], [t] and [tʰ], or [k] and [kʰ]. Of course, just the opposite is true in Khmer, where aspiration is distinctive (see section 3.1.4).

Other features provide for other contrasts. For example, we can capture the contrast between /t/ and /s/ in English with the feature [continuant]. Both /t/ and /s/ are voiceless and have an alveolar point of articulation. By viewing the relevant distinctive feature as [continuant], we can use the same feature to distinguish between /p/ and /f/, /b/ and /v/, and /d/ and /z/ (see table 3.26).

TABLE 3.26	Stop-fricative contrasts captured by a distinctive feature
[– continuant]	[+ continuant]
p	f
b	v
t	s
d	z

By systematically examining the phonemic contrasts of a language, we can extract the distinctive features and use them to describe the phonemic inventory.

Features, processes, and allophonic variation

A third reason for using features in phonology is that they enable us to describe allophonic variation more precisely. Viewed from the perspective of features, allophonic variation is not simply the substitution of one allophone for another but rather the environmentally conditioned change or specification of a feature or features. As we saw in section 3.1.6, for instance, English vowels have nasalized allophones when in front of [m], [n], or [ŋ]: [bãm] *bomb*, [ãn] *on*, [lãŋ] *long*, etc. Features allow an elegant statement of this generalization: vowels become [+nasal] in front of a [+nasal] consonant. (With a little bit of testing, you'll see that the nasal consonant not only has to follow the vowel; it also has to be in the same syllable. Say the words *an* and *any* with a finger on your nose.)

3.3.2 Feature representations

In this section, we present and define features that are needed to analyze the sound system of English, as well as of many other languages.

Binary features

Most features have labels that reflect traditional articulatory terms such as [voice], [consonantal], and [nasal]. They are written in lower case and are **binary**, with one of two values, + or –, each of which defines a particular class of sounds. For example, [+voice] sounds involve vibration or voicing in the larynx, while [–voice] sounds involve an open glottis and therefore no vibration or voicing.

- **Major class features** *features that represent the classes consonant, obstruent, and sonorant (nasal, liquid, glide, vowel)*

    [±consonantal] Sounds that are [+consonantal] are produced with a major obstruction in the vocal tract. All consonants are [+consonantal], except for the glottals [h] and [ʔ], which are produced at the glottis rather than in the vocal tract. Like glides and vowels, they are [–consonantal].

    [±syllabic] Sounds that can act as syllabic nuclei are [+syllabic]; this includes vowels, syllabic liquids, and syllabic nasals. All other sounds are [–syllabic].

    [±sonorant] All and only those sounds that are 'singable' are [+sonorant]; they include vowels, glides, liquids, and nasals (even if the sounds are devoiced). All non-singable sounds (namely, obstruents) are [–sonorant].

Table 3.27 illustrates how the major class features are used to divide sounds into classes. Note that nasals and liquids have the same values for the three major class features; to distinguish these two classes from each other, additional (manner) features are therefore needed.

TABLE 3.27 Use of major class features

	Obstruents	Nasals	Liquids	Glides	Vowels
[±consonantal]	+	+	+	–	–
[±syllabic]	–	–	–	–	+
[±sonorant]	–	+	+	+	+
Examples:	p d v tʃ	m n	l r	j w	i u

The manner features given next represent manners of articulation. Their use is particularly important in distinguishing the following classes: stops/affricates from fricatives ([±continuant]), affricates from stops ([±delayed release]), nasals from non-nasals ([±nasal]), and laterals from non-laterals ([±lateral]).

- **Manner features** *features that represent manner of articulation*

    [±continuant] Sounds produced with free or nearly free airflow through the oral cavity—vowels, glides, liquids, and fricatives—are [+continuant]. All other sounds are [–continuant]; these include nasal and oral stops as well as affricates.

    [±delayed release] ([±DR]) When an affricate sound such as [tʃ] is produced, the tongue is slower in leaving the roof of the mouth than when a stop like [t] is produced on its own. Hence, affricates are said to be produced with 'delayed release' of air. All and only affricates such as [tʃ] and [dʒ] are [+DR]. All other sounds are [–DR].

    [±nasal] Sounds produced with a lowered velum—nasal stops and all nasalized sounds—are [+nasal]. Sounds that are oral, and thus produced with a raised velum, are [–nasal].

    [±lateral] All and only varieties of *l* are [+lateral], with air escaping along the lowered sides of the tongue. All other sounds are [–lateral].

Voicing, aspiration, and glottal constriction are all the result of laryngeal activity. To represent different laryngeal states, we use the features [±voice], [±spread glottis], and [±constricted glottis].

- **Laryngeal features** *features that represent laryngeal activity*

    [±voice] All voiced sounds are [+voice]; all voiceless sounds are [–voice].

[**±spread glottis**] (**[±SG]**) All aspirated consonants and [h] are [+SG]; all others are [–SG]. The use of this feature reflects the fact that aspiration occurs when the vocal folds remain open (spread) after the release of a consonant's closure.

[**±constricted glottis**] (**[±CG]**) All sounds made with a closed glottis are [+CG]; all others are [–CG]. In English, only the glottal stop [ʔ] is [+CG].

Articulator features

A second set of features identifies the articulators that are active in the production of particular sounds. These **articulator features** are written in upper case and do not have + and – values: when they are inactive, they are simply not present in the representation. The three key articulator features are as follows:

> LABIAL, for articulations involving the lips
> CORONAL, for articulations involving the tongue tip or the tongue blade
> DORSAL, for articulations involving the tongue body

Articulator features are linked to specific binary features that capture details about manner and place of articulation relevant to the operation of the articulators.

Only the LABIAL articulator (the lips) can be rounded or unrounded ([±round]). And only the DORSAL articulator (tongue body and back) adopts [±high] or [±back] positions. These links make sense: the lips cannot be high or low, and the tongue body cannot be rounded. Here is a fuller description of the relationship between articulator features and binary features.

■ **Articulator features** *features that indicate the activity of the lips and tongue*

[**LABIAL**] This feature represents the labial articulator: any sound that is produced with involvement of one or both of the lips is [LABIAL].

[**±round**] A sound produced with the labial articulator may be produced by protruding the lips—such sounds are [+round] (rounded vowels and the rounded labiovelar glide [w]); labial sounds made with no lip protrusion are [–round] ([p, b, f, v]).

[**CORONAL**] This feature represents the coronal articulator: any sound that is produced with involvement of the tongue tip or blade is [CORONAL].

[**±anterior**] All coronal sounds articulated in front of the alveopalatal region (interdentals and alveolars) are [+anterior]; coronal sounds articulated at or behind the alveopalatal region are [–anterior].

[**±strident**] All 'noisy' coronal fricatives and affricates ([s, z, ʃ, ʒ, tʃ, dʒ]) are [+strident]; all other coronal fricatives and affricates ([θ, ð]) are [–strident].

[**DORSAL**] This feature represents the dorsal articulator: all sounds that are produced with involvement of the body of the tongue, including all vowels, are [DORSAL].

[**±high**] Dorsal consonants (velars and palatals) and vowels produced with the tongue body raised from a central position in the oral cavity are [+high]. Sounds produced with a neutral or lowered tongue body are [–high].

[**±low**] Vowels produced with the tongue body lowered from a central position in the oral cavity are [+low]. All other vowels are [–low]. The feature [low] is not needed for consonants in English, although it may be used in languages that have uvular or pharyngeal consonants.

[**±back**] Dorsal consonants and vowels produced with the tongue body behind the palatal region (hard palate) in the oral cavity are [+back]. Sounds produced with the tongue body at or in front of the palatal region are [–back].

[±tense] Vowels that are tense are [+tense]; vowels that are lax are [−tense]. In some analyses, the feature [tense] is replaced by the feature [advanced tongue root] ([ATR]), in recognition of the fact that the tongue root adopts a somewhat higher position in the vocal tract for tense vowels than for their lax counterparts.

[±reduced] The vowel schwa ([ə]) is a lax and exceptionally brief vowel and is therefore [+reduced]; all other vowels are [−reduced].

Using articulator features

To see exactly how the articulator features are used to represent the various places of articulation of the consonants found in English, let us look at table 3.28. In the feature representations, a checkmark indicates that the relevant articulator is active in the production of a sound. Where no checkmark is present, the articulator is inactive. Using [p] as an example, the feature representations in table 3.28 can be laid out as follows:

- [p] is produced with the lips in an unrounded state. It is therefore a [LABIAL], [−round] sound. The tongue blade and the tongue body are not used in the production of [p], and therefore [p] has no feature specifications for the coronal and dorsal articulators.

TABLE 3.28   Use of articulator features to represent some English consonants

	Labials		Dentals	Alveolars	Alveopalatals[3]	Palatals	Velars
	p	w	θ	s	ʃ	j	k
LABIAL	✓	✓					
[±round]	−	+					
CORONAL			✓	✓	✓		
[±anterior]			+	+	−		
[±strident]			−	+	+		
DORSAL	✓					✓	✓
[±high]	+					+	+
[±back]	+					−	+

- [θ s ʃ] are all [CORONAL] sounds because they are produced with the tongue blade. [θ s] are produced with the tongue blade in front of or at the alveolar ridge and are therefore [+anterior], while [ʃ] is produced with the tongue blade behind the alveolar ridge and is therefore [−anterior]. [θ] is produced with a quiet airflow and thus is [−strident], while [s ʃ] are produced with noisy airflow and thus are [+strident]. Since neither the lips nor the tongue body are used to produce these sounds, they have no specifications for the [LABIAL] or [DORSAL] features. (For further discussion of the representation of [ʃ] and other alveopalatal sounds, see note 3 at the end of the chapter.)

- [j k] are both produced with the tongue body and are therefore [DORSAL] sounds; both have a raised tongue body, so are [+high]. [j] is pronounced with the tongue body at the hard palate, so it is [−back]. In contrast, [k] is pronounced with the tongue body behind the hard palate, so it is [+back]. Finally, since neither the lips nor the tongue blade are used to produce these sounds, they have no specifications for the features [LABIAL] or [CORONAL].

- [w] is a labiovelar sound and is thus coarticulated: it is produced with both a tongue body that is raised and behind the hard palate *and* with lip rounding. This means that both the back of the tongue and the lips are used to produce [w], so it is executed with two articulators acting simultaneously. It is therefore both [LABIAL] and [DORSAL]; as a [LABIAL] sound, it is [+round], and as a [DORSAL] sound, it is [+high, +back]. Since the tongue blade is not used to produce this sound, it has no specifications for the [CORONAL] feature.

Table 3.29 exemplifies how the articulator features are used to represent vowels in English. All vowels are produced with an active tongue body and therefore are [DORSAL]. Vowels that involve lip rounding are also produced with the [LABIAL] articulator. [CORONAL] is never used in the feature representations of vowels. All vowels except schwa are unreduced and therefore specified as [–reduced].

TABLE 3.29	Use of articulator features to represent some English vowels			
	u	ɛ	ə	ɑ
LABIAL	✓			
[±round]	+			
DORSAL	✓	✓	✓	✓
[±high]	+	–	–	–
[±low]	–	–	–	+
[±back]	+	–	+	+
[±tense]	+	–	–	+
[±reduced]	–	–	+	–

- [u] is a high back tense vowel and is therefore specified as [+high], [+back], and [+tense]. Since it is round, it is [LABIAL, +round] in addition to being [DORSAL]. Since it is [+high], it is also [–low]. (Because the tongue body cannot be both raised and lowered at the same time, all [+high] vowels are also [–low].)

- [ɛ] is a mid front (non-back) lax unrounded vowel. Since it is unrounded, it does not use the labial articulator. As a mid vowel, it has neither a raised nor a lowered tongue body, so it is [DORSAL, –high, –low]. As a front vowel, it is [–back], and as a lax vowel, it is [–tense].

- [ə] is a mid central unrounded lax reduced vowel. As a mid vowel, it is [DORSAL, –high, –low]. As a central and therefore non-front vowel, it is [+back] (all central vowels are [+back] in feature representations). Being unrounded, it does not involve the labial articulator. Because it is a lax reduced vowel, it is [–tense] and [+reduced].

- [ɑ] is a low back unrounded tense vowel. Since it is produced with a lowered tongue body it is [DORSAL, +low]; because a lowered tongue body cannot be simultaneously raised, it is also [–high]. Since it is back, it is [+back]. Being tense, it is [+tense], and being unrounded, it has no labial specifications.

Feature notation does not provide a convenient way to distinguish diphthongs such as [aj], [aw], and [oj] from the other vowels. These diphthongs may be treated as vowel-glide sequences when using features.

Tables 3.30 and 3.31 provide the feature representations for all the consonants and vowels of English. As you go through these tables, notice that for every sound, features are listed in the following order: major class features, manner features, laryngeal features, and articulator features.

TABLE 3.30 Feature matrix for English consonants

		p	pʰ	b	t	tʰ	d	k	kʰ	g	f	v	s	z	θ	ð	ʃ	ʒ	tʃ	dʒ	m	n	ŋ	l	r	j	w	ʍ	h	ʔ
Major class features	[consonantal]	+	+	+	+	+	+	+	+	+	+	+	+	+	+	+	+	+	+	+	+	+	+	+	+	−	−	−	−	−
	[sonorant]	−	−	−	−	−	−	−	−	−	−	−	−	−	−	−	−	−	−	−	+	+	+	+	+	+	+	+	−	−
	[syllabic]	−	−	−	−	−	−	−	−	−	−	−	−	−	−	−	−	−	−	−	−	−	−	−	−	−	−	−	−	−
Manner features	[nasal]	−	−	−	−	−	−	−	−	−	−	−	−	−	−	−	−	−	−	−	+	+	+	−	−	−	−	−	−	−
	[continuant]	−	−	−	−	−	−	−	−	−	+	+	+	+	+	+	+	+	−	−	−	−	−	−	+	+	+	+	+	−
	[lateral]	−	−	−	−	−	−	−	−	−	−	−	−	−	−	−	−	−	−	−	−	−	−	+	−	−	−	−	−	−
	[DR]	−	−	−	−	−	−	−	−	−	−	−	−	−	−	−	−	−	+	+	−	−	−	−	−	−	−	−	−	−
Laryngeal features	[voice]	−	−	+	−	−	+	−	−	+	−	+	−	+	−	+	−	+	−	+	+	+	+	+	+	+	+	−	−	−
	[CG]	−	−	−	−	−	−	−	−	−	−	−	−	−	−	−	−	−	−	−	−	−	−	−	−	−	−	−	−	+
	[SG]	−	+	−	−	+	−	−	+	−	−	−	−	−	−	−	−	−	−	−	−	−	−	−	−	−	−	−	+	−
Articulator features	LABIAL	✓	✓	✓							✓	✓									✓						✓	✓		
	[round]	−	−	−							−	−									−						+	+		
	CORONAL				✓	✓	✓						✓	✓	✓	✓	✓	✓	✓	✓		✓		✓	✓					
	[anterior]				+	+	+						+	+	+	+	−	−	−	−		+		+	−					
	[strident]				−	−	−						+	+	−	−	+	+	+	+		−		−	−					
	DORSAL							✓	✓	✓													✓			✓	✓	✓		
	[high]							+	+	+													+			+	+	+		
	[back]							+	+	+													+			−	+	+		

Note: [low], [tense], and [reduced] are not used for English consonants.

TABLE 3.31 Feature matrix for English vowels		i	ɪ	e	ɛ	æ	ʌ	ə	ɑ/a*	u	ʊ	o
Major class features	[consonantal]	–	–	–	–	–	–	–	–	–	–	–
	[sonorant]	+	+	+	+	+	+	+	+	+	+	+
	[syllabic]	+	+	+	+	+	+	+	+	+	+	+
Manner feature	[continuant]	+	+	+	+	+	+	+	+	+	+	+
Laryngeal feature	[voice]	+	+	+	+	+	+	+	+	+	+	+
Articulator features	LABIAL									✓	✓	✓
	[round]									+	+	+
	DORSAL	✓	✓	✓	✓	✓	✓	✓	✓	✓	✓	✓
	[high]	+	+	–	–	–	–	–	–	+	+	–
	[low]	–	–	–	–	+	–	–	+	–	–	–
	[back]	–	–	–	–	–	+	+	+	+	+	+
	[tense]	+	–	+	–	–	–	–	+	+	–	+
	[reduced]	–	–	–	–	–	–	+	–	–	–	–

*Note: While [a] and [ɑ] are phonetically different, we give them the same phonological features. For languages and dialects in which they contrast phonemically, the two sounds would have distinct feature specifications.

Further discussion of how to determine feature representations is provided on the Companion Website.

3.4 Derivations and rules

As explained in section 3.1, the segments making up words can be associated with two different types of representations. On the one hand, there are phonological representations, consisting of phonemes, which contain just information about contrasts. On the other hand, there are phonetic representations, made up of allophones, which contain a great deal of additional information about the details of pronunciation.

> *tab*
> /tæb/   ← Phonological representation (contrasts only)
> [tʰæːb]   ← Phonetic representation (all details of pronunciation)

As already noted, one way to understand the difference between the two representations is to say that the phonological representation corresponds to what is in the mind while the phonetic representation corresponds to what comes out of the mouth. As we'll see next, general processes, often called **phonological rules**, apply to phonological representations to derive the phonetic representation by filling in the various predictable phonetic details that contribute to a word's actual pronunciation.

3.4.1 Derivations

Phonetic representations are created by rules that apply in a step-by-step fashion to the phonological representation (also called the **underlying representation**), resulting in a **derivation**. Figure 3.15 shows three derivations.

(UR = underlying representation; PR = phonetic representation).

FIGURE 3.15 The derivations of three English words	UR →	/tæp/ 'tap'	/pæd/ 'pad'	/slæp/ 'slap'
	Aspiration	tʰæp	pʰæd	—
	V-lengthening	—	pʰæːd	—
	PR →	[tʰæp]	[pʰæːd]	[slæp]

Two rules are at work in these examples. Aspiration applies to the syllable-initial voiceless stops in *tap* and *pad*, and vowel lengthening applies to the vowel in *pad*, which precedes a voiced obstruent in the same syllable. The end result—the phonetic representation—reflects the addition of predictable phonetic details to a less specific mental representation of the word.

Rule application

The environments in which aspiration and vowel lengthening apply (onset and pre-coda position, respectively) are entirely different. The two rules therefore do not interact or affect each other in any way; the order in which they apply makes no difference to the outcome of the derivation. As figure 3.16 shows, there is no difference in the outcome if the rules are applied in the reverse order compared to figure 3.15.

FIGURE 3.16 Aspiration and vowel lengthening applied in reverse order	UR →	/tæp/ 'tap'	/pæd/ 'pad'
	V-lengthening	—	pæːd
	Aspiration	tʰæp	pʰæːd
	PR →	[tʰæp]	[pʰæːd]

We therefore say that the rules of aspiration and vowel lengthening are unordered with respect to each other.

In some cases, though, order matters because the application of one rule creates an environment that makes possible the application of another rule. One such case involves the rule that devoices the liquids /l/ and /r/ when they occur in a syllable onset right after a syllable-initial voiceless stop. If you pronounce the words in (15) slowly while holding a finger on your larynx, you'll notice few if any vocal cord vibrations during the production of the liquid; vibrations don't begin in earnest until the start of the vowel. (We ignore aspiration here.)

(15) *pry* [pr̥aj] (compare to *rye*: [raj])
true [tr̥u] (compare to *rue*: [ru])
claw [kl̥ɑ] (compare to *law*: [lɑ])
etc.

In careful speech, the word *polite* in English is pronounced [pəlʌjt], but in colloquial speech the schwa in the first syllable is often deleted because it is unstressed and in an open syllable. This

FIGURE 3.17 Rule order in a derivation	UR →	/pəlajt/
	Stress assignment	pə.'lajt
	Schwa deletion	'plajt
	Liquid devoicing	'pl̥ajt

leaves the liquid /l/ directly after a voiceless stop, making it subject to the rule of liquid devoicing, as illustrated in figure 3.17.

The rule for assigning stress must apply before the rule for schwa deletion, since the deletion of schwa is sensitive to a word's stress pattern. And the rule of schwa deletion must apply before liquid devoicing, since the liquid occurs in a devoicing position only after the schwa has been deleted.

3.4.2 The form of rules

So far, we have been stating rules informally (e.g., a vowel is lengthened before a voiced obstruent in the same syllable). This is fine as a first step, but phonologists typically try to make rules more precise by stating them in a formal way, following the template in (16).

(16)   A → B / X ___ Y

In this notation, *A* stands for the input to the rule, *B* for the output of the rule, and *X* and *Y* for the environment in which the rule applies. The slash separates the statement of the change from the statement of the conditioning environment, and can be interpreted as 'in the environment'. The rule in (16) is therefore read as *A becomes B in the environment between X and Y*. (Some rules make reference only to the preceding environment and some only to the following environment, depending on which is relevant to the change.)

As an illustration of how this works, we can translate our informal generalization about vowel lengthening, which occurs before a voiced obstruent in the same syllable, as in *pad* (see section 3.2.6). The rule can be stated as follows, with σ signifying a syllable boundary.

(17)   V → long / ___ voiced obstruent σ

At an even greater level of precision, rules are written using a combination of symbols and features to make explicit the natural classes of sounds to which the rule is sensitive.

(18)   V → [+ long] / ___ $\begin{bmatrix} + \text{cons} \\ - \text{syllabic} \\ - \text{sonorant} \\ + \text{voice} \end{bmatrix}$ σ

Another example of a formal rule involves the phenomenon of vowel nasalization, whose effects are heard in words such as [ãn] *on* and [bæ̃n] *ban*, where a vowel comes right before a nasal consonant (see section 3.1.6).

(19)   V → [+ nasal] / ___ $\begin{bmatrix} + \text{cons} \\ + \text{nasal} \end{bmatrix}$

This rule describes the regressive assimilation that takes place here: the [+nasal] feature is added to the vowel under the influence of the [+nasal] feature in the adjacent consonant.

Yet another example involves liquid devoicing as in *pry* and *claw*, which we have been stating informally as follows.

(20)   Liquids become voiceless after syllable-initial voiceless stops.

We can now state this more formally as follows.

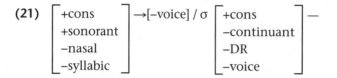

(21) $\begin{bmatrix} +\text{cons} \\ +\text{sonorant} \\ -\text{nasal} \\ -\text{syllabic} \end{bmatrix} \rightarrow [-\text{voice}] \ / \ \sigma \begin{bmatrix} +\text{cons} \\ -\text{continuant} \\ -\text{DR} \\ -\text{voice} \end{bmatrix} \underline{\quad}$

Using feature notation, this rule groups together the class of liquids (sounds that are [+consonantal, +sonorant, –nasal, –syllabic], as outlined in table 3.30), and states that they take on the [–voice] feature of a preceding syllable-initial stop. (As you can see by consulting table 3.30, voiceless stops have in common the features [+consonantal, –continuant, –DR, and –voice].)

Deletion and epenthesis as rules

We have already seen that English speakers (optionally) drop a schwa [ə] in an open syllable when it is followed by a stressed syllable, as in *police* [pl̩is] and *parade* [pr̩eːjd]. The rule can be formalized as follows. (The symbol V́ indicates stress.)

(22)   Schwa deletion in English:

[ə] → ø / C __ σ   CV́...

Now consider the reverse process of epenthesis, which adds a vowel where previously there was none. This can happen when an impermissible syllable structure is encountered in a borrowed word, as in the English pronunciation of the name *Dmitri* [dəmitri] in which [ə] is used to break up the first two consonants. In addition, there are dialects of English that do not permit a coda consisting of [l] and another consonant. In these dialects, *milk* is pronounced [mɪlək], *elm* [ɛləm], and *film* [fɪləm], in accordance with the following insertion rule.

(23)   Schwa insertion in English:

ø → [ə] / [+lateral] __ $\begin{bmatrix} +\text{cons} \\ -\text{syllabic} \end{bmatrix} \sigma$

Summing up

Phonology is the study of the contrasts and patterns that underlie the use of sounds to communicate meaning. The single most important unit in phonology is the **phoneme,** which consists of a group of phonetically similar sounds (its **allophones**) that do not contrast with each other but do contrast with other sounds. Phonemes are identified with the help of **minimal pairs,** while **complementary distribution** offers a key test for identifying allophones of the same phoneme.

Phonemes are grouped together into **syllables**, which consist of a **nucleus** and (optionally, depending on the language) an **onset** and a **coda**. Many phonological phenomena, including a great deal of allophonic variation, are sensitive to syllable structure, as is rhyming in poetry.

Phonemes can be broken down into **features**, which help define **natural classes** of sounds that behave alike with respect to phonological processes such as aspiration, nasalization, vowel lengthening, and so on.

The relationship between a word's **phonological representation** and its **phonetic representation** can be captured by formal rules, stated in terms of features, which capture significant generalizations about a language's sound pattern.

Notes

1. In some dialects of English, there is also a contrast between [ɑ] and the mid back rounded lax vowel [ɔ] in words like *cot* [kʰɑt] and *caught* [kʰɔt]. In Canadian English, these words and other analogous ones are both pronounced [kʰɑt].

2. In some dialects of English, the high tense vowels /i/ and /u/ are pronounced with strong off-glides—[ij] and [uw], respectively. In other dialects, these off-glides are very weak, and in still other dialects, they are not present at all. Since there is less variability in the pronunciation of the mid vowels, we focus on them in this section. To account for dialects with [ij, ej, uw, ow], the generalization given in (6) can be restated as follows: the non-low (high and mid) tense vowels of English are predictably followed by a glide that has the same backness and roundness.

3. Alveopalatals may pattern together with high front vowels and glides for the application of some rules. In such cases, we can assume that they are specified with the features [DORSAL, +high, −back] as well as [CORONAL, −anterior, +strident]. In other words, in such cases, alveopalatals require the activation of two articulators.

Recommended reading

Anderson, Stephen R. 1985. *Phonology in the Twentieth Century: Theories of Rules and Theories of Representations*. Chicago: University of Chicago Press.

Avery, Peter, B. Elan Dresher, and Keren Rice, eds. 2008. *Contrast in Phonology: Theory, Perception, Acquisition*. Berlin: Mouton de Gruyter.

Blevins, Juliette. 2004. *Evolutionary Phonology: The Emergence of Sound Patterns*. Cambridge: Cambridge University Press.

Carr, Philip, and Jean-Pierre Montreuil. 2013. *Phonology*. 2nd ed. London: Palgrave Macmillan.

Goldsmith, John A., ed. 1999. *Phonological Theory: The Essential Readings*. Malden, MA: Wiley-Blackwell.

Goldsmith, John, Jason Riggle, and Alan C.L. Yu, eds. 2011. *The Handbook of Phonological Theory*. 2nd ed. Hoboken, NJ: Wiley-Blackwell.

Odden, David. 2005. *Introducing Phonology*. Cambridge: Cambridge University Press.

Pellegrino, François, Egidio Marsico, Ioana Chitoran, and Christophe Coupé, eds. 2009. *Approaches to Phonological Complexity*. Berlin: Mouton de Gruyter.

Appendix: Hints for solving phonology problems

The task of solving a phonology problem is made easier if certain facts presented in this chapter and summarized here are kept in mind. The data that we consider below are taken from Tagalog (Filipino), a language spoken in the Philippines. (When phonetic data are presented as a set, square brackets are often dispensed with.)

1. In the following data, consider the sounds [h] and [ʔ] and determine whether they contrast or are allophones of one phoneme.

a) kahon	'box'	d) ʔariʔ	'property'
b) hariʔ	'king'	e) kaʔon	'to fetch'
c) ʔumagos	'to flow'	f) humangos	'to pant'

   In order to determine whether the sounds contrast, we begin by looking for minimal pairs. These establish which segments are contrastive. Minimal pairs occur in items a–e and b–d, and there is a near-minimal pair in c–f. We therefore have very good evidence that [h] and [ʔ] contrast with each other and belong to separate phonemes.

2. Now consider the following Tagalog data, and determine whether the two sounds [d] and [r] contrast or are allophones of one phoneme.

a) datiŋ	'to arrive'	f) daraʔiŋ	'will complain'
b) dami	'amount'	g) marumi	'dirty'
c) dumi	'dirt'	h) marami	'many'
d) daratiŋ	'will arrive'	i) daʔiŋ	'to complain'
e) mandurukot	'pickpocket'	j) mandukot	'to go pickpocketing'

   Since the data contain no minimal pairs that contrast [d] and [r] and because the two sounds are phonetically similar (both are voiced and produced in the alveolar region), we suspect that they are allophones of the same phoneme and we therefore must look to see whether they are in complementary distribution.

   In checking to see whether two (or more) sounds are in complementary distribution, the best thing to do is to list the environments in which the sounds occur:

[r] occurs:	[d] occurs:
–between two vowels (e.g., [marami])	–word-initially (e.g., [dami])
	–following a nasal (e.g., [mandukot])

   We quickly notice that the sounds occur in non-overlapping environments—[r] occurs between vowels, and [d] occurs elsewhere (at the beginning of a word, after a nasal consonant). We thus have complementary distribution, and we can conclude that the two sounds are allophones of the same phoneme.

   ```
                    /d/
                   /   \
                 [r]     [d]
          between vowels  elsewhere
   ```

The key to this step in the analysis is to make the most general statements allowed by the data about the distribution of the individual allophones. So when you notice that [r] occurs between two [u]s in (e), between two [a]s in (d, f, h), and between [a] and [u] in (g), look for what all three patterns have in common: the [r] is between two vowels. If [d] never occurs in this context (that is, if it only occurs elsewhere), you have complementary distribution.

3. In a more advanced analysis, it is common to write a rule that will derive the appropriate allophone(s) from the underlying phonemes. Such a rule in this case would look like this:

$$d \rightarrow r / V\_\_\_V$$

The process at work here is a form of assimilation, in that an underlying voiced stop consonant becomes a continuant sonorant when found between two continuant sonorants (vowels).

For even greater explicitness, the rule can be formulated using features.

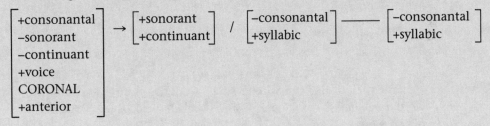

Here's a flow chart that summarizes the analytic steps described above.

Starting with two (or more)
sounds, ask:
'Are there minimal pairs involving these sounds?'

If yes:
The sounds contrast and belong to
two separate phonemes.

If no (and if the sounds are
phonetically similar), ask:
'Is there complementary distribution?'

If yes:
Summarize the
complementary
distribution using
the format illustrated
in step 2 above.

If no:
Recheck your work.
If you haven't missed
anything, you need more
data to proceed.

Write a rule that will
produce the appropriate
allophone.

In more advanced work (but not in the practice exercises that follow), you may have to deal with two additional factors—neutralization and free variation.

Neutralization involves the loss of a contrast between two phonemes in certain circumstances because of a shared allophone. For example, /t/ and /d/ are clearly distinct phonemes in English, as shown by minimal pairs such as *tie–die* and *mate–made*. Between vowels, however, both phonemes may be pronounced as the flap [ɾ]. This leads to the loss of the /t/–/d/ contrast in words such as *rating* and *raiding*, each of which is pronounced [rejɾɪŋ]. The resulting phonological system looks like this:

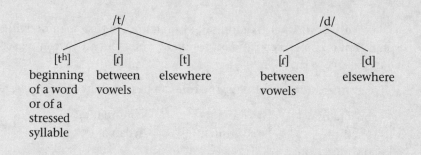

Free variation occurs when a single word has more than one pronunciation. The word *economics* is a case in point, since English speakers regularly pronounce it in either of two ways:

[ikənɑmɪks]   [ɛkənɑmɪks]

Although /i/ and /ɛ/ are distinct phonemes in English (that's why we interpret *beat* and *bet* as different words), either can be used in the word *economics* without creating a difference in meaning.

Free variation can also occur with allophones of a phoneme. At the end of a word, English stop consonants such as /p/ have several allophones—the default [p], an unreleased [p̚], in which the closure is maintained past the end of the word, and a [pˡ], in which the closure is vigorously released, with added aspiration.

stop: [stɑp], [stɑp̚], [stɑpˡ]

There's obviously no complementary distribution here—the three sounds occur in exactly the same position. But because they are phonetically similar and because they don't contrast with each other here or anywhere else (*stop* is the same word regardless of how the final 'p' is pronounced), they still count as allophones of the same phoneme.

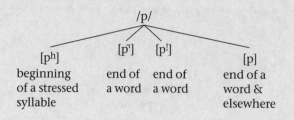

alophones of the same phoneme can't interchange (handwritten)

Exercises

All data are presented using IPA.

1. *Inuktitut* (Inuktitut is an indigenous language of Canada.)

   Consider the following data from Inuktitut.

   /a/ and /u/ and /i/ and /a/ (handwritten)

   /i/ and /u/ (handwritten)

   i u / a u / i a (handwritten, left margin)

a)	iglumut	'to a house'	h)	pinːa	'that one up there'
b)	ukiaq	'late fall'	i)	ani	'female's brother'
c)	aiviq	'walrus'	j)	iglu	'(snow)house'
d)	aniguvit	'if you leave'	k)	panːa	'that place up there'
e)	aglu	'seal's breathing hole'	l)	aivuq	'she goes home'
f)	iglumit	'from a house'	m)	ini	'place, spot'
g)	anigavit	'because you leave'	n)	ukiuq	'winter'

   a) List all the minimal pairs you can find in these data.

   b) For each minimal pair, identify the phonological contrast for which the pair of words provides evidence.

2. *Mokilese* (Mokilese is an Austronesian language of the South Pacific.)

   voiced i / voiceless i (handwritten)
   voiced u / voiceless u (handwritten)

   Examine the following data from Mokilese.

a)	pisan	'full of leaves'	g)	uduk	'flesh'
b)	tupukta	'bought'	h)	kaskas	'to throw'
c)	puko	'basket'	i)	poki	'to strike something'
d)	kisa	'we two'	j)	pil	'water'
e)	supwo	'firewood'	k)	apid	'outrigger support'
f)	kamwɔkiti	'to move'	l)	ludʒuk	'to tackle'

   Do [i] and [i̥] belong to separate phonemes, or are they allophones of the same phoneme? What about [u] and [u̥]? Be sure to justify your answer in the usual way.

3. *Gascon* (Gascon is spoken in southwestern France.)

   Consider the following data from Gascon. See table 2.29 in Chapter 2 for information about any unfamiliar IPA symbols.

   β between vowels   b = elsewhere (handwritten)
   d = word initial   nasalized   ð = between vowels (handwritten)

a)	brẽn	'endanger'	n)	gat	'cat'
b)	bako	'cow'	o)	lũŋg	'long'
c)	ũmbro	'shadow'	p)	saliβo	'saliva'
d)	krãmbo	'room'	q)	noβi	'husband'
e)	dilys	'Monday'	r)	aβe	'to have'
f)	dũŋko	'until'	s)	ʃiβaw	'horse'
g)	duso	'sweet'	t)	byðɛt	'gut'
h)	taldepãn	'leftover bread'	u)	eʃaðo	'hoe'
i)	pũnde	'to lay eggs'	v)	biɣar	'mosquito'
j)	dudze	'twelve'	w)	riɣut	'he laughed'
k)	guteʒa	'flow'	x)	agro	'sour'
l)	ẽŋgwãn	'this year'	y)	ʒuɣet	'he played'
m)	puðe	'to be able'			

Following the usual procedure, determine whether [b̪] and [β̞] belong to different phonemes or are allophones of the same phoneme. What about [d] and [ð]? And [g] and [ɣ]? Be sure to justify your analysis in the usual way.

4. *Korean* (Korean is the national language of Korea.)

   Consider the following data from Korean

a)	pʰul 풀	'glue'		f)	pap 밥	'food'
b)	pam 밤	'night'		g)	pʰal 팔	'arm'
c)	siɫpʰə 슬퍼	'sad'		h)	apʰə 아파	'hurt'
d)	pi 비	'rain'		i)	pul 불	'fire'
e)	pʰjo 표	'ticket'		j)	pan 반	'half'

   Do [p] and [pʰ] belong to separate phonemes in Korean, or are they allophones of one phoneme? Justify your analysis in the usual way.

5. *Hindi* (Hindi is an Indo-European language spoken in India.)

   Consider the segments [b] and [b̤] in the data below and answer the questions that follow. The segment transcribed [b̤] is a murmured voiced stop.

a)	bara	'large'		f)	b̤ɛd	'disagreement'
b)	b̤ari	'heavy'		g)	bais	'twenty-two'
c)	bina	'without'		h)	b̤əs	'buffalo'
d)	b̤ir	'crowd'		i)	bap	'father'
e)	bori	'sackcloth'		j)	b̤ag	'part'

   Are [b] and [b̤] allophones of the same phoneme, or do they belong to separate phonemes? Justify your analysis in the usual way.

6. *Swampy Cree* (Swampy Cree is an Indigenous language in Canada of the Algonquian family.)

   The following data from Swampy Cree show a number of different voiced and voiceless consonantal segments.

a)	niska	'goose'		l)	nisto	'three'
b)	kodak	'another'		m)	tʃiːgahigan	'axe'
c)	asabaːp	'thread'		n)	adim	'dog'
d)	waskoːw	'cloud'		o)	miːbit	'tooth'
e)	paskwaːw	'prairie'		p)	pimiː	'lard'
f)	niːgi	'my house'		q)	mide	'heart'
g)	koːgoːs	'pig'		r)	oːgik	'these'
h)	tahki	'often'		s)	tʃiːmaːn	'canoe'
i)	namwaːtʃ	'not at all'		t)	waːbos	'rabbit'
j)	ospwaːgan	'pipe'		u)	naːbeːw	'man'
k)	midʒihtʃij	'hand'		v)	miːdʒiwin	'food'

   i) Do [p] and [b] belong to separate phonemes, or are they allophones of one phoneme? What about [t] and [d], [k] and [g], and [tʃ] and [dʒ]? Justify your analysis in the usual way.

ii) Make a general statement about the relationship among all the consonantal pairs whose distribution you have examined.

7. *Korean* (Korean is the national language of Korea.)

   Consider the following data from Korean.

a)	pi	비	'rain'	m)	kæ 개	'dog'
b)	saŋdʒa 상자		'box'	n)	ip 입	'mouth'
c)	ta 다		'all'	o)	tʃa 자	'ruler'
d)	ɨmak 으악		'music'	p)	mat 맛	'taste'
e)	page 박에		'in the gourd'	q)	tʃogæ 조개	'clam'
f)	tʃunbi 준비		'preparation'	r)	podo 포도	'grape'
g)	melda 멀다		'far'	s)	ibul 이불	'comforter'
h)	madʒa 맞아		'correct'	t)	ilgə 일거	'read'
i)	tʃalba 짧다		'short'	u)	kanda 간다	'go'
j)	puldʒirɨda 불지르다		'set fire'	v)	paŋgɨm 방금	'just now'
k)	ipku 입구		'entrance'	w)	hakpu 학부	'undergraduate school'
l)	kɨktoro 극도		'extremely'			

   Following the usual procedures, determine whether [p] and [b] belong to different phonemes or are allophones of the same phoneme. What about [t] and [d]? [k] and [g]? [tʃ] and [dʒ]? Be sure to justify your answer in the usual way, by identifying either minimal pairs or complementary distribution.

8. Using the syllabification procedure outlined in section 3.2.2, draw the syllable structure for each of the following words.
   a) Hindi
   b) recent
   c) praying
   d) dinosaurs
   e) depth
   f) explanation

9. *English*

   Many speakers of English use two variants of [l]. One, called *clear l*, is transcribed as [l] in the following data. The other, called *dark l*, is transcribed as [ɫ]. Examine the data, and answer the questions that follow.

a)	lʌjf	'life'	g)	pʰıɫ	'pill'
b)	lip	'leap'	h)	fiɫ	'feel'
c)	luːz	'lose'	i)	hɛɫp	'help'
d)	ilowp	'elope'	j)	bʌɫk	'bulk'
e)	dilʌjt	'delight'	k)	sowɫd	'sold'
f)	slip	'sleep'	l)	fʊɫ	'full'

   Do [l] and [ɫ] belong to separate phonemes or are they allophones of the same phoneme? If you think they belong to separate phonemes, answer question (i). If you think they are allophones of the same phoneme, answer question (ii).

   i) State the evidence that makes your case for treating [l] and [ɫ] as separate phonemes.
   ii) State the distribution of [l] and [ɫ] in words.

10. *Canadian French*

   In the following data from Canadian French, the sounds in each pair are in complementary distribution.
   [i] and [ɪ] are allophones of one phoneme
   [y] and [ʏ] are allophones of a second phoneme
   [u] and [ʊ] are allophones of a third phoneme

   The symbol [y] represents a high front rounded tense vowel while [ʏ] represents a high front rounded lax vowel.

   Examine the data and answer the questions that follow.

a)	pilʏl	'pill'	o)	fini	'finished'
b)	griʃe	'to crunch'	p)	fɪj	'girl'
c)	grɪʃ	'it crunches'	q)	dzʏr	'hard'
d)	pətsi	'little (masc.)'	r)	tryke	'to fake'
e)	pətsɪt	'little (fem.)'	s)	fʊl	'(a) crowd'
f)	vitamɪn	'vitamin'	t)	plʏs	'more'
g)	saly	'hi'	u)	ru	'wheel'
h)	ʒʏp	'skirt'	v)	rʊt	'road'
i)	fyme	'smoke'	w)	suvã	'often'
j)	lynɛt	'glasses'	x)	trupo	'herd'
k)	tɔrdzy	'twisted'	y)	sʊp	'flexible'
l)	lʏn	'moon'	z)	tʊʃ	'touch'
m)	pɪp	'pipe'	aa)	fu	'crazy (masc.)'
n)	grimas	'grimace'	bb)	trʏk	'(a) trick'

   i)   With the help of reference to syllable structure, make a general statement about the distribution of [i] and [ɪ], [y] and [ʏ], [u] and [ʊ] in these words.

   ii) If you have completed the section on rule formalization, write a single rule that derives the allophones of each phoneme from the underlying form. Use features! Be sure to give your rule a name; use this name as you complete the derivations below.

   iii) Provide derivations for the words meaning 'vitamin' and 'glasses' (for a review of derivations, see section 3.4.1).

UR	/	/	'vitamin'	/	/	'glasses'
PR	[vitamɪn]			[lynɛt]		

11. *English*

   The following data contains both careful speech and fast speech forms. Note the differences and answer the questions that follow. Some phonetic detail irrelevant to the question has been omitted from the transcription. Remember that an asterisk before a form indicates that it is not acceptable to (most) native speakers.

Careful speech	Fast speech	Spelled form
a) æspərən	æsprən	aspirin
b) pɔrsələn	pɔrslən	porcelain
c) næʃənəlajz	næʃnəlajz	nationalize
d) rɪzənəbl̩	rɪznəbl̩	reasonable
e) ɪmædʒənətɪv	ɪmædʒnətɪv	imaginative
f) sɛpərəbɪlɪri	sɛprəbɪlɪri	separability
g) mɛmərajz	mɛmərajz (*mɛmrajz)	memorize
h) kənsɪdərejʃən	kənsɪdərejʃən (*kənsɪdrejʃən)	consideration

i) The deletion of schwa in rapid speech is constrained by a number of factors, one of which is illustrated in the examples given. State the simple generalization that distinguishes the acceptable instances of deletion in (a) to (f) from the unacceptable ones in (g) and (h).

ii) If you have completed the section on rule formalization, state your generalization using formal notation.

12. There are a number of natural classes in the vowel and consonant data below. Circle three natural classes in each set of sounds. Indicate which feature or features define the class, as in the example. The phone [x] is a voiceless velar fricative.

Example: [+voice]——(b   d   tʃ   k)   h ——[–continuant]

a) i   u
    e   o
        a

b) p   tʃ   k
          dʒ
    f   θ   ʃ   x
    m   ŋ

13. Name the single feature that distinguishes the sounds in each of the following pairs.

a) θ : ð	e) b : m	i) ʌ : ə
b) p : f	f) s : ʃ	j) s : θ
c) u : ʊ	g) i : ɪ	k) e : ɛ
d) i : e	h) k : g	l) u : o

14. Complete the feature matrix for each of the sounds indicated. The V abbreviates the features [+syllabic, –consonantal], and the C abbreviates the features [–syllabic, +consonantal].

a) [e]   V

$$\begin{bmatrix} +\text{sonorant} \\ \text{DORSAL} \\ -\text{high} \\ -\text{low} \end{bmatrix}$$

b) [ʃ]   C

$$\begin{bmatrix} -\text{sonorant} \\ -\text{voice} \\ -\text{nasal} \end{bmatrix}$$

c) [m]   C

$$\begin{bmatrix} +\text{sonorant} \\ \text{LABIAL} \end{bmatrix}$$

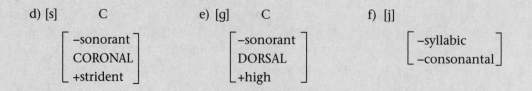

d) [s]   C

$$\begin{bmatrix} -\text{sonorant} \\ \text{CORONAL} \\ +\text{strident} \end{bmatrix}$$

e) [g]   C

$$\begin{bmatrix} -\text{sonorant} \\ \text{DORSAL} \\ +\text{high} \end{bmatrix}$$

f) [j]

$$\begin{bmatrix} -\text{syllabic} \\ -\text{consonantal} \end{bmatrix}$$

15. Change the following statements into rule notation. Be sure to name the process in question for each case. (See chapter 2, section 2.9.3, for a discussion of phonetic processes.)
    a) Stops and affricates become fricatives between vowels.
    b) A schwa is inserted between adjacent obstruents.
    c) Stops are nasalized in front of a nasal consonant.

16. Change each of the following rules to a statement, making reference to natural classes and common linguistic processes (# marks a word boundary).

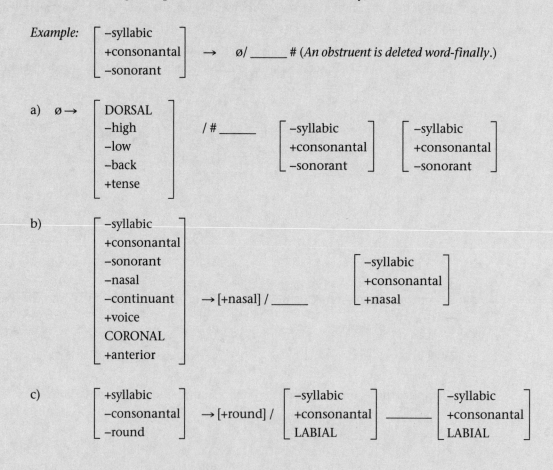

Example:
$$\begin{bmatrix} -\text{syllabic} \\ +\text{consonantal} \\ -\text{sonorant} \end{bmatrix} \rightarrow \emptyset/ \underline{\hspace{1cm}} \# \quad (\textit{An obstruent is deleted word-finally.})$$

a) $\emptyset \rightarrow \begin{bmatrix} \text{DORSAL} \\ -\text{high} \\ -\text{low} \\ -\text{back} \\ +\text{tense} \end{bmatrix} / \# \underline{\hspace{1cm}} \begin{bmatrix} -\text{syllabic} \\ +\text{consonantal} \\ -\text{sonorant} \end{bmatrix} \begin{bmatrix} -\text{syllabic} \\ +\text{consonantal} \\ -\text{sonorant} \end{bmatrix}$

b) $\begin{bmatrix} -\text{syllabic} \\ +\text{consonantal} \\ -\text{sonorant} \\ -\text{nasal} \\ -\text{continuant} \\ +\text{voice} \\ \text{CORONAL} \\ +\text{anterior} \end{bmatrix} \rightarrow [+\text{nasal}] / \underline{\hspace{1cm}} \begin{bmatrix} -\text{syllabic} \\ +\text{consonantal} \\ +\text{nasal} \end{bmatrix}$

c) $\begin{bmatrix} +\text{syllabic} \\ -\text{consonantal} \\ -\text{round} \end{bmatrix} \rightarrow [+\text{round}] / \begin{bmatrix} -\text{syllabic} \\ +\text{consonantal} \\ \text{LABIAL} \end{bmatrix} \underline{\hspace{1cm}} \begin{bmatrix} -\text{syllabic} \\ +\text{consonantal} \\ \text{LABIAL} \end{bmatrix}$

17. *Tamil* (Tamil is a Dravidian language spoken in southern India and Sri Lanka.)
In the following Tamil data, some words begin with glides while others do not. The symbol [ḍ] represents a voiced retroflex stop and the diacritic [ˌ] indicates dentals.

Initial j-glide		*Initial w-glide*		*No initial glide*	
a) jeli	'rat'	f) woḍi	'break'	k) arivu	'knowledge'
b) jiː	'fly'	g) woːlaj	'palm leaf'	l) aiṇṭu	'five'
c) jilaj	'leaf'	h) wuːsi	'needle'	m) aːsaj	'desire'
d) jeŋgeː	'where'	i) wujir	'life'	n) aːru	'river'
e) jiḍuppu	'waist'	j) woːram	'edge'	o) aːdi	'origin'

The occurrence of word-initial [w] and [j] is predictable. Using your knowledge of natural classes, make a general statement about the distribution of the glides.

To learn more about the topics discussed in this chapter, visit the Companion Website for *Contemporary Linguistic Analysis.*

Morphology: the analysis of word structure

Carve every word before you let it fall.

OLIVER WENDELL HOLMES, SR., *URANIA: A RHYMED LESSON* (1846)

NOTHING IS more important to language than words. Unlike phonemes and syllables, which are simply elements of sound, words carry meaning. And unlike sentences, which are created as needed and then discarded, words are permanently stored in a speaker's mental dictionary, or **lexicon**. They are the fundamental building blocks of communication.

The average high school student knows about sixty thousand basic words—items such as *read, language, cold*, and *near* whose meaning cannot be predicted from their component parts. Countless other words can be constructed and comprehended by the application of general rules to these items. For example, any speaker of English who knows the verb *phish* ('fraudulently obtain sensitive information via email') recognizes *phished* as its past tense form and can construct and interpret words such as *phisher, phishing*, and *unphishable.*

Linguists use the term **morphology** to refer to the part of the grammar that is concerned with words and word formation. As we will see, the study of morphology offers important insights into how language works, revealing the need for different categories of words, the presence of word-internal structure, and the existence of operations that create and modify words in various ways.

Language Matters How Many Words Does English Have?

The Oxford English Dictionary (20 volumes), whose stated goal is to present all of English vocabulary "from the time of the earliest records to the present day," contains a total of 616 500 word forms. But no dictionary can ever be up to date, because new words and new uses of old words are being added to the language all the time. *The online version of the Oxford English Dictionary* (www.oed.com) is updated on a quarterly basis and the online *Urban Dictionary* (www.urbandictionary.com) adds hundreds of new definitions EVERY DAY!

The Oxford English Dictionary, 2nd ed. (1989). By permission of Oxford University Press, www.oup.com

4.1 Words and word structure

As speakers of English, we rarely have difficulty segmenting a stream of speech sounds into words or deciding where to leave spaces when writing a sentence. What, though, is a word?

Linguists define the **word** as the smallest **free form** found in language. A free form is simply an element that does not have to occur in a fixed position with respect to neighbouring elements; in many cases, it can even appear in isolation. Consider, for instance, the following sentence.

(1) Dinosaurs are extinct.

We all share the intuition that *dinosaurs* is a word here and that the plural marker -*s* is not. But why? The key observation is that -*s* is not a free form: it never occurs in isolation and cannot be separated from the noun to which it belongs. (Elements that must be attached to something else are written here with a hyphen; an asterisk indicates unacceptability.)

(2) *Dinosaur are -s extinct.

In contrast, *dinosaurs* is a word because it can occur both in isolation, as in example (3), and in different positions within sentences, as in example (4):

(3) *Speaker A*: What creatures do children find most fascinating?
    Speaker B: Dinosaurs.

(4) *a.* Paleontologists study *dinosaurs*.
    b. *Dinosaurs* are studied by paleontologists.
    c. It's *dinosaurs* that paleontologists study.

Some words—like *are*—normally do not occur in isolation. However, they are still free forms because their positioning with respect to neighbouring words is not entirely fixed, as shown in (5).

(5) *a.* Dinosaurs *are* extinct.
    b. *Are* dinosaurs extinct?

4.1.1 Morphemes

Many words have an internal structure consisting of smaller units organized with respect to each other in a particular way. The most important component of word structure is the **morpheme**, the smallest unit of language that carries information about meaning or function. The word *builder*, for example, consists of two morphemes: *build* (with the meaning 'construct') and -*er* (which indicates that the entire word functions as a noun with the meaning 'one who builds'). Similarly, the word *houses* is made up of the morphemes *house* (with the meaning 'dwelling') and -*s* (with the meaning 'more than one').

Some words consist of a single morpheme. For example, the word *train* cannot be divided into smaller parts (say, *tr* and *ain* or *t* and *rain*) that carry information about the word's meaning or function. Such words are said to be **simple** and are distinguished from **complex** words, which contain two or more morphemes (see table 4.1).

TABLE 4.1	Words consisting of one or more morphemes		
One	**Two**	**Three**	**More than three**
and			
couple	couple-s		
hunt	hunt-er	hunt-er-s	
act	act-ive	act-iv-ate	re-act-iv-ate

Free and bound morphemes

A morpheme that can be a word by itself is called **free**, whereas a morpheme that must be attached to another element is **bound**. The morpheme *boy*, for example, is free because it can be used as a word on its own; plural *-s*, however, is bound.

Concepts that are expressed by free morphemes in English do not necessarily have the same status in other languages. For example, in Hare (an Athabaskan language spoken in Canada's Northwest Territories), morphemes that indicate body parts must always be attached to a morpheme designating a possessor, as shown in table 4.2. (The diacritic ´ marks a high tone.)

TABLE 4.2	Some body part names in Hare		
Without a possessor		**With a possessor**	
*fí	'head'	sefí	'my head'
*bé	'belly'	nebé	'your belly'
*dzé	'heart'	ʔedzé	'someone's heart/a heart'

In English, of course, body part names are free morphemes and do not have to be attached to another element.

Conversely, there are also some bound forms in English whose counterparts in other languages are free. For example, when attached to a verb, the bound morpheme *-ed* can express the notion 'past' or 'completed' (as in *I washed the car*, or *a washed car*). In Thai, in contrast, these notions are expressed by the free morpheme *lɛɛw*. As the following sentence shows, *lɛɛw* can even be separated from the verb by an intervening word. (Tone is not marked here.)

(6) Boon   thaan   khaaw   lɛɛw.
  Boon   eat   rice   past
  'Boon ate rice.'

Allomorphs

The variant pronunciations of a morpheme are called its **allomorphs**. The morpheme used to express indefiniteness in English has two allomorphs—*an* before a word that begins with a vowel sound and *a* before a word that begins with a consonant sound.

(7) an orange   a building
     an accent   a car
     an eel   a girl

Note that the choice of *an* or *a* is determined on the basis of pronunciation, not spelling, which is why we say <u>*an*</u> *M.A. degree* and <u>*a*</u> *U.S. dollar.*

Another example of allomorphic variation is found in the pronunciation of the plural morpheme *-s* in the following words.

(8) cats
     dogs
     judges

Whereas the plural is /s/ in *cats*, it is /z/ in *dogs*, and /əz/ in *judges*. Here again, selection of the proper allomorph is dependent on phonological facts. (For more on this, see section 4.6.)

Yet another case of allomorphic variation is found in the pronunciation of the prefix *in-*, with the meaning 'not'. The final consonant is pronounced as /n/ in most cases—*indirect, inactive*, and so on. But it is pronounced as /m/ in front of another labial consonant (*impossible, immodest*), as /l/ in front of another /l/ (*illegal*), and as /r/ in front of another /r/ (*irregular*). These changes are easy to spot because of the spelling, but remember that allomorphic variation involves pronunciation. In some cases, this is reflected in the spelling, but in other cases (such as plural *-s*), it is not.

4.1.2 Analyzing word structure

In order to represent the internal structure of words, it is necessary not only to identify each of the component morphemes but also to classify them in terms of their contribution to the meaning and function of the larger word.

Roots and affixes

Complex words typically consist of a **root** morpheme and one or more **affixes**. The root constitutes the core of the word and carries the major component of its meaning. Roots typically belong to a **lexical category**, such as noun (N), verb (V), adjective (A), or preposition (P).

Language Matters **Having Trouble Figuring Out a Word's Category?**

Here are some rules of thumb:

- ■ Nouns typically refer to people and things (*citizen, tree, intelligence*, etc.).
- ■ Verbs tend to denote actions, sensations, and states (*depart, teach, melt, remain*, etc.).
- ■ Adjectives usually name properties (*nice, red, tall*, etc.).
- ■ Prepositions generally encode spatial relations (*in, near, under*, etc.).

Unlike roots, affixes do not belong to a lexical category and are always bound morphemes. For example, the affix *-er* is a bound morpheme that combines with a verb such as *teach*, giving a noun with the meaning 'one who teaches'. The internal structure of this word can be represented as in figure 4.1. ('Af' stands for affix.)

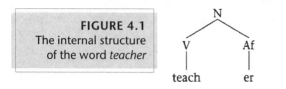

FIGURE 4.1
The internal structure of the word *teacher*

Figure 4.2 provides some additional examples of word structure.

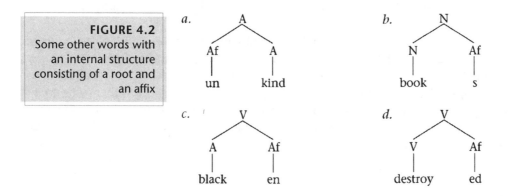

FIGURE 4.2
Some other words with an internal structure consisting of a root and an affix

The structural diagrams in figures 4.1 and 4.2 are often called **tree structures**. The information they depict can also be represented by using labelled bracketing—e.g., [$_A$ [$_{Af}$ un] [$_A$ kind]] for *unkind* and [$_N$ [$_N$ book] [$_{Af}$ s]] for *books*. (Because they are somewhat easier to read, we will generally use tree structures in this chapter.) Where the details of a word's structure are irrelevant to the point being considered, it is traditional to use a much simpler system of representation that indicates only the location of the morpheme boundaries: *un-kind, book-s*, and so on.

Bases

A **base** is the form to which an affix is added. In many cases, the base is also the root. In *books*, for example, the element to which the affix *-s* is added corresponds to the word's root. In other cases, however, the base can be larger than a root, which is always just a single morpheme. This happens in words such as *blackened*, in which the past tense affix *-ed* is added to the verbal base *blacken*—a unit consisting of the root morpheme *black* and the suffix *-en*.

FIGURE 4.3 A tree diagram illustrating the difference between a root and a base

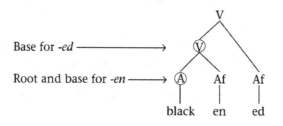

In this case, *black* is not only the root for the entire word but also the base for *-en*. The unit *blacken*, however, is simply the base for *-ed*.

Types of affixes

An affix that is attached to the front of its base is called a **prefix**, whereas an affix that is attached to the end of its base is termed a **suffix**. Both types of affix occur in English, as shown in table 4.3.

TABLE 4.3 Some English prefixes and suffixes	
Prefixes	**Suffixes**
de-activate	faith-*ful*
re-play	govern-*ment*
il-legal	hunt-*er*
in-accurate	kind-*ness*

We will consider the nature and properties of English affixes in more detail in sections 4.2.1 and 4.4.1.

Far less common than prefixes and suffixes are **infixes**, a type of affix that occurs within another morpheme. The data in table 4.4 from the Philippine language Tagalog contains examples of the infix *-in-*, which is inserted after the first consonant of the root to mark a completed event.

TABLE 4.4 Examples of the Tagalog infix *-in-*			
Base		**Infixed form**	
bili	'buy'	b-*in*-ili	'bought'
basa	'read'	b-*in*-asa	'read' (past tense)
sulat	'write'	s-*in*-ulat	'wrote'

Beginning students sometimes think that a morpheme such as *-en* in *black-en-ed* is an infix since it occurs between two other morphemes (*black* and *-ed*), but this is not right: *-en* is a suffix that combines with the adjective *black* to give the verb *blacken*, to which the suffix *-ed* is then added (see figure 4.3). To be an infix, an affix must occur *inside* another morpheme (as when Tagalog *-in-* appears inside *sulat* 'write'). Nothing of this sort happens in the case of *-en*.

A very special type of infixing system is found in Arabic and other Semitic languages, in which a typical root consists simply of three consonants. Various combinations of vowels are then inserted among the consonants to express a range of grammatical contrasts. (In the examples that follow, the segments of the root are written in boldface.)

(9) k**a**t**a**b**a**   k**u**t**i**b   **a**kt**u**b
    'wrote'   'has been written'   'am writing'

One way to represent the structure of such words is as follows, with the root and affixal vowels assigned to different **tiers**, or levels of structure, that combine with each other to give the word's pronunciation (see figure 4.4).

FIGURE 4.4
Two tiers used to represent the structure of the infixed word meaning 'has been written' in Arabic

Tagalog and Arabic offer examples of **non-concatenative morphology**, in which word building does not proceed in a linear, sequential manner, as happens in English words such as *travel-er-s* and *creat-iv-ity*.

Problematic cases

The majority of complex words in English are built from roots that are free morphemes. In the words *re-do* and *treat-ment*, for example, the root (*do* and *treat*, respectively) can itself be used as a word. Because most complex words work this way in English, English morphology is said to be **word-based**.

There is no such requirement in **morpheme-based systems**. In Japanese and Spanish, for instance, verbal roots are always bound and can therefore not stand alone: *camin* is not a word in Spanish, *arui* is not a word in Japanese, and so on. (In Spanish, the diacritic ´ marks a stressed syllable.)

(10) *a.* Spanish

camin-ó	**escuch**-ó	**limpi**-ó
walk-Pst	listen-Pst	wipe-Pst

b. Japanese

arui-ta	**kii**-ta	**hui**-ta
walk-Pst	listen-Pst	wipe-Pst

Although its morphology is overwhelmingly word-based, English too has a sizeable number of bound roots, as in words like *unkempt* and *inept*. Words like these each have their own story. In the case of *unkempt*, there was once a word *kempt* in English, with the meaning 'well-combed, neat'; it disappeared, leaving us with just *unkempt*. The word *inept* has a different history. It was borrowed into English as a whole word from Latin *ineptus* 'not suitable'; unknown to many, it is related to *apt* and *aptitude*, both from Latin *aptus* 'fitted, suited'.

Language Matters **Word Play**

The following excerpt from the humorous essay "How I Met My Wife", by Jack Winter, plays on the fact that certain English roots are bound and cannot be used as words:

I was **furling** my **wieldy** umbrella for the coat check when I saw her standing alone in the corner. She was a **descript** person, a woman in a state of total **array**. Her hair was **kempt**, her clothing **shevelled**, and she moved in a **gainly** way. (From *The New Yorker*, July 25, 1994).

Another class of words that are problematic for morphological analysis includes items such as *receive, deceive, conceive,* and *perceive,* or *permit, submit,* and *commit.* These items were borrowed into English from Latin (usually via French) as whole words, and their component syllables have no identifiable meaning of their own. Unlike the *in-* of *inept,* which retains the meaning of negation, the *re-* of *receive* does not have the sense of 'again' that it does in *redo,* and no specific meaning can be assigned to *-ceive* or *-mit.* For this reason, we will not treat these word parts as morphemes.

4.2 Derivation

Derivation uses an affix to build a word with a meaning and/or category distinct from that of its base. One of the most common derivational affixes in English is the suffix *-er,* which combines with a verb to form a noun with the meaning 'one who *V*s', as shown in table 4.5. (Do not confuse this suffix with the *-er* that applies to a noun in cases such as *Quebecer* and *islander,* or the *-er* that combines with an adjective in cases such as *taller* and *smarter.*)

TABLE 4.5	The derivational affix *-er*
Verb base	**Derived noun**
sell	sell-er (one who sells)
write	writ-er (one who writes)
teach	teach-er (one who teaches)
sing	sing-er (one who sings)
think	think-er (one who thinks)

Other examples of derivation include *treatment,* in which the suffix *-ment* combines with the verb *treat* to give the noun *treatment*; *unkind,* in which the prefix *un-* combines with the adjective *kind* to give a new adjective with a different meaning; and the other derived words illustrated in figure 4.5.

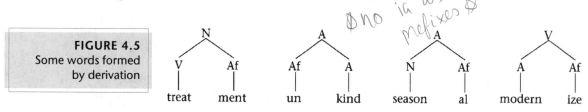

FIGURE 4.5
Some words formed by derivation

Once formed, derived words become independent lexical items that receive their own entry in a speaker's mental dictionary. As time goes by, they often take on special senses that are not predictable from the component morphemes. The word *writer,* for example, is generally used not simply for someone who can write but rather for someone who writes for a living (e.g., *She's a writer*); *comparable* (with stress on the first syllable) means 'similar' rather than 'able to be compared'; *profession* usually denotes a career rather than the act of professing; and so on.

4.2.1 Some English derivational affixes

Table 4.6 provides a partial list of English derivational affixes, along with information about the category of their usual base (ignoring bound roots) and of the resulting derived word. The entry for *-able* (line 7) states that it applies to a verb base and converts it into an adjective. Thus, if we add the affix *-able* to the verb *fix*, we get an adjective (with the meaning 'able to be fixed').

TABLE 4.6	Some English derivational affixes	
Affix	**Change**	**Examples**
Suffixes		
-al	V → N	refus-al, dispos-al, recit-al
-ant	V → N	claim-ant, defend-ant
-(at)ion	V → N	realiz-ation, assert-ion, protect-ion
-er	V → N	teach-er, work-er
-ing$_1$	V → N	the shoot-ing, the danc-ing
-ment	V → N	adjourn-ment, treat-ment, amaze-ment
-able	V → A	fix-able, do-able, understand-able
-ing$_2$	V → A	the sleep-ing giant, a blaz-ing fire
-ive	V → A	assert-ive, impress-ive, restrict-ive
-dom	N → N	king-dom, fief-dom
-ful	N → A	faith-ful, hope-ful, dread-ful
-(i)al	N → A	president-ial, nation-al
-(i)an	N → A	Arab-ian, Einstein-ian, Albert-an
-ic	N → A	cub-ic, optimist-ic, moron-ic
-ize$_1$	N → V	hospital-ize, crystall-ize
-less	N → A	penni-less, brain-less
-ous	N → A	poison-ous, lecher-ous
-ish	A → A	green-ish, tall-ish
-ate	A → V	activ-ate, captiv-ate
-en	A → V	dead-en, black-en, hard-en
-ize$_2$	A → V	modern-ize, national-ize
-ity	A → N	stupid-ity, prior-ity
-ness	A → N	happi-ness, kind-ness
Prefixes		
anti-	N → N	anti-abortion, anti-pollution
ex-	N → N	ex-president, ex-wife, ex-friend
de-	V → V	de-activate, de-mystify
dis-	V → V	dis-continue, dis-obey
mis-	V → V	mis-identify, mis-place
re-	V → V	re-think, re-do, re-state
un$_1$-	V → V	un-tie, un-lock, un-do
in-	A → A	in-competent, in-complete
un$_2$-	A → A	un-happy, un-fair, un-intelligible

Note: Unlike suffixes, English prefixes typically do not change the category of the base.

The category of the base to which an affix attaches is sometimes not obvious. In the case of *worker*, for instance, the base (*work*) is sometimes used as a verb (as in *They work hard*) and sometimes as a noun (as in *The work is time-consuming*). How then can we know the category of the base for *-er*? The key is to find words such as *teacher* and *writer*, in which the category of the base can be unequivocally determined. Because *teach* and *write* can only be verbs, we can infer that the base with which *-er* combines in the word *worker* is also a verb.

Complex derivations

Since derivation can apply to a word more than once, it is possible to create words with multiple layers of internal structure, as in the following example.

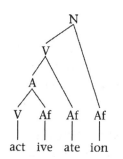

FIGURE 4.6
A word with a multilayered internal structure

As can be seen here, each layer of structure reflects the attachment of an affix to a base of the appropriate type. In the deepest layer, the affix *-ive* attaches to the verbal base *act* to give an adjective. In the next layer, *-ate* attaches to the adjective and converts it into a verb (*activate*). Finally, the affix *-ion* is added, converting the verb into the noun *activation*.

In some cases, the internal structure of a complex word may not be so transparent. How do we know, for instance, which of the two structures in figure 4.7 is the right one for the word *unhappiness*?

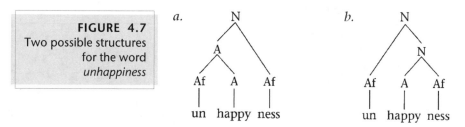

FIGURE 4.7
Two possible structures for the word *unhappiness*

The key observation is that the prefix *un-* combines quite freely with adjectives but not with nouns, as shown in table 4.7.

TABLE 4.7 The prefix *un-*	
***un*+ A**	***un* + N**
unable	*unknowledge
unkind	*unhealth
unhurt	*uninjury

This suggests that *un-* must combine with the adjective *happy* before it is converted into a noun by the suffix *-ness*, as depicted in figure 4.7a.

By contrast, in a word such as *unhealthy*, the prefix *un-* can be attached only AFTER the suffix has been added to the root. That is because *-y* turns nouns into adjectives (as in *wealthy* and *cloudy*), creating the category of word with which *un-* can combine (see figure 4.8).

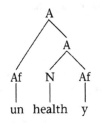

FIGURE 4.8
The internal structure of the word *unhealthy*

Constraints on derivation

Derivation is often subject to special constraints and restrictions. For instance, the suffix *-ant* (see table 4.6) can combine with bases of Latin origin, such as *assist* and *combat*, but not with those of native English origin, such as *help* and *fight*. Thus, we find words such as *assistant* and *combatant* but not **helpant* and **fightant*.

In other cases, derivation may be blocked by the existence of an alternative word. For instance, the word *cooker* (to mean 'one who cooks') is blocked by the existence of the word *cook*, which already has that meaning; *famosity* (from *famous*) is blocked by *fame*; and so on.

Sometimes, a derivational affix is able to attach only to bases with particular phonological properties. A good example of this involves the suffix *-en*, which can combine with some adjectives to create verbs with a causative meaning as shown in table 4.8 (*whiten* means roughly 'cause to become white').

TABLE 4.8   Restrictions on the use of *-en*

Acceptable	Unacceptable
whiten	*abstracten
soften	*bluen
madden	*angryen
quicken	*slowen
liven	*greenen

The contrasts illustrated here reflect the fact that *-en* can be attached only to a monosyllabic base that ends in a consonant other than the sonorants /l/, /r/, /m/, /n/, or /ŋ/. Thus, it can be added to *white*, *quick*, *mad*, and *live*, which are monosyllabic and end in a consonant of the right type. But it cannot be added to *abstract*, which has more than one syllable; to *slow* or *blue*, which end in a vowel; or to *green*, which ends in the wrong type of consonant.

4.2.2 Two classes of derivational affixes

It is common to distinguish between two types of derivational affixes in English. **Class 1 affixes** often trigger changes in the pronunciation of the base's consonants and vowels, and may affect stress placement as well. In addition, they often combine with bound roots, as in the last of the examples in table 4.9.

TABLE 4.9	Typical effects of Class 1 affixes	
Affix	**Sample word**	**Change triggered by affix**
-ity	san-ity; public-ity	vowel in the base changes from /e/ to /æ/ (cf. *s<u>a</u>ne*), final consonant of the base changes from /k/ to /s/, stress shifts to second syllable (cf. *públi<u>c</u>* vs. *publí<u>c</u>ity*)
-y	democrac-y	final consonant of the base changes from /t/ to /s/, stress shifts to second syllable (cf. *démocra<u>t</u>* vs. *demócra<u>cy</u>*)
-ive	product-ive	stress shifts to second syllable (cf. *próduct* vs. *prodúctive*)
-(i)al	part-ial	final consonant of the base changes from /t/ to /ʃ/ (cf. *par<u>t</u>* vs. *par<u>t</u>ial*)
-ize	critic-ize	final consonant of the base changes from /k/ to /s/ (cf. *criti<u>c</u>* vs. *criti<u>c</u>ize*)
-ion	nat-ion	final consonant of the base changes from /t/ to /ʃ/ (cf. *na<u>t</u>ive* vs. *na<u>t</u>ion*)

In contrast, **Class 2 affixes** tend to be phonologically neutral, having no effect on the segmental makeup of the base or on stress placement (see table 4.10).

TABLE 4.10	Some typical Class 2 affixes	
Affix	**Sample word**	**Change triggered by affix**
-ness	prompt-ness	None
-less	hair-less	None
-ful	hope-ful	None
-ly	quiet-ly	None
-er	defend-er	None
-ish	self-ish	None

As the following examples illustrate, a Class 2 affix cannot intervene between the root and a Class 1 affix.

(11) relat-ion-al   divis-ive-ness   *fear-less-ity   fear-less-ness
       ROOT 1 1   ROOT 1 2   ROOT 2 1   ROOT 2 2

All combinations of Class 1 and Class 2 affixes are found in English words, except one—a Class 2 suffix followed by a Class 1 suffix.

4.3 Compounding

Another common technique for word building in English involves **compounding**, the combination of two already existing words (see figure 4.9). With very few exceptions, the resulting compound word is a noun, a verb, or an adjective. (Possible examples of compound prepositions include the words *into* and *onto*.)

FIGURE 4.9
Some English
compounds

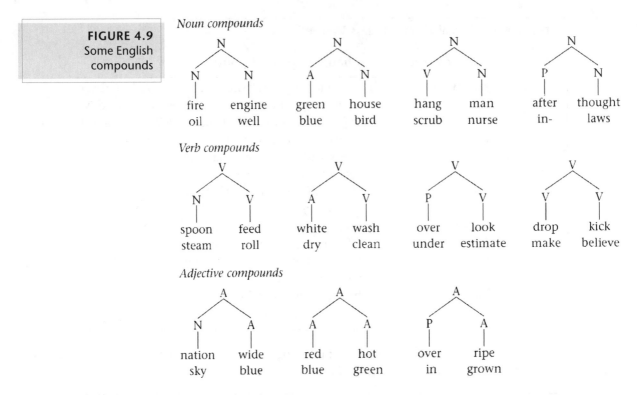

Noun compounds

N	N	N	N
N N	A N	V N	P N
fire engine	green house	hang man	after thought
oil well	blue bird	scrub nurse	in- laws

Verb compounds

V	V	V	V
N V	A V	P V	V V
spoon feed	white wash	over look	drop kick
steam roll	dry clean	under estimate	make believe

Adjective compounds

A	A	A
N A	A A	P A
nation wide	red hot	over ripe
sky blue	blue green	in grown

In the most common type of English compound, the rightmost morpheme determines the category of the entire word. Thus, *bluebird* is a noun because its rightmost component is a noun, *spoonfeed* is a verb because *feed* also belongs to this category, and *nationwide* is an adjective just as *wide* is. The morpheme that determines the category of the entire word is called the **head**.

Once formed, compounds can be combined with other words to create still larger compounds, as the examples in figure 4.10 show.

FIGURE 4.10
Compounds formed
from smaller
compounds

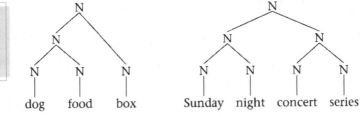

dog food box   Sunday night concert series

In addition, compounding can interact with derivation, yielding forms such as *election date*, in which the first word in the compound is the result of derivation, as shown in figure 4.11.

FIGURE 4.11
The interaction
of derivation
with compounding

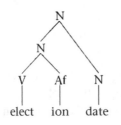

elect ion date

Compounding is an inexhaustible source of new words in English, as can easily be seen by perusing the new-word updates offered by Oxford Dictionaries Online. Recent additions include the following items, among many others.

TABLE 4.11 Some new compounds added to Oxford Dictionaries Online in the last several years

New compound	Meaning
bitcoin	a digital currency
buzzworthy	likely to arouse public interest and attention
binge-watch	watch multiple episodes of a TV program in rapid succession
digital detox	refraining from using electronic devices
hackerspace	a community-operated workspace where people with common interests can socialize and collaborate
sit ski	a ski with a seat fitted on top, designed to be used by skiers with limited or no mobility

4.3.1 Properties of compounds

English orthography is not consistent in representing compounds, which are sometimes written as single words, sometimes with a hyphen, and sometimes as separate words. In terms of pronunciation, however, an important generalization can be made (see table 4.12): adjective–noun compounds are characterized by more prominent stress on their first component. In non-compounds consisting of an adjective and a noun, in contrast, the second element is generally stressed.

TABLE 4.12 Compounds versus non-compounds

Compound word		Non-compound expressions	
greénhouse	'a glass-enclosed garden'	green hoúse	'a house painted green'
bláckboard	'a chalkboard'	black boárd	'a board that is black'
wét suit	'a diver's costume'	wet suít	'a suit that is wet'

A second distinguishing feature of compounds in English is that tense and plural markers can typically not be attached to the first element, although they can be added to the compound as a whole. (There are some exceptions, however, such as *craftsman* and *parks supervisor*.)

(12) *a.* Compound verb with internal tense:
   *The player [dropped kick] the ball through the goal post.

   b. Compound verb with external tense:
   The player [drop kick]ed the ball through the goal post.

(13) *a.* Compound noun with internal plural:
   *The [ducks hunter] didn't have a licence.

   b. Compound noun with external plural (different meaning):
   The [duck hunter]s didn't have a licence.

> **Language Matters Do You Say Brothers-in-Law or Brother-in-Laws?**
>
> Is it *governors-general* or *governor-generals*? *Maids-of-honour* or *maid-of-honours*? *Runners up* or *runner ups*? There is now variation on this point. For some people, at least some expressions of this type have become compounds, which is why the plural marker cannot occur inside, as it once had to.

4.3.2 Endocentric and exocentric compounds

In most cases, a compound denotes a subtype of the concept denoted by its head (the rightmost component). Thus, *dog food* is a type of food, a *caveman* is a type of man, *sky blue* is a type of blue, and so on. Such compounds are said to be (semantically) **endocentric**. In a smaller number of cases, however, the meaning of the compound does not follow from the meaning of its parts in this way. Thus, although *redneck* is a noun (like *neck*), it denotes a type of person, not a type of neck. Similarly, a *sabre-tooth* is a type of tiger rather than a type of tooth. Such compounds are **exocentric**.

A very striking difference between English endocentric and exocentric compounds sometimes shows up in cases where the head is a word like *tooth* or *foot*, which has an irregular plural form. Consider in this regard the examples in table 4.13.

TABLE 4.13 Pluralization in English compounds

In endocentric compounds	In exocentric compounds
wisdom t<u>ee</u>th	sabre-t<u>oo</u>th<u>s</u> (an extinct species of carnivore)
club f<u>ee</u>t	bigf<u>oo</u>t<u>s</u> (a mythical creature, or sasquatch)
policem<u>e</u>n	Watchm<u>an</u>s (a type of portable TV)
oak lea<u>ve</u>s	Maple Leaf<u>s</u> (Toronto's NHL hockey team)

Notice that whereas the endocentric compounds employ the usual irregular plural (*teeth*, *feet*, etc.), the exocentric compounds permit the regular plural suffix *-s*.

4.3.3 Compounds in other languages

The practice of combining words (especially nouns) to build a more complex word is very widespread in the languages of the world. With the exception of Tagalog, in which compounds are left-headed, the languages exemplified in table 4.14 all have compounds in which the rightmost element is the head. In right-headed Korean, for example, the head of *kot elum* 'icicle' is *elum* 'ice' since icicles are a type of ice, and the head of *nwun mwul* 'tears' is *mwul* 'water' since tears are a type of water. In left-headed Tagalog, in contrast, the head of *tubig-alat* 'sea water' is *tubig* 'water' since sea water is a type of water, and in *bayad-utang* 'debt payment', the head is *bayad* 'payment' since a debt payment is a type of payment.

TABLE 4.14	Noun compounds in various languages	
Korean		
kot elum straight ice 'icicle'	isul pi dew rain 'drizzle'	nwun mwul eye water 'tears'
Tagalog		
tubig-alat water salt 'sea water'	isip-lamok mind mosquito 'weak mind'	bayad-utang payment debt 'debt payment'
German		
Gast haus guest house 'inn'	Wort bedeutungs lehre word meaning theory 'semantics'	Fern seher far seer 'television'
Finnish		
lammas nahka turkki sheep skin coat 'sheepskin coat'	elin keino tulo vero laki life's means income tax law 'income tax law'	
Cree		
mishtikw naapeu wood man 'carpenter'	piyesuu upiiwiih duck feather 'duck feather'	ishkuteu utaapan fire vehicle 'train'
Source: "Compound Nouns," *East Cree Language Resources*, www.eastcree.org.		

4.4 Inflection

A large number of languages have contrasts such as singular versus plural and present versus past. Such contrasts are often marked with the help of **inflection**, the modification of a word's form to indicate grammatical information of various sorts.

4.4.1 Inflection in English

Inflection is most often expressed via **affixation**, the process of adding an affix to a base (The base to which an inflectional affix is added is sometimes called a **stem**.). Many languages (e.g., Japanese, Swahili, Inuktitut, and Finnish) have dozens of inflectional affixes. With only eight inflectional affixes (all suffixes), English is not a highly inflected language. Table 4.15 lists the inflectional affixes of English.[1]

TABLE 4.15	The English inflectional affixes
Nouns	
Plural -*s*	the book<u>s</u>
Possessive (genitive) -*'s*	John<u>'s</u> book
Verbs	
3rd person singular non-past -*s*	He read<u>s</u> well.
Progressive -*ing*	He is work<u>ing</u>.
Past tense -*ed*	He work<u>ed</u>.
Past participle -*en*/-*ed*	He has eat<u>en</u> /stud<u>ied</u>.
Adjectives	
Comparative -*er*	the small<u>er</u> one
Superlative -*est*	the small<u>est</u> one

Although most inflection in English involves affixation, some words mark inflectional contrasts in other ways. This is most obvious in the case of verbs, a number of which indicate past tense by substituting one form with another (as in *am-was* or *go-went*) or by internal changes of various sorts (e.g., *come-came, see-saw, fall-fell, eat-ate*). We will consider these processes in more detail in section 4.5.

4.4.2 Inflection versus derivation

Because inflection and derivation are both commonly marked by affixation, the distinction between the two can be subtle. Four criteria are commonly used to help distinguish between inflectional and derivational affixes.

Category change

Inflection does not change either the syntactic category or the type of meaning found in the word to which it applies.

FIGURE 4.12
The output of inflection: there is no change in either the category of the base or the type of meaning it denotes.

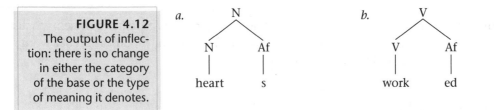

The form produced by adding the plural suffix -*s* in figure 4.12a is still a noun and has the same type of meaning as the base. Even though *hearts* differs from *heart* in referring to several things rather than just one, the type of thing(s) to which it refers remains the same. Similarly, a past tense suffix such as the one in figure 4.12b indicates that the action took place in the past, but the word remains a verb and it continues to denote the same type of action.

In contrast, derivational suffixes usually change the category and/or the type of meaning of the form to which they apply. Consider the examples of derivation given in figure 4.13.

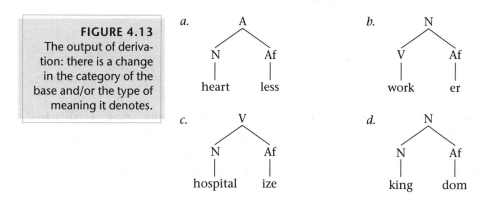

FIGURE 4.13
The output of derivation: there is a change in the category of the base and/or the type of meaning it denotes.

As figure 4.13a shows, *-less* makes an adjective out of a noun, changing the type of meaning it expresses from a thing (*heart*) to a property (*heartless*). Parallel changes in category and type of meaning are brought about by *-er* (V to N) and *-ize* (N to V). Matters are a little different in the case of *-dom*, which does not bring about a category change in the word *kingdom* since both the base and the resulting word are nouns. However, *-dom* does modify the type of meaning from a person (*king*) to a place (*kingdom*).

Order

A second property of inflectional affixes has to do with the order in which they are combined with a base relative to derivational affixes. As figure 4.14 illustrates, derivational affixes must be closer to the base than inflectional affixes (IA = inflectional affix; DA = derivational affix).

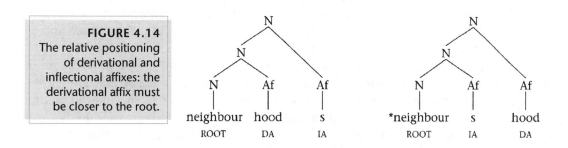

FIGURE 4.14
The relative positioning of derivational and inflectional affixes: the derivational affix must be closer to the root.

The positioning of inflectional affixes outside derivational affixes in these examples reflects the fact that inflection applies to the output of derivation.

Productivity

A third criterion for distinguishing between inflectional and derivational affixes has to do with **productivity**, the relative freedom with which they can combine with bases of the appropriate category. Inflectional affixes are typically more productive than derivational affixes. The suffix *-s*, for example, can combine with virtually any noun that allows a plural form (aside from a few exceptions such as *oxen* and *feet*). In contrast, derivational affixes characteristically apply to restricted classes of bases. Thus, *-ize* can combine with only certain adjectives to form a verb.

(14) modern-ize   *new-ize
       legal-ize   *lawful-ize
       final-ize   *last-ize

In the case of verbs, matters are somewhat more complicated, since many English verbs have irregular past tense forms (*saw*, *left*, *went*, and so on). Nonetheless, the inflectional affix *-ed* is much more generally applicable than a derivational affix such as *-ment*. All the verbs in table 4.16 can take the regular past tense ending, but only the first three are able to take the *-ment* suffix.

TABLE 4.16   Compatibility of verb bases with inflectional *-ed* and derivational *-ment*

Verb	With *-ed*	With *-ment*
confine	confined	confinement
align	aligned	alignment
treat	treated	treatment
arrest	arrested	*arrestment
straighten	straightened	*straightenment
cure	cured	*curement

Semantic transparency

Finally, the contribution of an inflectional affix to the word's meaning is usually completely transparent and consistent. Adding a plural suffix gives the meaning 'more than one' (*cat-cats*, *tree-trees*), adding a past tense suffix gives the meaning 'prior to the present' (*walk-walked*, *play-played*), and so forth.

Things are not always so straightforward in the case of derivation, where it is often not possible to predict the word's meaning from its parts. An *actor* is someone who acts, but a *professor* is not someone who professes. The word *teacher* often refers to someone who holds a teaching job, but no such implication is associated with *walker*. *Government* can be used to refer either to an institution (as in 'the government's agenda') or the act of governing (as in 'government by the people'), but *abandonment* lacks the first type of meaning.

4.4.3 Case and agreement

Inflection is a very widely used morphological process, and its effects can be seen in far more cases than can be discussed here. Nonetheless, two additional phenomena are worth mentioning, however briefly, because of their importance and frequency in languages of the world.

Case inflection indicates a word's grammatical role in the sentence (subject, direct object, and so on). A very simple example of this can be seen in English, where the pronoun form *he* is used for subjects and the form *him* is employed for direct objects. There is a comparable contrast between *I* and *me*, *she* and *her*, *we* and *us*, and *they* and *them*.

(15) He met the new professor.   The new professor met him.

      ↑   ↑

    subject   direct object

Agreement takes place when one word is inflected to match certain grammatical properties of another word. Especially common is agreement for **number** (singular vs. plural) and for **person** (first person—speaker; second person—addressee; third person—anyone else). Here again, English offers a simple example: the suffix *-s* appears on a present tense verb when the subject is third person singular.

(16) That woman speak**s** French.

(Compare: *I speak French* or *They speak French*, with no *-s* suffix.)

4.5 Other morphological phenomena

No introductory textbook can hope to offer a full survey of the processes that contribute to word formation in human language. The preceding sections have touched upon many of the most common and central processes, but a number of others merit consideration as well. We will divide these into two groups—those that pertain primarily to inflection and those that involve other sorts of phenomena.

4.5.1 Processes primarily related to inflection

Internal change

Internal change is a process that substitutes one non-morphemic segment for another to mark a grammatical contrast, as illustrated in the pairs of words in table 4.17.

TABLE 4.17 Internal change in English	
s**i**ng (present)	s**a**ng (past)
s**i**nk (present)	s**a**nk (past)
dr**i**ve (present)	dr**o**ve (past)
f**oo**t (singular)	f**ee**t (plural)
g**oo**se (singular)	g**ee**se (plural)

Verbs such as *sing, sink,* and *drive* form their past tense by changing the vowel (e.g., from *i* to *a* in the first two examples). The term **ablaut** is often used for vowel alternations that mark grammatical contrasts in this way.

Some internal changes reflect phonologically conditioned alternations from an earlier stage in the language's history. The irregular plurals *geese* and *feet* came about in this way: the original back vowel /o/ in the words *goose* and *foot* was fronted under the influence of the front vowel in the old plural suffix /i/, which was subsequently dropped. This type of change in English and other Germanic languages is known as **umlaut**.

(17) Old singular form of *goose*:   /gos/
Old plural form: /gos-i/
Umlaut: /gœs-i/(/œ/ is a front version of the vowel /o/)
Loss of the plural suffix: /gœs/
Later changes: /ges/ and then /gis/ 'geese'

Internal change differs from infixing in important ways. As shown by the Tagalog examples in table 4.4 (section 4.1.2), the base into which an infix is inserted typically exists as a separate form elsewhere in the language (compare *sulat* 'write' with *s-in-ulat* 'wrote'). Matters are quite different in the case of alternations such as *foot/feet* or *sing/sang* in English, since we have no form *ft* meaning 'lower extremity of the leg' or *sng* meaning 'produce words in a musical tone'. Moreover, in contrast to the situation in Tagalog, the segments that alternate when there is internal change are not systematically associated with a particular meaning and therefore do not count as morphemes: the *a* of *ran* and the *o* of *drove* do not in general carry the meaning 'past' in English any more than the *ee* of *geese* normally carries the meaning 'plural'.

Suppletion

Suppletion replaces a morpheme with an entirely different morpheme in order to indicate a grammatical contrast. Examples of this phenomenon in English include the use of *went* as the past tense form of the verb *go*, and *was* and *were* as the past tense forms of *be*. Table 4.18 provides examples of suppletion in some other European languages.

TABLE 4.18	Suppletion in some European languages	
Language	**Basic form**	**Suppletive form**
French	*avoir* 'to have'	*eu* 'had'
Spanish	*ir* 'to go'	*fue* '(s/he) went'
German	*ist* 'is'	*sind* 'are'
Russian	*xorošij* 'good'	*lučše* 'better'

In some cases, it is hard to distinguish between suppletion and internal change. For example, are the past tense forms of *think* (*thought*) and *seek* (*sought*) instances of suppletion or internal change? This type of alternation is sometimes treated as an extreme form of internal change, but the term **partial suppletion** is also used by some linguists.

Reduplication

A common morphological process in some languages involves **reduplication**, which marks a grammatical or semantic contrast by repeating all or part of the base to which it applies.

Repetition of the entire base yields **full reduplication**, as shown in the Turkish and Indonesian examples in table 4.19.

TABLE 4.19 Examples of full reduplication			
Base		**Reduplicated form**	
Turkish			
çabuk	'quick'	çabuk çabuk	'quickly'
yavaş	'slow'	yavaş yavaş	'slowly'
güzel	'beautiful'	güzel güzel	'beautifully'
Indonesian			
orang	'man'	orang orang	'men'
anak	'child'	anak anak	'children'
mangga	'mango'	mangga mangga	'mangoes'

In contrast, **partial reduplication** copies only part of the base. In the Tagalog examples in table 4.20, for instance, reduplication affects only the first consonant-vowel sequence rather than the entire word.

TABLE 4.20 Examples of partial reduplication in Tagalog			
Base		**Reduplicated form**	
takbo	'run'	tatakbo	'will run'
lakad	'walk'	lalakad	'will walk'
pili	'choose'	pipili	'will choose'

English makes limited use of partial reduplication in various semi-idiomatic expressions such as *hocus pocus, razzle dazzle,* and *nitty gritty,* but this process does not mark grammatical information and is not <u>productive</u>. → cannot be used in every word

Tone

In Mono-Bili (spoken in the Congo), **tone** is used to make the distinction between past and future tense, a process called **tone placement**. (A high tone is marked by ´ and a low tone by ` in table 4.21.)

TABLE 4.21 Past and future tense in Mono-Bili			
Past		**Future**	
dá	'spanked'	dà	'will spank'
zí	'ate'	zì	'will eat'
wó	'killed'	wò	'will kill'

4.5.2 **Other processes**

Cliticization

Some morphemes behave like words in terms of their meaning and function but are unable to stand alone as independent forms for phonological reasons. Called **clitics**, these elements must always be pronounced with another word (known as a **host**). A good example of this can be found in English, where certain verb forms have reduced variants (*'m* for *am*, *'s* for *is*, and *'re* for *are*) that cannot stand alone. Cliticization occurs, attaching these elements to the preceding word.

(18) *a.* I*'m* leaving now.
    b. Mary*'s* going to succeed.
    c. They*'re* here now.

Cliticization is also common in French, which has a set of unstressed clitic object pronouns that must be attached to the verb. The two are then pronounced as if they formed a single word (despite the way the second example is written).

(19) Jean *t'*aime.   Suzanne *les* voit.
    John you-likes   Suzanne them-sees
    'John likes you.'   'Suzanne sees them.'

Clitics that attach to the end of their host (as in the English examples) are called **enclitics**; those that attach to the beginning of their host (as in the French examples) are known as **proclitics**.

The effects of cliticization can bear a superficial resemblance to affixation: in both cases, a morpheme that cannot stand alone is attached to a word belonging to a syntactic category, such as a noun or a verb.

Conversion

Conversion is a process that assigns an already existing word to a new syntactic category. Even though it does not add an affix, conversion is often considered to be a type of derivation because of the change in category and meaning that it brings about. For this reason, it is sometimes called **zero derivation**. Table 4.22 contains examples of the three most common types of conversion in English. Less common types of conversion can yield a noun from an adjective (*the poor, millennials*) and even a verb from a preposition (*down a beer, up the price*).

TABLE 4.22 Examples of conversion		
V derived from N	**N derived from V**	**V derived from A**
ink (a contract)	(a long) run	dirty (a shirt)
butter (the bread)	(a hot) drink	empty (the box)
ship (the package)	(a pleasant) drive	better (the old score)
nail (the door shut)	(a brief) report	right (a wrong)
button (the shirt)	(an important) call	total (a car)
medal (in the Olympics)	(a big) ask	weird (someone out)

A notorious recent example of conversion involves the use of the noun *friend* as a verb to mean 'add someone as a friend on a social networking website', making it distinct from the already existent word *befriend*, which refers to a more conventional social relationship. The transition to verbhood in this case is confirmed by the appearance of derived words such as *unfriend* and *defriend*, created with the help of prefixes used for other verbs in the language (*untie, deactivate*).

Conversion is usually restricted to words containing a single morpheme, although there are some exceptions, such as *e-mail* (noun to verb) and *dirt-y* (adjective to verb). In addition, it is common in English to form nouns from verb + preposition combinations—a *toss-up*, a *slow-down*, a *dropout*, and so on. The result is a headless compound—the category of the entire word (noun) cannot be traced to either of its component parts, one of which is a verb and the other a preposition.

Stress placement provides a useful clue to the category of related bisyllabic words in English, regardless of which one is more basic. As the examples in table 4.23 show, the verb has stress on the final syllable while the corresponding noun is stressed on the first syllable. (Stress is represented here by ´.)

TABLE 4.23   Stress shift and conversion of two-syllable words

Verb	Noun
implánt	ímplant
impórt	ímport
presént	présent
subjéct	súbject
contést	cóntest
slow dówn	slówdown

Clipping

Clipping is a process that shortens a polysyllabic word by deleting one or more syllables. Some of the most common products of clipping are names—*Liz, Ron, Rob, Sue,* and so on. Clipping is especially popular in casual speech, where it has yielded forms like *prof* for *professor, psych* for *psychology, bot* for *robot, doc* for *doctor,* and *burger* for *hamburger.* However, clipped forms often become accepted in general usage: *app, ad, auto, lab, sub, deli, demo,* and *condo.*

Language Matters Some Cases of Clipping That Might Surprise You

zoo < zoological garden
fax < facsimile
fan (as in sports) < fanatic
flu < influenza
van < caravan
mob < mobile vulgus (Latin, for 'fickle crowd')

A popular twenty-first-century clip is *blog*, from *Web log*—a personal website-based log of events, comments, and links. Once coined (in the spring of 1999), *blog* quickly appeared in compounds (*blog archive, blog post*) and has undergone conversion to a verb (as in 'things to blog about'). The verb, in turn, has undergone derivation, resulting in the noun *blogger*. No wonder *blog* was voted the new word most likely to succeed at the 2003 meeting of the American Dialect Society!

Blending

Blending creates words from non-morphemic parts of two already existing items, usually the first part of one and the final part of the other. Innovations of this type include *froyo* from *frozen yogurt*, *wi-fi* from *wireless* and *hi-fi*, *bromance* from *brother* and *romance*, *sexting* from *sex* and *texting*, and *jeggings* from *jeans* and *leggings*. Older examples include *brunch* from *breakfast* and *lunch*, *smog* from *smoke* and *fog*, *motel* from *motor* and *hotel*, *instagram* from *instant camera* and *telegram*, *aerobicise* from *aerobics* and *exercise*, *chunnel* (for the underwater link between Britain and mainland Europe) from *channel* and *tunnel*, and *infomercial* from *information* and *commercial*. And where would we be without the word *toonie*, the affectionate name for Canada's two-dollar coin—a blend of *two* and *loonie*?

Another type of blend, common in languages of Asia, is strongly syllable-oriented: two or more words each contribute a syllable to the blend.

(20) *a.* Tagalog
tap-si-log < tapa sinangag itlog
breakfast combination (from 'dried meat – fried rice – egg')

b. Malay
pulada < pusat latihan darat
army training camp (from 'centre – training – army')

In Japanese, Korean, and Mandarin, nicknames for universities (among other words) are often created in this way.

(21) *a.* Korea Tayhakkyo > Kotay
Korea University

b. Tokyo Daigakku > Todai
Tokyo University

c. Beijing Da Xue > Beida
Beijing University

Sometimes, a word is formed by a process that is on the borderline between compounding and blending in that it combines all of one word with part of another. Examples of this in English include *perma-press, workaholic, medicare, guesstimate,* and *mansplain*. A fairly productive strategy of this type involves the creation of words that begin with *e*, from *electronic*: *e-mail, e-banking, e-waste, e-business, e-cigarette*, and so on.

Backformation

Backformation is a process that creates a new word by removing a real or supposed affix from another word in the language. *Resurrect* was originally formed in this way from *resurrection*. Other backformations in English include *enthuse* from *enthusiasm*, *donate* from *donation*, *liposuct* from *liposuction*, *liaise* from *liaison*, and *self-destruct* from *self-destruction*.

Language Matters Some Words That Originated as Blends

Some words become part of the language without most of its users having any idea of their origin. For example, all of the following words began as blends.

bit (unit of information in computer science) < binary + digit
modem < modulator + demodulator
pixel < picture + element
quasar < quasi + stellar
chortle < chuckle + snort
spam (the sandwich meat) < spiced + ham
cyborg < cybernetics + organism

Sometimes, backformation involves an incorrect assumption about a word's form: for example, the word *pea* was derived from the singular noun *pease*, whose final /z/ was incorrectly interpreted as the plural suffix.

Words that end in *-or* or *-er* have proven very susceptible to backformation in English. Because hundreds of such words are the result of affixation (*runner, walker, collector,* etc.), any word with this shape is likely to be perceived as a verb + *-er* combination. The words *editor, peddler, swindler,* and, more recently, *vapor* have all been (mis)analyzed in this way, with the results summarized in table 4.24.

TABLE 4.24   Some examples of backformation

Original word	Perceived structure	Verb formed by backformation
editor	edit + or	edit
peddler	peddle + er	peddle
swindler	swindle + er	swindle
vapor	vap + or	vape

Two other familiar backformations are *lase* and *tase*, from *laser* and *taser*, respectively, each of which have their own unusual origin (see "Acronyms and initialisms" on **page 126**).

Language Matters Word of the Year

Every year, Oxford Dictionaries picks a 'word of the year'. Among the winners in recent years was *selfie*—a root-plus-suffix combination that refers to a photo that one has taken of oneself, usually with a smart phone. Runner-ups included *showrooming* (a suffixed compound that describes the practice of examining a product in a store before buying it at a lower price online) and *twerk* (dance to popular music in a sexually provocative manner)—a word that Oxford lexicographers think may be a blend of *twist* or *twitch* and *work*.

Acronyms and initialisms

Acronyms are formed by taking the initial letters of (some or all) the words in a phrase or title and pronouncing them as a word. This type of word formation is especially common in names of organizations and in military and scientific terminology. Common examples include *UNICEF* for *United Nations International Children's Emergency Fund*, *CIDA* for *Canadian International Development Agency*, *NATO* for *North Atlantic Treaty Organization*, and *AIDS* for *acquired immune deficiency syndrome*. More recent innovations include *ASAP* 'as soon as possible', *YOLO* 'you only live once', *FOMO* 'fear of missing out', and *BOGO* 'buy one, get one (free)'.

Acronyms are to be distinguished from **initialisms** such as *PEI* for *Prince Edward Island* or *USA* for *United States of America*, not to mention *DIY* for *do it yourself*, *LOL* for *laugh out loud*, and *BYOB* for *bring your own booze*, all of which are pronounced as a series of letters rather than as a word. An intermediate case is *CD-ROM*, a compound consisting of the initialism *CD* (*compact disc*) and the acronym *ROM* (*read-only memory*).

Over time, acronyms can turn into ordinary lexical items as speakers become unaware of their origin. Four commonly used words of this type are *radar* (from *radio detecting and ranging*), *scuba* (*self-contained underwater breathing apparatus*), *laser* (*light amplification by stimulated emission of radiation*), and *taser* (named by its inventor after his hero, Tom Swift: *Thomas A. Swift's electrical rifle*)!

Onomatopoeia

All languages have some words that have been created to sound like the thing that they name. Examples of such **onomatopoeic words** in English include *buzz, hiss, sizzle,* and *cuckoo*. Since onomatopoeic words are not exact phonetic copies of noises, their form can differ from language to language, as shown in table 4.25.

TABLE 4.25	Onomatopoeia across languages	
English	**Japanese**	**Tagalog**
cock-a-doodle-doo	kokekokko	kuk-kukaok
meow	nyaa	ngiyaw
chirp	pii-pii	tiririt
bow-wow	wan-wan	aw-aw

English does not always have an equivalent for the onomatopoeic words found in other languages. The Athabaskan language Slavey, for instance, has the onomatopoeic word [sah sah sah] for 'the sound of a bear walking unseen not far from camp', [ðik] for 'the sound of a knife hitting a tree', and [tɬóòtʃ] for 'the sound of an egg splattering'.

Other sources of new words

Sometimes, a word may be created from scratch. Called **word manufacture** or **coinage**, this phenomenon is especially common in the case of product names, including *Kodak, Dacron, Orlon,* and *Teflon*. (Notice how the *on* of the final three words makes them sound more scientific, perhaps because an affix with this form occurs in science-related words of Greek origin such as *phenomenon* and *automaton*.)

New words can also sometimes be created from names, including those listed in table 4.26. Words created in this way are called **eponyms**.

TABLE 4.26	Some English words created from names
Word	**Name of the person**
watt	James Watt (late 18th-century scientist)
curie	Marie and Pierre Curie (early 20th-century scientists)
Fahrenheit	Gabriel Fahrenheit (18th-century scientist)
boycott	Charles Boycott (19th-century land agent in Ireland who was ostracized for refusing to lower rents)

In still other cases, brand names can become so widely known that they are accepted as generic terms for the product with which they are associated. The words *kleenex* for 'facial tissue' and *xerox* for 'photocopy' are two obvious examples of this, as is the verb *google* in the sense of 'conduct an Internet search'.

Finally, languages frequently look to other languages for new words. English has always been open to borrowing of this sort, and the language continues to absorb new words from many different sources—*latte* from Italian, *feng shui* from Chinese, *al Qaeda* from Arabic, and so forth.

Language Matters What's the Longest Word in English?

Is it

ANTIDISESTABLISHMENTARIANISM (28 letters)
(the belief that opposes removing the tie between church and state)?

Or is it

SUPERCALIFRAGILISTICEXPIALIDOCIOUS (34 letters)
('extremely wonderful' from the 1964 Disney movie *Mary Poppins*)?

Neither! The longest English word in any dictionary is

PNEUMONOULTRAMICROSCOPICSILICOVOLCANOCONIOSIS
(45 letters; also spelled ' . . . koniosis')
(a lung disease caused by breathing in particles of siliceous volcanic dust).

4.6 Morphophonemics

A word's pronunciation can be affected by morphological factors, including its internal structure. The study of these effects is known as **morphophonemics** (or **morphophonology**).

A well-known example of a morphophonemic phenomenon in English involves the plural suffix *-s*, which can be /s/, /z/, or /əz/, depending on the context, as mentioned in section 4.1.1.

(22) lip/s/
pill/z/
judg/əz/

This alternation is, in part, the result of phonetic factors: voiceless /-s/ occurs after voiceless sounds (such as /p/), voiced /-z/ occurs after voiced sounds (such as /l/), and the /-əz/ form shows up only when a vowel is needed to break up a non-English consonant cluster (no English syllable ends with the coda /dʒz/). What makes the alternation morphophonemic is its interaction with two additional factors.

First, the alternation involves separate phonemes—/s/ and /z/. In this, it differs from a purely phonetic alternation, such as aspiration of the /t/ in *top* but not *stop*, a variation that involves allophones of the same phoneme.

Second, morphological structure matters. It is perfectly possible to have /s/ after /l/ in English when they are both in the same morpheme, as in the word *pulse*. But when the 's' represents the plural as it does in *pills*, and is therefore a separate morpheme, only /z/ is permitted. Alternations like this that occur specifically at morpheme boundaries are sometimes referred to as **sandhi**, a Sanskrit word used to describe similar phenomena in the languages of India, where morphophonological analysis was being done in the 4th century BC.

Another example of morphophonemic alternation can be seen in the contrast illustrated in table 4.27.

TABLE 4.27   A contrast between two negative prefixes

Context	The prefix *in-*	The prefix *un-*
in front of a vowel	in-active	un-announced
in front of /p/	im-possible	un-proven
in front of /l/	il-legal	un-lawful
in front of /r/	ir-regular	un-readable

Here *in-* (but not *un-*) manifests a morphophonemic alternation involving the phonemes /n/, /m/, /l/, and /r/ at the boundary between the prefix and the root.

Summing up

This chapter has focused on the structure and formation of **words** in human language. **Morphemes** are the basic building blocks for words. These elements can be classified in a variety of ways (**free** versus **bound, root** versus **affix, prefix** versus **suffix**) and can be combined and modified under various conditions to build words.

The two basic types of word formation in English are **derivation** and **compounding**. **Inflection**, a change in the form of a word to convey grammatical information such as plurality or tense, can be expressed via **affixation, internal change, reduplication,** and **tone** placement. Other important morphological phenomena include **cliticization, conversion, clipping, blending,** and **backformation.**

Note

1. There are three *-ing* affixes in English: one inflectional and two derivational. Inflectional *-ing* combines with a verb to give another verb, as in *He is breathing*. One derivational *-ing* combines with a verb to give a noun (*The breathing of the runners*) and the other converts a verb into an adjective (*the sleeping giant*)—see table 4.6. There are also two types of *-en/-ed* suffix: one inflectional, as noted in table 4.15, and the other derivational. The latter converts verbs into adjectives so that they can appear in structures such as the following:

the *stolen* money

the *escaped* convict

Recommended reading

Anderson, Stephen. 1989. "Morphological Theory." In *Linguistics: The Cambridge Survey*. Vol. 1. Edited by Frederick J Newmeyer, 146–91. New York: Cambridge University Press.

Aronoff, Mark, and Kirsten Fudeman. 2010. *What Is Morphology?* 2nd ed. Boston: Wiley-Blackwell.

Bauer, Laurie. 2003. *Introducing Linguistic Morphology*. 2nd ed. Washington, DC: Georgetown University Press.

Bauer, Laurie, Rochelle Lieber, and Ingo Plag. 2013. *The Oxford Reference Guide to English Morphology*. Oxford, UK: Oxford University Press.

Booij, Geert. 2005. *The Grammar of Words*. Oxford, UK: Oxford University Press.

Gleason, Henry Allan. 1961. *An Introduction to Descriptive Linguistics*. Rev. ed. New York: Holt, Rinehart and Winston.

Katamba, Francis. 2006. *Morphology*. 2nd ed. New York: Palgrave Macmillan.

Pinker, Steven. 1999. *Words and Rules: The Ingredients of Language*. New York: Basic Books.

Appendix: How to identify morphemes in unfamiliar languages

An important part of morphological analysis involves identifying morphemes in unfamiliar languages and determining the nature of the information that they carry. (A number of the problems in the set of exercises at the end of this chapter will give you an opportunity to practise this type of analysis.) The key procedure for working on this sort of problem can be stated simply as follows:

■ Identify recurring strings of sounds and match them with recurring meanings.

Consider in this regard the small sample of data in table 4.28 from Turkish, consisting of four words along with their English translations.

TABLE 4.28 Some Turkish words

mumlar	'candles'
yollar	'roads'
adamlar	'men'
kitaplar	'books'

As you can probably see, the syllable *lar* occurs in all four items in our sample. From the translations of these items, you can see that a particular feature of meaning—namely, plurality—is present in all four cases as well. By matching the recurring string of sounds with the recurring meaning, we are able to hypothesize that *-lar* is the morpheme marking plurality in Turkish. Once this has been determined, we can then infer that *mum* in *mumlar* is also a morpheme (with the meaning 'candle'), that *yol* in *yollar* is a morpheme (with the meaning 'road'), and so on. A larger sampling of Turkish data would confirm the correctness of these inferences.

In doing morphological analysis in unfamiliar languages, a number of pitfalls must be avoided. For the type of data normally investigated at the introductory level, the following guidelines are especially important.

- Do not assume that the morpheme order in the language you are analyzing is the same as in English. In Korean, for example, morphemes indicating location (the rough equivalent of 'at', 'in', and so forth) follow rather than precede the noun (*hakkyo-eyse* 'at school' is literally 'school at').

- Do not assume that every semantic contrast expressed in English will also be manifested in the language you are analyzing. Turkish, for instance, has no equivalent for English *the* and *a*. Mandarin has no *he-she* distinction: the same pronoun form can be used to refer to a male or a female.

- Conversely, do not assume that every contrast expressed in the language you are analyzing is manifested in English. For example, some languages distinguish more than two number categories (Inuktitut distinguishes singular, dual, and plural), and some languages make multiple tense contrasts (ChiBemba has an eight-way distinction).

- Remember that a morpheme can have more than one form, or allomorph. For example, further study of Turkish would reveal that the plural suffix in this language can also be realized as *-ler*, depending on the vowel in the base to which the suffix is attached.

Exercises

Note: Data from languages other than English is sometimes presented in transcribed form (in which case it appears between slashes) and sometimes in the native orthography or romanization.

1. Consider the following words and answer the questions below.

a) fly	f) reuse	k) spiteful	p) preplan
b) desks	g) triumphed	l) suite	q) optionality
c) untie	h) delight	m) fastest	r) prettier
d) tree	i) justly	n) deform	s) mistreat
e) dislike	j) payment	o) disobey	t) premature

i) For each word, determine whether it is simple or complex.
ii) Circle all the bound morphemes. Underline all the roots.

2. The following problem, from the Lukunosh dialect of Mortlockese (a language of Micronesia), was prepared by Emerson Lopez Odango.

   a) ngiij   'my tooth'   e) ngiimam   'our (excl) tooth'
   b) ngiimw   'your (sg) tooth'   f) ngiimi   'your (pl) tooth'
   c) ngiin   'his/her/its tooth'   g) ngiir   'their tooth'
   d) ngiish   'our (incl) tooth'

   Note: incl = inclusive (the speaker and the addressee)
             excl = exclusive (the speaker and someone other than the addressee)
             pl = plural
             sg = singular

   i) Identify the morpheme corresponding to each of the following:

tooth _____ngii_____	our (incl) ___sh___
my _____j_____	our (excl) ___mam___
your (sg) ___mw___	your (pl) ___mi___
his/her/its ___n___	their ___r___

   ii) Given that the word for 'leg/foot' in Mortlockese is *peshe*, how would you say each of the following?

   your (sg) leg/foot ___peshemw___
   his/her/its leg/foot ___peshen___
   our (excl) leg/foot ___peshemam___

3. The following problem, from Irarutu (an Austronesian language spoken in West Papua, Indonesia) was provided by Jason Jackson.

   a) adena   'my mother'   d) ambamba   'my elder brother'
   b) odena   'your mother'   e) ombamba   'your elder brother'
   c) idena   'his/her mother'   f) imbamba   'his/her elder brother'

   g) afrag   'my hand'   j) atgrag   'my ear'   m) aftag   'my stomach'
   h) ofram   'your hand'   k) otgram   'your ear'   n) oftam   'your stomach'
   i) ifra   'his/her hand'   l) itgra   'his/her ear'   o) ifta   'his/her stomach'

   i) Irarutu has different strategies for expressing possession in the case of kinship and possession in the case of body parts. Based on the data above, identify the morphemes used to express each type of possession.

   ii) Given that *mce* means 'eye' and that *nfut* means 'younger sibling', how would you say each of the following in Irarutu?

   his/her younger sibling _____
   my eye _____
   his/her eye _____

4. Consider the following data from Kwakum, a Bantu language spoken in Cameroon.

   a) /sɛbɔmmɛ/   'We bought (a long time ago).'
   b) /sɛbɔmko/   'We bought (recently).'
   c) /sɛbɔmkowɛɛ/   'We did not buy (recently).'
   d) /nyebɔmmɛ/   'I bought (a long time ago).'

e) /ɔbɔmmɛ/   'You (sg) bought (a long time ago).'

f) /yebɔmko/   'They bought (recently).'

g) /nɛbɔmko/   'You (pl) bought (recently).'

h) /abɔmmɛwɛɛ/   'S/he did not buy (a long time ago).'

i) What are the Kwakum morphemes for each of the following concepts?

I ____   we ____

you (sg) ____   you (pl) ____

s/he ____   they ____

buy ____

negation (not) ____

recent past (recently) ____

remote past (a long time ago) ____

ii) How would you say the following in Kwakum?

I bought (recently). _____

I didn't buy (recently). _____

They bought (a long time ago). _____

5. All the following Persian words (presented in roman orthography) consist of two or more morphemes. (Note: *xar* means 'buy' and *-id* designates the past tense.)

a) xaridam   'I bought'

b) xaridi   'you (sg) bought'

c) xarid   '(he) bought'

d) naxaridam   'I did not buy'

e) namixaridand   'they were not buying'

f) naxaridim   'we did not buy'

g) mixarid   '(he) was buying'

h) mixaridid   'you (pl) were buying'

i) Match each of the following notions with a morpheme in the Persian data.

I ____   they ____

you (sg) ____   not ____

we ____   was/were + -ing (continuous) ____

you (pl) ____

ii) How would you say the following in Persian?

They were buying. _____

You (sg) did not buy. _____

You (sg) were buying. _____

6. Consider the following data from Zapotec.

a) racañeea   'I help'   racañeetonoo   'we help'

b) racañeelo   'you (sg) help'   racañeetoo   'you (pl) help'

c) racañeeni   's/he helps'   racañeeni   'they help'

d) cocañeea   'I helped'   cocañeetonoo   'we helped'

e) cocañeelo   'you (sg) helped'   cocañeetoo   'you (pl) helped'

f) cocañeeni	's/he helped'	cocañeeni	'they helped'
g) cacañeea	'I will help'	cacañeetonoo	'we will help'
h) cacañeelo	'you (sg) will help'	cacañeetoo	'you (pl) will help'
i) cacañeeni	's/he will help'	cacañeeni	'they will help'

Match each of the following notions with a Zapotec morpheme.

help ____	I ____	we ____
present ____	you (sg) ____	you (pl) ____
past ____	he/she/they ____	
future ____		

7. Consider the following data from Turkish, presented in phonemic transcription.

a) /lokanta/	'a restaurant'	/lokantada/	'in/at a restaurant'
b) /kapɨ/	'a door'	/kapɨda/	'in/at a door'
c) /randevu/	'an appointment'	/randevuda/	'in/at an appointment'
d) /baş/	'a head'	/başta/	'in/at a head'
e) /kitap/	'a book'	/kitapta/	'in/at a book'
f) /koltuk/	'an armchair'	/koltukta/	'in/at an armchair'
g) /taraf/	'a side'	/tarafta/	'in/at a side'

   i) What are the allomorphs for the Turkish morpheme meaning 'in/at'?
   ii) Describe the distribution of the allomorphs as generally as possible.

8. The following problem, from Serbian (a Slavic language), was prepared by Diana Stojanovic.

a) /hrabra/	'brave (fem sg)'	/hrabrija/	'braver (fem sg)'
b) /hrabro/	'brave (neut sg)'	/hrabrije/	'braver (neut sg)'
c) /pametna/	'smart (fem sg)'	/pametnija/	'smarter (fem sg)'
d) /pametno/	'smart (neut sg)'	/pametnije/	'smarter (neut sg)'
e) /sretçna/	'happy (fem sg)'	/sretçnija/	'happier (fem sg)'
f) /sretçno/	'happy (neut sg)'	/sretçnije/	'happier (neut sg)'
g) /lepo/	'beautiful (neut sg)'	/lepʃe/	'more beautiful (neut sg)'
h) /lako/	'light (neut sg)'	/lakʃe/	'lighter (neut sg)'

   i) Make a list of the morphemes in the above data and indicate the meaning of each.
   ii) If your analysis of the above data is correct, you will have noticed instances of allomorphic variation. Under what conditions does each allomorph occur?

9. Consider the following words.

a) desks	e) triumphed	i) prearrange	m) optionality
b) untie	f) ageless	j) smartest	n) prettier
c) insincere	g) loser	k) redistribute	o) mistreat
d) disprove	h) payment	l) disobey	p) resell

   i) Draw a tree structure for each word.
   ii) For the word *optionality*, what is the base for the affix *-ion*? What is the base for the suffix *-ity*? Are either of these bases also the root for the entire word? If so, which one?

10. The following problem, from Puyuma (a Formosan language, spoken in Taiwan), was prepared by Yen-hsin Chen.

a)	sanay	'a song'	semanay	'to sing'
b)	treli	'a decrease in weight'	tremeli	'to lighten'
c)	traetra	'a lock'	tremaetra	'to lock'
d)	sapuk	'a seedling'	semapuk	'to sow'
e)	seber	'a bud'	semeber	'to bud'
f)	garutr	'a comb'	gemarutr	'to comb'
g)	sungal	'a bow'	semungal	'to bow (to someone)'

i) What is the affix that converts nouns into verbs in Puyuma?
ii) What type of affix is it? *infix*

11. In this chapter, an argument was presented in favour of the following structure for the word *unhappiness*.

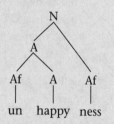

Using the same type of argument, draw and justify tree structures for the words *unresourceful, redisposal*, and *disinvestment*. (*Hint:* This will involve determining the type of syntactic category with which the affixes in these words can combine; see table 4.6.)

12. In English, the suffix *-er* can be added to a place name. Examine the words in the two columns below.

Column 1	Column 2
Long Islander	*Denverer
Vermonter	*Philadelphiaer
New Yorker	*Vancouverer
Newfoundlander	*Torontoer
Londoner	*Miamiaer

i) In general terms, what does the suffix *-er* mean in these words?
ii) How is this *-er* different in meaning from the *-er* found in the words *skater* and *walker*?
iii) State the constraint on the distribution of *-er* illustrated in this data set.
iv) Does this constraint also apply to the type of *-er* used in the word *skater*?

13. The following words have all been formed by compounding. Draw a tree structure for each word. If you are in doubt as to the lexical category of the compound, remember that the category of the head determines the category of the word.

a) football	d) in-crowd	g) freeze-dry
b) billboard	e) fast food	h) oversee
c) sunspot	f) softball	i) tree trunk

j) lead-free	o) potato peel	t) blueprint
k) home plate	p) bittersweet	u) red alert
l) girlfriend	q) hockey match	v) space ship
m) city centre	r) smartphone	w) exam day
n) failsafe	s) flower pot	

14. Examine the following compounds and answer the questions below.

a) loudmouth	i) pickpocket
b) skinhead	j) spoilsport
c) killjoy	k) laptop
d) junk mail	l) brain-dead
e) death blow	m) blow-dry
f) airhead	n) armchair
g) Walkman	o) lowlife
h) cutthroat	

   i) For each of the compounds determine whether it is endocentric or exocentric.

   ii) How do you form the plural of *lowlife*, *Walkman* (a portable music player popular in the 1980s), and *loudmouth*? (*Hint*: See table 4.13.) Also, compare the pronunciation of the plural forms of *life* and *mouth* as independent words with their pronunciations in the plural forms of the compounds *lowlife* and *loudmouth*. What difference do you notice?

15. English contains many verbal expressions that consist of a verb plus a preposition:

   hold up (a bank)
   carry on (a conversation)
   drop out (of school)
   back down (from a challenge)
   take over (a company)

   Should these sorts of expressions be considered compounds? In answering this question, be sure to refer to the properties of compounds discussed in section 4.3.

   Now consider the nouns that are derived from these verbal expressions via conversion: *a holdup, a dropout, a takeover*. According to the criteria you used to answer the preceding question, should they be considered compounds?

16. Indicate whether the words in each of the following groups are related to one another by process of inflection or derivation.

   a) go, goes, going, gone
   b) discover, discovery, discoverer, discoverable, discoverability
   c) lovely, lovelier, loveliest
   d) inventor, inventor's, inventors, inventors'
   e) democracy, democrat, democratic, democratize

17. The following sentences contain both derivational and inflectional affixes. Underline all of the derivational affixes and circle the inflectional affixes.

   a) The farmer's cows escaped.
   b) It was raining.
   c) She noted his impoliteness.
   d) José needs the newer copy.
   e) The strongest rower continued.
   f) The pitbull has bitten the cyclist.
   g) She quickly closed the book.
   h) The alphabetization went well.

18. Each of the following columns illustrates a different way of marking inflection.

Column 1	Column 2	Column 3
a) mouse/mice	f) go/went	k) record/recorded
b) dive/dove	g) is/was	l) arrive/arrived
c) take/took	h) good/better	m) start/started
d) man/men	i) she/her	n) discuss/discussed
e) eat/ate	j) am/are	o) try/tried

i) How is inflection expressed in column 1? column 2? column 3?

ii) Think of at least one more English example to add to each column.

19. Consider the following data from Samoan, presented in the native orthography. (The reversed apostrophe represents a glottal stop.)

a) mate	'he dies'	mamate	'they die'
b) nofo	'he stays'	nonofo	'they stay'
c) galue	'he works'	galulue	'they work'
d) tanu	'he buries'	tatanu	'they bury'
e) alofa	'he loves'	alolofa	'they love'
f) ta'oto	'he lies'	ta'o'oto	'they lie'
g) atama'i	'he is intelligent'	atamama'i	'they are intelligent'

i) What morphological process is used to express the inflectional contrast between singular and plural here?

ii) Describe how it works in your own words.

iii) If 'he is strong' is *malosi* in Samoan, how would you say 'they are strong'?

20. The following words from Chamorro, spoken in Guam and the Mariana Islands, all involve derivation. (Data are presented in Chamorro orthography.)

I. Root		*Derived word*	
a) adda	'mimic'	aadda	'mimicker'
b) kanno	'eat'	kakanno	'eater'
c) tuge	'write'	tutuge	'writer'

II. Root		*Derived word*	
d) atan	'look at'	atanon	'nice to look at'
e) sangan	'tell'	sanganon	'tellable'
f) guaiya	'love'	guaiyayon	'lovable'
g) tulaika	'exchange'	tulaikayon	'exchangeable'
h) chalek	'laugh'	chalekon	'laughable'
i) ngangas	'chew'	ngangason	'chewable'

III. Root		*Derived word*	
j) nalang	'hungry'	nalalang	'very hungry'
k) dankolo	'big'	dankololo	'very big'
l) metgot	'strong'	metgogot	'very strong'
m) bunita	'pretty'	bunitata	'very pretty'

Like inflection, derivation can be expressed in a variety of ways—including by affixation of various types (prefixation, suffixation, infixation) and by reduplication.

i) What morphological process is manifested in I? in II? in III?

ii) Formulate a general statement that describes how the derived words in I are formed. Do the same for II and III.

iii) One of these derivational processes consists of affixation involving allomorphs. What is the distribution of the allomorphs?

21. The following words can be either nouns or verbs.

a) record   f) outline   k) report

b) journey   g) convict   l) assault

c) exchange   h) imprint   m) answer

d) remark   i) reply   n) import

e) surprise   j) retreat   o) access

i) For each word, determine whether stress placement can be used to make the distinction between noun and verb.

ii) Think of two more English examples illustrating the process of stress shift to mark a category distinction.

22. Indicate the morphological phenomenon illustrated by each item in column 2.

Column 1	*Column 2*
a) automation	→ automate ~~backformation~~
b) plastic	→ <u>non</u>plastic ~~derivational~~
c) information, entertainment	→ infotainment ~~blending (chunks are removed and put together)~~
d) love, seat	→ loveseat ~~compounding~~
e) prógress	→ progréss ~~tone placement so conversion changes the category~~
f) typographical error	→ typo ~~Clipping~~
g) cannabis, business	→ cannabusiness ~~blending & compounding?~~
h) act	→ deactivate ~~derivational~~
i) extra virgin olive oil	→ EVOO ~~Acronym~~
j) perambulator	→ pram ~~clipping (removing alot)~~
k) (the) comb	→ comb (your hair) ~~conversion~~
l) beef, buffalo	→ beefalo
m) random access memory	→ RAM
n) megabyte	→ meg
o) Europe, Asia	→ Eurasia
p) applications (for a computer)	→ apps
q) do you	→ d'you
r) Goods and Services Tax	→ GST

23. Here are ten instances where a new word is needed. Create a word for each of these definitions in the manner indicated.

a) Use an acronym ... for your uncle's second oldest brother.

"We visited my _____ at Christmas."

b) Use onomatopoeia ... for the sound of a coffee percolator at work.

"I can't concentrate because my perc is _____ ing."

c) Use conversion ... for wrapping something breakable in bubbles.

"You'd better _____ that ornament or else it might break."

d) Use a compound . . . for the annoying string of cheese stretching from a slice of hot pizza to one's mouth.

"As the _____ hung precariously from my lips, our eyes met!"

e) Use backformation . . . for the action of backformation.

"We had to _____ words in linguistics class today."

f) Use a product name . . . for the act of cleaning a mirror with Windex.

"I _____ ed the the mirror to get rid of the fingerprints."

g) Use a proper name . . . for the act of breaking dishes, which Jonathan does regularly.

"He's going to _____ all of my best dishes."

h) Use clipping . . . for a course in ovinology (the study of sheep).

"Have you done your _____ assignment yet?"

i) Use derivation . . . for being able to be contacted.

"The counsellor is not very _____."

j) Use a blend . . . for a hot drink made with chocolate and ginseng.

"I'll have a _____ and two peanut butter cookies, please."

24. In Korean, /p/ and /m/ are distinct phonemes, as shown by contrasts such as the following:

/pap/ 'food'   /pam/ 'night'

However, under the circumstances illustrated below, /p/ is converted to /m/.

/pap/ 'food' + /məkə/ 'eat' becomes /pamməkə/ 'eat food'
/sip/ 'ten' + /njən/ 'year' becomes /simnjən/ 'ten years'
/ip/ 'mouth' + /man/ 'only' becomes /imman/ 'mouth only'

i)   What type of phenomenon is this?

ii) Describe the process that is involved in terms of the change that takes place and the context in which it occurs.

iii) Now consider the following additional data.

/hak/ 'school' + /njən/ 'year' becomes /haŋnjən/ 'school year'
/ot/ 'clothes' + /mana/ 'be many' becomes /onmana/ 'there are many clothes'

Based on this data, how would you modify the statement that you made in response to question (ii)?

To learn more about the topics discussed in this chapter, visit the Companion Website for *Contemporary Linguistic Analysis*.

WILLIAM O'GRADY

Syntax: the analysis of sentence structure

. . . the game is to say something new with old words

RALPH WALDO EMERSON, *JOURNALS*, 1849

NOT MUCH can be said with a single word. If we are to use language to express complex thoughts and ideas, we must be able to combine and organize words into sentences. Not just any combination of words will do, however: the pattern in (1) is not permissible, even though the same words can be combined in a different way to form the acceptable sentence in (2).

(1) *House painted student a the.
(2) A student painted the house.

We say that an utterance is **grammatical** if native speakers judge it to be a possible sentence of their language. Hence, (2) is grammatical, but (1) is not.

This chapter will focus on **syntax**, the component of grammar that is concerned with the form of grammatical sentences. There are in fact two very different ways to approach syntax in contemporary linguistics.

One way is to describe sentences in terms of their most evident properties, especially the form and linear arrangement of words. This approach, which is often called 'descriptive syntax', is especially useful for the analysis of previously unstudied languages or for work that seeks to compare a large number of languages. An introduction to descriptive syntax can be found on the Companion Website, Chapter 5.

A second approach to syntax, which is outlined in this chapter, focuses not just on the form and order of words but also on the way in which they are organized into larger hierarchically arranged units. This approach is often referred to as 'formal syntax' and is especially important for work in linguistic theory. A defining goal of work on formal syntax is to create a system of rules and operations that can produce ('generate') the grammatical sentences of a languages. Such a system is called a **generative grammar**.

The starting point for work on generative grammar is the universally accepted idea that words belong to categories of different types (nouns, verbs, and so on) and that these categories can be combined in particular ways to form phrases—and ultimately, sentences. One widely accepted way to represent the internal structure of sentences makes use of 'tree diagrams', like the simplified one in figure 5.1.

FIGURE 5.1
A simplified syntactic structure (tree diagram)

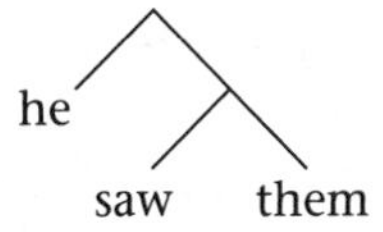

he

saw them

As we will see a little later in this chapter, structures like this are built by two interacting operations. A **Merge** operation combines words to create larger phrases and sentences, and a **Move** operation can carry an element to a new position within the structure. Before examining these operations, however, it is necessary to have a look at words and the categories to which they belong.

Language Matters What's the Longest Sentence in English?

George Bernard Shaw wrote one that was 110 words long. William Faulkner's novel *Absalom, Absalom!* includes a 1300-word sentence. James Joyce managed to produce a 4391-word sentence (which goes on for forty pages) in *Ulysses*. But even that's not the longest known sentence—*The Rotter's Club*, by Jonathon Coe, contains a sentence that is 13 955 words long!

The bottom line is that there's no such thing as the world's longest sentence—any sentence can be made longer. That's because the operations that combine words can be used over and over again, without limit.

It's the right answer.
I think it's the right answer.
You know I think it's the right answer.
Harry said you know I think it's the right answer.

....

a book
a book on the table
a book on the table near the bookcase
a book on the table near the bookcase in the office

The application of an operation to its own output to create an ever more complex structure is called **recursion**, and it's an essential part of our ability to build sentences.

5.1 Categories and structure

A fundamental fact about words in all human languages is that they can be grouped together into a relatively small number of classes called **syntactic categories** or **parts of speech**. This classification reflects a variety of factors, including the types of meaning that words express, the types of affixes that they take, and the types of structures in which they can occur.

5.1.1 Categories of words

Table 5.1 provides examples of the word-level categories that are most central to the study of syntax. The four most studied syntactic categories are **noun (N)**, **verb (V)**, **adjective (A)**, and **preposition (P)**. These elements, which are often called **lexical categories**, play a very important role in sentence formation, as we will soon see. A fifth and less studied lexical category consists of **adverbs (Adv)**, most of which are derived from adjectives.

Languages may also contain **non-lexical** or **functional categories**, including **determiner (Det)**, **auxiliary verb**, **conjunction**, and **degree word (Deg)**. Such elements generally have meanings that are harder to define and paraphrase than those of lexical categories. For example, the meaning of a determiner such as *the* or an auxiliary such as *would* is more difficult to describe than the meaning of a noun such as *hill* or a verb such as *sell*.

TABLE 5.1 Syntactic categories	
Lexical categories ('content words')	**Examples**
Noun (N)	Harry, boy, wheat, policy, moisture, bravery
Verb (V)	arrive, discuss, melt, hear, remain, dislike
Adjective (A)	good, tall, old, intelligent, beautiful, fond
Preposition (P)	to, in, on, near, at, by
Adverb (Adv)	slowly, quietly, now, always, perhaps
Non-lexical categories ('functional categories')	**Examples**
Determiner (Det)	the, a, this, these, no (as in *no books*)
Degree word (Deg)	too, so, very, more, quite
Auxiliary	
Modal	will, would, can, could, may, must, should
Non-modal	be, have, do
Conjunction	and, or, but

A potential source of confusion in the area of word classification stems from the fact that some items can belong to more than one category.

(3) *comb* used as a noun:
The woman found a comb.

comb used as a verb:
The boy should comb his hair.

(4) *near* used as a preposition:
The child stood near the fence.

near used as a verb:
The runners neared the finish line.

near used as an adjective:
The nearer car is mine.

How then can we determine a word's category?

Meaning

One criterion involves meaning. For instance, nouns typically name entities ('people and things'), including individuals (*Elsa, Björn*) and objects (*book, desk*). Verbs characteristically designate actions (*run, jump*), sensations (*feel, hurt*), and states (*be, remain*). Consistent with these tendencies, *comb* in (3) refers to an object when used as a noun but to an action when used as a verb.

The typical function of an adjective is to designate a property or attribute of the entities denoted by nouns. Thus, when we say *that tall building*, we are attributing the property 'tall' to the building designated by the noun.

In a parallel way, adverbs typically denote properties and attributes of the actions, sensations, and states designated by verbs. In the following sentences, for example, the adverb *quickly* indicates the manner of Janet's leaving, while the adverb *early* specifies its time.

(5) Janet left quickly.
Janet left early.

A word's category membership does not always bear such a straightforward relationship to its meaning, however. For example, nouns such as *difficulty, truth,* and *likelihood* do not name entities in the strict sense. Moreover, even though words for actions tend to be verbs, some nouns also express this type of meaning (e.g., *push* in *give someone a push* and *run* in *have a run*).

Matters are further complicated by the fact that in some cases, words with very similar meanings belong to different categories. For instance, the words *like* and *fond* are very similar in meaning (as in *Mice like/are fond of cheese*), yet *like* is a verb and *fond* is an adjective.

Inflection

Most linguists believe that meaning is only one of several criteria that enter into determining a word's category. As shown in table 5.2, inflection can also be very useful for distinguishing among different categories of words.

TABLE 5.2	Lexical categories and their inflectional suffixes in English	
Category	**Inflectional affix**	**Examples**
Noun	plural -*s*	books, chairs, doctors
	possessive -*'s*	John's, (the) man's
Verb	past tense -*ed*	arrived, melted, hopped
	progressive -*ing*	arriving, melting, hopping
	third person singular -*s*	arrives, melts, hops
Adjective	comparative -*er*	taller, faster, smarter
	superlative -*est*	tallest, fastest, smartest

However, even inflection does not always provide the information needed to determine a word's category. In English, for example, not all adjectives can take the comparative and superlative suffixes (**intelligenter, *beautifulest*) and some nouns cannot be pluralized (*moisture, bravery, knowledge*).

Distribution

A third and often more reliable criterion for determining a word's category involves its **distribution**—the type of elements, especially functional categories, with which it can co-occur.

For example, nouns can typically appear with a determiner, verbs with an auxiliary, and adjectives with a degree word in the patterns illustrated in table 5.3.

TABLE 5.3	Distributional properties of nouns, verbs, and adjectives	
Category	**Distributional property**	**Examples**
Noun	occurrence with a determiner	a car, the wheat
Verb	occurrence with an auxiliary	has gone, will stay
Adjective	occurrence with a degree word	very rich, too big

In contrast, a noun cannot occur with an auxiliary, and a verb cannot occur with a determiner or degree word.

(6) a noun with an auxiliary:
*will destruction

a verb with a determiner:
*the destroy

a verb with a degree word:
*very arrive

Distributional tests for category membership are simple and highly reliable. They can be used with confidence when it is necessary to categorize unfamiliar words.

Language Matters A Poem That Syntacticians Love

Thanks to distributional and inflectional clues, it's often possible to identify a word's category without knowing its meaning. The poem "Jabberwocky," by Lewis Carroll, illustrates this point in a particularly brilliant way—it's interpretable precisely because readers are able to figure out that *gyre* is a verb (note the auxiliary verb to its left), that *borogoves* is a noun (it's preceded by a determiner and takes the plural ending), and so on.

'Twas brillig, and the slithy toves
Did gyre and gimble in the wabe;
All mimsy were the borogoves,
And the mome raths outgrabe.

"Beware the Jabberwock, my son!
The jaws that bite, the claws that catch!
Beware the Jubjub bird, and shun
The frumious Bandersnatch!"

5.1.2 Phrase structure

Sentences are not formed by simply stringing words together like beads on a necklace. Rather, they have a hierarchical design in which words are grouped together into ever larger structural units called **phrases**—*the door, to the door, go to the door*, and so on.

The blueprint

As a first approximation, it is often suggested that the internal structure of phrases complies with the blueprint (called the **X' Schema**) shown in figure 5.2 (X' is pronounced 'X-bar').

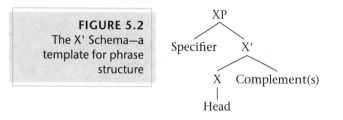

FIGURE 5.2
The X' Schema—a template for phrase structure

Heads

The **head** is the obligatory nucleus around which a phrase is built. For now, we will focus on four categories that can function as the head of a phrase—nouns (N), verbs (V), adjectives (A), and prepositions (P).

FIGURE 5.3
Some examples of heads

N	V	A	P
|	|	|	|
picture	arrive	certain	in

Specifiers

Specifiers have no single semantic function or grammatical category. Structurally, though, they are alike in that they occur at the edge of a phrase. As illustrated in table 5.4, the specifier position in English is at a phrase's left margin (the beginning).

TABLE 5.4   Some specifiers

Head	Specifier	Examples
N	Determiner (Det) *the, a, some, this, those . . .*	*a picture*, *the map*, *those people* *some guests*
V	Preverbal adverb (Adv) *never, perhaps, often, always, almost . . .*	*never quit*, *perhaps go*, *often failed*, *almost forgot*
A or P	Degree word (Deg) *very, quite, more, almost . . .*	*very smart*, *quite rich*, *almost in*

Note: Almost can be either an adverb or a degree word.

Syntax is a fast-moving field and it is not uncommon for ideas to be modified over time, sometimes radically. As we will see in section 5.5.5, the notion of specifier has been rethought in recent years, forcing us to rethink the status of determiners too.

Complements

Complements, which are always phrases, provide information about entities and locations implied by the meaning of the head. For example, the meaning of *protect* implies something that is protected (*protect the environment*); the meaning of *in* implies a location (*in the house*); the meaning of *map* implies an area that is depicted, as in *a map of Canada*; and so on.

As illustrated in figure 5.4, the X' Schema ensures that when a phrase includes both a specifier and a complement in addition to the head, the specifier will occur higher than the complement. To simplify here, we don't show the internal structure of the complement phrases.

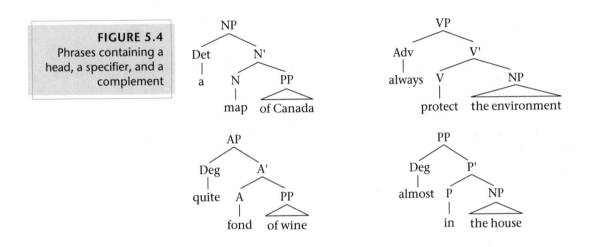

FIGURE 5.4
Phrases containing a head, a specifier, and a complement

However, it is common (and practical!) to represent tree structures in an abbreviated way, without the intermediate X', when there is no specifier and/or complement, as shown in figures 5.5 and 5.6.

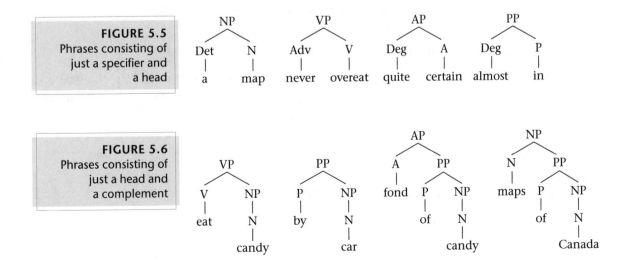

FIGURE 5.5
Phrases consisting of just a specifier and a head

FIGURE 5.6
Phrases consisting of just a head and a complement

Only when the phrase contains both a specifier and a complement in addition to the head is it necessary to make use of the intermediate X' level.

In the interests of being able to consider the largest number of patterns possible, we will adopt two common additional assumptions. First, we will treat both names (*Nuria, Paolo*, etc.) and pronouns (*she, he, him, her*, etc.) as instances of the N category that do not normally take either specifiers or complements.

FIGURE 5.7
Names and pronouns

a. Name

NP
|
N
|
Nuria

b. Pronoun

NP
|
N
|
she

c. Pronoun

NP
|
N
|
him

Second, we will assume that possessives (e.g., *the child's, Nirmala's, his*, etc.) are NPs that occur in the specifier position of a larger NP.

FIGURE 5.8
Possessives: NPs inside
NPs

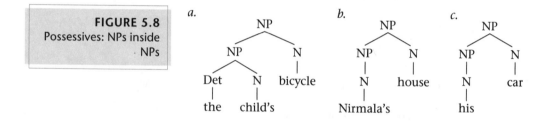

An appendix at the end of the chapter offers detailed instructions on how to draw tree structures; exercises 3 and 4 provide an opportunity to practice.

The Merge operation

We can now formulate the following operation for sentence building.

(7) *Merge*
  Combine words in a manner compatible with the X' Schema.

As illustrated in figure 5.9, the Merge operation is able to take a determiner such as *the* and combine it with the N *house* to form the NP *the house*. It is then able to take a preposition such as *in* and combine it with the NP *the house* to form the PP *in the house*.

FIGURE 5.9
The Merge operation in
action

a.

NP
Det   N
| |
the house

b.

PP
P   NP
| Det   N
in | |
    the house

Further application of the Merge operation to additional words can lead to the formation of phrases and sentences of unlimited complexity.

Language Matters **The Mirror Image**

Many languages have a head-complement order that is the mirror image of the one found in English—the complement occurs on the left side of the head rather than on the right side. (In both types of language, the specifier appears on the left side of the head.) Japanese works that way: the V occurs at the end of the VP, the P at the end of the PP, and so on.

[sono gakkō]-ni	[sono hon] yonda
that school at	that book read (Pst)
'at that school'	'read that book'

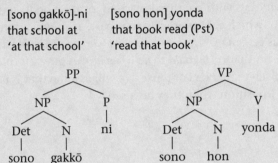

The version of the X' Schema needed for these languages looks like this—with the head to the right of its complement:

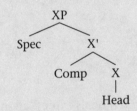

About half of the world's languages use this version of the X' Schema.

5.1.3 Sentences

The largest unit of syntactic analysis is the sentence. Sentences typically consist of an NP (often called 'the **subject**') and a VP that are linked together by an abstract category dubbed 'T' (for '**tense**'). As illustrated in figure 5.10, T serves as the head of the sentence, taking the VP as its

FIGURE 5.10
The structure of a
typical sentence

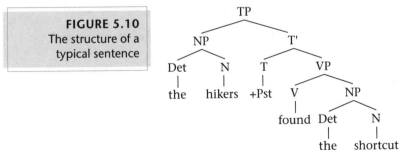

+Pst = past, −Pst = non-past

complement and the subject NP as its specifier. What we think of as a sentence or a sentential phrase, then, is really a TP.

The tense feature in T must be compatible with the form of the verb. So a sentence like the one above, whose head contains the feature +Pst, must contain a verb marked for the past tense (hence, *found* rather than *find*).

Although somewhat abstract, this analysis has the advantage of giving sentences the same internal structure as other phrases (with a specifier, a head, and a complement), making them consistent with the X' Schema. Moreover, because T, like all heads, is obligatory, we also account for the fact that all sentences have tense (i.e., they are all past or non-past).

The TP structure also provides us with a natural place to locate modal auxiliaries such as *can, may, will*, and *must*, most of which are inherently non-past, as shown by their incompatibility with time adverbs such as *yesterday*: **He can/will/must work yesterday*. (The modals *could* and *would* can be either past or non-past: *He could swim when he was three/He could swim tomorrow*.). Because modals are themselves markers of tense, we will assume that it is not necessary to have the feature ±Pst in the T position when they are used.

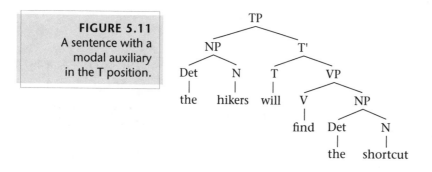

FIGURE 5.11
A sentence with a modal auxiliary in the T position.

This structure neatly accounts not only for the fact that modals express an inherent tense but also for their positioning between the subject (the specifier) and the VP (the complement)—in the position reserved for the head of the sentence. (We will consider the non-modal auxiliary verbs *be* and *have* in section 5.4.1.)

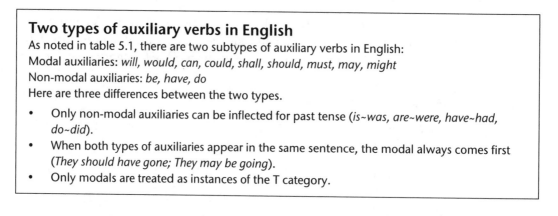

Two types of auxiliary verbs in English

As noted in table 5.1, there are two subtypes of auxiliary verbs in English:

Modal auxiliaries: *will, would, can, could, shall, should, must, may, might*

Non-modal auxiliaries: *be, have, do*

Here are three differences between the two types.

- Only non-modal auxiliaries can be inflected for past tense (*is~was, are~were, have~had, do~did*).
- When both types of auxiliaries appear in the same sentence, the modal always comes first (*They should have gone; They may be going*).
- Only modals are treated as instances of the T category.

The appendix at the end of the chapter outlines a procedure that will help you assign the right structure to sentences. Exercise 5 provides an opportunity to practice this procedure.

5.1.4 **Tests for phrase structure**

How can linguists be sure that they have grouped words together into phrases in the right way? The syntactic units, or **constituents**, found in tree structures can be verified with the help of special tests. Consider, for instance, the tree structure that the X' Schema requires for the sentence *The children will stop at the corner.*

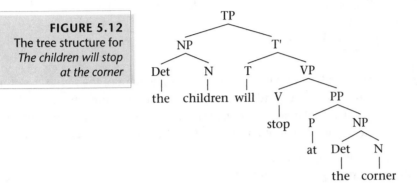

FIGURE 5.12
The tree structure for
*The children will stop
at the corner*

The substitution test

One piece of evidence for syntactic units comes from the fact that they can often be replaced by an element such as *they, she, he, it, do so,* and so on. (This is called a **substitution test**.)

As illustrated in (8), *the children* can be replaced by *they*, and *stop at the corner* can be replaced by *do so*—confirming that each is a syntactic unit, just as the tree structure shows.

(8) [NP The children] will [VP stop at the corner]. *They* always *do so*.
(*they = the children; do so = stop at the corner*)

A substitution test also confirms that *at the corner* is a unit, as it can be replaced by a single word in a sentence such as (9).

(9) The children stopped [PP at the corner] and we stopped *there* too.
(*there = at the corner*)

Elements that do not form a constituent cannot be replaced in this way. Thus, there is no word in English that we can use to replace *children stopped*, for example, or *at the*.

The movement test

A second indication that *at the corner* forms a constituent in figure 5.12 is that it can be moved as a single unit to a different position within the sentence. (This is called a **movement test**.) In (10), for instance, *at the corner* can be moved from a position after the verb to the beginning of the sentence.

(10) They stopped [PP at the corner]. ⟶ [PP At the corner], they stopped.

Of course, *at the*, which is not a syntactic unit, cannot be fronted in this manner (**At the, they stopped corner*).

The coordination test

Finally, we can conclude that a group of words forms a constituent if it can be joined to another group of words by a conjunction such as *and, or,* or *but*. (This is known as the **coordination test** since patterns built around a conjunction are called **coordinate structures**.) The sentence in (11) illustrates how coordination can be used to help establish that *stop at the corner* is a constituent.

(11)   The children will [$_{VP}$ stop at the corner] *and* [$_{VP}$ look both ways].

5.2 Complement options

How can we be sure that individual words will occur with a complement of the right type in the syntactic structures that we have been building? Information about the complements permitted by a particular head is included in that head's entry in a speaker's lexicon. For instance, the lexicon for English includes an entry for *devour* that indicates that it requires an NP complement.

(12)   *a. devour* with an NP complement:
            The child devoured [$_{NP}$ the sandwich].

   b. devour without an NP complement:
            *The child devoured.

The term **subcategorization** is used to refer to information about a word's complement options, such as the fact the verb *devour* belongs to a verb subcategory that requires an NP complement.

5.2.1 Complement options for verbs

Table 5.5 illustrates some of the more common complement options for verbs in English. The subscripted prepositions indicate subtypes of PP complements, where this is relevant. *Loc* stands for any preposition expressing a location (such as *near, on,* and *under*).

TABLE 5.5	Some examples of verb complements	
Complement option	**Sample heads**	**Example**
Ø	vanish, arrive, die	The rabbit vanished.
NP	devour, cut, prove	The professor proved [$_{NP}$ *the theorem*].
AP	be, become	The man became [$_{AP}$ *very angry*].
PP$_{to}$	dash, talk, refer	The dog dashed [$_{PP}$ *to the door*].
NP NP	spare, hand, give	We handed [$_{NP}$ *the man*] [$_{NP}$ *a map*].
NP PP$_{to}$	hand, give, send	He gave [$_{NP}$ *a diploma*] [$_{PP}$ *to the student*].
NP PP$_{for}$	buy, cook, reserve	We bought [$_{NP}$ *a hat*] [$_{PP}$ *for Andy*].
NP PP$_{loc}$	put, place, stand	He put [$_{NP}$ *the muffler*] [$_{PP}$ *on the car*].
PP$_{to}$ PP$_{about}$	talk, speak	I talked [$_{PP}$ *to a doctor*] [$_{PP}$ *about Talisha*].
NP PP$_{for}$ PP$_{with}$	open, fix	We opened [$_{NP}$ *the door*] [$_{PP}$ *for Amit*] [$_{PP}$ *with a crowbar*].

The verbs in the first line of table 5.5 (*vanish, arrive*, and *die*) don't take a complement, those in the second line take an NP complement, and so on.

When a verb's complement options include an NP, as in the case of *devour, give, buy*, and so on, it is said to be **transitive**, and its NP complement is often referred to as its **direct object**. Verbs like *vanish, arrive*, and *dash* that don't have an NP complement are called **intransitive**.

A word can belong to more than one subcategory. The verb *eat*, for example, can occur either with or without an NP complement and therefore belongs to both of the first two subcategories in table 5.5.

(13) After getting home, they ate (a snack).

Of course, not all verbs exhibit this flexibility. As we have already seen, *devour*—although similar in meaning to *eat*—requires an NP complement and therefore belongs only to the second subcategory in our table.

As the examples in table 5.5 also show, some heads can take more than one complement. The verb *put* is a case in point, since it requires both an NP complement and a PP complement (or a locative adverb such as *there*).

(14) *a.* *put* with an NP complement and a PP complement:
The librarian put [NP the book] [PP on the shelf].

b. *put* without an NP complement:
*The librarian put [PP on the shelf].

c. *put* without a PP complement:
*The librarian put [NP the book].

The VP *put the book on the shelf* has the structure in figure 5.13, in which the VP consists of the head *put* and two complements—the NP *the book* and the PP *on the shelf*.

FIGURE 5.13
A verb with two complements

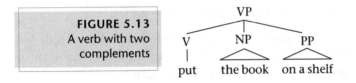

5.2.2 Complement options for other categories

Various complement options are also available for Ns, As, and Ps. Tables 5.6, 5.7, and 5.8 provide examples of just some of the possibilities.

TABLE 5.6	Some examples of noun complements	
Complement option	**Sample heads**	**Example**
Ø	car, boy, electricity	the car
PP$_{of}$	memory, failure, death	the memory [PP *of a friend*]
PP$_{of}$ PP$_{to}$	presentation, donation	the presentation [PP *of a medal*] [PP *to the winner*]
PP$_{with}$ PP$_{about}$	argument, discussion, conversation	an argument [PP *with Stella*] [PP *about politics*]

TABLE 5.7 Some examples of adjective complements

Complement option	Sample heads	Example
Ø	tall, green, smart	very tall
PP$_{about}$	curious, glad, angry	curious [$_{PP}$ *about China*]
PP$_{to}$	apparent, obvious	obvious [$_{PP}$ *to the student*]
PP$_{of}$	fond, full, sick	fond [$_{PP}$ *of chocolate*]

TABLE 5.8 Some examples of preposition complements

Complement option	Sample heads	Example
Ø	near, away, down	(he got) down
NP	in, on, by, near	in [$_{NP}$ *the house*]
PP	down, up, out	down [$_{PP}$ *into the cellar*]

Here again, subcategorization ensures that particular heads can appear in tree structures only if there is an appropriate type of complement. Thus, the adjective *afraid* can take an *of*-PP as its complement, while the adjective *paranoid* cannot.

> (15) *a.* afraid [$_{PP}$ of the future]
> *d.* paranoid [$_{PP}$ about the future] (compare: *paranoid of the future)

A good deal of what we know about our language consists of information about words and the type of complements with which they can appear. Much of this information must be stored in the lexicon, since it cannot be predicted from a word's meaning.

5.2.3 Complement clauses

All human languages allow sentential phrases (or 'clauses', as they are often called) to function as complements. A simple example of this from English is given in (16).

(16)

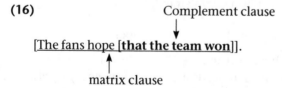

The bold-faced bracketed phrase in (16) is called a **complement clause**; the larger underlined phrase in which it occurs is called the **matrix clause**. Words such as *that, whether,* and *if* are known as **complementizers** (Cs). Together with their TP complement, they form a CP (complementizer phrase), as depicted in figure 5.14.

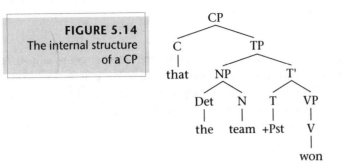

FIGURE 5.14
The internal structure of a CP

When a CP occurs in a sentence such as (16), in which it serves as complement of the verb *hope*, the entire sentence has the structure in figure 5.15.

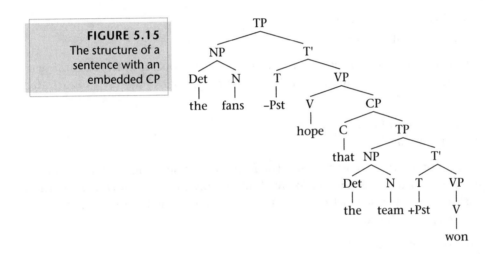

FIGURE 5.15
The structure of a sentence with an embedded CP

There is no limit on the number of embedded clauses that can occur in a sentence, as (17) shows.

(17) Harry said [CP that you know [CP that I think [CP that . . .

Table 5.9 provides examples of some verbs that are often found with a CP complement.

TABLE 5.9   Some verbs permitting CP complements

Complement(s)	Sample heads	Example
CP	believe, know, think, remember	They believe [CP *that Eric left*].
NP CP	persuade, tell, convince, promise	They told [NP *Sabina*] [CP *that Eric had left*].
PP$_{to}$ CP	confess, admit	They admitted [PP *to Sabina*] [CP *that Eric had left*].

5.3 Move

As we have seen, it is possible to build a very large number of different sentences by allowing the Merge operation to combine words and phrases in accordance with the X' Schema and the subcategorization properties of individual words. Nonetheless, there are still many kinds of sentences that we cannot yet build. This section considers two such patterns and discusses the sentence-building operation needed to accommodate them.

5.3.1 *Yes-no* questions

The sentences in (18) are examples of *yes-no* **questions** (so called because the expected response is usually 'yes' or 'no').

(18) *a.* **Should** those guys leave?
    b. **Can** we meet at the library?

A defining feature of *yes-no* questions is that the auxiliary verb occurs at the beginning of the sentence rather than in its more usual position to the right of the subject, as illustrated in (19).

(19) *a.* Those guys **should** leave.
    b. We **can** meet at the library.

How does the word order in (18) come about? The formation of question structures requires the use of an operation that we can call **Move**. Traditionally known as a **transformation** because it transforms an existing structure, Move transports the item in the T position to a new position to the left of the subject.

(20) Should those guys _ leave?

This analysis has at least two advantages. First, it allows us to avoid positing two types of modal auxiliary verbs in English: one that occurs between the subject and the VP and one that occurs to the left of the subject. Thanks to Move, all modal auxiliaries belong in the same place—in the T position, from which they can then be moved to the left of the subject in order to signal a question.

Second, the use of Move automatically captures the fact that the sentence *Should those guys leave?* is the question structure corresponding to *Those guys should leave*. According to the analysis presented here, both sentences initially have the same basic composition. They differ only in that the Move operation has applied to the T category in the question structure.

A landing site for T

In what position does the modal auxiliary 'land' when it is moved to the left of the subject? One promising idea assumes that all TPs occur within a larger CP 'shell' and that the C position can carry information about whether the sentence is a statement or a question. For the sake of illustration, we use the symbol +Q to indicate a question; sentences with the feature –Q in their C position will be interpreted as statements.

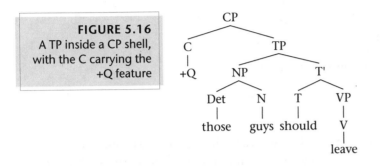

FIGURE 5.16
A TP inside a CP shell, with the C carrying the +Q feature

In some languages, the Q feature is 'spelled out' as a separate morpheme (see the example from Yoruba in the box on page 156). In languages like English, where there is no such morpheme, the feature must attract another element to its position. The modal auxiliary in the T position is that element. As illustrated in figure 5.17, T is drawn to the C position, where it attaches right next to the +Q feature.

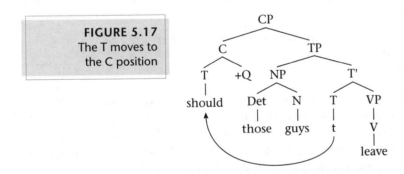

FIGURE 5.17
The T moves to the C position

A Move operation can do no more than change an element's position. It does not change the categories of any words and it cannot eliminate any part of the structure created by the Merge operation. Thus, *should* retains its T label even though it is moved into the C position (it changes its address, not its name). Moreover, the position that T formerly occupied remains in the tree structure. Called a **trace** and marked by the symbol *t*, it records the fact that the moved element comes from the head position within TP.

The Move operation used for *yes-no* questions is often informally called **Inversion**; it can be formulated as follows.

(21) *Inversion*
Move T to the C position.

Interesting evidence that T does in fact end up in the C position comes from patterns such as (22), which contain an embedded CP.

(22) I wonder [CP whether those guys should leave].

Here, the C position in the embedded clause is occupied by the complementizer *whether*.

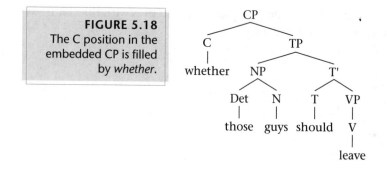

Assuming that no more than one word can occur in a head position, we predict that Inversion should not be able to apply in the embedded clause since there is nowhere for the moved auxiliary verb to land. The ungrammaticality of (23) shows that this is correct.

(23) Attempted inversion when there is a complementizer—the landing site is full:
*I wonder [CP **whether** those guys *t* leave].
*should

Crucially, the acceptability of Inversion improves quite dramatically when there is no complementizer in the C position.

(24) Inversion in an embedded CP that does not have a complementizer:
I wonder [CP should those guys *t* leave].

To summarize before continuing, we have introduced two changes into our system of syntactic analysis. First, we assume that TPs occur inside CP shells even when there is no overt complementizer. Second, we assume that the Inversion transformation moves T (and its contents) to the C position in order to indicate a question. In addition to giving the correct word order for the question structure, this analysis helps explain why the result of applying Inversion sounds so unnatural when the C position is already filled by another element, as in (23).

Language Matters Another Way to Ask a *Yes-No* Question

Although Inversion is a widely used question-marking strategy around the world, many languages go about things in an entirely different way. Instead of moving something to the C position, they place a special question morpheme there to begin with. Yoruba (a Benue-Congo language spoken in Nigeria) works that way.

Yoruba
Ṣé Olú wá?
+Q Olu come
'Did Olu come?'

```
        CP
       /  \
      C    TP
      |    /\
      Ṣé  Olú wá
```

Source: Adapted from Oluseye Adesola, *Yoruba: A Grammar Sketch*, Version 1.0, www.africananaphora.rutgers.edu.

5.3.2 *Wh* questions

Consider now the question construction exemplified in (25). These sentences are called **wh questions** because of the presence of a question word that (in English) usually begins with *wh*. A *wh* question asks for a specific type of information (the identity of a person, a thing, a place, a time, or a reason); it requires more than a yes/no answer.

(25) *a.* [NP Which languages] can Radha speak?
  b. [NP What] will they talk about?

TABLE 5.10	The syntactic category of *wh* words	
Wh word	**Syntactic category**	**Examples**
who	N	***Who*** *did you contact?*
what	N, when it occurs by itself	***What*** *did you see?*
	Det, when it occurs with a noun	***What*** *movie do you want to see?*
which	N, when in occurs by itself	***Which*** *do you prefer?*
	Det, when it occurs with a noun	***Which*** *car do you prefer?*
where	Adv	***Where*** *are you going?*
when	Adv	***When*** *did you move to Canada?*
why	Adv	***Why*** *did you leave the room?*
how	Adv, when it asks about a verb	***How*** *did they escape?*
	Deg, when it occurs with an adjective	***How*** *rich are they?*

There is reason to believe that the *wh* elements at the beginning of sentences such as those in (25) have been moved there from the positions indicated in (26).

(26) *a.* Radha can speak [NP which languages]
  b. They will talk about [NP what]

As illustrated here, *which languages* corresponds to the complement of *speak* (compare: *Radha can speak many languages*) and *what* corresponds to the complement of *about* (compare: *They will talk about politics*).

How, then, do the *wh* phrases end up at the beginning of the sentence? The answer is that they are attracted there by the +Q feature, which triggers the application of a Move operation known as **Wh Movement**.

(27) *a.* **[Which languages]** can Radha speak *t*?
    ⬆ *Wh* Movement ⌐

  b. **[What]** will they talk about *t*?
    ⬆ *Wh* Movement ⌐

A landing site for *wh* words

A moved *wh* phrase ends up as the specifier of CP—the only available position, since the modal occupies the C position. We can make this idea precise by formulating the *Wh* Movement operation as follows.

(28) Wh *Movement*
  Move a *wh* phrase to the specifier position under CP.

The sentence *Which languages can Radha speak?* can now be analyzed in steps, the first of which involves formation of the structure in figure 5.19a, which includes an unfilled specifier position under CP. *Wh* Movement and Inversion then apply, as depicted in figures 5.19b and 5.19c.

a. The structure produced by the Merge operation, with *which languages* functioning as complement of *speak*

FIGURE 5.19
Steps for forming the sentence Which *languages can Radha speak?*

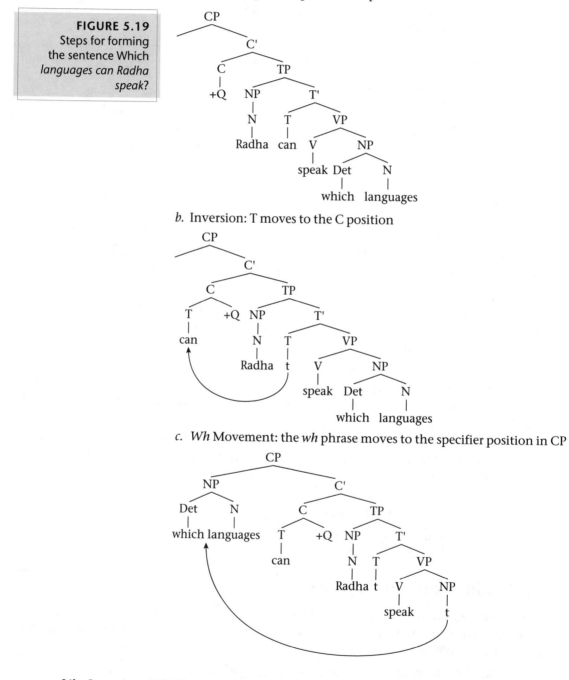

b. Inversion: T moves to the C position

c. Wh Movement: the *wh* phrase moves to the specifier position in CP

Like Inversion, *Wh* Movement cannot eliminate any part of the previously formed structure. The position initially occupied by the *wh* phrase is therefore not lost. That is because the Move operation leaves behind an empty category (a trace) that marks the earlier position of the moved element. In the case at hand, the trace indicates that the NP *which languages* originates as the complement of the verb *speak*.

Here's a second example, involving sentence (27b).

a. The structure produced by the Merge operation

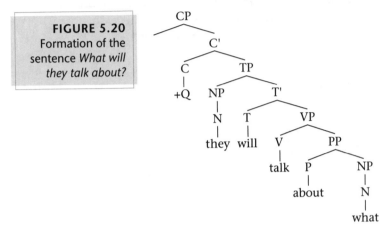

FIGURE 5.20
Formation of the sentence *What will they talk about?*

b. Inversion and *Wh* Movement (compressed here into a single step to save space)

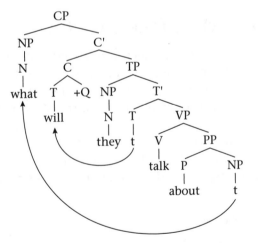

Language Matters **Pied Piping**

In more formal varieties of English, there is a second possibility—the entire PP containing the *wh* word can undergo *Wh* Movement.

Movement of the PP *about what*:

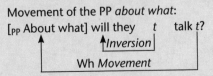

[PP About what] will they   *t*   talk *t*?

This phenomenon is known as 'pied-piping', a whimsical reference to the folk tale *The Pied Piper of Hamelin*, in which (in the words of Robert Browning) "the Piper advanced and the children followed."

In the examples considered so far, the *wh* word originates as the complement of a verb or preposition. In sentences such as the following, however, the wh word asks about the subject (the person who will walk the dog).

(29) Who will walk the dog?

The *wh* word in these patterns originates in the subject position. For the sake of generality, we assume that it subsequently moves to the specifier position in CP, even though the actual order of the words in the sentence does not change as a result of this movement (see figure 5.21). (We will assume that there is no Inversion in this type of question structure.)

FIGURE 5.21
Movement of a subject
wh phrase

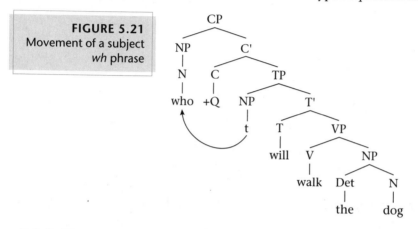

5.3.3 Deep structure and surface structure

The preceding examples show that two distinct types of mechanisms are involved in structure building. The first is the Merge operation, which creates tree structures by combining categories in a manner consistent with their subcategorization properties and the X' Schema. The second is the Move operation, which can modify these tree structures by moving an element from one position to another.

In the system sketched here, all instances of the Merge operation take place before any instances of the Move operation. This yields two distinct levels of syntactic structure, as shown in figure 5.22. The first, called **deep structure** (or **D-structure**), is formed by the Merge operation.

FIGURE 5.22
Structure-building
operations

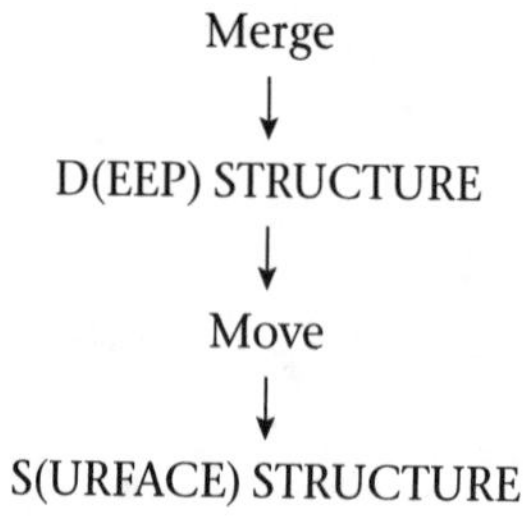

Merge
↓
D(EEP) STRUCTURE
↓
Move
↓
S(URFACE) STRUCTURE

The second level of syntactic structure corresponds to the final syntactic form of the sentence. Called **surface structure** (or **S-structure**), it results from applying whatever Move operations are appropriate for the sentence in question.

5.4 Universal Grammar and parametric variation

An intriguing aspect of work on syntax is the emphasis on **Universal Grammar (UG)**, the system of categories, operations, and principles shared by all languages. The key idea is that despite the many superficial differences among languages, there are certain commonalities with respect to how syntax works, including categories such as noun and verb, structure-building operations such as Merge and Move, and general constraints such as those imposed by the X' Schema.

This does not mean that languages must be alike in every way, though. Universal Grammar leaves room for variation, allowing individual languages to differ with respect to certain **parameters**. (You can think of a parameter as the set of options that UG permits for a particular phenomenon.) We have already seen one example of this sort of variation with regard to the X' Schema: the Head-Complement Parameter allows the head to precede its complement (as in English) or to follow it (as in Japanese; see section 5.1.2).

> **(30)** *The Head-Complement Parameter*
> Option a: The head precedes its complement.
> Option b: The head follows its complement.

Another parameter involves the placement of *wh* words. As we have seen, *wh* words move to the specifier position under CP in simple *wh* questions in English. In Chinese, though, they stay in their 'original' position.

> **(31)** Ni mai le **shenme**?
> you buy past what
> 'What did you buy?'

This suggests the existence of a *Wh* Movement Parameter with the two options summarized in (32).

> **(32)** *The* Wh *Movement Parameter*
> Option a: *Wh* words move to the specifier position in CP.
> Option b: *Wh* words don't move.

The next section presents yet another example of parametric variation, this one involving verb movement.

Language Matters **When *Wh* Words Don't Move in English**

English requires *Wh* Movement when the question is a simple request for information but not in certain other types of questions.

1. *Incredulity questions, expressing disbelief or surprise*. Such questions usually have a high-rising intonation and heavy stress on the *wh* word.

> Speaker A: The Prime Minister appointed the Queen to the Senate.
> Speaker B: The Prime Minister appointed WHO to the Senate?!!

2. *Pure echo questions, which request a repetition due to partial unintelligibility*. They also manifest a rising intonation and stress on the *wh* word, although generally less extreme than in the case of incredulity questions.

> Speaker A: The Prime Minister appointed [mumble, mumble] to the Senate.
> Speaker B: The Prime Minister appointed WHO to the Senate?

3. *Quizmaster questions, sometimes used by courtroom attorneys and quiz program announcers*. They have a flat or falling intonation.

> Now, Mr. Smith, you said you were where the night the Stanley Cup was stolen?
> For $15,000, the Fathers of Confederation met in Charlottetown in what year?

Source: Adapted from J.-Marc Authier, "Nonquantificational *Wh* and Weakest Crossover," *Linguistic Inquiry* 24, 1 (1993): 161–68.

5.4.1 Verb Raising

Consider the contrast between the following two English sentences.

(33) *a.* Paul always works.
   b. *Paul works always.

The ungrammaticality of the second sentence is expected since the preverbal adverb *always* functions as specifier of the verb and therefore should occur to its left, as in (33a). Surprisingly, however, the equivalent adverb must follow the verb in French, even though specifiers in French normally precede the head, just as they do in English.

(34) *a.* If the adverb precedes the verb, the sentence is ungrammatical:
   *Paul **toujours** travaille. (= English [33a])
   Paul always work
   'Paul always works.'

   b. If the adverb follows the verb, the sentence is grammatical:
   Paul travaille **toujours**. (= English [33b])
   Paul work always
   'Paul always works.'

Why should this be? One possibility is that the tense feature in the T category attracts the verb to the T position in French, just as the Q feature can attract T to the C position in some languages. As a result, French has the Verb Raising rule outlined in (35).

(35) *Verb Raising*

Move V to the T position.

This Move operation brings about the change depicted in figure 5.23, adjoining the verb to the tense feature with which it is associated.

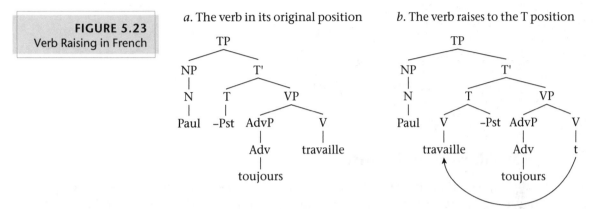

FIGURE 5.23
Verb Raising in French

a. The verb in its original position

b. The verb raises to the T position

An important piece of independent evidence for the existence of Verb Raising in French comes from Inversion. As we have already seen (section 5.3.1), this operation moves the T category to the C position. In English, only auxiliary verbs occur in the T position, which explains why only they can undergo Inversion.

(36) *a.* Inversion of an auxiliary verb in English:

Will you *t* stay for supper?

b. Inversion of a non-auxiliary verb in English:

*Stay you *t* for supper?

In French, however, ordinary verbs can occur in the T position, thanks to Verb Raising. This predicts that Inversion in French should be able to apply to these verbs as well as to auxiliaries. This is correct. Like English, French can form a question by moving an auxiliary leftward (when the subject is a pronoun).

(37) Inversion of an auxiliary:

As-tu *t* essayé?

have you tried
'Have you tried?'

However, unlike English, French also allows inversion of non-auxiliary Vs.

(38) Inversion of a non-auxiliary verb:

Vois-tu *t* le livre?

see you the book
'Do you see the book?'

Figure 5.24 depicts the interaction between Verb Raising and Inversion: the V first raises to the T position; the T complex then moves to the C position.

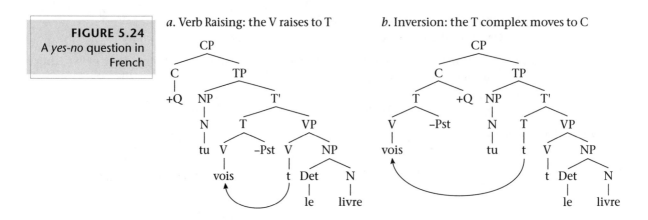

FIGURE 5.24
A *yes-no* question in French

a. Verb Raising: the V raises to T

b. Inversion: the T complex moves to C

Verb Raising in English

At this point, it might seem that there is a simple Verb Raising parameter with two options—raising (as in French) and no raising (as in English). This neatly accounts for the facts that we have considered so far, but matters are not so simple. As we'll see next, Verb Raising can apply in English, but only to *have* and *be*.

To begin, consider the sentences in (39), which contain two auxiliaries—one modal and one non-modal.

(39) *a.* The students should have finished the project.

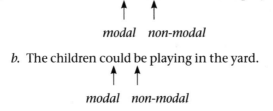

modal   non-modal

b. The children could be playing in the yard.

modal   non-modal

As we have already seen, modal auxiliaries occur under T, but what about non-modal auxiliaries? As depicted in figure 5.25, they are considered to be a special type of V that takes a VP complement.

FIGURE 5.25
Structures containing a modal auxiliary and a non-modal auxiliary

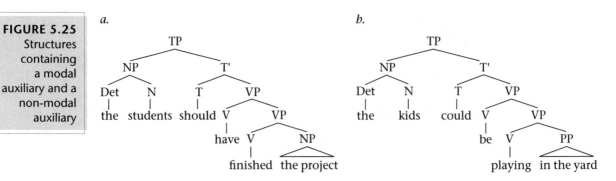

As expected, only the modal auxiliary can undergo Inversion in these structures.

(40) *a.* The modal auxiliary verb moves to the C position (grammatical):
[CP Should [TP the students *t* have finished the project]]?

b. The non-modal auxiliary moves to the C position (ungrammatical):

*[CP Have [TP the students should *t* finished the project]]?

Crucially, however, a non-modal auxiliary can undergo Inversion when there is no modal.

(41) Inversion of a non-modal auxiliary in the absence of a modal auxiliary:

[CP Have [TP the students *t* finished the project]]?

(from: The students have finished the project.)

Since Inversion involves movement from T to C, the auxiliary in (41) must have moved to the T position, and from there to the C position, as depicted in figure 5.26.

FIGURE 5.26
The V moves to the T position (Verb Raising); the T complex then raises to C (Inversion).

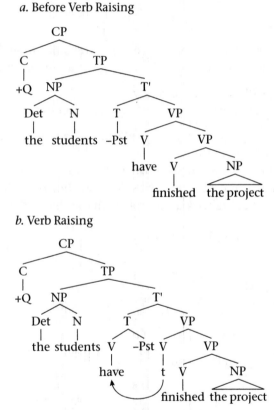

a. Before Verb Raising

b. Verb Raising

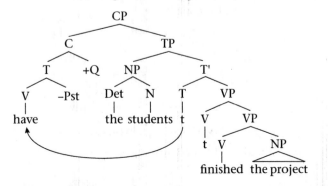

c. Inversion (raising of the T complex to C)

In sum, then, it appears that the two options permitted by the Verb Raising parameter should be stated as follows.

(42) *The Verb Raising Parameter*
Option a: Any type of verb raises to T (French).
Option b: Only auxiliary verbs raise to T (English).

5.5 Some additional structures

Now that we have in place a basic system for forming sentences, it is possible to extend it to encompass various other syntactic phenomena, four of which will be considered here.

5.5.1 Modifiers

Words and phrases that denote properties of heads are called **modifiers**. For example, adjective phrases (APs) commonly serve as modifiers of Ns, while adverb phrases (AdvPs) modify Vs.

(43) *a.* a [$_{AP}$ good] friend of the family
b. always read the instructions [$_{AdvP}$ very carefully]

The AP *good* denotes a property of the friend, while the AdvP *very carefully* describes the manner in which the reading occurred.

How do modifiers fit into phrase structure? For the purposes of this introduction to syntax, we will assume (as most syntacticians do) that they occur in an intermediate position, lower than specifiers but higher than complements, as illustrated in figure 5.27.

FIGURE 5.27
The place of modifiers in phrase structure

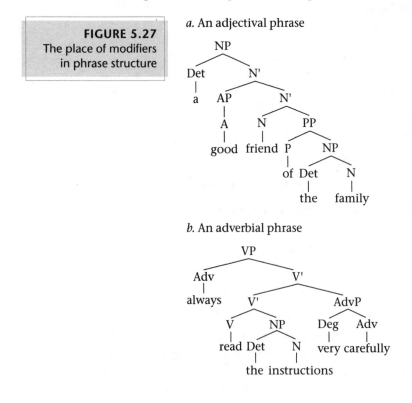

a. An adjectival phrase

b. An adverbial phrase

In figure 5.27a, the modifier (on the left side of the head) occurs lower than the specifier (the determiner *a*), but higher than the complement (the PP *of the family*), creating two intermediate levels in the phrase. In figure 5.27b, the modifier (the adverbial phrase) occurs on the right side of the head, once again above the complement but below the specifier.

5.5.2 Relative clauses

Sometimes even CPs can serve as modifiers. In the following sentence, for instance, a special type of CP called a **relative clause** provides information about the N to its left.

(44) *a.* The friend [$_{CP}$ who Hadassah visited *t*] lives in Saskatchewan.
      b. the choice [$_{CP}$ which most people prefer *t*]

Relative clause structures resemble *wh* questions in two respects. First, they can begin with a *wh* word such as *who* or *which* (a so-called **relative pronoun**).[1] Second, there is an empty position within the sentence from which the *wh* phrase has apparently been moved. (In [44a] and [b], that position occurs right after the transitive verb.)

The first step in the formation of the relative clause in (44a) involves the D-structure in figure 5.28; the +Rel feature in the C position indicates that the CP is a relative clause. (The CP here includes an open specifier position for subsequent use as a landing site for *Wh* Movement.)

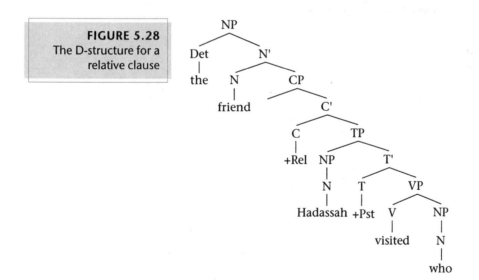

FIGURE 5.28
The D-structure for a relative clause

Here, the *wh* word *who* occurs as complement of the verb *visit* since it corresponds to the direct object (the person who was visited). The next step involves the application of *Wh* Movement (triggered by the +Rel feature in the C position) to give the structure in figure 5.29, with the *wh* word ending up in the specifier position within CP.

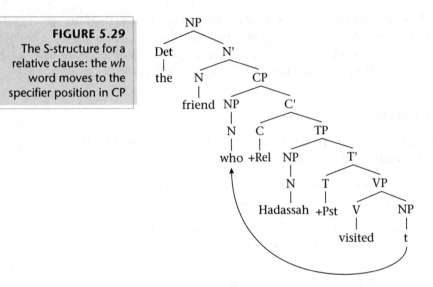

FIGURE 5.29
The S-structure for a relative clause: the *wh* word moves to the specifier position in CP

In the preceding example, the *wh* word originates in the direct object position. In (45), in contrast, it originates in the subject position.

(45) Gabriella met some people [CP who live in Alberta].

Here *who* corresponds to certain people who live in Alberta. The D-structure for this sentence therefore has the *wh* word in the subject position. Like other *wh* words, it subsequently moves to the specifier position within CP even though the actual order of the words in the sentence does not change as a result of this movement.

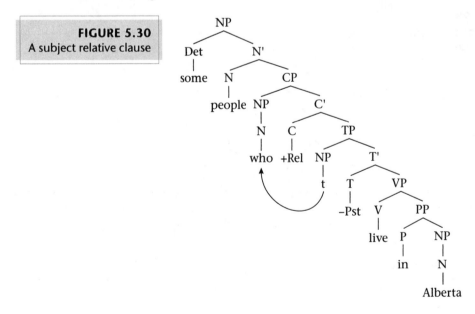

FIGURE 5.30
A subject relative clause

5.5.3 Passives

Another important syntactic phenomenon involves the relationship between the two sentence types exemplified in (46). (The first type is called **active** because the subject denotes the 'agent' or 'instigator' of the action denoted by the verb, while the second is called **passive**.)

(46) *a.* Active sentence type:
A thief stole the painting.

b. Passive sentence type:
The painting was stolen (by a thief).

We will focus here on two key properties of passive constructions. First, passive constructions involve a major reduction in the importance of the agent. Whereas the agent serves as subject of an active clause, it is not expressed at all in the vast majority of passive sentences in English.

(47) The painting was stolen.

Second, some other NP—usually the direct object of the corresponding active sentence—functions as subject in the passive sentence and therefore is interpreted as what the sentence is about. This too can be seen in example (47), where the NP *the painting* serves as direct object in the active sentence and as subject in the passive sentence.

The D-structure for a passive sentence such as *The painting was stolen* is depicted in figure 5.31. (Remember that the auxiliary *be* is treated as a V that takes a VP complement.) We include an empty subject position under TP. (When the agent is expressed as part of a PP [e.g., *by the thief*], the PP is attached to the lower VP, to the right of the verb's NP complement.)

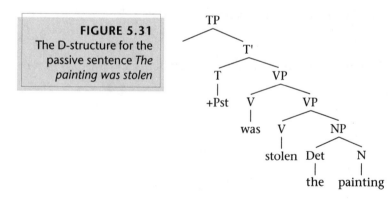

FIGURE 5.31
The D-structure for the passive sentence *The painting was stolen*

This D-structure is obviously very abstract—it does not sound like any sentence that we actually utter. However, it neatly captures the two key properties of passive constructions. First, the agent is not expressed, leaving the subject position open. Second, the verb has a direct object that can take over as subject.

The D-structure in figure 5.31 is converted into an S-structure with the help of the Move operation in (48).

(48) *NP Movement*
Move NP into the specifier position in TP.

Movement of the NP *the painting* to the subject position gives the S-structure depicted in figure 5.32.

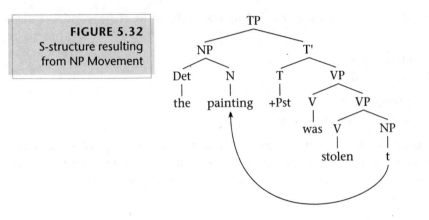

FIGURE 5.32
S-structure resulting
from NP Movement

5.5.4 **VP-internal subjects**

As we have just seen, the subject in a passive sentence originates in the complement position within the VP. Interestingly, there is reason to think that (contrary to what we have been assuming up to this point) subjects of active sentences also originate inside the VP—in the specifier position. (If this is right, then preverbal adverbs such as *perhaps* and *always* would have to be treated as modifiers rather than as specifiers of VP—a relatively minor adjustment.)

Sentence (49) provides a preliminary illustration of how this works.

(49) Children are playing in the yard.

As illustrated in figure 5.33, the sentence's subject (*children*) occurs in the specifier position in VP in D-structure.

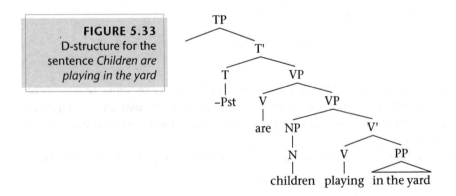

FIGURE 5.33
D-structure for the
sentence *Children are
playing in the yard*

It subsequently moves (via NP Movement) to the specifier position in TP.

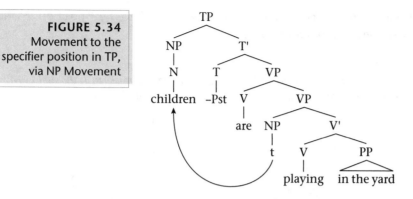

FIGURE 5.34
Movement to the specifier position in TP, via NP Movement

Various facts make this analysis attractive; we will mention just two here.

First, there are patterns in which the would-be subject is trapped inside the VP, in the specifier position. One such pattern is illustrated in (50), where the subject position is occupied by *there*—a special place-filling NP with no meaning of its own.

(50) [TP There are [VP children playing in the yard]].

As illustrated in figure 5.35, the presence of *there* in the specifier position in TP forces the NP that would otherwise be the subject (*children*) to remain in its point of origin—the specifier position inside VP.

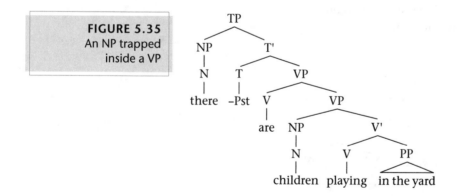

FIGURE 5.35
An NP trapped inside a VP

Second, we now have a tantalizing explanation for patterns in which the verb comes before the subject—the preferred word order in about 10 percent of the world's languages. The following example is from Welsh.

(51) Gwelodd Sion ddraig.
     saw   Sion dragon
     'Sion saw a dragon.'

It is hard to see how this order can be accommodated in tree structures that place subjects in the specifier position within TP. However, a straightforward analysis is possible if subjects originate inside VP: instead of raising the subject to the specifier position in TP as English does, languages like Welsh leave the subject where it is but raise the verb to the T position. As illustrated in figure 5.36, this gives verb–subject order.

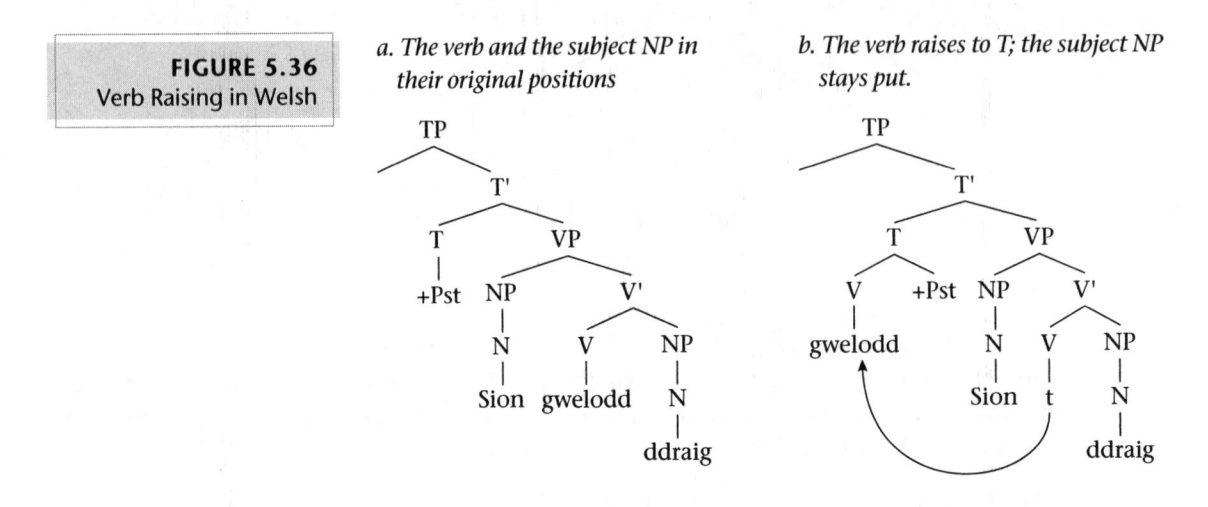

FIGURE 5.36
Verb Raising in Welsh

a. The verb and the subject NP in their original positions

b. The verb raises to T; the subject NP stays put.

This idea makes a crucial prediction: the verb should have to stay inside the VP in cases where the T position is already filled. This seems to be exactly right: when the T position is occupied by the special auxiliary verb *gwnaeth* 'do', the main verb *gwelodd* 'saw' remains inside the VP, to the right of the subject *Sion*.

(52) Gwnaeth Sion gwelodd ddraig.
      did   Sion saw   dragon
      'Sion saw a dragon.'

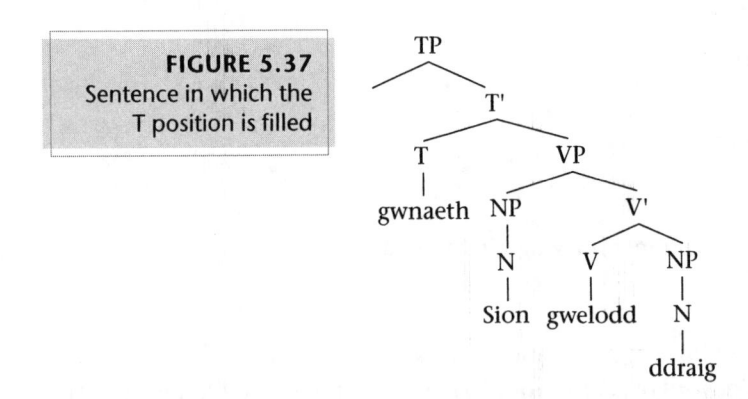

FIGURE 5.37
Sentence in which the
T position is filled

Of course, if we decide that the specifier position within VPs is reserved for the subject, we will have to make adjustments elsewhere in our grammar. In particular, words like *always, never,* and *perhaps* can't be treated as specifiers any more, contrary to what we assumed in table 5.4. The usual practice these days is to treat them as modifiers and to locate them in a position that is lower in phrase structure than the specifier position (see section 5.5.1). Your instructor will decide whether you should revise the way you draw tree structures or whether the VP-internal subject analysis should be set aside for now.

5.5.5 **Rethinking specifiers**

The VP-internal subject hypothesis underlines a puzzling fact about specifiers: with the exception of determiners, they are always phrasal. This is true for subjects (e.g., **The children** *left*), regardless of whether they occur as specifiers of TP or VP. It is also true for *wh* phrases, which occur in the specifier position of CP, as in **Which languages** *can Radha speak?* (see section 5.3.2). It is even true for possessives such as *the child's* in **the child's** *bicycle* (see section 5.1.2) Why are determiners so different?

The likely answer is that they have been misanalyzed and that they are really just heads that take an NP as their complement and project up to a DP (determiner phrase). So the right structure for *a map of Canada* is actually the one depicted in figure 5.38a rather than figure 5.38b. (In order to highlight this new perspective, the label for Determiner is written as 'D' rather than 'Det'.)

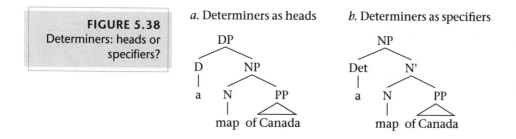

FIGURE 5.38
Determiners: heads or specifiers?

a. Determiners as heads

b. Determiners as specifiers

Generalizing this idea, it is often suggested that all NPs occur inside a DP 'shell' (just as all TPs occur inside a CP). In order to make this idea work, the determiner will sometimes be invisible, just as the C is sometimes invisible in CP structure. We see examples of DPs with an empty D position in figure 5.39.

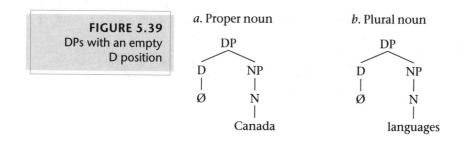

FIGURE 5.39
DPs with an empty D position

a. Proper noun

b. Plural noun

Of course, these D positions could be filled (as in **the** *Canada of the 1950s* or **these** *languages*), but they don't have to be.

One advantage of this approach is that it reveals similarities between languages that would not otherwise be noticed. At first glance, French seems to be very different from English since it requires (overt) determiners in patterns with a proper name or a plural noun: *le Canada* and *les langues*. But if all NPs occur inside DPs, the difference between English and French becomes less striking: they differ only with regard to whether the determiner is overtly expressed.

DPs can even have DP specifiers, as in the following possessive pattern.

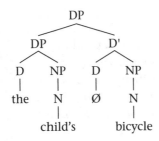

FIGURE 5.40
The DP *the child's* functions as specifier of the larger DP *the child's bicycle.*

In the above example, the head of the larger DP is invisible. But there's reason to believe that it's there nonetheless. In fact, it can even be filled in certain patterns, as shown in figure 5.41.

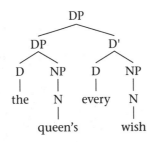

FIGURE 5.41
The D position in a possessive pattern is filled by the determiner *every.*

Language Matters The World's Most Controversial Language

In 2005, a startling report was published on Pirahã, a language spoken by a few hundred mostly monolingual tribespeople in the rainforest of northwestern Brazil. Pirahã, it was reported, lacks complex syntactic structure in general, including complement clauses and coordination: unlike every other known language, it supposedly permits only short, simple sentences. (It is also said to lack colour terms, numerals, and quantity-denoting expressions such as 'every' and 'some'.) Although the report has received widespread attention in the media, its conclusions are being hotly debated within linguistics. A great deal of additional research and scrutiny will be required before a consensus is reached on the status of this fascinating language.

Sources: Andrew Nevins, David Pesetsky, and Cilene Rodrigues, "Pirahã Exceptionality: A Reassessment," *Language* 85, 2 (2009): 355–404; Daniel Everett, "Pirahã Culture and Grammar: A Response to Some Criticisms," *Language* 85, 2 (2009): 405–442; John Colapinto, "The Interpreter," *The New Yorker*, April 16, 2007, 118–37.

Summing up

Syntactic structure is built by two basic operations. A **Merge** operation combines words in accordance with their **syntactic category** and their **subcategorization** properties, creating a representation called **D(eep) Structure**. D-structure must comply with the **X' Schema**, which stipulates the place of **heads**, **specifiers**, and **complements** in phrase structure. **Move** operations can modify D-structure by moving words and phrases in particular ways to produce an **S(urface) structure**.

Although the form of sentences can vary considerably from language to language, **Universal Grammar** appears to provide all languages with the same general type of syntactic mechanisms. Differences among languages can, for the most part, be attributed to a small set of **parameters**, each of which makes available a variety of alternatives from which individual languages may choose.

Note

1. A relative clause can also begin with the complementizer *that*, in which case the relative pronoun must be deleted (*the friend [that Leslie visited t]*). Except in the case of subject relative clauses, it is even possible to delete both the complementizer and the relative pronoun (*the friend [Leslie visited t]*).

Recommended reading

Carnie, Andrew. 2012. *Syntax: A Generative Introduction*. 3rd ed. Boston: Blackwell.
Tallerman, Maggie. 2015. *Understanding Syntax*. New York: Routledge.

Appendix: How to build tree structures

Note: This review of structure building is based on the system introduced in the sections of this chapter up to 5.5.4. In building a tree structure from scratch for a phrase or sentence that you are analyzing, you will probably find it easiest to proceed in steps, working from the bottom up and from right to left. As an illustration, let us first consider the phrase *a picture of Akira*.

Using Merge to build simple phrases

The first step involves assigning each word to the appropriate category, as depicted in figure 5.42.

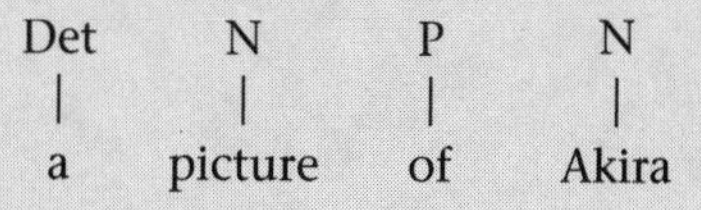

```
Det      N       P       N
 |       |       |       |
 a     picture   of    Akira
```

FIGURE 5.42 The first step: determining the word-level categories

Then, working from right to left, the appropriate phrasal structure is built above each, starting with an NP above the N *Akira*.

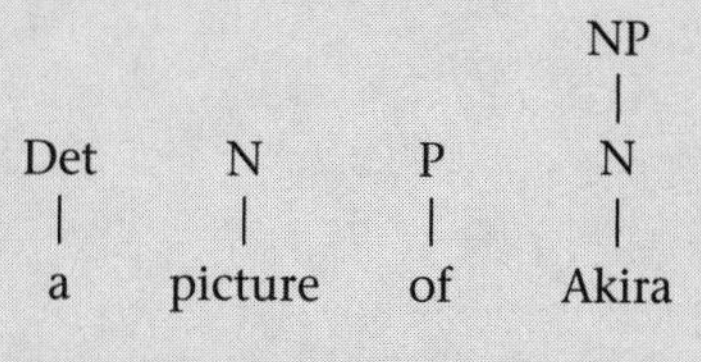

```
                         NP
                          |
Det      N       P        N
 |       |       |        |
 a     picture   of     Akira
```

FIGURE 5.43 Construction of the NP

Next, we carry out the same procedure for the P *of*, combining it with the NP *Akira* (its complement), as depicted in figure 5.44.

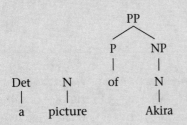

FIGURE 5.44 Combination of the P *of* with its complement NP, resulting in a PP

Next, the N *picture* combines with the PP, to give an N'.

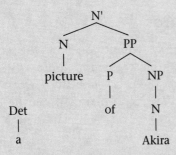

FIGURE 5.45 Combination of the N *picture* with its complement PP

Finally, the determiner is added as specifier of the N, giving the full NP depicted in figure 5.46.

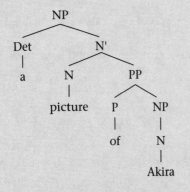

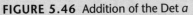

FIGURE 5.46 Addition of the Det *a*

Using Merge to build sentence structure

Consider now how we proceed in the case of a complete sentence such as *The dog might bite that man*. Assignment of each word to the appropriate category gives the structure depicted in figure 5.47.

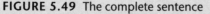

Det	N	T	V	Det	N
the	dog	might	bite	that	man

FIGURE 5.47 Category assignment

Then, working from right to left, it is easy to see that *bite that man* forms a VP.

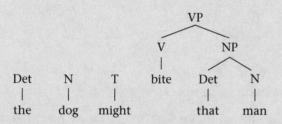

FIGURE 5.48 The VP *bite that man*

Next, the T *might* combines with the VP, creating a T', which is then merged with the subject NP *the dog*. The resulting TP is then embedded in a CP, whose head carries the feature –Q, indicating a statement rather than a question.

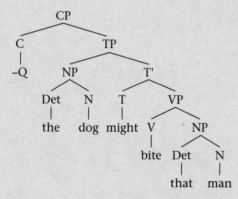

FIGURE 5.49 The complete sentence

Using Move

Recognizing that a Move operation such as Inversion or *Wh* Movement has applied is relatively simple: if a sentence contains an auxiliary verb to the left of the subject, then Inversion has applied; if it begins with a *wh* word, then *Wh* Movement has applied. In the sentence *What should the farmers plant?*, then, both operations have applied.

In order to represent the deep structure, we must place the auxiliary verb in its normal position under T and we must determine the position from which the *wh* word has been moved. Since the *wh* word in the sentence *What should the farmers plant?* asks about the complement of the verb (the thing that is planted), we place *what* in the complement position within VP in deep structure. This gives the deep structure depicted in figure 5.50.

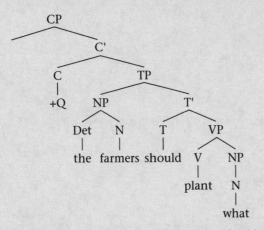

FIGURE 5.50 The D-structure for *What should the farmers plant?*

Attracted by the +Q feature, *should* then moves to the C position (Inversion) and *what* moves to the specifier position under CP (*Wh* Movement), yielding the complete S-structure depicted in figure 5.51.

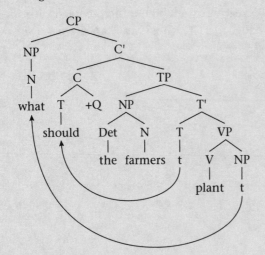
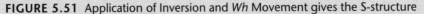

FIGURE 5.51 Application of Inversion and *Wh* Movement gives the S-structure

Some things to remember
- A sentence is a TP, with a T as its head.
- The T position contains either a modal auxiliary (if there is one) or the ±Pst tense feature.
- Every T takes a VP as its complement.
- Every T has an NP specifer (the subject).
- Every TP occurs inside a CP shell (although this is sometimes not represented for reasons of space).

Exercises

1. Place an asterisk next to any of the sentences that are ungrammatical for you. Then try to identify what makes these sentences ungrammatical.
   a) The instructor told the students to study.
   b) The instructor suggested the students to study.
   c) The customer asked for a cold beer.
   d) The customer requested for a cold beer.
   e) He gave the Red Cross some money.
   f) He donated the Red Cross some money.
   g) The pilot landed the jet.
   h) The jet landed.
   i) A journalist wrote the article.
   j) The article wrote.
   k) Jerome is satisfied of his job.
   l) Jerome is tired of his job.

2. Indicate the category of each word in the following sentences. (It may help to refer back to section 5.1.1.)
   a) That glass broke.
   b) A jogger ran toward the end of the lane.
   c) These tall trees are blocking the road.
   d) The detective looked through the records.
   e) The peaches never appear quite ripe.
   f) Jeremy will play the trumpet and the drums in the orchestra.

3. Each of the following phrases consists of a specifier and a head. For each example, build a tree structure that complies with the X' Schema.
   a) the zoo   f) this house
   b) always try   g) very competent
   c) so witty   h) quite cheap
   d) perhaps pass   i) never surrender
   e) less bleak   j) those books

4. The following phrases include a head, a complement, and (in some cases) a specifier. For each example, build a tree structure that complies with the X' Schema, following the same abbreviatory conventions adopted in the chapter.
   a) into the house
   b) fixed the telephone
   c) full of mistakes
   d) more towards the window
   e) a film about pollution
   f) always study this material
   g) perhaps earn the money
   h) that argument with Owen
   i) the success of the program

5. Drawing on the X' Schema, create trees for each of the following sentences.
   a) Those guests should leave.
   b) Maria never ate a brownie.
   c) That shelf will fall.
   d) The glass broke.
   e) The student lost the debate.
   f) The manager may offer a raise.
   g) The judge never jails shoplifters.
   h) The teacher often organized a discussion.
   i) A psychic will speak to this group.
   j) Marianne could become quite fond of Larry.

6. Apply the substitution test to determine which of the bracketed sequences in the following sentences form constituents.
   a) [The news] upset the entire family.
   b) They hid [in the cave].
   c) The [computer was very] expensive.
   d) [The houses] will be rebuilt.
   e) Jane will [leave town].
   f) The goslings [swam across] the lake.

7. Apply the movement test to determine which of the bracketed sequences in the following sentences form constituents.
   a) We ate our lunch [near the river bank].
   b) Vijay looked [up the number] in the book.
   c) The [island has been] flooded.
   d) I love [peanut butter and bacon sandwiches].
   e) The environmental [movement is gaining momentum].

8. Lexical categories are divided into subcategories on the basis of their complements. For each of the following words, two potential complement options are given.
   i) For each word, determine which one of the two options better matches its subcategorization requirements.
   ii) Justify your choice by creating a sentence using that complement option.

Verb	*Options*	*Verb*	*Options*
a) expire	Ø *or* NP NP	e) clean	NP PP_{for} *or* NP NP
b) destroy	NP *or* Ø	f) mumble	NP *or* NP NP
c) observe	NP *or* PP_{to} PP_{about}	g) throw	Ø *or* NP PP_{loc}
d) discuss	NP *or* Ø	h) paint	NP PP_{to} *or* NP PP_{for}

Noun	*Options*
i) debate	PP_{of} PP_{to} *or* PP_{with} PP_{about}
j) hammer	Ø *or* PP_{with} PP_{about}
k) success	PP_{of} PP_{to} *or* PP_{of}
l) transfer	PP_{with} PP_{about} *or* PP_{of} PP_{to}
m) sickness	Ø *or* PP_{with} PP_{about}

	Adjective	*Options*
n)	strong	Ø *or* PP_{about}
o)	sick	NP *or* PP_{of}
p)	happy	PP_{with} *or* PP_{of}
q)	knowledgeable	PP_{to} *or* PP_{about}
r)	small	PP_{of} *or* Ø

9. The following sentences all contain embedded clauses that function as complements of a verb. Draw a tree structure for each sentence.
   a) The reporter said that an accident injured a woman.
   b) The fishermen think that the company polluted the bay.
   c) Bill reported that a student asked whether the eclipse would occur.

10. The derivations of the following sentences involve the Inversion transformation. Give the deep structure and the surface structure for each sentence.
    a) Will the boss hire Hillary?
    b) Can the dog fetch the frisbee?
    c) Should the student report the incident?
    d) Must the musicians play that sonata?
    e) Might that player leave the team?

11. The following sentences involve the rules of *Wh* Movement and Inversion. Draw the trees to show the deep structure and the surface structure for each of these sentences.
    a) Who should the director call?
    b) Who should call the director?
    c) What can Joanne eat?
    d) Who will the visitors stay with?
    e) What might Terry bake?
    f) What could Anna bring to the gathering?

12. The following data illustrates the formation of *yes-no* questions in German.
    a) Das Kind wird die Schwester lehren.
       the child will the sister teach
       'The child will teach the sister.'
    b) Wird das Kind die Schwester lehren?
       will the child the sister teach
       'Will the child teach the sister?'
    c) Der Mann liebt die Frau.
       the man loves the woman
       'The man loves the woman.'
    d) Liebt der Mann die Frau?
       loves the man the woman
       'Does the man love the woman?'

    Assuming that German makes use of the same Inversion operation as English (i.e., 'Move T to the C position'), what does the above data tell us about whether German employs the Verb Raising operation?

13. Draw the structure for the following sentences, each of which contains one or more modifiers. (Because no movement is involved in any of these sentences, the deep structure and surface structure will be alike.)
    a) The efficient workers finished very quickly.
    b) A very clever engineer designed this new car.
    c) The large tiger suddenly leapt into the tree.

14. Each of the following phrases contains a relative clause. Draw the deep structure and the surface structure for each.
    a) the girl who Jane befriended
    b) the girl who Ismael talked to
    c) the cyclist who the hiker met
    d) the cyclist who met the hiker
    e) the tree which the Queen stood under

To learn more about the topics discussed in this chapter, visit the Companion Website for *Contemporary Linguistic Analysis*.

Semantics: the study of meaning

In every object there is inexhaustible meaning.

THOMAS CARLYLE, *THE FRENCH REVOLUTION* (1848)

EVERY TIME we hear a sentence or a word, we try to assign a meaning to it. Usually, we're successful. But how, exactly, do we determine what an utterance means? **Semantics** is the component of grammar that is concerned with the meaning of words and sentences.

Take a sentence like *Malik hired Su-Ying yesterday*. It is clear what it means, but it is less obvious why it has the meaning that it does. Different factors are involved. For example, the order of the words is important: the sentence obtained by switching the order of subject and object (as in *Su-Ying hired Malik yesterday*) expresses a very different meaning. Lexical choices also contribute to the meaning of the sentence. If we replace the verb *hired* with *fired* (as in *Malik fired Su-Ying yesterday*), we also obtain a sentence expressing a very different meaning.

Finally, when a sentence is uttered by a particular speaker, the **context** in which the utterance occurs also affects the meaning that is expressed. If the speaker utters the sentence *Malik hired Su-Ying yesterday* on January 15, 2019, the sentence means that Malik hired Su-Ying on January 14, 2019. But if the utterance occurs on February 9, 2019, it means that Malik hired Su-Ying on February 8, 2019.[1]

6.1 Meaning and logic

6.1.1 Logical relations among sentences

If you know the meaning of a sentence, then you know what follows or does not follow from the truth of that sentence. In other words, you know what relation that sentence bears to certain other possible sentences of the language. In this section, we explore four logical relations that can hold between sentences: logical entailment, logical equivalence, logical contradiction, and logical contrariety.

Logical Entailment

The relation of **logical entailment** holds when the truth of one sentence requires the truth of another. More specifically, given two sentences *p* and *q*, *p* logically entails *q* if the truth of *p* requires the truth of *q*. In other words, if *p* is true, *q* cannot be false. Take the following two sentences.

(1) *a.* Arjun buttered the toast with a knife.
　　 b. Arjun buttered the toast.

The sentence in (1a) logically entails the one in (1b) because if (a) is true, then it must be the case that (b) is true as well. If Arjun buttered the toast with a knife, then it must be true that Arjun buttered the toast.

The entailment relation in (1) allows both (a) and (b) to be false, as in a situation where Arjun did not butter the toast with a knife, and he did not butter it at all. It is also consistent with a situation in which (a) is false, but (b) is true: Arjun may have buttered the toast with a spoon rather than knife. What logical entailment rules out is a situation where (a) is true and (b) is false.

To test whether one sentence entails another, we can use the **contradiction test**: if we join sentence *p* with the negation of sentence *q* and the result is contradictory, then we know that *p* entails *q*. What happens when we apply this test for the sentences in (1)? (We use # to indicate that although the sentence is grammatical, it is semantically unacceptable.)

(2) #Arjun buttered the toast with a knife but he did not butter the toast.

This sentence is contradictory, which confirms that (1a) entails (1b): you cannot assert the truth of (1a) while asserting the falsity of (1b).

Consider another example of entailment.

(3) *a.* Snoopy is a beagle.
　　 b. Snoopy is a dog.

The sentence in (3a) logically entails the one in (3b) because if (a) is true, then (b) must be true. Even though you may never have seen Snoopy, if you know what a beagle is and you know what a dog is, then you know that if Snoopy is a beagle, then Snoopy is also a dog. The contradiction test confirms this: sentence (4) is semantically unacceptable.

(4) #Snoopy is a beagle but he is not a dog.

Logical Equivalence

The sentences *p* and *q* have a relation of **logical equivalence** just in case *p* entails *q* and *q* entails *p*. This rules out two types of situation: (i) situations where *p* is true and *q* is false, and (ii) situations where *q* is true and *p* is false. Thus, *p* and *q* are logically equivalent only if *p* and *q* are both true or if *p* and *q* are both false. Here is an example of logically equivalent sentences.

(5) *a.* Edward is a bachelor.
　　 b. Edward is an unmarried man.

You might not know whether Edward is or is not a bachelor. However, if you know the meaning of these two sentences (that is, if you know what *bachelor* and *unmarried man* mean), then you know that either both sentences are true or both sentences are false.

Logical Contradiction

The sentences *p* and *q* have a relation of **logical contradiction** just in case they have opposite truth values: *p* is true and *q* is false, or *p* is false and *q* is true. Examples of pairs of sentences in a relation of contradiction are given in (6) and (7).

(6) *a.* Snoopy is a dog.
  b. Snoopy is not a dog.

(7) *a.* Someone loves Charlie.
  b. Nobody loves Charlie.

The negation in (6b) switches the truth value of the corresponding positive sentence in (6a). This guarantees that (a) and (b) will be contradictory. If it is true that Snoopy is a dog, then it is false that Snoopy is not a dog. And if it is false that Snoopy is a dog, then it is true that Snoopy is not a dog. Similarly, if you know what (7a) means, then you know that if (7a) is true, then (7b) is false and if (7a) is false, then (7b) is true.

Logical Contrariety

The sentences *p* and *q* have a relation of **logical contrariety** just in case *p* and *q* cannot both be true: if *p* is true, then *q* must be false. Unlike two sentences in a relation of contradiction, two sentences in a relation of contrariety can both be false. Furthermore, while two contradictory sentences exhaust the realm of possibilities (Snoopy is either a dog or he is not a dog), contraries do not.

Here is an illustration.

(8) *a.* Lucy is more courageous than Charlie.
  b. Lucy is less courageous than Charlie.

The two sentences in (8) cannot both be true. However, they could both be false because there is a third possibility: Charlie and Lucy might be equally courageous. Adjectives like *courageous* are called **scalar adjectives** because they are associated with a scale of degrees (more courageous, less courageous, as courageous). Pairs of scalar adjectives such as *tall/short*, *good/bad*, or *big/small* are typical cases of logical contraries.

6.1.2 Logical relations between words

Pairs of words can also be classified into logical relations. Four such relations are subordination, equivalence, incompatibility, and complementarity.

Subordination

Words can have a relation of **logical subordination**. Recall the pair of sentences used above to illustrate logical entailment between sentences, repeated in (9).

(9) *a.* Snoopy is a beagle.
  b. Snoopy is a dog.

If you know what the words *beagle* and *dog* mean, then you know that (9a) logically entails (9b). This is because to know the meanings of *beagle* and *dog* is to know that the word *beagle* is subordinate to the word *dog*.

One way to represent this relation is to think of the meanings of words like *dog* and *beagle* as representing sets: the meaning of *dog* represents the set of things to which the word *dog* refers—that is, the set of dogs; similarly, the meaning of *beagle* represents the set of things to which the word *beagle* refers—that is, the set of beagles. Thus, to say that one word is subordinate to another word is to say that the first word (e.g., *beagle*) denotes a subset of the set denoted by the second word (e.g., *dog*), as shown in figure 6.1.

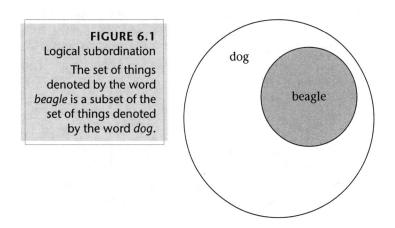

FIGURE 6.1
Logical subordination

The set of things denoted by the word *beagle* is a subset of the set of things denoted by the word *dog*.

The following pair provides another example of logical subordination between two expressions.

(10) *a.* Alex is Cesar's sister.
       b. Alex is Cesar's sibling.

Sentence (10a) logically entails (10b): if it is true that Alex is Cesar's sister, then it is true that Alex is Cesar's sibling. This is because the word *sister* is a subordinate of the word *sibling*: the set of sisters is a subset of the set of siblings.

Equivalence

The terms A and B have a relation of logical equivalence just in case A and B have the same meaning. Recall the pair of sentences used above to illustrate logical equivalence between sentences, repeated in (11).

(11) *a.* Edward is a bachelor.
       b. Edward is an unmarried man.

These two sentences are logically equivalent because they are either both true or both false.

Equivalence can hold at the word (or smaller-than-sentence) level as well. In fact, the reason why (11a) and (11b) are logically equivalent is that the terms *bachelor* and *unmarried man* are equivalent: that is, they have the same meaning. Using the notion of sets again, we can say that *bachelor* and *unmarried man* are equivalent because they refer to exactly the same set of things.

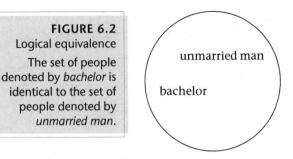

FIGURE 6.2
Logical equivalence

The set of people denoted by *bachelor* is identical to the set of people denoted by *unmarried man*.

Complementarity

The terms A and B have a relation of **logical complementarity** just in case the meanings of A and B do not overlap and together exhaust the set of relevant possibilities. Assuming that all things are either animate or inanimate, for example, we can represent the complementarity relation between the words *animate* and *inanimate* as shown in figure 6.3.

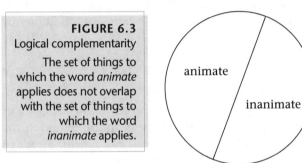

FIGURE 6.3
Logical complementarity

The set of things to which the word *animate* applies does not overlap with the set of things to which the word *inanimate* applies.

Incompatibility

The terms A and B have a relation of **logical incompatibility** just in case the meanings of A and B do not overlap but do not exhaust the set of relevant possibilities. The terms in each line in (12) are incompatible.

(12) *a.* blue-eyed, brown-eyed
    b. dog, cat

Take the two terms in (12b): *dog* and *cat* are incompatible because an animal cannot be both a *dog* and a *cat* and because there are other possibilities (an animal could, for example, be a rabbit).

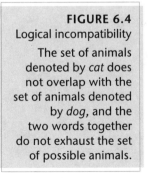

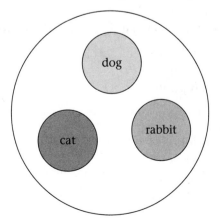

FIGURE 6.4
Logical incompatibility

The set of animals denoted by *cat* does not overlap with the set of animals denoted by *dog*, and the two words together do not exhaust the set of possible animals.

As we saw earlier, pairs of scalar adjectives like *good/bad* are also logically incompatible in that someone cannot be both good and bad at something, but he could be neither good nor bad. For example, consider the following sentences.

(13) *a.* As for arithmetic, Alicia is good at it.
       b. As for arithmetic, Alicia is bad at it.
       c. As for arithmetic, Alicia is neither good nor bad. She's average.

Given that we are talking about Alicia's ability in arithmetic, (13a) and (13b) cannot both be true. However, they could both be false if Alicia is neither good nor bad at arithmetic, as in (13c).

6.2 Words and the multiplicity of meanings

One interesting property of a natural language like English is that its words do not just have one single meaning. When a word has more than one meaning we say that the word is **ambiguous.** If a word is ambiguous, the sentence containing the word will be ambiguous too. Let's consider two ways in which ambiguity manifests itself in language—homonymy and polysemy.

6.2.1 Homonymy   *no relation whatsoever*

Two words are **homonyms** if they have different meanings but either sound the same or have the same written form. In the first case, the two words are **homophones**, and in the second case, they are **homographs.** For example, the noun *bark* has two meanings: it can refer to the outer covering of a tree or to the vocal sound that dogs make. Note that $bark_1$ and $bark_2$ are both homophones and homographs—they are pronounced the same and spelled the same.

Some additional examples of homonyms can be found in table 6.1. As you can see, homonyms do not have to belong to the same grammatical category; moreover, some homonyms are both homophones and homographs, and some are just one or the other.

Homonyms exemplify **lexical ambiguity**—that is, ambiguity at the level of the word.

TABLE 6.1   Homophones and Homographs

Homophones and homographs
   $band_1$: a group of musicians
   $band_2$: a thin, flat piece of material that is put around something else

   $spring_1$: the season following winter
   $spring_2$: a piece of coiled metal

Homophones but not homographs
   two: 2
   too: also

Homographs but not homophones
   $tear_1$: a drop of liquid from the eye
   $tear_2$: a hole in a piece of material

Language Matters Hypernyms and Related Relations

In addition to the relations discussed thus far, there are various less-known relations among words, such as the relationship between the word *dog* and the words for various types of dogs (*spaniel, collie, beagle*, etc.). The word for the general class (here, *dog*) is called the *hypernym*, whereas the words for the members of that class are its *hyponyms*. Of course, *dog* also has a hypernym—the word *animal*.

Meronyms designate the parts of a whole, and a *holonym* is the whole to which parts belong. Meronyms for dog include *head, nose, paws, tail*, and so on. Conversely, *dog* is the holonym for those parts.

You can find a large online database of these relations at Princeton University's *WordNet: A Lexical Database for English* (wordnet.princeton.edu).

6.2.2 Polysemy

Polysemy, a pervasive phenomenon of natural language, holds when a word has two or more related meanings, as shown in (14). (In the case of homonymy, in contrast, the meanings are unrelated to each other.)

(14) *a.* cap
  meaning 1: a piece of clothing worn on the head
  meaning 2: a cover placed on the top of a bottle
b. mole
  meaning 1: a small animal that lives and hides underground
  meaning 2: a spy
c. book
  meaning 1: a bound collection of pages
  meaning 2: the act of reserving a seat for an event ← why? how are they related?

Language Matters The Pinnacle of Polysemy

The most ambiguous word in English may well be the word *set*. In an entry that extends over nineteen pages, the *Oxford English Dictionary* lists more than 150 meanings and uses. Here are some examples:
  Set the box on the floor.
  Set the wood on the fire.
  Set the table.
  Let's play a *set* of tennis.
  a *set* of golf clubs
  a *set* time

Both homonymy and polysemy are different from **vagueness** and context-dependence. Intuitively, a word is vague if the corresponding concept has fuzzy boundaries. Scalar adjectives are examples of vague terms. Suppose you see a time-lapse video of a plant growing: initially, it is clearly small, and after a certain amount of time, it is clearly big, but when did it exactly transition from small to not-small? That is a very hard question to answer, and there are numerous ways to fix the boundary between small and not-small.

To fix the relevant boundary, we often require contextual information. This results in scalar adjectives having different interpretations in different contexts. For example, in *Mercury is small*, the adjective is normally interpreted relative to the average size of a planet, whereas in *The Fiat 500 is small*, it is normally interpreted relative to the average size of a car. Does it follow that there are at least two distinct meanings for the adjective *small*, depending on whether we are talking about planets or cars? This does not seem right because once the information about the class of object in question is understood, we see that the adjective *small* actually means the same thing in both sentences—below some standard of size for the class of object in question. We will discuss the notion of context-dependence in more detail in section 6.4.2.

6.2.3 Synonymy and antonymy

Two words are **synonyms** if they have the same (or almost the same) meaning, as in the case of *happy* and *content,* or *smart* and *intelligent*. Most cases of synonymy involve a partial overlap in their range of possible meanings. For instance, *positive* and *optimistic* are synonyms when we are discussing attitudes about the future, but not when *positive* is used to mean 'certain' (as in *I'm positive that I saw her*).

Two words are **antonyms** if they have opposite meanings. Antonymy corresponds to the logical relation of incompatibility. Incompatible scalar adjectives like *good/bad* or *tall/short* are antonyms, and so are complementary words such as *dead/alive*. Examples of non-adjectival antonyms are *above/below, buy/sell, give/take, student/teacher*.

6.3 Verb phrases and meaning

In this section, we look at verb phrases with a focus on two aspects of their interpretations—thematic roles and aspectual properties.

Language Matters Meaning and the Body

The meanings of many words are tightly integrated with physical experience. Indeed, studies have shown that exposure to verbs denoting various physical actions triggers involuntary activation of the part of the brain responsible for controlling those actions. Seeing the word *chew* leads to activation of the part of the brain that controls movement of the mouth, seeing *kick* stimulates the part of the brain associated with leg movements, and so on.

Sources: F. Pulvermüller, M. Härle, and F. Hummel, "Walking or Talking? Behavioral and Neurophysiological Correlates of Action Verb Processing," *Brain and Language* 78 (2001): 143–68; O. Hauk, I. Johnsrude, and F. Pulvermüller, "Somatotopic Representation of Action Words in Human Motor and Premotor Cortex," *Neuron* 41, 2 (2004): 301–7.

6.3.1 Thematic roles

Intuitively, when we know the meaning of the sentence *Celeste kicked the ball,* we know that it is about an event involving two 'participants'—Celeste and the ball. Moreover, we know that these two participants stand in different relations with respect to the kicking: Celeste is the **agent**—that is, the participant doing the kicking—and the ball is the **patient**—that is, the participant undergoing and being affected by Celeste's action. These relations are described with the help of a set of semantically defined labels called **thematic roles**. The NP to which a thematic role is assigned is called an **argument**.

TABLE 6.2 Some thematic roles	
Thematic role	**Definition**
Agent	The entity that intentionally performs an action
Patient (also often called '**theme**')	The entity that is affected by an action
Experiencer	The entity that experiences a psychological state
Stimulus	The trigger of a psychological state
Benefactive	The entity that benefits from an action
Goal	The entity toward which an action is directed
Source	The entity from which something is moved by performing an action *location*

The following sentences illustrate the thematic roles listed in table 6.2.

(15) *a.* Everyone dove (into the water).
          agent
      b. Salome bought the ball.
          agent   patient
      c. Aviva devoured the sandwich.
          agent   patient
      d. Ann sent the letter to Jonas.
          agent   patient   goal
      e. Fred realized the answer.
          experiencer   stimulus
      f. LiMing borrowed "The Lord of the Rings" from the library.
          agent   patient   source

We can represent the information about the thematic roles associated with particular verbs within angled brackets, creating what is often called a **thematic grid**, as illustrated in (16).

(16) *Verb*   *Thematic roles*
       dive   <agent>
       kick   <agent, patient>
       devour   <agent, patient>
       sent   <agent, theme, goal>
       realize   <experiencer, theme>
       borrow   <agent, patient, source>

If the requirements of the thematic grid are not satisfied, the resulting sentence is ungrammatical.[2]

(17) *a.* *Frida bought.
      b. *Ivor devoured.

(18) *a.* *The visitors dove their friends.
      b. *Meena realized the truth to Vijay.

All of the sentences in (17) and (18) have the wrong number of arguments. The sentences in (17) are ungrammatical because they do not have enough arguments—there is no NP to which the patient role can be assigned. In contrast, the sentences in (18) are ungrammatical because they have too many arguments; there is no thematic role for *their friends* in (18a) or for *Vijay* in (18b). A sentence is grammatical only if each thematic role is assigned to an argument, and each argument receives a thematic role. This generalization is often called the **Theta Criterion**.

> **(19)** *The Theta Criterion*
>   *a.* Each thematic role is assigned to exactly one argument.
>   *b.* Each argument is assigned exactly one thematic role.

6.3.2 Aspectual properties of predicates

Now that we have discussed verbs, we can introduce a widely used way of classifying verb phrases—or **predicates**—according to their **aspectual properties**: that is, the properties of the event or situation they denote.[3] For example, consider the contrast between the predicates *read a book* and *eat ice cream*. The former seems to describe an event that can proceed until its 'natural' end point is reached—that is, until the whole book is read. In contrast, the second predicate does not seem to have a stated end point.

The system of classification of predicates is built on three basic contrasts:

■ An event is **telic** if it has a natural end point and **atelic** otherwise.

■ An event is **durative** if it develops over (at least some) time, and is otherwise **instantaneous**.

■ An event is **static** if it is durative and uniform (with no natural beginning and end). An event that is not static is said to be **dynamic**.

These contrasts allow us to define four classes of verb phrases:

(20) Activities: durative, atelic, and dynamic
  a. RUN: Julian ran.
  b. WALK: Mathilda walked.
  c. SWIM: Greta swam.
  d. DRIVE A CAR: Bill drove a car.

(21) Accomplishments: durative, telic, and dynamic
  a. DRAW A PICTURE: Julian drew a picture.
  b. RUN A MILE: Mathilda ran a mile.
  c. GROW UP: Greta grew up.
  d. DRIVE TO SCHOOL: Bill drove to school.

(22) Achievements: instantaneous, telic, and dynamic
  a. REACH THE TOP: Julian reached the top.
  b. FIND THE CURE: Mathilda found the cure.   *almost either he did or not*
  c. WIN THE RACE: Greta won the race.
  d. DIE: Bill died.

(23) States: durative, static
  a. BE HAPPY: Julian is happy.
  b. WANT A VACATION: Mathilda wants a vacation.
  c. KNOW THE ANSWER: Greta knows the answer.
  d. BE SICK: Bill is sick.

In order to distinguish among the four verb classes, linguists employ various diagnostic tests. We outline a number of tests below and explain how they are used, beginning with the ones that help identify stative predicates.

States versus events

TABLE 6.3 Diagnostic tests to identify stative predicates

Diagnostic test	Applied to stative predicate
1 Statives are incompatible with the progressive form.	#Bill is being sick.
2 Statives do not have a habitual interpretation when in the present tense.	Julian knows the answer. (not habitual)
3 Statives are not acceptable with verbs like *force* and *persuade*.	#Greta persuaded Bill to know the answer.
4 Statives are not acceptable in imperative clauses.	#Know the answer!
5 Statives are not acceptable in the sentence pattern 'What X did was __'.	#What John did was know the answer.

To apply the first diagnostic tool, try changing the verb in a particular VP to the progressive form. Of the four predicate types, only **stative predicates** (that is, predicates that describe a state) are incompatible with the progressive form (*be V-ing*) in English.

> **(24)** *a.* Julian is running. (activity)
> *b.* Mathilda is drawing a picture. (accomplishment)
> *c.* Greta is winning the race. (achievement)
> *d.* #Bill is being sick. (state)

As illustrated in in (24d), the progressive aspect is incompatible with the property of being static, which only stative predicates have.

The second diagnostic has to do with habitual action. When an activity or an accomplishment predicate occurs in the present tense in English, as in (25a) and (b), the sentence acquires a **habitual interpretation**: that is, the sentence is about some event that happens regularly. Sentence (25c) shows that no such interpretation arises with a state.

> **(25)** *a.* Julian runs. (activity)
> (means that Julian habitually runs)
> *b.* Julian drives to school (accomplishment)
> (means that Julian habitually drives to school)
> *c.* Julian knows the answer. (state)
> (does not mean that Julian habitually knows the answer)

The third diagnostic is based on the fact that only non-statives, such as (26a–c), can occur with verbs like *persuade* and *force*. Stative predicates are incompatible with such verbs, as (26d) illustrates.

(26) *a.* Mathilda persuaded Julian to drive. (activity)
      b. Mathilda persuaded Greta to solve the problem. (accomplishment)
      c. Mathilda persuaded Bill to reach the top. (achievement)
      d. #Greta persuaded Bill to know the answer. (state)

The incompatibility of stative predicates with verbs like *persuade* has to do with the lack of agentivity in states. Although you may have done something to find out the answer, *knowing the answer* is not something you do: it is a state that you are in *after* having done something. If someone persuades you to do something, however, you intentionally proceed to do it.

To apply the fourth diagnostic, try changing a stative predicate to an imperative, as in (27d). Note that only non-stative predicates, such as (27a–c), occur in imperatives.

(27) *a.* Run! (activity)
      b. Solve the problem! (accomplishment)
      c. Find the key! (achievement)
      d. #Know the answer! (state)

Language Matters Being Good: A State or an Activity?

Stative predicates like *be good* or *be stubborn* sometimes appear to be compatible with the progressive form (e.g., *Amanda is being good* or *Shivan is being stubborn*) and with the imperative form (*Be good!* or *Don't be stubborn!*). Notice, though, that in these examples, the predicate is interpreted as 'acting in a good way/behaving well' or 'acting in a stubborn way/behaving stubbornly'. Thus, *Mary is being good* and *Be good!* are interpreted as *Mary is behaving well* and *Behave well!* respectively. The predicate *be good* has been reinterpreted as an activity in these cases, and is therefore compatible with the progressive and imperative forms.

Fifth, only non-statives, such as (28a–c), can occur in sentences of the form *What x did was _____* .

(28) *a.* What Matsuko did was run. (activity)
      b. What Liam did was solve the problem. (accomplishment)
      c. What Cherie did was find the key. (achievement)
      d. #What John did was know the answer. (state)

Like the third diagnostic, the fourth and fifth diagnostic tools are again related to agentivity. In (27d), you can't be ordered to know the answer: you either know it or you don't. And the sentence in (28d) doesn't work because knowing the answer is not something you *do*.

Distinguishing among events: activities versus accomplishments

As noted above, activities are durative, dynamic, and atelic, whereas accomplishments are durative, dynamic, and telic. Thus, the key factor that distinguishes activities from accomplishments is that only the latter are telic. Table 6.4 lists two diagnostic tools that can be used to test for telicity in order to determine if a VP is an activity predicate or an achievement predicate.

TABLE 6.4 Diagnostic tests to distinguish between activities and achievements	
Diagnostic test	**Applied to activity and achievement predicates**
1 Activities take *for*-adverbials. Accomplishments take *in*-adverbials.	Omar built a house in a month/#for a month. Roberta swam for an hour/#in an hour.
2 Activities have the subinterval property. Accomplishment do not.	Roberta swam for an hour. *(She was swimming at most/all points in the hour.)* Omar built a house in a month. *(He was not building at most/all points in the month.)*

The first test concerns the compatibility of these predicates with *in*-adverbials and *for*-adverbials. Whereas accomplishments take the former kind of adverbials, activities take the latter.

(29) *Accomplishments* (acceptable with *in*-adverbials but not with *for*-adverbials):
   a. Omar built a house in a month/#for a month.
   b. Omar drove to the office in an hour/#for an hour.

   Activities (acceptable with *for*-adverbials but not with *in*-adverbials):
   c. Roberta swam for an hour/#in an hour.
   d. Roberta ate potato chips for an hour/#in an hour.

Second, only activities have the so-called **subinterval property**. To understand this property, consider the following example with the activity verb *swim*.

(30) Roberta swam for an hour. (activity)

If it is true that Roberta swam for an hour, then it is true that Roberta swam at most points during the one-hour interval. Thus, *swim* has the subinterval property because if it is true that Roberta swam for an hour, then it is true that Roberta swam at most (if not all) points throughout that period.

Now compare *swim* with the predicate *build a house*.

(31) Omar built a house in one month. (accomplishment)

Suppose that this sentence is true and ask yourself if it is also true that at most points during that month-long interval Omar built a house. Our intuition is that it is not true. The sentence means that Omar built only one house, which was completed only at the end of the month-long interval.

The contrast between (30) and (31) is related to the fact that activities and accomplishments allow different inference patterns. If the sentence *Roberta is now swimming* (an activity) is true, we can infer that Roberta has swum (for a few moments at least). But if the sentence *Omar is now building a house* (an accomplishment) is true, we can infer that he has not (yet) built it.

Distinguishing among events: achievements versus accomplishments

To distinguish between achievements and accomplishments, we can use the '*almost* test.' The adverb *almost* gives rise to an ambiguity with accomplishments but not with achievements.

(32) *a.* Nguyen almost drove to school. (accomplishment)
     b. Nguyen almost died. (achievement)

Sentence (32a) is ambiguous. In one interpretation, Nguyen almost started driving to school. This would be true if he planned to drive to school but then at the last minute changed his mind and decided to take the bus. In the other interpretation, Nguyen drove toward the school but never reached it. This would be true in a situation where he drove for a while toward the school, but then realized he had forgotten his backpack and had to turn around and go back home, never reaching his intended destination. The following continuations disambiguate the sentence.

(33) *a.* Nguyen almost drove to school but in the end decided that, given the approaching storm, it was safer to take the bus.
     b. Nguyen had almost driven to school when he realized he had left his backpack at home. He turned around and went back home.

There is no such ambiguity in *Nguyen almost died*. This sentence can only mean that Nguyen was on the verge of death.

Before concluding this section, a final point must be stressed: it is whole verb phrases that we classify as states, activities, accomplishments, or achievements—not just the verb but the entire predicate. Even minimal changes to any part of the predicate can affect its aspectual properties. Consider the examples in (34).

(34) *a.* Miriam ate an apple.
     b. Miriam ate apples.

If you run the tests described above, you will see that while the verb phrase *ate an apple* patterns like an accomplishment, the verb phrase *ate apples* patterns like an activity.

6.4 Meaning and context

Some components of an utterance's meaning depend on the particular context in which the utterance is produced—who is participating in the conversation, when and where the conversation is taking place, what the goal of the conversation is. While engaged in conversations, speakers routinely use contextual information to enrich the literal meaning of the sentences they utter. To illustrate how this works, we will discuss pronouns, demonstratives, indexical pronouns and adverbs, scalar (gradable) adjectives, presuppositions, and implicatures.

6.4.1 Pronouns

Pronouns (words like *he*, *she*, *him* and *her*) can be interpreted in different ways. Under some circumstances a pronoun can be interpreted by associating it with the referent of another NP (called its **antecedent**), which often appears in the same sentence, as in *The child lost her toy*. However, as the following sentences illustrate, pronouns do not require this type of antecedent.

(35) *a.* He tried to kick the football.
     b. Lucy tricked him.

The intended referents of the pronouns *he* and *him* in (35) are either mentioned somewhere in the preceding discourse or are salient in the general conversational context. The exchange in (36) illustrates the first possibility.

(36) A: Charlie should not trust Lucy.

B: Why?

A: Because she will trick him.

Here, we understand *she* as referring to Lucy and *him* as referring to Charlie. This is because we normally understand a sentence to be relevant to previous sentences in the same discourse and to be about the same topic of conversation. This fact, together with the fact that *Charlie* and *Lucy* match the gender and number features on the pronouns *he* and *she*, respectively, makes them suitable antecedents for those pronouns.

Table 6.5 lists some of the different types of pronoun in English.

TABLE 6.5 Types of pronoun			
Pronoun		**Gender**	**Character**
3rd person	singular: *he, she, it* plural: *they*	marked only in the singular	*she*: the referent is a female individual distinct from speaker and addressee. An appropriate character for the other third person pronouns can be constructed in a similar way
1st, 2nd person	singular: *I, you* plural: *we, you*	not marked	*I*: the speaker *you*: the addressee(s) *we*: a group of people including the speaker
demonstratives	singular: *this, that* plural: *these, those*	not marked	*this*: the referent is in the proximity of the speaker *that*: the referent is distant from the speaker

In English, third person pronouns are marked for gender and number. First and second person pronouns are marked for number but not for gender. Moreover, all these pronouns (first, second, and third person) have an extra layer of meaning called **character** that functions as an 'instruction' about how to find the referent of the pronoun.

Pronouns that have a character are often called **indexical**. For example, as shown in table 6.5, the character of the indexical pronoun *I* is 'the author of the utterance' (the speaker); the character of *you* is 'the person(s) the author of the utterance is addressing' (the addressee or the hearer); the character of *she* is 'the person in the context of utterance who is female and distinct from the speaker and the addressee.'

To illustrate the importance of character to a sentence's meaning, consider a situation in which Peppermint Patty and Linus are having the conversation shown in (37).

(37) Peppermint Patty: I like Charlie Brown.

Linus: I like Charlie Brown too.

What is the meaning of these two utterances? The indexical pronoun *I* occurs in both, but refers to a different individual in each. It refers to Peppermint Patty when she speaks and to Linus when he speaks. This is because the indexical *I* does not have a fixed referent. However, the character of *I* ensures that it is correctly interpreted as the speaker in both utterances.

In addition to indexical pronouns, languages have **indexical adverbs** such as *now, today, here,* and *there,* whose interpretation depends on the time and place they are uttered (see table 6.6).

TABLE 6.6 Indexical adverbs	
Indexical adverbs	**character**
now	the time of the utterance
today	the day of the utterance
here	the location where the utterance is made
there	a place distant from the location where the utterance is made

6.4.2 Context-dependent adjectives

Another area where we see the contribution of contextual information is in the interpretation of scalar adjectives. Consider the following examples.

(38) *a.* Max is tall.
      b. The CN Tower is tall.

Both statements could be true even though Max and the CN Tower are very different in height. Adjectives of this type are **context-dependent** in that their interpretation involves a **contextual standard of comparison**. Thus, when the speaker is talking about Max, the contextual standard of comparison is the height of other people, and *tall* is interpreted as follows. When we are talking about buildings, the contextual standard of comparison will be the height of the other buildings, and that information will be reflected in the interpretation of the sentence.

To sum up, scalar adjectives like *tall, new, young, old, big, small, large,* and so on are interpreted relative to the context of utterance. More precisely, they are interpreted relative to a standard of comparison that has been made salient in the context of the utterance. This allows us to capture the multiplicity of interpretations that arises with this kind of adjective without postulating the existence of multiple meanings for each adjective.

6.4.3 Presuppositions

In section 6.1.1, we introduced and defined the notion of entailment: given two sentences *p* and *q*, *p* logically entails *q* if the truth of *p* requires the truth of *q*. In the following example, sentence (39a) entails (39b).

(39) *a.* Snoopy chased the ball in the park.
      b. Snoopy chased the ball.

We can show this entailment by using the contradiction test we introduced earlier. When we conjoin (39a) with the negation of (39b), we obtain a contradiction, as shown in (40).

(40) #Snoopy chased the ball in the park but Snoopy did not chase the ball.

But now notice what happens to the entailment relation when (39a) is negated, as shown in (41)?

(41) Snoopy did not chase the ball in the park.

Notice that the entailment relation no longer exists. That is, it does not follow from the truth of (41) that Snoopy chased the ball. We can show that this intuition is correct by using the contradiction test: conjoining (41) with the negation of (39b) does not give a contradictory result.

(42) Snoopy did not chase the ball in the park; (in fact) Snoopy did not chase the ball (at all).

The conclusion is that the entailments of a sentence *p* are not entailments of the negation of *p*.

Sometimes, however, the entailment of a sentence *p* survives even when *p* is negated. In such cases, the entailment is called a **presupposition**. Consider the following example.

(43) *a.* Corinne regrets firing Yusuf.
     b. Corinne fired Yusuf.

Sentence (43a) entails (43b), as shown by the fact that it is contradictory to say *Corinne regrets firing Yusuf but she didn't fire Yusuf.* However, unlike the case of Snoopy chasing the ball above, the negated sentence *Corinne does not regret firing Yusuf* also entails *Corinne fired Yusuf.* When we try the contradiction test, the resulting sentence sounds contradictory too.

(44) #Corinne doesn't regret firing Yusuf but she didn't fire Yusuf.

In this case, we have a presupposition: *Corinne fired Yusuf.* The conclusion, then, is that given two sentences *p* and *q*, *p* presupposes *q* just in case both *p* and *not p* entail *q*. Another example illustrates the same point. Suppose A asks the question *Has John quit smoking?* Whether B answers *Yes, John has quit smoking* or *No, John has not quit smoking*, the presupposition is *John is a smoker.*

When A asks B whether Corinne regrets firing Yusuf, the information A is seeking is whether Corinne feels regret or not. The use of *regret* indicates that A takes for granted that both A and B believe that Corinne fired Yusuf. In other words, the use of *regret* signals that the speaker takes it to be part of the participants' **common ground** that Corinne fired Yusuf, where the common ground is all the information that the participants in the conversation (knowingly) share.

Presuppositions, then, are part of the common ground shared by the participants. They are **old information**. Thus, we can divide the content of the sentence *Corinne regrets firing Yusuf* into two parts. The first part is what is new—that is, the novel contribution of the utterance itself. In our example, the novel contribution is that Corinne feels regret. The second part is the old information, which is already part of the common ground: that Corinne fired Yusuf. The novel part is what the sentence asserts; the old part is what the sentence presupposes.

A presupposition is triggered by a lexical item in the sentence. For example, the presupposition that Corinne fired Yusuf in the sentence *Corinne regrets firing Yusuf* is triggered by the verb *regret.* And the presupposition that John was a smoker in *John quit smoking* is triggered by the verb *quit.* In the next section, we will look at different kinds of triggers and the presuppositions they bring about.

Definite articles and possessives

Suppose that Finbarr and Bree are standing in the same corner of a classroom. In the opposite corner, there are ten chairs. Bree turns to Finbarr and, without pointing, says "Can you please bring the chair here?" It is very likely that this question would confuse Finbarr and that he would feel unable to meet Bree's request. His response would most likely be "Which chair?"—a request for further clarification. Why would he feel this way?

The intuition we have is that Bree's use of the definite article *the* in her question, along with the singular *chair*, presupposes that there is a unique chair in the room and that the sentence is odd because this presupposition is not met in the context of the utterance. Let us call this the **uniqueness presupposition**—the presupposition that an entity to which a speaker refers is unique.

Now consider the following question-and-answer sequence.

(45) A: Is the king of France bald?
      B_1: Yes, the king of France is bald.
      B_2: No, the king of France isn't bald.

Both the positive answer (*The king of France is bald*) and the negative answer (*The king of France isn't bald*) are odd because they both presuppose that there is a king of France, even though there isn't. Here the definite article triggers what we call the **existence presupposition**—the presupposition that an entity to which a speaker refers exists.

Possessive phrases trigger a similar presupposition, as in the following example in which *his* refers to Charlie.

(46) $Charlie_1$ went ice skating with his_1 friends.

If you try the question test that we used above (*Did Charlie go ice skating with his friends?*), you can see that whether you answer positively (*Yes, Charlie went ice skating with his friends*) or negatively (*No, Charlie did not go ice skating with his friends*), you are still committed to the proposition that Charlie has friends. This is because possessive phrases trigger an existence presupposition.

Factive predicates

Factive predicates are verbs or adjectives that take a sentential complement that is presupposed to be true. (For the purposes of our discussion, a sentential complement is simply a clause that functions as direct object.) Factive predicates include *know, discover, find out, regret, be glad*, and *be sorry*. In (47), the complement is designated by square brackets.

(47) *a.* Lucy knows [that Charlie will try to kick the football].
      b. Linus discovered [that the Great Pumpkin does not exist].
      c. Snoopy is glad [that Woodstock is his best friend].

The sentence in (47a), with the main verb *know*, presupposes that it is true that Charlie will try to kick the football. No such presupposition is associated with the verb *believe*, as shown by the difference in the results of the contradiction test.

(48) *a.* Lucy believes that Charlie will try to kick the football but she is wrong about it.
      b. #Lucy knows that Charlie will try to kick the football but she is wrong about it.

A similar test can be done with (47b) and (c) to show that the verb *discover* and the predicate *be glad* require that their complement be true.

(49) *a.* #Linus discovered that the Great Pumpkin does not exist but the Great Pumpkin does exist.
      b. #Snoopy is glad that Woodstock is his best friend but Woodstock is not his best friend.

Aspectual verbs

So-called **aspectual verbs** like *continue, stop*, and *quit*, which help indicate that an action is ongoing or complete, also trigger presuppositions. This is why all the examples in (50) and

(51) entail that Linus is or was waiting for the Great Pumpkin, regardless of whether the aspectual verb is negative.

> **(50)** *a.* Linus continued to wait for the Great Pumpkin.
> *b.* Linus didn't continue to wait for the Great Pumpkin.

> **(51)** *a.* Linus quit waiting for the Great Pumpkin.
> *b.* Linus didn't quit waiting for the Great Pumpkin.

To sum up, different kinds of triggers give rise to various types of presuppositions. The definite article creates both an existence presupposition and a uniqueness presupposition, as do possessive phrases. Factive predicates give rise to the presupposition that their complements are true, while aspectual verbs give rise to presuppositions about the temporal properties of the event described by the predicate.

6.4.4 Conversational implicatures

Many utterances convey a layer of meaning that is neither entailed nor presupposed by the utterance itself. Consider the following examples.

> **(52)** A: Do you want to come to the movies tonight?
> B: I have a test tomorrow.

> **(53)** A: What would you like for your graduation?
> B: Alice Munro's new collection of short stories just came out.

The key observation has to do with how we interpret B in these two dialogues. In (52), B asserts that she has a test tomorrow, but her intention is to communicate that she will not go to the movies tonight. Similarly, in (53), B's utterance asserts that a certain book just came out, but it also conveys a desire to receive that book for her graduation. How does this extra meaning arise, and how does it relate to what the speaker said?

In conversations, we often convey more than we say. This is because speakers follow an implicit principle called the **Cooperative Principle**.

> **(54)** *The Cooperative Principle*
> Make your contribution to the conversation as required by the goal of the conversation.

The Cooperative Principle can be divided into the four maxims described in table 6.7.

TABLE 6.7 The four maxims associated with the Cooperative Principle	
Cooperative Principle	
Maxim of Relevance	Be relevant to the goal of the conversation.
Maxim of Quantity	Say as much as is required by the goal of the conversation. Do not say too much and do not say too little.
Maxim of Quality	Do not say what you think is false and do not say what you lack evidence for.
Maxim of Manner	Make your contribution as clear as possible. Avoid obscurity and ambiguity, be brief, and be orderly.

Because every conversational participant is assumed to follow the Cooperative Principle (and therefore the four maxims), hearers interpret a speaker's flouting of one of the maxims as an intentional conversational move designed to invite a certain inference. An inference derived in this way is called a **conversational implicature**.

In (52) above, the literal content of B's assertion violates the maxim of relevance since A's and B's utterances appear to be about different topics. However, A assumes that B is following the maxims and will therefore reason as follows:

> *In order to make B's assertion relevant to my question, I must assume that having a test tomorrow is relevant to the question I asked. Since normally when you have a test, you need to prepare for it, B intends me to understand that she will need to prepare for the test tonight and therefore will not be able to go to the movies.*

This information—that B will not go to the movies because she needs to prepare for the test—is the conversational implicature that A must compute in order to make B's contribution relevant to the conversation.

A similar reasoning explains what is going on in (53): what A understands is that B would like Alice Munro's new collection of short stories for her graduation gift. In order to reconcile B's utterance with the maxim of relevance, A will reason as follows:

> *B's utterance is relevant to the conversation (i.e., it answers my question) only if I assume that B would like to receive Munro's new collection for her graduation gift.*

Thus, in the context of the conversation in (53), B's utterance will have the conversational implicature that B would like to receive Munro's new collection of short stories as her graduation gift.

The following dialogue illustrates an apparent violation of the maxim of manner. Suppose Kim walks into Darren's house and smells baking. She says, "It smells good in here. Have you baked a cake?" and Darren responds, "Well, I've mixed flour, eggs, sugar, and milk together and shoved the whole thing into the oven." What Darren clearly intends to communicate to Kim is that his attempt at baking might not have been successful.

How do we derive this implicature? Instead of simply answering, "Yes, I have," Darren chose to refer to his baking in a rather long and unusual way, appearing to flout the maxim of manner. Kim must therefore reason that the only way to reconcile this behaviour with the assumption that all participants obey the Cooperative Principle is to assume that Darren believes that his activity does not amount to proper baking.

Unlike entailments and presuppositions, conversational implicatures can be suspended or cancelled, as shown by B's response in (55).

(55) A: What would you like for your graduation?
      B: Alice Munro's new collection of short stories just came out, but that is not what I want for my graduation.

Here, B's addition of the phrase *but that is not what I want for my graduation* stops the hearer from drawing the implicature that B wants Munro's new collection for her graduation gift. Suspending this conversational implicature does not cause a contradiction, unlike what would happen if we were trying to cancel an entailment or a presupposition (see sections 6.1.1 and 6.4.3, respectively).

6.5 The role of structure in interpretation

Syntactic structure plays a major role in the interpretation of sentences. In this section, we consider several examples of how structure can affect meaning.

6.5.1 Structural ambiguity

Many sentences are ambiguous not because of the meaning of their individual words, but because the words can be grouped together in more than one way. This type of ambiguity is called **structural ambiguity**. Take the sentence *The company wants to hire young engineers and mathematicians*. With a little thought, you'll realize that the sentence is ambiguous depending on how the phrase *young engineers and mathematicians* is interpreted: one interpretation is that both engineers and mathematicians are young and another is that just the engineers are young. We can represent this with the simplified tree structures in figure 6.5.

FIGURE 6.5
Capturing structural
ambiguity

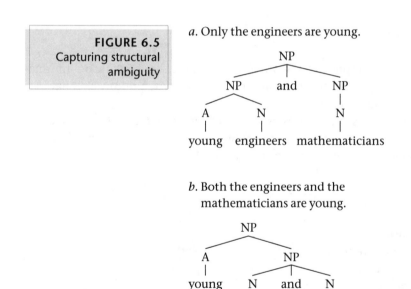

a. Only the engineers are young.

b. Both the engineers and the
mathematicians are young.

A second example of structural ambiguity is found in cases like the following, with the structure of the two interpretations shown in (56a) and (b), and represented in Figure 6.6.

(56) Hadley caught the frog with the hat.
   a. Hadley [caught [the frog with the hat]]
   b. Hadley [caught [the frog] with the hat]

In (a), the frog was carrying or wearing a hat; in (b), Hadley caught the frog by using a hat.

a. The frog had the hat.

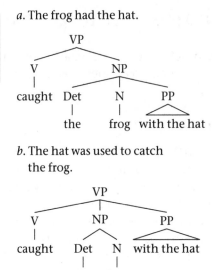

b. The hat was used to catch
the frog.

6.5.2 Pronouns

As we saw in section 6.4.1, the interpretation of pronouns often requires drawing on information from the context in which they occur. However, syntactic structure can also have an important role to play in pronoun interpretation.

We can divide English pronouns into two classes based on their morphological composition—**plain pronouns** like *I, you, she, he*, and **reflexive pronouns** like *myself, yourself, herself, himself*. They are organized according to their different features in table 6.8.

TABLE 6.8 English pronouns				
ENGLISH PRONOUNS	**Plain (non-reflexive) pronouns**		**Reflexive pronouns**	
	singular	*plural*	*Singular*	*plural*
1st person	I, me	we, us	myself	ourselves
2nd person	you	you	yourself	yourselves
3rd person	she, her	they, them	herself	themselves
	he, him		himself	
	it		itself	

The most salient characteristic of pronouns is that they do not have a meaning all by themselves. We know that the referent of *she* must be a single female individual different from the speaker and the hearer. However, this is as much as we can get from the pronoun itself, which is not enough to figure out who *she* refers to. In many cases, the interpretation of a pronoun depends on another linguistic expression—its antecedent.

Consider the following illustration.

(57) Sonia believes that the CEO will hire her.

This sentence can be interpreted as asserting that Sonia believes that the CEO will hire Sonia. In this case, we say that *Sonia* is the antecedent for the pronoun *her* and that the two are **co-referential** since they refer to the same person. The sentence could also be interpreted as asserting that Sonia believes that the CEO will hire some other female individual. In this case, the listener must resort to non-linguistic information in order to determine who the pronoun refers to since there is no antecedent in the sentence.

A phrase can be the linguistic antecedent of a pronoun only if certain structural constraints are satisfied. Consider the following sentences. (In these and other examples, we use subscripts, called 'indices', to indicate that a particular pronoun takes a particular NP as its antecedent.)

(58) *a.* John$_1$ will hire him$_{2/*1}$.
   b. Bill$_1$ believes [that John$_2$ will hire him$_{1/*2}$].

As a first approximation, these sentences suggest that non-reflexive pronouns need to have their antecedent outside their clause. This is why *him* can refer to Bill but not to John in the sentences above. (An asterisk next to an index shows that an NP and a co-indexed pronoun cannot be co-referential.)

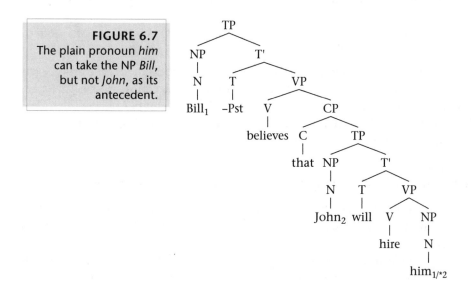

FIGURE 6.7
The plain pronoun *him* can take the NP *Bill*, but not *John*, as its antecedent.

The situation is reversed for reflexive pronouns. As the next examples show, a reflexive pronoun must have a linguistic antecedent within its clause: *himself* can refer to John but not to Bill.

(59) *a.* John$_1$ will hire himself$_1$.
   b. Bill$_1$ believes [that John$_2$ will hire himself$_{2/*1}$].

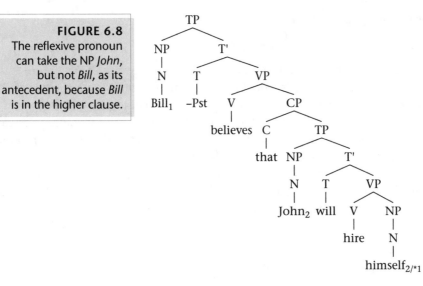

At this point, we have the following two simple generalizations.

(60) *a.* A reflexive pronoun must have an antecedent in the same clause.
　　b. A plain pronoun cannot have an antecedent in the same clause.

These generalizations are not quite right, however, as you can see by considering the following sentence.

(61) [[*The girl's*]$_1$ *father*]$_2$ *congratulated her1/herself$_{2/*1}$.*

Here, the plain pronoun *her* can refer to the girl, but the reflexive pronoun *herself* cannot, even though the pronoun and the potential antecedent are in the same clause. This is the exact opposite of what our previous examples appeared to show. How can this be?

In order to explain these facts, we need to introduce an important linguistic notion: the structural concept of **c-command**.

(62) *C-command*
　　NP$_i$ c-commands NP$_j$ if and only if the first category above NP$_i$ contains NP$_j$.

In figures 6.7 and 6.8, you'll see that the antecedent that we were considering (*John*) c-commands the pronoun in the same clause: the first category above the NP *John* (TP) also contains the pronoun *him* or *himself*.

Let's revise our generalizations to take this into account. We'll also give the new generalizations their official names. Taken together, the two principles make up what is sometimes called **Binding Theory**.

(63) *a. Principle A*
　　Reflexive pronouns must have a c-commanding antecedent in the same clause.
　　b. Principle B
　　Plain pronouns cannot have a c-commanding antecedent in the same clause.

So far, so good. But what about the problematic example in (61), with the tree structure depicted in figure 6.9?

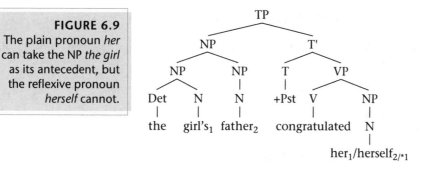

FIGURE 6.9
The plain pronoun *her* can take the NP *the girl* as its antecedent, but the reflexive pronoun *herself* cannot.

Notice that the NP *the girl* does not c-command the pronoun in this structure, since the first category above it (the NP *the girl's father*) does not contain the pronoun. This means that *the girl* can serve as the antecedent for *her* without violating Principle B. But it cannot serve as the antecedent for the reflexive pronoun *herself*, which requires a c-commanding antecedent, according to Principle A. (The NP *the girl's father* does c-command the reflexive pronoun, of course, and could, in principle, be its antecedent were it not for the gender mismatch.) Things now work just as they should.

But there's one more problem to consider. In (64), the possessive pronoun *his* can take the c-commanding NP *Harry* as its antecedent, even though both are in the same clause (see figure 6.10).

(64) Harry$_1$ admires [his$_1$ teacher].

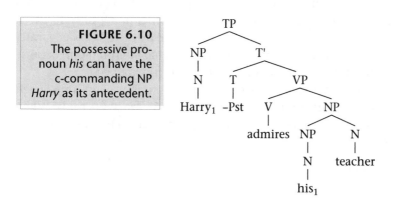

FIGURE 6.10
The possessive pronoun *his* can have the c-commanding NP *Harry* as its antecedent.

Why isn't this a violation of Principle B?

Possessive pronouns are special in being able to function as either a reflexive pronoun or a plain pronoun, depending on the context. In figure 6.10, *his* behaves like a reflexive pronoun in having a c-commanding antecedent in the same clause. In a sentence such as *I admire his teacher*, in contrast, it behaves like a plain pronoun in that it can have an antecedent outside the sentence.

6.5.3 **Quantificational noun phrases**

A quantificational noun phrase (QNP) has a **quantifier** such as *every, each, some, a, no, most,* or *one* in its determiner position.

(65) Every farmer is hard-working.

In patterns such as those in (66), the QNP c-commands a pronoun, leading to an intriguing interpretive phenomenon.

(66) [Every farmer]$_1$ worried about his$_1$ crop.

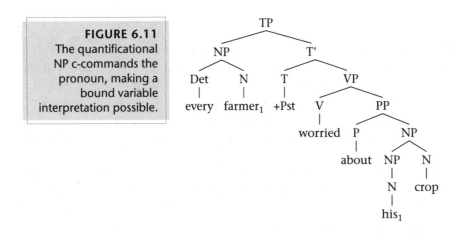

FIGURE 6.11
The quantificational NP c-commands the pronoun, making a bound variable interpretation possible.

The pronoun here can have two quite different interpretations. On one hand, it can refer to a specific individual not mentioned in the sentence: perhaps all the farmers were worried about Bao's crops because Bao was ill and unable to work. On the other hand, the referent of the pronoun can also co-vary with the individuals in the set denoted by the QNP: each farmer could be worried about his own crop. This is called the **bound variable** interpretation because the referent of the pronoun is variable, although not completely unconstrained.

An intriguing feature of the bound variable interpretation is that it is available only when the quantificational NP c-commands the pronoun, as happens in (66) (see figure 6.11). When there is no such relationship, as in (67), *his* can only refer to a specific person not mentioned in the sentence (see figure 6.12).

(67) His crop worried every farmer.

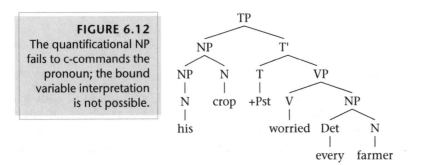

FIGURE 6.12
The quantificational NP fails to c-commands the pronoun; the bound variable interpretation is not possible.

6.5.4 Ambiguities with quantifiers (Advanced)

When two QNPs occur in the same sentence, interesting things happen, as exemplified in (68).

(68) Every child likes a beagle.

This sentence is **ambiguous**: it has two distinct interpretations. To see this, consider the following situation: unlike all other beagles, Snoopy (a beagle) is liked by every child. If I utter (68) in this situation, this sentence is true because there is one particular beagle—namely Snoopy—who is liked by every child. Now imagine a different situation: there is no agreement among the children and, while they each like a different beagle, there is no one beagle that they all like. Even though this latter situation is incompatible with the former (in which one beagle was liked by all the children), you could still utter the sentence in (68) truthfully.

We can disambiguate (68) by adding the continuations in (69).

(69) *a.* 'Single dog' reading: Every child likes a beagle, *namely Snoopy*.
    b. 'Multiple dog' reading: Every child likes a beagle, *but not the same one*.

The interpretation of (68) depends on the relation between the two QNPs in the sentence—*every child* and *a dog*. In the 'multiple dog' reading, which particular beagle is liked varies with each child. In the 'single dog' reading, one specific beagle is liked by all the children. This dependence relation between two QNPs is called **scope**. When the indefinite QNP has the multiple interpretation, it is said to have **narrow scope** with respect to the QNP on which it depends. When the indefinite QNP has the single interpretation, it is said to have **wide scope** with respect to the QNP on which it depends.

The sentence in (68) illustrates a case where a sentence is ambiguous because both types of scope relation can exist between two QNPs. Ambiguities can also arise when a QNP occurs with negation in the same sentence. For example, consider the ambiguous sentence in (70), which contains negation and the QNP *more than two questions*.

(70) Carlo didn't answer more than two questions.

According to one interpretation, it is not the case that Carlo answered more than two questions: in other words, Carlo answered two or fewer questions. We call this interpretation the narrow scope interpretation of *more than two questions* with respect to the negation. According to a second interpretation, there are more than two questions that Carlo did not answer: in other words, Carlo might have failed to answer three or more questions. We call this reading the wide scope interpretation of *more than two questions*.

Now, imagine a situation where Carlo took a test with ten questions on it and he managed to answer six of the ten questions. In this situation, (70) is only true if it is understood with the wide scope interpretation of *more than two questions*: there are more than two questions (four in our situation) that Carlo did not answer. In other words, (70) would not be true if understood with the narrow scope interpretation of *more than two questions* (according to which Carlo answered two or fewer questions) because in our hypothetical situation Carlo did answer six questions.

To sum up, sentences with QNPs can be ambiguous: that is, they can have more than one interpretation. This can happen in sentences where multiple QNPs occur or in sentences where a QNP occurs with negation. For more on quantifiers, see the recommended readings at the end of the chapter.

Summing up

Semantics is the study of meaning at the level of words, sentences, and larger chunks of speech. The meaning of a sentence depends on the component words and how they are put together, as well as on the context of the utterance.

A word can have a multiplicity of meanings and can be in a logical relation with other words. Four such relations are **subordination**, **equivalence**, **complementarity**, and **incompatibility**. Sentences, too, can occur in logical relations, including **entailment**, **equivalence**, **contradiction**, and **contrariety**.

The semantics of verb phrases, or **predicates**, includes the assignment of **thematic roles** such as **agent**, **patient**, **goal**, and **source** to the **arguments** of the verb. Predicates have **aspectual properties**: predicates are **telic** or **atelic**, **durative** or **instantaneous**, and **static** or **dynamic**. Depending on its properties, a predicate can be categorized as a **state**, an **achievement**, an **accomplishment**, or an **activity**.

When we engage in a conversation, we sometimes have to derive meaning with the help of **presuppositions**, the **Cooperative Principle**, and **conversational implicatures**. The context of an utterance is often critical to its meaning. The interpretation of **indexical pronouns**—including **plain pronouns** and **reflexive pronouns**—is heavily dependent on their linguistic or situational context. Structural constraints are also important, as illustrated by the importance of the notion of **c-command**, which helps explain the interpretation of pronouns (**Principles A** and **B**) and the computation of scope.

Notes

1. In this chapter, we explore various factors that contribute to a sentence's meaning. There are many different ways to do this, and this chapter differs somewhat in its approach from the semantics chapter in earlier editions of this book. For those who prefer a slightly less formal introduction to semantics, the earlier chapter is available on the Companion Website, Chapter 6.

2. There are seemingly intransitive uses of transitive verbs that are acceptable, for example in *John wanted to open the door, so <u>he kicked and kicked</u> until the door opened*; or *We need to do the dishes but we don't have much time. The most efficient way is if I wash and you dry*. Our intuition is that in these cases, the missing object (*the door* and *the dishes*) is implicit and retrievable from the context of utterance.

3. Recall that a verb phrase is the phrase formed by a verb with its complements, if any. See chapter 5 for more on phrases.

Recommended reading

Bach, Emmon. 1989. *Informal Lectures on Formal Semantics*. Albany, NY: SUNY Press.

Cruse, Alan. 2011. *Meaning in Language: An Introduction to Semantics and Pragmatics*. 3rd ed. Oxford, UK: Oxford University Press.

Elbourne, Paul. 2011. *Meaning: A Slim Guide to Semantics*. Oxford, UK: Oxford University Press.

Green, Georgia M. 1996. *Pragmatics and Natural Language Understanding*. 2nd ed. Mahwah, NJ: Lawrence Erlbaum.

Kearns, Kate. 2011. *Semantics*. 2nd ed. London, UK: Palgrave Macmillan.
Löbner, Sebastian. 2013. *Understanding Semantics*. 2nd ed. New York: Routledge.
Portner, Paul H. 2005. *What Is Meaning? Fundamentals of Formal Semantics*. Oxford, UK: Blackwell.

Exercises

1. What is the logical relation between the sentences in each of the following pairs? Is it logical entailment, equivalence, contradiction, contrariety, or none of the above?
   a) Mary read a book about Ancient Rome and she wrote a report about it.
      Mary read a book about Ancient Rome. *entailment (additional info makes it that and not equivalence)*
   b) Mary is my maternal aunt. *equivalence*
      Mary is my mother's sister.
   c) Bill knows more about logic than John. *contrariety*
      Bill knows less about logic than John.
   d) Sue read a newspaper yesterday. *none of the above (not logically related = knowledge acquisition?)*
      Sue will read a newspaper tomorrow.
   e) No student is taller than Mary. *equivalence or none of the above*
      Every student is shorter than Mary.
   f) Every student paper received a prize. *contradiction*
      A student paper did not receive a prize.

2. What is the logical relation between the words in the following pairs? Is it subordination, equivalence, incompatibility, complementarity, synonymy, polysemy, or antonymy?
   a) early, late *antonym*
   b) mare, female horse *not written in same context synonymy*   ππ
   c) armchair, sofa *incompatibility*
   d) human, man *subordination*

3. Determine the thematic role for each NP (underlined) in the following sentences.
   a) <u>Mary</u> gave <u>a book</u> to <u>John</u>. *agent, patient, goal*
   b) <u>The boat</u> sailed under <u>the bridge</u>. *patient, location*
   c) <u>The child</u> ate <u>the apple</u>. *agent, patient*
   d) <u>Fred</u> likes <u>history books</u>. *experiencer, stimulus*
   e) <u>Sue</u> knows <u>logic</u>. *experiencer, stimulus*
   f) <u>John</u> is happy. *agent experiencer*

4. Determine whether each verb phrase in the following sentences describes an activity, accomplishment, achievement, or state. Use the diagnostics described in section 6.3.2 to support your answers.
   a) Fred <u>biked to school</u>.
   b) The children <u>swam</u>.
   c) The plant <u>died</u>.
   d) The boat <u>crossed the river</u>.

5. The following sentences contain context-dependent adjectives. For each sentence, create a context for which the sentence is true and a context for which the sentence is false.
   a) This spaceship is small.
   b) This butterfly is fast.
   c) The kindergarten children in room #102 are tall.

6. For each pair of sentences, determine whether sentence (b) is a presupposition of sentence (a). Use the tests discussed in section 6.4.3 to justify your answer.
   i)   a. Wilma knows that Fred is driving home.
        b. Fred is driving home.
   ii) a. The doctor believes this is a case of measles.
        b. This is a case of measles.
   iii) a. The students are sad that the holidays are over.
        b. The holidays are over.
   iv) a. The website reported that the Blue Jays won the game.
        b. The Blue Jays won the game.
   v)   a. Charlie managed to pass the test.
        b. Charlie passed the test.
   vi) a. Sue remembered to close the door.
        b. Sue closed the door.
   vii) a. The doctor is on call again.
        b. The doctor was on call before.

7. For each sentence below, find the presupposition trigger and identify the class it belongs to (e.g., definite article, possessive phrase, factive predicate, aspectual verb).
   a) Despite the housing prices, John continues to want to live in the city.
   b) John's friends are all in town.
   c) Mary realized that the painting is a fake.
   d) The police stopped searching for the missing key.

8. What is the conversational implicature of sentence (b) in the following exchange? Explain your answer in terms of the Cooperative Principle and its maxims (see section 6.4.4).
   A: Did you go to Fred's pool party?
   B: I can't swim.

9. In light of what you learned about Binding Theory, explain the interpretive possibilities indicated by the indices in the following sentences.
   a) $Mary_1$ saw $herself_1$/her_{*1} in the mirror.
   b) $John_1$ believes that $Fred_2$ likes $him_{1/*2}$.

10. In this chapter, the reciprocal expression *each other* was not discussed. Based on the following examples, determine which principle of Binding Theory *each other* is subject to. In other words, does it function like a plain pronoun or a reflexive pronoun? Explain your reasoning.
    a) The $children_1$ admire each $other_1$.
    b) *The $children_1$ said that Fred admires each $other_1$.
    c) *The $children's_1$ teacher congratulated each $other_1$.
    d) The $children_1$ believe that their $mothers_2$ admire each $other_{2/*1}$.

11. The following sentences are ambiguous. Identify the source of the ambiguity, and then paraphrase the two readings of each sentence.
    a) Every raccoon searched a garbage can.
    b) A raccoon searched each garbage can.
    c) At Jane's request, every girl nominated her teacher for a prize.

ALEKSANDRA STEINBERGS | WILLIAM O'GRADY

7

The classification of languages

Everything it is possible for us to analyze
depends on a clear method which distinguishes
the similar from the not similar.

LINNEUS, *GENERA PLANTARUM* (1754)

There are more than 7000 languages in the world today, each with its own sound patterns, syntax, and vocabulary. But underlying these differences are similarities that allow languages to be classified and grouped in various ways. This chapter focuses on the methods of classification used by linguists and on some of the similarities and differences that have been uncovered in comparative research on the world's languages. First, though, some preliminary discussion is in order.

7.1 Basic issues and concerns

In an attempt to bring some order to the linguistic diversity found in the world's speech communities, linguists attempt to distinguish dialect from language and to classify languages in various ways. In this section, we explore some of the results of their work, as well as the alarming threat to the survival of a large number of the world's languages.

7.1.1 Dialect and language

It is sometimes difficult to determine whether two linguistic communities speak different languages or merely different dialects of the same language. One test that linguists use to decide this involves the criterion of **mutual intelligibility**. Mutually intelligible varieties of the same language can be understood by speakers of each variety. According to this criterion, the English of Toronto, the English of Milwaukee, and the English of London qualify as dialects of the same language. In contrast, if two speakers cannot understand one another, then linguists normally conclude that they are speaking different languages. The Italian of Florence and the French of Paris are examples of varieties of speech that are not mutually intelligible.

Political, cultural, social, historical, and religious factors frequently interfere when determining linguistic boundaries. (In fact, it is sometimes said that a language is just a dialect with an army and a navy!) For example, Serbs and Croats—with their different histories, cultures, and religions—often claim that they speak different languages. However, even though Serbian and Croatian are written with different alphabets, they are actually mutually intelligible dialects of the same language, which linguists call Serbo-Croatian. In contrast, people often speak of Chinese as if it were a single language, even though it is actually a number of individual, mutually unintelligible languages (Mandarin, Cantonese, Taiwanese, Wu, and so on), each with a multitude of dialects of its own.

In addition to the problems presented by these non-linguistic considerations, complications arise when we try to divide a continuum of mutually intelligible dialects whose two endpoints are not intelligible. Dutch and German, for example, are mutually intelligible around the border area between Germany and the Netherlands; however, the Dutch of Amsterdam and the German of Munich are not. Similarly, Palestinian Arabic and Syrian Arabic are mutually intelligible, but Moroccan Arabic and Saudi Arabian Arabic are not.

7.1.2 The threat to human linguistic diversity

Taking these considerations into account, exactly how many languages are spoken in the world today? The best available estimate, from the Ethnologue organization (www.ethnologue.com), places the figure at 7097, with the geographic distribution shown in table 7.1.

TABLE 7.1 The geographical distribution of the world's living languages		
Region	**Number of languages**	**% of the total**
The Americas	1 060	14.9
Africa	2 143	30.2
Europe	288	4.1
Asia	2 300	32.4
The Pacific	1 306	18.4
Total	**7 197**	

Source: www.ethnologue.com. Used by permission, © SIL.

Table 7.2 presents the estimated speaker populations for the world's twenty most-spoken languages. (Except where otherwise indicated, estimates include only native speakers; L2 = second language.) These are large numbers, but they are not typical. In 2016, UNESCO reported that 2124 languages have fewer than 100 000 speakers, and 1749 have fewer than 10 000 speakers; in 2019, Ethnologue reported that 467 languages had fewer than 100 speakers. According to a 2003 UNESCO report, 96 percent of the world's languages are spoken by just 3 percent of the world's population, leaving much of the world's linguistic diversity in the hands of a very small number of speakers.

Ask the average person to name a dead language, and he or she is likely to mention Latin. In fact, Latin did not really die; rather, it evolved over a period of centuries into French, Spanish, Italian, Portuguese, Romanian, and the other modern-day Romance languages (see section 7.3.1).

TABLE 7.2 The world's twenty most-spoken languages and estimated number of speakers (in millions) as of 2018

Mandarin	909
Spanish	442
English	378
Hindi-Urdu	329.2
Bengali	243
Portuguese	223
Russian	154
Japanese	128
Punjabi (India and Pakistan)	92.7
Javanese (Indonesia)	84.4
Wu (China)	80.7
Turkish	78.5
Korean	77.2
French	76.8
German	76
Telugu (India)	74.8
Yue (China)	73.4
Marathi (India)	71.8
Urdu	69.2
Vietnamese	68

Source: www.ethnologue.com. Used by permission, © SIL.

Contrast this with the situation of Manx, a Celtic language indigenous to the Isle of Man, a small island midway between Ireland and Great Britain. Its last speaker, Ned Maddrell, died in 1974. Just one hundred years earlier, 12 000 people had spoken Manx. Now no one does. Manx didn't just change over time; it eventually ceased to be spoken. A similar fate befell the Eyak language of Alaska in 2008 and the language Bo (once spoken in India's Andaman Islands) in 2010. The last native speaker of the Salish language Klallam (Washington State) died in early 2014, at the age of 103. Alban Michael, the last known speaker of the Nuchatlaht dialect of Nuučaan'uł (British Columbia), passed away in 2016.

On average, a language is lost every three months, accelerating a process that has been underway for several centuries. According to the most recent estimates, more than 40 percent of the world's languages are at risk, with few, if any, children learning them. The situation is grim in many different areas of the world. Of the sixty Indigenous languages once spoken in Canada, very few have large enough speaker populations to have a good chance of surviving over the long term. Of the 300 languages spoken in the area corresponding to the United States at the time of Columbus, only 175 were still spoken in 2010, and many of these are on the verge of disappearing. Ninety percent of Australia's 250 Aboriginal languages are near extinction. You can find up-to-date information on the plight of hundreds of endangered languages at www.endangeredlanguages.com.

The death of languages is lamentable for a variety of reasons. From a purely linguistic perspective, the loss of linguistic diversity means that we have much less information about how language works and about the different forms that it can take. For example, when the last speaker of Ubykh (a North Caucasian language spoken in Turkey) died in 1992, linguists lost the opportunity to study a very unusual phonological system—Ubykh had eighty-one consonants and just three vowels. (In contrast, a typical variety of Canadian English has twenty-four consonants and around sixteen vowels and diphthongs.)

At the level of the community that once spoke the language, its loss can be even more serious. Language often helps define a community's sense of identity, serving as a source of solidarity and group membership. A 2007 study of youth suicides in Indigenous communities in British Columbia reported that rates were far lower in communities where at least half the population could still speak their traditional language than in communities with low language-retention rates.

How and why do languages die? In some cases, they die because the people who speak them perish as the result of war or disease. Indeed, according to some estimates, up to 95 percent of the Indigenous population of North America died from diseases brought to their continent by European colonists.

More commonly these days, however, languages die because their speakers gradually use them less and less in favour of a language that appears to offer greater economic or educational opportunities. English, Spanish, and French are obvious examples of international languages that acquire new speakers in this way, but many other languages are dominant on a more local scale: Mandarin Chinese, Thai, Bahasa Indonesia, the East African language Swahili, and Filipino (also called Tagalog) are all threats to smaller languages in their respective territories. The classic pattern of language loss involves three generations: the parents are monolingual, their children become bilingual by adopting a new language, and their children's children grow up monolingual in the new language—unable to speak to their own grandparents.

With about 7000 languages in the world today and only about 200 countries, the vast majority of the world's languages do not have the protection of a national government. Smaller linguistic communities are therefore often left without the economic or educational resources needed to compete with the larger languages that surround them.

The ongoing pervasive threat to the world's linguistic diversity is of great concern to linguists, many of whom are actively involved in studying and documenting languages on the verge of extinction. Where feasible, linguists are also seeking ways to improve the prospects for endangered languages by participating in linguistic, social, and educational programs designed to promote and protect the use of indigenous languages.

7.1.3 Types of classification

Within the field of linguistics, three different approaches to language classification are used.

A first approach, **linguistic typology**, classifies languages according to their structural characteristics. For example, typologists might group together languages with similar sound patterns or those with similar grammatical structures. Typological studies also endeavour to identify **linguistic universals**: that is, structural characteristics that occur in all or most languages. We discuss linguistic typology further in section 7.2.

A second approach, **genetic classification**, categorizes languages according to their descent. Languages that developed historically from the same ancestor language are grouped together and are said to have a **genetic relationship**. This ancestor may be attested (that is, texts written in this language have been discovered or preserved, as in the case of Latin), or it may be a reconstructed proto-language for which no original texts exist (as is the case for Proto-Indo-European). Section 7.3 of this chapter and the Companion Website present an overview of a few hundred languages and the families to which they belong.

Language Matters Language Immersion to the Rescue?

In the 1960s, a group of Canadian parents and educators, taking advantage of children's natural abilities as language learners, launched "French immersion"—a wildly successful program that made French the language of instruction for English-speaking school children. This same idea underlies a series of exciting immersion initiatives whose goal is the survival of indigenous languages. Following the pioneering effort of the Maori in New Zealand in the early 1980s, immersion programs have been implemented with varying degrees of success for many endangered languages, including Hawaiian, Blackfoot, Navajo, and Mohawk.

Sources: Leanne Hinton and Ken Hale, eds., *The Green Book of Language Revitalization in Practice* (San Diego: Academic Press, 2001); Pūnana Leo Preschools, *'Aha Pūnana Leo*, www.ahapunanaleo.org "Mohawk Immersion Pilot Programs," *Kanatsiohareke Mohawk Community*, www.mohawkcommunity.com.

Genetically related languages need not look alike. For example, both Latvian and English belong to the European branch of the Indo-European family, but their morphological structure is quite different. Indeed, the English sentence *It has to be figured out* can be expressed in Latvian by the single word *ja-izgudro*. Of course, Latvian and English are very distantly related, and languages that are more closely related typically manifest greater similarity. At the same time, even languages that are totally unrelated may be similar in some respects. For instance, English, Thai, and Swahili, which are unrelated to each other, all employ subject-verb-object word order in simple declarative sentences.

(1) Swahili
    Maria anapenda   Anna.
    Maria likes   Anna
    'Maria likes Anna.'

(2) Thai
    Roudbuntuk   ding roud.
    truck   push car
    'Trucks push cars.'

Finally, **areal classification** identifies characteristics shared by languages that are in geographical contact. Under these circumstances, languages often borrow words, sounds, morphemes, and even syntactic patterns from one another. As a result, neighbouring languages can come to resemble each other, even though they may not be genetically related. (For example, contour tones are found in many unrelated languages in East and Southeast Asia, including Thai, Vietnamese, and Chinese.) Areal classification is a challenging endeavour that requires detailed knowledge of a region's speech communities and their languages. For reason of space, we will not be able to discuss this type of research further in this chapter.

7.2 Typological classification

Typological studies group languages together on the basis of similarities in their syntactic patterns, morphological structure, and/or phonological systems. An important area of research within the study of linguistic typology is the search for linguistic universals. Structural patterns and traits that occur in all languages are called **absolute universals** (one such universal is that all languages have syntactic structure), while those that occur in most languages are known as **universal tendencies.**

Many typological generalizations involve **implicational universals,** which specify that the presence of one trait implies the presence of another (but not vice versa). For instance, if a language has nasal vowels, as does Portuguese (e.g., *mãe* 'mother'), it must also have oral vowels. In such situations, we say that oral vowels are **unmarked** (or more basic), and nasal vowels are **marked** (less basic).

Implicational universals such as the one exemplified in table 7.3 allow us to make predictions about what types of languages are possible and impossible. The following sections present some of the typological generalizations and universals that have been proposed in the areas of phonology, morphology, and syntax.

TABLE 7.3 Oral and nasal vowel phonemes: nasal vowels imply oral vowels.		
Nasal vowels	**Oral vowels**	
no	yes	possible (English, Japanese)
yes	yes	possible (French, Portuguese)
yes	no	**impossible**

7.2.1 Phonology

In this section, we represent vowel and consonant systems phonemically. However, the exact phonetic realization of these systems may vary in the individual languages.

Vowel systems

Languages are often classified according to the size and pattern of their vowel systems. The most common vowel system has five phonemes—two high vowels, two mid vowels, and one low vowel (see figure 7.1). The front vowels are unrounded, as is the low vowel, and the back vowels are rounded. About half the world's languages—including Basque (spoken in Spain), Hawaiian, Hebrew, Spanish, and Swahili—have such a system.

FIGURE 7.1
The most common vowel system

```
i            u

e            o

      a
```

The majority of the world's other languages have vowel systems with three to nine different vowels (disregarding contrasts based on length or nasalization, which can double or triple the number of vowel phonemes). Languages with fewer than three or more than nine distinctive vowels are rare. Some typical vowel systems are presented in figure 7.2.

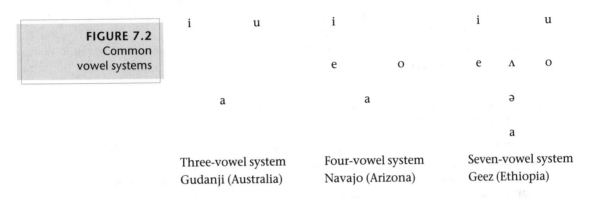

FIGURE 7.2
Common vowel systems

i	u	i		i		u
		e	o	e	ʌ	o
a		a		ə		
				a		

Three-vowel system
Gudanji (Australia)

Four-vowel system
Navajo (Arizona)

Seven-vowel system
Geez (Ethiopia)

Analysis of many languages has led to the discovery of a number of universal tendencies pertaining to vowel systems. Some of these tendencies are listed here, along with a description of the most commonly occurring vowels.

- The most commonly occurring vowel phoneme is /a/, which is found in almost all the languages of the world. The vowels /i/ and /u/ are almost as common as /a/.
- Front vowel phonemes (e.g., /i, e, ɛ, æ/) are generally unrounded, while non-low back vowel phonemes (e.g., /ɔ, o, u/) are generally rounded.
- Low vowels (e.g., /æ, a, ɑ/) are generally unrounded.

Although English has an above-average number of vowels, they all conform to the above tendencies. Thus, English has only front unrounded vowels, all the low vowel phonemes are unrounded, and all of the back, non-low vowels are rounded. The vowel system of Canadian English is represented in figure 7.3.

FIGURE 7.3
The vowel system of Canadian English

i		u
ɪ		ʊ
e		o
ɛ	ʌ	
æ		ɑ

As already noted with respect to nasal and oral vowels, the relationship between certain contrasting vowel types can be expressed in terms of implicational universals, since the presence of one vowel phoneme type implies the presence of another (but not vice versa).

- As already noted, if a language has nasal vowel phonemes, then it will also have oral vowel phonemes. For example, French contrasts different nasal vowels—as in *long* /lɔ̃/ 'long' versus *lent* /lã/ 'slow'. And it contrasts oral vowels with nasal vowels, as in *là* /la/ 'there' versus *lent* /lã/ 'slow'. Predictably, French also contrasts different oral vowels, as in *clos* /klo/ 'shut' versus *clou* /klu/ 'nail'. English shows contrasts among oral vowels but does not contrast nasal vowels with oral vowels. There are no contrasts in English like /bɑt/ 'bought' and */bɑ̃t/.
- If a language has long vowel phonemes, then it will also have short vowel phonemes. For example, Finnish has contrasting long vowels, and, predictably, contrasting short vowels (see table 7.4).

TABLE 7.4	Finnish vowel contrasts	
Long versus long	/viːli/ 'junket'	/vaːli/ 'election'
Short versus short	/suka/ 'bristle'	/suku/ 'family'
Short versus long	/tuli/ 'fire'	/tuːli/ 'wind'

The reverse is not necessarily the case—in fact, a language need not have long vowel phonemes at all. English works that way, since it has no phonemic contrast between long and short vowels.

TABLE 7.5	Long and short vowel phonemes: long vowels imply short vowels.	
Contrasting long vowels	**Contrasting short vowels**	
no	yes	possible (English)
yes	yes	possible (Finnish)
yes	no	**impossible**

Consonant systems

It is not particularly useful to classify languages according to the number of consonants that they contain, since there is a great deal of variation in the size of consonant inventories (see the Language Matters box, "Record-Breaking Languages," on page 222). Nevertheless, typological analysis of consonant systems has produced a number of well-substantiated universals:

- All languages have stops.
- The most common stop phonemes are /p, t, k/. Very few languages lack any one of these, and there are no languages that lack all three. If any one of these three stops is missing, it will probably be /p/; for example, Aleut (Alaska), Tlingit (British Columbia), and Chipewyan (Northwest Territories), have no /p/ phoneme. The most commonly occurring phoneme of the three is /t/.
- The most commonly occurring fricative phoneme is /s/. If a language has only one fricative, it is most likely to be /s/. It is the only fricative found in Nandi (Kenya) and Weri (Papua New Guinea). The next most common fricative is /f/.
- The vast majority of languages have at least one nasal phoneme. In cases where a language has only one nasal phoneme, that phoneme is usually /n/ (as in Arapaho, spoken in Wyoming). If there are two contrasting nasals, they are normally /m/ and /n/.

- Most languages have at least one phonemic liquid. However, a relatively small number of languages have none at all: for example, Blackfoot and Dakota (North American Indigenous languages), Efik (Nigeria), and Siona (Ecuador). English, of course, has two: /l/ and /r/.

Consonant phonemes are also subject to various implicational universals:

- If a language has voiced obstruent phonemes (stops, fricatives, or affricates), then it will almost always have corresponding voiceless obstruent phonemes (see table 7.6). The reverse is not necessarily true; for example, Ainu (a language of northern Japan) has only voiceless obstruent phonemes: /p, t, k, tʃ, s/.

TABLE 7.6 Obstruent phonemes: voiced obstruents imply voiceless obstruents.

Voiced obstruents	Voiceless obstruents	
no	yes	possible (Ainu)
yes	yes	possible (English)
yes	no	**very rare** (Canela-Krahô [Brazil])

- Sonorant consonants are generally voiced. Very few languages have voiceless sonorant phonemes such as /l̥/; those that do always have voiced sonorant phonemes as well (see table 7.7). For example, Burmese contrasts voiced and voiceless nasals and laterals.

TABLE 7.7 Sonorant phonemes: voiceless sonorants imply voiced sonorants.

Voiceless sonorants	Voiced sonorants	
no	yes	possible (English)
yes	yes	possible (Burmese)
yes	no	**impossible**

- If a language has fricative phonemes, then it will also have stop phonemes (see table 7.8). There are no languages that lack stops; however, there are some languages that lack fricatives. For example, Gilbertese (Gilbert Islands) Akuntsú (Brazil), and Nuer (southeastern Sudan) have no fricatives.

TABLE 7.8 Stop and fricative phonemes: fricatives imply stops.

Fricatives	Stops	
no	yes	possible (Nuer)
yes	yes	possible (English)
yes	no	**impossible**

- Languages that have affricates will also have fricatives and stops (see table 7.9). This is not surprising, since an affricate is, in essence, a sequence of a stop followed by a fricative. However, many languages lack affricate phonemes altogether. For example, French has fricative and stop phonemes, but no affricate phonemes. In contrast, English has all three consonant types.

TABLE 7.9 Types of obstruent phonemes: affricates imply fricatives; fricatives imply stops.

Affricates	Fricatives	Stops	
yes	yes	yes	possible (English)
no	yes	yes	possible (French)
no	no	yes	possible (Akuntsú)
yes	yes	no	**impossible**
no	yes	no	**impossible**
yes	no	no	**impossible**

Language Matters Record-Breaking Languages

There are no official 'world records' within linguistics, but it's natural to wonder about languages that are 'extreme' in some way. Here are some languages that are frequently mentioned for the unusual size (large or small) of their phonological inventory.

- *Fewest consonants*: Rotokas has just 6 consonant phonemes. (Rotokas has about 11 600 speakers in Papua New Guinea.)
- *Most consonants*: !Kung, a language with a speaker population of about 20 000 in Namibia and Angola, has 96 consonant phonemes.
- *Fewest vowels*: Some dialects of Abkhaz have just 2 vowel phonemes. (This North Caucasian language has approximately 106 000 speakers, mostly in the Republic of Georgia.)
- *Fewest overall number of phonemes*: Rotokas again (11).
- *Greatest overall number of phonemes*: By some counts, !Xóõ has 77 consonant phonemes, including dozens of clicks, and 31 vowel phonemes. To hear a brief sample of !Xóõ, which is spoken by about 2500 people in Botswana, go to the Companion Website.

Suprasegmental systems

Languages can also be classified according to their suprasegmental (or prosodic) type. Languages that use pitch to make meaning distinctions between words are called **tone languages**. As illustrated in table 7.10, Mandarin has four contrastive tones.

TABLE 7.10 Tone contrasts in Mandarin

High tone	dā	'build'
Low rising tone	dá	'achieve'
Falling rising tone	dǎ	'hit'
High falling tone	dà	'big'

The other Chinese languages, as well as many languages of Southeast Asia, Africa, and the Americas, are also tone languages. A few tone languages are also found in Europe; for example, one of the dialects of Latvian makes a three-way tonal distinction (see table 7.11).

TABLE 7.11	Tone contrasts in Latvian			
Falling tone		loks	[lùoks]	'arch, bow'
Level (high) tone		loks	[lūoks]	'green onion'
Rising falling (broken) tone		loks	[lûoks]	'window'

There are two types of tones: level tones and contour tones. Tone languages most often contrast only two tone levels (usually high and low). However, contrasts involving three tone levels (such as high, low, and mid) are also relatively common. Five or more levels of tonal contrast are practically unknown.

Tone systems, too, exhibit various universal tendencies:

- If a language has contour tones (such as rising or falling tones), then it will also have level tones (such as high, mid, or low tones), as outlined in table 7.12. Burmese, Crow (spoken in Montana), Latvian, and Mandarin are examples of languages that fit this pattern. The reverse pattern (languages with contour tones but no level tones) is extremely rare; Dafla, spoken in northern India, has such a system.

TABLE 7.12	Tone contrasts: contour tones imply level tones.	
Contour tones	**Level tones**	
no	yes	possible (Sarcee)
yes	yes	possible (Mandarin)
yes	no	**very rare** (Dafla)

Differences in stress are also useful in classifying languages. Fixed stress languages are those in which the position of stress on a word is predictable. For example, in Modern Hebrew and K'iché (a Mayan language), stress always falls on the last syllable of a word; in Polish, Swahili, and Samoan, stress falls on the penultimate (second-to-last) syllable of words, while in Czech, Finnish, and Hungarian, the stressed syllable is always the first syllable of a word. In **free stress** languages, the position of stress varies. Free stress is also called phonemic stress because of its role in distinguishing between words. Russian is an example of a language with free stress, as shown in table 7.13.

TABLE 7.13	Stress contrasts in Russian		
múka	'torture'	muká	'flour'
zámok	'castle'	zamók	'lock'
rúki	'hands'	rukí	'hand's' (possessive singular)

Syllable structure

The CV and V syllable types are unmarked. They are found in all languages (with the possible exception of the Australian language Arrernte, which seems to have only the VC and V types) and are learned first by children.

In any given language, onsets may be structured differently from codas. For example, in English, a nasal + stop sequence is permitted in the coda (in a word like *hand*) but not in the onset (no English words begin with the sequence *nd*). However, Swahili has precisely the opposite restrictions: the *nd* sequence is permitted in onset position (in words like *ndizi* 'banana') but not in coda position. In fact, Swahili syllables are codaless—they can only end in vowels.

Two examples of implicational universals for syllable structure are presented below.

■ If a language permits sequences of consonants in the onset, then it will also permit syllables with single consonant onsets (see table 7.14).

TABLE 7.14   Onsets: multiple consonant onsets imply single consonant onsets.

Multiple C onsets	Single C onsets	
no	yes	possible (Hawaiian)
yes	yes	possible (English)
yes	no	**impossible**

■ If a language permits sequences of consonants in the coda, then it will also permit syllables with single consonant codas and syllables with no coda at all (see table 7.15).

TABLE 7.15   Codas: multiple consonant codas imply single consonant codas/no codas.

Multiple C codas	Single C codas/no codas	
no	yes	possible (Cantonese)
yes	yes	possible (English)
yes	no	**impossible**

7.2.2 Morphology

Both words and morphemes are found in all languages. However, there are clear differences in whether and how individual languages combine morphemes to form words. Four types of systems can be distinguished.

The isolating type

An **isolating** (or **analytic**) language avoids affixes, using free forms to express notions such as tense and number. Mandarin shows strong isolating tendencies, as exemplified by the fact that the morpheme used to indicate past tense (roughly) is a word rather than an affix and can therefore appear in more than one position in the sentence.

(3) *a.* Ta chi fan **le**.
    he eat meal past
    'He ate the meal.'

   b. Ta chi **le** fan.
    he eat past meal
    'He ate the meal.'

Other languages that are primarily isolating include Cantonese, Vietnamese, Laotian, and Khmer (Cambodian).

The agglutinating type

An **agglutinating** language makes widespread use of affixes, each of which typically expresses a single piece of grammatical information. The following examples are from Turkish (GEN = genitive, an affix used to mark a possessor).

(4) *a.* köy
    'village'

   b. köy-ler
    village-PL
    'villages'

   c. köy-ler-in
    village-PL-GEN
    'of the villages'

As can be seen here, Turkish words can have a complex morphological structure, but each morpheme typically has a single, clearly identifiable function. In (4c), for instance, *-ler* marks plurality and *-in* marks possession, giving the meaning 'of the villages'.

The fusional type

Words in a **fusional** or **inflectional** language can also consist of root + affix combinations. However, in contrast to agglutinating systems, the affixes in fusional languages often express several bits of grammatical information simultaneously. In Russian, for example, a single inflectional suffix marks the noun's gender class (masculine, feminine, or neuter), its number (singular or plural), and its grammatical role (subject, direct object, and so on). This is illustrated in (5) for the suffix *-u* (ACC = accusative, an affix used to mark the direct object; FEM = feminine; SG = singular).

(5) My vidim ruk-u.
    we see hand-FEM.SG.ACC
    'We see a/the hand.'

The polysynthetic type

In a **polysynthetic** language, single words can consist of long strings of roots and affixes that often express meanings associated with entire sentences in other languages. The following word from Inuktitut illustrates this.

(6) Ayagciqnillruyugnarquq.

ayag	-ciq	-ni	-llru	-yugnarqe	-u		-q
go	FUT	claim	PAST	probably	INDIC.INTR		3SG

'He probably said he would go.'

Polysynthesis is common in many Indigenous languages in North America, including Inuktitut, Cree, and Tsúut'ína.

Mixed types

Many (perhaps most) languages do not belong exclusively to any of the four categories just outlined. For example, English employs isolating patterns in many verbal constructions, where each notion is expressed by a separate word. The future, for instance, is indicated by the independent word *will* (rather than by an affix) in structures such as *I will leave*. However, English exhibits considerable agglutination in derived words, such as *re-en-act-ment*, which consist of a series of clearly identifiable morphemes, each with its own unique meaning and function. Furthermore, the English pronoun system is largely fusional, since a single form can be used to indicate person, number, gender, and case. The word *he*, for instance, is used to express a third person, singular, masculine subject.

Since many, if not most, of the world's languages exhibit mixed patterns, it has been suggested that terms like *isolating*, *agglutinating*, and *fusional* should be used to refer not to a language as a whole but to particular structures within a language. It is also important to recognize that these classifications do not take into consideration morphological processes such as compounding (e.g., English *greenhouse*), reduplication (e.g., Tagalog *sulat* 'write' versus *susulat* 'will write'), grammatical use of stress or tone (e.g., the noun *présent* versus the verb *presént* in English), and internal word change (e.g., vowel ablaut, as in English *run* versus *ran*).

Implicational universals: morphology

A variety of generalizations can be made about word structure in human language.

- If a language has inflectional affixes, it will also have derivational affixes. For example, English has not only inflectional suffixes such as the past tense *-ed* and plural *-s* but also derivational suffixes like *-ment* (*treatment*, *discernment*) and *-able* (*doable*, *readable*).

- If a word has both a derivational and an inflectional affix, the derivational affix is closer to the root (see table 7.16).

TABLE 7.16   The ordering of derivational and inflectional affixes

English

friend-ship-s			*friend-s -ship		
Root	DA	IA	Root	IA	DA

Turkish

iş	-çi	-ler	*iş	-ler	-çi
work	-er	-PL	work	-PL	-er
Root	DA	IA	Root	IA	DA

DA = derivational affix; IA = inflectional affix

- If a language has only suffixes, it will also have only **postpositions**. (In languages that place the head at the end of the phrase, postpositions are the equivalent of prepositions.) Turkish, for example, has only suffixes; as expected, it also has postpositions rather than prepositions. This is illustrated in the following sentence.

(7) Hasan   Ebru   için   kitap   al-dı.
Hasan   Ebru   for   book   buy-PST
'Hasan bought a book for Ebru.'

7.2.3 Syntax

Work on syntactic universals often takes as its starting point the relative order of the subject (S), the direct object (O), and the verb (V) in simple declarative sentences such as *The men built the house*. The three most common word orders (in descending order of frequency) are SOV, SVO, and VSO. Of languages with an identifiable basic order, about 47.5 percent employ SOV, 41 percent use SVO, and 8 percent prefer VSO.

(8) SOV (Turkish)
Hasan   öküz-ü   al-dı.
Hasan   ox-ACC   buy-PST
'Hasan bought the ox.'

(9) SVO (English)
The athlete broke the record.

(10) VSO (Welsh)
Lladdodd   y   ddraig   y   dyn.
killed   the   dragon   the   man
'The dragon killed the man.'

SOV, SVO, and VSO patterns all have one trait in common: the subject appears before the direct object. The prevalence of the S-before-O pattern (more than 95 percent of the languages studied) may be due to the fact that the subject usually coincides with the topic of the sentence (i.e., what the sentence is about) and therefore is more useful at an early point in the utterance.

While an overwhelming majority of the world's languages place the subject to the left of the direct object in their basic word order, this pattern is not universal. There are a small number of VOS languages, of which the best-known example is Malagasy.

(11) VOS (Malagasy)
Nahita   ny   mpianatra   ny   vehivavy.
saw   the   student   the   woman
'The woman saw the student.'

In addition, there are a very few OVS and OSV languages, all of which seem to be found in South America:

(12) OVS (Hixkaryana)
Kana   janɨmno   bɨrjekomo.
fish   caught   boy
'The boy caught a fish.'

(13) OSV (Apuriña)
Anana   not   apa.
pineapple   I   fetch
'I fetch a pineapple.'

Word order universals

Sometimes, the order of elements within one kind of structure has implications for the order of elements in other structures. Many of these implications concern the relationship between the verb and its (direct) object.

- If a language has VO word order, then it will almost always have prepositions rather than postpositions. Languages of this type include Berber (Morocco), Hebrew, Maori (New Zealand), Maasai (Kenya), Welsh, and Irish Gaelic.

(14) Irish Gaelic
   a. VSO pattern:
      Chonaic   mé   mo   mháthair.
      saw   I   my   mother
      'I saw my mother.'

   b. Preposition pattern:
      sa teach
      in house
      'in the house'

- If a language has OV word order, then it will probably have postpositions rather than prepositions. Languages with this structural pattern include Basque, Burmese, Hindi, Japanese, Korean, Quechua (spoken in the Andean regions of South America), Turkish, and Guugu Yimidhirr, an Indigenous language of Australia (ERG = ergative, an affix used for the subject of a transitive verb).

(15) Guugu Yimidhirr
   a. SOV pattern:
      Gudaa-ngun   yarrga   dyindaj.
      dog-ERG   boy   bit
      'The dog bit the boy.'

   b. Postposition pattern:
      yuwaal   nganh
      beach   from
      'from the beach'

- Prepositional phrases (PPs) almost always precede the verb in OV languages and usually follow the verb in VO languages (NOM = nominative, an affix used to mark the subject of the sentence).

(16) Japanese
   a. SOV pattern:
      Gakusei-ga   hon-o   yonda.
      student-NOM   book-ACC   read
      'The student read a book.'

    b. PP precedes verb:
        Taroo-ga   [pp nitiyoobi   ni] tsuita.
        Taroo-NOM   Sunday   on   arrived
        'Taroo arrived on Sunday.'

(17) English
    a. SVO pattern:
        I like candy.

    b. PP follows verb:
        George left [pp on Sunday].

■   Manner adverbs overwhelmingly precede the verb in OV languages and generally follow the verb in VO languages.

(18) Japanese (SOV pattern, as seen in [16a])
    Manner adverb precedes verb:
    Joozu   hasiru.
    well   run
    '(He) runs well.'

(19) English (SVO pattern, as seen in [17a])
    Manner adverb follows verb:
    John runs well.

■   There is an overwhelming preference for Possessor + N order in OV languages, and a (somewhat weaker) preference for N + Possessor order in VO languages.

(20) Japanese (SOV pattern, as seen in [16a])
    Possessor precedes head N:
    Taroo-no   hon
    Taroo-GEN   book
    'Taroo's book'

(21) French
    a. SVO pattern:
        Pierre   aime   Marie.
        'Pierre   likes   Marie.'

    b. Possessor structure follows head N:
        la   maison   de   Marie
        the   house   of (GEN) Marie
        'Marie's house'

English, although an SVO language, exhibits both Possessor + N and N + Possessor patterns:

(22) *a.* Possessor + N pattern:
        the country's laws

    b. N + Possessor pattern:
        the laws of the country

Grammatical hierarchies

Implicational universals are often stated in terms of hierarchies of categories or relations. One of the most important hierarchies of this type refers to the grammatical relations of subject and direct object.

(23) The grammatical relation hierarchy:
subject > direct object > other

According to this hierarchy, a process that applies only to subjects is less marked than a process that applies to direct objects. In other words, if a particular phenomenon applies to direct objects, it should also apply to subjects. In contrast, it would not be surprising to find a process that applies to subjects but not direct objects.

Among the many typological phenomena that conform to this hierarchy is verb agreement. As the following examples show, in some languages, the verb agrees only with the subject, and in others, it agrees with both the subject and the direct object (3 = 3rd person; SG = singular; PL = plural).

(24) Agreement with subject only (Spanish):

Subject		
Juan	ley-ó.	dos libros.
Juan	read-SG.PST	two books
'Juan read two books.'		

(25) Agreement with subject and direct object (Swahili):

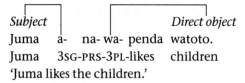

Subject				*Direct object*
Juma	a-	na- wa-	penda	watoto.
Juma	3SG-PRS-3PL-likes			children
'Juma likes the children.'				

However, as predicted by the hierarchy, there are no languages in which the verb agrees only with the direct object.

Language Matters The Ergative Way

In some languages, the verb agrees with the subject of an intransitive verb and the direct object of a transitive verb, but not with the subject of a transitive verb. The following example (provided by Farooq Babrakzai) is from Pashto, one of the major languages of Afghanistan.

    a. Agreement with the 3rd person subject of an intransitive verb:

        xəza   də-daftar -na   raɣ-**a.**
        woman   POSS-office-from   came-3FS*
        'The woman came from the office.'

    b. Agreement with the 3rd person direct object of a transitive verb:

        ma **xəza**   wəlid-**a.**
        I   woman saw-3FS
        'I saw the woman.'

A grammatical rule that treats the subject of an intransitive verb and the direct object of a transitive verb alike is said to be **ergative**. The existence of such phenomena suggests that the grammatical hierarchy in (23) may represent just one option—although a very common one—for creating syntax.

*3 FS = third person feminine singular

7.2.4 Explaining universals

Linguists are still uncertain about how to explain the existence of many linguistic universals. Nonetheless, a number of interesting proposals have been made, and it is worthwhile to consider some of them here.

Phonology

Perceptual factors play a role in shaping phonological universals. For example, the fact that /s/ is the most commonly occurring fricative may have to do with its acoustic prominence: varieties of /s/ are inherently louder and more strident than other kinds of fricatives.

Vowel systems (discussed in section 7.2.1) develop so as to keep vowel phonemes as different from each other as possible. A three-vowel system such as the one in figure 7.4 allows for plenty of 'space' around each vowel, which probably makes each vowel easier to distinguish from the others.

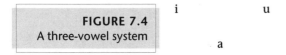

FIGURE 7.4
A three-vowel system

The distribution of stop phonemes is also sensitive to perceptibility. The reason that /p/, /t/, and /k/ are the three most common stops in languages is probably that they occur at three maximally distant places of articulation within the supralaryngeal vocal tract. These three stops are much easier to distinguish perceptually than a sequence of dental, alveolar, and palatal stops, for example, all of which are produced in the central region of the oral cavity.

It has been suggested that consonant systems in general respond to the articulatory pressures that give rise to unmarked sounds and systems. Articulatorily basic obstruents such as /p/, /t/, and /k/ are found much more commonly than more complex articulations such as /tɬ/ and /qw/. Table 7.17 presents the set of obstruents that is most widely used across human languages.

TABLE 7.17 Obstruents most often found cross-linguistically			
p	t	k	ʔ
b	d	g	
f	s		h
	tʃ		

Languages tend to have consonant systems that consist of about 70 percent obstruents and 30 percent sonorants, no matter what the total size of their consonant inventories may be. These figures reflect the articulatory possibilities available for contrast: more distinctions can be made among obstruents than among sonorants. There are, for example, no nasal fricatives, because the air pressure needed to force air through a narrow opening (which is necessary for the production of fricatives) cannot be built up when so much air is flowing through the nasal passage at the same time.

Morphology

Other types of explanations are appropriate for morphological universals. For example, the fact that languages with suffixes but no prefixes always have postpositions (section 7.2.2) may have a historical explanation. Because suffixes often evolve from postpositions, the co-existence of the two types of morphemes is expected.

An example of this very phenomenon can be seen in the closely related languages Finnish and Estonian. Their ancestor language (Proto-Balto-Finnic) contained a postposition **kanssa* 'with', which is still evident in Standard Finnish but has evolved into the suffix *-ga* in Estonian (see table 7.18; COM = comitative, a case expressing accompaniment; an asterisk is used to indicate that a word has been reconstructed with the help of data from related languages).

TABLE 7.18   Proto-Balto-Finnic postposition *kanssa* becomes suffix *-ga*

Standard Finnish: postposition *kanssa* 'with'

poja	'boy'	poja-n	kanssa	'with the boy'
		boy-GEN	with	

Estonian: case suffix-*ga*

poja	'boy'	poja-ga		'with the boy'
		boy-COM		

The requirement that derivational affixes occur closer to the root than inflectional affixes has another type of explanation. Derivation typically forms new words, while inflection marks the subclass (for example, plural for Ns, past tense for Vs) to which a word belongs. Given that a word must be formed before its subclass can be determined, it follows that derivational processes will precede inflection. This is reflected in word structure, where derivational affixes appear closer to the root than inflectional markers. In figure 7.5, for instance, the verbal root *treat* is converted into a noun by the affix *-ment* before the plural inflectional marker is added.

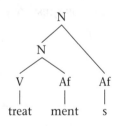

FIGURE 7.5
The structure of a word containing a derivational affix and an inflectional affix

Syntax

At least some syntactic universals may be explained in terms of the way that the human brain processes sentence structure. Consider the summary of word order patterns in table 7.19, which is based on the implicational universals discussed in section 7.2.3.

TABLE 7.19	Word order patterns	
Constituents	Order in VO language	Order in OV language
P & NP	preposition-NP	NP-postposition
V & PP	verb-PP	PP-verb
V & manner Adv	verb-manner Adv	manner Adv-verb
Poss & N	noun-possessor	possessor-noun

One explanation as to why word order properties cluster together involves the contrast between right-branching and left-branching languages. In right-branching languages, the more elaborate part of a phrase's structure occurs on its right branch; in left-branching languages, it occurs on the left. Thus, a verb-object pattern is right-branching since a phrasal constituent (an XP) appears on its right branch, but an object-verb pattern is left-branching, as shown in figure 7.6.

FIGURE 7.6
Right-branching and left-branching patterns

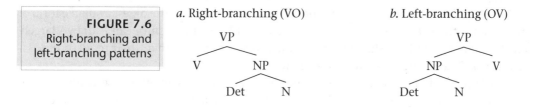

As you can easily determine for yourself, the P-NP, V-PP, V-Adv, and N-Poss patterns commonly associated with VO languages are also all right-branching. (Possessors are a type of NP, and manner adverbs are a type of AdvP.) In contrast, the NP-P, PP-V, Adv-V, and Poss-N patterns typically found in OV languages are all left-branching.

Language Matters Typology and Geography

Thanks to the collaboration of dozens of linguists, there is now a major online source of information on the distribution of various linguistic features (vowel inventories, morphological structure, word order, and so on) throughout the world. *The World Atlas of Language Structures*, with more than 140 maps and data from more than 2500 languages, can be accessed at wals.info/.

7.3 Genetic classification

The goal of genetic classification is to group languages into families based on evidence of a common origin established through use of the comparative method. This work is challenging for a variety of reasons.

Perhaps the biggest problem is simply the amount of data that must be collected before linguists can be confident about the status of a group of languages. For example, it is only in the last few decades that enough information has been accumulated to propose a detailed classification of the languages of Africa. Moreover, many of the languages of South America, New Guinea, and Australia are still relatively unknown.

Matters are further complicated by the fact that entirely unrelated languages may be similar in various ways. This is particularly likely if the languages have been in contact long enough to have borrowed a large number of words, sounds, morphemes, or syntactic structures from one another.

Even languages that are related may not look that similar. The more distant the genetic relationship between languages, the less likely that a large number of obvious similarities will be found, especially since sound changes can obscure relationships between words that descended from a common source—as happened with English *water* and Russian *vodka* 'little water' and with French *eau* and Spanish *agua* (both meaning 'water'), among many other examples.

Research is also made difficult by the fact that words that may be excellent indicators of a genetic relationship can drop out of the lexicon. For example, Old English had a word *leax* 'salmon' (which was cognate with German *Lachs* and Yiddish *lox*), but this lexical item has since been lost from the native English lexicon. (*Lox* has been borrowed back into some varieties of English as the name for brined salmon, a popular delicatessen food.)

Since word loss is a common occurrence, linguists prefer to use the oldest available form of a language for their research. Thus, our knowledge of Proto-Indo-European is drawn largely from the study of Old English, Sanskrit, Latin, and so on, rather than their modern descendants such as English, Hindi-Urdu, and French.

Some language families contain many hundreds of languages. In other cases, only one language may remain to represent a family. In still other cases, families have become extinct. The following section summarizes some of what we know about the Indo-European family of languages. Although it might appear to be overly Eurocentric to focus on this particular family, you will see that the homelands of the various Indo-European languages extend well beyond Europe into the Middle East and India. It is also worth noting that a number of languages spoken in Europe (Finnish, Hungarian, and Basque, to name three) do not belong to the Indo-European family.

7.3.1 The Indo-European family

If we consider only living languages, the Indo-European family currently has nine branches, which are listed in table 7.20.

TABLE 7.20 Main branches of the Indo-European family		
Germanic	Hellenic	Baltic
Celtic	Albanian	Slavic
Italic (Romance)	Armenian	Indo-Iranian

Germanic

The Germanic branch of Indo-European can be divided into three sub-branches: East, North, and West. The East Germanic branch included Gothic, the oldest Germanic language for which written texts exist (dating from the fourth century AD). Gothic and any other languages belonging to this branch of Germanic have long been extinct.

The North Germanic (or Scandinavian) branch originally included Old Norse (also known as Old Icelandic), which was the language of the Vikings and the ancestor of modern Icelandic, Norwegian, Faroese (spoken on the Faroe Islands, north of Scotland), Swedish, and Danish.

The West Germanic branch includes English, German, Yiddish, Dutch, Afrikaans, and Frisian. Afrikaans is descended from the Dutch spoken by seventeenth-century settlers (known as Boers) in South Africa. Frisian, generally thought to be the language most closely related to English, is spoken on the north coast of Holland and on the Frisian Islands just off the coast, as well as on the northwestern coast of Germany. English descended from the speech of the Angles, Saxons, and Jutes—Germanic tribes who lived in northern Germany and southern Denmark (in an area just east of the Frisians) before invading England in 449 AD and settling there.

The organization of the Germanic family of languages is illustrated in table 7.21. (In this and other tables, parentheses are used to indicate languages that no longer have any native speakers. The tables are intended to illustrate the membership and organization of the families; they do not necessarily provide a complete list of the languages in each family.)

TABLE 7.21 The Germanic family		
(East Germanic)	**North Germanic**	**West Germanic**
(Gothic)	Icelandic	English
	Faroese	German
	Norwegian	Dutch
	Danish	Frisian
	Swedish	Afrikaans
		Yiddish

Although we use tables to represent family groupings in this book, trees of the sort illustrated in figure 7.7 are widely used as well.

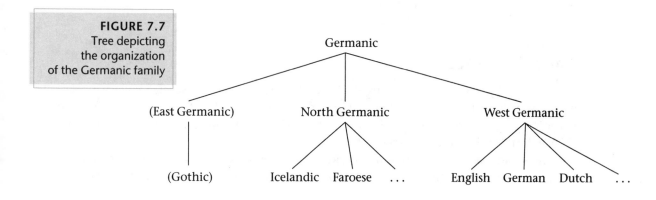

FIGURE 7.7
Tree depicting the organization of the Germanic family

Language Matters A Sister for English?

Although Frisian is generally considered to be the closest living relative of English, there is another contender for that title. Scots (also call Lallands), the language of the famed eighteenth-century Scottish poet Robert Burns, has been spoken for centuries in the Lowlands and Northern Isles of Scotland. Not to be confused with Scottish English or with Gaelic, it is sometimes claimed to be a language in its own right. Is Scots distinct enough from English in terms of mutual intelligibility to merit status as a distinct language rather than a dialect? To decide for yourself, listen to the sample of Scots in the YouTube video "The Scots Language"; for the URL, go to the Companion Website. You can find out more about Scots from the website of the Scots Language Centre: www.scotslanguage.com.

Celtic

The Celtic branch of Indo-European (see table 7.22) has two main sub-branches: Insular and Continental (now extinct). Gaulish, a member of the Continental branch, was once spoken in France (the Gauls were the tribe Julius Caesar defeated), but it has long been extinct.

The Insular sub-branch can be subdivided into two groups of languages: Brythonic or British (also called P-Celtic) and Goidelic or Gaelic (also called Q-Celtic). Brythonic languages include Welsh and Breton (which is spoken in northwestern France) as well as Cornish, which was once spoken in southwest Britain but no longer has any native speakers. The Goidelic branch contains Irish (or Irish Gaelic), which is still spoken natively in the western parts of Ireland; the now extinct Manx; and Scots Gaelic, which is spoken in parts of northwestern Scotland (especially the Hebrides Islands) and, to a lesser extent, on Cape Breton Island in Nova Scotia.

TABLE 7.22 The Celtic family

Insular		(Continental)
Brythonic	*Goidelic*	
Welsh	Irish [= Irish Gaelic]	(Gaulish)
Breton	Scots Gaelic	
(Cornish)	(Manx)	

Italic (Romance)

The Italic family originally had a number of branches, which included several now-extinct languages spoken in the area corresponding roughly to modern-day Italy. The only Italic languages that are presently spoken all descended from Latin, the language of the Roman Empire (hence the term 'Romance languages').

These languages are commonly divided into four groups. Ibero-Romance includes Portuguese and Spanish, while Gallo-Romance contains French, Catalan (spoken in northeastern Spain, around Barcelona), and Romansch (one of the four official languages of Switzerland). The Italo-Romance branch includes Italian and Sardinian; Romanian is the best-known language in the Balkano-Romance group (see table 7.23).

TABLE 7.23 The Romance family			
Ibero-Romance	**Gallo-Romance**	**Italo-Romance**	**Balkano-Romance**
Spanish Portuguese	French Catalan Romansch	Italian Sardinian	Romanian

Hellenic

The Hellenic branch of Indo-European has only one living member, Greek. All modern Greek dialects are descended from the classical dialect known as Attic Greek, which was the speech of Athens during the Golden Age of Greek culture (approximately 500 to 300 BC).

Hellenic Greek, which was used in subsequent centuries, was the language of commerce throughout the Middle East. (Hellenic Greek was also Cleopatra's native language; she was descended from one of Alexander the Great's generals, and Egyptian was long extinct by her time.)

Albanian

The Albanian branch of Indo-European has only one member, Albanian, which is spoken not only in Albania but also in parts of the former Yugoslavia, Greece, and Italy.

Armenian

The Armenian branch also has only one member, Armenian. This language is centred in the Republic of Armenia but is also spoken in Turkey, Iran, Syria, Lebanon, and Egypt.

Baltic

The Baltic branch contains only two surviving languages, Latvian (or Lettish) and Lithuanian. They are spoken in Latvia and Lithuania (located just west of Russia and northeast of Poland). Lithuanian has an elaborate case system, which resembles the one proposed for Proto-Indo-European.

Slavic

The Slavic branch of Indo-European can be divided into three sub-branches: East, West, and South. The East Slavic branch is made up of Russian (also called Great Russian), Ukrainian, and Belarusian (or White Russian). The latter is spoken in Belarus, which is just east of northern Poland. The West Slavic branch includes Czech, Slovak, and Polish. The South Slavic branch includes Bulgarian, Macedonian, Serbo-Croatian, and Slovene (or Slovenian).

The organization of the Slavic group of languages is represented in table 7.24.

TABLE 7.24 The Slavic family		
East Slavic	**South Slavic**	**West Slavic**
Russian	Serbo-Croatian	Polish
Ukrainian	Bulgarian	Czech
Belarusian	Macedonian	Slovak
	Slovene	

Indo-Iranian

The Indo-Iranian branch of Indo-European is divided into the Iranian and Indic sub-branches. The Iranian sub-branch contains about two dozen different languages, including Modern Persian (also called Parsi or Farsi, spoken in Iran), Pashto (the principal language of Afghanistan), and Kurdish (found in Iran, Iraq, Turkey, and Syria). Other Iranian languages are spoken in Pakistan, Afghanistan, Tajikistan, and parts of Turkey, Russia, and China.

There are about thirty-five Indic languages. Most of the languages spoken in northern India, Pakistan, and Bangladesh belong to this branch of Indo-European. Some of the most widespread (in terms of number of speakers) are Hindi-Urdu, Bengali, Marathi, and Gujarati. Although there is a high degree of mutual comprehensibility between colloquial Hindi and Urdu (sometimes jointly referred to as Hindustani), they have totally different writing systems and are associated with different cultures since the Urdu variety is spoken principally in Pakistan by Muslims while the Hindi variety is spoken primarily in India by Hindus.

A less-known Indic language is Romany, or Gypsy. It is now believed that the Gypsies (or Roma) fled to Turkey from northwestern India during the Middle Ages, after being defeated by Islamic invaders. Subsequently they spread throughout Europe: Gypsies are found as far west as Ireland and as far east as Russia. Many now also live in North America. Romany contains many borrowed words—particularly from Greek, which was widely spoken in Turkey during the Middle Ages.

Table 7.25 depicts the organization of Indo-Iranian.

TABLE 7.25 The Indo-Iranian family	
Iranian	**Indic**
Persian	Hindi-Urdu
Pashto	Bengali
Kurdish	Marathi
	Gujarati
	Romany [= Gypsy]

The map in figure 7.8 illustrates the geographic location of the Indo-European families identified in this chapter.

FIGURE 7.8
Location of Indo-European languages

1 Celtic
2 Germanic
3 Romance
4 Hellenic
5 Slavic
6 Albanian
7 Armenian
8 Indo-Iranian
9 Baltic

Solid lines indicate linguistic boundaries

Source: Adapted from Thomas Pyles and John Algeo, *Problems in the Origins and Development of the English Language*, 2nd ed., p. 84. © 1972 Heinle/Arts & Sciences, a part of Cengage Learning, Inc. Reproduced by permission. www.cengage.com/permissions.

7.3.2 Some other families

Although no introductory text could hope to present a complete survey of all of the world's language families, you can find additional information on this topic on the Companion Website. Among the families discussed there are Uralic (which includes Finnish and Hungarian), Altaic (Turkish, and possibly Japanese and Korean), Austronesian (Samoan, Fijian, Filipino, and Indonesian), Austro-Asiatic (Vietnamese and Khmer), Afro-Asiatic (Arabic and Hebrew), and Niger-Congo (Swahili), in addition to the dozens of language families indigenous to the Americas.

Not all of the world's languages have been placed in families at this point in time. Languages with no known relatives are called **isolates**. Basque (spoken in northern Spain and southwestern France), Ainu (northern Japan), Burushaski (Pakistan), Kutenai (British Columbia), Gilyak (Siberia), Tarascan (Mexico), and Yukagir (Siberia) are among the languages that are widely considered to be isolates.

7.3.3 Language phyla

In recent years, attempts have been made to place many of the world's language families in even larger groupings called **macrofamilies** or **phyla** (singular 'phylum').

One of the best known of the proposed phyla is Nostratic (also called Eurasiatic). Supposedly dating back 20 000 years, this hypothetical phylum includes Indo-European, Uralic, Altaic, and (depending on the proposal) various other languages and language families. This proposal is controversial, however, and most linguists remain very skeptical about the evidence and conclusions associated with comparative research involving a time depth greater than eight or ten thousand years because phonetic changes over longer periods obscure the similarities needed for meaningful comparative work.

Language Matters Could All Languages Be Related?

Some linguists have even gone so far as to begin reconstructing a single common ancestor for all human languages. Called Proto-World, or Proto-Sapiens, it is assumed to have been spoken approximately 60 000 to 70 000 years ago. Here is a proposed reconstruction of one word:

Proto-World *mena 'to think (about)'

Possible cognates: Latin *men(s)* 'mind', Basque *munak* (pl) 'brains', Hungarian *mon(-d)* 'say', Telugu *manavi* 'prayer, humble request', Shawnee *menw* 'prefer, like', Bambara *mɛ* 'know', Tumale *aiman* 'think', Songhai *ma* 'understand', Masa *min* 'wish'.

Work along these lines is both intriguing and entertaining, but its validity is not currently accepted by most professional linguists.

For more on this topic, read "Quest for the Mother Tongue," by Robert Wright (The Atlantic Monthly, April 1991).

Source: List of cognates compiled from information in John D. Bengtson and Merritt Ruhlen, "Global Etymologies," in On *the Origin of Languages: Studies in Linguistic Taxonomy*, edited by Merritt Ruhlen (Stanford: Stanford University Press, 1994), 312–13.

Summing up

The focus of this chapter is on the criteria that linguists use to classify languages and on the enormous variety of languages found throughout the world. Linguists sometimes attempt to classify languages solely in terms of their structural similarities and differences (that is, in terms of their **linguistic typology**). Analysis of cross-linguistic data has identified a number of **linguistic universals** indicating the most common characteristics of human language. The other major type of classificatory work in linguistics is concerned with **genetic relationships**—establishing language families such as Indo-European whose members are descended from a common ancestor. While research in this area is hampered by both the large number of languages involved and the scarcity of data, a sizable portion of the world's several thousand languages have been placed in families.

Recommended reading

Campbell, Lyle, Raina Heaton, Eve Okura, Sean Simpson, Alex Smith, and John Van Way. 2013. "New Knowledge: Findings from the Catalogue of Endangered Languages (ELCat)." Paper presented at the annual meeting of the Linguistic Society of America.

Comrie, Bernard. 1989. *Language Universals and Linguistic Typology*. 2nd ed. Oxford: Blackwell.

Croft, William. 2003. *Typology and Universals*. 2nd ed. New York: Cambridge University Press.

Dryer, Matthew S., and Martin Haspelmath, eds. 2013. *The World Atlas of Language Structures Online*. Leipzig, Germany: Max Planck Institute for Evolutionary Anthropology. Available online at wals.info. Contains information about the distribution of dozens of linguistic features in more than 2500 languages.

Lewis, M. Paul, Gary F. Simons, and Charles D. Fennig, eds. 2019. *Ethnologue: Languages of the World*. 22nd ed. Dallas, TX: SIL International. Available online at www.ethnologue.com. The most complete and up-to-date catalogue of the world's languages, locations, and speaker numbers.

Lyovin, Anatole V., Brett Kessler, William R. Leben. 2017. *An Introduction to the Languages of the World*. 2nd ed. New York: Oxford University Press.

Newmeyer, Frederick. 2008. "Universals in Syntax." *The Linguistic Review* 25: 35–82.

Palosaari, Naomi, and Lyle Campbell. 2011. "Structural Aspects of Language Endangerment." In *The Cambridge Handbook of Endangered Languages*, edited by Peter K. Austin and Julia Sallabank, 100–19. Cambridge: Cambridge University Press.

Ruhlen, Merritt. 1994. *On the Origin of Languages: Studies on Linguistic Taxonomy*. Stanford, CA: Stanford University Press.

The Case for Linguistic Diversity. 2011. *Terralingua Langscape* 2, 8.

UNESCO. 2003. "Language Vitality and Endangerment." Document submitted to the International Expert Meeting on UNESCO Programme Safeguarding of Endangered Languages, Paris, March 10–12.

Exercises

The data for exercises 1 to 3 are from Merritt Ruhlen, *A Guide to the Languages of the World* (Stanford, CA: Stanford University, Language Universals Project, 1976).

1. Which tendencies and universals are manifested in the following vowel systems?

   a) Afrikaans (South Africa) ([y] and [ø] are front rounded vowels)

i	y		u
	ø	ə	o
ɛ			ɔ
		a	

   b) Sḵwx̱wú7mesh (Squamish) (British Columbia)

i		u
	ə	
	a	

2. As noted in section 7.2.1, the presence of long and nasal vowel phonemes is governed by implicational universals. Do the vowel systems below comply with the implicational universals that make reference to length and nasality?

   a) Maltese Arabic

i	u	iː	uː
e	o	eː	oː
	a		aː

   b) Awji (North New Guinea)

i	u		ĩ	ũ
e	ə	o	ẽ	ə̃	õ
	a		ã	

3. Consider the following consonant systems. Do these consonant systems comply with the implicational universals mentioned in this chapter?

   a) Tahitian (Tahiti)

p	t	ʔ
f		h
v	r	
m	n	

   b) Palauan (Palau Islands)

	t	k	ʔ
b			
	ð		
	s		
m		ŋ	
	1, r		

   c) Nengone (Loyalty Islands, South Pacific)—Stop and nasal system only

pʰ	tʰ	ʈʰ		kʰ	ʔ
b	d	ḍ		g	
m	n		ɲ	ŋ	
m̥	n̥			ŋ̊	

   (*Note*: The diacritic [̣] indicates a retroflex consonant; [̥] marks a voiceless nasal; [ɲ] represents a palatal nasal.)

   d) Mixe (South Mexico)

p	t		k	ʔ
	d		g	
	ts	tʃ		
	s		x	h
v			ɣ	
m	n			

   (*Note*: /x/ is a voiceless velar fricative, and /ɣ/ is a voiced velar fricative)

4. Describe the morphological characteristics of the patterns in each of the following languages in terms of the four-way system of classification outlined in section 7.2.2.
   a) Siberian Yupik
      Angya-ghlla-ng-yug   -tuq.
      boat -big   -get -want-3sG
      'He wants to get a big boat.'

   b) Latvian

las-u	las-ām	rakst-u	rakst-ām
read-1SG.PRES	read-1PL.PRES	write-1SG.PRES	write-1PL.PRES
'I read'	'we read'	'I write'	'we write'

   c) Japanese
      Gakusei-wa   home-rare-na-i.
      student-TOPIC   praise-PASSIVE-NEG-PRES
      'The student is not praised.'

5. Do a morphological analysis of the following data from Latvian. After you have segmented and identified the morphemes, describe how the data reflect the implicational universals in section 7.2.2.
   a) lidotājs   'aviator (nominative)'
   b) lidotāju   'aviator (accusative)'
   c) lidotājam   'to the aviator (dative)'
   d) lidot   'to fly'
   e) rakstītājs   'writer (nominative)'
   f) rakstītāja   'writer's (genitive)'
   g) rakstīt   'to write'

6. Note the following data from Malagasy, an Austronesian language spoken on the island of Madagascar. The data are from Catherine J. Garvey, *Malagasy: Introductory Course* (Washington: Center for Applied Linguistics, 1964). Does Malagasy comply with all the word order tendencies mentioned in section 7.2.3?
   a) amin' ny restauranta
      to the restaurant
      'to the restaurant'

   b) Enti'n   ny   labiera   ny   mpiasa.
      brings   the beer   the waiter
      'The waiter brings the beer.'

   c) Avy   any   Amerika   izy.
      come   from America   he
      'He comes from America.'

To learn more about the topics discussed in this chapter, visit the Companion Website for *Contemporary Linguistic Analysis*.

Historical linguistics: the study of language change

Many men sayn that in sweveninges
Ther nys but fables and lesynges;
But men may some swevenes sene
Whiche hardely that false ne bene,
But afterwarde ben apparaunt.

CHAUCER, *THE ROMANCE OF THE ROSE* (C. 1370)

LANGUAGE CHANGE is both obvious and rather mysterious. The English of the late fourteenth century is so different from Modern English that without special training it is difficult to understand the opening lines to *The Romance of the Rose* cited above.[1] Not only would these sentences have a foreign sound, but words and structures such as *sweveninges, lesynges*, and *false ne bene* are unfamiliar. The existence of such differences between early and later variants of the same language raises questions as to how and why languages change over time.

Historical linguistics is concerned with both the description and explanation of language change. In this chapter we examine the nature and causes of language change and survey phonological, morphological, syntactic, lexical, and semantic change. We also explore techniques used to reconstruct linguistic pre-history and briefly discuss related research into language acquisition and linguistic universals.

8.1   The nature of language change

All languages change over time. English has undergone continuous and dramatic change throughout its three major periods: Old English (roughly from 450 to 1100 AD), Middle English (from 1100 to 1500), and Modern English (from 1500 to the present). Although Chaucer's Middle English is at least partially comprehensible today, Old English looks like a completely foreign language. The following is an extract from an eighth-century Old English document, a translation of Bede's Latin history of England. (The letter þ, called 'thorn', represented the phoneme /θ/ in Old English; here and elsewhere in this chapter, the symbol ˉ over a vowel marks a long vowel in the orthography.)

(1) and Seaxan þā sige geslōgan.
and Saxons the victory won
'And the Saxons won the victory.'

þā sendan hī hām ǣrenddracan.
then sent they home messenger
'Then they sent home a messenger.'

The Old English sentences in (1) differ from their Modern English counterparts in many respects. In terms of pronunciation, for instance, the Old English word *hām* [haːm] 'home' in the second sentence became [hɔːm] in Middle English, and then [howm] in Modern English. In its morphology, Old English differed significantly from Modern English. The suffix *-an* on the Old English word for 'sent' indicates both past tense and plurality of the subject (*hī* 'they'). Differences in word order are also readily apparent, with the verb following both the subject and the direct object in the first sentence and preceding both the subject and the direct object in the second. Neither of these word orders would be acceptable in the Modern English forms of these sentences.

In addition, some Old English words have disappeared from use, as the unfamiliar *ærenddracan* 'messenger' and *sige* 'victory' indicate. Still other words have been maintained, but with a change in meaning. For example, the Old English word *geslōgan* (which we translated as 'won') is the past tense of the verb *slēan*, the Old English predecessor of our word *slay*. Although the Modern English meaning of this word in normal usage is restricted to the act of killing, the Old English verb could also mean 'to strike, beat, coin (money), and forge (weapons)'. As these examples imply, all components of the grammar, from meaning (semantics) to individual sounds (phonology), are subject to change.

8.1.1 Systematicity of language change

A striking fact about language change in general is its regularity and systematicity. For example, the development of a fixed subject-verb-direct object (SVO) word order in English did not affect just a few verbs; all verbs in Modern English appear before rather than after the direct object. Similarly, the changes affecting the vowel in the word *hām* did not occur in that word only; they represent the regular development of the Old English vowel *ā* ([aː]). (See table 8.1.)

TABLE 8.1 Changes affecting Old English [aː]			
Old English	**Middle English**	**Modern English**	
[baːt]	[bɔːt]	[bowt]	'boat'
[aːθ]	[ɔːθ]	[owθ]	'oath'
[staːn]	[stɔːn]	[stown]	'stone'

8.1.2 **Causes of language change**

The inevitability of language change is guaranteed by the way in which language is passed on from one generation to the next. Children must learn the language of their parents based on their exposure to it. In such a situation, it is hardly surprising that differences arise, even if only subtle ones, from one generation to the next. Moreover, since all children draw on the same physiological and cognitive endowment in learning language, it is to be expected that the same patterns of change will be consistently and repeatedly manifested in all languages. Following is a brief overview of the principal causes of language change.

Articulatory simplification

As might be expected, most sound changes have a physiological basis. Since such sound changes typically result in **articulatory simplification**, they have traditionally been related to the idea of 'ease of articulation'. Although this notion is difficult to define precisely, we can readily identify cases of articulatory simplification in our everyday speech, such as the deletion of a consonant in a complex cluster or, in some dialects, the insertion of a vowel to break up a complex cluster (see table 8.2).

TABLE 8.2 Simplification of complex clusters		
Deletion of a consonant		
[fɪfθs] →	[fɪfs]	'fifths'
Insertion of a vowel		
[æθlit] →	[æθəlit]	'athlete'

Spelling pronunciation

Not all changes in pronunciation have a physiological motivation. A minor, but nevertheless important, source of change in English and other languages is **spelling pronunciation**. Since the written form of a word can differ significantly from the way it is pronounced, a new pronunciation can arise that seems to reflect more closely the spelling of the word. A case in point is the word *often*. Although this word was pronounced with a [t] in earlier English, the voiceless stop was subsequently lost, resulting in the pronunciation [ɑfən] (parallel to *soften*). However, since the letter *t* was retained in the spelling, [t] has been reintroduced into many speakers' pronunciation of this word.

Another case in point is the pronunciation of [s] in words such as *assume* and *consume*. Although in earlier English, such words were pronounced with [s], the presence of the high vowel [u] resulted in a pronunciation with [ʃ] (still heard in *assure*). However, similar to the case of *often* above, the influence of the spelling (which remained unchanged) led to the reintroduction of the pronunciation with [s].

Analogy and reanalysis

Cognitive factors also play a role in change in all components of the grammar. Two sources of change that have a cognitive basis are **analogy** and **reanalysis**. Analogy reflects the preference of speakers for regular patterns over irregular ones. It typically involves the extension or generalization of a regularity on the basis of the inference that if elements are alike in some respects, they should be alike in others as well. Both phonological and semantic characteristics can serve as a basis for analogy. For example, on the basis of its phonological similarity with verbs such as *sting/stung* and *swing/swung*, in some dialects the form *brung* has emerged as the past tense of *bring*, as in *I brung it into the house*. The effects of analogy can also be observed in the speech of children, who often generalize the regular *-ed* past tense form to produce forms such as *goed* and *knowed*. As we will see shortly, analogy plays a very important role in morphological change as well.

Reanalysis is particularly common in morphological change. Morphological reanalysis typically involves an attempt to attribute a compound or root + affix structure to a word that formerly was not broken down into component morphemes. A classic example in English is the word *hamburger*, which originally referred to a type of meat patty that derived its name from the city of Hamburg in Germany. This word has been reanalyzed as consisting of two components, *ham + burger*. The latter morpheme has since appeared in many new forms including *fishburger, chickenburger*, and even as the free morpheme *burger*. (Note that the reanalysis need not be correct. There is usually no ham in a burger—especially a *veggie burger*!)

Language contact

Another cause of language change is **language contact**. Language contact refers to the situation where speakers of a language frequently interact with the speakers of another language or dialect. As a consequence, extensive **borrowing** can occur, particularly where there are significant numbers of bilinguals or multilinguals. Although borrowing can affect all components of the grammar, the lexicon is typically most affected. English, for example, has borrowed many words from Indigenous languages, including *Canada, moccasin, totem, tomahawk, chinook, moose,* and *skunk*.

Among the effects that borrowing can have on the sound system are the introduction of new phonemes or allophones and changes in their distribution. For example, some English speakers pronounce the name of the classical composer *Bach* with the final velar fricative [x] found in the German pronunciation. If there are a significant number of borrowings from another language, a foreign segment can eventually become a new phoneme. In the early Middle English period, the London dialect had [f] but not [v] in word-initial position. The [v] was introduced later as a result of contact with other English dialects and with French, in which it did occur word-initially. This contact was a likely factor in the development of a contrast between /f/ and /v/ word-initially, as found in Modern English pairs such as *file* and *vile*.

Language (as well as dialect) contact also results in another minor but nevertheless important source of language change, **hypercorrection**. Hypercorrection occurs when a speaker who is attempting to speak another dialect or language overgeneralizes particular rules. For example, most Canadians speak a dialect in which no distinction is made between intervocalic [t] and [d] so that words such as *latter* and *ladder* are both pronounced with an intervocalic flap [ɾ]. If a speaker from such a dialect attempts to emulate the pronunciation of a speaker from another dialect who does distinguish the two stops intervocalically, hypercorrection could result in the use of intervocalic [t] in words where [d] should be used; for example, the pronunciation *pro*[t]*igy* for *pro<u>d</u>igy*.

Another example of hypercorrection is the use of *I* in constructions such as *He saw John and I*. This usage is an overgeneralization of the rule that one should use *I*, not *me*, in *John and I are going*. For some speakers, hypercorrection has resulted in the belief that all coordinate phrases (and not just those in subject position) require *I*.

8.2 Sound change

Although all components of the grammar are susceptible to change over time, some types of change yield more obvious results than others. Variation and change are particularly noticeable in the phonology of a language. Several common types of sound change can be distinguished.

Most sound changes begin as subtle alterations in the sound pattern of a language in particular phonetic environments. The linguistic processes underlying such **phonetically conditioned** change are identical to the ones found in the phonology of currently spoken languages. The application of such processes usually brings about an articulatory simplification, and over time, significant changes in the phonology of a language can result.

Although all aspects of a language's phonology (e.g., tone, stress, and syllable structure) are subject to change over time, we will restrict our attention here to change involving segments.

8.2.1 Change based on articulatory factors

Most sound changes are based on articulatory factors such as voicing, place or manner of articulation, and so on. Table 8.3 lists many of the most common articulation-based changes.

TABLE 8.3 Sound changes based on articulatory factors	
Assimilation	**Weakening and deletion**
Place assimilation	*Vowels*
Manner assimilation	Vowel reduction
Palatalization	Syncope
Affrication	Apocope
Nasalization	*Consonants*
Umlaut	Degemination
Voicing assimilation	Voicing
Dissimilation	Frication
Epenthesis	Deaffrication
Metathesis	Rhotacism
	Deletion

Assimilation

The most common type of change based on articulatory factors is **assimilation**, which has the effect of increasing the efficiency of articulation through a simplification of articulatory movements. We will focus here on the seven types of assimilation indicated in table 8.3.

Partial assimilation involving **place** or **manner of articulation** is a very common change that, over time, can result in total assimilation. In the Spanish and Latin examples in table 8.4, the nasal assimilated in place of articulation to the following consonant.

TABLE 8.4 Assimilation (place of articulation) in Spanish and Latin[2]				
Old Spanish	se<u>md</u>a	Modern Spanish	se<u>nd</u>a	'path'
Early Latin	i<u>np</u>ossibilis	Later Latin	i<u>mp</u>ossibilis	'impossible'

The first of the Old English examples in table 8.5 shows **voicing assimilation** and the second illustrates nasal assimilation (with /f/ becoming /m/ in front of /n/).

TABLE 8.5 Assimilation in Old English		
Early Old English	**Later Old English**	
slæ<u>pd</u>e	slæ<u>pt</u>e	'slept'
ste<u>fn</u>	ste<u>mn</u>	'stem (of a plant)'

In the Italian examples in table 8.6, a stop assimilated totally to a following stop, resulting in a geminate, or extra long, consonant.

TABLE 8.6 Total assimilation in Italian		
Latin	**Italian**	
o<u>ct</u>o (*c* = [k])	o<u>tt</u>o	'eight'
se<u>pt</u>em	se<u>tt</u>e	'seven'
da<u>mn</u>um	da<u>nn</u>o	'damage'

Another type of assimilation is **palatalization**—the effect that front vowels and the palatal glide [j] typically have on velar, alveolar, and dental stops, making their place of articulation more palatal. If you compare your pronunciation of *keep* and *cot*, you will notice that the pronunciation of [k] in *keep* is much more palatal than in *cot* due to the influence of [i]. Palatalization is often the first step in **affrication**, a change in which palatalized stops become affricates: [ts] or [tʃ] if the original stop was voiceless, and [dz] or [dʒ] if the original stop was voiced (see table 8.7).

TABLE 8.7 Palatalization/affrication induced by front vowels and [j]					
Examples from the Romance languages					
Latin	<u>c</u>entum [k]	Italian	<u>c</u>ento	[tʃ]	'one hundred'
Latin	me<u>d</u>ius [d]	Italian	me<u>zz</u>o	[dz]	'half'
Latin	<u>g</u>entem [g]	Old French	<u>g</u>ent	[dʒ]	'people'

Nasalization refers to the nasalizing effect that a nasal consonant can have on an adjacent vowel. This change occurred in both French and Portuguese, with the subsequent loss of the nasal consonant. (The pronunciation of the vowels in the examples in table 8.8 underwent additional changes in French.)

TABLE 8.8 Nasalization in Portuguese and French			
Latin	**Portuguese**	**French**	
bon-	bom [bõ]	bon [bɔ̃]	'good'
un-	um [ũ]	un [œ̃]	'one'

Although assimilation is probably most common in the case of adjacent segments, it can also apply at a distance. A case in point is **umlaut**, the effect that a vowel or sometimes a glide in one syllable can have on the vowel of another syllable, usually a preceding one. Umlaut (resulting in the front rounded vowels [y] and [ø]) played an important role in Old English and is the source of irregular plurals such as *goose/geese* and *mouse/mice* in Modern English. The plural of the pre-Old English words *gōs* 'goose' and *mūs* 'mouse' was formed by adding the suffix [-i]. As a result, umlaut of the vowel in the preceding syllable occurred in the plural forms (see pre-Old English stages 1 and 2 in table 8.9) but not in the singular forms. By early Old English, the suffix [-i] had been lost in a separate change, leaving the umlauted vowel as the marker of the plural form. (Subsequent changes included the derounding of the umlauted vowels [ȳ] and [ø̄], yielding [ī] and [ē] respectively by Middle English, and the Great Vowel Shift as described in section 8.2.3.)

TABLE 8.9 Umlaut in English Plurals							
Pre-Old English 1		**Pre-OE 2**		**Early OE**		**Modern English, after subsequent changes**	
[gōs]	>	[gōs]	>	[gōs]	>	[gus]	'goose'
[gōsi]	>	[gø̄si]	>	[gø̄s]	>	[gis]	'geese'
[mūs]	>	[mūs]	>	[mūs]	>	[maws]	'mouse'
[mūsi]	>	[mȳsi]	>	[mȳs]	>	[majs]	'mice'
Note: It is traditional in historical linguistics to use the sign > to mean 'changed into'.							

Dissimilation

Dissimilation, the process whereby one segment is made less like another segment in its environment, is much less frequent than assimilation. This type of change typically occurs when it would be difficult to articulate or perceive two similar sounds in close proximity. The word *anma* 'soul' in Late Latin, for example, was modified to *alma* in Spanish, thereby avoiding two consecutive nasal consonants. Like assimilation, dissimilation can also operate at a distance to affect non-adjacent segments. For instance, the Latin word *arbor* 'tree' became *arbol* in Spanish and *albero* in Italian, thereby avoiding two instances of *r* in adjacent syllables. (By contrast, dissimilation did not occur in French, where *arbre* has retained both instances of *r*.)

Epenthesis

Another common sound change, **epenthesis**, involves the insertion of a consonant or vowel into a particular environment (see table 8.10). In some cases, epenthesis results from the anticipation of an upcoming sound.

TABLE 8.10 Epenthesis in Old English

Earlier form	Change			Later form	
ga<u>nr</u>a	VnrV	>	VndrV	ga<u>ndr</u>a	'gander'
si<u>ml</u>e	VmlV	>	VmblV	si<u>mbl</u>e	'always'
æ<u>mt</u>ig	VmtV	>	VmptV	æ<u>mpt</u>ig	'empty'

In these examples, the epenthetic [d], [b], and [p] have the place of articulation of the preceding nasal but agree with the following segment in terms of voice and nasality. The epenthetic segment therefore serves as a bridge for the transition between the segments on either side (see table 8.11).

TABLE 8.11 The nature of epenthesis

[m]	[b]	[l]	[m]	[p]	[t]
labial	labial	non-labial	labial	labial	non-labial
nasal	non-nasal	non-nasal	nasal	non-nasal	non-nasal
voiced	voiced	voiced	voiced	voiceless	voiceless

In other cases, vowel epenthesis serves to break up a sequence of sounds that would otherwise be difficult to pronounce or even inconsistent with the phonotactic patterns of the language. As mentioned above, some English speakers avoid [θl] clusters by inserting an epenthetic [ə] in their pronunciation of words such as *athlete* as *ath*[ə]*lete*. In the history of Spanish, word-initial [sk] clusters were avoided by adding a vowel before the cluster (see table 8.12).

TABLE 8.12	Examples of epenthesis			
Latin	s<u>ch</u>ola [sk]	Spanish	<u>e</u>scuela [esk]	'school'
Latin	<u>scr</u>ībere [sk]	Spanish	<u>e</u>scribir [esk]	'write'

Metathesis

Metathesis involves a change in the relative positioning of segments. This change, like assimilation and dissimilation, can affect adjacent segments (see table 8.13) or segments at a distance.

TABLE 8.13	Metathesis of adjacent segments in Old English	
Earlier form	**Later form**	
wæ<u>ps</u>	wæ<u>sp</u>	'wasp'
þ<u>ri</u>dda	þ<u>ir</u>dda	'third'

Metathesis at a distance is found in the change from Latin *mīrāculum* 'miracle' to Spanish *milagro*, in which [r] and [l] have changed places although they were not adjacent (see figure 8.1).

FIGURE 8.1
Metathesis of non-adjacent segments in Spanish

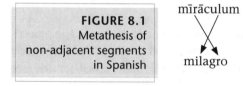

Language Matters Metathesis in Sign Language

Although users of signed languages do not use their oral articulators to produce speech sounds, they do nonetheless *articulate*. The difference is that they use the shape, position, and orientation of the hands to create meaning. These gestures are subject to processes very much like the ones found in speech. For example, the sign for *deaf* in American Sign Language was originally made by touching the jaw beside the ear with the index finger, and then touching the cheek beside the mouth. Over time, the order was reversed (cheek, then jaw), especially when following a sign that ended near the jaw. Today, both versions are acceptable.

Weakening and deletion

Both vowels and consonants are also susceptible to outright **deletion** as well as to various **weakening** processes. We will first treat the effects of these processes on vowels and then turn to their effects on consonants.

Vowel deletion commonly involves a word-final vowel (**apocope**) or a word-internal vowel (**syncope**) (see table 8.14). A vowel in an unstressed syllable is particularly susceptible to deletion, especially when a nearby neighbouring syllable is stressed.

TABLE 8.14   Vowel deletion in French

Apocope

Latin	*French*	
cúra	cure [kyʁ]	'cure'
ōrnáre	orner	'decorate'

Syncope

Latin	*French*	
pérdere	perdre	'lose'
vívere	vivre	'live'

Language Matters **Frequency Contributes to Shortening**

More frequent words are, in general, more likely to have a shortened pronunciation than are less common words. That's why the middle vowel in *every* is far more likely to be dropped than the middle vowel in *summery* (in the sense of 'summerlike'). Words such as *memory* and *family*, which are intermediate in frequency, permit more variation in terms of whether the middle vowel is lost or retained.

Vowel deletion is commonly preceded by **vowel reduction**, in which a full vowel is reduced to a schwa-like vowel (i.e., short lax central [ə]). Vowel reduction typically affects short vowels in unstressed syllables and may affect all or only a subset of the full vowels (see figure 8.2).

FIGURE 8.2
Vowel reduction

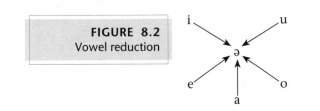

Vowel reduction with subsequent deletion (syncope and apocope) occurred in Middle English and Early Modern English, as shown in table 8.15.

TABLE 8.15 Vowel reduction and deletion in English

Syncope

Old English		Middle English (vowel reduction)		Early Modern English (syncope)	
stānas (pl)	[a]	stones	[ə]	stones	Ø
stānes (poss)	[e]	stones	[ə]	stone's	Ø

Apocope

Old English		Middle English (vowel reduction)		Early Modern English (apocope)	
nama	[a]	nāme	[ə]	name	Ø
talu	[u]	tāle	[ə]	tale	Ø

Note: The vowel [a] in the first syllable of Old English *nama* and *talu* underwent vowel lengthening. The Middle English long vowels were subsequently affected by the Great English Vowel Shift (see section 8.2.3).

Consonant deletion is also a very common sound change. For example, the word-initial cluster [kn] was found in Old and Middle English, as the spelling of such words as *knight, knit, knot*, and *knee* implies, but the [k] was subsequently lost, giving us our modern pronunciation. The loss of word-final consonants has played a major role in the evolution of Modern French. The final letters in the written forms of the words in table 8.16 reflect consonants that were actually pronounced at an earlier stage of the language.

TABLE 8.16 Consonant loss in French

French spelling (masculine form)	Current pronunciation	
gros	[gro]	'large'
chaud	[ʃo]	'warm'
vert	[vɛr]	'green'

Just as vowel reduction can be identified as a weakening process since it represents an intermediate step on the pathway from a full vowel to deletion of the vowel, so too can pathways of **consonant weakening** be identified. The scale of **consonantal strength** in figure 8.3 can be helpful in identifying cases of weakening.

FIGURE 8.3
Scale of consonantal strength

Consonantal strength

stronger ↑ voiceless stops
voiceless fricatives, voiced stops
voiced fricatives
nasals
liquids
weaker ↓ glides

Note: Geminate, or long, consonants are stronger than their non-geminate counterparts.

Geminates weaken to non-geminates (**degemination**), stops weaken to fricatives (**frication**), and voiceless stops or voiceless fricatives weaken to voiced stops or voiced fricatives, respectively (**voicing**).[3] Weakening can ultimately result in the deletion of the consonant. Figure 8.4 is a typical pathway of weakening. (We use a double consonant here to represent gemination.)

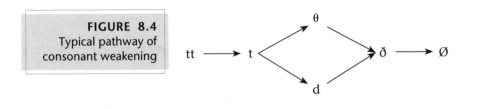

FIGURE 8.4
Typical pathway of consonant weakening

Consonants are particularly subject to weakening in an intervocalic environment. Parts of the pathway of consonantal weakening are exemplified in table 8.17 with developments from the Romance languages.

TABLE 8.17   Consonantal weakening in Romance

Degemination (tt > t):	Latin	mi<u>tt</u>ere	Spanish	me<u>t</u>er	'to put'
Voicing (t > d):	Latin	mā<u>t</u>ūrus	Old Spanish	ma<u>d</u>uro	'ripe'
Frication (d > ð):	Old Spanish	ma<u>d</u>uro	Spanish	ma<u>d</u>uro [ð]	'ripe'
Deletion (ð > Ø):	Old French	[maðyr]	French	mûr	'ripe'

Rhotacism is a relatively common type of weakening that typically involves the change of [z] to [r]. Often rhotacism is preceded by a stage involving the voicing of [s] to [z]. Within the Germanic family of languages, for instance, [s] first became [z] in a particular intervocalic environment. This [z] remained in Gothic but became [r] in other Germanic languages such as English, German, and Swedish. The effects of the latter part of this change can be seen in the standard spellings of the words in table 8.18.

TABLE 8.18   Rhotacism in English, German, and Swedish

Gothic	English	German	Swedish
maiza	more	mehr	mera
diuzam	deer	Tier	djur
huzd	hoard	Hort	—

In Modern English, rhotacism is the source of the alternation between [z] and [r] in *was* and *were*. The [r] resulted from earlier [z], which was originally intervocalic.

Deaffrication

Segments such as affricates are considered to be complex sounds because they represent the fusing of a stop plus a fricative into a single segment: e.g., [dʒ] or [ts]. Such complex segments are commonly subject to simplification (a type of weakening). A very common type of segmental simplification is **deaffrication**, which has the effect of turning affricates into fricatives by eliminating the stop portion of the affricate (see table 8.19).

TABLE 8.19	Deaffrication in French					
Old French	<u>c</u>ent	[ts]	French	<u>c</u>ent	[s]	'one hundred'
Old French	<u>g</u>ent	[dʒ]	French	<u>g</u>ent	[ʒ]	'people, tribe'

Since deaffrication of [tʃ] (or [dʒ]) has not occurred in English, early borrowings from French maintain the affricate, while later borrowings have a fricative (see table 8.20).

TABLE 8.20	Borrowing from French
Early borrowings (before deaffrication occurred in French)	
Old French [tʃ]	***English*** [tʃ]
<u>ch</u>aiere	<u>ch</u>air
<u>ch</u>aine	<u>ch</u>ain
Note: Compare Modern French [ʃ] in <u>*chaire*</u> 'throne, seat' and <u>*chaîne*</u> 'chain'.	
Later borrowings (after deaffrication occurred in French)	
Modern French [ʃ]	***English*** [ʃ]
<u>ch</u>andelier	<u>ch</u>andelier
<u>ch</u>auffeur	<u>ch</u>auffeur

8.2.2 Change based on auditory factors

Although articulatory factors (particularly relating to 'ease of articulation') are of central importance in sound change, as indicated in the discussion above, auditory factors also play a role. **Substitution** is a type of auditorily-based change involving the replacement of one segment with another similar-sounding segment. A common type of substitution involves [f] replacing other voiceless non-strident fricatives, such as velar [x] and interdental [θ]. Earlier in the history of English, [f] replaced [x] in some words in standard varieties of English while [f] replaced [θ] in Cockney, a non-standard dialect spoken in London (see table 8.21).

TABLE 8.21	Auditorily based substitution			
[x] > [f]	Middle English	laugh [x]	Standard English	laugh [f]
[θ] > [f]	English	thin [θ]	Cockney English	[fɪn]

So far we have treated sound changes without consideration of their effect on the sound pattern of the particular language as a whole. All the foregoing sound changes can lead both to new types of allophonic variation and to the addition or loss of phonemic contrasts. Examples of such cases are presented in the next section.

8.2.3 Phonetic versus phonological change

The sound changes outlined in the previous sections can affect the overall sound pattern (phonology) of a language in different ways. Commonly, the first stage of a sound change results in the creation of a new allophone of an already existing phoneme. The term **phonetic sound change** can be used to refer to this stage.

A good example of phonetic sound change involves the laxing of high vowels that has developed in Canadian French (see table 8.22). This change can be seen in closed word-final syllables, among other environments.

TABLE 8.22	Vowel laxing in Canadian French	
European French	**Canadian French**	
Closed syllable		
[vit]	[vɪt]	'quick'
[libʁ]	[lɪbʁ]	'free'
[ekut]	[ekʊt]	'listen'
[pus]	[pʊs]	'thumb'
Open Syllable		
[vi]	[vi]	'life'
[li]	[li]	'bed'
[vu]	[vu]	'you'
[lu]	[lu]	'wolf'

Whereas Canadian French has the lax vowels [ɪ] and [ʊ] in closed word-final syllables, European French has kept the tense vowels [i] and [u]. Both dialects of French retain [i] and [u] in open syllables. This suggests that Canadian French has developed the rule in figure 8.5.

FIGURE 8.5
Vowel laxing rule in Canadian French

$$\begin{bmatrix} V \\ +high \\ +tense \end{bmatrix} \rightarrow [-tense] \ / \ \_\_C\,(C)\,\#$$

Although this rule did introduce an allophone not present in European French, it did not create any new phonemes because there was no contrast between lax vowels and their tense counterparts in Canadian French.[4]

Splits

Sometimes sound change can lead to changes in a language's phonological system by adding, eliminating, or rearranging phonemes. Such **phonological change** can involve **splits**, **mergers**, or **shifts**.

In a phonological split, allophones of the same phoneme come to contrast with each other, often because of the loss of the conditioning environment, with the result that one or more new phonemes are created. The English phoneme /ŋ/ was the result of a phonological split (see table 8.23). Originally, [ŋ] was simply the allophone of /n/ that appeared before a velar consonant. During Middle English, consonant deletion resulted in the loss of [g] in word-final position after a nasal consonant, leaving [ŋ] as the final sound in words such as *sing*.

TABLE 8.23 Phonological split resulting in /ŋ/	
Original phonemic form	/sɪng/
Original phonetic form	[sɪŋg]
Deletion of [g]	[sɪŋg] > [sɪŋ]
New phonemic form	/sɪŋ/

The loss of the word-final [g] created minimal pairs such as *sin* (/sɪn/) and *sing* (/sɪŋ/), in which there is a contrast between /n/ and /ŋ/. This example represents a typical phonological split. When the conditioning environment of an allophonic variant of a phoneme is lost through sound change, the allophone is no longer predictable and thus becomes contrastive (i.e., phonemic). The original phoneme (in figure 8.6, /n/) splits into two phonemes (/n/ and /ŋ/).

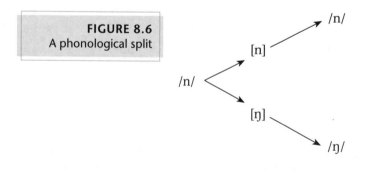

FIGURE 8.6
A phonological split

Mergers

In a phonological merger, two or more phonemes collapse into a single one, thereby reducing the number of phonemes in the language. The case of auditorily-based substitution discussed above has this effect in Cockney English, where all instances of the interdental fricative /θ/ have become /f/ (see figure 8.7). Consequently, the phonemes /θ/ and /f/ have merged into /f/ and words such as *thin* and *fin* have the same phonological form (/fɪn/). Similarly, /v/ and /ð/ have merged (e.g., /smuv/ for *smooth*).

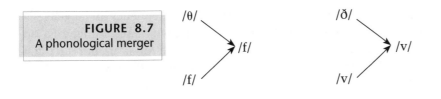

FIGURE 8.7
A phonological merger

Shifts

A phonological shift is a change in which a series of phonemes is systematically modified so that their organization with respect to each other is altered. A well-known example of such a change is called the **Great English Vowel Shift**. Beginning in the Middle English period and continuing into the eighteenth century, the language underwent a series of modifications to its long vowels (see table 8.24).

TABLE 8.24   The Great English Vowel Shift

Middle English	Great Vowel Shift			Modern English	
/tiːd/	/iː/	>	/aj/	/tajd/	'tide'
/luːd/	/uː/	>	/aw/	/lawd/	'loud'
/geːs/	/eː/	>	/iː/	/gis/	'geese'
/sɛː/	/ɛː/	>	/iː/	/si/	'sea'
/goːs/	/oː/	>	/uː/	/gus/	'goose'
/brɔːkən/	/ɔː/	>	/oː/	/brokən/	'broken'
/naːmə/	/aː/	>	/eː/	/nem/	'name'

Figure 8.8 illustrates the changes that gradually affected the English long vowels.

FIGURE 8.8
Changes brought about by the Great English Vowel Shift

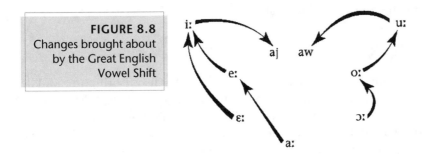

Another well-known shift, Grimm's Law, is discussed later, in section 8.7.3.

8.2.4 Explaining phonological shift

The causes and even the details of the Great English Vowel Shift remain unclear. In fact, the causes of phonological shift in general are not well understood. A possible motivation in some cases may involve the notion of phonological space. Although the vowel systems of languages can be arranged in various ways (see chapter 7), there is a tendency for languages to maximize the use of space in the vowel quadrangle (i.e., the oral cavity). Accordingly, if a language has only three vowel phonemes, they will likely be /i/, /a/, and /o/ or /u/, not (for example) /i/, /e/, /ɛ/. Similarly, if a language has five vowel phonemes, they will typically be distributed throughout the phonological space as /i/, /e/, /a/, /o/, /u/ rather than, say, /u/, /ʊ/, /a/, /o/, /ɔ/ (see figure 8.9).

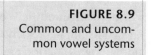
FIGURE 8.9
Common and uncommon vowel systems

a. Typical distribution of vowels in phonological space

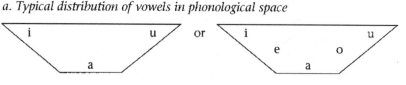

b. Atypical distribution of vowels in phonological space

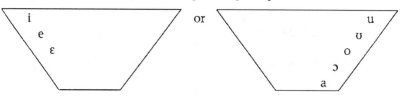

Languages with seven (or more) vowels (e.g., English at the starting point of the Great English Vowel Shift illustrated in figure 8.8) often undergo **diphthongization**. This can be seen as a reaction to the overcrowding of the phonological space, since the effect of the diphthongization of a pair of vowels is to reduce a seven-vowel system to a five-vowel system. (Think of the two diphthongs as not infringing on the space of the simple vowels.)

8.3 Morphological change

In this section, we discuss morphological changes resulting from analogy and reanalysis as well as changes involving the addition or loss of affixes.

8.3.1 Addition of affixes

Borrowing has been a very important source of new affixes in English. During the Middle English period, many French words containing the suffix *-ment* (e.g., *accomplishment, commencement*) made their way into the language. Eventually, *-ment* established itself as a productive suffix in English and was used with bases that were not of French origin (e.g., *acknowledgement, merriment*). The ending *-able*, which converts a verb into an adjective (e.g., *readable, lovable*, etc.), followed a similar pattern. Although words with this ending (e.g., *favourable, conceivable*) were initially borrowed into English as whole units, eventually the suffix became productive and was used with new bases.

Not all new affixes are the result of borrowing. Lexical forms can become grammatical forms over time through a process called **grammaticalization**. Grammaticalized forms often undergo dramatic phonological reduction, as well as semantic change in which they can lose much of their original content; for example, the Latin word *habeō* '(I) have, hold, grasp' is the source of the Italian future suffix *-ō*. In the first stage of grammaticalization, *habeō* remained an independent word but underwent semantic reduction and functioned as an auxiliary verb indicating future tense: for example, *amāre habeō* 'I will love'. When two words are frequently adjacent, over time they can become fused together to form a single unit consisting of a base and an affix. This specific type of grammaticalization, where words develop into affixes (either prefixes or suffixes), is called **fusion** (see table 8.25).

TABLE 8.25 Fusion		
word word	>	base + affix (suffixation)
word word	>	affix + base (prefixation)

A number of Modern English suffixes have been derived from earlier words by means of fusion (see table 8.26).

TABLE 8.26   English suffixes resulting from fusion

Suffix		Old English word	
-hood (childhood)	<	hād	'state, condition, rank'
-dom (freedom)	<	dōm	'condition, power'
-ly (fatherly)	<	(ge-)līc	'similar, equal, like'

8.3.2 Loss of affixes

Just as affixes can be added to the grammar, they can also be lost. Sometimes affixes simply fall into disuse for no apparent reason. For example, a number of Old English derivational affixes, including *-oþ* and *-estre*, are no longer used (see table 8.27).

TABLE 8.27 Affixes no longer found in English		
V + oþ	>	N (e.g., *hunt-oþ* 'hunting' from *hunt-ian* 'to hunt')
V + estre	>	N (e.g., *luf-estre* 'lover' from *luf-ian* 'to love')

It is also very common for affixes to be lost through sound change. For example, Old English had a complex system of affixes marking case and gender. Nouns were divided into three gender classes—**masculine, neuter,** and **feminine.** Assignment to a class was based on grammatical gender; for example, the word for *stone* (Old English *stān*) and even a word for *woman* (*wīfmann*) were masculine, the word for *sun* (*sunne*) was feminine, and another word for *woman* (*wīf*) was neuter. Each gender class was associated with a different set of case endings (see table 8.28).

TABLE 8.28   Old English case affixes

	Masculine	Neuter	Feminine
	hund 'dog'	dēor 'animal'	gief 'gift'
Singular			
Nominative	hund	dēor	gief-u
Accusative	hund	dēor	gief-e
Genitive	hund-es	dēor-es	gief-e
Dative	hund-e	dēor-e	gief-e
Plural			
Nominative	hund-as	dēor	gief-a
Accusative	hund-as	dēor	gief-a
Genitive	hund-a	dēor-a	gief-a
Dative	hund-um	dēor-um	gief-um

The following Old English sentence contains all four case categories.

(2) Se cniht   geaf   gief-e   þæs hierd-es   sun-e.
    the youth-NOM   gave   gift-ACC   the shepherd-GEN   son-DAT
    'The youth gave a gift to the shepherd's son.'

By the fifteenth century, English case endings had changed radically. Consonant deletion resulted in the loss of the earlier [m] of the dative plural suffix, and through vowel reduction, all the unstressed vowels of the case endings were reduced to the short lax vowel [ə] (which was later lost through vowel deletion). Consequently, many of the earlier case and gender distinctions were obliterated. (The examples in table 8.29 also include changes to the stem-internal vowels as the result of various processes, including the Great English Vowel Shift.)

TABLE 8.29   The loss of case affixes through sound change (in English *hound*)

	Old English	Middle English (e = [ə])	Modern English
Singular			
Nominative	hund	hund	hound
Accusative	hund	hund	hound
Genitive	hund-es	hund-(e)s	hound's
Dative	hund-e	hund-(e)	hound
Plural			
Nominative	hund-as	hund-(e)s	hounds
Accusative	hund-as	hund-(e)s	hounds
Genitive	hund-a	hund-(e)	hounds'
Dative	hund-um	hund-(e)	hounds

Whereas Old English had five distinct suffixes for cases, Middle English had only two suffixes, -*e* and -*es*, which, with the loss of schwa, were ultimately reduced to a single suffix -*s*, still used in Modern English for the plural and the possessive. This represents a typical example of how sound change can result in modification to the morphological component of the grammar.

8.3.3 From synthetic to analytic to synthetic

Since languages vary greatly in the complexity of their morphology, linguists often make a distinction between **analytic** and **synthetic** languages. Whereas analytic languages have very few inflectional affixes (e.g., Modern English), synthetic languages have many (e.g., Latin, Old English).

Even in the absence of borrowing, sound change and fusion ensure that there is an endless transition in the morphology of a language over time. As we have seen, due to the loss of case endings through sound change, English has developed from a synthetic language with many inflectional affixes to a more analytic one with very few, as the above discussion of nouns such as *hound* indicates.

By contrast, fusion ensures the rise of new synthetic forms. Fusion can be observed in some Modern English dialects in forms such as *coulda* (e.g., *I coulda won*), which represents the fusion of *could* and *have*. For many speakers, the -*a* is treated as a suffix that is no longer related to *have*, as evident in spellings such as *coulda*. Through fusion, a language with an analytic morphology can become more synthetic over time.

8.3.4 Analogy

The drastic effects that sound change can have on the morphology of a language are often alleviated through analogy. For example, the plural of Old English *hand* 'hand' was *handa*. Vowel reduction and apocope applying to *handa* would have yielded a Modern English plural form identical to the singular form, namely *hand* (see table 8.30).

TABLE 8.30   Potential sound changes applied to Old English *handa* 'hands'

handa	
handə	vowel reduction
hand	apocope

The Modern English plural *hands* is obviously not the consequence of sound change. Rather, it is the result of earlier analogy with words such as Middle English *hund* 'hound' (see table 8.29), which formed the plural with the suffix -*s*. This suffix, whose earlier form -*as* was predominant even in Old English, was extended by analogy to all English nouns with a few exceptions (such as *oxen, men, geese,* etc.). Other plural forms besides *hands* that were created on the basis of analogy include *eyes* (*eyen* in Middle English) and *shoes* (formerly *shooen*).

Continuing analogy along these lines is responsible for the development of the plural form *youse* (from *you*) in some English dialects. Each generation of English-speaking children temporarily extends the analogy still further by producing forms such as *sheeps*, *gooses*, and *mouses*. To date, however, these particular innovations have not been accepted by adult speakers of Standard English and are eventually abandoned by young language learners.

8.3.5 Reanalysis

As mentioned in section 8.1.2, reanalysis can result in a new morphological structure for a word. It can affect both borrowed words and, particularly in cases where the morphological structure of the word is no longer transparent, native words. Reanalysis can result in new productive patterns (as in the case of *burger*, discussed in section 8.1.2) or it can remain quite isolated, affecting perhaps only one word. Since the type of reanalysis exemplified by *hamburger* is not based on a correct analysis of a word (at least from a historical perspective) and does not usually involve a conscious or detailed study of the word on the part of the speaker, it is often called **folk etymology** (see table 8.31).

TABLE 8.31 Folk etymology in English (native words and borrowings)	
Modern word	**Source**
belfry	Middle English *berfrey* 'bell tower' (unrelated to *bell*)
bridegroom	Middle English *bridegome* (unrelated to *groom*; cf. Old English *brȳd* 'bride' and *guma* 'man')
muskrat	Algonquian *musquash* (unrelated to either *musk* or *rat*)
woodchuck	Cree *otchek* (unrelated to either *wood* or *chuck*)

In other cases, folk etymology commonly involves changes in pronunciation that reflect the new morphological analysis. For example, the Modern English word *earwig* derives from Old English *ēarwicga* [ǽərwidʒa], a compound consisting of 'ear' and 'insect'. Taking into consideration sound change alone, the expected Modern English pronunciation of this word would be *earwidge* [ɪrwɪdʒ]. However, the second part of the compound was lost as an independent word by Middle English, so speakers could no longer associate it with the meaning of 'insect'. Subsequently, reanalysis associated the second part of the compound with the verb 'wiggle', resulting in Middle English *arwygyll* (literally 'ear + wiggle'). The end result is Modern English *-wig* and not *-widge*.

Although reanalysis of individual words is common, affixes can also be affected, sometimes with new productive morphological rules developing as a result. This is the case of the Modern English adverbial suffix *-ly* (from Old English *-lic-e*). In Old English, adjectives could be derived from nouns by adding the suffix *-lic*. Adverbs, in turn, could be derived by adding the suffix *-e* to adjectives (including those derived with *-lic*) (see table 8.32). At some point, the entire complex suffix *-lic+e* was reanalyzed as an adverbial suffix (rather than as an adjectival suffix *-lic* plus an adverbial suffix *-e*). It was then used by analogy to derive adverbs from adjectives in forms where it was not used before, resulting in Modern English *deeply* and other such words.

TABLE 8.32 The derivation of Old English adjectives and adverbs

Formation of an adjective from a noun				
dægN	+ -lic	→	dæglicA	'daily' (e.g., as in 'daily schedule')
Formation of an adverb from an adjective				
dēopA	+ -e	→	dēopeAdv	'deeply'
Formation of an adverb from a derived adjective with *-lic*				
dæg+licA	+ -e	→	dægliceAdv	'daily' (e.g., as in 'she ran daily')

8.4 Syntactic change

Like other components of the grammar, syntax is also subject to change over time. Syntactic changes can involve modifications to phrase structure (such as word order) and to transformations, as the following examples illustrate.

8.4.1 Word order

All languages make a distinction between the subject and direct object. This contrast is typically represented through either case marking or word order. Since Old English had an extensive system of case marking, it is not surprising that its word order was somewhat more variable than that of Modern English. In unembedded clauses, Old English placed the verb in second position (much like Modern German). Thus we find subject-verb-object order in simple transitive sentences such as the following.

(3) S   V   O
Hē   geseah þone mann.
'He saw   the man.'

When the clause began with an element such as *þa* 'then' or *ne* 'not', the verb preceded the subject as in the following example.

(4)   V   S   O
þa   sende sē cyning þone disc.
then sent   the king   the dish
'Then the king sent the dish.'

Although this word order is still found in Modern English, its use is very limited and subject to special restrictions, unlike the situation in Old English.

(5)   V S   O
       Rarely has he ever deceived me.

When the direct object was a pronoun, the subject-object-verb order was typical.

(6) S   O   V
    Hēo   hine lǣrde.
    She   him   advised
    'She advised him.'

The subject-object-verb order also prevailed in embedded clauses, even when the direct object was not a pronoun.

(7)   S   O   V
   þa   hē þone cyning sōhte, hē bēotode.
   when he the king   visited he boasted
   'When he visited the king, he boasted.'

After case suffixes were lost during the Middle English period through sound change, fixed subject-verb-object order became the means of marking grammatical relations. As table 8.33 shows, a major change in word order took place between 1300 and 1400, with the verb-object order becoming dominant.

TABLE 8.33 Word order patterns in Middle English

Year	1000	1200	1300	1400	1500
Direct object before the verb (%)	53	53	40	14	2
Direct object after the verb (%)	47	47	60	86	98

From SOV to SVO

Just as languages can be classified in terms of their morphology, they can also be grouped on the basis of the relative order of subject (S), object (O), and verb (V) in basic sentences. Almost all languages of the world fall into one of three types: SOV, SVO, or VSO, with the majority of languages being one of the first two types. Just as languages change through time from one morphological type to another, they can also change from one syntactic type to another. A case in point is found in the history of English, which shows the development from SOV to SVO syntax.

Evidence indicates that the earliest form of Germanic from which English descended was an SOV language. Indeed, this order can be seen in one of the earliest recorded Germanic sentences, which was inscribed on a golden horn (now called the Golden Horn of Gallehus) about 1600 years ago.

(8) Horn of Gallehus

			S		O	V
ek	HlewagastiR	HoltijaR			horna	tawido
I	Hlewagastir	of Holt			horn	made

'I, Hlewagastir of Holt, made the horn.'

Another type of evidence for an earlier SOV order is found in morphological fusion (see section 8.3.1). Since fusion depends on frequently occurring syntactic patterns, it can sometimes serve as an indicator of earlier syntax. The OV compound, very common in Old English (as well as in Modern English), likely reflects an earlier stage of OV word order (see table 8.34).

TABLE 8.34	Old English compounds with OV structure	
mans/æht	'man' + 'strike'	'manslaughter, murder'
æppelbǣre	'apple' + 'bear'	'apple-bearing'

If the earliest Germanic was SOV and Modern English is firmly SVO, then Old English represents a transitional syntactic type. In developing from SOV syntax to SVO syntax, languages seem to follow similar pathways. For example, Modern German, which developed from the same Germanic SOV source as English, shares two signature characteristics of Old English. Not only is the verb typically placed in the second position of the sentence in main clauses, preceded by the subject or some other element (such as an adverb), but SOV order is also employed for embedded clauses.

(9) Modern German word order

    a. Verb in second position in unembedded clauses
       (Compare the Old English sentence in [4].)

	V	S		O
Gestern	hatte	ich	keine	Zeit.
yesterday	had	I	no	time

       'I had no time yesterday.'

    b. SOV in embedded clauses
       (Compare the Old English sentence in [7].)

	S	O	V
Als	er	den Mann	sah . . .
when	he	the man	saw

       'When he saw the man . . .'

The change from SOV to SVO is not restricted to English and other Germanic languages. The same change is evident in completely unrelated languages such as those of the Bantu family of Africa. Since linguists are still not sure why languages change from one syntactic type to another, the causes of such change will undoubtedly remain an important area of investigation, especially since the relative order of verb and object (OV versus VO) has been closely linked with other word order patterns.

8.4.2 Inversion in the history of English

In Old and Middle English, Inversion (the operation that moves auxiliary verbs to the left of the subject in yes-no questions) could apply to all verbs, not just auxiliaries, yielding forms that would be unacceptable in Modern English.

>   **(10)** Speak they the truth?

During the sixteenth and seventeenth centuries, the Inversion rule was changed to apply solely to auxiliary verbs.

>   **(11)** *Inversion   (old form)*
>   Any type of verb can move to the left of the subject
>   They speak → Speak they?
>   They can speak → Can they speak?
>
>   *Inversion   (new form)*
>   Only an auxiliary verb can move to the left of subject
>   They speak → *Speak they?
>   They can speak → Can they speak?

With this change, structures such as *Speak they the truth?* were no longer possible. The corresponding question came to be formed with the auxiliary *do* as in *Do they speak the truth?*[5]

8.5 Lexical and semantic change

Another obvious type of language change involves modifications to the lexicon. Since we have already dealt with some changes relating to derivational and inflectional morphology in section 8.3, the main focus here will be on lexical change involving entire words. Simply stated, there are two possible types of lexical change: addition and loss. The addition or loss of words often reflects cultural changes that introduce novel objects and notions and that eliminate outmoded ones.

8.5.1 Addition of lexical items

Addition is frequently the result of technological innovations or contact with other cultures. Such developments result in **lexical gaps** that can be filled by adding new words to the lexicon. New words are added either through the word formation processes available to the language or through borrowing.

Word formation

The most important word formation processes are compounding and derivation, although other types, including conversion, blending, backformation, clipping, and acronyms can play a significant role.

Compounding and derivation have always been available to English speakers for the creation of new words. In fact, much of the compounding and derivation in Old English seems very familiar (see table 8.35).

TABLE 8.35 Compounding and derivation in Old English

Noun compounds

| N + N | sunbēam | 'sunbeam' |
| A + N | middelniht | 'midnight' |

Adjective compounds

| N + A | blōdrēad | 'blood-red' |
| A + A | dēadboren | 'stillborn' |

Derived nouns

| bæc$_V$ | -ere | → | bæcere | 'baker' |
| frēond$_N$ | -scipe | → | frēondscipe | 'friendship' |

Derived adjectives

| wundor$_N$ | -full | → | wundorfull | 'wonderful' |
| cild$_N$ | -isc | → | cildisc | 'childish' |

Just as speakers of Modern English can use compounding and derivational rules to create new words (e.g., the N + N compound *airhead*), so could Old English speakers create new words such as the poetic N + N compound *hwælweg*, literally 'whale' + 'path', to mean 'sea'.

Language Matters Dictionaries as Historical Records

The *Oxford English Dictionary* provides a window on language change. A lexical entry includes not only definitions of the word but also examples of how the word has been used in written documents over many years. Consider the citations for the word *linguist*:

> 1591. Shakespeare, *Two Gentlemen of Verona*. "Seeing you are beautiful, with goodly shape; and by your owne report A Linguist."
> 1695. Edwards, *Perfect Script*. "Here linguists and philologists may find that which is to be found no where else."

The Oxford English Dictionary, 2nd ed. (1989): Definition of "linguist." By permission of Oxford University Press.

Even though many Old English compounding and derivational patterns have been maintained in Modern English, words that were acceptable in Old English are not necessarily still in use in Modern English, despite the fact that they are often quite understandable (see table 8.36).

TABLE 8.36	Old English compound and derived forms that are no longer used	
Noun compounds		
N + N	bōccræft ('book' + 'craft')	'literature' (compare *witchcraft*)
A + N	dimhūs ('dim' + 'house')	'prison'
Adjective compounds		
N + A	ælfscīene ('elf' + 'beautiful')	'beautiful as a fairy'
A + A	eallgōd ('all' + 'good')	'perfectly good'
Derived nouns		
sēam$_V$ -ere → sēamere		'tailor' (compare *seamster, seamstress*)
man$_N$ -scipe → manscipe		'humanity' (compare *friendship*)
Derived adjectives		
word$_N$ -full → wordfull		'wordy' (compare *wonderful*)
heofon$_N$ -isc → heofonisc		'heavenly' (compare *childish*)

Not all word formation processes available to Modern English speakers were found in Old English. For example, conversion (as in Modern English [summer]$_N$ → [summer]$_V$) was not possible in Old English. In fact, this process is typically not available to (synthetic) inflectional languages such as Old English, since change in a word's category in such languages is usually indicated morphologically; by definition, conversion does not involve the use of affixes.

Borrowing

As discussed in section 8.1.2, language contact over time can result in an important source of new words: borrowing. Depending on the cultural relationship holding between languages, three types of influence of one language on the other are traditionally identified: **substratum, adstratum**, and **superstratum** influence.

Substratum influence is the effect of a politically or culturally non-dominant language on a dominant language in the area. Both Canadian and American English and Canadian French, for instance, have borrowed vocabulary items from Indigenous languages (see examples in section 8.1.2). From a much earlier period in the history of English, the influence of a Celtic substratum is also evident, particularly in place names such as *Thames, London*, and *Dover*. Substratum influence does not usually have a major impact on the lexicon of the borrowing language. Borrowed words are usually restricted to place names and unfamiliar items or concepts. This situation reflects the fact that it is usually the speakers of the substratum language who inhabited the area first.

Superstratum influence is the effect of a politically or culturally dominant language on another language or languages in the area. For example, the Athabaskan language Gwich'in (spoken in Canada's Northwest Territories) has borrowed a number of governmental terms and expressions from English, including *bureaucratic, constituents, program, business, development,* and *political.*

In the case of English, Norman French had a superstratum influence. The major impact of French on the vocabulary of English is related to a historical event—the conquest of England by French-speaking Normans in 1066. As the conquerors and their descendants gradually learned English over the next decades, they retained French terms for political, judicial, and cultural notions (see table 8.37). These words were in turn borrowed by native English speakers who, in trying to gain a place in the upper middle class, were eager to imitate the speech of their social superiors. Not surprisingly, borrowing was especially heavy in the vocabulary areas pertaining to officialdom: government, the judiciary, and religion. Other areas of heavy borrowing include science, culture, and warfare.

TABLE 8.37	Some French loan words in English
Government	tax, revenue, government, royal, state, parliament, authority, prince, duke, slave, peasant
Religion	prayer, sermon, religion, chaplain, friar
Judiciary	judge, defendant, jury, evidence, jail, verdict, crime
Science	medicine, physician
Culture	art, sculpture, fashion, satin, fur, ruby
Warfare	army, navy, battle, soldier, enemy, captain

Language Matters **Getting Rid of French**

The following whimsical piece, from *The Christian Science Monitor*, gives us an idea of what English would be like without the influence of French.

> The Franco-American ~~dispute~~ *falling out* over the best ~~approach~~ *way* to ~~disarming Iraq~~ *take away Iraq's weapons* has resulted in perhaps the highest ~~level of~~ anti-French feeling in the United ~~States~~ *Lands* since 1763.
>
> A French-owned ~~hotel~~ *innkeeping* firm, Accor, has taken down the ~~tricolor~~ *three-hued* flag. In the House of ~~Representatives~~ *Burghers*, the ~~chairman~~ *leader* of the ~~Committee~~ *Body* on ~~Administration~~ *Running Things* has ~~renamed~~ *named anew* French fries "freedom fries" and French toast "freedom toast" in House ~~restaurants~~ *eating rooms*.
>
> It is time for English-speaking ~~peoples~~ *folk* to throw off this cultural ~~imperialism~~ *lording-it-over-others* and ~~declare~~ *say* our linguistic freedom. It is time to ~~purify~~ *clean* the English ~~language~~ *tongue*. It will take some ~~sacrifices~~ *hardship* on everyone's part to get used to the new ~~parlance~~ *speech*. But think of the ~~satisfaction~~ *warm feeling inside* on the day we ~~are all able to~~ *can all* stare the *Académie Française* in the eye and say without fear of ~~reprisal~~ *injury*: "Sumer is icumen in . . ."

In some cases, French loan words were used in conjunction with native English words to convey distinctions of various sorts. For a minor crime, for example, the English word *theft* was employed, but for a more serious breach of the law, the French word *larceny* was used. The English also kept their own words for domestic animals, but adopted the French words for the meat from those creatures (see table 8.38).

TABLE 8.38   French loan words used in conjunction with native English words

English origin	French origin
cow	beef
calf	veal
sheep	mutton
pig	pork

Adstratum influence refers to the situation where two languages are in contact and neither one is clearly politically or culturally dominant. In a city such as Montréal, with its large number of bilingual speakers, English and French inevitably influence each other (see table 8.39).

TABLE 8.39   French influence on Montréal English

Montréal English	
subvention	'subsidy'
metro	'subway'
autoroute	'highway'

Language Matters **Multiple Borrowings**

Languages have been known to borrow back their own words. For example, the French word *biftek* comes from the English word *beefsteak*. However, earlier, English borrowed the French word *boeuf* as *beef*.

Earlier in the history of English, when the Scandinavians settled part of England beginning in 800 AD, there was substantial contact between the speakers of English and Old Norse (from which Icelandic, Norwegian, Danish, and Swedish descended), resulting in an adstratum relationship. As evident in the examples in tables 8.39 and 8.40, adstratum contact usually results in the borrowing of common, everyday words. In fact, without consulting a dictionary, most English speakers could not distinguish between borrowings from Scandinavian languages and native English words.

TABLE 8.40   Some loan words from Old Norse and other Scandinavian languages

anger, cake, call, egg, fellow, gear, get, hit, husband, low, lump, raise, root, score, seat, skill, skin, take, their, they, thrust, ugly, window, wing

---

Borrowed words from many other languages attest to various types of cultural contact and often serve to fill the lexical gaps such contact inevitably brings (see table 8.41).

TABLE 8.41   Some lexical borrowings into English

Italian	motto, artichoke, balcony, casino, mafia, malaria
Spanish	comrade, tornado, cannibal, mosquito, banana, guitar, vigilante, marijuana
German	poodle, kindergarten, seminar, noodle, pretzel
Dutch	sloop, cole slaw, smuggle, gin, cookie, boom
Slavic languages	czar, tundra, polka, intelligentsia, robot
Indigenous languages	toboggan, opossum, wigwam, chipmunk, Ottawa, Toronto
Hindi	thug, punch (a drink), shampoo, chintz

Although borrowing has been a very rich source of new words in English, it is noteworthy that loan words are least common among the most frequently used vocabulary items. This reflects a general tendency for highly frequent words to be relatively resistant to loss or substitution (see table 8.42).

TABLE 8.42   Origin of the 5000 most frequent words in English

Degree of frequency	Source language (%)			
	English	*French*	*Latin*	*Other*
First 1000	83	11	2	4
Second 1000	34	46	11	9
Third 1000	29	46	14	11
Fourth 1000	27	45	17	11
Fifth 1000	27	47	17	9

8.5.2 Loss of lexical items

Just as words can be added to the lexicon, they can also be lost. Changes in society play an important role in the loss of words, as lexical items often fall into disuse because the object or notion they refer to has become obsolete (see table 8.43).

TABLE 8.43   Some Old English words lost through cultural change

dolgbōt	'compensation for wounding'
þeox	'hunting spear'
eafor	'tenant obligation to the king to convey goods'
flȳtme	'a blood-letting instrument'

Language Matters Borrowing Phrases

Sometimes languages borrow simple phrases or expressions and translate them word-for-word. The following are all examples of common English phrases that came from another language.

English phrase	Source phrase
brainwashing	Chinese *xiù naùo*
flea market	French *marché aux puces*
antibody	German *Antikörper*
moment of truth	Spanish *el momento de la verdad*

8.5.3 Semantic change

Although changes in word meaning take place continually in all languages, words rarely jump from one meaning to an unrelated one. Typically, the changes occur step by step and involve one of the following phenomena.

Semantic broadening is the process in which the meaning of a word becomes more general or more inclusive than its historically earlier form (see table 8.44).

TABLE 8.44   Semantic broadening

Word	Old meaning	New meaning
bird	'small fowl'	'any winged creature'
barn	'place to store barley'	'farm building for storage and shelter'
aunt	'father's sister'	'father or mother's sister'

Semantic narrowing is the process in which the meaning of a word becomes less general or less inclusive than its historically earlier meaning (see table 8.45).

TABLE 8.45   Semantic narrowing

Word	Old meaning	New meaning
hound	'any dog'	'a hunting breed'
meat	'any type of food'	'flesh of an animal'
fowl	'any bird'	'a domesticated bird raised for food'
disease	'any unfavourable state'	'an illness'

Language Matters Dictionaries Help Track Meaning Changes

The word *girl* in Middle English was used to refer to a child of either sex. Note the following definition from the *Oxford English Dictionary*:

> Girl. A child or young person of either sex; a youth or maiden.
> 1290. "And gret prece of gurles and men comen hire."
> ('And a great throng of children and men came here.')

The Oxford English Dictionary, 2nd ed. (1989): Definition of "girl" By permission of Oxford University Press.

In **amelioration**, the meaning of a word becomes more positive. The opposite change, **pejoration**, also occurs (see tables 8.46 and 8.47).

TABLE 8.46 Amelioration

Word	Old meaning	New meaning
pretty	'tricky, sly, cunning'	'attractive'
knight	'boy'	'a mounted man-at-arms'

TABLE 8.47 Pejoration

Word	Old meaning	New meaning
silly	'happy, prosperous'	'foolish'
wench	'girl'	'wanton woman, prostitute'

Semantic shift is a process in which a word loses its former meaning and takes on a new, but often related, meaning (see table 8.48). Sometimes a series of semantic shifts occurs over an extended period of time, resulting in a meaning that is completely unrelated to the original sense of a word. The word *hearse*, for example, originally referred to a triangular harrow (a farming implement). Later, it denoted a triangular frame for church candles and later still it was used to refer to the device that held candles over a coffin. In a subsequent shift, it came to refer to the framework on which curtains were hung over a coffin or tomb. Still later, *hearse* was used to refer to the coffin itself before finally taking on its current sense of the vehicle used to transport a coffin.

TABLE 8.48 Semantic shift

Word	Old meaning	New meaning
immoral	'not customary'	'unethical'
bead	'prayer'	'prayer bead, bead'

One of the most striking types of semantic change is triggered by **metaphor**, a figure of speech based on a perceived similarity between distinct objects or actions. Metaphorical change usually involves a word with a concrete meaning taking on a more abstract sense, although the word's original meaning is not lost. The meanings of many English words have been extended through metaphor (see table 8.49).

TABLE 8.49 Some examples of metaphor in English	
Word	**Metaphorical meaning**
grasp	'understand'
yarn	'story'
high	'on drugs'

8.6 The spread of change

Up to this point, we have been concerned with the causes and description of linguistic change. Still to be dealt with is the question of how linguistic innovations spread. This section focuses on two types of spread, one involving the way in which an innovation is extended through the vocabulary of a language and the other involving the way in which it spreads through the population.

8.6.1 Diffusion through the language

Some linguistic change first manifests itself in a few words and then gradually spreads through the vocabulary of the language. This type of change is called **lexical diffusion**. A well-attested example in English involves an ongoing change in the stress pattern of words such as *convert*, which can be used as either a noun or a verb. Although the stress originally fell on the second syllable regardless of lexical category, in the latter half of the sixteenth century three such words, *rebel, outlaw,* and *record,* came to be pronounced with the stress on the first syllable when used as nouns. As figure 8.10 illustrates, this stress shift was extended to an increasing number of words over several centuries.

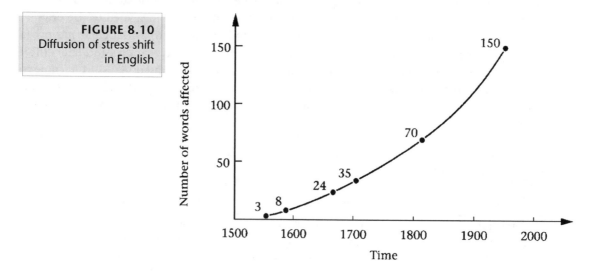

FIGURE 8.10
Diffusion of stress shift in English

This change still has not diffused through the entire vocabulary of English. There are about a thousand nouns of the relevant sort that still place the stress on the second syllable (e.g., *report, mistake,* and *support*). Table 8.50 illustrates the spread of this change to date.

TABLE 8.50	Stress shift in English (nouns)		
Before the 16th century	**During the 16th century**	**During the 18th century**	**Today**
rebél	rébel	rébel	rébel
affíx	affíx	áffix	áffix
recéss	recéss	recéss	récess
mistáke	mistáke	mistáke	mistáke

This ongoing change can be observed in progress today. The noun *address*, for example, is pronounced by many people with stress on the first syllable as [ǽdrɛs], although the older pronunciation [ədrés] is still heard. Some speakers alternate between the two pronunciations. This change may continue to work its way through the language until all nouns in the class end up with stress on the first syllable.

The changes discussed in the section on analogy also spread word by word. For example, the transition of strong (irregular) verbs (the *sing/sang/sung* type) to the weak verb class (regular verbs with past tense *-ed*) is an ongoing change. Both strong and weak past tense forms of original strong verbs such as *dive* and *shine* are heard in current English: *dove/dived* and *shone/shined*.

However, not all linguistic change involves gradual diffusion through the vocabulary of a language. Sound changes typically affect all instances of the segment(s) involved. For example, in some dialects of Spanish (such as Cuban), [s] weakened to [h] in syllable-final position. Although the change was gradual, it affected syllable-final [s] in all words to the same degree along the way. The relevant rule can be stated as in figure 8.11.

FIGURE 8.11
Consonant weakening of [s] to [h] in certain Spanish dialects

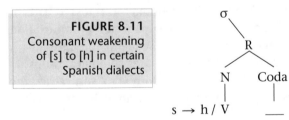

This rule has resulted in changes such as those exemplified in table 8.51.

TABLE 8.51	The effects of the [s] to [h] change in Spanish dialects	
Standard pronunciation	**New pronunciation**	
[felismente]	[felihmente]	'happily'
[estilo]	[ehtilo]	'type'
[espaɲa]	[ehpaɲa]	'Spain'

This change is entirely regular, affecting all instances of syllable-final [s] in the speech of individuals who adopt it.

Two types of language change can thus be identified. One, exemplified by the stress shifts in bisyllabic English nouns of the type we have discussed, affects individual words one at a time and gradually spreads through the vocabulary of the language. The other, exemplified by the consonant weakening of syllable-final [s] to [h] in some dialects of Spanish, involves an across-the-board change that applies without exception to all words.

8.6.2 Spread through the population

For a language change to take place, the particular innovation must be accepted by the linguistic community as a whole. For example, although children acquiring English often use *drived* as the past tense of *drive*, it is eventually displaced by *drove*. In contrast, *thrived* has managed to push out *throve* as the past tense form of *thrive*. It's no coincidence that the irregular form that survived is from a frequent verb, and the one that was lost is from a verb that is less commonly used. The frequency with which irregular forms are heard and used is a major determinant of their longevity.

Just as change sometimes begins with a small number of words, the effects of a change often appear first in the speech of only a small number of people. Social pressures often play an important role in whether a particular innovation will spread through the entire linguistic community. Since speakers can consciously or subconsciously alter the way they speak to approximate what they perceive to be a more prestigious or socially desirable variety of speech, once a change has taken hold in the speech of a particular group it may gradually spread to other speakers and ultimately affect the entire linguistic community.

There have been numerous examples of this in the history of English, notably the loss of postvocalic [r] along the east coast of the United States. This change, which led to an 'r-less' pronunciation of words such as *far* as [faː], originated in parts of England in the seventeenth and eighteenth centuries. At that time, postvocalic [r] was still pronounced throughout English-speaking settlements in North America. Two factors accounted for its loss in parts of this continent. First, the children of the New England gentry picked up the new pronunciation in British schools, where they were sent for their education, and subsequently brought it back to the colony. Second, the speech of newly arrived immigrants, including colonial administrators and church officials who enjoyed high social status in the colony, typically lacked the postvocalic [r]. As a result, the innovation was widely imitated and ultimately spread along much of the east coast and into the south.

Social pressures were also involved in limiting the spread of this innovation. It did not penetrate Pennsylvania or the other midland states since the most prestigious group of settlers there were Quakers from northern England, an area that retained the postvocalic [r]. Similarly, in Canada, the influence of Scottish and Irish settlers, whose dialects did not undergo the change in question, helped ensure the survival of postvocalic [r] in all but a few areas where contact with New England was strongest, most notably Lunenburg County in Nova Scotia and Grand Manan Island in New Brunswick. More recently, the 'r-less' pronunciation has become stigmatized in some areas, even where it was previously firmly entrenched, and we now see a trend to restoration of [r] in environments where it had been deleted.

8.7 Language reconstruction

When we compare the vocabulary items of various languages, we cannot help but notice the strong resemblance certain words bear to each other. By systematically comparing languages, we can establish whether two or more languages descended from a common parent and are therefore **genetically related**. The **comparative method** refers to the procedure of reconstructing earlier forms on the basis of a comparison of later forms. In this way, it is possible to reconstruct properties of the parent language with a great degree of certainty.

8.7.1 Comparative reconstruction

The most reliable sign of family relationships is the existence of **systematic phonetic correspondences** in the vocabulary items of different languages. Many such correspondences can be found in the sample of vocabulary items in table 8.52 from English, Dutch, German, Danish, and Swedish, all of which are members of the Germanic family of languages.

TABLE 8.52	Some Germanic cognates			
English	**Dutch**	**German**	**Danish**	**Swedish**
man	man	Mann	mand	man
hand	hand	Hand	hånd	hand
foot	voet	Fuß (β = [s])	fod	fot
bring	brengen	bringen	bringe	bringa
summer	zomer	Sommer	sommer	sommar

Since the relationship between the phonological form of a word and its meaning is mostly arbitrary, the existence of systematic phonetic correspondences in the forms of two or more languages must point toward a common source. Conversely, where languages are not related, their vocabulary items fail to show systematic similarities. This can be seen by comparing words from Turkish (see table 8.53), which is not related to the Germanic languages, with their counterparts in the languages cited in the table above.

TABLE 8.53	Some words in Turkish, a non-Germanic language (orthographic transcription)
adam	'man'
el	'hand'
ayak	'foot'
getir	'bring'
yaz	'summer'

Words that have descended from a common source (as shown by systematic phonetic correspondences and, usually, semantic similarities) are called **cognates**. Cognates are not always as obvious as the Germanic examples in table 8.52. Where languages from the same family are only distantly related, the systematic correspondences may be considerably less striking. This is exemplified in the data in table 8.54 from English, Russian, and Hindi, all of which are distantly related to each other. Forms from the unrelated Turkish are included to emphasize the similarities among the first three languages.

TABLE 8.54 Some distantly related cognates compared to non-related Turkish			
English	**Russian**	**Hindi**	**Turkish**
two	dva	dō	iki
three	tri	tīn	üç
brother	brat	bhāī	kardeş
nose	nos	nahī̃	burun

Once the existence of a relationship between two or more languages has been established, an attempt can be made to reconstruct the common source. This reconstructed language, or **proto-language**, is made up of **proto-forms**, which are written with a preceding asterisk (e.g., *hand*) to indicate their hypothetical character as reconstructions of earlier forms that have not been recorded or are not directly observable.

8.7.2 Techniques of reconstruction

Reconstruction can be undertaken with some confidence because (as discussed in the previous sections) the processes underlying language change are systematic. Once the processes are uncovered by linguists, they can be reversed in order to allow us to infer earlier forms of the language. Although it is possible to reconstruct all components of a proto-language (its phonology, morphology, syntax, lexicon, and semantics), we will focus here on phonological reconstruction, the area in which linguists have made the most progress.

Reconstruction strategies

Reconstruction of a proto-form makes use of two general strategies. The most important one is the **phonetic plausibility strategy**, which requires that any changes posited to account for differences between the proto-forms and later forms must be phonetically plausible. (Table 8.3 in section 8.2 presents a catalogue of phonetically plausible sound changes.) If the matter cannot be decided by phonetic plausibility, linguists often rely on a **majority rules strategy**, which selects the segment that is found in the majority of cognates.

Consider the cognates in table 8.55 (somewhat simplified) from members of the Romance family.

TABLE 8.55 Romance cognates				
French	**Italian**	**Romanian**	**Spanish**	
si	si	ʃi	si	'yes'

The data exemplify a correspondence between [s] and [ʃ] before the vowel [i]. To account for this, we could assume either that Romanian underwent a change that converted [s] to [ʃ] before [i] or that the other three languages underwent a change converting [ʃ] to [s] before [i], as shown in figure 8.12.

FIGURE 8.12 Hypotheses for reconstructing Proto-Romance 'yes'	*Hypothesis A*
	Proto-form *si
	Sound change (Romanian only) *s > ʃ / ___ i
	Hypothesis B
	Proto-form *ʃi
	Sound change (French, Italian, and Spanish) *ʃ > s / ___ i

Both reconstruction strategies favour hypothesis A. Most importantly, the phonetic change that is needed to account for the Romanian pronunciation involves palatalization before [i]. Since palatalization in this context is a very common phenomenon in human language, it is reasonable to assume that it occurred in Romanian. It would be much more difficult to argue that the proto-language contained [ʃ] before [i] and that three languages underwent the change posited by hypothesis B, since depalatalization before [i] would be an unusual phonetic process. (Moreover, the reconstructed *s posited in hypothesis A is also compatible with the majority rules strategy since three of the four languages in the data have [s] before [i].)

Reconstructing Proto-Romance

Consider now the slightly more complex example in table 8.56 involving data from several languages of the Romance family.

TABLE 8.56 Some Romance cognates

Spanish	Sardinian	French	Portuguese	Romanian	Original meaning
riba [riβa]	ripa	rive [ʁiv]	riba	rîpă	'embankment'
amiga [amiɣa]	amica	amie [ami]	amiga	–	'female friend'
copa	cuppa	coupe [kup]	copa	cupă	'cup, goblet'
gota	gutta	goutte [gut]	gota	gută	'drop'

Note: Orthographic *c* represents [k] in all the above examples. Romanian ă and î represent the central vowels [ə] and [ɨ], respectively. [β] is a voiced bilabial fricative and [ɣ] is a voiced velar fricative. [ʁ] is a voiced uvular fricative. Some details of vowel quality have been ignored.

Our goal here is to reconstruct the proto-forms for these words in Proto-Romance, the parent language of the Modern Romance languages, which stands very close to Latin.

Let us first consider the reconstruction of the Proto-Romance form for 'embankment'. Since the first two segments are the same in all the cognate languages, we can reconstruct Proto-Romance *r and *i on the basis of the majority rules strategy. In the case of the second consonant, however, there are differences between the cognates (see table 8.57).

TABLE 8.57	Systematic correspondences in the cognates for 'embankment'			
Spanish	**Sardinian**	**French**	**Portuguese**	**Romanian**
-β-	-p-	-v	-b-	-p-

It is most important that we first think in terms of phonetic plausibility. In the absence of evidence to the contrary, we will assume that one of the segments found in the cognates ([p], [b], [v], or [β]) should be reconstructed for Proto-Romance. Logically possible changes ranked with respect to their phonetic plausibility are found in table 8.58.

TABLE 8.58	Changes based on phonetic plausibility	
Change (in V__V)	**Name of change**	**Phonetic plausibility**
p > b	voicing	high
p > v	voicing (p > b) and frication (b > v)	high
p > β	voicing (p > b) and frication (b > β)	high
b > p		low
β > p		low
v > p		low

In terms of plausibility, the only possible reconstruction for Proto-Romance is *p. Proto-Romance *p underwent no change in Sardinian and Romanian, but in Portuguese it underwent intervocalic voicing and in Spanish it underwent both voicing and frication (that is, weakening) (see table 8.59). (We assume that voicing preceded frication in Spanish and French, since Portuguese shows voicing but no frication.) If we assume that the final vowel of the proto-form was still present in French when the consonant changes took place, we can conclude that voicing and frication occurred in this language as well. (In its written form, *rive* retains a sign of the earlier reduced vowel [ə].) These changes are phonetically plausible and thus expected.

TABLE 8.59	Summary of the changes affecting Proto-Romance *p	
*p > p / V__V	no change in Sardinian or Romanian	
*p > b / V__V	voicing in Portuguese	
*p > b > β / V__V	voicing and frication in Spanish	
*p > b > v / V__V	voicing and frication in French	

Turning now to the final vowel, we note that three languages have full vowels, Romanian has [ə], and French has no vowel at all (see table 8.60). Since vowel reduction and apocope are identified as phonetically plausible changes in table 8.3, it is appropriate to posit a full vowel for the proto-language. Furthermore, since the three languages with a full vowel all have [a], we can posit this vowel on the basis of the majority rules strategy. Accordingly, the reconstructed proto-form is *ripa.

TABLE 8.60	Summary of the changes affecting Proto-Romance *a	
Language	**Change (word final)**	**Name of change(s)**
Romanian	*a > ə	vowel reduction
French	*a > ə > Ø	vowel reduction and apocope

We can now outline the evolution of this word in French, which has the most complicated development of the six languages (see table 8.61).

TABLE 8.61	Evolution of French *rive* from **ripa*	
Change	**ripa*	**Name of change**
p > b / V __ V	riba	voicing
b > v / V __ V	riva	frication
a > ə / __ #	rivə	vowel reduction
ə > Ø / __ #	riv	apocope

In the case of the cognates for 'female friend' (the second row of table 8.56), the first three segments are the same in all the languages in the data. According to the majority rules strategy we can reconstruct them as *ami-. In the reconstruction of the second consonant, however, we must appeal to our strategy of phonetic plausibility (see table 8.62).

TABLE 8.62	Systematic correspondences in the second consonant of the cognates for 'female friend'			
Spanish	**Sardinian**	**French**	**Portuguese**	**Romanian**
-ɣ-	-k-	-Ø	-g-	–

Once again, since intervocalic voicing, frication, and deletion are phonetically plausible changes, it is most appropriate to posit *k for the proto-form (see table 8.63).

TABLE 8.63	Summary of the changes affecting Proto-Romance *k	
Language	**Change (in V_V)**	**Name of change(s)**
Portuguese	*k > g	voicing
Spanish	*k > g > ɣ	voicing and frication
French	*k > g > ɣ > Ø	voicing, frication, and deletion

In the case of the final vowel, we have the same situation we had in the previous form. The full vowel is found in Spanish, Sardinian, and Portuguese, but there is no vowel in French. We can therefore assume the full vowel *a for the proto-form, with subsequent vowel reduction and apocope in French. Consequently, we arrive at the proto-form *amika.

Finally, applying the same procedure to the cognates in the final two rows of table 8.56 yields the proto-forms *kuppa* 'cup' and *gutta* 'drop'. All the languages in the data retain the initial consonant of both proto-forms. The vowel *u* is reconstructed on the basis of the majority rules strategy, since we have no phonetic grounds for choosing either [u] or [o] as the older vowel.[6] The systematic correspondences involving the intervocalic consonants are given in table 8.64.

TABLE 8.64	Systematic correspondences of the medial consonants of *kuppa* and *gutta*			
Spanish	**Sardinian**	**French**	**Portuguese**	**Romanian**
-p-	-pp-	-p	-p-	-p-
-t-	-tt-	-t	-t-	-t-

Regardless of whether we are dealing with original *pp* or *tt*, the same pattern is evident in the case of both geminate types. There is a geminate stop consonant in Sardinian and a single consonant in Spanish, French, Portuguese, and Romanian. Since degemination is an expected sound change (see table 8.3), we assume that the proto-forms contained geminate consonants that underwent degemination except in Sardinian. This is an example of a case where the phonetic plausibility strategy overrules the majority rules strategy (since four of the five languages have [p]/[t] whereas only one language has [pp]/[tt]). As far as the final vowels are concerned, the same pattern found in the previous examples is once again evident. Proto-Romance *a* was retained in Spanish, Sardinian, and Portuguese, reduced to [ə] in Romanian, and deleted in French (see table 8.60).

Of the languages exemplified here, Sardinian is considered the most conservative since it has retained more of the earlier consonants and vowels. (In fact, the Sardinian words in the examples happen to be identical with the proto-forms, but this state of affairs would not be maintained in a broader range of data.) In the case of the other Romance languages and changes we have discussed, the most to least conservative are Portuguese (degemination and voicing) and Romanian (degemination and vowel reduction); Spanish (degemination, voicing, and frication); and French (degemination, voicing, frication, consonant deletion, vowel reduction, and apocope).

Although Proto-Romance is not identical with Classical Latin (the latter is a literary language, whereas the former corresponds to the spoken language of the time), close similarity is expected. Accordingly, the fact that our reconstructions are so close to the Latin words gives us confidence in our methods of reconstruction (see table 8.65).

TABLE 8.65	Comparison of Latin and Proto-Romance forms
Proto-Romance form	**Latin**
*ripa	rīpa
*amika	amīca (c = [k])
*kuppa	cuppa
*gutta	gutta

It is sometimes not possible to reconstruct all the characteristics of the proto-language. For example, on the basis of our data we were not able to reconstruct vowel length (Latin had a distinction between long and short vowels) since there was no evidence of this characteristic in the cognate forms.

It is also worth noting that we are not always so fortunate as to have written records of a language we expect to be very close to our reconstructed language. In the case of the Germanic languages, for example, there is no ancient written language equivalent to Latin. We must therefore rely completely on our reconstruction of Proto-Germanic to determine the properties of the language from which the modern-day Germanic languages descended. Furthermore, for many languages of the world we have no written historical records at all from any time period, making our task all the more difficult.

In summary, when the forms of two or more languages appear to be related, we can, through a consideration of systematic phonetic correspondences among cognates, reconstruct the common form from which all the forms can be derived by means of phonetically plausible sound changes. The reconstructed forms are proto-forms, and a reconstructed language, a proto-language.

Language Matters **Going Farther**

The search for a way to reconstruct ever more distant genetic relationships continues. One strategy is to focus on words that are frequently used in everyday speech, in the belief that they evolve slowly enough to permit reliable identification of cognates at great time depths. (Among the possible words of this type are *I, you, not, this, who, what, hand,* and *fire.*) Some researchers claim that this method allows the detection of linguistic relationships as old as 15 000 years—well beyond what was previously thought possible for the comparative method. Using this approach, they have postulated the existence of a Eurasian superfamily consisting of several smaller language families that had not previously been thought to be related to each other. Work of this type remains controversial, however, and is not yet widely accepted within linguistics.

For more information, see Mark Pagel, Quentin D. Atkinson, Andreea S. Calude, and Andrew Meade, "Ultraconserved Words Point to Deep Language Ancestry across Eurasia," *Proceedings of the National Academy of Sciences* 110 (2013): 8471–76.

8.7.3 The discovery of Indo-European

The late eighteenth-century discovery that Sanskrit (an ancient language of India) was related to Latin, Greek, Germanic, and Celtic revolutionized European linguistic studies. Sir William Jones, a British judge and scholar working in India, summed up the nature and implications of the findings in his 1786 address to the Royal Asiatic Society, a part of which follows:

> *The Sanscrit language, whatever be its antiquity, is of a wonderful structure; more perfect than the Greek, more copious [having more cases] than the Latin, and more exquisitely refined than either, yet bearing to both of them a stronger affinity, both in the roots of verbs and in the forms of grammar, than could possibly have been produced by accident; so strong indeed, that no philologer could examine them all three, without believing them to have sprung from some common source, which, perhaps, no longer exists: there is a similar reason . . . for supposing that both the Gothick and the Celtick . . . had the same origin with the Sanscrit; and the old Persian might be added to the same family.*

This discovery led to several decades of intensive historical-comparative work and to important advances in historical linguistics during the nineteenth century. By studying phonetic correspondences from an ever-increasing number of languages, linguists eventually ascertained that most of the languages of Europe, Persia (Iran), and the northern part of India belong to a single family, now called Indo-European. By applying the techniques of the comparative method, they began reconstructing the grammar of the proto-language from which these languages evolved, **Proto-Indo-European (PIE)**.

A number of individuals advanced this research. In 1814, the Danish linguist Rasmus Rask carefully documented the relationships among cognates in a number of Indo-European languages, and at the same time established the methods that would govern the emerging science of historical-comparative linguistics. He wrote:

> *When agreement is found in [the most essential] words in two languages, and so frequently that rules may be drawn up for the shift in letters [sounds] from one to the other, then there is a fundamental relationship between the two languages; especially when similarities in the inflectional system and in the general make-up of the languages correspond with them.*

Rask worked without access to Sanskrit. The first comparative linguistic analysis of Sanskrit, Greek, Persian, and the Germanic languages was conducted by the German scholar Franz Bopp in 1816. In 1822 another German, Jacob Grimm, extended Rask's observations and became the first person to explain the relationships among the cognates noted by Rask in terms of a **sound shift**—a systematic modification of a series of phonemes. Some of the correspondences on which he based his work are given in table 8.66.

TABLE 8.66   Some Indo-European phonetic correspondences

Greek	Latin	English
patér	pater	father
treîs	trēs	three
hekatón	centum [k]	hundred

The crucial observation is that where English has [f], [θ], and [h] (here, in word-initial position), Greek and Latin have [p], [t], and [k]. Grimm tabulated a series of consonant shifts for Proto-Germanic that differentiated it from other Indo-European languages. **Grimm's Law** is the name given to the special set of consonant shifts that affected the Germanic language family (see table 8.67).

TABLE 8.67   The sound shifts underlying Grimm's Law

Proto-Indo-European	p	t	k	b	d	g	bh	dh	gh
Proto-Germanic	f	θ	x	p	t	k	b	d	g

Note: [x] underwent a subsequent change to [h]. The symbols *bh, dh,* and *gh* represent aspirated stops.

Language Matters The Brothers Grimm

Jacob Grimm is well known for the collection of fairy tales and songs that he compiled with his brother Wilhelm. Stories such as "Snow White" and "Sleeping Beauty" were first recorded in writing by the Brothers Grimm. However, the two siblings were also scholars. Wilhelm focused on literary studies and Jacob, who developed Grimm's Law, was a philologist.

Some additional examples of the relationships captured by these shifts follow in table 8.68. The Proto-Indo-European consonants were either maintained in Sanskrit, Greek, and Latin or, in some cases, underwent changes different from those found in Germanic (represented here by English).

TABLE 8.68   Some examples of the consonant shifts underlying Grimm's Law

Shift in Germanic	PIE	Sanskrit	Greek	Latin	English
p > f	*ped	pād-	pod-	ped-	foot
t > θ	*ténhus	tanu-	tanaós	tenuis	thin
k > x (> h)	*k̑mtóm	çatam	hekatón	centum	hundred
d > t	*dékmt	daça	déka	decem	ten
g > k	*hég̑ros	ajras	agrós	ager	acre
bh > b	*bhrā́tar	bhrātā	phrā́tēr	frāter	brother
dh > d	*hwidhéwh	vidhavā	ḗitheos	vidua	widow
gh > g	*g̑hans	hansas	khḗn	(h)ānser	goose

Note: [x] underwent a subsequent change to [h]; k̑ represents a palatal velar stop.

It should also be noted here that borrowing must be taken into consideration in comparative reconstruction. For example, English has many words that do not show the effects of Grimm's Law (see table 8.69).

TABLE 8.69   English words not showing the effects of Grimm's Law

Expected by Grimm's Law	Latin	English
p > f	ped-	pedestrian
t > θ	tenuis	tenuous
k > x (> h)	canalis	canal

The apparent failure of Grimm's Law here stems from the fact that the English words were borrowed directly from Latin or French many centuries after the sound shifts described by Grimm's Law had taken place. The task of reconstruction can often be complicated by such borrowings.

Subsequent developments

By the middle of the nineteenth century, the study of language had made great strides, especially in the field of phonetics, which opened the way for the detailed comparison of linguistic forms. One influential hypothesis at that time was that sound laws operated without exception. A group of linguists known as the Neogrammarians adopted this idea and made many important contributions to the fledgling science of linguistics by applying it to new and more complicated data. Although such factors as lexical diffusion and social pressures were more or less ignored by the Neogrammarians, their hypothesis represented an important and daring advance in the scientific study of language.

Language Matters Reviving Indo-European

A non-profit organization in Europe, Academia Prisca, is devoted to reviving Indo-European and promoting its use as the main official language of the European Union and as a major international language. To read more about this project, go to the organization's website at academiaprisca.org, which includes a proposed grammar of 'Modern Indo-European', a variety of texts translated into the language, a self-learning guidebook, and an audio recording of a fable told in Indo-European.

The nineteenth century also saw major advances in the classification of languages. A German scholar, August Schleicher, developed a classification for the Indo-European languages in the form of a genealogical tree. This type of genetic classification is discussed in more detail in the chapter on language typology.

Work in comparative reconstruction is far from finished. In particular, linguists are now considering the possibility of superfamilies. One such proposed family is Nostratic, which includes Indo-European, Afro-Asiatic (e.g., Arabic, Hebrew), Altaic (e.g., Japanese, Korean, Turkic), and Uralic (e.g., Finnish, Hungarian). Comparative reconstruction is also playing an important role in determining the genetic relationships of the hundreds of North American Indigenous languages, a topic that still remains highly controversial.

8.7.4 Reconstruction and typology

Since the 1800s, when a considerable amount of reconstruction of Proto-Indo-European was carried out, linguists have accumulated vast amounts of information on thousands of languages. This is in part due to the explosion of studies in the field of linguistic typology, which is concerned with the investigation of structural similarities among languages that are not genetically related. Even languages that do not belong to the same family can have striking similarities. For example, in addition to shared word order patterns, SOV languages commonly exhibit a strong tendency toward agglutinating morphology (a type of complex affixation). Typological studies play an important role in the linguist's search for universals of language—statements that are true for all languages.

The extensive information on the languages of the world available to modern linguists was, of course, not available when the initial attempts at reconstructing Proto-Indo-European were made. Modern linguists involved in comparative reconstruction now take a keen interest in typological studies, and the role of **typological plausibility** in reconstruction has become an important topic. For example, a linguist would be very reluctant to propose a reconstruction that violates a universal property of language or that has no parallel in any known language.

Some linguists have argued that the traditional reconstruction of the PIE consonant system (given in table 8.70) should be rejected on the basis of typological plausibility. This reconstruction is typologically questionable in at least two respects. First, reconstructed forms with PIE *b are extremely rare (as is indicated by the parentheses in table 8.71), almost as if there were a very unusual gap in the labial system. Typically, if there is an aspirated voiced stop, there is also a plain voiced stop. Second, the traditional reconstruction posits a series of voiced aspirated stops but no corresponding series of voiceless aspirated stops, even though some typologists have argued that all languages that have a voiced series also have the voiceless one.

TABLE 8.70   The traditional reconstruction of the Proto-Indo-European consonants

p	t	ḱ [c]	k	k^w	(voiceless stops)
(b)	d	ǵ [ɟ]	g	g^w	(voiced stops)
bh	dh	ǵh	gh	g^wh	(voiced aspirated stops)
	s				

Note: ḱ, ǵ, and ǵh are palatal stops, and ^{w} indicates a labialized consonant.

Such facts have led some linguists to propose what they believe is a more typologically plausible reconstruction of Proto-Indo-European involving a voiceless stop series, an ejective series, and a voiced stop series (as well as *s as in the traditional reconstruction; see table 8.71).[7]

TABLE 8.71   A recent reconstruction of the Proto-Indo-European consonants

p	t	ḱ	k	k^w	(voiceless stops)
(p')	t'	ḱ'	k'	k'^w	(ejectives)
b	d	ǵ	g	g^w	(voiced stops)
	s				

Not only does this reconstruction avoid the problem with aspirates, it is also common for languages with an ejective series to lack the labial ejective. From this perspective, this reconstruction seems much more plausible than the traditional one.

Both reconstructions have their supporters, and it is difficult to come to a definitive decision on the basis of typological considerations, since it is common for universal tendencies to have exceptions. A few languages have been found with the characteristics attributed to Proto-Indo-European by the traditional reconstruction. For example, some languages have labial gaps in the voiced series (e.g., North American Indigenous languages of the Athabaskan and Caddoan families), and some have a voiced aspirated series but no voiceless counterpart (e.g., Madurese, an Indonesian language). As long as the traditional reconstruction is linguistically possible, it seems hasty to reject it simply because the phonological system proposed is a rare one.

Typological plausibility will likely continue to play a secondary role in reconstruction until linguists can draw a clear line between what is linguistically possible and what is not possible. Nevertheless, as our knowledge and understanding of language universals continues to improve, it is certain that linguists involved in the reconstruction of proto-languages will maintain an interest in typological plausibility.

8.8 Language change and naturalness

A striking fact about language change is that the same patterns of change occur repeatedly, not only within a particular language at different periods in its history but also across languages. Both the similarity of changes across languages as well as the directionality of language change suggest that some changes are more natural than others. This notion of **naturalness** is implicit in the phonetic plausibility strategy introduced in the section on comparative reconstruction.

If naturalness is a factor in language change, its manifestations should also be found in language acquisition and in language universals. This does seem to be the case. As a specific example, let us consider the frequently made claim that the CV syllable is the most natural of all syllable types. At least three different kinds of evidence support this claim. First, in terms of universals, virtually all languages of the world have CV syllables in their syllable type inventory, and some languages only have CV syllables. Second, a variety of sound changes have the effect of reducing less natural syllable types to the more natural CV type (see table 8.72).

TABLE 8.72	Sound changes yielding CV syllables						
Deletion							
CCV	>	CV	Old English	cnēow	English	knee	/ni/
CVC	>	CV	Old Spanish	non	Spanish	no	
Vowel epenthesis							
CCVCV	>	CVCVCV	Italian	croce	Sicilian	kiruci	'cross'

By contrast, such changes rarely, if ever, apply to a CV syllable to yield a different syllable type. Deletion of the C in a word-initial CV syllable is extremely rare, as is vowel epenthesis in a CV syllable or a sequence of CV syllables.

Third, in terms of language acquisition, the CV syllable type is one of the first syllable types to be acquired and many phonetic processes found in child language have the effect of yielding CV syllables, just like the sound changes listed above (see table 8.73).

TABLE 8.73	Phonetic processes in language acquisition yielding CV syllables	
CCV → CV	tree → [ti]	(simplification of consonant clusters)
CVC → CV	dog → [dɑ]	(deletion of final consonants)

The precise effects of linguistic naturalness are not yet fully understood. Mysteries remain, since some known sound changes produce less natural syllables. For instance, syncope has the effect of reducing a sequence of CVCVCV syllables to the less natural CVCCV. Usually in such cases, a different motivation can be identified, such as the preference for shorter phonological forms over longer forms. But given the complexity of human language, not to mention human behaviour in general, it should not be surprising that there are many different parameters of linguistic naturalness and that these can, in turn, lead to apparently conflicting changes in language over time. It remains an important task of the linguist to identify, rank, and ultimately explain relations of linguistic naturalness. The study of language change will continue to make an important contribution to this area.

Summing up

Historical linguistics studies the nature and causes of language change. The causes of language change find their roots in the physiological and cognitive makeup of human beings. Sound changes usually involve articulatory simplification, as in the case of the most common type, **assimilation. Analogy** and **reanalysis** are particularly important factors in morphological change. **Language contact** resulting in **borrowing** is another important source of language change.

All components of the grammar, from phonology to semantics, are subject to change over time. A change can simultaneously affect all instances of a particular sound or form, or it can spread through the language word by word by means of **lexical diffusion**. Sociological factors can play an important role in determining whether or not a linguistic innovation is ultimately adopted by the linguistic community at large. Since language change is systematic, it is possible, by identifying the changes that a particular language or dialect has undergone, to reconstruct linguistic history and thereby posit the earlier forms from which later forms have evolved. Using sets of **cognates, comparative reconstruction** allows us to reconstruct the properties of the parent or **proto-language** on the basis of **systematic phonetic correspondences**.

Studies in historical linguistics can provide valuable insights into relationships among languages and shed light on prehistoric developments. Furthermore, historical studies of language are of great importance to our understanding of human linguistic competence. In fact, it has often been stated that language change provides one of the clearest windows into the workings of the human mind. Furthermore, the study of language change contributes to our understanding of how social, cultural, and psychological factors interact to shape language. Finally, the integration of studies on language change, language acquisition, and language universals remains one of the most important challenges facing linguists today.

Notes

[1] The translation for the passage is as follows:

Many men say that in dreams
There is nothing but talk and lies
But men may see some dreams
Which are scarcely false
But afterward come true.

[2] In these and other examples throughout this chapter, orthographic forms are given where these clearly reflect the sound change(s) in question. If required, partial or full phonetic transcriptions are provided.

[3] Since voicing commonly occurs between voiced segments, it can also be considered a type of assimilation. It is treated here as weakening since it is often part of a larger pattern of change involving various weakening processes.

[4] A fully phonemic contrast between lax and tense vowels appears to be developing in Canadian French. Borrowings from English are contributing to this development (e.g., *poule* 'hen', pronounced [pʊl] in colloquial speech, versus *pool*).

[5] We have simplified here in two respects. First, we ignore the fact that the verbs *be* and *have* can undergo Inversion even when they do not function as auxiliaries.

Are they here?

Have you no sense?

Second, we have not discussed the emergence of the auxiliary verb *do* in the formation of questions.

[6] In fact, the assumption of umlaut would be a very good working hypothesis; that is, **u* became [o] in Spanish and Portuguese due to the lowering influence of the word-final low vowel **a*. However, a larger dataset would show that this type of umlaut did not occur in these languages.

[7] Ejectives are produced by closing the glottis and raising the larynx.

Recommended reading

Anttila, Raimo. 1989. *Historical and Comparative Linguistics.* 2nd ed. Amsterdam: John Benjamins.

Brinton, Laurel J., and Leslie K. Arnovick. 2017. *The English Language: A Linguistic History.* 3rd ed. Oxford: Oxford University Press.

Campbell, Lyle. 2013. *Historical Linguistics: An Introduction.* 3rd ed. Cambridge, MA: MIT Press.

Gelderen, Elly van. 2014. *A History of the English Language.* Rev. ed. Amsterdam: John Benjamins.

Hock, Hans Henrich. 1991. *Principles of Historical Linguistics.* 2nd ed. Amsterdam: Mouton de Gruyter.

Hock, Hans Henrich, and Brian D. Joseph. 2009. *Language History, Language Change, and Language Relationship: An Introduction to Historical and Comparative Linguistics.* 2nd ed. New York: Mouton de Gruyter.

Hogg, Richard M., ed. *The Cambridge History of the English Language.* 1992–2001. Six volumes. Cambridge, UK: Cambridge University Press.

Hopper, Paul J., and Elizabeth Closs Traugott. 2003. *Grammaticalization.* 2nd ed. Cambridge, UK: Cambridge University Press.

Joseph, Brian D., and Richard D. Janda, eds. 2003. *The Handbook of Historical Linguistics*. Oxford: Blackwell.

Koerner, E.F., and R.E. Asher, eds. 1995. *Concise History of the Language Sciences: From the Sumerians to the Cognitivists*. New York: Pergamon.

Labov, William. 1994. *Principles of Linguistic Change, Vol. 1: Internal Factors*. Oxford: Wiley Blackwell.

Labov, William. 2001. *Principles of Linguistic Change, Vol. 2: Social Factors*. Oxford: Blackwell.

Lass, Roger. 1997. *Historical Linguistics and Language Change*. Cambridge, UK: Cambridge University Press.

Lehmann, Winfred P. 1992. *Historical Linguistics*. 3rd ed. New York: Routledge.

McMahon, April M.S. 1994. *Understanding Language Change*. Cambridge, UK: Cambridge University Press.

Trask, R.L. 2015. *Trask's Historical Linguistics*. 3rd ed. Revised, edited, and compiled by Robert McColl Millar. London: Routledge.

Exercises

1. Identify the following sound changes with reference to the discussion of sound change in sections 8.2.1 and 8.2.2 table 8.3. In each pair of examples, focus on the segment(s) in bold only. The form on the left indicates the original segment(s) before the change and the form on the right indicates the segment(s) after the change. (The orthography is supplemented with IPA, in square brackets, where the intended pronunciation is not otherwise clear.)

a)	Sanskrit	s**n**eha	Pali	si**n**eha	'friendship'
b)	Old English	**hl**āf	English	**l**oaf	
c)	Pre–Old English	*lū**si**	Old English	lȳ**s** [yː]	'lice'
d)	English	triath**l**on	dialect	triath[ə]**l**on	
e)	Latin	vi**du**a [dw]	Spanish	viu**da** [wd]	'widow'
f)	Sanskrit	sa**pt**a	Pali	sa**tt**a	'seven'
g)	Latin	turtu**r**	English	turtl**e**	
h)	Pre-Spanish	*ve**nr**é	Spanish	ve**ndr**é	'I will come'
i)	Italian	mun**d**o	Sicilian	mun**n**u	'world'
j)	Old French	cire [**ts**]	French	cire [**s**]	'wax'
k)	Latin	pā**n**-	French	pai**n** [ɛ̃]	'bread'
l)	Latin	mu**lg**ēre	Italian	mu**ng**ere	'to milk'
m)	Latin	pa**c**are [k]	Italian	pa**g**are	'to pay'
n)	Old Spanish	ni**d**o	Spanish	ni**d**o [ð]	'nest'
o)	Latin	pe**cc**ātum [kk]	Spanish	pe**c**ado [k]	'sin'
p)	Pre-Latin	*honō**s**is	Latin	honō**r**is	'honor (gen sg)'
q)	Old French	rai**ge** [dʒ]	French	ra**ge** [ʒ]	'rage'
r)	English	**coffee**	Chipewyan	[**kapi**]	
s)	Latin	mar**e**	Portuguese	mar	'sea'
t)	Latin	vī**c**īnitās	Spanish	ve**c**indad	'neighbourhood'
u)	Gothic	**þl**iuan [θ]	English	**fl**ee	
v)	Old English	(ic) sin**ge**	English	(I) sin**g**	
w)	Latin	su**mm**a	Spanish	su**m**a	'sum, gist'
x)	Latin	ōr**n**āmentum	Old French	orn**e**ment [ə]	'ornament'

2. a) Describe the difference between the two French dialects in the following data. Assume that the data are in phonetic transcription. (*Note*: [ø] is a mid front tense round vowel; [y] is a high front tense round vowel.)

   b) What sound change(s) would you posit here? Why?

   c) State the sound change in the form of a rule.

	European French	*Acadian French*	
i)	okyn	otʃyn	'none'
ii)	kør	tʃør	'heart'
iii)	ke	tʃe	'wharf'
iv)	kɛ̃ːz	tʃɛ̃ːz	'fifteen'
v)	akyze	atʃyze	'accuse'
vi)	ki	tʃi	'who'
vii)	kav	kav	'cave'
viii)	kɔr	kɔr	'body'
ix)	kurir	kurir	'run'
x)	ɑ̃kɔːr	ɑ̃kɔːr	'again'

3. a) What sound changes differentiate Guaraní from its parent language, Proto-Tupí-Guaraní, in the following data? (*Note*: [ɨ] is a high central unrounded vowel.)

   b) State these changes in rule form.

	Proto-Tupí-Guaraní	*Guaraní*	
i)	jukɨr	jukɨ	'salt'
ii)	moajan	moajã	'push'
iii)	puʔam	puʔã	'wet'
iv)	meʔeŋ	meʔẽ	'give'
v)	tiŋ	tʃĩ	'white'
vi)	potiʔa	potʃiʔa	'chest'
vii)	tatatiŋ	tatatʃĩ	'smoke'
viii)	kɨb	kɨ	'louse'
ix)	men	mẽ	'husband'

4. a) Describe the three changes that took place between Proto-Slavic and Bulgarian in the following data. (The symbol ˘ over a vowel indicates that it is short.)

   b) State these changes as rules and indicate, as far as possible, the order in which they must have applied.

   c) Apply these rules to the Proto-Slavic word for 'adroit' to show how the Bulgarian form evolved.

	Proto-Slavic	*Bulgarian*	
i)	gladŭka	glatkə	'smooth'
ii)	kratŭka	kratkə	'short'
iii)	blizŭka	bliskə	'near'
iv)	ʒeʒĭka	ʒeʃkə	'scorching'
v)	lovŭka	lofkə	'adroit'
vi)	gorĭka	gorkə	'bitter'

5. Determine all the sound changes required to derive the later form from the proto-form. Where necessary, give the chronology of the sound changes.

   a) *feminam   Old French   femme (final e = [ə])   'woman'
   b) *lumine   Spanish   lumbre   'fire'
   c) *tremulare   Spanish   temblar   'tremble'
   d) *stuppam   Spanish   estopa   'tow'
   e) *populu   Romanian   plop   'poplar'

6. Taking into consideration the Great English Vowel Shift, give all the changes necessary to derive the Modern English forms from the Old English forms. (*Note*: Assume, simplifying somewhat, that the Old English forms were pronounced as they are written.)

Old English	*Modern English*
a) brōde	brood [brud]
b) cnotta (c = [k])	knot [nɑt]
c) wīse	wise [wajz]
d) hlǣfdige	lady [lejdi]

7. Place names are often subject to spelling pronunciation. Transcribe your pronunciation of the following words and then compare your pronunciation with that recommended by a good dictionary. Do you think any of your pronunciations qualify as spelling pronunciations?

   a) Worcestershire
   b) Thames
   c) Edinburgh (Scotland; compare Edinburgh, Texas)
   d) Cannes (France)
   e) Newfoundland

8. Compare the Old English singular and plural forms:

Singular	*Plural*	
bōc	bēc	'book(s)'
āc	ǣc	'oak(s)'

   Although the Old English words have a plural form that was brought about by umlaut (as in Old English gōs/gēs 'goose/geese'), the Modern English forms do not. Explain how the change in plural formation in Modern English could have come about.

9. All of the following English words at one time had meanings that are quite different from their current ones. Identify each of these semantic changes as an instance of narrowing, broadening, amelioration, pejoration, weakening, or shift.

Word	*Earlier meaning*
a) moody	'brave'
b) uncouth	'unknown'
c) write	'scratch'
d) butcher	'one who slaughters goats'
e) witch	'male or female sorcerer'
f) sly	'skilful'
g) accident	'an event'

h)	argue	'make clear'
i)	carry	'transport by cart'
j)	grumble	'murmur, make low sounds'
k)	shrewd	'depraved, wicked'
l)	praise	'set a value on'
m)	ordeal	'trial by torture'
n)	picture	'a painted likeness'
o)	seduce	'persuade someone to desert his or her duty'
p)	box	'a small container made of boxwood'
q)	baggage	'a worthless person'
r)	virtue	'qualities one expects of a man'
s)	myth	'story'
t)	undertaker	'one who undertakes'
u)	hussy	'housewife'
v)	astonish	'strike by thunder'

10. Look up the following words in a good dictionary or in the Online Etymology Dictionary. What was the original meaning of the second component of each compound?
    a) wed<u>lock</u>
    b) witch<u>craft</u>
    c) stead<u>fast</u>
    d) after<u>ward</u>

11. Consider the following lyrics from the Middle English song "Sumer is i-cumen in." Compare the Middle English lyrics with the Modern English translation and answer the questions that follow.

    Original text
    Sumer is i-cumen in;
    Lhude sing, cuccu!
    Grōweþ sēd, and blōweþ mēd,
    And springþ þe wude nū.

    Transcription
    [sʊmər ɪs ɪkʊmən ɪn
    luːdə sɪng kʊkku
    grɔːwəθ seːd and blɔːwəθ meːd
    and sprɪŋgθ ðə wʊdə nuː]

    Translation
    'Summer has come in;
    Loudly sing, cuckoo!
    Seed grows and meadow blooms
    And the wood grows now.'

    a) What affix converted the adjective *loud* into an adverb in Middle English?
    b) What accounts for the difference between the Middle English and Modern English pronunciation of the vowel in *loud*?
    c) What other words in this poem reflect this general shift?
    d) How has the relative ordering of the subject and verb changed since this was written?
    e) How has the third person singular present tense suffix changed since Middle English?

12. The following words found in various Cree dialects were borrowed from French as the result of contact between the two groups on the Canadian prairies. (Notice that the French determiner was not treated as a separate morpheme and was carried along with

the borrowed word.) What types of considerations could one plausibly assume played a role in the borrowing of these words into Cree?

	Cree	French	
a)	/labutoːn/	le bouton	'button'
b)	/lɪːbot/	les bottes	'boots'
c)	/lamilaːs/	la mélasse	'molasses'
d)	/lapwiːl/	la poêle	'frying pan'
e)	/litɪː/	le thé	'tea'

13. The following Latin roots are found in words that have been borrowed into English. Since these words were borrowed after Grimm's Law had applied, they do not show its effects. All of these roots, however, do have Germanic cognates that did undergo Grimm's Law. On the basis of your knowledge of this law and the meaning of the borrowing, try to determine the Modern English (Germanic) cognate for each root. Consult a good dictionary if you need help. (*Note*: Focus on the portion of the Latin word in bold only; you can ignore vowel changes.)

	Latin root	Related borrowing	English cognate
a)	**ped**is	pedestrian	*foot*
b)	**nep**os	nepotism	____
c)	**pisc**es	piscine	____
d)	**ager**	agriculture	____
e)	**corn**u	cornucopia	____
f)	**duo**	dual	____
g)	**ed**ere	edible	____
h)	**gen**us	genocide	____

14. Reconstruct the Proto-Romance form for each set of cognates. Give all the changes necessary to derive each of the modern forms from the proto-forms. If you are not sure how to proceed, return to section 8.7. (*Note*: The Spanish and Romanian spelling 'ie' represents the sequence /je/, and the Romanian spelling 'ia' represents the sequence /ja/. In Spanish, orthographic *h* is not pronounced word initially.)

	Spanish	Sardinian	Romanian	
a)	vida	—	vită (ă = [ə])	'life'
b)	sí	si	și (ș = [ʃ])	'yes'
c)	riso	rizu	rîs	'laugh'
d)	miel	mele	miere	'honey'
e)	hierro	ferru	fier	'iron'
f)	piedra	pedra	piatră (ă = [ə])	'stone'
g)	hierba	erva	iarbă (ă = [ə])	'grass'
h)	oso	ursu	urs	'bear'
i)	roto	ruttu	rupt	'broken'
j)	lecho	lettu	–	'bed'

To learn more about the topics discussed in this chapter, visit the Companion Website for *Contemporary Linguistic Analysis*.

Indigenous languages in Canada

Language is our unique relationship to the Creator, our attitudes, beliefs, values, and fundamental notions of what is truth. Our languages are the cornerstone of who we are as a People. Without our languages we cannot survive.

ASSEMBLY OF FIRST NATIONS, TOWARDS LINGUISTIC JUSTICE FOR FIRST NATIONS (1990)

THE STUDY of languages spoken by the descendants of the original inhabitants of North America has made a number of significant contributions to the development of linguistics. In practically every book that the student of linguistics reads, the impact of work in this area is evident. It would be no exaggeration to say that the lasting and profound influence of such eminent pioneers of linguistics as Franz Boas, Edward Sapir, and Leonard Bloomfield is due in large part to the seminal work they did on structurally diverse Indigenous languages in North America, especially in Canada.

The value of current research on North American Indigenous languages stems in part from the light that it can shed on the nature of human linguistic competence. Besides refuting the popular misconception that these languages are somehow primitive, this work has also uncovered certain structural and semantic phenomena that are not found in more widely studied languages such as English, French, Mandarin, and so on. Another compelling reason for the study of Indigenous languages is that it can yield clues (sometimes the only ones available) to help resolve problems in archaeology and anthropology (especially ethnohistory) relating to the origin and migration of the Indigenous peoples of the Americas. It is also important to recognize that Indigenous languages in North America are in a grave state of decline, so that an urgency underlies their study, whether theoretical or historical.

9.1 Ethnolinguistic overview

How many Indigenous languages are there? How are they related genetically? How are they distributed? Although definitive answers cannot yet be given to any of these questions, the current tentative consensus is briefly outlined in the next two sections prior to a comment on the decline of Indigenous languages in Canada. A discussion of the structural characteristics of these languages then follows.

9.1.1 Genetic classification

John Wesley Powell's work of 1891, which represents the first attempt at a comprehensive genetic classification of the Indigenous languages of North America, recognizes fifty-eight families. Although this classification was preceded by and indebted to many other classifications, it is considered one of the most valuable works in Native American linguistics. Powell's classification of hundreds of different languages into fewer than sixty families was a remarkable achievement, but it was really only a first step toward a definitive genetic classification.

In the years following Powell's work, many linguists came to assume that all of the Indigenous languages of North America ultimately originated from a small number of mother languages. Consequently, they began trying to place the known language families into larger **stocks** and still larger **phyla**. The best-known classification from this perspective was proposed by Edward Sapir in 1929. In this far-reaching analysis—which owes a great deal to earlier work by Alfred Kroeber and Ronald Dixon, among others—all Indigenous language families of Canada, the United States, and parts of Central America were grouped into stocks that, in turn, were organized into six super-stocks (also known as macrofamilies or phyla). Although not adequately substantiated in all details, this proposal stimulated a great deal of research aimed at the further classification of Indigenous languages.

A more realistic classification was proposed in 1964. Following Sapir's scheme, 221 languages were grouped into 42 families and 31 isolates (languages with no known relatives), which were then classified into 9 phyla. A great deal more has been learned since this proposal was made, and some aspects of this work are now out of date. Certain languages that were earlier treated as isolates have since been shown to be related. For example, Yurok and Wiyot of California, originally considered isolates, have not only been found to be related to each other but have been placed in the Algonquian family (as claimed by Sapir as early as 1913). Similarly, studies of Tlingit (Łingít) suggest a distant relationship to Dene/Athabaskan languages and Eyak.

There is also strong evidence that what were formerly considered dialects of one language should be treated as separate languages. For example Tłı̨chǫ Yatıì (formerly Dogrib), Bear Lake (Sahtúgot'ıné), and Hare (K'áshogot'ıné) of the Dene/Athabaskan family were once believed to be dialects of the same language, but their status has since been reconsidered. The identity of Tłı̨chǫ Yatıì as a separate language is now well established, and the possibility that Bear Lake and Hare are separate languages is under consideration. Several of the proposed phyla also remain in question; in fact, many linguists have chosen to retreat from such large-scale classification until the histories of the individual families are better understood. (A more up-to-date and more widely accepted classification appeared in the seventeenth volume of the Smithsonian's *Handbook of North American Indians*; see 'Recommended reading' at the end of this chapter.)

> #### Language Matters The Amerind Hypothesis
>
> A relatively new and daring classification has been widely entertained in popular media and in interdisciplinary research. Highly controversial, this classification recognizes the Inuit-Yupik-Unangan family and Na-Dene—a stock consisting of the Dene/Athabaskan family, Tlingit, Eyak, and perhaps Haida—but places all other Indigenous languages of the Americas into a single large group, labelled Amerind.

(Continued)

9.1.2 Languages in Canada

Indigenous peoples in Canada fall into three distinct political groupings: First Nations, Inuit, and Métis. Although there is no agreement on the details of genetic classification, there is some consensus that Canada's First Nations represent no less than eight language families and several isolates, that the Inuit represent a separate language family, and that the Métis represent a unique mixed language.

The map in figure 9.1 shows the geographic distribution of the widely accepted Indigenous language families and isolates of Canada discussed in this chapter (each symbol marks a community of speakers). Of course, the political border between Canada and the United States is not a linguistic boundary; the traditional homeland of many Indigenous groups includes portions of both countries.

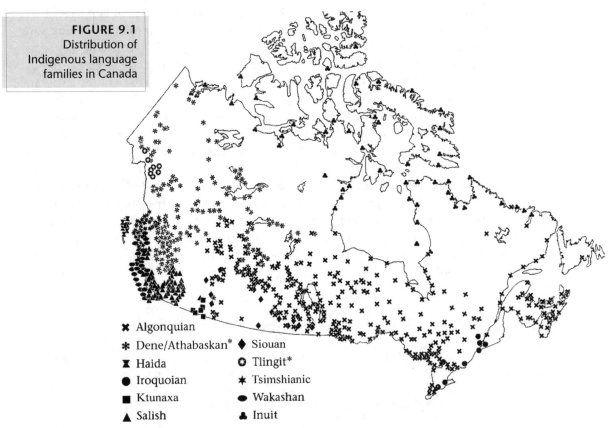

FIGURE 9.1
Distribution of Indigenous language families in Canada

✖ Algonquian
✳ Dene/Athabaskan*
✠ Haida
● Iroquoian
■ Ktunaxa
▲ Salish
◆ Siouan
✪ Tlingit*
✴ Tsimshianic
⬬ Wakashan
♣ Inuit

Note: For the purposes of this map, we treat Dene/Athabaskan and Tlingit separately, even though they are now often considered to be members of the larger Na-Dene family.

Languages and affiliations are introduced below in descending order of size (in Canada). Slashes (/) indicate alternative names for languages or dialects. Although some of the names provided may appear exotic, they are in fact the ones preferred by the Indigenous peoples to identify themselves. Note, too, that there are no exact figures on speaker populations. Figures suggested here are informed estimates based primarily on mother tongue and home language data from the Statistics Canada 2016 census, but also drawing on a variety of other sources. (See the Sources section at the end of this book.) The dash means 'not applicable'. Where data from the 2016 census is not available, we mark our estimates with an asterisk.

Algonquian

Two of the most widely spoken Indigenous languages in Canada, Cree and Ojibwe, belong to the Algonquian family (see table 9.1). Dialects of both languages are spoken in British Columbia, Alberta, Saskatchewan, Manitoba, Ontario, and Québec. Cree is also represented in Labrador by the Innu dialects. Maliseet-Passamaquoddy and Mi'kmaq are spoken in the Atlantic provinces. (Here and elsewhere, speaker populations outside Canada are provided to give an idea of the overall size of the various Indigenous linguistic communities. Of the Algonquian languages, only Ojibwe is widely spoken outside Canada.)

TABLE 9.1　The Algonquian languages spoken in Canada		
Language	Estimated number of speakers in Canada	Estimated number of speakers in the United States
Cree 　Dialects: Plains (nēhiyawēwin), 　Swampy, Woods, Moose, 　At(t)ikamek(w), Montagnais 　and Naskapi Innu	102 785	870
Ojibwe/Anishinaabemowin 　Dialects: Odawa, Saulteau(x), 　Ojibwa/Chippewa, Algonquin, 　Severn/Oji-Cree	37 580	10 700
Mi'kmaq/Micmac	7 730	205
Blackfoot	4 945	600*
Maliseet-Passamaquoddy	495	845
Potawatomi/Neshnabémwen	4*	3–4*
Munsee Delaware	3*	–
Western Abenaki	2*	2–3*

Inuit-Yupik-Unangan

Only the Inuit branch of this family (formerly Eskimo-Aleut) is represented in Canada, by a dialect continuum that spans the Far North, from northern Labrador (Nunatsiavut) to the northwestern part of the Northwest Territories (Inuvialuit). The major dialects are Inuktitut, Inuvialuktun, and Canadian Iñupiaq (see table 9.2). There are 42 710 speakers in total, mostly of

Inuktitut. Of those with Inuktitut as their mother tongue, almost a third live in northern Québec (Nunavik) and almost two-thirds live in Nunavut, Canada's newest and largest territory. A syllabary for writing Inuktitut, adapted from Cree, is now in wide use, especially in Nunavut.

TABLE 9.2 The Inuit Languages		
Variety	Estimated number of speakers in Canada	Estimated number of speakers outside of Canada
Inuktitut	39 030	Greenland/Denmark
Inuvialuktun		Inuktun: 800
Natsilingmiutut	1 785*	Greenlandic: 61 932
Inuinnaqtun	1 060	Alaska
Siglitun	420	Inupiaq: 2 583
Uummarmiutun (Iñupiaq)	120	

Na-Dene

This family exhibits the greatest internal diversity, with seventeen distinct languages in this country alone (see table 9.3). They are spoken in British Columbia, the Yukon, the Northwest Territories, Alberta, Saskatchewan, and Manitoba. All except Tlingit belong to the Dene/Athabaskan subfamily.

TABLE 9.3 The Na-Dene languages spoken in Canada		
Language	Estimated number of speakers in Canada	Estimated number of speakers in the United States
Łingít/Tlingit	165	500
Dene/Athabaskan:		–
Dakelh/Carrier	1 285	–
Dënesųłiné/Chipewyan	11 785	–
Slave(y), including Hare	2 210	–
Tłıchǫ Yatıì/Dogrib	2 060	–
Tsilhqot'in/Chilcotin	820	–
Gwich'in/Kutchin	295	300
Kaska	240	–
Tutchone (Northern, Southern)	225	–
Dunneza/Beaver	190	–
Tahltan	180	–
Witsuwet'en Babine/Nedut'en	135	–
Tsúut'ína/Sarcee	110	–
Sekani	105	–
Upper Tanana	10*	40*
Hän	2*	6*
Tagish	2*	–

Siouan

The Siouan language family is represented by three Dakotan languages in Canada: (1) Îyethka/Isga (Stoney Nakoda/Nakota), spoken in Alberta; (2) Assiniboine (Hohe Naḱoda/Nakota), spoken in Saskatchewan; and (3) Dakota-Lakota (formerly Sioux), a continuum of three dialects: Teton Lakota (T̄itoŋwaŋ Laḱot̄a) and Yankton Dakota (Ihaŋktoŋwaŋ Daḱot̄a), spoken in Saskatchewan; and Santee Dakota (Isaṇt̄i Dakota/Daḱot̄a), spoken in Saskatchewan and Manitoba. (See table 9.4; separate figures are not available for Yankton and Santee, which are commonly grouped together as Dakota.)

TABLE 9.4   The Siouan languages spoken in Canada

Language	Estimated number of speakers in Canada	Estimated number of speakers in the United States
Îyethka/Isga/Stoney (Nakoda/Nakota)	3 215	–
Dakota-Lakota: Yankton and		
Santee (Dakota)	1 195	17 855
Teton (Lakota)	3*	2 000*
Assiniboine (Hohe Naḱoda/Nakota)	34*	75

Salish

The Salish family has ten languages centred in British Columbia. Its total speaker population is estimated at 3670 (see table 9.5).

TABLE 9.5   The Salish languages spoken in Canada

Language	Estimated number of speakers in Canada	Estimated number of speakers in the United States
Nsyilxcən/Nsilxcín/Okanagan	490	230
nɬeʔkèpmxcín/Nlaka'pamuxtsn/ Thompson	295	–
Éy7á7juuthem/Ayeahjuthum/ Comox-Sliammon	400*	–
Secwepemctsín/Shuswap	835	–
St'át'imcets/Lillooet	525	–
Halkomelem/Halq'eméylem/ Hul'q'umin'um'/hən'q'əmin'əm'	685	–
Nuxalk/Bella Coola	100*	–
Saanich/SENĆOŦEN/Straits/Malchosen/ Lekwungen/Semiahmoo/T'Sou-ke	280	–
S̲kwx̲wú7mesh/Squamish	160	–
Shashishalhem/Sechelt	10*	–

Tsimshianic

Tsimshianic languages are located in northwestern British Columbia (see table 9.6). This family is believed to be distantly related to a dozen other language families of the American Pacific Coast, under a proposed phylum called Penutian.

TABLE 9.6 The Tsimshianic languages spoken in Canada		
Language	**Estimated number of speakers in Canada**	**Estimated number of speakers in the United States**
Nass-Gitksan	Gitksan/Gitsenimx̱: 970	25*
	Nisga'a: 700	100*
Tsimshian	Sm'algy̱ax/Coast Tsimshian: 200	40
	Klemtu/South Tsimshian: 1*	–

Iroquoian

Another major group of Indigenous languages represented in Canada is the Iroquoian family, which is found in southwestern Québec and southern Ontario, as well as in adjoining parts of the United States (see table 9.7).

TABLE 9.7 The Iroquoian languages spoken in Canada		
Language	**Estimated number of speakers in Canada**	**Estimated number of speakers in the United States**
Kanien'kéha/Kanyen'kéha/Mohawk	1715	1945
Onʌyota'a:ka/Onʌyotaʔa·ka/Oneida	180	12*
Goyogohó:nǫʼ/Cayuga	105	3*
Onǫda'géga'/Onoňda'géga'/Onondaga	5*	2*
Onöndowá'ga:'/Seneca	3*	30*
Skarù·rę'/Sgarooreh'/Tuscarora	2*	3*

Wakashan

The Wakashan family, which is spoken principally on Vancouver Island and the adjacent British Columbia coast, consists of five languages in Canada (see table 9.8). (A sixth Wakashan language, Makah, has about twenty speakers in Washington State, opposite Vancouver Island.)

TABLE 9.8 The Wakashan languages spoken in Canada

Language	Estimated number of speakers
Nuučaan'uɫ/Nuu-chah-nulth/Nootka	345
Kwak̓wala	375
X̄enaksialak'ala/Henaksiala-X̄a'islak̓ala/Haisla	135
Hailhzaqvla/Híɫzaqv/Heiltsuk-'Uik̓ala/Oowekyala	Heiltsuk: 60
	Oowekyala: 6*
diiʔdiitidq/Diitiidʔaatx̱/Ditidaht/Nitinat	10*

Isolates

Certain Indigenous language families in Canada have a single member. One such isolate is Inuit Sign Language, which is still known by some 35 Deaf Inuit and by a few others in each of their families. Other Indigenous sign languages include Plateau Sign Language and Plains Sign Talk (see below). Two other language isolates are spoken in Canada: X̱aad Kil (Haida), spoken in Haida Gwaii (formerly the Queen Charlotte Islands) off the northern coast of British Columbia, and Ktunaxa, spoken in the Canadian Rockies in southeastern British Columbia (see table 9.9).

TABLE 9.9 Language isolates of Canada

Language	Estimated number of speakers/signers in Canada	Estimated number of speakers/signers in the United States
Inuit Sign Language	100*	15
X̱aad Kil/X̱aaydaa Kil/Haida	35*	
Ktunaxa/Kootenay-Kinbasket	35*	10

Contact languages

Contact languages resist genetic classification in terms of language families or isolates, because they do not descend from a single parent language. Michif is a fascinating example of a contact language unique to the Métis Nation, members of which are (mostly) descendants from Cree or Ojibwe women and French-Canadian fur trappers. Michif nouns, prepositions, and negation markers are mostly of French origin, whereas its verbs, personal pronouns, question words, demonstratives, and adverbial particles are mostly Cree. Still, Michif is not mutually intelligible with either Cree or French. According to the 2016 Canadian census, there are about 645 speakers of Michif in the Canadian Prairie Provinces and another 75 in North Dakota and Montana in the United States. Crucially, many of these speakers do not know Cree or French. Here is an example of a Michif sentence (words in italics derive from Cree; the others derive from French). Unless otherwise noted, all examples of sentences and words in Indigenous languages in this chapter are written using IPA.

(1) *eːgwanɪ-gi*   liː   savaːz   *kiːpaːʃamwak*   la   vjãd
    they   the   Indigenous people   dried   the   meat
    'The Indigenous people dried the meat.'

Historically, Canada also had its share of trade **jargons** or **pidgins**, characterized by rudimentary grammars and limited vocabularies. For example, at one time or another Inuktitut was mixed with Basque, French, and Montagnais in Labrador-Inuit Pidgin; with Cree and Montagnais in Hudson Strait Pidgin Inuktitut; with English in Inuktitut-English Pidgin (which was used until the mid-twentieth century); and with Dene/Athabaskan languages in Loucheux Jargon.

Chinook Jargon, which originated as a lingua franca in the Pacific Northwest, drew many basic words from Nuu-chah-nulth (Nuučaan'uɬ) and from Canadian French. Its use peaked in the nineteenth century with an estimated 100 000 speakers representing more than 100 mother tongues. There are now probably no more than a dozen speakers of Chinook Jargon in Canada, mostly in British Columbia.

A form of communication using the hands, Plains Sign Talk, was more commonly used as a lingua franca in the Plains area; its use also appears to have peaked in the nineteenth century in Alberta, Saskatchewan, and Manitoba. It is still known by a few Cree, Blackfoot, and Dakota—some deaf, and others hearing—who use it to accompany their oral narratives.

Language Matters Confusing Signs

The Plains sign for 'big belly' involves moving the right hand outward and down, fingers pointing left. The sign for 'waterfall' is similar but with fingers pointing forward. Eighteenth-century Cree and French speakers apparently mixed these signs and began referring to the 'Falls Indians', whom they encountered on the Canadian Prairies, as 'Big-Bellied Indians'. The Algonquian-speaking Gros Ventres—'Big Bellies' in French—now reside in Montana.

Source: Based on Andrew Cowell, Allan Taylor, and Terry Brockie, "Gros Ventre Ethnography and Place Names: A Diachronic Perspective," *Anthropological Linguistics* 58, 2 (2016): 132–70; see p. 132.

9.1.3 Decline of Indigenous languages

Epidemics (especially smallpox), famines, and innumerable wars reduced the Indigenous population of North America from over five million at the time of Columbus (the late fifteenth century) to fewer than half a million at the beginning of the twentieth century. Fortunately, Indigenous peoples are now recovering rapidly from these historical disasters: the Indigenous population in Canada has grown from 120 000 in 1925 to a million today.

Nonetheless, many Indigenous languages in (what is now) Canada were lost when their last speakers died, including Laurentian (Iroquoian, Québec) in the late 1500s; Beothuk (isolate, Newfoundland) in 1829; Nicola (Dene/Athabaskan, British Columbia) in the late 1800s; Huron-Wendat (Iroquoian, Québec) and Tsetsaut/Ts'ets'aut (Dene/Athabaskan, British Columbia) in the early 1900s; and Pentlatch (Salish, British Columbia) around 1940. (Beothuk appears to have been an isolate; as such, it represents yet another language lineage in Canada.)

Of the languages that remain in Canada, many are critically endangered. Notably, the Algonquian languages Munsee Delaware and Western Abenaki, the Dene/Athabaskan languages Hän and Tagish, and the Iroquoian languages Tuscarora and Seneca each have only a few remaining speakers. Dialects, too, are disappearing, such as the Ts'ooke and Songish dialects of Northern Straits Salish. This state of affairs resulted in part from deliberate action: Indigenous language use was generally forbidden in the church- and government-run residential schools to which Indigenous children were sent from the 1880s to the 1970s.

Other Indigenous languages with more speakers are nonetheless rapidly becoming obsolete under the influence of English and French, which have become the languages of the nursery and the living room in most of Canada due in part to the influence of mass media. Recently, however, many Indigenous communities have sought to counteract the loss of their ancestral languages. With the help of government agencies, museums, and universities, they have launched programs to retain and promote their languages and cultures. As a result of this renaissance movement, some languages (such as Tsilhqut'in, Ktunaxa, and Secwepemctsín) have seen the establishment of an orthography for the first time, and others have become part of school curricula or even a medium of instruction in lower grades. The long-term effect of this effort on the survival of Indigenous languages remains to be seen. In the meantime, linguists can assist Indigenous communities who wish to preserve their languages by becoming involved in the development of sociolinguistic surveys, curriculum material, and resource materials such as dictionaries, grammars, and texts.

Linguists can also help by dispelling counterproductive ideas and policies with research evidence. There is a pervasive ideology of monolingualism in North America that encourages Indigenous parents and other caregivers to raise children with a single language—English or French. According to this ideology, parents are told it is irregular and perhaps disadvantageous to raise children with one or more Indigenous languages alongside English and/or French: it may expose them to prejudice or discrimination; it may strain their growing brains, causing delays or even disorders of a linguistic, cognitive, or social nature; it may confuse the children, causing them to mix or fuse languages, and even to fail to master any language fully; they may fall behind their monolingual peers and not 'fit in'; and so on.

In reality, research suggests that young children exposed to multiple languages develop separate and complete linguistic systems, simultaneously, without effort or confusion (see Chapter 12). Proficient speakers may mix languages, but only in fluent speech, by rapidly shifting between systems, as caregivers and others around them do.

9.1.4 Reclamation of Indigenous languages in Canada

It is remarkable that in spite of the difficulties confronting them, certain Indigenous languages in Canada remain relatively healthy. For instance, speakers of Dënesųłiné abound in parts of Saskatchewan (9065). Nine out of every ten people who have grown up speaking this Dene/ Athabaskan language continue to use it regularly at home. It therefore continues to be acquired by children as a first language in many northern communities, such as Fond du Lac, Black Lake, and La Loche. A similar situation holds in Québec among speakers of Inuktitut (12 250), Innu-aimun (9770), and Atikamekw (6600). Children raised in homes with these Inuit and Algonquian languages all but guarantee the continued existence of their Indigenous linguistic heritage.

In the 2016 census, 228 765 people reported speaking an Indigenous language at home. Interestingly, a large number of them reported having acquired the Indigenous language as a second or third language, after English or French. Moreover, many such second-language speakers of Indigenous languages report using it regularly at home, in addition to their mother tongues (e.g., Cree: 14 630; Anishinaabemowin [Ojibwe]: 7030; Inuktitut: 2845; Dënesųłiné: 460). The number of Indigenous language learners continues to grow among youth in particular, many of whom already or may soon have children of their own. Their multilingual households may significantly improve the long-term viability of Indigenous languages—even ones discouragingly termed 'near-extinct'.

For instance, while only two dozen elderly fluent speakers of X̱aad Kil remain (on Haida Gwaii in British Columbia), 150 youth and adults on Haida Gwaii are currently learning this language isolate and using it regularly at home. Especially promising is that a dozen of these second-language learners are already semi-fluent, and some of them are now raising their children in X̱aad Kil. Similarly, there are only 60 elderly native speakers of Goyogóhó:nǫ' (Cayuga), but there are 200 second-language learners on the Six Nations Reserve in Ontario, and 15 of their children are growing up bilingual. Another uniquely compelling case is Huron-Wendat: its last mother-tongue speakers in Canada passed away a century ago, but dozens of new speakers—a few of whom claim fluency—were created anew in Wendake, Québec, as part of a million-dollar-per-year project called Yawenda ('Voice'), which ran from 2007 to 2013.

It can be very difficult to learn a new language, and to find opportunities to use it regularly after childhood. Indigenous youth and adults who take up this challenge often ascribe their drive to a sense of duty, honour, and pride. Most describe their heritage tongue as a sacred trust—their forebears' will and testament of cultural and historical survival. Moreover, many regard their ancestral languages as essential to forming healthy identities and relationships and to their social, physical, and spiritual health. There is indeed increasing evidence that Indigenous language use correlates with physical and mental well-being. This correlation bodes well for Indigenous peoples and their languages, as they continue to recover from historical, political, economic, social, and cultural upheavals.

9.2 Structural features

Since there are so many apparently unrelated languages in Canada, it is not surprising to find a great deal of typological variation. Although it is impossible to present even a synopsis of the structural characteristics of these languages, a small selection of those that the reader might consider strikingly different and interesting will be given.

9.2.1 Phonology

The Algonquian languages (such as Cree and Blackfoot) and the Dene/Athabaskan languages (such as Tsúut'ína and Dënesųłiné) have long been in contact in the Prairie Provinces of Canada. However, the phonological differences between these two language families are striking. For example, Cree (an Algonquian language) has one of the simplest phonemic inventories while Dënesųłiné (Dene/Athabaskan) has one of the most complex.

Cree vowels may be either short or long, except for /eː/, which is always long. The Cree consonantal system is also simple and straightforward, with no aspiration or glottalization. Consonant clusters are rare, and the most common syllable types are CV, CVC, and V. The vowel and consonant systems of Cree are given in table 9.10.

TABLE 9.10 Vowel and consonant phonemes in Cree

Vowel phonemes		Consonant phonemes	Bilabial	Alveolar/ Palatal	Velar	Glottal
i, iː	o, oː	Obstruents	p	t	k	
				ts		
eː	a, aː			s		h
		Sonorants	m	n		
				j	w	

In contrast, Dënesųłiné has five tense vowels, each of which may be either oral or nasal, as well as a lax vowel, which has no nasal counterpart. The Dënesųłiné consonant system has four times more phonemes than does Cree. It is characterized by a large and symmetrical class of obstruents, particularly affricates, as shown in table 9.11. Another characteristic of Dënesųłiné phonology is the presence of contrastive tone, which, along with nasality, makes for many more syllable types in Dënesųłiné than in Cree.

TABLE 9.11　Vowel and consonant phonemes in Dënesųłiné

Vowel phonemes

	Oral			*Nasal*	
i		u	ĩ		ũ
e	ə	o	ẽ		õ
	a			ã	

Consonant phonemes

	Labial	*Interdental*	*Alveolar*	*Alveolar*
Plain	p	tθ	t	ts
Aspirated		tθ^h	t^h	ts^h
Glottalized		tθ'	t'	ts'
		ð		z
		θ		s
	m		n	r

	Lateral	*Alveopalatal*	*Velar*	*Labiovelar*	*Glottal*
Plain	tɬ	tʃ	k	(k^w)	
Aspirated	tɬ^h	tʃ^h	k^h	(k^{wh})	
Glottalized	tɬ'	tʃ'	k'	(k$^{w'}$)	ʔ
	l	j	ɣ	w	
	ɬ	ʃ	x	(x^w)	h

Note: ɬ is a voiceless alveolar lateral fricative, ɣ is a voiced velar fricative, and x is a voiceless velar fricative.

Putting aside the elements in parentheses (whose phonemic status is questionable), there are thirty-five consonantal phonemes in Dënesųłiné, most of which are obstruents. Several sets of stops, affricates, and fricatives constitute the core system. There are two very conspicuous phonological characteristics: a three-way contrast (plain versus aspirated versus glottalized) involving six sets of stops and affricates, and a large inventory of affricates in four series (interdental, alveolar, lateral, and alveopalatal). Particularly worthy of note here are the interdental and lateral affricates, which are seldom found in other language families, as well as the paucity of bilabial stops. The syllable structure is either CV or CVC.

The examples in table 9.12 illustrate CV and CVC syllable types as well as a contrast between oral and nasal vowels and between high tone (marked by the diacritic ´) and low tone.

TABLE 9.12	Vowel and tone contrasts in Dënesųɫiné			
Low tone/high tone	ɫu	'fish'	ɫú	'white fish'
	kʰūe	'house'	kʰūé	'town'
	teskʰoθ	'I cough'	teskʰóθ	'I am wide'
Oral/nasal	ti	'prairie chicken'	tĩ(ɣĩ)	'four'
	tsʰá	'beaver'	tsʰą́	'excrement'
	si	'I'	sĩ	emphatic particle

In Dënesųɫiné, consonant clusters are avoided in syllable margins, and every syllable has a vowel; as already noted, syllables are maximally CVC. Some consonant clusters are allowed in Cree syllables: for example, /amisk/ 'beaver', /ospwa:kan/ 'pipe'. Consonant clusters that are considerably more complex are found in other Indigenous languages in Canada. In particular, Blackfoot (Algonquian) allows words like /niʔtssksksínitaksini/ 'one minute', and Oowekyala (Wakashan) and Nuxalk (Salish) are notorious for allowing all-consonant utterances, as in (2) and (3).

(2) tɫxҳspstɫkts (Oowekyala)
'This (here with me, not visible) will be a nice thwart.'

(3) ts'ktskʷts' (Nuxalk)
'He arrived.'

9.2.2 Morphology

Equally interesting characteristics of North American Indigenous languages are seen in their morphology, whose complexity has fascinated linguists for many years. We can illustrate some of these intricacies with the help of several Indigenous languages spoken in Canada.

Polysynthesis

The term *polysynthetic* is often used to underscore the morphological complexities that are easily observable in many Indigenous languages. **Polysynthetic languages** are characterized by morphologically complex words whose component morphemes often express meanings that would be expressed by separate words in such languages as English and Mandarin. In Inuktitut, for instance, a typical word consisting of a root followed by one or more bound morphemes can be the equivalent of an entire sentence in English. The following utterances, transliterated into the Roman alphabet, are each considered to consist of a single word. (There is allomorphic variation involving the morpheme *gik/rik* meaning 'good'.)

(4) *a.* Iglu-gik-tuq.
house-good-has.3SG
'He has a good house.'

b. Qayaq-rik-tuq.
kayak-good-has.3SG
'He has a good kayak.'

The following words further illustrate polysynthesis in Slave, a Dene/Athabaskan language, and Blackfoot, an Algonquian language.

(5) ts'e-   kʰu-   nĭ-   wa (Slave)
preverb   them   you   wake
'You woke them.'

(6) máát-   á-   akahkayi-   wa (Blackfoot)
not   be   go home   he
'He is not going home.'

Person and number

Most English speakers are familiar with a three-way contrast involving person (first person—speaker; second person—addressee; third person—other party) and a two-way contrast involving number (unmarked singular versus marked plural). In many Indigenous languages in Canada, however, a much more elaborate system of contrasts is encountered. For instance, Inuktitut has three subcategories of number—singular (one), dual (two), and plural (three or more). The following two sets of examples illustrate how these subcategories are marked in nouns and verbs.

(7) iglu   'an igloo (house)'   niriyu-q   'he ate'
iglu-k   'igloos (two)'   niriyu-k   'they (two) ate'
iglu-t   'igloos (three or more)'   niriyu-t   'they (three or more) ate'

The Algonquian languages have an especially elaborate system of person and number marking, as the verb paradigm from Cree in table 9.13 illustrates.

TABLE 9.13 Person and number marking in Cree verbs		
pimisin 'to lie down'		
1st singular	ni-pimisin-in	'I lie down'
2nd singular	ki-pimisin-in	'you (sg) lie down'
3rd singular (proximate)	pimisin	'he or she lies down'
4th singular (obviative)	pimisin-ijiwa	'the other lies down'
1st plural (inclusive)	ki-pimisin-inaw	'we (including you) lie down'
1st plural (exclusive)	ni-pimisin-inaːn	'we (excluding you) lie down'
2nd plural	ki-pimisin-inaːwaːw	'you (pl) lie down'
3rd plural	pimisin-wak	'they lie down'

These examples exhibit a contrast in the first person plural between the so-called **inclusive** and **exclusive**. This contrast is found not only in Algonquian languages, but also in languages in the Iroquoian, Siouan, and Wakashan families. The inclusive verb form indicates that the addressee is to be included in the interpretation of the morpheme corresponding to English *we*. Thus, /ki-pimisin-inaw/, the inclusive first person plural form, means 'you and I (and possibly others) lie down'. In contrast, the exclusive form /ni-pimisin-inaːn/ indicates that the addressee is to be excluded. In English, the phrase 'we lie down' is potentially ambiguous because the grammatical distinctions observed in Cree are not made.

The grammatical distinction between **proximate** and **obviative** (sometimes called third person and fourth person, respectively) is made in all Algonquian languages, as well as in the isolate Ktunaxa. It is difficult to describe, but an example may help illustrate its function. Suppose you and I are talking about two male persons other than ourselves and that one of us uses the sentence *He lay down.* In English it is unclear which of the two people *he* refers to. Cree speakers avoid this ambiguity by choosing one 'third person' as the focus of the conversation and marking this choice grammatically. One of the ways that this choice can be signalled is by using the focused person's name as subject of a proximate form of the verb. Subsequent references to that person can then be made by means of a proximate verb form. Thus, when a Cree speaker uses the proximate form /pimisin/ to express the meaning 'he lay down', listeners know that he or she is talking about the person chosen as the focus of the conversation. Reference to any other person requires use of the obviative form /pimisin-ijiwa/.

Gender

Several Iroquoian languages (Mohawk, Oneida, and Onondaga) divide third-person pronominals into **masculine, feminine**, and **neuter**, in the manner of English (*he, she, it*) and other Indo-European languages. (The following Kanien'kéha/Mohawk examples are written using the language's orthography.)

(8) Wa<u>h</u>ahnekí:ra'.
'<u>He</u> drank it.'

Wa'<u>e</u>hnekí:ra'.
'<u>She</u> drank it.' (This can also be used for unspecified sex: 'someone drank it'.)

Wa'<u>ka</u>hnekí:ra'.
'<u>It</u> drank it.' (This can also be used for some female persons: 'she drank it'.)

In contrast, grammatical gender in Cree and other Algonquian languages distinguishes between animate and inanimate. This contrast can be seen in the two different forms of the Cree plural suffix: /-ak/ for animate nouns and /-a/ for inanimate ones (see table 9.14).

TABLE 9.14	Animate and inanimate nouns in Cree			
	Singular		**Plural**	
Animate	si:si:p	'duck'	si:si:p-ak	'ducks'
	na:pe:w	'man'	na:pe:w-ak	'men'
	ospwa:kan	'pipe'	ospwa:kan-ak	'pipes'
Inanimate	mi:nis	'berry'	mi:nis-a	'berries'
	astotin	'cap'	astotin-a	'caps'
	a:tsimo:win	'story'	a:tsimo:win-a	'stories'

As the assignment of /ospwa:kan/ 'pipe' to the animate class illustrates, this distinction can be sensitive to culture-specific factors whose motivation may no longer be obvious, especially to outsiders.

9.2.3 Syntax

Indigenous languages in Canada show great diversity in word order. For example, Wakashan languages such as Oowekyala have a strict VSO order. Salish languages and the isolate Ktunaxa are also verb-initial. By contrast, Siouan languages such as Dakota are rigidly SOV; Dene/Athabaskan languages are also verb-final.

(9) Verb-initial (Wakashan languages)
daduqʷla wism-aχi   w'ats'-iaχi (Oowekyala)
saw   man-the/a dog-the/a
'The/a man saw the/a dog.'

(10) Verb-final (Dene/Athabaskan languages)

tʰatʰaŋka pʰeʒi jutapi (Dakota)   k'ɔt'íníʔí mitʃàdikòdí ìɣálà (Tsúut'ína)
bison   grass eat   man   beaver   kill
'Bison eat grass.'   'The man killed a beaver.'

The word order in many other Canadian Indigenous languages is remarkably free. This is the case in Inuktitut, in Iroquoian languages such as Mohawk, in Algonquian languages such as Cree, and in Michif. All six orderings in each of (11) and (12) are grammatical and the literal meaning does not change. (The function of the morpheme *ne* in the VOS and OVS patterns in [12] is not yet understood.)

(11) 'The children killed the ducks.' (Cree)

SVO	awa:sisak nipahe:wak si:si:pa	'children killed ducks'
SOV	awa:sisak si:si:pa nipahe:wak	'children ducks killed'
VSO	nipahe:wak awa:sisak si:si:pa	'killed children ducks'
VOS	nipahe:wak si:si:pa awa:sisak	'killed ducks children'
OVS	si:si:pa nipahe:wak awa:sisak	'ducks killed children'
OSV	si:si:pa awa:sisak nipahe:wak	'ducks children killed'

(12) 'Sak likes her dress.' (Mohawk; written in Mohawk orthography)

SVO	Sak ra-nuhwe'-s ako-atya'tawi.	'Sak likes her-dress'
SOV	Sak ako-atya'tawi ra-nuhwe'-s.	'Sak her-dress likes'
VSO	Ra-nuhwe'-s Sak ako-atya'tawi.	'likes Sak her-dress'
VOS	Ra-nuhwe'-s ako-atya'tawi ne Sak.	'likes her-dress Sak'
OVS	Ako-atya'tawi ra-nuhwe'-s ne Sak.	'her-dress likes Sak'
OSV	Ako-atya'tawi Sak ra-nuhwe'-s.	'her-dress Sak likes'

Also of interest is the oft-repeated claim that many of Indigenous languages in Canada (especially those in the Salish, Wakashan, and Iroquoian families, as well as Inuktitut) lack a distinction between the syntactic categories of noun and verb. This claim is controversial, but most linguists agree that the noun/verb distinction is weak in the syntax of these languages. For example, in the Wakashan language Nuu-chah-nulth (Tseshaht dialect), /quːʔas/ 'man' has not only the noun-like use in (13a) but also the verb-like use in (13b). (Verbs come at the beginning of the sentence in Nuu-chah-nulth.)

(13)   *a.*   Noun-like use of *quːʔas*   *b.*   Verb-like use of *quːʔas*

           mamuːk-ma   quːʔas-ʔi   quːʔas-ma   mamuːk-ʔi

           work-3sɢ   man-the   man-3sɢ   work-the

           'The man is working.'   'The working one is a man.'

Summing up

This chapter outlines genetic classifications, geographic distributions, and speaker populations of Indigenous languages in Canada and presents a selection of phonological and grammatical characteristics of these languages. Even this brief discussion illustrates just how much languages can differ from each other. It is important to remember that despite their differences and occasionally unusual properties, these and other languages can still be described in terms of universal categories and processes (phonemes, morphemes, inflection, derivation, phrase structure, and so on). For this reason, the structural diversity of Indigenous languages in Canada offers the linguist opportunities to reaffirm familiar principles, as well as to discover new insights into the nature of human language.

Recommended reading

Campbell, Lyle. 1997. *American Indian Languages: The Historical Linguistics of Native America.* Oxford: Oxford University Press.

Goddard, Ives, ed. 1996. *Handbook of North American Indians, Vol. 17: Languages.* Washington, DC: Smithsonian Institution.

Mithun, Marianne. 2001. *The Languages of Native North America.* Cambridge, UK: Cambridge University Press.

Voegelin, C.F., and F.M. Voegelin. 1965. "Classification of American Indian Languages." Languages of the World, Native America Fascicle 2, section 1.6, *Anthropological Linguistics* 7: 121–50.

To learn more about the topics discussed in this chapter, visit the Companion Website for *Contemporary Linguistic Analysis.*

First language acquisition

The only language that [people] learn perfectly
is acquired [in] childhood when no one can
teach [them].

MARIA MONTESSORI, *THE ABSORBENT MIND* (1949)

A MAJOR LANDMARK in human development is the acquisition of language. Most children acquire language quickly and effortlessly, giving the impression that the entire process is simple and straightforward. However, the true extent of children's achievement becomes evident when we compare their success with the difficulties encountered by adults who try to learn a second language. Understanding how children the world over are able to master the complexities of human language in the space of a few short years has become one of the major goals of contemporary linguistic research.

This chapter provides a brief overview of the progress that has been made in this area. We will begin by considering the research strategies used by linguists and psychologists in the study of linguistic development. We will then describe some of the major findings concerning children's acquisition of the various parts of their language—phonology, vocabulary, morphology, syntax, and semantics. The chapter concludes with a brief examination of the contribution of the linguistic environment to language acquisition, the relationship between the emergence of language and cognitive development, and the possible existence of inborn linguistic knowledge.

10.1 The study of language acquisition

Although we commonly refer to the emergence of language in children as 'language acquisition', the end result of this process is actually a **grammar**—the mental system that allows people to speak and understand a language. There are at least two reasons for believing that the development of linguistic skills must involve the acquisition of a grammar.

First, mature language users are able to produce and understand an unlimited number of novel sentences. This can only happen if, as children, they have acquired the grammar for their language. Simple memorization of a fixed inventory of words and sentences would not equip learners to deal with previously unheard utterances—a basic requisite of normal language use.

A second indication that children acquire grammatical rules comes from their speech errors, which often provide valuable clues about how the acquisition process works. Even run-of-the-mill errors such as *doed, *runned, and *goed can be informative. Since adults don't talk that way, such errors tell us that children don't just imitate what they hear. Rather, they create rules of their own to capture the regularities that they observe in the speech of those around them.

10.1.1 Methods

Two complementary methods of data collection are used in the study of child language—naturalistic observation and experimentation.

Two approaches

In the **naturalistic approach**, investigators observe and record children's spontaneous utterances. One type of naturalistic investigation is the so-called **diary study**, in which a researcher (often a parent) keeps daily notes on a child's linguistic progress. Here's a short example, drawn from a diary tracking a child's early vocabulary development.

Date	Child's word	Adult word	Comment
June 9, 2003	krakuh	cracker	said several times to refer to Japanese crackers; used a few days later to refer to graham crackers
June 24, 2003	G	MG	said on several occasions while pointing at the MG symbol on her father's shirt; used on July 24 to refer to an actual MG roadster

---

Language Matters Darwin the Linguist

One of the first language diarists was Charles Darwin, who kept a detailed record of the development of his son. Among the observations in "A Biographical Sketch on an Infant" (1877) is the following anecdote: "At exactly the age of a year, he invented a word for food, namely *mum*. . . . And now instead of beginning to cry when he was hungry, he used the word in a demonstrative manner or as a verb, implying 'Give me food'."

In *The Descent of Man*, Darwin wrote that language "has justly been considered as one of the chief distinctions between man and the lower animals."

Sources: Charles Darwin, "A Biographical Sketch on an Infant," *Mind* 2 (1877): 285–94; Charles Darwin, *The Descent of Man, and Selection in Relation to Sex* (New York: D. Appleton, 1882), 84.

Another way to collect naturalistic data involves regular taping sessions, often at biweekly intervals, to gather samples (usually an hour at a time) of the child interacting with his or her caregivers. Detailed transcripts are then made for subsequent analysis. A great deal of data of this type is available through CHILDES (the Child Language Data Exchange System), which can be accessed online at childes.talkbank.org. Here is a small excerpt from a CHILDES transcript containing a fragment of a conversation between Adam (aged 2 years, 5 months) and his mother:

*CHI:	car
*MOT:	one is a car and one is a what?
*CHI:	truck
*CHI:	(a)nother one truck
*CHI:	(a)nother one
*CHI:	train
*CHI:	Adam drop it train
*CHI:	choo-choo train . . .
*CHI:	drop it choo-choo train
*MOT:	oh
*MOT:	Adam dropped the choo choo train?
*CHI:	yep
*CHI:	choo-choo train
*CHI:	choo-choo [8 times]
*CHI:	train
*CHI:	train coming

The CHILDES database includes thousands of hours of data from more than twenty languages.

Naturalistic studies tend to be **longitudinal** in that they examine language development over an extended period of time (sometimes as long as several years). As the name suggests, longitudinal studies take a long time to conduct, but they have the advantage of permitting researchers to observe development as an ongoing process in individual children.

Naturalistic data collection provides a great deal of information about how the language acquisition process unfolds, but it also has its shortcomings. The most serious of these is that particular structures and phenomena may occur rarely in children's everyday speech, making it difficult to gather enough information from natural speech samples to test hypotheses or draw firm conclusions. This problem is further compounded by the fact that speech samples from individual children capture only a small portion of their utterances at any given point in development. Because of the amount of time required to transcribe and analyze recordings, researchers typically have to be content with hour-long samples taken at weekly or biweekly intervals.

In **experimental** studies, researchers typically make use of specially designed tasks to elicit linguistic activity relevant to the phenomenon that they wish to study. The child's performance is then used to formulate hypotheses about the type of grammatical system acquired at that point in time.

Experimental research is typically **cross-sectional** in that it investigates and compares the linguistic knowledge of different children at a particular point in time. A typical cross-sectional study might involve conducting a single experiment with a group of two-year-olds, a group of four-year-olds, and a group of six-year-olds, taking each of these groups to be representative of a particular stage or 'cross-section' of the developmental process.

Types of experimental studies

Experimental studies usually employ tasks that test children's comprehension, production, or imitation skills. One widely used method for testing comprehension calls for children to judge the truth of statements that are made about particular pictures or situations presented to them

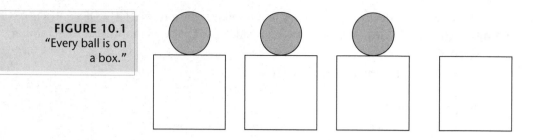

FIGURE 10.1
"Every ball is on a box."

by the experimenter. Figure 10.1 offers an example of one such task. When asked whether every ball is on a box, many preschool children respond by saying 'no', justifying their answer by noting that one of the boxes doesn't have a ball on it!

A second method for testing comprehension involves supplying children with an appropriate set of props and then asking them to act out the meaning of a sentence—perhaps a passive structure such as *The truck was bumped by the car*. Children's responses can provide valuable clues about the type of grammatical rules being used to interpret sentences at various stages of development.

In a typical production task, the experimenter presents the child with a situation that calls for a particular type of statement or question. In order to determine whether three-year-old children correctly order the auxiliary verb and the subject when asking *yes-no* questions, for instance, a researcher might design a game in which the child asks a puppet for his opinion about various pictures, as in the example in Figure 10.2.

FIGURE 10.2
"Ask the puppet if the dog is smiling."

If all goes well, the child will respond by asking a question, which allows us to look for signs of Inversion—the operation that places the auxiliary verb to the left of the subject, as in *Is the dog smiling?*

Although production tasks can be useful for assessing certain types of linguistic knowledge, many structures are hard to elicit, even from adults, because they are used only in special contexts. (For example, passive sentences such as *The house was painted by students* are quite rare and are reserved for situations in which the speaker wants to highlight the 'under-goer' of an action.) Moreover, because children's ability to comprehend language is often more advanced than their ability to produce sentences of their own, production tasks can provide an overly conservative view of linguistic development unless they are accompanied by other types of tests.

Experiments that have children imitate model sentences can also provide important clues about grammatical development. Although imitation might appear to be easy, it has been found that children's ability to repeat a particular structure provides a good indication of how well they have mastered it. For instance, a child who has not yet acquired auxiliary verbs will repeat the sentence *Mickey is laughing* as *Mickey laughing*.

The principal advantage of the experimental approach is that it allows researchers to collect data of a very specific sort about particular phenomena or structures. Experimentation is not without its pitfalls, however. In addition to the difficulty of designing a good experiment, there is always the possibility that a child's performance will be affected by extraneous factors, such as inattention, shyness, or a failure to understand what is expected. Nonetheless, by using experimental techniques together with naturalistic observation, linguists and psychologists have made significant progress toward understanding the language acquisition process. This chapter is devoted to a survey of this progress, beginning with the development of speech sounds.

10.2 Phonological development

Children seem to be born with a perceptual system that is especially designed for listening to speech. Newborns respond differently to human voices than to other sounds, they show a preference for the language of their parents over other languages by the time they are two days old, and they can recognize their mother's voice within a matter of weeks.

From around one month of age, children exhibit the ability to distinguish among certain speech sounds. In one experiment, infants were presented with a series of identical [ba] syllables. These were followed by an occurrence of the syllable [pa]. A change in the children's sucking rate (measured by a specially designed pacifier) indicated that they perceived the difference between the two syllables and that they were therefore able to distinguish between [p] and [b].

10.2.1 Babbling

The ability to produce speech sounds begins to emerge around six months of age, with the onset of babbling. Babbling provides children with the opportunity to experiment with and begin to gain control over their vocal apparatus—an important prerequisite for later speech. Children who are unable to babble for medical reasons (because of the need for a breathing tube in their throat, for example) can subsequently acquire normal pronunciation, but their speech development is significantly delayed.

Language Matters **Hearing It All**

Infants are even able to distinguish between sounds in unfamiliar languages. In one experiment, six- to eight-month-old infants who were being raised in English-speaking homes could hear contrasts among unfamiliar consonants in Hindi and Nlaka'pamuxtsn (an Indigenous language spoken on parts of Canada's West Coast). By the time they were ten to twelve months old, though, this ability had begun to diminish.

Sources: P. Iverson, P.K. Kuhl, R. Akahane-Yamada, E. Diesch, Y. Tohkura, A. Kettermann, and C. Siebert, "A Perceptual Interference Account of Acquisition Difficulties for Non-native Phonemes," *Cognition* 87, 1 (2003): B47–57; P.K. Kuhl, K.A. Williams, F. Lacerda, K.N. Stevens, and B. Lindblom, "Language Experience Alters Phonetic Perception in Infants by Six Months of Age," *Science* 255 (1992): 606–8; Janet Werker, Valerie Lloyd, Judith Pegg, and Linda Polka, "Putting the Baby in the Bootstraps: Toward a More Complete Understanding of the Role of the Input in Infant Speech Processing," in *Signal to Syntax*, ed. J. Morgan and K. Demuth (Mahwah, NJ: Erlbaum, 1996), 427–47; Katherine Yoshida, Ferran Pons, Jessica Maye, and Janet Werker, "Distributional Phonetic Learning at Ten Months of Age," *Infancy* 15 (2010): 420–33.

Despite obvious differences among the languages to which they are exposed, children from different linguistic communities exhibit significant similarities in their babbling. The tendencies in table 10.1 are based on data from fifteen different languages, including English, Thai, Japanese, Arabic, Hindi, and K'iche'. (We focus here on consonant sounds, for which the data is somewhat more reliable than for vowels.)

TABLE 10.1 Cross-linguistic similarities in babbling	
Frequently found consonants	**Infrequently found consonants**
p b m	f v θ ð
t d n	ʃ ʒ tʃ dʒ
k g	l r ŋ
s h w j	

Such cross-linguistic similarities suggest that early babbling is at least partly independent of the particular language to which children are exposed. In fact, even deaf children babble, although their articulatory activity is somewhat less varied than that of hearing children.

10.2.2 Developmental order

Babbling increases in frequency until the age of about twelve months, at which time it begins to give way to intelligible words. By the time children have acquired fifty words or so (usually by around eighteen months of age), they begin to adopt fairly regular patterns of pronunciation.

Although there is a good deal of variation from child to child in terms of the order in which speech sounds are mastered in production and perception, the following general tendencies seem to exist.

- As a group, vowels are generally acquired before consonants (by age three).
- Stops tend to be acquired before other consonants.
- In terms of place of articulation, labials are often acquired first, followed (with some variation) by alveolars, velars, and alveopalatals. Interdentals ([θ] and [ð]) are acquired last.
- New phonemic contrasts manifest themselves first in word-initial position. Thus, the /p/-/b/ contrast, for instance, is manifested in pairs such as *pat-bat* before *cap-cab*.

By age two, a typical English-speaking child has the inventory of consonant phonemes shown in table 10.2.

TABLE 10.2 Typical consonant inventory at age two				
Stops			**Fricatives**	**Other**
p	b	m	f	w
t	d	n	s	
k	g			

By age four, this inventory is considerably larger and typically includes the sounds shown in table 10.3.

TABLE 10.3	Typical consonant inventory at age four			
Stops			**Fricatives**	**Affricates**	**Other**

Stops			**Fricatives**		**Affricates**	**Other**	
p	b	m	f	v	tʃ dʒ	w	j
t	d	n	s	z		1	r
k	g	ŋ	ʃ				

Many children do not acquire the interdental fricatives [θ] and [ð] and the voiced alveopalatal fricative [ʒ] until still later.

In general, the relative order in which sounds are acquired reflects their distribution in the world's languages. The sounds that are acquired early tend to be found in more languages whereas the sounds that are acquired late tend to be less common across languages.

10.2.3 Early phonetic processes

Children's ability to perceive the phonemic contrasts of their language develops well in advance of their ability to produce them. So even children who are unable to produce the difference between words like *mouse* and *mouth*, *cart* and *card*, or *jump* and *dump* may nonetheless be able to point to pictures of the correct objects in a comprehension task. Moreover, as the following experimenter's report vividly illustrates, children even seem to know that their pronunciations are sometimes not yet 'right'.

> *One of us spoke to a child who called his inflated plastic fish a fis. In imitation of the child's pronunciation, the observer said: "This is your fis?" "No," said the child, "my fis." He continued to reject the adult's imitation until he was told, "That is your fish." "Yes," he said, "my fis."*

The child's reaction to the adult's initial pronunciation of *fish* shows that he could perceive the difference between /s/ and /ʃ/ and that he had correctly represented the word as /fɪʃ/ in his lexicon even though he could not yet produce it himself.

What precisely is responsible for the special character of the sound patterns in children's early speech? The key seems to lie in the operation of a limited number of universal phonetic processes.

Syllable deletion

Because syllables bearing primary or secondary stress are more noticeable than their unstressed counterparts, they tend to be more salient to children in the early stages of the language acquisition process. As a result, stressed syllables are more likely to be retained in children's pronunciation than are unstressed syllables (see table 10.4).

TABLE 10.4   Differences in the retention of stressed and unstressed syllables

Word	Child's pronunciation
hip po pó ta mus	[pɑs]
spa ghé tti	[gɛ]
hé li còp ter	[ɛlkɑt]
kan ga róo	[wu]
té le phòne	[fow]

Note: ´ = primary stress; ` = secondary stress

However, unstressed syllables in final position tend to be retained, probably because the ends of words are easier to remember (see table 10.5).

TABLE 10.5   Retention of unstressed syllables in final position

Word	Child's pronunciation
po tá to	[tejdo]
ba ná na	[nænə]
to má to	[mejdo]
él e phant	[ɛlfən]

Syllable simplification

Another frequent process in children's speech involves the systematic deletion of certain sounds in order to simplify syllable structure. In the data in table 10.6, typical of the speech of two- and three-year-old children, consonant clusters are reduced by deleting one or more segments.

TABLE 10.6   Reduction of consonant clusters

[s] + stop (strategy: delete [s])
stop → [tɑp]
small → [mɑ]
desk → [dɛk]

stop + liquid (strategy: delete liquid)
try → [taj]
crumb → [gʌm]
bring → [bɪŋ]

fricative + liquid (strategy: delete liquid)
from → [fʌm]
sleep → [sip]

nasal + voiceless stop (strategy: delete nasal)
bump → [bʌp]
tent → [dɛt]

Yet another common deletion process in early child language involves the elimination of final consonants, as in the following examples.

(1) dog   [dɑ]
    bus   [bʌ]
    boot   [bu]

Both the reduction of consonant clusters and the deletion of final consonants have the effect of simplifying syllable structure, bringing it closer to the consonant-vowel (CV) template that is universally favoured by children and that is the most widely found pattern in human language in general.

Substitution

One of the most widespread phonetic processes in early language involves substitution—the systematic replacement of one sound by an alternative that the child finds easier to articulate (see table 10.7). Common substitution processes include **stopping**, the replacement of a fricative by a corresponding stop; **fronting**, the moving forward of a sound's place of articulation; **gliding**, the replacement of a liquid by a glide; and **denasalization**, the replacement of a nasal stop by a non-nasal counterpart.

TABLE 10.7   Substitution in early speech

Process	Example	Change
Stopping (continuant → stop)	sing → [tɪŋ]	s → t
	sea → [ti]	s → t
	zebra → [dibrə]	z → d
	thing → [tɪŋ]	θ → t
	this → [dɪt]	ð → d, s → t
	shoes → [tud]	ʃ → t, z → d
Fronting	ship → [sɪp]	ʃ → s
	jump → [dzʌmp]	dʒ → dz
	chalk → [tsɑːk]	tʃ → ts
	go → [dow]	g → d
Gliding	lion → [jajn̩]	l → j
	laughing → [jæfɪŋ]	l → j
	look → [wʊk]	l → w
	rock → [wak]	r → w
	story → [stowi]	r → w
Denasalization	spoon → [bud]	n → d
	jam → [dæb]	m → b
	room → [wub]	m → b

Assimilation

Still another widespread phonetic process in child language is assimilation—the modification of one or more features of a segment under the influence of neighbouring sounds. In the following examples, initial consonants have been voiced in anticipation of the following vowel.

(2) tell [dɛl]
    pig [bɪg]
    push [bʊs]
    soup [zup]

Assimilation is also observed in children's tendency to maintain the same place of articulation for all of the consonants or vowels in a word. This can lead to the pronunciation of *doggy* as [gɑgi] (with identical consonants), and [bibi] for *baby* (with identical vowels in both syllables). Other examples include [fɛlf] for *self*, [kæklɪn] for *Cathleen*, and [næns] for *dance*.

10.3 Vocabulary development

By age eighteen months or so, the average child has a vocabulary of fifty words or more. Common items include the words listed in table 10.8.

TABLE 10.8   Common items in the first fifty words
Entities
Words referring to people: *daddy, mommy, baby* food/drink: *juice, milk, cookie, water, toast, apple, cake* animals: *dog, cat, duck, horse* clothes: *shoes, hat* toys: *ball, blocks* vehicles: *car, boat, truck* other: *bottle, key, book*
Properties
hot, allgone, more, dirty, cold, here, there
Actions
up, sit, see, eat, go, down
Personal-social
hi, bye, no, yes, please, thank-you

As table 10.8 shows, noun-like words make up the single largest class in the child's early vocabulary, with verb- and adjective-like words being the next most frequent category types. Among the most frequent words are expressions for displeasure or rejection (such as *no*) and various types of social interaction (such as *please* and *bye*). Over the next months, this vocabulary grows rapidly, sometimes by as much as ten or twelve words a day. By age six, most children have mastered about 13 000 or 14 000 words.

Children seem to differ somewhat in the types of words that they focus on, especially in the early stages of language acquisition. One of these differences is reflected in the number of nouns in early vocabulary. Whereas some children have a relatively high proportion of such words (75 percent or more) by age two, other learners exhibit a much lower percentage of nouns (50 percent or less). Making up for the smaller number of nouns is a larger vocabulary of socially useful expressions such as *bye, go-away, stop-it, thank-you, I-want-it*, and so on. (Hyphens are used here to indicate that these expressions are not yet segmented into their component words.)

Language Matters **Moving Along**

Every child develops at his or her own pace, of course, but to the extent that we can depict a 'typical' profile for vocabulary development, it would look something like this. Note the relatively slow start (just fifty words in eighteen months), followed by a rapid acceleration that is sustained over a multi-year period.

18 mos.	6 yrs.	17 yrs.
- - - 10 words per day	up to 20 words per day	- - -
↑	↑	↑
50 words	14 000 words	60 000 words

10.3.1 Strategies for acquiring word meaning

Children seem to draw on certain strategies when trying to determine the meaning of a new word. This is perhaps easiest to illustrate in the case of noun-type meanings, for which the following strategies appear to be employed.

(3) Three strategies for learning the meanings of new words:

The Whole Object Assumption
A new word refers to a whole object.

The Type Assumption
A new word refers to a type of thing, not just to a particular thing.

The Basic Level Assumption
A new word refers to objects that are alike in basic ways (appearance, behaviour, etc.).

To see how these strategies work, imagine that a mother and her eighteen-month-old daughter are driving through the countryside and they encounter a sheep munching on the grass. The mother points to the animal and says "sheep." What does the child think the word means? Does it mean 'white', or does it mean 'woolly'? Does it refer to the animal? Or to parts of the animal? Or does it refer to the fact that a particular animal is munching on grass?

The Whole Object Assumption allows the child to infer that the word *sheep* refers to the animal itself, not to its parts, not to its whiteness, and not to its woolliness. The Type

Assumption allows her to infer that *sheep* refers to a type of animal, not to just one particular sheep. And the Basic Level Assumption leads her to guess that *sheep* is used to refer just to white, four-legged, woolly animals, and not to animals in general.

Contextual clues

Another major factor in vocabulary development is the child's ability to make use of contextual clues to draw inferences about the category and meaning of new words. For instance, from early in the language acquisition process, children can use the presence or absence of determiners to distinguish between names and ordinary nouns. Two-year-old children who are told that a new doll is *a dax* will apply this label to similar-looking dolls as well. However, if they are told that the new doll is *Dax*, they assume that it refers just to the doll they have actually been shown. Like adults, these children treat *dax* as an ordinary noun when it is preceded by *a*, but as a name when there is no determiner.

In another experiment, three- and four-year-old children were asked to act out the meaning of sentences such as 'Make it so there is *tiv* to drink in this glass (of water)'. The only clues about the interpretation of *tiv* came from the meaning of the rest of the sentence and from the child's understanding of the types of changes that can be made to a glass of water. Not only did more than half the children respond by either adding or removing water, but some even remembered what *tiv* 'meant' two weeks later!

For children to benefit from this sort of experience, they have to have some sense of what other speakers are talking about. The meaning of a new word can hardly be learned if the speaker is referring to one thing and the child is focused on another. Somehow, children have to be 'in sync' with other humans—noticing what they notice and thinking what they are thinking.

This is no trivial matter. In fact, psychologists often note that being able to sense the intentions and thoughts of others in this way requires a 'theory of mind'—an understanding of how other people think and see the world. This is part of what it takes to be a social creature—to 'fit in' to a family and a society.

(4) *The Social Strategy*
To figure out what new words mean, think like other people think.

A variety of experiments help illustrate how children use this strategy. In one experiment involving two-year-old children, an adult looked at and named a toy (saying, "Look! A modi!") just as the child's attention was drawn to another toy by lighting it up. When the children were then asked to retrieve the 'modi', they consistently chose the object that the adult had been looking at. Somehow, the children knew that the adult was naming the toy that he was looking at when he spoke, regardless of what else was happening. That's how language is used in ordinary social situations, and part of learning a language involves realizing that simple fact.

10.3.2 Meaning errors

The meanings that children associate with their early words sometimes correspond closely to the meanings employed by adults. In many cases, however, the match is less than perfect. The two most typical semantic errors involve overextension and underextension.

Language Matters **Fast Mapping**

How many times does a child have to hear a new word in order to learn it? In one study, eighteen-month-old children were able to learn pairs of new words after just three exposures. In a study of somewhat older children (two- to five-year-olds), a single encounter with a new word led to impressive success: 81 percent of the children could identify the word's referent the next time they heard it. The rapid learning of new words is called *fast mapping*.

Sources: C. Dollaghan, "Child Meets Word," *Journal of Speech and Hearing Research* 28 (1985): 449–54; C. Houston-Price, K. Plunkett, and P. Harris, "Word Learning Wizardry at 1:6," *Journal of Child Language* 32 (2005): 175–90.

Overextensions

In cases of **overextension**, the meaning of the child's word is more general or inclusive than that of the corresponding adult form. The word *dog*, for example, can be overextended to include horses, cows, and other four-legged animals. Similarly, *ball* is sometimes used for any round object, including a balloon, an Easter egg, a small stone, and so on. As many as one-third of children's words may be overextended at the fifty-word stage of vocabulary development (see table 10.9).

TABLE 10.9   Examples of overextension

Word	First referent	Subsequent extensions
tick tock	watch	clocks, gas meter, fire hose on a spool, scale with round dial
fly	fly	other small insects, specks of dirt, dust, child's toes, crumbs of bread
quack	duck	all birds and insects, flies, coins (with an eagle on the face)
candy	candy	cherries, anything sweet
apple	apples	balls, tomatoes, cherries, onions, biscuits
turtle	turtles	fish, seals
cookie	cookies	crackers, any dessert
kitty	cats	rabbits, any small furry animal
box	boxes	elevators
belt	belts	watch strap

Physical similarities seem to be a critical factor in children's first hypotheses about word meanings. As a result, children often overextend a word to include a set of perceptually similar objects that they know to have diverse functions. For example, one child used the word *moon* for the moon, grapefruit halves, and a crescent-shaped car light. Another child used the word *money* for a set of objects ranging from pennies to buttons and beads. If you reconsider the examples of overextension given in table 10.9, you will see that they too can be explained in terms of visible similarities.

Many overextensions may be deliberate attempts to compensate for vocabulary limitations. One indication of this is that particular overextensions often disappear as soon as children learn the right word for the objects that they have been mislabelling. For example, two-year-old Allen was using the word *dog* for dogs, cats, sheep, and other four-legged mammals, but he stopped doing so as soon as he learned the words *cat* and *sheep*. If he thought that *dog* meant 'animal', he could still have sometimes referred to cats and sheep as *dogs* (just as adults sometimes refer to them as animals). The fact that he didn't suggests that he never thought *dog* meant 'animal'; he had just been 'borrowing' it until the right word came along.

A further indication that many overextensions are designed to compensate for vocabulary limitations comes from the fact that children seem to overextend more in their production than in their comprehension. Even children who sometimes use *dog* to refer to cows or horses typically point to the right animal when asked to point to the dog (see Figure 10.3). This is not what one would expect if children thought that *dog* meant 'animal'.

FIGURE 10.3
A sample
overextension test

Underextensions

Another possible type of word-meaning error in early language involves **underextension**, the use of lexical items in an overly restrictive fashion. Thus, *kitty* might be used to refer to the family pet but not to other cats. Or the word *dog* might be used for collies, spaniels, and beagles but not for teacup chihuahuas.

Underextension errors often reflect children's propensity to focus on prototypical or core members of a category. The potential referents of many words differ in terms of how well they exemplify the properties associated with a particular concept. For example, among the potential referents of the word *dog*, golden retrievers and spaniels have more of the properties associated with the concept 'dog' (long hair, relative size, type of bark, and so on) than do ultra-tiny teacup chihuahuas. While the preference for a prototype can be overruled by factors such as the presence of a non-typical category member in the child's everyday experience (e.g., a chihuahua as a family pet), the internal structure of concepts can have an important influence on semantic development.

Verb meanings

Meaning errors also occur with verbs. For example, some preschool children believe that *fill* means 'pour' rather than 'make full'. So, when asked to decide which of the two series of pictures in Figure 10.4 is an example of filling, they choose the second series—even though the glass remains empty!

FIGURE 10.4
Sample pictures used to test children's understanding of *fill*

Not surprisingly, children who make this sort of mistake tend to use *fill* in the wrong syntactic patterns as well.

(5) And fill the little sugars up in the bowl . . . (Mark, at age 4 yrs., 7 mos.)
    Can I fill some salt into the [salt shaker]? (E, at age 5 yrs.)

These errors disappear as children come to realize that *fill* means 'make full' rather than 'pour into'.

Dimensional terms

Terms describing size and dimensions are acquired in a relatively fixed order, depending on their generality (see table 10.10). The first adjectives of this type to be acquired, *big* and *small*, are the most general in that they can be used for talking about any aspect of size (height, area, volume,

TABLE 10.10 Order of acquisition for dimensional adjectives

Step	Words	What they describe
1	*big-small*	any aspect of size
2	*tall-short, long-short, high-low*	a single dimension
3	*thick-thin, wide-narrow, deep-shallow*	a secondary dimension

and so on). In contrast, the second group of adjectives to emerge—*tall, long, short, high,* and *low*—can only be used for a single dimension (height or length). The remaining modifiers (*thick-thin, wide-narrow,* and *deep-shallow*) are still more restricted in their use since they describe the secondary or less extended dimension of an object. For instance, the dimension of a stick that we describe in terms of width or thickness is almost always less extended than the dimension that we describe in terms of height or length, which tends also to be perceptually more salient.

The difficulty of dimensional adjectives for children is also evident in experimental tasks. In one experiment children aged three to five were shown pairs of objects—sometimes a big one and a tall one (pair [a] below) and sometimes a big one and a long one (pair [b] below). Younger children did well when asked to choose 'the big one'. However, when asked to choose 'the tall one' or 'the long one', they often picked the big one instead. This suggests that they are initially more sensitive to overall size than to a single dimension like height or length.

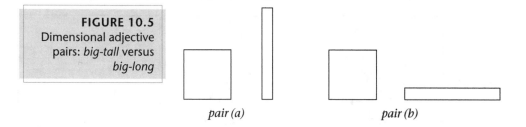

FIGURE 10.5
Dimensional adjective pairs: *big-tall* versus *big-long*

pair (a)   *pair (b)*

10.4 Morphological development

As is the case with the sound pattern of language and with vocabulary, the details of morphological structure emerge over a period of several years. Initially, affixes are systematically absent and most words consist of a single root morpheme.

10.4.1 Overgeneralization

Because many common words have irregular inflection in English (*went* as the past tense form of *go, ran* as the past form of *run, men* as the plural form of *man*), children sometimes begin by simply memorizing inflected words on a case-by-case basis without regard for general patterns or rules. As a result, they may initially use irregular forms such as *men* and *ran* correctly. However, when they subsequently observe the generality of *-s* as a plural marker and *-ed* as a past tense marker (usually around age two and a half), they sometimes use these suffixes for the irregular forms—producing words such as *mans* and *runned*. (Errors that result from the overly broad application of a rule are called **overgeneralizations** or **overregularizations**.) Even occasional mixed forms such as *felled*, a blend of *fell* and *falled*, may occur during this period. (See table 10.11.)

TABLE 10.11	The development of affixes
Stage 1:	Case-by-case learning (plural *boys, men*, etc.; past tense *walked, ran*, etc.)
Stage 2:	Overuse of general rule (plural *mans*; past tense *runned*)
Stage 3:	Mastery of exceptions to the general rule (plural *men*; past tense *ran*)

One of the best indications that children have mastered an inflectional rule comes from their ability to apply it to forms they have not heard before. In a classic experiment, children were shown a picture of a strange creature and told, "This is a wug." A second picture was then presented and the children were told, "Now, there's another wug. There are two of them. Now, there are two . . . ?" (see Figure 10.6). Even four- and five-year-old children did well with the plural forms of '*wug* words', demonstrating that the general rules for inflection have been learned by that time, despite the occurrence of occasional errors.

<table>
<tr><td>

FIGURE 10.6
The '*wug* test'

</td><td>

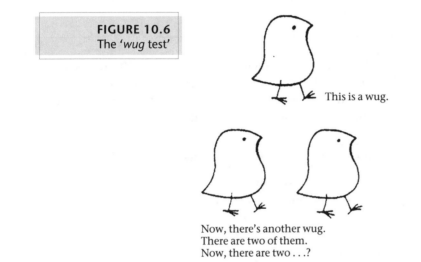

This is a wug.

Now, there's another wug.
There are two of them.
Now, there are two . . .?

</td></tr>
</table>

Source: Jean Berko, "The Child's Learning of English Morphology," *Word* 14 (1958): 150–77.
Reprinted courtesy of Jean Berko Gleason.

Although inflectional overgeneralizations such as *runned* for *ran* and *foots* for *feet* are very noticeable in children's speech, the rate at which they occur varies significantly from child to child. Moreover, there is also variation from word to word, depending in part on their relative frequency: for example, many children learn the past tense of *see* earlier than the past tense of the much less common verb *win*.

Language Matters How Many Times Does It Take to Get It Right?

How many times does a child have to hear the adult form of an irregular verb before all overregularizations are eliminated? Up to a hundred times, according to one estimate. That's why children are often relatively quick at figuring out the right past tense form for frequently heard irregular verbs like *go* and *see*, but take much longer to master less common verbs such as *sink* or *win*.

Source: Michael Maratsos, "More Overregularizations After All: New Data and Discussion on Marcus, Pinker, Ullman, Hollander, Rosen and Xu," *Journal of Child Language* 27 (2000): 183–212.

10.4.2 A developmental sequence

An important result of early work on child language was the discovery that the development of bound morphemes and functional categories (such as determiners and auxiliaries) takes place in an orderly fashion that is quite similar across children. In a pioneering study of three children between the ages of twenty and thirty-six months, the developmental sequence in table 10.12 was found to be typical.

TABLE 10.12 Typical developmental sequence for English non-lexical morphemes	
1. *-ing*	5. past tense *-ed*
2. plural *-s*	6. third person singular *-s*
3. possessive *-'s*	7. auxiliary *be*
4. *the, a*	

An interesting feature of this developmental sequence is that it seems to be at least partly independent of the frequency with which the various morphemes occur in adult speech (see table 10.13). For example, the determiners *the* and *a* are the most frequent morphemes in the children's environment but are nonetheless acquired relatively late.

TABLE 10.13 Typical relative frequency of morphemes in parental speech	
1. *the, a*	5. possessive *-'s*
2. *-ing*	6. third person singular *-s*
3. plural *-s*	7. past tense *-ed*
4. auxiliary *be*	

This shows that frequency by itself cannot explain developmental order for these morphemes, although it does have a significant role to play in many other cases. It's also clear that pronunciation by itself is not decisive either, since the three *-s* morphemes are acquired at different times.

What, then, determines the order of acquisition of non-lexical categories and bound morphemes? Research on a variety of languages suggests that several factors are involved.

1. ***Frequent occurrence, especially in utterance-final position*** Children show a greater tendency to notice and remember elements that occur at the end of the utterance than those found in any other position.

2. ***Syllabicity*** Children seem to take greater notice of morphemes such as *-ing*, which can constitute syllables on their own, than the plural or possessive suffix *-'s*, whose principal allomorphs (/-s/ and /-z/) are single consonants.

3. ***Absence of homophony*** Whereas the word *the* functions only as a determiner in English, the suffix *-s* can be used to mark any one of three things: plural number in nouns, third person singular in verbs, or possession. The resulting complication in the relationship between form and meaning may impede acquisition.

4. ***Few or no exceptions in the way it is used*** Whereas all singular nouns form the possessive with *-'s*, not all verbs use *-ed* to mark the past tense (*saw, read, drove*). Such exceptions hinder the language acquisition process.

5. ***Allomorphic uniformity*** Whereas the affix *-ing* has the same form for all verbs, the past tense ending *-ed* has three allomorphs—/-t/ for verbs such as *chase*, /-d/ for forms such as *love*, and /-əd/ for verbs such as *decide*. This type of allomorphic variation, which also

occurs with the plural, possessive, and third person singular affixes in English, slows morphological development.

6. ***Clearly discernible semantic function*** Whereas morphemes such as plural -*s* express easily identifiable meanings, some morphemes (such as the third person singular -*s*, as in *She works hard*) make no obvious contribution to the meaning of the sentence. Acquisition of this latter type of morpheme is relatively slow.

10.4.3 Word formation processes

The major word formation processes in English—derivation and compounding—both emerge early in the acquisition of English. The first derivational suffixes to show up in children's speech are the ones that are most common in the adult language (see table 10.14).

TABLE 10.14 Suffixes in the speech of a child prior to age four		
Ending	**Meaning**	**Example**
-*er*	'doer'	walk<u>er</u>
-*ie*	'diminutive'	dogg<u>ie</u>
-*ing*	'activity'	Runn<u>ing</u> is fun.
-*ness*	'state'	happi<u>ness</u>
Note: The suffix -*er* can also have an 'instrument' meaning, as in *cutter* 'something used for cutting', but this is less frequent in children's early speech.		

Children as young as three demonstrate an ability to use derivation to make up names for agents when presented with questions such as the following.

> *"I've got a picture here of someone who crushes things. What could we call someone who crushes things? Someone who crushes things is called a . . ."*

Children exhibit a propensity for forming compounds, especially of the N-N type. When asked "What would you call a boy who rips paper?", they don't hesitate to respond "a paper ripper." However, some of the compounds found in the spontaneous speech of three- and four-year-olds do not follow the usual pattern for English compounds (e.g., the verb-noun pattern **open man* for 'someone who opens things' and **cutter grass* for 'grass cutter'), but these disappear by age five. Other early compounds have the right structure but are inappropriate because English already has words with the intended meaning (see table 10.15).

TABLE 10.15 Some innovative compounds	
Child's word	**Intended meaning**
car-smoke	'exhaust'
cup-egg	'boiled egg'
firetruck-man	'fire fighter'
plant-man	'gardener'
store-man	'clerk'
leg-pit	'area behind the knee'

Language Matters It Takes a While

The full system of derivational morphology continues to develop well into the school years. Even ten-year-olds have some difficulty using suffixes to recognize the category of unfamiliar words, as when they are asked which of four words best fits in a sentence such as the following:

You can _____ the effect by turning off the lights.

intensify   intensification
intensity   intensive

They have even more trouble when the possible words are made up rather than real:

I wish Dr. Who would just _____ and get it over with.

transumpation   transumpative
transumpate   transumpatic

Source: A. Tyler and W. Nagy, "The Acquisition of English Derivational Morphology," *Journal of Memory and Language* 28 (1989): 649–67.

Children's creativity with compounds points to a preference for building words from other words, perhaps because this places less demand on memory than does learning an entirely new word for each concept.

Even the subtlest properties of word formation seem to be acquired in the preschool years. One such property involves the fact that an inflectional suffix such as the plural cannot occur inside compounds (compare *dogs catcher* with *dog catcher*). In one study, children as young as three years of age produced compounds that obeyed this constraint. Thus, when asked a question such as "What do you call someone who eats cookies?", they responded by saying *cookie eater* rather than *cookies eater*.

10.5 Syntactic development

Like phonological and morphological development, the emergence of syntactic structure takes place in an orderly manner and reveals much about the nature of the language acquisition process. We will briefly survey some of the milestones in this developmental process here.

10.5.1 The one-word stage

As noted earlier, children begin to produce one-word utterances between the ages of twelve and eighteen months. A basic property of these one-word utterances is that they can be used to express the type of meaning that is associated with an entire sentence in adult speech. Thus, a child might use the word *dada* to assert 'I see Daddy', *more* to mean 'Give me more juice', and *up* to mean 'I want to be picked up'. Such utterances are called **holophrases** (literally 'whole sentences').

In forming holophrastic utterances, children seem to choose the most informative word that applies to the situation at hand. A child who wants juice, for example, would say *juice* rather than *want* since *juice* is more informative in this situation. Similarly, a child who notices a new doll would be more likely to say *doll* than *see*, referring to the most novel feature of the situation he or she is trying to describe.

Table 10.16 presents examples of the types of holophrastic meaning that children commonly express during the one-word stage.

TABLE 10.16 Semantic relations in children's one-word utterances		
Semantic relation	**Utterance**	**Situation**
Agent of an action	*dada*	as father enters the room
Action or state	*down*	as child sits down
Undergoer (or 'theme')	*door*	as father closes the door
Location	*here*	as child points
Recipient	*mama*	as child gives mother something
Recurrence	*again*	as child watches lighting of a match

Comprehension appears to be considerably in advance of production in the one-word stage, and children are also able to understand many multi-word utterances during this period. One indication of this comes from an experiment in which children in the one-word stage listened to sentences such as *Big Bird is hugging Cookie Monster* as an experimenter tracked their gaze toward competing pictures: the children preferred to look at a depiction of Big Bird hugging Cookie Monster rather than the reverse situation.

10.5.2 The two-word stage

Within a few months of their first one-word utterances, children begin to produce two-word 'mini-sentences'. Table 10.17 provides a sampling of these utterances and the types of meaning they are commonly used to express. (Although these examples are from English, similar patterns are found in the early development of all languages.)

TABLE 10.17 Some patterns in children's two-word speech		
Utterance	**Intended meaning**	**Semantic relation**
Baby chair	'The baby is sitting on the chair.'	agent-location
Doggy bark	'The dog is barking.'	agent-action
Ken water	'Ken is drinking water.'	agent-theme
Hit doggy	'I hit the doggy.'	action-theme
Daddy hat	'Daddy's hat'	possessor-possessed

Early multi-word utterances tend to exemplify a relatively small number of 'slot-and-frame' patterns: *It's-a__, more__, no__, see__,* and so on. It is unclear whether children have acquired syntactic categories such as noun, verb, and adjective at this point in their development. This is because the markers that help distinguish among syntactic categories in adult English (e.g., inflection such as the past tense suffix and functional categories such as determiners and auxiliary verbs) are absent during this period. To complicate matters still further, the relative shortness of the utterances produced during the two-word stage means that the positional differences associated with category distinctions in adult speech are often not manifested. Thus, words such as *busy* (an adjective in adult speech) and *push* (a verb) may appear in identical patterns.

(6) Mommy busy.
Mommy push.

While this does not show that children lack syntactic categories, it makes it difficult to demonstrate that they possess them. For this reason, researchers are split over whether to describe children's utterances in terms of the syntactic categories of adult speech.

A notable feature of children's two-word utterances is that they almost always exhibit the appropriate word order, and there is some reason to think that learners have a general word order rule by the time they are three years old. Not only do they use the right subject–verb–direct object order in their own speech, they are reluctant to abandon this pattern, even when experimenters present them with verbs used in novel orders. In one experiment, for instance, children aged two to four were taught made-up verbs (such as *tam, gop*, and *dack*) for novel actions involving puppet characters. The verbs were presented using the following orders:

(7) *subject-verb-object order*: Elmo tammed the apple.
subject-object-verb order: Elmo the apple gopped.
verb-subject-object order: Dacked Elmo the apple.

Even very young children were far more likely to reproduce the experimenter's utterance when it contained the standard word order, and they rarely adopted an unusual word order for new verbs.

10.5.3 The telegraphic stage

After a period of several months during which their speech is largely limited to one- and two-word utterances, children begin to produce longer and more complex grammatical structures, drawing on an ever-growing store of words. As illustrated in the following examples from children's speech, a defining feature of these patterns is the frequent absence of bound morphemes and non-lexical categories.

(8) Chair broken.
Daddy like book.
What her name?
Man ride bus today.
Car make noise.
Me wanna show Mommy.
I good boy.

Linguists often call such speech **telegraphic**, thanks to its resemblance to the clipped style of language found in the now-defunct telegram (a pre-texting form of written communication that required paying by the word).

Although it is certainly true that many important morphemes are missing from children's early speech, these items do not go entirely unnoticed. As noted in section 10.3.1, for instance, children as young as seventeen months can infer from the presence or absence of a determiner whether a novel word refers to a type of object (e.g., a doll) or to a particular object. Eighteen-month-olds pay more attention to sentences containing an *is* + *V-ing* pattern (e.g., *she is playing*) than to one containing the ungrammatical *she can playing*. And infants as young as eleven months of age are surprised when *a* or *the* is replaced by a nonsense syllable, or when it is used in the wrong place, as in *book the*.

The **telegraphic stage** is characterized by the emergence of quite elaborate types of phrase structure. As the examples in (8) show, children can form phrases consisting of a head and a complement (*like book, ride bus, show mommy*), phrases that include a modifier (such as *today* and *good*), and even full-fledged sentences.

TABLE 10.18	The development of phrase structure	
Stage	**Approx. age**	**Developments**
Holophrastic	1–1.5 yrs.	single word utterances; no structure
Two-word	1.5–2 yrs.	early word combinations; presence of syntactic categories unclear
Telegraphic	2–2.5 yrs.	emergence of phrase structure

Language development from this point onward is rapid. As the examples in table 10.19 illustrate, in a matter of just a few months children move from relatively primitive two- and three-word utterances at the beginning of the telegraphic stage to a broad range of morphologically and syntactically intricate sentence types.

TABLE 10.19	Sample utterances from a child's speech over an 11-month period
Age	**Sample utterances**
28 mos.	What doing? Tape recorder Like some?
30 mos.	Take a button off. Dis a other one. Dat's a my pencil. Hand me a piece of paper.
32 mos.	This is heavy. You going faster? Where horses go? Go down right side.
34 mos.	Let me have one. Some kind fishing rod. Want some milk in it. Heard you talking. Look at that train Ursula brought. Is this goes over here?
36 mos.	Do you want me eat with that fork? I want to sit on steps. I'm going give Robin that pencil. Why not he have ball? You going bring raisin tomorrow?

(Continued)

| 38 mos. | I want to see what's going on in there.
Let's have something to read.
Mommy cook something eat.
I just went to sleep.
I don't want to go to bed again.
Mommy, I better go outside and hang yours outside . . . |

10.5.4 Later development

In the months following the telegraphic stage, children continue to acquire the complex grammar that underlies adult linguistic competence, including the operations that move various words and phrases to non-basic positions in the sentence.

Yes-no questions

In the very early stages of language acquisition, children signal *yes-no* questions by means of rising intonation alone. (Recall that auxiliary verbs are a relatively late development.)

(9) See hole?
I ride train?
Ball go?
Sit chair?

Even after individual auxiliary verbs make their appearance, there is often a delay of a few months before Inversion takes place in *yes-no* questions. In one study, for example, a young boy began using the auxiliary verb *can* at age two years, five months, but he did not use it in the pre-subject position until six months later.

An interesting—but infrequent—error in children's early use of Inversion in both *yes-no* and *wh* questions is exemplified in (10).

(10) *Can* he *can* look?
What *shall* we *shall* have?
Did you *did* came home?

In these sentences, the auxiliary verb occurs twice—once to the left of the subject and once to the right. It has been suggested that this pattern reflects an error in the use of Inversion that involves leaving a copy of the moved auxiliary behind in its original position.

Wh questions

Wh questions emerge gradually between the ages of two and four. The first *wh* words to be acquired are typically *what* and *where*, followed by *who, how,* and *why; when, which,* and *whose* are relatively late acquisitions.

(11) Where that?
What me think?
Why you smiling?
Why not me drink it?

With the acquisition of auxiliary verbs, Inversion becomes possible. Interestingly, some children appear to find Inversion easier in *yes-no* questions, where it is the only movement operation, than in *wh* questions, where the *wh* word must also be moved. (For some reason, this is especially true in the case of *why* questions.) The following examples from children's speech all show the effects of moving the *wh* word but not the auxiliary verb.

(12) What I did yesterday?
Where I should sleep?
Why that boy is looking at us?
Why she doesn't like bananas?
Why unicorns are pretend?

10.5.5 The interpretation of sentence structure

The interpretation of sentences draws heavily on various features of syntactic structure. In this section, we will briefly consider some aspects of the acquisition of two interpretive phenomena that rely on information about syntactic structure.

Passives

Children learning English are able to use word order clues to interpret sentences at a very early point in the acquisition process. By the time their average utterance length is two words, they are able to respond correctly about 75 percent of the time to comprehension tests involving simple sentences such as (13), in which *the truck* is the agent and *the car* is the undergoer (or 'theme').

(13) The truck bumped the car.

However, children find it much harder to interpret certain other types of sentences correctly. This is especially true for passive sentences such as the one in (14), in which more than just word order matters—the form of the verb and the presence of *by* jointly indicate that the first NP refers to the undergoer rather than the agent.

(14) The car was bumped by the truck.

Although children produce passive sentences in their own speech from around age three, they have continuing difficulty responding appropriately to passive constructions in comprehension tests (see table 10.20).

TABLE 10.20	Accurate interpretation of passive constructions
Group	**Percentage correct**
Nursery School	20
Kindergarten	35
Grade 1	48
Grade 2	63
Grade 3	88

Why should this be so? One possibility is that children expect the first NP in a sentence to refer to the agent. This is sometimes called the **Canonical Sentence Strategy**.

(15) *The Canonical Sentence Strategy*
    NP ... V ... NP is interpreted as
    agent – action – undergoer

The Canonical Sentence Strategy works for active sentences such as *The truck bumped the car*, but not for passive sentences, where the first NP refers to the undergoer and the second NP to the agent.

(16) Active sentence: The truck bumped the car.
                                         agent   undergoer
         Passive sentence: The car was bumped by the truck.
                                         undergoer   agent

Children employing the Canonical Sentence Strategy associate the first NP with the agent and the second NP with the undergoer, so when they hear the passive sentence in (16), they think the car bumped the truck.

As the data in table 10.20 show, this strategy is applied much less consistently by grade one children, who have evidently begun to realize that word order is not the only thing that determines a sentence's interpretation—the verbal construction (*was bumped*) and the presence of a preposition such as *by* also matter. A year or so later, children's scores start to rise dramatically, indicating that they have come to recognize the special properties of the passive construction.

Pronouns

Sometimes, even more abstract features of sentence structure are relevant for comprehension. For example, a defining feature of reflexive pronouns (*myself, himself, herself,* and so on) is that they look to a structurally higher NP for their interpretation. (This NP is called the 'antecedent'; a structurally higher NP is said to 'c-command' a structurally lower item.)

A sentence's structure can be represented in different ways, but everyone agrees that subjects are always higher than direct objects, no matter what else might be in the sentence, as illustrated in the following somewhat simplified tree diagram.

FIGURE 10.7
Subjects above direct
objects in sentence
structure

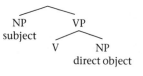

For that reason, it's possible for the antecedent to be the subject and for the reflexive pronoun to be the direct object, but not vice versa.

(17) *a.* Direct object reflexive pronouns with subject antecedent:
            I hurt ***myself*** with the stapler.

      b. Subject reflexive pronoun with direct object antecedent:
            ****Myself*** hurt ***me*** with the stapler.

But even this is not enough—not only does the antecedent have to be higher, it has to be in the same clause.

(18) *I said [someone hurt ***myself*** with the stapler].

Things work the opposite way for plain pronouns such as *me, him*, and *her*: they can't have a higher antecedent in the same clause, but they can take an antecedent outside their clause.

(19) *a.* A plain pronoun with a higher antecedent in the same clause:
*I hurt *me* with the stapler.

b. A plain pronoun with an antecedent outside its clause:
I said [someone hurt *me* with the stapler].

Despite the abstractness of these constraints, children appear not to have trouble using either type of pronoun in their own speech. In one study of the use of *me* and *myself* in speech transcripts from three children aged two to five, researchers found a few errors of the following type.

(20) Sample pronoun errors:
Mistake involving *me*: I see *me*. (Adam, age 34 mos., looking through a telescope)
Mistake involving *myself*: You hurt *myself*. (Abe, age 34 mos.)

Overall though, the children misused *me* only about 5 percent of the time and made errors with *myself* less than 1 percent of the time. We will return to this point in section 10.6.4.

10.6 What makes language acquisition possible?

In the preceding sections, we have seen that the language acquisition process extends over a period of several years. It is relatively easy to describe what takes place during these years, but it is much more difficult to explain *how* it happens. The sections that follow focus on some of the factors that may contribute to an eventual understanding of how the language acquisition process works.

10.6.1 The role of experience

First and foremost, children need to be exposed to language; they need to observe it being used by those around them as often as possible. One very clear indication of this comes from a two-and-a-half-year study of parental speech to forty-two children, who were seven to nine months old when the project began. The key finding revealed the consequences of limited exposure to speech in a very striking manner: children who hear a lot of language develop much faster than children who do not (see table 10.21).

TABLE 10.21   Effects of exposure to language on development

High-level exposure to language				
Words/hour	Words/day	Utterances/day	Utterances/year	After three years
2 100	29 000	7 250	2.5 million+	7.5 million
Average vocabulary size at age thirty months: 766 words				
Average number of words learned in the next six months: 350				

Low-level exposure to language				
Words/hour	Words/day	Utterances/day	Utterances/year	After three years
620	8 680	2 170	800 000	2.5 million
Average vocabulary size at age thirty months: 357 words				
Average number of words learned in the next six months: 168				

Not only do children who are exposed to large amounts of speech know twice as many words at age thirty months than children who have fewer opportunities to hear language, but they also go on to do significantly better in school. One of the most important things that parents and other caregivers can do is speak to their children.

Do parents need to make special adjustments to their speech when talking to children? Probably not, although many subconsciously make some changes, producing what is sometimes called **motherese** or **caregiver speech**. Table 10.22 summarizes the principal features of the caregiver speech used by middle-class English-speaking caregivers.

TABLE 10.22 Some features of English caregiver speech
Phonetic
Slow, carefully articulated speech   Higher pitch   Exaggerated intonation and stress   Longer pauses
Lexical and semantic
More restricted vocabulary   Concrete reference to the here and now
Syntactic
Few incomplete sentences   Short sentences   More imperatives and questions
Conversational
More repetitions   Few utterances per conversational turn

Caregiver speech could be helpful to children in various ways. For example, exposure to slow, carefully articulated speech may make it easier for children to pick out words and to learn their pronunciation. (Remember that sentences consist of a continuous stream of speech sounds; there are generally no pauses between words.) Moreover, the acquisition of meaning may be facilitated by the fact that caregiver speech tends to concentrate on the here and now, especially the child's surroundings, activities, and needs. The examples in table 10.23 help illustrate this. Exposure to language of this type may well make it easier to match morphemes, words, and phrases with meanings—a major part of the language acquisition process.

TABLE 10.23 Some examples of caregiver speech	
Caregiver's utterance	**Context**
That's right, pick up the blocks.	the child is picking up a box of building blocks
That's a puppy.	the child is looking at a young dog
The puppy's in the basket.	the child is examining a puppy in a basket

Although potentially *helpful*, caregiver speech may not actually be *necessary* to the language acquisition process. In Western Samoa, for instance, speech to children is not simplified in the way it often is in North America, and caregivers do not try to reformulate children's unintelligible speech or make any special attempt to understand it. Yet Samoan children have no trouble learning Samoan. Evidently, the speech style typical of middle-class caregivers in North America is not essential for language acquisition.

Moreover, even in cultures where it is common, caregiver speech seems to have very selective effects on child language. For instance, the number of *yes-no* questions in caregiver speech seems to be correlated with the rate at which auxiliary verbs develop—apparently because auxiliaries occur in the salient sentence-initial position in *yes-no* questions (*Can Jennifer go?*). At the same time, though, many other features of caregiver speech seem *not* to affect child language. As we saw earlier (in section 10.4.2), for example, the relative frequency of bound morphemes and non-lexical categories in caregiver speech apparently does not determine their order of acquisition.

Language Matters Do Children Learn by Imitating?

Popular opinion holds that children learn language simply by imitating the speech of those around them. This cannot be right, however. Not only do children tend not to repeat the speech of others, but they are typically unable to imitate structures that they have not yet learned. For instance, children who have not yet started to invert the auxiliary verb and the subject in questions will avoid Inversion in their imitations.

>   Model sentence: Why can't kitty stand up?
>   Child's imitation: Why kitty can't stand up?

Children's own grammar, not the model provided by adult speech, determines what they will say at any given point of development.

10.6.2 The role of feedback

It is sometimes suggested that parents help their children learn language by correcting their 'mistakes'. However, studies of actual interactions between parents and children point in a quite different direction. In general, parents tend to be more concerned with the truth of children's utterances than with their grammaticality—one transcript of a parent-child conversation includes *That's right* as a response to the grammatical monstrosity *Mama isn't boy, he's a girl!*

Moreover, even when adults do attempt to correct children's grammatical errors, their efforts often have little effect. The following exchange between a child and his father is typical in this regard.

(21) *Child*:   Want other one spoon, Daddy.
     Father: You mean, you want the other spoon.
     Child: Yes, I want other one spoon, please Daddy.
     Father: Can you say "the other spoon"?
     Child: other . . . one . . . spoon.
     Father: Say "other."
     Child: other.
     Father: "spoon."
     Child: spoon.
     Father: "other spoon."
     Child: other . . . spoon. Now give me other one spoon?

Interestingly, however, some research suggests that subtler forms of feedback may have a role to play in the language acquisition process.

Recasts

Adults often respond to a child's utterance by repeating it, making adjustments to its form and/or content. (Responses of this sort are called **recasts**.)

(22) *Child*:   Daddy here.
     Mother: Yes, Daddy is here.
     Child: Him go.
     Mother: Yes, he is going.
     Child: Boy chasing dog.
     Mother: Yes, the boy is chasing the dog.
     Child: The dog is barking.
     Mother: Yes, he is barking at the kitty.

Recasts provide children with potentially useful information—adding a missing verb (*is* in the first example), changing the form of a pronoun (*him* to *he* in the second example), and so on. However, parents usually don't correct errors, and sometimes they actually reformulate their children's *grammatical* utterances (as in the final example), so recasts also have the potential to be misleading.

It is not yet clear what role recasts play in language learning, and studies to date have yielded conflicting results. For instance, a study of the acquisition of *the* and *a* by three children revealed no link between the frequency of recasts and the rate at which their use of determiners increased—no matter how many recasts children heard, the rate of development stayed the same.

A quite different result emerged from an experiment in which four- and five-year-olds were taught made-up verbs with irregular past tense forms—for example, *pell* (with *pold* as its past tense). When the children first learned what the verbs meant (they were linked to various funny actions, such as hitting someone with a beanbag attached to a string), they heard only the *-ing* forms ('This is called *pelling*'). They therefore had no idea what the past tense forms should be. Just hearing an adult use *pold* to refer to a past pelling action had little or no effect, but being allowed to make 'mistakes' such as *pelled* and then hearing an adult recast the sentence using *pold* had a major impact. In fact, a single recast was often enough to permit learning of the irregular form, which suggests that certain types of feedback have a role to play in the language acquisition process after all.

10.6.3 The role of cognitive development

Because there are dramatic changes in both linguistic and non-linguistic abilities during the first years of life, it is tempting to think that the two are somehow linked. Yet there is considerable evidence to suggest that language acquisition is to a large extent independent of other types of cognitive development. One such piece of evidence comes from the study of individuals whose general cognitive development is deficient but whose language is highly developed. For example, Rick performed so poorly at age fifteen on a variety of non-linguistic tasks that his general cognitive level was estimated to be that of a preschool child. Yet, as the following examples illustrate, his speech manifests considerable syntactic and morphological sophistication—with appropriate use of affixes, non-lexical categories, and word order.

(23) She must've got me up and thrown me out of bed.
     She keeps both of the ribbons on her hair.
     If they get in trouble, they'd have a pillow fight.
     She's the one that walks back and forth to school.
     I wanna hear one more just for a change.

At the same time, there are documented cases of individuals who suffer from a genetic disorder involving the FOXP2 gene that leaves their intellects relatively intact (although their non-verbal IQ is somewhat below average) but seriously impairs certain aspects of their speech, including the use of inflection for the past tense and the plural, as illustrated in (24).

(24) The boys eat four cookie.
     It's a flying finches, they are.
     The neighbours phone the ambulance because the man fall off the tree.

Language Matters A Linguistic Savant

A particularly celebrated case of a dissociation between language and cognitive development involves Christopher. Now an adult, Christopher can read, write, and communicate in about twenty languages (including English, Danish, Dutch, Finnish, French, German, Modern Greek, Hindi, Italian, Norwegian, Polish, Portuguese, Russian, Spanish, Swedish, Turkish, and Welsh). He learned some of these languages as a child (based on minimal exposure) and taught himself others as an adolescent and adult, often with amazing speed, as the following account of his encounter with Dutch illustrates.

> Shortly before he was due to appear on Dutch television, it was suggested that he might spend a couple of days improving his rather rudimentary Dutch with the aid of a grammar and dictionary. He did so to such good effect that he was able to converse in Dutch—with facility if not total fluency—both before and during the programme. (p. 18)

Christopher has a non-verbal IQ (depending on the test) of between 56 and 76, and a mental age of 9 years, 2 months. He has trouble with addition (he can handle simple cases such as 12 + 13, but not 'carrying over' as in 14 + 19); he is very bad at drawing; and he can't figure out how tic-tac-toe works. He is unable to care for himself and lives in a home for adults with special needs.

Source: Neil Smith and Ianthi-Maria Tsimpli, *The Mind of a Savant* (Oxford: Blackwell, 1995). A short video (4:33) on Christopher is available on YouTube and further information can be found in Neil Smith, Ianthi Tsimpli, Gary Morgan, and Bencie Woll, *The Signs of a Savant: Language against the Odds* (Cambridge, UK: Cambridge University Press, 2011).

Case studies such as these suggest that certain aspects of language (in particular, morphology and syntax) are independent of non-linguistic types of cognitive development. This in turn implies that the mental mechanisms responsible for the acquisition of those parts of the grammar are relatively autonomous and that their operation neither follows from nor guarantees general cognitive development.

10.6.4 The role of inborn knowledge

There can be no doubt that some special quality of the human mind facilitates the acquisition of language. The only real question has to do with precisely what that special quality is.

A very influential view among linguists is that children are born with prior knowledge of the type of categories, operations, and principles that are found in the grammar of any human language. They therefore know, for example, that the words in the language they are acquiring will belong to a small set of syntactic categories (N, V, and so on) and that they can be combined in particular ways to create larger phrases (NP, VP, etc.). The set of inborn categories, operations, and principles common to all human languages makes up what is often referred to as **Universal Grammar (UG)**.

Although the idea dates back several centuries, modern theories of UG owe a great deal to the work of Noam Chomsky. Chomsky's basic claim is that the grammars for human language are too complex and abstract to be learned on the basis of the type of experience to which children have access. Therefore, he argues, significant components of the grammar must be inborn. To illustrate this, we must consider a relatively complex example involving the notion of c-command alluded to earlier.

Principles A and B

As we have seen (section 10.5.5), the interpretation of pronouns such as *himself* and *him* is regulated by two quite abstract principles.

> **(25)** *Principle A*
> A reflexive pronoun must have a c-commanding antecedent in the same clause.
>
> *Principle B*
> A plain pronoun must not have a c-commanding antecedent in the same clause.

These principles have played an important role in the study of language acquisition, and three arguments have been put forward in support of the claim that they are inborn.

First, the notion of c-command is quite abstract. It is not the type of concept that we would expect young children to discover simply by listening to sentences. Since we also know that no one teaches them about c-command, it makes sense to think that this notion is inborn and therefore does not have to be discovered or taught.

Second, the c-command relation seems to be universally relevant to the interpretation of pronouns. The universality of this restriction would be explained if Principles A and B were innate and hence part of the inborn linguistic knowledge of all human beings.

Third, as we saw earlier in this chapter, Principles A and B seem to be available to children from a very early stage in their development—even three-year-olds appear to have mastered the distinction between reflexives and plain pronouns in their own speech (although they do sometimes make mistakes in comprehension). Given the complexity of these principles, this provides additional evidence for the claim that they are inborn.

Parameters

Of course, not every feature of a language's grammar can be inborn. Its vocabulary and morphology must be learned, and so must at least part of its syntax. For example, UG stipulates that a phrase can include a head and its complements, but it does not specify the relative order of these elements. This differs from language to language, so that a child acquiring English must learn that heads precede their complements, whereas a child acquiring Korean must learn the reverse order.

(26) Head-complement order in English and Korean:
   a. English (head–complement)
      read [that book]

   b. Korean (complement–head)
      [ku chayk] ilke
      that book read

UG includes a parameter for word order that offers a choice between head-initial and head-final order. (We ignore the positioning of specifiers for the purposes of the illustration in table 10.24.)

TABLE 10.24 The word order parameter	
Stipulated by UG	**Resulting options**
A phrase consists of a head and a complement	Head–Complement order [head-initial—English] Complement–Head order [head-final—Korean]

There are also phonological parameters: for example, languages can differ from each other in terms of whether they allow two or more consonants in the onset of a syllable—English does (e.g., *gleam, sprint*), whereas Japanese and Hawaiian do not.

All of this suggests that part of the language acquisition process involves **parameter setting**—that is, determining which of the options permitted by a particular parameter is appropriate for the language being learned.

10.6.5 Is there a critical period?

One of the most intriguing issues in the study of language acquisition has to do with the possibility that normal linguistic development is possible only if children are exposed to language during a particular time frame or **critical period**. Evidence for the existence of such a period comes from the study of individuals who do not experience language during the early part of their lives.

One such individual is the much-discussed Genie, who was kept in a small room with virtually no opportunity to hear human speech from around age two to age thirteen. After many years of therapy and care, Genie's non-linguistic cognitive functioning was described as 'relatively normal' and her lexical and semantic abilities as 'good'. In terms of syntax and morphology, however, many problems remained, as evidenced in the sample utterances in table 10.25.

TABLE 10.25 Some of Genie's utterances	
Utterance	**Meaning**
Applesauce buy store.	'Buy applesauce at the store.'
Man motorcycle have.	'The man has a motorcycle.'
Want go ride Miss F. car.	'I want to go for a ride in Miss F.'s car.'
Genie have full stomach.	'I have a full stomach.'
Mama have baby grow up.	'Mama has a baby who grew up.'

As these examples show, Genie makes word order errors (the first two examples) and her speech does not contain non-lexical categories or affixes.

Another revealing case study involved Chelsea, a deaf child who was misdiagnosed as mentally disabled and emotionally disturbed. Chelsea grew up without language and was not exposed to speech until the age of thirty-one, when she was finally fitted with hearing aids. After intensive therapy, she is able to hold a job and to live independently. However, her vocabulary consists of only 2000 words and her sentences are badly formed, as the following examples help show.

(27)   The woman is bus the going.
Combing hair the boy.
Orange Tim car in.
The girl is gone the ice cream shopping buying the man.

Based on case studies such as these, it is now widely believed that the ability to acquire a first language in an effortless and ultimately successful way begins to decline from age six and becomes increasingly compromised with each passing year.

Summing up

This chapter has been concerned with the problem of how children acquire the **grammar** of their first language. Research in this area deals with two major issues: the nature of the developmental sequence leading to the emergence of mature linguistic competence in the areas of phonology, vocabulary, morphology, and syntax, and the factors that make it possible for children to acquire a complex grammar. A number of factors may contribute to the child's acquisition of language, including the properties of **caregiver speech, recasts,** and inborn linguistic knowledge (**Universal Grammar**). We look to future research for deeper insights into the precise role of these and other factors.

Recommended reading

Ambridge, Ben, and Elena V.M. Lieven. 2011. *Child Language Acquisition: Contrasting Theoretical Approaches*. Cambridge, UK: Cambridge University Press.

Berko Gleason, Jean, and Nan Bernstein Ratner. 2016. *The Development of Language*. 9th ed. Upper Saddle River, NJ: Pearson.

Blom, Elma, and Sharon Unsworth, eds. 2010. *Experimental Methods in Language Acquisition Research*. Amsterdam: John Benjamins.

Bloom, Paul. 2002. *How Children Learn the Meanings of Words*. Cambridge, MA: MIT Press.

Clark, Eve V. 2016. *First Language Acquisition*. 3rd ed. Cambridge, UK: Cambridge University Press.

Hirsh-Pasek, Kathy, and Roberta Golinkoff. 2012. "How Babies Talk: Six Principles of Early Language Development." In *Re-visioning the Beginning: Developmental and Health Science Contributions to Infant/Toddler Programs for Children and Families Living in Poverty*. Edited by S.L. Odom, E. Pungello, and N. Gardner-Neblett, 77–101. New York: Guilford Press.

Lust, Barbara. 2006. *Child Language: Acquisition and Growth*. Cambridge, UK: Cambridge University Press.

O'Grady, William. 2005. *How Children Learn Language*. Cambridge, UK: Cambridge University Press.

Exercises

1. One piece of evidence that children acquire a grammar is their production of over-regularized past tense forms such as *doed, leaved*, and *goed*. Based on this model, what type of evidence should we look for in order to show that children have acquired the rule that creates comparative forms such as *bigger, richer*, and *taller*? (Hint: Think about adjectives that have irregular comparative forms in the adult language.)

2. In one naturalistic study, a search for passive structures in a sample of 18 000 utterances from sixty children yielded only nineteen examples produced by twelve of the children.
   a) Does this mean that the other forty-eight children had not yet learned the passive structure?
   b) How are the disadvantages of the naturalistic method exemplified here?

3. The following transcriptions represent the pronunciation of a two-year-old child. Indicate which phonetic processes have applied in each case.

a)	skin	[kɪd]	h)	thin	[tɪn]
b)	spoon	[bun]	i)	teddy	[dɛdi]
c)	zoo	[du]	j)	brush	[bʌt]
d)	John	[dɑn]	k)	lump	[wʌp]
e)	bath	[bæt]	l)	play	[pwej]
f)	other	[ʌdə]	m)	breakfast	[brɛkpəst]
g)	Smith	[mɪt]			

4. Drawing on the phonetic processes posited for the preceding exercise, predict one or more plausible immature pronunciations for each of the following words.

a)	show	e)	juice
b)	please	f)	thumb
c)	spit	g)	zero
d)	under	h)	ring

5. Consider the following examples of overextensions, all of which have actually been observed in children's speech. What is the apparent basis for each of these overextensions?

Word	*First referent*	*Overextensions*
a) sch	sound of a train	music, noise of wheels, sound of rain
b) bow-wow	dog	sheep, rabbit fur, puppet
c) baby	baby	people in pictures
d) sizo	scissors	nail file, knife, screwdriver, spoon
e) policeman	policeman	mailman, sailor, doctor
f) strawberry	strawberry	grapes, raspberry
g) fireworks	fireworks	matches, light, cigarette
h) Batman	Batman logo on a T-shirt	any logo on a T-shirt

6. Since children have a tendency to focus on the prototypical members of categories in the acquisition of words, how might you expect children to underextend the following words? What members of the category might you expect children not to include?
   a) bird
   b) pet
   c) toy

7. The allomorphic variation associated with the 3rd person singular verbal ending *-s* is identical to that found with plural *-s*.
   a) Make up a test parallel to the '*wug* test' discussed in section 10.4.1.
   b) If possible, give your test to children between the ages of three and seven. Are your results similar to the ones discussed in the chapter?

8. Based on the discussion in section 10.4.2 about the developmental sequence of morpheme acquisition, consider the acquisition in other languages of the morphemes corresponding to those listed in table 10.12. Would you predict that these morphemes would be acquired in exactly the same order as their English equivalents? Why or why not?

9. Considering children's tendency to overgeneralize morphological rules, what might we expect a young child to use in the place of the following adult words? Justify your choice in each case.
   a) fish (plural)   f) geese
   b) went   g) brought
   c) mice   h) hit (past tense)
   d) ate   i) himself
   e) has   j) women

10. Each of the following utterances is from the speech of a child in the two-word stage. Identify the semantic relation expressed by each of these utterances.

Intended meaning	*Child's utterance*
a) Jimmy is swimming.	Jimmy swim.
b) Ken's book	Ken book
c) Daddy is at his office.	Daddy office.
d) You push the baby.	Push baby.
e) Mommy is reading.	Mommy read.

11. Consider the following data from Jordie, a two-and-a-half-year-old child, in light of the list of morphemes in table 10.12.

Intended meaning	*Jordie's utterance*
a) Where's my blanket?	Where my blanket?
b) Does it go right here, Mommy?	Go right here, Mommy?
c) It's running over.	Running over.
d) Here, it goes here.	Here, go here.
e) No, that's mine.	No, that mine.
f) Dinosaurs say gronk.	Dinosaur say gronk.
g) There's more.	There more.

   i) Which of the morphemes in table 10.12 are missing in Jordie's sentences but present in the equivalent adult utterance?

   ii) List the morphemes that are present in both the adult interpretations and in Jordie's speech.

12. Now consider the following utterances from a child named Krista.

Intended meaning	*Krista's utterance*
a) My name is Krista.	Mine name Krista.
b) My sister's name is Peggy.	Sister name Peggy.
c) The tape is right there.	Tape right there.
d) Daddy's book	Daddy book
e) I've got a book.	I'm got a book.
f) Read me a story.	Read me story.
g) I'll do it.	I'm do it.
h) He went outside.	He went outside.
i) Open the gate, please.	Open a gate, please.
j) Gramma's house	Gramma's house
k) Smell the flowers.	Smell flowers.
l) My shoes are on.	Shoes on.
m) The wee boy fell down.	Wee boy fell down.
n) That's my ball.	That's mines ball.

   i) Which morphemes are missing in Krista's speech but present in the adult version of the sentence?

   ii) Krista uses the past tense twice in the above utterances. Do you think this is evidence that she has fully acquired the past tense morpheme? Why or why not?

   iii) Comment on Krista's difficulty with possessive pronouns.

   iv) Do you think she has acquired possessive -'s? Why or why not?

13. The following utterances were produced spontaneously by Holly, age three years.

   a) I learned about loving moms.
   b) Put him in the bathtub.
   c) We eated gummy snakes.
   d) Thank you for giving these books us.
   e) I don't know.
   f) He bited my finger. (When corrected, she said: He bitted my finger.)

g) I runned in the water.

h) I rided on a elephant.

i) Has Holly acquired the past tense morpheme? How do you know?

ii) What is the evidence in Holly's speech that she has learned phrases that consist of a head, a complement, and/or a specifier?

iii) What is the evidence that she has acquired the category noun? the category verb?

14. It has been reported that hearing children growing up in homes with non-speaking deaf parents cannot learn spoken language from radio or even television (see p. 278 of *The Language Instinct* by Steven Pinker [New York: Morrow, 1994]).

a) Can you think of any reasons for this?

b) What are the implications of these findings for our understanding of the type of experience that is required for language acquisition?

To learn more about the topics discussed in this chapter, visit the Companion Website for *Contemporary Linguistic Analysis*.

Second language acquisition

When we talk about acquisition in SLA research, we are not talking about acquisition in the sense that one acquires polo ponies, Lladró figurines, or CBS, but rather in the sense that one acquires vicious habits, a taste for Brie, or a potbelly.

KEVIN R. GREGG, *LINGUISTIC PERSPECTIVES ON SECOND LANGUAGE ACQUISITION* (1989)

THE FIELD of **second language acquisition** (SLA) research investigates how people attain proficiency in a language that is not their mother tongue. Whether we are talking about someone learning to read Greek in university, or someone becoming fluent in a third language in their forties, or a child acquiring a new language after moving to a new country, we refer to it as second language acquisition. The interesting phenomenon of children simultaneously acquiring two languages is generally investigated in the field known as **bilingualism**, which will be discussed in Chapter 12. In this chapter, we will primarily be concerned with second language acquisition in adults.

Over the years, the study of second language acquisition has been undertaken from a variety of different perspectives. In the 1950s and 1960s, the primary objective was pedagogic. Researchers were interested in trying to improve the way in which second languages were taught. Therefore, they were interested in discovering how those languages were learned. From the 1970s on, the focus moved from the teacher to the learner, and the field of second language (L2) instruction became somewhat separate.

This change in perspective was related to what was going on in linguistics, psychology, and first language acquisition research. All three of these areas shifted focus from the external to the internal in the 1960s. Linguistics became concerned with the mental grammar of the speaker, not just the description of the linguistic structures of a given language. Psychology shifted from behaviourism (which denied the importance of mental representations) to cognitive psychology, and research on first language acquisition focused on children's internal grammars rather than just their verbal production. These fields are also crucial to the study of SLA. Linguistics gives us a sophisticated and accurate description of what people are trying to learn (the second language) and what they already know (the first language). Psychology can provide us with a learning theory to account for how people acquire knowledge. Finally, the field of first language acquisition (which has been around longer than the field of second language acquisition) offers various findings that can be productively applied to SLA. For example, we know that children who are acquiring their first language (L1) have systematic grammars and that their utterances are not just bad imitations of the adult target. As we will see, second language learners, too, are developing a grammar that is systematic even if it is not nativelike.

11.1 The study of second language acquisition

In the case of first language acquisition, we may ascribe the difference between child and adult grammars to either cognitive or biological immaturity in the child. In the case of second language learning by adults, however, we cannot say that the learners are either cognitively or biologically immature. Rather, they are subject to an influence that is absent from the child's situation: the first language itself.

FIGURE 11.1 Linguistic influences on an interlanguage grammar

L1 → Interlanguage Grammar ← L2

Figure 11.1 illustrates the fact that second language learners have a systematic **interlanguage (IL) grammar**—so called because it is a system of mental representations influenced by both the first and the second language and has features of each.

The form in table 11.1, produced by French speakers, reflects the fact that French lacks the phoneme /h/, while the pronunciation associated with German speakers can be traced to the fact that German includes a rule of syllable-final obstruent devoicing (which changes the [v] to a [f]).

TABLE 11.1 Phonological transfer: French and German

English target	French speaker	German speaker
have [hæv]	[æv]	[hæf]

The term **transfer** is used to describe the process whereby a feature or rule from a learner's first language is carried over to the IL grammar. Other examples can be seen in table 11.2.

TABLE 11.2 More phonological transfer: Spanish, English, and French

L1	L2	Example	Comment
Spanish	English	I espeak Espanish.	Spanish does not allow s + consonant sequences word-initially.
English	French	[ty] (you) → [tu]	English does not have the front rounded vowel [y]. The English speaker substitutes the [u] sound.
Québec French	English	Over dere.	French has no [ð] sound, so it is replaced by [d].
European French	English	Over zere.	French has no [ð] sound, so it is replaced by [z].
English	Spanish	[ɾio] 'river' → [rio]	Since English does not use [ɾ] word-initially, an [r] is substituted.

11.1.1 The role of the first language

One of the most easily recognizable traits of a second language learner's speech is that it bears a certain resemblance to the learner's L1. Thus, someone whose first language is French is likely to sound different from someone whose first language is German when they both speak English. We have already seen an example of this in the typical pronunciation of the English word *have* by speakers of French and German, as illustrated in table 11.1.

11.1.2 The nature of an interlanguage

The first language is not the only influence on the interlanguage grammar, since some properties of the IL can be traced to aspects of the L2. In the case of a German speaker who is learning English, for example, the IL grammar will contain some features of both German and English. Consider how a German speaker learning Canadian English might pronounce the word *eyes*. As illustrated in table 11.3, the learner first applies the rule of syllable-final obstruent devoicing (transferred from German), changing /ajz/ to [ajs]. But the learner also has acquired some knowledge of the language being learned (called the **target language**)—in this case, the rule of Canadian Raising (discussed in chapter 3), which converts /aj/ to [ʌj] before a voiceless consonant. Thanks to application of the devoicing rule, the input form now ends in a voiceless consonant ([s]), which triggers Canadian Raising and results in the learner pronouncing 'eyes' as 'ice'.

TABLE 11.3	One possible pronunciation of the English word *eyes* by a German-speaking learner	
Target form	**Result of syllable-final obstruent devoicing**	**Result of Canadian Raising**
/ajz/	[ajs]	[ʌjs]

This example shows us something about the nature of an interlanguage: it contains features of both the L1 and the L2. The speech of second language learners can exhibit non-nativelike characteristics in any linguistic domain, as shown in table 11.4. When the interlanguage grammar stops changing, it is said to have **fossilized** (or reached a plateau).

11.1.3 The final state

So far we have been talking about the characteristics of the intermediate grammar. But a discussion of what an IL grammar looks like must consider the target: that is, what is to be acquired. The field of SLA, then, must address the issue of actual proficiency or **communicative competence**. Although knowledge of a language's grammar allows us to distinguish between grammatical and ungrammatical sentences, successful communication requires

TABLE 11.4	Types of errors found in the acquisition of English		
L1	**Example**	**Error type**	**Comment**
Spanish	Juana is <u>embarrassed</u>. (meaning 'pregnant')	lexical	Spanish *embarazada* = 'pregnant'
Various	I live in a two-bedroom <u>department</u>.	lexical	The speaker chooses the wrong word.
Various	I <u>didn't took</u> the car yesterday.	morphological	English doesn't mark the past tense on both auxiliary and main verbs.
Various	She <u>get ups</u> late.	morphological	The speaker adds the agreement marker to the preposition, not the verb.
French	He <u>drinks frequently</u> tea.	syntactic	French places the main verb before the adverb.
Various	There's the man that I saw <u>him</u>.	syntactic	Some languages (e.g., Arabic, Turkish) allow pronouns in this position in a relative clause.

much more than this. The learner must also be able to use the language in a way that is appropriate to the situation or context. As figure 11.2 illustrates, both grammatical accuracy and communicative ability are part of communicative competence.

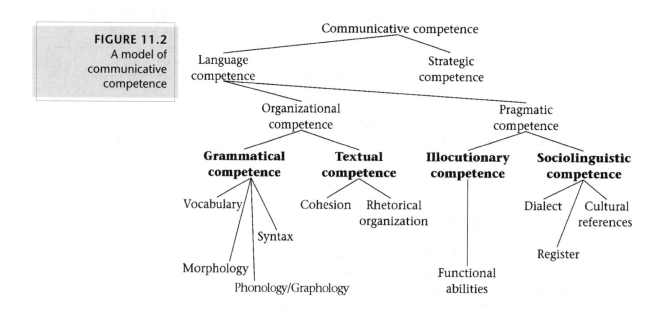

FIGURE 11.2
A model of communicative competence

> ### Language Matters Even Though They Are Natural, L2 Mistakes Can Be Embarrassing
>
> "It's those tiny details that do you in: a vowel here, a consonant there. Who would think it would make such a difference? Like the time I thought I was telling my roommate that the sink was plugged again. I said *kinor*. I meant *kiyor* . . . big deal. But Ruthie had no idea what I was trying to say. I ask you, how hard can it be to figure out that I meant *sink* and not *violin*? Oh, and there was the time her friends came calling, and asked if she was *yeshna* (there). I thought they were asking if she was *yeshena* (sleeping). I said yes and closed the door. They thought I was nuts. Fortunately, she woke up and explained that I was only Canadian."
>
> Janet McDonald on speaking Hebrew

What the model depicted in figure 11.2 captures graphically is that the skills required to function in a second language go beyond the core domains of linguistics: phonetics, phonology, morphology, syntax, and semantics. **Textual competence** recognizes the ability to string sentences together appropriately. **Sociolinguistic competence** involves the ability to use the linguistic register appropriate to the situation. **Illocutionary competence** showcases the ability to convey a particular meaning via a variety of linguistic forms.

In sum, communicative competence is a model of proficiency that allows us to measure second language knowledge and ability, to construct second language proficiency tests, and to design balanced second language courses.

11.1.4 Variation in performance

An important goal of L2 research is to integrate the study of competence (linguistic knowledge) and **performance** (actual language use in particular situations). One of the characteristics of the output of second language learners is that it is quite variable. For example, a learner might well produce the following sentence:

(1) I **didn't** like **th**at movie so I told her I **no** want to go **d**ere.

In this (hypothetical) example, the learner is inconsistent, getting one of the two negatives right and correctly pronouncing one of the two interdental fricatives. The question that intrigues researchers has to do with what causes this sort of variation. We usually think of knowledge as fairly stable within an individual. For example, if a person makes a mistake while speaking in his or her native language, we tend not to question the speaker's competence in that language but rather to assume that some kind of performance error was made. So how do we account for learners who behave as if they know how to negate a verb or pronounce [ð] on some occasions but not others? Do they have the knowledge or don't they?

It is difficult to answer this question, in part because of considerations involving error frequency. We would probably say that a non-native speaker who gets the English past tense correct 10 percent of the time does not know the past tense and that someone who gets it right 90 percent of the time does. But what of someone who gets it right somewhere between those two scores? This is a complex research question. The (admittedly simplistic) view adopted in this chapter is that variation falls into the realm of linguistic performance—it reflects the imperfect use of linguistic knowledge rather than deficits in the knowledge itself.

Linguistic performance clearly involves the interaction of a number of cognitive systems and has much in common with other skills. A crucial notion for the study of how skills develop involves the distinction between controlled and automatic processing. When acquiring a new skill (e.g., playing golf), we begin by having to devote a lot of conscious or controlled processing to the activity: feet apart, head down, elbow straight, white shoes, and so on. Once we become proficient, we 'just' hit the ball; the activity has become automatic.

We need to shift processing from controlled to automatic because, as humans, we have a fixed processing capacity. We can't consciously process everything at once. Shifting some material into automatic processing frees up space for additional controlled processing. Consider an example from reading. When we first learn how to read, we devote much of our cognitive processing to determining what the written symbols stand for. When we are focusing on decoding the letters, we do not have the processing capacity to deal with things like reading for prejudice or bias. After a time, though, letter recognition happens automatically in our first language, and we can devote more of our cognitive capacity to higher-level skills.

That native speakers do this kind of thing automatically can be seen by the difficulty many of us have in proofreading. It is hard to suppress the information we're getting from the context since the mind tries to make sense of what it's reading. Conversely, when we are forced by exceptional circumstances to devote a lot of energy to decoding the print (e.g., a bad photocopy or a small phone screen), our higher-level processing slows down; we can't focus as much on the message when we are focusing on the form.

All of this is relevant to second language acquisition in that it can help explain the variable performance of L2 learners. When learners are focusing on the form of the L2 utterance, they may be able to produce it accurately. However, when there are extra demands, such as trying to communicate a complex thought or carry on a conversation in a noisy room, errors may occur. This suggests that the learner has a mental representation of the form in question (say, a negated verb or an interdental fricative) but can have difficulty implementing or accessing it under certain conditions.

11.2 Interlanguage grammars

Let us turn now to a discussion of the specifics of what is acquired when learning the phonology, morphology, and syntax of a second language. The general question we are trying to answer here is, What is the structure of an interlanguage? Second language learners are acquiring grammars, and those grammars involve mental representations. Therefore, we can investigate the nature of those representations within the various subdomains of linguistic theory. We begin with phonology.

> ### Language Matters The Subtleties in Learning New Lexical Items
>
> "I suppose hearing a language is a different way of feeling the words. I don't suppose there are synonyms really. I wonder if *moon* means exactly the same thing as *luna*? I don't suppose it does; there's a slight difference. There should be—in every word. So that to learn any language is to find out different ways of viewing, of sensing the universe, the world, or ourselves."
>
> Jorge Luis Borges
> The Royal Society of Arts, October 5, 1983

11.2.1 L2 phonology

Let us consider what is to be acquired in the domain of phonology. Broadly speaking, we can distinguish between segmental and prosodic phonology. Segmental phonology has to do with the characteristics of phonological segments, like consonants and vowels. Prosodic phonology, however, has to do with phonological phenomena that affect more than a single segment (e.g., syllables and stress).

Segmental phonology

Languages vary in their segmental inventory in that they choose a subset of the sounds found in human languages. There is thus a good chance that anyone learning a second language will have to learn to produce and perceive some sounds that are not found in the learner's native language.

   One of the most obvious characteristics of adult second language speech is that it is 'accented' as the result of phonological and phonetic transfer from the native language. This is why native speakers of English can usually distinguish French-accented English from German-accented English. Consider the examples in table 11.5.

TABLE 11.5	Examples of French- and German-accented English	
English target	**Québec French speaker**	**German speaker**
[ðə] 'the'	[də]	[zə]

Since both French and German lack the interdental fricative [ð], native speakers of those languages substitute a sound from their L1 that shares some features with the target sound. French speakers substitute a voiced alveolar stop, while German speakers substitute a voiced alveolar fricative. Particularly at a beginning level of proficiency, L2 learners pronounce words using their L1 phonological system.

   A similar phenomenon can be seen in the phonology of loan words. When a word is borrowed from another language, its pronunciation is modified to suit the phonological system of the receiving language. For example, when English borrowed the word *pterodactyl* from Greek, the initial consonant was dropped from the /pt/ onset, which conforms to Greek syllable structure but not to that of English. However, no such change was made in the word *helicopter* (with the same Greek root *pter* 'wing') since it already complied with the phonological pattern of English, thanks to the syllable break between /p/ and /t/.

Markedness

One question that has received a lot of attention in SLA research is why some sounds are harder to acquire in a second language than others. Perhaps some sounds are simpler than others. Or perhaps some sound systems are easier for speakers of a certain language to acquire. Which would be easier for a Japanese speaker to acquire, English or Vietnamese? As might be expected, these are not simple issues. We cannot talk about the ease or difficulty of entire languages, but we may have something to say about individual sounds.

When linguists consider the notions of ease or simplicity, they make use of the notion of 'markedness'. Structures that are simple and/or especially common in human language are said to be **unmarked**, while structures that are complex or less common are said to be **marked**. So we might say that a sound that is found in relatively few of the world's languages (e.g., [θ]) is marked, while a sound that occurs in many of the world's languages (e.g., [t]) is unmarked.

Markedness is commonly approached from the perspective of language typology, which is concerned with the comparative study of similarities and differences among languages. Researchers have discovered certain implicational universals of the form 'if a language has *x*, it will also have *y*'. For example, if a language has nasal vowel phonemes (e.g., /ã/), then it will also have oral vowel phonemes (e.g., /a/). Crucial to the understanding of implicational universals is the fact that the implication is unidirectional. Thus a language that has oral vowel phonemes does not necessarily have nasal vowel phonemes. This allows us to identify /a/ as less marked than /ã/, in accordance with the following generalization.

(2) *X* is more marked than *y* if the presence of *x* implies the presence of *y*, *but not vice versa*.

Do IL grammars obey such implicational universals, and can these universals help to explain the relative ease or difficulty of learning an L2?

The **Markedness Differential Hypothesis** provides a possible answer to these questions.

(3) *Markedness Differential Hypothesis*
Structures that are typologically marked will be more difficult than their unmarked counterparts for second language learners.

Remember the earlier example of syllable-final obstruent devoicing in German, which explains why a word like *Hund* 'dog' is pronounced with a [t] at the end. German speakers learning English typically transfer this devoicing rule into their IL (producing [hæt] for [hæd] 'had') and must learn to make the contrast between [t] and [d] at the ends of words. We might be tempted to think that the principle underlying this phenomenon is something like 'it's hard to learn to make contrasts that your L1 doesn't make'. But German does contrast /t/ and /d/ in other positions—just not at the ends of words. Furthermore, when we look at another set of data, we see that this hypothetical principle isn't supported.

French makes a contrast between [ʃ] and [ʒ] in places where English does not, as table 11.6 indicates. If it were invariably difficult for second language learners to make contrasts that are not found in their L1, we would expect English speakers to have difficulty learning to

	English [ʃ]/[ʒ]	French [ʃ]/[ʒ]
TABLE 11.6 The [ʃ]/[ʒ] contrast in English and French		
Initial	<u>s</u>ure [ʃ]/*[ʒ][1]	<u>ch</u>ant [ʃ]/<u>g</u>ens [ʒ] 'song' 'people'
Medial	a<u>ss</u>ure [ʃ]/a<u>z</u>ure [ʒ]	bou<u>ch</u>er [ʃ]/bou<u>g</u>er [ʒ] 'to fill up' 'to move'
Final	lea<u>sh</u> [ʃ]/lie<u>g</u>e [ʒ]	ha<u>ch</u>e [ʃ]/a<u>g</u>e [ʒ] 'h' 'age'

produce [ʒ] at the beginning of words. But they don't. English speakers seem able to learn to pronounce French words like *jaune* 'yellow' and *jeudi* 'Thursday' without trouble.

The notion of markedness can be used to explain why German speakers have difficulty making a new contrast in English, while English speakers don't have difficulty making a new contrast in French. The typological situation is as follows:

- If a language has a voicing contrast word-finally, it will also have one word-medially and word-initially (e.g., English).
- If a language has a voicing contrast word-medially, it will also have one word-initially, but not necessarily word-finally (e.g., German).
- If a language has a voicing contrast word-initially, it will not necessarily have one word-medially or word-finally (e.g., Sardinian).

These generalizations allow us to formulate the general implicational universal in (4).

(4) The presence of a voicing contrast in final position implies the presence of a voicing contrast in medial position, which in turn implies the presence of a voicing contrast in initial position.

We can represent this universal graphically as follows (The symbol > can be read as 'is implied by'.):

(5) initial > medial > final
     A   B   C

The presence of C implies the presence of B and A (but not vice versa), and the presence of B implies the presence of A (but not vice versa). Therefore, C is the most marked and A is the least marked.

This markedness differential explains the differing degrees of difficulty exhibited by the German and English L2 learners. The German speakers learning English are attempting to acquire a contrast in a universally more marked position (final) whereas the English speakers learning French are attempting to acquire a contrast in a universally unmarked position (initial).[2]

Acquiring new features

One question that often comes up in the field of second language phonology is whether one can learn material that is not found in one's first language. Some have argued that if a phonological feature is lacking in the L1, then acquiring L2 contrasts based on that feature will be impossible. One study compared the relative success of Chinese learners of the English /l/ versus /r/ contrast and the lack of success of Japanese learners attempting to acquire the same contrast. Both Mandarin Chinese and Japanese lack the /l, r/ contrast but, it was argued, Mandarin has the appropriate phonological *feature* ([lateral]) in the L1, whereas Japanese lacks it. (The specific feature is not important for our discussion.) However, it appears that this is too strong a stance. In some cases, L2 learners *can* acquire contrasts based on features absent from their L1. We will give two brief examples.

First, Japanese learners of Russian can acquire Russian /r/ (even though they have difficulty with English /r/). How could this be possible if they are lacking the appropriate phonological feature? Second, it has been shown that English learners of Japanese can acquire the distinction between long (or geminate) and short consonants, even though English does not have that distinction. The details of why either of these feats of acquisition are possible are complex (involving such things as phonetic salience), but the main point is that features that are absent from the L1 can be acquired in the L2.

Language Matters Foreign Accent Syndrome

There have been several documented cases of what has become known as *foreign accent syndrome*, in which people have been known to suddenly acquire what sounds like a non-native accent. A British English speaker, for example, may start to sound as if she has a Spanish accent. Or an American English speaker may acquire a British accent. The cases all result from underlying brain damage (from a stroke or some sort of cerebral trauma), but it appears that there is no one brain area that is related to this syndrome. In 2006, the *Journal of Neurolinguistics* (vol. 19, no. 5) devoted an entire issue to this subject. To hear an actual example of foreign accent syndrome, go to the Companion Website, Chapter 11.

Prosodic phonology

In addition to the segmental inventory, second language learners also have to acquire the prosodic phonology of the target language. For example, they have to acquire the principles of syllabification and stress assignment. We will now look at each in turn.

L2 syllabification

Syllables have the hierarchical structure shown in figure 11.3.

FIGURE 11.3
The internal structure of the syllable

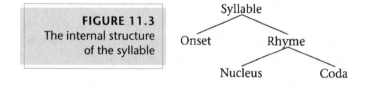

The languages of the world vary in the type of syllable structures that they permit. For instance, some languages, such as most varieties of Arabic, do not allow more than one consonant at the beginning of a syllable, so that the longest possible syllable is CVC. When speakers of Arabic start learning English as a second language, they add the vowel /i/ after 'extra' consonants.[3]

(6) *English target*   *Non-native speaker's version*
    plant   [pi.lan.ti]
    Fred   [fi.rɛd]
    translate   [ti.ran.si.let]

Research on the acquisition of English by Mandarin Chinese speakers sheds light on the different types of repair strategies that are available to a learner whose L1 does not allow syllables of the same type and complexity as those found in the second language. (Mandarin Chinese allows only /n/ and /ŋ/ in coda position, but English allows many options, including consonant clusters.) There are two possible repair strategies: deletion and epenthesis.

(7) *Target word*   *Deletion strategy*   *Epenthesis strategy*
    seed   [si]   [sidə]
    big   [bɪ]   [bɪgə]
    went   [wɛ]   [wɛntə]

As learners' proficiency increases, they make more epenthesis repairs than deletion repairs—a positive development because the epenthesized version is easier for listeners to understand.

Illusory Vowels

Following up our discussion of epenthesis and deletion, we turn now to how L1 properties can affect both perception and production. It might seem that the production by an L2 learner of an English word like 'street' as [istrit] simply reflects the articulatory complexity of having three consonants in a row. But this would not tell the whole story. A number of studies have demonstrated that the L1 phonology influences perception as well as production. Studies done on learners from a range of L1s (such as Japanese, Thai, and Brazilian Portuguese) have shown that when these learners listen to an English word like 'stop' they *hear* [istɑp]—even when there is no [i] in the acoustic input.

A look at the methodology involved in these experiments will help explain what is occurring. One experimental paradigm (known as an auditory discrimination task) has subjects listen to two audio files and indicate whether the sounds are the same or different. They might press one computer key if they are the same (S) and another key if they are different (D). This is a methodology that can be used to investigate segmental perception, as in (8).

(8) [rɑk]   [lɑk]   Same or Different?

Studies done with L2 learners whose L1s do not allow [s]+consonant clusters (such as [st], [sn], [sl]) reveal that perceptual accuracy is low in experimental tasks such as (9).

(9) [istɑp]   [stɑp]   Same or Different?

The Japanese, Thai, and Brazilian Portuguese subjects had error rates ranging between 50 percent and 72 percent in perceiving these clusters. They heard an *illusory* vowel in these stimulus items. For these subjects, it seems that their non-targetlike production stems from non-targetlike perception. And the non-targetlike perception results from a non-targetlike interlanguage grammar.

There are also cases, though, where production and perception do not match up quite so nicely. Persian is a language that does not allow [s]+consonant clusters in syllable onsets. Predictably, Persian speakers of English often insert epenthetic vowels, producing English words like *fly* as [felaj] or *snow* as [esnow]. And yet studies have shown that the L1 Persian subjects are very accurate when it comes to perceiving the difference between, say, 'stop' and 'estop'. The reason why Persian listeners are more accurate than, say, Japanese or Brazilian Portuguese listeners is complex but probably has something to do with the fact that Persian allows complex codas (in words like *xatm* 'funeral') and this gives them an advantage when acquiring L2 English complex onsets (in words like 'stop'). Japanese (and Brazilian Portuguese) do not allow these complex sequences in their codas.

Stress assignment

L2 learners also have to acquire the stress patterns of the language they are trying to learn. Consider an example from Polish, a language in which word-level stress is always assigned to the penultimate (second-to-last) syllable. The transfer of this L1 principle results in one of the characteristics of a Polish accent in English: the tendency to place stress on the penultimate syllable of English words. The following examples illustrate a non-native stress pattern in which the second-to-last syllable is always stressed.

> **(10)** *English target*   *Non-native form*
> astónish   astónish
> maintáin   máintain
> cábinet   cabínet

11.2.2 L2 syntax

L2 learners also have to acquire the syntax of their new language. In this section, we will look at two facets of syntactic structure: the Null Subject Parameter and Verb Raising.

Null subjects

According to the theory of Universal Grammar, the human language faculty includes both universal principles that account for what all natural languages have in common and parameters that account for cross-linguistic variation. Parameters are like linguistic switches (often binary) that can be set to a particular value as a result of the linguistic input. One of the first parameters to be proposed by researchers was the Null Subject (or Pronoun-Drop) Parameter. Essentially, this parameter is designed to account for the contrast between languages like French and English, which require overt subjects (e.g., *He speaks French/*Speaks French*), and languages like Spanish and Italian, which allow subjects to be omitted (e.g., Spanish *El habla español/Habla español* '[S/he] speaks Spanish').

> **(11)** *The Null Subject Parameter*
> The subject of a clause with a verb marked for tense [may/may not] be null.

Languages that allow null subjects (i.e., [+null subject] languages) tend to have other associated grammatical traits. For one, they tend to allow declarative sentences with the word order verb + subject as well as subject + verb, as in the following examples from Spanish.

(12)   *a.* Juan llegó.
John arrived

b. Llegó Juan.
arrived John

Secondly, they tend to allow sentences like the following, in which a complementizer (here *que* 'that') is immediately followed by the trace (*t*) of a moved *wh* word.

(13)   Quién   dijo usted   que *t*   llegó?
who   said you   that   arrived
'Who did you say arrived?'

As (14) shows, such sentences are unacceptable in English, which is [–null subject].

(14)   *Who did you say [CP that [TP *t* arrived]]?
(deep structure = *you did say that who arrived*)

Studies on L2 learners of English show that Spanish speakers are more likely to judge subjectless English sentences to be grammatical than are French speakers. This is consistent with the assumption that L1 parameter settings are transferred into the IL grammar, at least in the early stages. Learning a second language can be seen as involving the resetting of parameters that have different values in the L1 and the L2.

Moreover, when Spanish subjects are given a task that requires them to change a declarative sentence into a question, they are more likely to produce a sentence that contains a *that*-trace sequence than are French subjects. For example, if Spanish subjects are given a sentence like *Joshua believed that his father would be late* and asked to form a question asking about the underlined element, they are more likely than French subjects to produce a sentence like *Who did Joshua believe that* t *would be late?* This points toward the possibility that the admissibility of null subjects and the acceptability of *that*-trace sequences are somehow both related to the Null Subject Parameter (i.e., speakers of null subject languages are more likely to permit *that*-trace sequences).

However, there are complications. Remember that the Spanish and French subjects in the study we have been considering had to actually create their own sentences. Another study had both French and Spanish L2 learners simply judge the grammaticality of English sentences with a *that*-trace violation. Both groups were quite able to reject those sentences as ungrammatical. For some reason, there is a stronger L1 influence when learners have to form new sentences themselves.

Verb Raising

French and English differ in the setting of the Verb Raising Parameter (which is slightly simplified here).

(15)   *The Verb Raising Parameter*
A main verb marked for tense [raises/does not raise] to T.

The transformation of Verb Raising takes a verb from within the VP and moves it to T (see figure 11.4). English does not allow Verb Raising (as the operation is articulated here) but French does. Thus, in French the verb raises to T past a preverbal adverb, but in English it does not. This difference can be seen in the sentences in (16), in which movement of the verb over the adverb separating it from the T position gives an ungrammatical result in English but a grammatical one in French.

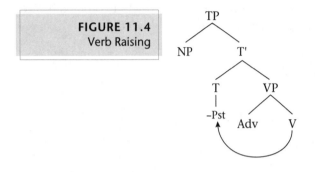

FIGURE 11.4
Verb Raising

(16) *a.* *Marie watches often *t* television.
      b. Marie regarde souvent *t* la télévision.

Studies have shown that French speakers learning English initially assume that English allows Verb Raising and produce sentences like (16a). To become more proficient in English, they have to reset the value of the Verb Raising Parameter.

Markedness and the Subset Principle

Another interesting facet of a parameter-setting approach to SLA has to do with whether adult L2 learners can reset their parameters and whether the direction of difficulty posited by the Markedness Differential Hypothesis (see section 11.2.1) can be captured in a parameter-setting model. The Null Subject Parameter can be used to address these questions. To understand how, we must first consider how a parameter-setting model instantiates the notion of markedness.

If we consider the two settings of the Null Subject Parameter (+/−), we can see that the different values result in different grammars, as shown in the following sentences from English and Spanish.

(17) [−null subject]: He speaks Spanish.
                  *Speaks Spanish.
    [+null subject]: El habla español.
                  Habla español.

As shown in (17), the [+null subject] setting generates more grammatical utterances than the [−null subject] setting does. Therefore the [−] setting is said to be a subset of the [+] setting. Graphically, this can be represented as in figure 11.5.

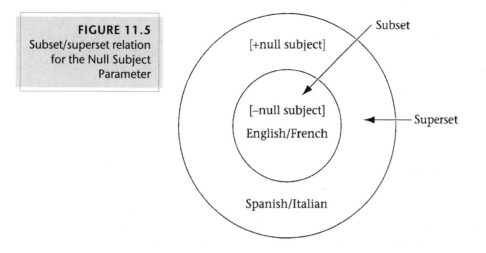

FIGURE 11.5
Subset/superset relation for the Null Subject Parameter

Subset

[+null subject]

[−null subject]
English/French

Superset

Spanish/Italian

The **Subset Principle**, which relates to first-language learning, can be stated as follows.[4]

(18) *The Subset Principle*

The initial, or default, setting of a parameter will correspond to the most restrictive option (i.e., the option that permits the fewest patterns).

When attempting to reset from subset to superset or from superset to subset, second language learners need access to different types of evidence. Imagine a native speaker of English (who has the [−null subject] setting) trying to learn Spanish. The learner's initial assumption will be the L1 parameter setting, which leads to the expectation that all sentences will have overt subjects. When faced with Spanish input, the learner will be exposed to grammatical utterances in the L2 that do not have overt subjects (e.g., *Hablo español* '[I] speak Spanish'), which indicates that the L1 setting is incorrect and needs to be reset. Data like this, which involves grammatical utterances to which one is actually exposed, is referred to as **positive evidence**.

Now imagine a learner whose L1 is Spanish ([+]) who is trying to learn English ([−]). The learner's initial assumption will be that English is [+null subject], like the L1. The learner's IL grammar will allow both sentences with overt subjects and sentences without. Crucially, there will be no positive evidence in the English input directed at this learner to show that the L1 parameter setting is wrong. The learner will hear sentences with overt subjects, which are sanctioned by the current IL grammar, but there will be no direct indication that sentences with null subjects are not allowed. There is no pressure to reset the parameter. In this case, the learner will have to rely on **negative evidence** (i.e., observations about what is missing or ungrammatical in the data) to reset the parameter. In particular, the learner would either have to be explicitly told what is ungrammatical (**direct negative evidence**), or infer that it is ungrammatical on the basis of the fact that no one else ever says it (**indirect negative evidence**).

Given that positive evidence is available in one case (English → Spanish) and negative evidence is required in the other (Spanish → English), we might predict that it will be harder for Spanish speakers to learn the English value of the Null Subject Parameter than vice versa. In fact, the prediction is borne out. Studies have shown that it is easier for English speakers to reset to the Spanish value of the Null Subject Parameter than it is for Spanish subjects to reset to the English setting.

Let us now consider how an approach based on typological universals would treat the same phenomenon.

(19) *Null Subject Implicational Universal*
   If a language has null subjects, it will also have overt subjects, but not vice versa.

According to this formulation, null subjects are more marked than overt subjects. The Markedness Differential Hypothesis predicts that structures that are more marked typologically will cause difficulty in second language acquisition. The Subset Principle, on the other hand, predicts that structures that are more marked will not cause difficulty because there will be clear evidence that the L1 setting is wrong. For example, if learners start with the assumption that a language (say, Spanish) allows only overt subjects, they will quickly encounter sentences with null subjects (as well as sentences with overt subjects) and will be able to make the appropriate adjustment to their interlanguage grammar.

11.2.3 L2 morphology

The study of second language morphology has a slightly different flavour than that of either L2 phonology or L2 syntax. L2 phonology has been studied for a long time, though the analyses have changed to reflect changes in linguistic theory. L2 syntax is a much younger field, and much of it has been informed by current linguistic theory. By contrast, L2 morphology has been studied more or less in a theoretical vacuum. In the 1970s, a number of studies collected data on the accuracy of second language learners on a variety of morphemes. This research drew on previous studies in the field of first language acquisition that had attempted to determine the order of acquisition of morphemes in L1 development and found the developmental sequence in table 11.7.

TABLE 11.7 Developmental order for first language acquisition	
Morpheme	**Example**
1. *-ing*	She is work*ing*.
2. plural *-s*	bottle*s*
3. irregular past	She *taught* French.
4. possessive *-'s*	a child*'s* toy
5. copula *be*	I *am* happy.
6. articles	A man read *the* book
7. regular past	She walk*ed* quickly.
8. 3rd person singular *-s*	She walk*s* quickly.
9. auxiliary *be*	She *is* working.

Research on second language acquisition focused on whether the developmental sequence in L2 learning was the same as for L1 learning, and found the order in table 11.8.

TABLE 11.8	Developmental order for second language acquisition	
1. *-ing*	4. auxiliary *be*	7. regular past
2. copula *be*	5. plural *-s*	8. 3rd person singular *-s*
3. articles	6. irregular past	9. possessive *-'s*

There are many similarities in the two orders, but also some differences. For example, note that auxiliary and copula *be* are acquired at relatively earlier points in L2 than in L1 and that the possessive morpheme *-'s* is acquired later in L2 than in L1. To attempt to explain these patterns, we need to look a little more closely at the structures involved.

Children acquire *be* as a copula verb before they acquire *be* as an auxiliary verb. So they produce sentences that have only a copula verb (e.g., *He is hungry*) before they produce sentences that include an auxiliary plus a main verb (e.g., *He is working*). The syntactic structures for these sentences are shown in figure 11.6.

FIGURE 11.6
Sentence structure for copula versus auxiliary *be*

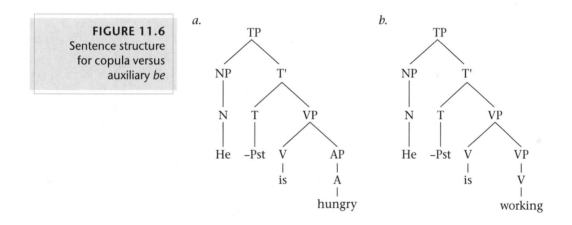

The structure in *b* has an extra level of complexity in that it has one VP within another. Differences in the L1 and L2 acquisition of *be* seem to arise from this complexity. In contrast to child L1 learners, adult L2 learners appear to be able to use both the simple copula and auxiliary verbs quite early on, presumably because they have both types of structure available to them from their L1.

Remember that children learning English as their first language acquire the three *-s* morphemes in the order plural, possessive, third person singular. Phonetically, these morphemes have the same realization, so we can't say that the order reflects phonological complexity. The order might be explained by noting that noun plurality is a word-level phenomenon (e.g., *dogs*), possessive is a phrase-level phenomenon (e.g., [*the king of England*]'*s horse*, not **the* [*king*]'*s of England horse*), and third-person marking involves a relation between the verb and a phrase (the subject) elsewhere in the sentence (e.g., [*That man*] *usually watches TV*). Like the pattern noted for the development of copula and auxiliary *be*, children seem to be acquiring structures in order of complexity, as shown in figure 11.7.

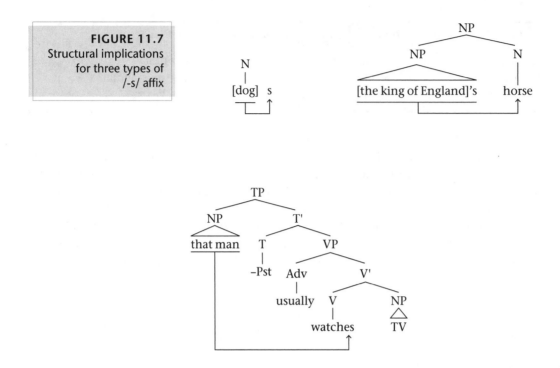

FIGURE 11.7
Structural implications for three types of /-s/ affix

In contrast, adult second language learners acquire the plural quite early but seem to get both the possessive and the third person marking quite late—perhaps for reasons involving processing. (When concentrating on getting the words right, we do not always have the processing capacity to produce well-formed higher-level structures.) Interestingly, the adults do not seem to find interphrasal morphology (like third-person marking) more difficult than phrasal morphology (like possessives). This may be because the adults have already acquired the grammar for their first language, which most likely has both phrase-level and interphrasal morphological phenomena. In contrast, children could conceivably be building a sentence's structure from the bottom up (words → phrases → sentences).

In summary, we note that the phenomenon of developmental order is intriguing in both first and second language acquisition, even though we await a conclusive explanation of the facts. There will probably not be a single explanation, however, given that the morphemes under investigation include both verbal and nominal elements.

11.2.4 Morphology and syntax

We conclude this section with a discussion of a recent theoretical approach that looks at the interaction of morphology and syntax in second language learners in an attempt to answer one of the questions we have already posed in this chapter: If someone leaves something out, does it really mean he or she doesn't have a representation for it? To answer this question, we will consider what second language learners know about tense.

It is well known that non-native speakers often make mistakes with the tense of a sentence, as exemplified in (20).

(20) You know, I *call* Bill this morning and nobody *answer*. And I *start* to worry . . . He either *stay* in Eliotville, because he said he *call* me last night, and he never did.

The lack of overt tense marking might tempt us to conclude that this learner lacks knowledge of tense. Two alternative theoretical positions have been put forward. The first is the **Impaired Representation Hypothesis**, which argues that the learners have some sort of underlying representational deficiency (i.e., problems with the representation of tense).

(21) *Impaired Representation Hypothesis*
    The interlanguage grammar is lacking certain grammatical features.

The second position is the **Missing Surface Inflection Hypothesis**, which argues that the learners have the correct underlying functional categories but have difficulty mapping surface inflectional forms onto those categories.

(22) *Missing Surface Inflection Hypothesis*
    Even though L2 learners may omit inflection at times, they are nonetheless sensitive to the relevant grammatical contrasts.

How can we decide between these two hypotheses? We will use the data from a longitudinal case study to build our argument for the Missing Surface Inflection Hypothesis. The subject, known as Patty in the literature, is a native Mandarin (and Hokkien) speaker who first acquired English as an adult. An example of her English is given in (20) above. At the time of the first recording, she had been in the United States for about ten years. She was recorded three times over the next nine years. During that period, she was virtually immersed in English, and yet, as shown in table 11.9, she often does not mark her past tense forms in obligatory contexts. Note that she supplies the past tense marking in about 34 percent of the contexts where native speakers do. Although Patty is clearly not placing the proper inflectional morphology on her verbs, we will argue that she does have targetlike knowledge of the tense feature.

TABLE 11.9 Patty's past-tense marking in obligatory contexts

Recording #	Suppliance/contexts	%
1	24/69	34.78
2	191/548	34.85
3	46/136	33.82

The subject of a tense-bearing verb in English receives **nominative** case. In contrast, the subjects of verbs that lack tense marking do not receive nominative case, as can be seen by comparing the pronouns in the sentences in (23).

(23) *a.* I believe that [he   is a liar].
                    NOM   [tense marked]

    b. I believe [him   to be a liar].
               ACC   [no tense]

In (23a) the second verb (*is*) is marked for tense and the pronoun has nominative case. In (23b), in contrast, the second verb lacks tense (*to be*) and the preceding pronoun does not have nominative case. Note that *him* is not the object of the verb *believe*—you don't believe him; in fact, you think he's a liar. The point is that there is a connection between tense and nominative case marking.

Let us return to our two hypotheses about Patty. The Impaired Representation Hypothesis holds that because Patty does not use tense marking on her verbs, she should be unable to make the connection between tense and nominative case marking. In contrast, the Missing Surface Inflection Hypothesis suggests that Patty has the category of tense but has trouble with the overt morphological marking; it therefore predicts that she will demonstrate a connection between tense and case marking. So what does she do? The data in table 11.10 clearly show that Patty correctly assigns nominative case to all pronominal subjects of a tense-bearing verb.

TABLE 11.10 Patty's use of nominative case on pronominal subjects		
Recording #	**Nominative subject pronouns/Past tense contexts**	**%**
1	49/49	100
2	378/378	100
3	76/76	100

Furthermore, Patty does not *incorrectly* mark pronouns in other contexts, as her sentences in (24) demonstrate. Note that in non-finite contexts she correctly uses the accusative form.

(24) It's best for *me* to stay in Shanghai.
It is possibility for *me* to get out.
That doesn't have anything to do with *me* leaving home.
She asked *him* to go to this place.

These considerations suggest that Patty does have a mental representation of tense that governs case assignment, even though she has fossilized with respect to its morphological expression on verbs.

11.2.5 Variation at the Interfaces

We have already noted that production of L2 morphology can be variable. It has been argued that we see the greatest variation when morphosyntactic forms are conditioned by pragmatic factors. For example, Italian is a null-subject language. The grammaticality of a null subject in a sentence is a syntactic property, and L2 learners of Italian (learners whose first language is [−null subject]) learn to use null subjects with considerable accuracy. By contrast, the acceptability of using an overt subject pronoun in Italian is governed by contextual or pragmatic features. The use of an overt pronoun signals a shift of topic or focus. So, in an Italian sentence like *Laura hugged Maria and then she went out*, the use of the overt pronoun *she* indicates that while the focus of the main clause is Laura, the focus in the adjoined clause is Maria and thus *she* can refer only to Maria. L2 learners of [+null subject] languages have greater difficulty (as evidenced by greater variation in accuracy) in acquiring such constructions.

11.3 Factors affecting SLA

So far, we've looked at some of the characteristics of an IL grammar. Now let's turn to a variety of non-linguistic factors that can influence second language acquisition. It is clear that there is much more variation in the IL grammars of people learning second languages than in the developing grammars of children learning first languages. This brings us to the question of what factors might help to account for that variation.

11.3.1 Age

One of the obvious ways in which language learners vary is in their age. People start learning second languages at different points in their lives. Could the age of onset of L2 learning cause different levels of final proficiency?

This is a question usually considered under the hypothesis that there is a **critical period** during which children must be exposed to language if the aqcuisition process is to be fully successful. We know that biologically based critical periods exist in other species. For example, some birds can learn the song of their species only if exposed to it during a particular window of opportunity. If they only begin to hear the song after a certain period of development, then learning will not take place.

Is second language learning like this? Is there an optimal time (or critical period) to acquire a second language? The answer appears to be 'yes and no'. Proficiency in a language is a remarkably complex thing (see the discussion of communicative competence in section 11.1.3). Usually, discussion of a possible critical period focuses on the area of phonological competence. Although people who begin SLA as adults tend to retain non-nativelike phonology in the target language, it is much more difficult to predict knowledge or ability in any of the other areas of communicative competence (syntax, cohesion, sociolinguistics, etc.) based upon age of acquisition.

In fact, even L2 phonology is not so straightforward as it might first appear to be. We can predict with a fair degree of certainty that people who start learning their L2 before the age of seven will have nativelike L2 speech and that people who start learning after fourteen or fifteen will probably have non-nativelike speech. But the results for people who start learning between the ages of seven and fourteen are much more varied. Some end up with accents, and some do not.

This is not to say that the age of first significant exposure to the second language does not have any effect. A number of studies (from the Centre for Bilingualism in Stockholm) have shown that although listeners may judge subjects to be nativelike, more detailed linguistic analysis (e.g., acoustic or experimental) may reveal subtle differences in performance between those who started learning at a younger age and those who started at a later age. However, other work has demonstrated that there is no single feature (e.g., aspiration or restrictions on the interpretation of reflexive pronouns) that is unacquirable by all late learners. This has been coined the *universal learnability hypothesis* (everything is learnable by someone). So, while there is variation in the proficiency levels achieved by adult L2 learners, it is not the case that some linguistic elements cannot be learned after a certain age.

Still more recently, a reanalysis of many influential studies on the age of acquisition has shown that age of significant first exposure may not be an accurate measure of the quantity of input that a learner receives over the years. Many studies had assumed that all learners who started learning at, say, age eight would receive the same quantity of input. However, it turns out that many factors (such as family circumstances, social factors, etc.) can influence the quantity of input a particular eight-year old would receive. Thus, age of acquisition is only one of many factors that may explain the variability in L2 learners' levels of proficiency.

There is no current evidence of anything biological that prevents adults from acquiring proficiency in a second language. Factors that have been considered in the past (like brain lateralization) are now thought to have little predictive value in determining L2 ability. Recent research demonstrates that people who start learning their second language as adults *are* able to reach a final state that is indistinguishable from native speakers. One study in the syntactic domain shows that near-native speakers perform like native speakers when it comes to speed and accuracy in grammaticality judgment tasks (involving sentences such as *Who did Mary meet the man after she saw* t*?*).

Similarly, studies have shown that some people (admittedly a minority, but they do exist) can start learning their second language as adults and perform within the range of native speakers when it comes to their pronunciation. When native-speaker judges listen to tapes of both native and non-native speakers (not knowing which is which) and give a global accent rating, there are always some native speakers who do not get a perfect rating and some non-native speakers who can score more highly than these subjects. Currently, the critical period debate in SLA research is usually couched in terms of the question, Do adults have access to Universal Grammar? Rather than looking for changes in the brain that coincide with aging, researchers now look to see whether IL grammars are governed by the same constraints as human languages in general.

If adults are engaged in the same kind of developmental process as children, then we would expect their IL grammars to be describable in terms of the same principles and parameters of UG that we use to describe all languages. Conversely, if adults are acquiring their second languages using qualitatively different learning mechanisms than are used to acquire an L1 (e.g., if they use general problem-solving abilities), then we might expect them to adopt hypotheses that are not sanctioned by Universal Grammar. Something like this may in fact happen in the acquisition of gender in French.

Children learning French as a first language seem to have very little trouble learning grammatical gender as they learn the words themselves (e.g., *le livre*, 'the book', is masculine; *la table*, 'the table', is feminine; and so on). However, adults whose first language does not have grammatical gender often have great difficulty learning French gender. They seem to set up complex (but incorrect) rules for predicting the gender of a given noun. For example, they may assume that words naming parts of the body (or some other semantic category) are all of one gender, or that words that end with a certain sound sequence are of another. Rules like this sometimes allow non-native speakers to guess the gender correctly, but they still perform significantly differently from native speakers. This is an example of how adults' greater capacity to formulate general rules can sometimes lead them down the wrong path.

11.3.2 Individual differences

Learners vary in ways other than age. Broadly speaking, the researcher asks the question, If learners have a particular quality *x*, does this make them better at second language acquisition? For example, we might look at the effect of inhibition, left-handedness, or some other individual trait on L2 ability. As intuitively appealing as this avenue is, it is one that must be taken carefully. In particular, we must be explicit about three points:

- how we define and measure *x*
- what it means to be *better*
- what aspect of communicative competence we are referring to

Consider in this regard a trait like empathy. It has been argued that people who are empathetic are better language learners. This is an intuitively appealing notion. People who are empathetic can imagine what it feels like to be in someone else's shoes and they can look at things from another perspective. And second language learning certainly involves looking at things from a different perspective. But in SLA research, we need to find a more precise way to evaluate this hypothesis.

There are tests that claim to measure a person's empathy, but how well defined is the notion of 'empathy'? Is one simply empathetic or not, or are there degrees of empathy? If there are degrees, do we see a correlation between degree of empathy and degree of L2 learning success? And what does it mean for empathetic learners to be better language learners than people who aren't empathetic? Do they make fewer errors? Less serious errors? Should we expect people with greater empathy to be better at everything in the L2? Or maybe just at phonology and sociolinguistic competence? On what basis could we make a prediction? These are not simple issues. We raise them not to argue that research in individual variation is misguided but to show some of the complex areas that need to be addressed before we can hope to establish a causal connection between a particular personality trait and success at second language learning.

Let us look at one set of factors that may influence second language learning.

Affective factors

Affective factors have to do with the emotional side of learning a second language. Clearly there can be a great deal at stake emotionally when learning a second language, and it is possible that emotions affect how successful an L2 learner is. Affective factors that have been studied include empathy, anxiety, inhibition, and risk-taking. In this section, we will look at one such factor: motivation.

Learners can vary with respect to the amount or type of motivation they have to learn a second language. If someone is highly motivated to learn, will that person do better at learning? In order to answer this question, we need to say a bit more about what it means to be motivated.

Traditionally, two types of motivation have been proposed: **instrumental** and **integrative**. Instrumental motivation involves wanting to learn the L2 for a specific goal or reason. For example, someone might need to pass a language requirement in order to get a graduate degree or a job with a government agency. Integrative motivation, in contrast, involves wanting to learn the L2 in order to learn more about a particular culture or fit into it better. For instance, someone might want to learn Japanese in order to learn more about a fascinating culture.

Studies have shown that the degree of integrative motivation correlates with the degree of success in language learning. That is, subjects who score highly on tests of integrative motivation do better on certain language tests than comparable subjects who score poorly on the same motivation tests. However, subjects with instrumental rather than integrative motivation can also do well under the right circumstances. One study found that subjects who were offered a cash reward if they obtained a certain score on a language test performed much the same as subjects with high integrative motivation. All of this seems to suggest that degree of motivation is a better predictor of future learning success than is type of motivation.

Language Matters **Exceptional Language Learning Ability**

Daniel Paul Tammet (born January 31, 1979, in London, England) is a high-functioning autistic savant who is gifted with a facility for mathematics problems, sequence memory, and natural language learning. He was born with congenital childhood epilepsy. He can't drive a car or tell right from left, but he holds the European record for memorizing and recounting *pi* to 22 514 digits in just over five hours.

Tammet can speak several languages, including English, French, Finnish, German, Spanish, Lithuanian, Romanian, Estonian, Icelandic, Welsh, and Esperanto. He particularly likes Estonian because it is rich in vowels, and he is creating a new language called Mänti. Mänti has many features related to Finnish and Estonian, both of which are Finno-Ugric languages.

Tammet is capable of learning new languages very quickly. To prove this for a television documentary, he was challenged to learn Icelandic, a language viewed by some as one of the world's most difficult, in one week. Seven days later, he appeared on Icelandic television conversing in Icelandic, with his Icelandic language instructor saying it was "incredible."

For more information, go to www.danieltammet.net.

11.4 Third Language Acquisition

Until now, we have been considering the acquisition of a single additional language—what we have called the L2. However, it is common for people to acquire a third language as well. In probing the nature of an L3 grammar, we must consider more than the possible influence of the L1, since the L2 could also have an impact on the L3 interlanguage grammar (see figure 11.8).

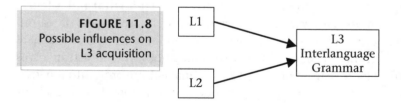

FIGURE 11.8
Possible influences on
L3 acquisition

Questions arise, then, as to when and how each of L1 and L2 might influence the acquisition of L3. A number of theoretical stances are worth exploring.

11.4.1 The L1 Factor Model

It could be argued that the L1 will always be privileged because it is the most cognitively entrenched language of the three and will therefore be more heavily relied upon. If the L2 is weaker or less advanced than the L1, it will be less likely to transfer into the L3 interlanguage. One study looked at subjects who spoke Chinese as their L1, English as their L2, and Norwegian as their L3. Chinese allows null object constructions (we have already discussed null subjects in this chapter). Note how in (25) the object of the verb *see* is not overtly expressed but the interpretation is clearly 'the thief thought nobody saw the thief' (as indicated by the subscript *i* linking the subject and object).

> **(25)** xiaotou$_1$ yiwei mei ren kanjian e$_1$.
> thief   think no   man see
> 'The thief$_1$ thought nobody saw (him$_1$)'.

Neither English (L2) nor Norwegian (L3) allows null objects. Yet the Chinese participants were quite accepting of Norwegian sentences with null objects, even though they were aware that their L2, English, did not allow null objects. It seems, then, that their L1 grammar was having more influence on their L3 grammar than their L2 grammar was.

11.4.2 The L2 Status Factor Model

Others have argued that in certain situations, the L2 influences the L3 more than the L1 does. One such circumstance appears to be sequential classroom learning of L2 and L3. If the L2 knowledge has been acquired through explicit teaching, and hence with some degree of meta-linguistic awareness, then that knowledge is likely to transfer to the grammar of the L3 if it too is being taught in a classroom.

Consider, for example, an L1 English/L2 Spanish speaker learning L3 Mandarin. Spanish has two verbs (*ser/estar*) that can be translated as English *be*. *Ser* is typically used for permanent states (e.g., *I am* a man) while *estar* is used for temporary states (e.g., *I am* sad). An L3 Mandarin learner would also have to learn two verbs that can be translated as to *be—shi* and *zai*. *Shi* is used for personal attributes (e.g., *I am* a professor) while *zai* is used for locations (e.g., *I am* at school). The L1 English learner who transfers the Spanish patterns onto the Mandarin grammar would be privileging the L2 grammar.

11.4.3 The Typological Primacy Model

Let us imagine a situation where either the L1 or the L2 (but not both) are typologically related to the L3—for example, L1/L2 French, Japanese (in either order), and L3 Spanish. French and Spanish belong to the same language family (Romance), but Japanese (Altaic) does not. Proponents of the Typological Primacy Model suggest that the learner is able to assess whether the L1 or the L2 is more closely related (or linguistically similar) to the L3. On the basis of that decision, the learner will use the grammar of *that* language as the starting point for learning L3.

Clear support for this approach comes from the lexicon. Imagine L3 learners of Spanish confronting a lexical gap and wondering if they should try using a French word or a Japanese word (L2) in the Spanish sentence (L3). It seems highly likely that, believing French to be more closely related to Spanish, they would use the French word (whether French is the L1 or the L2) for 'flower' (*fleur*) rather than the Japanese one (*hana*), thus producing (26a) rather than (26b).

(26) *a.* Yo tengo una *fleur*.
'I have a flower.'

b. Yo tengo una *hana*.
I have a flower.

In other linguistic domains, the question is less straightforward. Imagine a scenario of L1 English, L2 Spanish, and L3 French. The Typological Proximity Model predicts that the learner, perceiving that Spanish is more closely related to French than English is, might set up L2 Spanish as the initial state for acquiring the L3. However, Spanish allows null subjects, while neither English nor French do. L3 learners who rely on their knowledge of Spanish will therefore wrongly assume that French is a null subject language and produce sentences such as (27).

(27) *Parlent français.
speaks French

11.4.4 The Linguistic Proximity Model

For a variety of reasons, researchers have proposed models that do *not* assume across-the-board transfer of the grammar of *either* L1 or L2. One such model is the Linguistic Proximity Model, which assumes that learners are able to do a case-by-case, or structure-by-structure, assessment to choose the elements for the initial L3 grammatical state.

To illustrate the Linguistic Proximity Model, imagine a learner who is L1 English, L2 French, and L3 Spanish. The learner notices that Spanish stress (which is variable) is more like English stress (also variable) than like French stress (always word-final) and that Spanish lexical items look more like French than like English (e.g., Spanish *libro*, French *livre*, English *book*). In yet another area, the learner decides that Spanish reflexive verbs (*él **se afeita** todos los días* 'he [himself] shaves every day') are more like French (*il **se rase** tous les jours*) than like English (*he **kicks himself** every time he thinks of that day*). This learner is approaching L3 acquisition not by choosing either the L1 or L2 grammar as an initial state for L3 learning but by assessing various components of the language individually.

The field of L3 acquisition is in its very early stages, and we cannot yet conclude which model most accurately reflects actual L3 learning. All of the above types of transfer do occur, however, and we continue to search for the best explanatory model.

11.5 The L2 classroom

It has been flippantly said that people have been successfully acquiring second languages for thousands of years, but when teachers get involved, the success rate plummets. This comment is probably more a reflection of people's unfortunate experience in certain types of language classrooms (which may have been dull or even physically threatening, depending on the century) than it is a statement about the usefulness of teaching. However, the fact remains that language classrooms can be sheltered environments where students can benefit from being given the opportunity to learn and practise without being subject to the penalties for failure that can be imposed outside the classroom.

We should acknowledge at this point that there is really no such thing as *the* second language classroom. In reality, all classrooms are different because they have different people in them (both students and teachers).

11.5.1 Focus on form

One of the most obvious characteristics of a second language class is the presence of a teacher who may provide explicit instruction about the actual form of the target language. Let us look at what we can learn from the research on what is known as 'focus on form'. The term *focus on form* encompasses two distinct practices that tend to occur in most L2 classrooms: instruction about the language and explicit correction.

Most second language classes present the students with some sort of information about the language—noting, for example, that English has two different types of 'th' sound (i.e., voiced and voiceless) or that French has nasal vowels. Instruction of this type is designed to improve the form (or accuracy) of the student's L2. In all likelihood, other activities that happen in the class will focus on giving the student a chance to improve **fluency** or particular sociolinguistic skills.

Error correction is also designed to improve the form of the student's L2. Regardless of the methodology used, in most classes today there is some instruction about the language and some error correction. The interesting research question is whether either of these practices can be shown to have a positive effect on the learner. Do students who get corrected do better than students who don't?

The question may not be as straightforward as it appears. Remember that it has frequently been argued in first language acquisition research that attempts at error correction are relatively infrequent and don't really affect children's grammars. Could it be different for adult second language learners? The learning environment is different in that adult learners (unlike children) are usually exposed to a fair amount of error correction. But does that make a difference? Not surprisingly, this question is difficult to answer. Some studies have argued that second language learners who receive correction develop at about the same pace as those who do not. Other studies have shown certain increases in accuracy as the result of correction.

These results may not be as contradictory as they seem. The areas where correction seems to be most useful involve the use of lexical items. Feedback concerning certain structural phenomena may not be as effective. For example, the previously mentioned study of French speakers learning about the limited scope of Verb Raising in English (see section 11.2.2) found that while there were short-term improvements in the learners who were explicitly taught the relevant facts, there were no significant long-term effects. When the learners were tested a year later, they had reverted to their pre-instructional performance. Part of the reason for this poor performance may have been that the explicit instruction was not connected to a meaningful context.

Language Matters It Can Be Comforting to Hear Your Native Language

A seven-year-old Siberian tiger named Boris moved from a zoo near Montréal to a zoo in Edmonton. At first, zookeepers found him shy and aloof. Then one zookeeper began to speak to him in French. Immediately, the tiger came over to her and seemed much friendlier. It's not just humans who get used to a particular language!

Source: Canadian Press, "Bonjour Boris! Edmonton Zoo Discovers Quebec-Born Tiger Misses La Belle Langue," *CBC News*, May 30, 2007, www.cbc.ca.

But this doesn't mean that there is no place for explicit instruction in the classroom. Students benefit most when focus on form happens within a meaningful interaction. Research has shown that what is known as *spontaneous* focus on form can be beneficial to students' overall proficiency. There is a difference between *reactive* focus on form (when the teacher responds to an erroneous utterance with instruction) and *pre-emptive* focus on form (when a teacher or another student draws a learner's attention to a form that is anticipated to be problematic). An example of reactive focus on form would be the following exchange:

> *Student*: Sometimes they complain that.
> *Teacher*: They complain *about* that.

An example of pre-emptive focus on form can be seen in the following exchange:

> *Teacher*: Do you know what *ballet* is?
> *Student*: Ah, the classical music, the ladies . . .
> *Teacher*: Men and women, it's dance, it's a type of dance. Ballet.

This is coded as pre-emptive (though it looks a bit like interrupting) because the student has not actually produced an erroneous utterance. The teacher assumed that the student was going to say that ballet was a type of music. This distinction can help to explain some of the seemingly conflicting research results insofar as pre-emptive focus on form is more effective than reactive focus on form. Studies that didn't take this difference into account might have reached different conclusions.

In sum, adult students usually expect error correction, and teachers are accustomed to providing it. Assuming that the class is not devoted entirely to instruction that focuses on form (with no opportunity for meaningful practice), error correction doesn't seem to cause any harm. In a class with activities that focus on both form and fluency, the students tend to emerge with greater accuracy. Teachers who provide opportunities for interactions with both pre-emptive and reactive focus on form are serving the learners well.

11.5.2 Pronunciation Instruction

Our final topic in this chapter has to do with the goal of second language acquisition in the domain of pronunciation. Many teachers strive to have their students attain nativelike pronunciation. Indeed, the goal of many language learners is to be able to pronounce the L2 like a native speaker.

While we know that L2 learners can acquire new phonology, morphology, syntax, and semantics, it is also evident that the vast majority of learners are not mistaken for native speakers of the L2; they have accents. Canadian linguist Murray Munro has aptly noted that "nativelikeness is both uncommon and unnecessary." His statement is supported by a body of research demonstrating that accentedness is not directly related to intelligibility. Someone speaking with a heavy accent can often be easily understood. The term *intelligibility* refers to the ability of the listener to accurately recover the intended meaning of the speaker. It is highly unlikely that someone who says "I vant to see dat movie" will be misunderstood.

Second language accents are part of the human condition. Certain employers may have the right to demand intelligibility from their employees in the service industry, but they have no right to demand a nativelike accent. L2 students need to be on guard against the view that an accent is pathological and needs to be 'eliminated'.

The view of accent given here has implications for the L2 classroom, since it suggests that the goal of instruction should be intelligibility rather than nativelikeness. This is a much more manageable goal for both student and teacher.

Summing up

This chapter has dealt with a number of issues in the field of second language acquisition. We investigated the notion of an **interlanguage grammar** and the influence of both the source and target languages on this grammar in terms of **transfer** and developmental errors. Proficiency in a second language requires both knowledge and ability, something captured in a model of **communicative competence**. A learner must both acquire knowledge in all linguistic domains (phonetics, phonology, morphology, syntax, and semantics) and develop the ability to use that knowledge in a variety of social contexts.

What is easy or difficult to acquire in a second language has been investigated from a variety of perspectives. We focused on Universal Grammar (the **Subset Principle**) and typological universals (the **Markedness Differential Hypothesis**). However, it is not just universals that influence second language learning; the specific characteristics of an individual can also affect the process. Affective factors influence second language learning, as do factors such as focus on form.

The field of second language acquisition is remarkably diverse, in part because of what is involved in L2 learning. Someone who is attempting to learn an additional language must acquire new mental representations and develop facility at accessing those representations in a variety of circumstances. The field of SLA research must therefore draw on philosophy (theories of mind), psychology (theories of learning, theories of performance), linguistics (theories of linguistic structure), and pedagogy (theories of instruction). This is probably the main reason why we have not established anything like a comprehensive theory of how second languages are learned. But bit by bit, piece by piece, we're starting to put together some pieces of the puzzle.

Notes

[1] The asterisk indicates that this sound is not allowed in initial position (except in a few words that have been borrowed from French—e.g., *genre*, *gendarmes*, and so forth).

[2] Note that English phonology in general complies with the implicational universal given in (4), as can be seen with the phonemes /s/ and /z/, which contrast in all three positions: sip/ zip, racer/razor, race/raze. The lack of contrast of [ʃ]/[ʒ] in initial position is an **accidental gap**. Even with this gap, however, it seems that English speakers respect the universal when learning the phonology of a second language. The voicing contrast is easier to acquire in the universally unmarked position.

[3] This might also happen in a native Arabic word if two morphemes are put together and, as a result, two consonants occur adjacent to each other.

[4] As we will see, linguists infer the initial setting of a parameter on the basis of the kind of input or evidence available to the language learner. This leads to the hypothesis that the initial setting is [−null subject], yet, children's early sentences in English often lack overt subjects, which might lead us to believe that children begin with the [+] setting. However, the early sentences of English-speaking children do not contain the other structures associated with the [+null subject] parameter setting: *that*-trace patterns and VS order in declaratives. Given the complexity of this issue, we will assume the relationship shown in figure 11.5 when discussing second language learners.

Recommended reading

Archibald, John, ed. 2000. *Second Language Acquisition and Linguistic Theory*. Oxford: Blackwell.

Grosjean, François. 2010. *Bilingual: Life and Reality*. Cambridge, MA: Harvard University Press.

Hawkins, Roger. 2001. *Second Language Syntax: A Generative Introduction*. Oxford: Blackwell.

Herschensohn, Julia, and Martha Young-Scholten, eds. 2013. *The Cambridge Handbook of Second Language Acquisition*. Cambridge, UK: Cambridge University Press.

Meisel, Jürgen M. 2011. *First and Second Language Acquisition: Parallels and Differences*. Cambridge, UK: Cambridge University Press.

Ritchie, William C., and Tej K. Bhatia. 2013. *The New Handbook of Second Language Acquisition*. Boston: Brill.

White, Lydia. 2003. *Second Language Acquisition and Universal Grammar*. Cambridge, UK: Cambridge University Press.

Exercises

1. Consider the changes that would result if a particular L1 transferred aspects of its phonology to the L2. Apply the changes to the following sentence: *The bad guys tried to climb out and thought they had made it until they saw the dog.*
   a) Devoice final stops.
   b) Turn interdental fricatives into alveolar fricatives.
   c) Delete the second consonant of a consonant cluster.
   d) Insert an epenthetic vowel such as [ə] after a coda consonant.
   e) Delete glottal fricatives.

2. Indicate the type of error (phonological, morphological, syntactic, or lexical) found in the following sentences.
   a) She play tennis almost every day.
   b) I no get on the train on time.
   c) The house old needs painting.
   d) I'm not a very good cooker.
   e) You should get your hairs cut.
   f) Look at that goose with antlers!
   g) I miss the bus, yesterday.
   h) Tank you very much.

3. Some dialects of Arabic break up clusters by inserting the epenthetic vowel [i] to the *left* of a problematic consonant (unlike the dialect discussed in this chapter). How would a speaker of this dialect pronounce the words *plant*, *transport*, and *translate*? Draw the syllable structure for the resulting pronunciation of *plant*.

4. In your second language learning experience, can you think of an example of an L2 property that seemed very different from your L1 and that you found easy to learn? Can you think of an example of something different that you found hard to learn? What do you think might have led to the difference in ease of learning?

5. In second language learners whose first language does not allow coda consonants, we sometimes see variation in the production of English codas. Examine the following phrases and propose an explanation as to why some stops in coda position are deleted and others are produced. Segments in **boldface** are produced while ~~struckthrough~~ segments are deleted. Focus only on either boldface or struckthrough segments for this question.
   a) cu**p** of coffee
   b) ba~~ck~~ to work
   c) me**t** on the train
   d) ba~~d~~ with numbers

6. In the following sentences produced by the same speaker, why might we find variation in the accuracy of the production of the interdental fricative? (Hint: Consider aspects of the complexity of the two sentences.)
   a) Put [ð]at box over [ð]ere.
   b) Not having been swamped by [d]e waves, [d]eir yacht crossed [d]e line first.

7. Consider a Spanish learner of English and an English learner of Spanish. Do you think it would be more difficult for an English speaker to learn to drop pronominal subjects and produce grammatical Spanish sentences like "No speak French" or for a Spanish speaker to learn that pronominal subjects cannot be dropped and hence to avoid producing ungrammatical English sentences like "No speaks German"? What factors led you to your answer?

8. What explanation would you give for a native speaker of French producing the English sentence *I drink frequently coffee*? How could you explain the fact that when the same speaker produces the sentence *He is frequently late*, it is grammatical? Do any other English verbs have the same properties as *be*? For assistance, see chapter 5, section 5.4.1.

9. Consider the possible responses of a teacher when a student produces the following ungrammatical sentence: *Why he should bring a sweater?*
   Teacher A: *That should be "why should he bring a sweater?"*
   Teacher B: *He should?*
   Teacher C: *Think about what you know about WH questions with modals in them.*
   Teacher D: *Because it might be cold in the theatre.*

   What do you see as the pros and cons of each of the responses? What might influence your response?

10. Imagine that you are teaching English to a group of L2 learners. How might you respond to the following non-targetlike utterances? What do you think the intended utterance was? If you tried to explain the nature of the errors, what would you say?
    a) I like to fish eat.
    b) He said that he late would arrive.
    c) I was disgusted for the film.
    d) What did you see the man read the book that was on?
    e) Me, I'll not go ever to that place!
    f) Is raining.
    g) I bought in Japan.

11. If a teacher is striving for intelligibility in the students' speech (rather than nativelikeness), it has been suggested that they focus on phonological contrasts that have what has been called a high functional load. For example, the contrast [ɛ/æ] has many minimal pairs in English, and hence a high functional load; this contrast could be said to be doing 'a lot of work'. By contrast, not many minimal pairs rely on the contrast [t/θ]. This contrast is said to have a low functional load (it doesn't do much work). For each of the following contrasts, try to list three minimal pairs. The contrasts are listed in descending functional load:

    1. [æ/ɑ]   4. [p/b]
    2. [i/ɪ]   5. [v/ð]
    3. [ɑ/aw]   6. [f/θ]

🐁 To learn more about the topics discussed in this chapter, visit the Companion Website for *Contemporary Linguistic Analysis*.

Bilingualism and bilingual acquisition

Bilingualism is extremely widespread and is the norm in today's world (and not the exception).

FRANÇOIS GROSJEAN

WHAT is bilingualism? We can distinguish between **societal bilingualism** and individual bilingualism. Bilingualism at the societal level refers to communities, regions, or nations where two languages are spoken by the residents and might be used in government institutions, the legal system, and schools. In a bilingual region, many, but not necessarily all, individuals speak both languages. In the Canadian context, parts of New Brunswick, Québec, and Ontario constitute bilingual regions, although only in New Brunswick are French and English official languages of government.

A popular belief about individual bilingualism is that the label 'bilingual' must be reserved only for those who have complete mastery of two languages. Former Canadian prime minister Pierre Elliot Trudeau is often used as an example of this kind of 'perfect bilingualism'. In contrast to this popular belief, linguists employ a broader definition of bilingualism at the individual level: being bilingual simply means having some proficiency in more than one language, whether in reading, writing, speaking, and listening (comprehension) or in just some of these domains. For example, someone in Vancouver who grew up speaking Cantonese at home might lack literacy skills in that language but is still bilingual. An anglophone student in Calgary who learned French through immersion education might be more proficient in English than French but is still bilingual. In addition, bilingualism is a dynamic concept because a bilingual individual's proficiency in each language can shift and change across the lifespan.

Like bilingualism, **multilingualism** can apply at the societal level to mean a community, region, or nation where more than two languages are spoken and may be used in government, the legal system, or schools. South Africa is a multilingual nation with eleven official languages. But societal multilingualism does not mean that every individual speaks all the languages in that area. A multilingual individual, sometimes called a 'polyglot', is someone who has proficiency in more than two languages.

385

12.1 Is Canada a bilingual country?

A widespread misperception outside of Canada is that all Canadians speak both French and English. According to the Statistics Canada 2016 census, English and French are indeed the most widely spoken languages in the country, but they are not always spoken by the same people. Some statistics from that census clarify the picture:

- 86.2 percent of Canadians can hold a conversation in English (97.4 percent outside Québec)
- 29.8 percent of Canadians can hold a conversation in French (94.5 percent inside Québec)
- 17.9 percent of Canadians can hold a conversation in *both* French and English, with 85.7 percent of these people living in Québec and bordering areas in Ontario and New Brunswick

This demographic information raises the question, Is Canada a bilingual country? In order to answer this question, we will first examine the official policies regarding languages in Canada. Then we will look in more detail at the multilingual composition of this country.

French and English are the dominant, European colonial languages of Canada, and the notion of linguistic duality has played a role in Canadian society and government since Confederation in 1867. In 1969, the Official Languages Act was passed, enshrining the status of French and English as the **official languages** of the federal government and legal system and making other languages 'non-official', including both immigrant and Indigenous languages.

The 1982 Canadian Charter of Rights and Freedoms also reinforces the primacy of French and English as official languages and, consequently, the prestige of French-English bilingualism. The Charter guarantees the rights of people to receive government services in both official languages. It also guarantees the rights of francophone children in French-speaking communities outside Québec to be taught in their native language—that is, to receive their education in French, which needs to be distinguished from French immersion programs (see section 12.7).

From the 1970s onwards, Canada has also had policies recognizing the multicultural composition of the country, which includes immigrant and Indigenous communities. The Canadian Multiculturalism Act, passed in 1988, offers some protection to minority cultural and linguistic rights while maintaining the distinction between official and non-official languages.

Language Matters **Multiculturalism and Official Languages in Canada**

It was the view of the royal commission, shared by the government and, I am sure, by all Canadians, that there cannot be one cultural policy for Canadians of British and French origin, another for the original peoples and yet a third for all others. For although there are two official languages, there is no official culture, nor does any ethnic group take precedence over any other. No citizen or group of citizens is other than Canadian, and all should be treated fairly.

Pierre Elliott Trudeau, House of Commons, October 8, 1971

Source: "Documents," *Canada History*, www.canadahistory.com, © 2013.

The current linguistic landscape of Canada is more diverse than is suggested by official language policies. Non-official languages can be separated into Indigenous and immigrant languages. **Indigenous languages** are those spoken by the Indigenous peoples—First Nations, Métis, and Inuit. **Immigrant languages** are those spoken by the newcomers who have been arriving in waves since the initial period of French and English colonization.

The number of individuals who speak Indigenous languages in Canada is far smaller than those who speak immigrant languages. In 2016, a total of 228 765 people spoke an Indigenous language as their main or secondary home language while 7 749 115 spoke an immigrant language as their main or secondary home language. In that same year, the most widely spoken Indigenous languages in Canada were Cree, Inuktitut, Ojibwe, Oji-Cree, and the Dene/ Athabaskan languages. The ten most widely spoken immigrant languages in Canada were Mandarin, Cantonese, Punjabi, Tagalog, Spanish, Arabic, Italian, German, Urdu, and Portuguese.

Bilingualism in Canadian households varies according to mother tongue. Only 5.2 percent of those who speak English as their first language (L1) use another language at home, but 13.3 percent of French L1 speakers use another language at home. This difference is consistent with the fact that francophones are more likely to speak English than anglophones are to speak French. By a large margin, speakers of immigrant languages are the most likely to live in bilingual households, since 54.6 percent of them use English (or French) together with the immigrant language at home. Individuals who speak immigrant languages are increasingly becoming multilingual—able to speak both French and English in addition to their own language—especially in Montréal. Figure 12.1 displays the linguistic diversity in Canada's largest cities.

In sum, Canada is a multilingual society with linguistic layers: colonial official languages (French and English), Indigenous languages, and immigrant languages. At the individual level, most bilinguals speak either French and English, or English or French paired with a non-official language.

12.2 Different kinds of bilinguals

Bilingual individuals fall into different categories depending on the timing of their introduction to the second language (L2) and on the sociolinguistic status of their L1 and their L2. The primary distinction is between early and late bilinguals. **Early bilinguals** are those who learned two languages in childhood, and **late bilinguals** are those who began to learn an L2 in adolescence or adulthood. In this chapter, we discuss only early bilinguals.

Among early bilinguals, we make a distinction between simultaneous and sequential bilinguals. This distinction is based on age of acquisition of the two languages. **Simultaneous bilinguals** begin to learn their L1 and L2 before two to three years of age. In contrast, early **sequential bilinguals** are child L2 learners who begin to learn their L2 between the age of two to three years and adolescence. The languages of simultaneous bilinguals who learn two languages from birth are sometimes referred to as L_a and L_b, because there really is no L1 and L2.

The sociolinguistic status of a language affects a bilingual child's acquisition process and outcomes. One of a bilingual child's languages is usually a **majority language**—that is, a language that is widely spoken in a community, region, or nation; has high status; and is used in government institutions and schools. English is a majority language across Canada, but French is a majority language only in Québec.

A **minority language** is less widely spoken, has lower status, and is used in a limited way or not at all in government institutions and schools. Languages are on a continuum with respect to minority and majority status. Both Vietnamese and Mandarin are minority languages in Edmonton. However, Vietnamese is closer to the minority end of the continuum because it has fewer speakers than Mandarin, and there is a Mandarin bilingual program in Edmonton Public Schools but not a Vietnamese bilingual program. Even though French is a minority

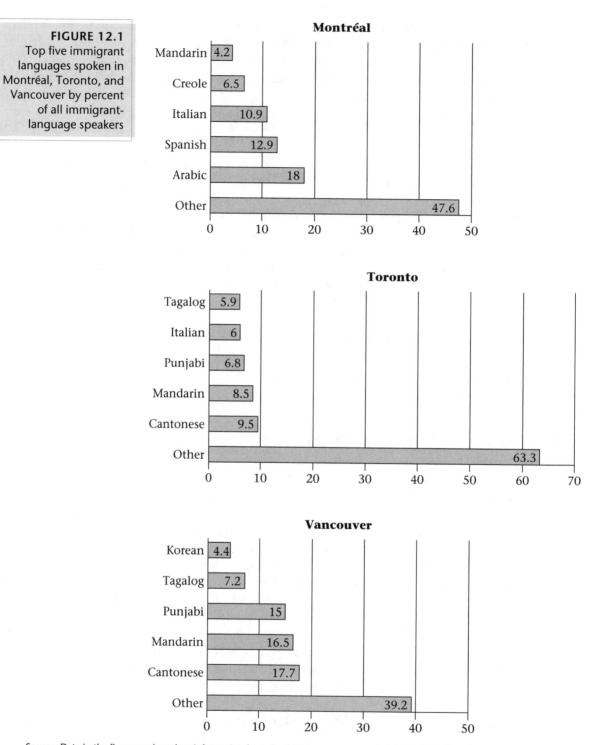

FIGURE 12.1
Top five immigrant languages spoken in Montréal, Toronto, and Vancouver by percent of all immigrant-language speakers

Source: Data in the figure are based on information from the 2016 census as reported in Statistics Canada, *Linguistic Diversity and Multilingualism in Canadian Homes*, catalogue no. 98-200-X2016010, 2017, and Statistics Canada, *Immigrant Languages in Canada* (infographic), catalogue no. 11-627-M, 2017. Retrieved from www.statcan.gc.ca.

language in western Canada, it has higher status than other minority languages because it is one of Canada's official languages. Therefore, in western Canada, French is closer than other minority language to the majority end of the continuum.

Let us illustrate the concepts of simultaneous/sequential and majority/minority with some examples:

■ A child who grows up in Montréal learning French from a francophone parent and English from an anglophone parent is a simultaneous bilingual acquiring two majority languages. Each language is widely spoken and has high status regionally and nationally. This child has strong potential for developing a high level of proficiency in both languages.

■ A child who acquires English as the L1 in Winnipeg and then learns French as an L2 through French immersion schooling is a sequential bilingual with a majority L1 and a minority L2. This child is likely to have greater proficiency in English than in French (see section 12.7).

■ A child who speaks an immigrant language like Korean at home until entering kindergarten in Vancouver is a sequential bilingual with a minority L1 and a majority L2. The child might be at risk for losing the L1 before adulthood (see section 12.5).

Figure 12.2 summarizes the different categories of bilinguals discussed in this section.

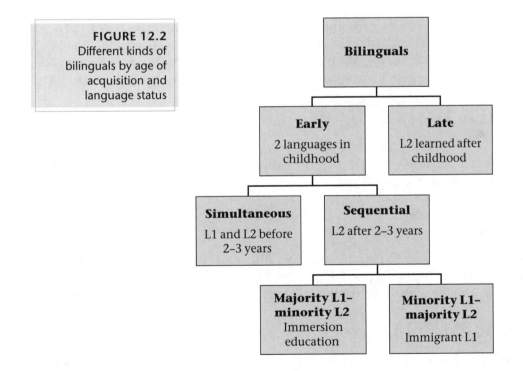

FIGURE 12.2 Different kinds of bilinguals by age of acquisition and language status

12.3 Early bilingual acquisition

It has been estimated that globally, the majority of children become bilingual before the age of twelve. The multilingual nature of Canadian society means that bilingualism is common among Canadian children. For this reason, understanding early bilingual acquisition is arguably as important as understanding monolingual L1 acquisition.

12.3.1 Developmental sequences in early bilingualism

Simultaneous bilinguals go through similar stages in their language development as monolingual children do. The character of their babbling, their phonological processes, and the morphosyntactic structure of their early utterances are all similar to what we see for monolingual children acquiring those same languages. Differences mostly occur when the two languages of a bilingual child interact with each other in acquisition, a topic covered in section 12.4.

In L1 acquisition, children tend to acquire morphosyntactic structures in a certain developmental sequence. Developmental sequences are different across languages, so a particular morphosyntactic structure might be acquired early in one language but late in another.

Overall, simultaneous bilinguals show developmental sequences that mirror those of monolinguals acquiring the languages in question. For example, English-speaking two-year-olds freely produce transitive sentences with object pronouns like *him*, *her*, or *it*, as in (1a). In contrast, French-speaking two-year-olds often omit object pronouns (*le*, *la*, *les*, *l'*) in transitive sentences, as in (1b).

(1) Object pronouns in English L1 and French L1 acquisition
 a. Mommy (is) hugging <u>her</u>.
 b. Maman embrasse. (instead of *Maman <u>l'</u>embrasse*)
    Mommy hugging.

The reason for this difference is the positioning of object pronouns in French. Both French and English sentences have a basic subject-verb-object word order, as shown in (2a) and (3a). In English, when the object of the verb is a pronoun, sentences still have this order, as in (2b). But, in French, when the object is a pronoun, it appears before the verb, as in sentence (3b).

(2) English: All direct objects follow immediately after the verb.
 a. Caroline is eating <u>an orange</u>.
 b. Caroline is eating <u>it</u>.

(3) French: Noun direct objects follow the verb; pronoun direct objects precede the verb.
 a. Caroline mange <u>une orange</u>.
    'Caroline is eating an orange.'
 b. Caroline <u>la</u> mange.
    'Caroline is eating it.'

This difference makes French object pronouns a little more difficult to learn than English object pronouns, so a French-English bilingual two-year-old might produce English sentences with the object pronoun placed correctly but French sentences with the pronoun omitted.

12.3.2 Language dominance

It is possible for children to be balanced bilinguals, which means they have equal proficiency in both languages. However, balanced bilingualism is rare and both child and adult bilinguals tend to have a **dominant language**. This does not mean that they cannot speak or understand their non-dominant language; rather, it means that when proficiency in the two languages is compared, one comes out on top. Different factors play a role in how we determine which is the dominant language for bilingual children (see figure 12.3).

One factor is the amount of input in each language. This is typically expressed as a percentage of the total language input the child receives in both languages: for example, a child might hear

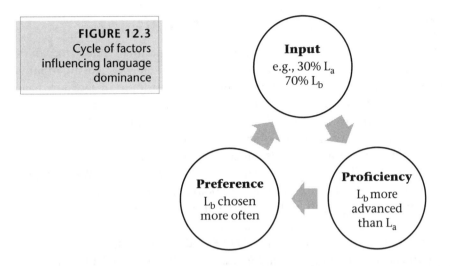

FIGURE 12.3
Cycle of factors influencing language dominance

English 65 percent of the time and French 35 percent of the time. Another factor is proficiency: In which language does the child have a bigger vocabulary or more advanced morphosyntax? Preference is a third factor. The child will generally choose one language more often than the other when communicating with family members, using media, and playing with friends. These three factors usually align with one another, all pointing to the same language as the dominant one.

For sequential bilinguals who speak an immigrant language as their L1, their dominant language usually starts as their L1 but changes to the L2 because this is the majority language of the community. For children who are born in the host country, this process, called *dominant language shift*, often begins with exposure to the majority language when they enter the school system. So Canadian-born children who only speak Farsi when beginning junior kindergarten in Toronto would probably shift to being English-dominant before grade 3 and would certainly shift to English dominance by grade 6.

Language Matters **Estimating Language Input**

How do researchers know the amount of input in each language that a bilingual child receives? They typically give parents a questionnaire to measure how often each language is spoken to the child by family members. Below are examples of questions with rating-scale answers. When these answers are compiled across all family members, researchers can estimate how much of each language a child hears.

1. What language does the mother speak to the child?

1	2	3	4	5
English never French always	English seldom French usually	English 50% French 50%	English usually French seldom	English always French never

2. What language does the father speak to the child?

1	2	3	4	5
English never French always	English seldom French usually	English 50% French 50%	English usually French seldom	English always French never

Source: Questionnaire example is based on information in Johanne Paradis, "Individual Differences in Child English Second Language Acquisition: Comparing Child-Internal and Child-External Factors," *Linguistic Approaches to Bilingualism* 1, 3 (2011): 213–37.

12.3.3 Rate of language acquisition in bilinguals

Simultaneous-bilingual children learn two languages in the same amount of time as monolinguals learn one. During the waking hours of the day, bilingual children's linguistic input is divided between their two languages, and they therefore receive less input in each language than a monolingual child would. We know from monolingual acquisition that the amount of time children spend hearing and using language has an impact on their rate of acquisition. Is this also true of bilingual children learning two languages simultaneously?

Let us start with language development milestones. Monolingual children produce their first word at around twelve months, and by eighteen to twenty-four months of age, they produce word combinations—phrases and short sentences. Bilingual children reach these milestones at approximately the same ages, but only in their dominant language.

When we look at vocabulary size and morphosyntactic development in the preschool years, simultaneous bilinguals, as a group, tend to lag behind monolingual children of the same age. When one considers that bilingual children have to build two linguistic representations in the same amount of time that monolinguals take to build one, it makes sense that they might lag behind. Nevertheless, bilinguals do not take twice as long as monolinguals to acquire each of their languages.

Language dominance matters when assessing the rate of vocabulary and morphosyntactic development in bilingual children. Bilingual children are more likely to have vocabulary sizes and morphosyntactic abilities closer to the monolingual average in their dominant language.

12.4 Cross-language interactions in early bilingualism

Bilingual infants start to separate their two languages perceptually during the first year of life. Infants can hear the voicing difference between pairs of consonants like [p] and [b] before they begin to speak. Bilingual infants can also hear the fine-grained phonetic differences between consonants and vowels within and across the two languages they are exposed to. Young bilinguals show developmental sequences in each language very similar to those of monolingual children. However, just because the languages are separate does not mean that they do not interact with each other during acquisition.

12.4.1 Cross-linguistic influence

Because a bilingual child's two languages are interconnected, **cross-linguistic influence** is almost inevitable: a phonological or morphosyntactic rule from one language is often transferred to the other. For example, in English, adjectives denoting colour come before the noun, but in French, they come after the noun. Cross-linguistic influence in a French-English bilingual child may result in occasional errors.

> **(4)** Adjective order and French-English bilinguals
>> *a.* English: the <u>red</u> house [adj-N]
>> *b.* French: la maison <u>rouge</u> [N-adj]
>>> the house red
>> *c.* Possible language transfer: *the house red* or *la rouge maison* (neither of which is acceptable in the target language)

How can we predict when cross-linguistic influence will occur? One factor is dominance, as determined by the child's transfer tendencies. Children often transfer phonological and morphosyntactic rules from their dominant to their non-dominant language. A bilingual child who says *the house red* is probably French-dominant.

Another reason for cross-linguistic influence is structural overlap between the two languages. For example, in English, the possessive construction is expressed in two different ways, shown in (5a) and (5b) below. French only has the equivalent of the English option in (5b).

(5) Possessive construction in English
    a. my friend's house [possessor-possessed]
    b. the house of my friend [possessed-possessor]

(6) Possessive construction in French
    la maison de mon ami [possessed-possessor]
    'the house of my friend'

English speakers prefer to use option (5a), but French-English bilingual children might use option (5b) more often when speaking English than monolingual children would. In this sense, the structural overlap between French and English 'invites' the use of the less preferred English option.

Signs of cross-linguistic influence have been observed in the speech of every bilingual child studied, although only in a minority of their utterances. Most of their utterances are similar to those of monolingual children in that language. Cross-linguistic influence signals the interconnectedness of bilingual developing grammars, but it is not pervasive in individual children's speech.

Language Matters Cross-Linguistic Influence in an English-Cantonese Bilingual Child

What can we make of the question "Where's the Santa Claus give me the gun?", uttered by an English-Cantonese bilingual child? This question is actually a complex construction containing a relative clause—a clause that modifies and provides additional information about a noun in the larger sentence.

In English, a relative clause is positioned after the noun it modifies, but in Cantonese, it occurs before the noun. In the question above, the bilingual child has placed the relative clause (*the Santa Claus give me*) before the noun it modifies (*the gun*), mixing Cantonese syntax with English vocabulary.

Mixed English-Cantonese: Where's [*the Santa Claus give me*] <u>the gun</u>?
English equivalent: Where's <u>the gun</u> [*that Santa Claus give me*]?

Source: Data are based on information in Victoria Yip and Stephen Matthews, *The Bilingual Child: Early Development and Language Contact* (Cambridge: Cambridge University Press, 2007), p. 164.

12.4.2 Code-switching

Code-switching is the use of words or morphemes from two languages in one sentence or stretch of discourse. Code-switching is different from cross-linguistic influence because it involves overt interaction between a bilingual's two languages. When adult bilinguals code-switch, this is frequently viewed negatively; somewhat pejorative labels like *franglais* or *Spanglish* are a reflection of this. However, linguistic research has shown that code-switching is not a random mish-mash of two languages, nor is it a sign of laziness on the part of speakers.

Code-switching is highly skilled language use and is part of the full communicative competence of bilingual adults. It serves specific functions and follows rules governing how the two languages can be combined. Adult bilinguals code-switch to emphasize or introduce a new topic in the discourse, to assert identity, or to use a word or phrase that comes to mind more quickly or conveys the meaning more accurately in one language than the other. They also tailor their code-switching according to their interlocutor's preferences and level of bilingualism. How does this skilled language use develop over time in bilingual children?

All bilingual children do some code-switching, even when they grow up in one-parent monolingual families. The code-switching of bilingual children aged two to four years is generally driven by their proficiency in each language: they tend to code-switch more when speaking their non-dominant language and when they know the word for an object in one language but not the other. For example, if a bilingual child says "Want play with *mon minou* [my kitty]" to her anglophone parent, the source of the code-switching could be that the child does not know, or cannot quickly recall, the word *kitty* in English.

Even with constraints related to dominance and lexical gaps, two-year-old children are sensitive to their interlocutor in their choice of language. Bilingual two-year-olds will use more French with their francophone parent and more English with their anglophone parent in a play session, which shows they are aware of the preferences of their parental interlocutors. Bilingual two- and three-year-olds also show this awareness when speaking with an unfamiliar adult: they will take the cue about which language to use from an adult they have never met before who is visiting their home. They will even code-switch more or less depending on how much code-switching the adult is doing.

Language Matters: **Code-Switching in a French Minority Context**

A study of French-English bilingual four-year olds in Edmonton found that the children code-switched freely with francophone adults but rarely with anglophone adults. This was true even for French-dominant children whose English abilities were limited. What explains this asymmetry? It is probably due to Edmonton being an English majority city with a small francophone minority population. In the children's experience, francophone adults are almost always bilingual, and anglophone adults are mainly monolingual. By age four, these bilinguals knew that they needed to stick to English only when speaking with anglophone adults. This suggests that by age four, bilinguals have an awareness of their broader sociolinguistic context.

Source: Based on information from Johanne Paradis, and Elena Nicoladis, "The Influence of Dominance and Sociolinguistic Context on Bilingual Preschoolers' Language Choice," *International Journal of Bilingualism and Bilingual Education* 10 (2007): 1–21.

Code-switching within sentences can involve single word insertions (e.g., *I ate some frites* 'I ate some fries') or syntactic switches of an entire phrase or clause (e.g., *She was driving trop vite dans le voisinage* 'She was driving too fast in the neighbourhood'). Examples of both types are presented in table 12.1. The most common code-switches in the speech of both child and adult bilinguals are single word insertions; sentences with syntactic switches are less common.

TABLE 12.1 Codeswitching within sentences by French-English bilingual children

Single Word Switches	Syntactic Switches
Where's the <u>mitaine</u> go?	*I'm talking <u>en anglais</u>.*
'Where's the mitten go?'	'I'm talking in English'.
I <u>plie</u> it.	*And the police was sitting <u>à coté de moi</u>.*
'I am folding it'.	'And the police was sitting beside me'.
Tintin's <u>caché</u>.	*We bring <u>saucisses à la garderie</u> yesterday.*
'Tintin's hidden'.	'We bring sausages to the daycare yesterday'.
Look at all these <u>brilliants</u> on her.	*That is <u>l'escalier</u>.*
'Look at all these sparkles on her'.	'That is the stairs'.
I want to <u>range</u> the lego.	*But we eat <u>les animaux</u>.*
'I want to put away the lego'.	'But we eat the animals'.
Ça a <u>popp</u>-é!	*Il y a <u>my toesie there</u>.*
'That popped!'	'There is my toe there'.
Comme <u>dark</u> bleu.	*Elle coupe <u>her hair</u>.*
'Like dark blue'.	'She cuts her hair'.
J'ai <u>almost</u> brisé.	*He <u>a pomme</u>.*
'I almost broke'.	'He has apple'.

Source: Data are based on information in Johanne Paradis, and Elena Nicoladis, "The Influence of Dominance and Sociolinguistic Context on Bilingual Preschoolers' Language Choice," *International Journal of Bilingualism and Bilingual Education* 10 (2007): 1–21; and Johanne Paradis, Elena Nicoladis, and Fred Genesee, "Early Emergence of Structural Constraints on Code-Mixing: Evidence from French-English Bilingual Children," *Bilingualism: Language and Cognition* 3 (2000): 245–61.

Congruence between the two languages often determines whether syntactic code-switching occurs in bilinguals' speech. For example, in French and English, code-switching *between* an auxiliary verb and its participle, as in (7a), is much less common than code-switching *before* the auxiliary and the participle, shown in (7b). This is because the auxiliary verb is part of the meaning of the verb, and the meaning is not the same in the two languages. For example, even though the phrase *ont regardé* in French translates as 'have watched' on a word-for-word basis, it does not mean *have watched* (as in the English sentence *The kids have already watched that movie*). Instead, it means the same as the simple past tense *watched* in English. Because of this semantic incongruence, English-French bilinguals rarely code-switch between an auxiliary verb and its participle.

(7) *a.* The kids have <u>regardé le film hier.</u>
    'The kids watched the film yesterday'.
b. The kids <u>ont regardé le film hier.</u>

Bilingual two- and three-year-olds do sometimes violate adult rules for syntactic code-switches, but by the time they reach age four, they generally exhibit rule-governed, adult-like code-switching patterns.

12.5 Heritage languages and bilingualism

Heritage languages are minority languages spoken in a community or region with a majority language. This means that heritage languages have fewer speakers and lower sociolinguistic status than the majority language.

Typically, heritage languages arise because of migration and colonialism. In Canada, for example, the languages spoken by immigrants and refugees count as heritage languages, as do the languages spoken by Indigenous peoples.

Waves of migrants from different regions across the globe affect the ranking of the heritage languages most widely spoken in Canada. For example, migration in the early twentieth century from Central and Eastern Europe caused Ukrainian and Yiddish to be among the top ten immigrant heritage languages spoken in Canada in 1941. Census data was not even collected on Tagalog and Punjabi until 1981, but these are now among the top ten immigrant heritage languages spoken, and Ukrainian and Yiddish have dropped from that list.

Immigrant heritage languages are typically only spoken for three generations. The first generation consists of the foreign-born speakers who migrated to the host country; the second generation, the speakers who were born in the host country; and the third generation, the grandchildren of the first generation. A 2006 Statistics Canada report found that just 32 percent of second-generation immigrants spoke the heritage language in their own homes when they became adults, and only 11 percent of their children, the third generation, spoke the heritage language at all.

Some linguistic/cultural communities, however, have a stronger track record for retaining their languages than others. The same Statistics Canada report says that languages very likely to be passed on to the second and third generations include Punjabi, Cantonese, and Greek. Languages that are unlikely to be passed on included Dutch, Tagalog, and Niger-Congo languages.

Bilingual children who grow up speaking two majority languages, like French and English, often experience **additive bilingualism** because both their languages are supported sociopolitically, as well as in the education system and media. In contrast, since heritage languages are minority, non-official languages, children who grow up with a heritage L1 and majority L2 often experience **subtractive bilingualism**: where the heritage language is not supported socio-politically or in the education system and media, children's opportunities to hear and use the L1 are limited.

Figure 12.4 illustrates the differential development of proficiency in a heritage L1 and a majority L2 that can occur for many bilingual children. Gradual loss of proficiency in the heritage language is referred to as heritage language attrition.

A hallmark characteristic of heritage language acquisition is variation among individuals. On an individual basis, proficiency in the heritage language can be higher or lower than is illustrated in figure 12.4. Some bilingual children grow up to be as proficient in their heritage L1 as in the majority L2 and so are balanced bilinguals. Other children might lose their heritage language completely as they grow up, or they may retain the ability to understand it but not to speak it.

In between these two extremes are children who have functional proficiency in the heritage language but also show differences in their vocabulary and morphosyntax when

FIGURE 12.4 Differential development of the heritage L1 and majority L2 across the lifespan

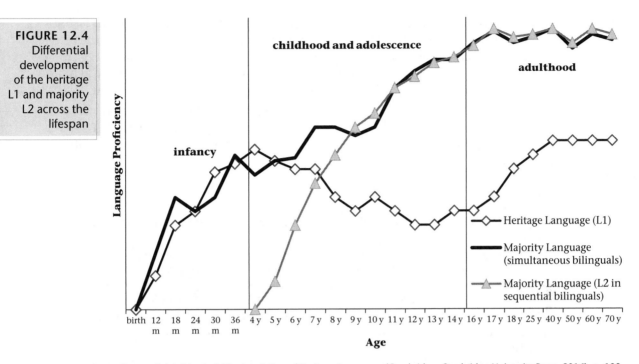

Source: Sylvia Montrul, *The Acquisition of Heritage Languages* (Cambridge: Cambridge University Press, 2016), p. 100.

compared with child speakers of that language in the home country. For example, we might expect child heritage speakers of Spanish to make more gender errors in noun phrases with determiners and adjectives than monolingual Spanish-speaking children the same age, as shown in table 12.2. Of course, not all aspects of vocabulary and morphosyntax differ in child heritage speakers and monolingual speakers, and individual heritage speakers can fluctuate between accurate and inaccurate use of morphology in their speech.

TABLE 12.2   Correct and incorrect gender agreement in Spanish

Spanish Noun Phrase			**Gender agreement**
Determiner + Noun + Adjective			Determiner and adjective must have the same gender (feminine or masculine) as noun
la	*casa*	*roja*	Correct gender agreement
the (fem)	house (fem)	red (fem)	
la	*casa*	***rojo***	Error in gender agreement
the (fem)	house (fem)	**red (masc)**	
el	*casa*	*roja*	Error in gender agreement
the (masc)	house (fem)	red (fem)	

Source: Data are created by the author but concepts are based on information from Sylvia Montrul, *The Acquisition of Heritage Languages* (Cambridge: Cambridge University Press, 2016).

Various factors contribute to proficiency in a heritage language. One important factor is age of acquisition. The older a child is when starting to learn the majority language, the better the chances of maintaining strong proficiency in the heritage language into adulthood. Other important factors are how much parents use the heritage language with their children at home and whether they place their children in heritage language classes and involve them in community activities. Some parents believe that continuing to speak the heritage language could impede their children's academic success and integration into Canadian society. Others place a high value on passing on the heritage language and culture and on maintaining ties with the home country.

Language Matters: Profiles of Two Heritage Language Children

Stefka is acquiring Bulgarian from her mother and English from her father in Regina, Saskatchewan. Stefka only receives Bulgarian input from one parent and from her grandmother in Bulgaria via video chat. Stefka's mother speaks Bulgarian to her because it feels more natural and she wants Stefka to be able to communicate with her grandmother. But she does not believe that Stefka needs to grow up knowing Bulgarian well. Both parents want Stefka to attend a French immersion school because they believe French is a more important language in Canada than Bulgarian.

Sandeep is acquiring Punjabi from both her parents in Abbotsford, British Columbia. She receives Punjabi input at home from her parents and siblings and from family members in India via video chat. She also has the opportunity to hear and use Punjabi in the community, and she attends religious and cultural activities that take place in Punjabi. Sandeep's parents grew up in the multilingual context of India, and they promote bilingualism for their daughter. They want her to know English well so she can succeed in school and in Canadian society. They also want her to grow up with the Punjabi language and culture and to be able to communicate with her cousins in India.

12.6 Cognitive consequences of bilingualism

Children who are learning two languages instead of one tend to show precocious development of **metalinguistic awareness**. Metalinguistic awareness involves being able to access and manipulate explicit knowledge of linguistic structures and to intentionally separate linguistic structures from their meanings. This skill usually emerges in children in general between the ages of four to six years.

A young monolingual child knows the word *dog* and its referent in the real world, but might not realize that there is no inherent connection between a word and its meaning. In contrast, this will be evident to a young bilingual child who knows the word for 'dog' in two languages (see figure 12.5 below). It is thought that this insight enables bilingual children to develop metalinguistic awareness earlier than monolingual children.

Metalinguistic awareness is an important cognitive skill for learning to read, since written words are symbols for spoken words and for their referents in the real world and are composed of smaller parts (letters). Early bilingualism in children can give them an edge when it comes to learning to read because of their enhanced metalinguistic awareness.

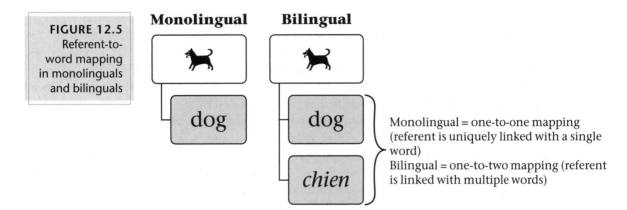

FIGURE 12.5 Referent-to-word mapping in monolinguals and bilinguals

Monolingual = one-to-one mapping (referent is uniquely linked with a single word)

Bilingual = one-to-two mapping (referent is linked with multiple words)

Cognitive abilities like attentional control might also be enhanced in children who are bilingual. Attentional control refers to the ability to focus on desired information and ignore salient but distracting information. Consider the following example of a task that demands attentional control. Children are given a deck of cards that have blue triangles, blue squares, red triangles, or red squares on them. Children are first asked to sort the cards according to shapes, so they sort them into piles of triangles and squares, ignoring the colours. They are then asked to sort the cards according to colours, and they make piles of red and blue cards, ignoring the shapes. Children might also be asked to switch the sorting citerion from shape to colour in the middle of the task.

Bilingual children typically show superior performance on this threefold task—especially in the ability to switch back and forth between the sorting criteria. It is thought that the bilingual advantage in attentional control is rooted in their experiences of switching between two languages, since they need to ignore distracting information from L_b when speaking L_a and vice versa.

12.7 Immersion and bilingual education

Children who have a heritage L1 typically become bilingual by learning the majority language as their L2 at school. It is also possible for children who speak a majority L1, like English in Alberta, to learn a minority language, like French, as their L2 at school. For example, students can take 'core' L2 courses, offered for one to two hours per week, as a subject in school. In English Canada, the core L2 model usually yields low proficiency in French. More effective models for children to acquire proficiency in an L2 are immersion and bilingual programs.

In an **immersion program**, all or almost all of the academic content is taught through the L2 in the early grades, with the percentage of content instruction in the L1 gradually being increased in senior grades. In a bilingual program, the academic content is taught in two languages and is often divided relatively equally between students' L1 and L2. The key feature of immersion and bilingual programs is that students learn some or all the academic content (e.g., science or math) through their L2, as opposed to having the L2 taught as a separate subject, as it is in core L2 programs.

12.7.1 French immersion

The first French immersion program in Canada was in St. Lambert, south of Montréal, in the 1960s. Since then, French immersion programs have become a popular choice for parents of anglophone children in all ten provinces. The highest enrolments in French immersion are in the Maritime provinces and Québec, and the lowest enrolments are in western Canada.

One of the most common questions asked about immersion programs is, What effect does a French immersion program have on the students' English and their academic achievement? In early immersion, students are taught exclusively in French until English language arts is introduced as a subject in the mid-elementary school grades. By the end of elementary school, these students' English skills for speaking, listening, reading, and writing are remarkably similar to those of students who have attended an English-only program. In addition, the academic achievement of French immersion students at the end of elementary and secondary school is very strong and sometimes even superior to students in English-only programs. Therefore, attending French immersion does not diminish either children's proficiency in their L1 or their academic achievement.

Another common question is, How proficient are French immersion students in French? French immersion students' proficiency in French is much stronger for receptive skills like listening and reading than for expressive skills like speaking and writing. They can have an English accent in their spoken French or make grammatical errors when they speak—for example, they may make gender errors like *ma [fem] crayon* instead of *mon [masc] crayon* 'my pencil'. But when compared with students in core French, students in French immersion have significantly greater overall proficiency in French, which is the primary goal of French immersion education.

Retention of French after immersion education can be a struggle for those students who are in English-majority regions of Canada. Many individuals who completed their entire education from kindergarten to grade 12 in French immersion report that they do not feel comfortable holding a conversion in French by the age of twenty-five. The maxim "Use it or lose it" applies to any L2 we learn, even one that was the language of instruction in our education program.

12.7.2 Heritage language education

Bilingual education programs in immigrant and Indigenous languages include content instruction in the majority language, which could be the children's L2, and in a minority language. Bilingual education programs have many benefits, including the following:

- They strengthen students' sense of identity and confidence and smooth the transition from the home culture and language to the school culture and language.

- They increase proficiency in the minority language, thus reducing heritage language attrition.

- They establish proficiency in an endangered language, thus promoting language revitalization.

Bilingual education programs in immigrant languages are aimed at creating an additive bilingual experience for children who might otherwise experience subtractive bilingualism. Edmonton Public Schools offers bilingual programs in Arabic, German, Mandarin, Spanish, and Ukrainian. Across many regions of the United States, Spanish-English bilingual programs are offered. As with French immersion students, students in heritage language bilingual programs are as proficient in the majority language as students in English-only programs, and their academic skills are similar to the skills of those students as well.

One challenge faced by heritage language programs is that students entering the program can have very different levels of proficiency in the L1. The need to include all proficiency levels complicates lesson planning and finding appropriate teaching materials. Another challenge faced by heritage language programs is the shift over time with respect to which immigrant languages are widely spoken (see section 12.5). For example, Ukrainian used to be in the top ten languages spoken in Canada, but the number of Ukrainian speakers is decreasing. This could impact enrolment numbers in a Ukrainian bilingual program.

Among non-official languages, Indigenous languages are less widely spoken in Canada than immigrant languages, and the transmission of these languages across generations has been seriously disrupted by colonialism, in general, and the residential school system, in particular. Therefore, education programs that include an Indigenous language as a medium of instruction could be key components of Indigenous language revitalization. One model for such programs is Kativik Ilisarniliriniq, the school board of Nunavik in northern Québec. Schools governed by this board provide bilingual education in Inuktitut and either French or English, and the educational approach is consistent with the values of the Inuit culture.

In some Indigenous communities, students are monolingual speakers of English or French and are learning the Indigenous language as an L2. A 2016 Statistics Canada report found that although 28 155 Indigenous youth aged fifteen to twenty-four could conduct a conversation in an Indigenous language, only 20 880 actually had an Indigenous mother tongue. This indicates that many Indigenous youth are learning their ancestral language as an L2, which may contribute to the revitalization of Indigenous languages in Canada.

Indigenous bilingual education programs also face challenges, however. If the number of speakers of the language is small, as it often is, it can be difficult to find enough proficient speakers to operate the program. For immigrant languages, teachers can be recruited among those who have come directly from the home country, but where, outside of Canada, would a school find a teacher who is proficient in Cree?

Summing up

With two **official languages** and many **heritage languages** (**immigrant** and **Indigenous languages**), Canada is more a multilingual country than a bilingual one. Many Canadians speak more than one language—perhaps the two **official languages**, or perhaps just French or English plus a **heritage language** (an **immigrant** or **Indigenous language**).

Age of acquisition, how the L1 and L2 are learned, and the sociolinguistic status of a language (whether it is a **majority** or **minority language**) can affect the prospects of successful bilingual acquisition. Young bilinguals, whether **simultaneous** or **sequential bilinguals**, are seldom balanced in their abilities in both languages; they usually have a **dominant language**. Bilingual children reach developmental milestones for language at about the same age as monolingual children, but only in their dominant language.

Almost all bilingual children experience **cross-linguistic influence** and engage in **code-switching**. Young bilinguals can show superior abilities in cognitive skills like **metalinguistic awareness** and attentional control.

Children can learn an L2 as a 'core' subject in school or through an **immersion program** or bilingual program. The latter two methods produce much better results in terms of overall

L2 proficiency. However, participation in heritage bilingual programs can positively influence students' development and maintenance of their heritage language.

Indigenous languages in Canada were seriously disrupted by colonization, and especially by the residential school system. There are hopeful signs that language revitalization is occurring, with many Indigenous young people learning their ancestral language as an L2. However, the revitalization process faces immense challenges, including the lack of native speakers in the case of some Indigenous languages.

Recommended reading

Grüter, Theres, and Johanne Paradis, J. (eds.) 2014. *Input and Experience in Bilingual Development*. Amsterdam: John Benjamins.

Montrul, Silvina. 2016. *The Acquisition of Heritage Languages*. Cambridge, UK: Cambridge University Press.

Murphy, Victoria A. 2014. *Second Language Learning in the Early School Years: Trends and Contexts*. Oxford, UK: Oxford University Press.

Paradis, Johanne, Fred Genesee, and Martha B. Crago. 2011. *Dual Language Development and Disorders: A Handbook on Bilingualism and Second Language Learning*. Baltimore: Brookes.

Yip, Virginia, and Stephen Matthews. 2007. *The Bilingual Child: Early Development and Language Contact*. Cambridge, UK: Cambridge University Press.

Exercises

1. In pairs or groups, ask each other these questions. Compile the information to establish the language demographics for the entire class.
   a) Are you monolingual or bilingual?
   b) If bilingual:
      What is your L1? your L2?
      Are you a simultaneous or sequential bilingual?
      If sequential, are you an early or late bilingual?
   c) For French immersion students: Can you still carry on a conversation in French?
   d) For heritage L1 speakers: Can you still carry on a conversation in your heritage language?

2. Respond to these questions with reference to figure 12.1 on immigrant languages spoken in major Canadian cities.
   a) The top immigrant languages vary by city, but which is the most spoken language across all cities? How did you determine this?
   b) Why do you think there is a higher concentration of Arabic and Creole speakers in Montréal than in Toronto and Vancouver?
   c) Why do you think there is a higher concentration of Punjabi speakers in Toronto and Vancouver than in Montréal?

3. English compound words like *toothbrush* consist of [modifier + head]: *toothbrush* has the modifier noun *tooth* and the head noun *brush*. We know *brush* is the head noun because a toothbrush is a type of brush, not a type of tooth. In French, compounds have the reverse

order, [head + modifier], with *de* or *à* in between: for example, *brosse à dents* brush of teeth 'toothbrush'.

The following compound nouns were produced in English by French-English bilingual children. Which ones show cross-linguistic influence from French?

a) chair-flower: meaning a chair with a floral pattern
b) shark-balloon: meaning a balloon in the shape of a shark
c) bed-baby: meaning a crib for a doll
d) bunny-sheets: meaning sheets with pictures of bunnies on them
e) opener-box: meaning a tool for opening boxes

4. Below are examples of intra-sentential code-switches. Indicate which ones are single word insertions and which ones are syntactic code-switches.

I'm going with her to the dépanneur.	It has two strings, mon cerf-à-volant.
The bonhomme is flying dans le ciel.	The shark nage in there.
C'était le pink foncé.	We went chez les grandparents hier.
Then we stopped parce qu'il pleuvait.	Regarde the stripes!

5. Imagine that a simultaneous Russian-English bilingual two-year-old is playing with her father, who speaks only Russian to her. She speaks mostly Russian to him, but sometimes uses English words. How would you explain why she does not stick to only using Russian?

6. Fill in the table based on the language background of the bilingual children described below.

Child	Simultaneous or sequential bilingual?	Likely dominant language?	L1 majority or minority/ heritage?	L2 majority or minority/ heritage?
Maxime				
Khadija				
Emma				
Youssef				
Eleni				
Noah				

a) Maxime: Age five. Born in Ottawa with an anglophone mother and francophone father. He heard both French and English from birth and now attends a French language school.
b) Khadija: Age eight. Born in Toronto and spoke mainly Urdu at home until beginning junior kindergarten in English at age four.
c) Emma: Age ten. Born in Halifax and spoke English at home until entering French immersion kindergarten at age five.
d) Youssef: Age eight. Born in Syria and arrived in Montréal at age six. He speaks only Arabic at home with his family. He has been attending a French language school for one year.

e) Eleni: Age seven. Born in Vancouver to second-generation Greek parents and grew up speaking Greek and English at home. She attends an English language school.

f) Noah: Age six. Born in Saskatoon. He spoke mainly English with his parents but his grandmother spoke mainly Cree to him. He attends a Cree-English bilingual program at school.

7. Consider the concepts of majority, minority, and heritage languages and additive versus subtractive bilingualism. Define each and explain how they are related to each other.

8. Suppose children heard sentences like (1) *Apples grows on trees* and (2) #*Apples grow on arms*. Sentence (1) is ungrammatical because of the [-s] on *grow*. Sentence (2) is grammatically correct but semantically strange (as indicated by #). Bilingual children would be better than monolinguals at detecting that sentence (1) is ungrammatical and sentence (2) is grammatical (even if a bit strange). Monolinguals might think sentence (2) was ungrammatical. Use what you learned from section 12.6 to explain this finding.

9. Based on what you have learned about immersion/bilingual education programs from section 12.7, how would you respond to these statements?

a) "It is the school system's job to make sure that immigrant children learn English as quickly as possible. They cannot succeed in Canada if we encourage them to speak their own languages."

b) "I'm afraid to place my child in French immersion because her English skills might suffer and then how would she cope in university? I can see why French might be important in Ottawa or Montréal, but we live in Calgary."

c) "We chose the Mandarin bilingual program for our son because, even though we speak Mandarin at home, we want him to be able to read and write well in Mandarin. But we are a little worried about how he will perform academically when there are two languages, instead of one, at school."

Psycholinguistics: the study of language processing

Words! Mere words! How terrible they were! How clear, and vivid, and cruel! One could not escape from them. And yet what subtle magic there was in them!

OSCAR WILDE, *THE PICTURE OF DORIAN GRAY* (1891)

WE ENGAGE in language processing every day of our lives. This processing takes place when we watch television, listen to the radio, read a passing billboard while driving, or discuss the weather. Usually these language activities are carried out with great ease and in a completely subconscious manner. We might sometimes be aware that we are searching for a word, composing a sentence, or straining to understand someone else, but we are never aware of the actual mechanisms and operations involved in producing and understanding language.

Psycholinguistics is the study of these language-processing mechanisms. Psycholinguists study how word meaning, sentence meaning, and discourse meaning are computed and represented in the mind. They study how complex words and sentences are composed in speech and how they are broken down into their constituent parts in the acts of listening and reading. In short, psycholinguists seek to understand how language is 'done'.

We begin this introduction to the field of psycholinguistics by discussing some methods used by psycholinguists to probe language representation and processing in the mind. This is followed by a summary of recent research on language processing in the domains of phonetics, phonology, morphology, and syntax. Finally, we discuss how these various aspects of linguistic processing work together to make the everyday acts of speaking, listening, and reading appear so simple and effortless. Although psycholinguists study both production and comprehension, this chapter focuses primarily on language processing during comprehension and therefore draws mostly on data from listening and reading.

13.1 Methods of psycholinguistic research

The key fact that guides psycholinguistic methodology is that language users are unaware of the details of language processing. Simply paying attention to what you are doing will not provide reliable insights into how you access words or build sentences. Perhaps the reason for this is that in normal use, language processing must occur very quickly. By shielding mental linguistic operations from the conscious mind, the language-processing system may be maximizing its ability to operate with speed and efficiency.

In order to get a sense of just how subconscious language processing is, you might try the following exercise. Give a friend a page of text to read silently and sit opposite him or her. Carefully observe your friend's eyes as they move across the text. You will notice that the eyes do not move smoothly from left to right but rather proceed in a series of jerks called **saccades**. Like most of us, your friend probably has the subjective impression that his or her eyes are moving very evenly across the page. But that subjective impression is incorrect. We are simply not constructed to be able to monitor many of our automatic activities, including language processing.

A substantial additional challenge for the psycholinguistic researcher comes from the fact that most of language processing involves not observable physical events such as eye movement but rather mental events that cannot be observed directly. Research in this field therefore requires that mental language-processing events be inferred from observable behaviour. Consequently, a large part of psycholinguistic research is concerned with the development of new (and often very clever) techniques to uncover how language processing is accomplished. Some of these techniques are presented in the following sections.

13.1.1 Field methods: slips of the tongue

Some of the earliest and most influential studies of language processing examined the spontaneous slips of the tongue produced during speech. Slips of the tongue are also known as **spoonerisms**—after Reverend William A. Spooner, who was head of New College, Oxford between 1903 and 1925. Reverend Spooner was famous for producing a great many, often humorous, speech errors. Here are some of his more well-known mistakes.

(1) What he intended: You have missed all my history lectures.
What he said: You have hissed all my mystery lectures.

(2) What he intended: noble sons of toil
What he said: noble tons of soil

(3) What he intended: You have wasted the whole term.
What he said: You have tasted the whole worm.

(4) What he intended: the dear old Queen
What he said: the queer old dean

In the 1960s, Victoria Fromkin began to study these and other naturally occurring slips of the tongue and noted that they can be very revealing of the manner in which sentences are created in speech. For instance, as can be seen in the examples above, the characteristic pattern in Reverend Spooner's errors is a tendency to exchange the initial consonants of words in the utterance. When these segment exchanges create new words (as opposed to non-words as in *fire and brimstone* → *bire and frimstone*), the result is often humorous. But here's the important psycholinguistic point: in order for these exchanges to occur, the sentence would have to be planned out before the person begins to say it. Otherwise, how would it be possible in example (1) for the first segment of the sixth word *history* to be transported backwards so that it becomes the first segment of the third word (<u>m</u>*issed* → <u>h</u>*issed*)?

Another important observation that Fromkin made was that speech errors also often involve 'mixing and matching' morphemes within words. Consider the following slips of the tongue.

(5) Intended: rules of word formation
    Produced: words of rule formation

(6) Intended: I'd forgotten about that.
    Produced: I'd forgot aboutten that.

(7) Intended: easily enough
    Produced: easy enoughly

All these errors involve morphemes being exchanged within a sentence. As is the case for sound exchange errors, these slips of the tongue provide evidence that a sentence must be planned out to some degree before speech begins. They also provide evidence that the morpheme, rather than the word, is the fundamental building block of English sentence production. Note how in example (5) the inflectional suffix *-s* remains in its original place, while the nouns *rule* and *word* reverse positions. In examples (6) and (7), it is the suffixes that move while the stems remain in their original positions. These examples all suggest that morphological components of words can function independently during sentence planning (and also in sentence mis-planning).

As can be seen from these examples, slips of the tongue can offer a fascinating window into the mechanisms involved in language production and into the role that linguistic units such as phonemes and morphemes play in that production. But because slips of the tongue are naturally occurring events, the researcher has no control over when and where they will occur and must simply wait for them to happen. In this way, the analysis of slips of the tongue is a **field technique** and differs from the **experimental paradigms** discussed in the following sections. In these experimental paradigms, the researcher takes an active role in controlling the circumstances under which language is processed, the stimuli to which the experimental participants are exposed, and the ways in which participants may respond to these stimuli.

13.1.2 Experimental methods: words in the mind

One of the most intense areas of psycholinguistic research has been the investigation of how words are organized in the mind. We are all in possession of a vocabulary that forms the backbone of our ability to communicate in a language. In many ways, this vocabulary must be used the way a normal dictionary is used. It is consulted to determine what words mean, how they are spelled, and what they sound like. But the dictionary in our minds, our mental lexicon, must also be substantially different from a desktop or electronic dictionary. It must be much more flexible, accommodating the new words that we learn with ease. It must be organized so that words can be looked up extremely quickly—word recognition takes less than one-third of a second and the average adult reads at a rate of about 250 words per minute. It must allow us to access entries in terms of a wide variety of characteristics. The tip-of-the-tongue phenomenon—that is, being temporarily unable to access a word—is particularly revealing with respect to how flexible access to the mental lexicon can be. We have all experienced episodes in which we eventually retrieve a word based on its meaning, sound, spelling, first letter, or even what it rhymes with.

Language Matters **Early Research and Experimentation**

Sigmund Freud (1856–1939) allowed his patients to speak as freely as possible, recorded their utterances, and sought to find meaning in unintentional speech errors, which he called *Fehlleistungen* ('faulty actions'). In his 1901 book *The Psychopathology of Everyday Life*, Freud discusses numerous speech errors, which he analyzed as revealing unconscious desires, memories, or conflicts—the infamous 'Freudian slips'.

Early experimentation

Although primarily interested in memory, Hermann Ebbinghaus (1850–1909) may be considered the first to have conducted psycholinguistic experiments. In 1885, he reported his use of nonsense syllables (e.g., *bim*, *lup*) as the basis of investigations into human learning, retention, and recall.

Many psycholinguists conceive of the mental lexicon as a collection of individual units as in figure 13.1. In this figure, the lexicon is shown as a space in which entries of different types are stored and linked together. The main questions that are asked about the mental lexicon are these: (1) How are entries linked? (2) How are entries accessed? (3) What information is contained in an entry?

FIGURE 13.1
Units in the mental lexicon

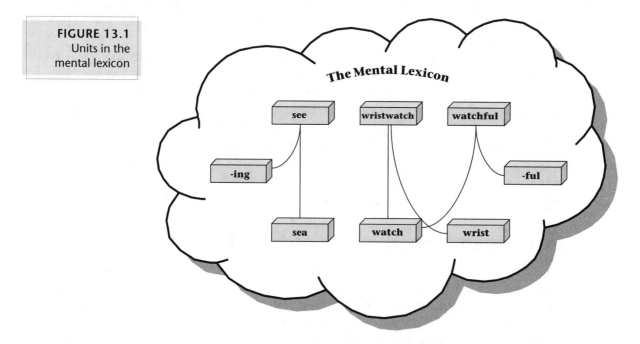

Although these questions are simple and straightforward, there is no way to answer them directly because the human mental lexicon cannot be observed. So the psycholinguist must use special experimental methods to understand how words are organized and represented in the mind and how they are accessed. We will briefly discuss the two most common of these methods—**lexical decision** and **priming**.

Lexical decision

In the lexical decision paradigm, the experimental participant (in this example, a native speaker of English) is seated in front of a computer screen. A word appears in the middle of the screen and the participant must judge as quickly as possible whether the word is a real English word and press a button labelled 'yes' or a button labelled 'no' (see figure 13.2).

FIGURE 13.2
A lexical decision experiment

This task is very easy for participants to carry out. They typically see and judge hundreds of words in a single fifteen-minute session. In most lexical decision experiments, there are two **dependent variables**—that is, things that are being measured: the time that it takes for a participant to respond (**response latency**) and the accuracy of the participant's judgment (**response accuracy**). A response is judged as correct if a participant responds 'yes' to a real word such as *glove* or *sadness* and 'no' to a non-word such as *blove* or *sadding*.

Lexical decision experiments usually involve comparing participants' performance on one set of words to their performance on another set of words. The key to the importance of the experimental paradigm is that in order for a participant to respond 'no' to a stimulus such as *blove* or 'yes' to a real word such as *glove*, the participant's mental lexicon must be accessed. The lexical decision task can therefore be used to measure the speed and accuracy with which words in the mental lexicon are accessed. It has been found in many experiments that participants take about half a second (500 milliseconds) to press the 'yes' button for frequently used words such as *free* but almost three-quarters of a second to press the 'yes' button for less common words such as *fret*. This finding has been called the **frequency effect**. Assuming that longer response times reflect more difficult or complex processing, this finding suggests that our mental dictionaries are organized so that words that we typically need more often (the frequent words) are more easily and quickly available to us.

Another way in which the lexical decision task can be used to explore language representation and processing is to investigate the speed and accuracy with which participants press the 'no' button for different types of stimuli. It has been found, for example, that pronounceable non-words such as *plib* show slower 'no' response times than unpronounceable non-words such as *nlib*. Thus, participants' lexical decisions seem to take into account the phonotactic constraints of the language. It has also been found that non-words that sound like real words (e.g., *blud*, *phocks*) take longer to reject than stimuli that are non-words both visually and phonologically. Again this tells us that aspects of phonology are automatically activated during word reading. (Note that in the lexical decision task, the participant never has to pronounce the word aloud.)

The priming paradigm

The priming paradigm very often involves the lexical decision task and can be considered an extension of it. Recall that in lexical decision tasks, different categories of stimuli (e.g., concrete versus abstract words) are compared in terms of participants' response latency and accuracy. Priming experiments typically involve the same procedure as the lexical decision task except that the word to be judged (now called the **target**) is preceded by another stimulus (called the **prime**). What is measured is the extent to which the prime influences the participant's lexical decision performance on the target stimulus, in terms of either accuracy or response time.

The priming paradigm is an excellent technique for probing how words are related in the mind. One of the first experiments using this paradigm showed that response time is faster when a target is preceded by a semantically related prime (e.g., *cat-dog*) as compared to when it is preceded by an unrelated prime (e.g., *bat-dog*). Results of this sort lead us to the view that words are connected in the mind in terms of networks. On the basis of evidence from these priming experiments, psycholinguists reason that when a word such as *cat* is seen, its representation is activated in the mind, and that activation spreads to semantically related words in the lexical network (e.g., *dog*). Because the mental representation for *dog* has already been activated through the prime, it is in a sense 'warmed up' so that when the participant later sees it on the screen as the target, response time is faster than it otherwise would have been. This is called the **priming effect** (as shown in figure 13.3).

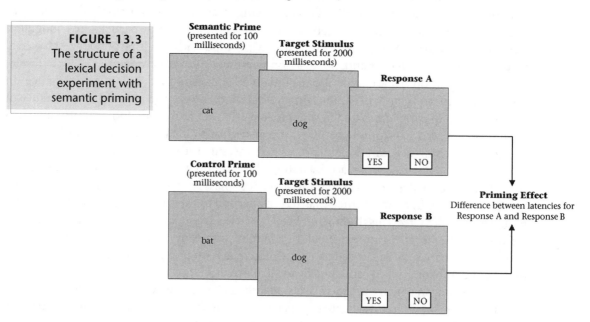

FIGURE 13.3
The structure of a lexical decision experiment with semantic priming

Semantic Prime (presented for 100 milliseconds)

cat

Target Stimulus (presented for 2000 milliseconds)

dog

Response A

YES   NO

Control Prime (presented for 100 milliseconds)

bat

Target Stimulus (presented for 2000 milliseconds)

dog

Response B

YES   NO

Priming Effect
Difference between latencies for Response A and Response B

In recent years, the priming paradigm has been used to explore many aspects of the representation of words in the mind, and researchers have explored many types of priming in addition to the semantic priming described above. For example, priming effects have been found for orthographically similar words (e.g., *couch-touch*), for phonologically similar words (e.g., *light-bite*), and for word roots and complex forms (e.g., *legal-illegality*). This last finding, which suggests that words are represented in the mind in terms of their constituent morphemes, will be discussed further in section 13.2.2.

13.1.3 Experimental methods: sentence processing

The lexical decision and priming paradigms offer interesting insights into how words are processed but are of limited use in exploring the processing of sentences. The main reason for this is that the types of questions asked about sentence processing tend to be different from those asked about the mental lexicon. Because every sentence is different, sentence processing must rely on a particular type of computation (as opposed to a particular type of storage, in the case of words). It is presumed that in sentence processing (i.e., in reading or listening), a sentence is understood through both the analysis of the meanings of its words and the analysis of its syntactic structure. Psycholinguists refer to this type of subconscious sentence analysis as **parsing**. Much of the research on sentence processing is concerned with the principles and steps in parsing, its speed, and the manner and conditions under which it can break down.

In this section, we review two groups of experimental paradigms that have been used extensively to study sentence processing: timed-reading experiments and eye-movement experiments.

Timed-reading experiments

Timed-reading experiments begin with the assumption that the more difficult sentence processing is, the longer it will take to read the sentence. Therefore, by timing how long it takes participants to read particular sentence types or parts of sentences, we can study the determinants of sentence-processing difficulty.

One of the more common and revealing timed-reading experimental paradigms is the bar-pressing paradigm, in which participants are seated in front of a computer screen and read a sentence one word at a time. The participant begins by seeing the first word of the sentence in the middle of the screen. When the participant presses a bar on the keyboard, the first word disappears and the second word of the sentence appears in its place. This process continues until all the words in the sentence have been read. The dependent variable in these experiments is the amount of time it takes participants to press the bar after seeing a particular word (i.e., the amount of time they need to process that word).

Bar-pressing experiments can be very revealing about how sentence processing occurs. Rather than producing equal bar-pressing times across a sentence, participants show a pattern that reflects the syntactic structure of the sentence. An example of such a pattern is shown in figure 13.4, which displays bar-pressing times for the sentence *The Chinese, who used to produce kites, used them in order to carry ropes across the rivers.*

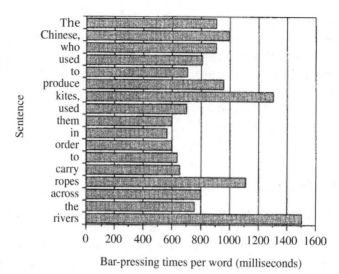

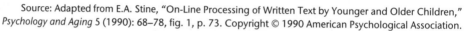

FIGURE 13.4
Bar-pressing times in
sentence reading

Bar-pressing times per word (milliseconds)

Source: Adapted from E.A. Stine, "On-Line Processing of Written Text by Younger and Older Children," *Psychology and Aging* 5 (1990): 68–78, fig. 1, p. 73. Copyright © 1990 American Psychological Association.

As can be seen in figure 13.4, participants show longer bar-pressing times for processing content words such as nouns and verbs and relatively less time for words such as determiners, conjunctions, and prepositions. Of particular interest is the length of the pause at the clause boundaries—especially at the end of the relative clause (*kites*) and the end of the full sentence (*rivers*). This increased processing time is interpreted as reflecting the extra amount of time required to integrate preceding information into a complete clause structure.

Eye movements

We have already noted that sentence reading involves a series of jerky eye movements called saccades. A number of events occur during these jerky movements. When the eyes are at rest they take a 'snapshot' of two or three words. These snapshots usually last from 200 to 250 milliseconds. While the snapshot is being taken, the language-processing system calculates where to jump to next. During a jump to the next fixation location (usually about eight letters to the right), the reader is essentially blind.

The details of eye movements in sentence reading are studied with sophisticated laboratory procedures in which a participant is often seated in front of a computer screen on which text is displayed. Eye movements are tracked by a device that illuminates the participant's eyes with low-intensity infrared light and records the reflection. The eye-position data are linked to the position of text on the screen so that it is possible to determine how the eyes move from one text position to another.

This technique has revealed that fixation times are typically longer for less frequent and less predictable words and that the points of fixation are typically centred on words such as nouns and verbs, rather than on function words such as determiners and conjunctions. Difficult sentence structures create longer fixation times as well as many more **regressive saccades**—backward jumps in a sentence that are usually associated with mis-parsing or mis-comprehension and with the need to reanalyze the sentence. On average, regressive saccades make up 10 to 15 percent of the saccades in sentence reading. But syntactically complex sentences and semantically anomalous sentences (e.g., *The pizza was too hot to drink*) create many more regressive saccades. It has also been found that slower and less accurate readers jump back and forth through sentences much more often than more skilled readers do.

13.1.4 Brain activity: event-related potentials

Perhaps the most exciting new technique to be used in psycholinguistic research is the study of **event-related potentials (ERPs)** produced by the brain during language processing. As a research technique, the ERP paradigm has the same basic advantage as eye-movement studies. The participant simply sits in front of a computer screen and reads. This is a relatively natural language-processing activity that, unlike lexical decision or bar pressing, is similar to what participants do in normal language-processing situations.

ERP experiments measure electrical activity in the brain. Electrodes are placed on a participant's scalp and recordings are made of voltage fluctuations resulting from the brain's electrical activity. There is a significant difference between ERP recordings and the more familiar EEG (electro-encephalogram) recordings. In the EEG, all the electrical activity of the brain is recorded. This electrical activity results from a very large number of background brain activities that are always going on. The advantage of the ERP approach is that it uses a computer to calculate what part of the brain's electrical activity is related to a stimulus event (in our case, words or sentences on a screen). This is done by a process of averaging. The computer records the instant at which a stimulus is presented and compares the voltage fluctuation immediately following the stimulus presentation to the random background 'noise' of the ongoing EEG. By repeating this process many times with stimuli of a particular type, random voltage fluctuations are averaged out and the electrical potentials related to that stimulus type can be extracted. The resulting wave forms are the event-related potentials.

The ERP pattern is typically presented as a line graph in which time is shown from left to right; voltage is shown on the vertical axis, with negative values on top and positive values on the bottom. An example of an ERP graph is provided in figure 13.5. (The horizontal line after 'The pizza was too hot to' represents zero voltage. Any point above the line is negative and any point below it is positive.)

FIGURE 13.5
ERPs elicited by sentence-final words that are congruent, incongruent, and very incongruent with the sentence context

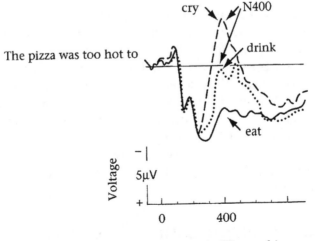

Source: Marta Kutas and Steven A. Hillyard, "Contextual Effects in Language Comprehension," in *Language, Communication, and the Brain*, edited by Fred Plum, 87–100, ARNMD (New York: Raven Press, 1988), fig. 5, p. 93. Reprinted with permission from Lippincott Williams & Wilkins, Philadelphia, PA.

Figure 13.5 also displays one of the most interesting psycholinguistic findings using ERPs. It turns out that in the processing of implausible sentences, the brain displays a characteristic ERP sign of surprise. Consider the following sentences, arranged in order of semantic plausibility:

(8) *a.* The pizza was too hot to eat.
    b. The pizza was too hot to drink.
    c. The pizza was too hot to cry.

As can be seen in figure 13.5, the unexpected words *drink* and *cry* elicited what is called an N400 wave—a wave running in a negative direction that occurs 400 milliseconds after the onset of the word. The word *drink*, which is semantically related to *eat*, evoked a much weaker N400 than *cry*, which is completely incongruous with the rest of the sentence and elicited a very strong N400.

The N400 effect can be obtained not only at the ends of sentences but in any sentence position. This fact suggests that sentence processing is immediate and online. When reading a sentence, we do not wait until the entire string is complete; rather, we are constantly building interpretations of the sentence as it unfolds. Whenever what we see or hear contradicts our expectations based on our ongoing interpretive processes, an N400 ERP component is observed.

Language Matters   Simple Experiments Can Be Very Revealing

One of the most revealing psycholinguistic experiments requires no laboratory and no special equipment. In fact, you can try it with a friend: simply tell your friend that in this experiment, you will say a word out loud and his or her task (as a participant in the experiment) is to try as hard as possible to not understand the word. You can give fair warning by counting down "3, 2, 1," and then saying the word (e.g., *water*). Of course, as long as the participant can actually hear the word, it is impossible to not understand it. This is probably the fundamental truth of language processing: it is automatic and obligatory.

The N400 was the first stable language-related ERP wave to be extensively documented. More recently, a number of other ERP signature waves have been isolated. These include the P600, which is a positive wave that typically reaches its peak at 600 milliseconds following stimulus onset. The P600 has been linked to the processing of syntactic anomaly (e.g., *The men is here*), in contrast to the semantic anomaly marked by the N400 wave.

Another ERP component related to syntactic anomalies that has emerged as very important is the ELAN (Early Left Anterior Negativity). As the name suggests, this is a negative wave that is associated with electrodes placed on the left front areas of the scalp. A key reason for the importance of this ERP wave is how early it can be seen. This is often less than 200 milliseconds after stimulus onset. This suggests that certain aspects of syntactic processing occur very early.

13.1.5   Language corpora and databases

Recent technological advances have enabled the creation of databases of many millions of words. These new databases and language corpora make it possible for psycholinguists to incorporate many more variables concerning language use into their experimental analyses. Thus, in addition to the word frequency variable, for example, researchers are able to analyze factors such as how early in life a particular word is typically acquired (age of acquisition), the number of different syntactic contexts in which it can occur, the number of complex words that have that word as a morphological constituent (morphological family size), and the semantic properties of the words that it has as neighbours in both speech and writing. This expanded analytical capability has greatly increased the sophistication of both the design and statistical analysis of recent psycholinguistic investigations. Finally, projects such as the English Lexicon Project have created databases of words that can be used as stimuli in psycholinguistic experiments and databases of lexical decision response times that have been obtained over multiple experiments using those words. (See the English Lexicon Project home page at elexicon.wustl.edu.)

Google Ngram is an interesting and very easy-to-use tool that demonstrates the power of large corpora built from the millions of books that Google has digitized. With the Google Ngram Viewer, anybody can examine the relative frequency of words or phrases in written English, over years or centuries. The tool also allows users to analyze differences in lexical category and analyze words with different inflections. Figure 13.6 provides an example of how Google Ngram can be used.

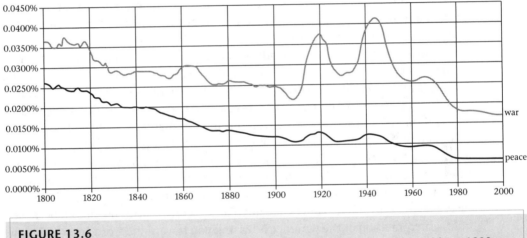
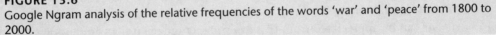

FIGURE 13.6
Google Ngram analysis of the relative frequencies of the words 'war' and 'peace' from 1800 to 2000.

As can be seen in Figure 13.6, the frequency of the words 'war' and 'peace' over the period 1800 to 2000 are closely linked in American English. Furthermore, by following the lighter line on top, it is easy to see that sudden increases in the use of the word 'war' correspond to times of war. The War of 1812 and the American Civil War (1861–65) show small bumps, and the two world wars (1914–18 and 1939–45) show huge rises in the frequency of the word 'war'.

13.2 Language processing and linguistics

In the preceding sections, we discussed some of the methods that psycholinguists use to investigate how language is processed. One of the most important results of such psycholinguistic investigations is that many of the concepts and principles used by linguists to describe and understand the structure of language in terms of phonetics, phonology, morphology, and syntax have been found to also play an important role in understanding how language is produced and comprehended during activities such as speaking, listening, reading, and writing. In this section, we will focus on these points of contact between theoretical linguistics and psycholinguistics.

13.2.1 Phonetics and phonology

The study of phonetics and phonology has revealed that the sound system of language is richly structured and contains different levels of representation. Thus, as discussed in chapters 2 and 3, individual segments can be characterized in terms of place and manner of articulation and described using phonological features. Sequences of sounds can be grouped into syllabic structures, and allophonic variation can be analyzed in terms of underlying phonemes and surface allophones. How much of this structure plays a role in language processing? The simple answer is all of it! The more complex answer, and of course also the more accurate answer, is that although the study of language processing shows evidence that features, phonemes, and syllable structure all capture some aspects of the way in which we process language, speech production and perception is a complex activity that involves much more than these phonetic and phonological representations.

To see why this is the case, consider what might occur when you hear the sentence *The dog bit the cat.* Because the utterance unfolds in time, you will first hear the segment /ð/ and then the segment /ə/. (In fact, you do not hear these segments separately; rather, you create them out of a continuous sound stream.) As soon as these segments are identified, you have already accessed the representation for the word *the* in your mental lexicon. When the next segment comes up in the sound stream, you already know that it is the beginning of a new word and you also know that this word will probably be a noun. The phonetic analysis that follows identifies the segments [d], [ɑ], and [g] and the corresponding lexical entry *dog*. Now come the first segments of the word *bit*. In principle, the first two phonemes /bɪ/ could be the first two segments of the word *believe*, but you are not likely to consider this possibility because your developing interpretation of the sentence is biasing you toward the word *bit*, which is associated in your mind with *dog*.

As can be appreciated from this example, language processing involves the interplay of information that develops simultaneously at many different levels of analysis. The person hearing the sentence *The dog bit the cat* is performing a phonetic analysis to isolate phonemes and word boundaries and to relate these to items in the mental lexicon. This inductive analysis is referred to as **bottom-up processing**. But we do not wait until we have analyzed all the phonemes in a sentence before we begin to try to understand it. Rather, we begin interpretation of a sentence spontaneously and automatically on the basis of whatever information is available to us. For this reason, by the time we get to the word *bit*, we are not only recognizing it using bottom-up processing but are also employing a set of expectations to guide phonetic processing and word recognition. This is called **top-down processing**. In normal language use, we are always engaged in both bottom-up and top-down activities. We never just process features, or phonemes, or syllables. We process language for the purpose of understanding each other.

In section 13.3 of this chapter, we will discuss how phonetic and phonological analysis fits into other processes involved in speaking and listening. For now, however, we will concentrate on three levels of linguistic structure that seem fundamental to phonetic and phonological representation: features, phonemes, and syllables.

Features

In both theoretical linguistics and psycholinguistics, the term *feature* is used to refer to characteristics of individual phonemes (e.g., [± voice], [± continuant], etc.). Features represent the most basic level of representation and are therefore always associated with bottom-up processing in language. The most straightforward evidence concerning the role of features comes from slips of the tongue. Some examples are presented in table 13.1.

TABLE 13.1 The role of features in speech errors	
Intended	**Actually produced**
a. big and fat	pig and vat
b. Is Pat a girl?	Is bat a curl?
c. Cedars of Lebanon	Cedars of Lemanon

The errors in table 13.1 follow a pattern, but that pattern can only be understood with reference to a system of phonological features. In all three examples, the errors involve a phonological feature. In example *a*, the feature [voice] has been exchanged between the words *big* and *fat* to create the new words *pig* and *vat* (remember that /b-p/ and /f-v/ only differ in the feature [voice]).

This same pattern of an exchange in the feature [voice] can be seen in example *b*, where *Pat* becomes *bat* and *girl* becomes *curl*. Finally, the error in *c* is particularly intriguing because it involves just a single feature change: the voiced labial stop /b/ becomes [+nasal] under the influence of the /n/ in the next syllable, yielding an /m/ and the pronunciation *Lemanon*. Such examples offer evidence that language production makes use of the individual feature components of phonemes and that the phonemes that we produce in speech may actually be put together 'on the fly' out of bundles of such features.

Segments

We saw in section 13.1.1 that spoonerisms show evidence of entire segments being misplaced during sentence planning. The segmental unit of representation also plays a central role in psycholinguistic models of speech processing, such as the **cohort model** proposed by William Marslen-Wilson in the 1980s. This model states that in word comprehension, words are analyzed by hearers from beginning to end. So, for example, when we hear the word *glass*, we initially consider all the words that begin with the sound [g]. When the next sound [l] is recognized, the number of possible words (the **cohort**) is reduced to those words that begin with [gl]. This process continues until the cohort of possible words is reduced to one—the word that is being recognized. In a number of experiments, Marslen-Wilson investigated whether this beginning-to-end analysis of spoken words proceeds one segment at a time, one cluster at a time, or one syllable at a time. He and his colleagues found that the segment seems to be the fundamental unit of auditory word recognition.

Syllables

Although in the cohort model, the phoneme rather than the syllable seems to be the fundamental unit of auditory word recognition, other evidence points to the syllable playing an important role in speech perception. In one study, participants were presented with disyllabic words (e.g., *bullet*) and disyllabic non-words (e.g., *sullet*) and were asked to press a button if a particular target unit was in the stimulus. The target units were either syllables (e.g., *let*) or segments (e.g., *t*). It was found for both words and non-words that participants were significantly faster at identifying syllable targets than at identifying single segment targets. The researchers concluded that syllable identification was faster because in normal auditory analysis, participants first break down stimuli into syllables and then into individual segments as the situation demands.

Another source of evidence concerning the role of the syllable in language processing comes from observing participants' performance on word-blending tasks. In such tasks, participants are given two monosyllabic words such as *bug* and *cat* and are required to blend the words together to make a new word. Participants have two options: (*bug* + *cat* = *bat*) or (*bug* + *cat* = *but*)?

FIGURE 13.7
Comparing a blend that respects syllabic constituents with one that does not.

a. Respects syllable constituents

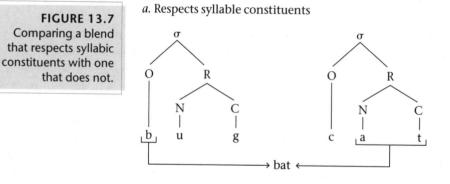

b. Does not respect syllable constituents

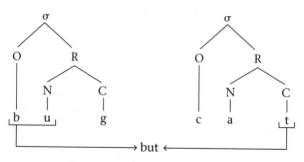

Notice that option *a* in Figure 13.7 aligns with the internal syllable structure of the two words: it combines the onset of the first word/syllable with the rhyme (nucleus plus coda) of the second word/syllable. Option *b*, in contrast, combines the first two sounds of the first word (thus breaking up the rhyme of the word) with the last sound of the second word. Typically, participants prefer option *a*: that is, they more frequently create word blends that make use of syllable structure than those that don't. This suggests that words are represented in speakers' minds in terms of their syllables and syllable constituents.

Language Matters SPAM: A Morphological Blend

In 1937, the luncheon meat Spam was introduced. The previous name for the product was Hormel Spiced Ham and it was produced by the Hormel Foods Corporation. In 1936, the company had a contest offering one hundred dollars for the best new name for the product. The prize was won by Kenneth Daigneau, the brother of the company's vice-president. Like the participants in the psycholinguistic experiments discussed above, Mr. Daigneau chose to combine the onset of the first word *spiced* and the rhyme of the second word <u>*ham*</u>.

13.2.2 Morphological processing

Morphology is the component of the grammar that is concerned with the structure and interpretation of words. The psycholinguistic study of morphology seeks to understand how word structure plays a role in language processing. In the following sections, we will summarize some psycholinguistic research that reveals how morphological structures and principles play a substantial role in how words are processed and recognized.

Morpheme activation

Words such as *blackboard*, *happiness*, and *watching* are all made up of two morphemes. In the case of the compound *blackboard*, both these morphemes are roots. In the case of *happiness*, one morpheme is a root and the other is a derivational suffix. Finally, in the case of *watching*, one morpheme is a root and the other is an inflectional affix. The first question we will address is whether the individual morphological components of words play a role in processing.

The answer to this question seems to be a straightforward 'yes'. For most multimorphemic words, individual morphemes are automatically activated during word recognition. Lexical decision experiments have shown that multimorphemic words will prime semantic associates of their constituents. Thus, when a participant is exposed to a multimorphemic word such as *suntan*, the activation of that word in the mind will facilitate the recognition of *moon*, which is highly associated with the initial morpheme *sun* but not with the whole compound word. The facilitation, therefore, must arise from independent activation of the morphemes within the word.

One very active domain of psycholinguistic research focuses on understanding such activation of constituent morphemes. This research has led to some very interesting explanations. The first and most straightforward explanation is that an integral component of a speaker's knowledge of a word such as *suntan* is the knowledge that it contains the elements *sun* and *tan*. Thus, we can say that a compound word such as *suntan* has a morphologically structured representation in the minds of speakers of English and that this morphological structuring is the source of the priming effect.

The morphological structuring explanation seems very reasonable for compounds such as *suntan*, which is **semantically transparent**—that is, its morphological constituents contribute to the meaning of the whole word in a clear manner. But what about more challenging

semantically opaque compound words such as *grapefruit* or *ladybug,* for which the meanings of the parts do not obviously accord with the meaning of the whole compound? Are these compounds also morphologically structured in the minds of English speakers? Are constituent morphemes of these words activated as well? The current research consensus is that they are.

This leads us to the interesting question of why this should be the case. The word *grape* in *grapefruit* does not really help a speaker of English in any way. Neither does the word *lady* in *ladybug.* However, the other morphemes do help a lot: The fact that *fruit* is the morphological head of *grapefruit* enables language users to know that it is a type of fruit, even when they are encountering the word for the first time. Similarly, the constituent *bug* as the morphological head of *ladybug* puts it in the correct semantic field (as does one of its other variants, *ladybeetle*).

Because recognizing even a part of a word can be so helpful in understanding what it means and what other words it is associated with, some psycholinguists have claimed that morphological processing is both automatic and obligatory. Perhaps the most dramatic evidence of automatic and obligatory morphological decomposition comes from a set of experiments that have investigated priming effects among words that look multimorphemic but are not. An example of such a word is *corner*. It looks like it contains a root *corn* and a suffix *-er*. But, of course, it does not mean 'someone who corns'. In a series of priming experiments, it was found that a word such as *corner* primes *corn* in much the same way that a truly multimorphemic word such as *hunter* primes *hunt*. In contrast, words such as *scandal*, which do not look like root + suffix combinations, do not create a priming effect. Seeing *scandal* does not improve participants' response times to *scan*. The *corner* example indicates that morphological decomposition can occur even when it is not appropriate and when the activated element is not a true morphological constituent of the word. This is consistent with the view that morphological decomposition is a very automatic process that is 'on the lookout' for all legal morphological strings.

Language Matters: **Word Histories Can Take Strange Twists and Turns**

Could a *grapefruit* just as easily have been called a *potatofruit*? Could a *ladybug* have been called a *womanbug*? In principle, yes! Words such as these come into the English language 'with a story.' Over time, the story fades away, but the words remain.

Most etymologists think that *grapefruit* was so named because it grows in bunches like grapes. Another theory is that *grapefruit* is actually a mispronunciation of *greatfruit*, so named because of the fruit's size. The word *ladybug* was named to refer to the mother of Jesus (as in, 'Our Lady'). One reason that has been given for this is that Mary is often depicted in a red cloak (in German, a ladybug is called a *Marienkäfer*—literal translation: 'Mary Beetle').

Selectional restrictions

The studies reviewed above point to the view that even for apparently simple multimorphemic words, a considerable amount of mental computation is involved in working out how morphemes do and do not fit together. To complete our brief discussion of this issue, let us consider the fact that not all roots and affixes combine freely in the formation of new words. For instance, the suffix *-ize* attaches to adjectives and nouns to form verbs (e.g., *nationalize, hospitalize*), but it cannot apply to a word that is already a verb (e.g., **understandize*). The question for psycholinguistic research is, Do these restrictions play a role in the way in which native speakers of English process new words?

In an experiment in morphological processing, participants were presented with nonsense roots (e.g., *birm*) that had prefixes and suffixes attached to them. Because they contained nonsense roots, none of these words made much sense (e.g., *rebirmable, rebirmize, rebirmity*). But notice that, as is shown in figure 13.8, *rebirmable* and *rebirmize* are morphologically legal, whereas *rebirmity* violates a morphological constraint—the prefix *re-* attaches to a verb to create another verb (as in *redo*), and the suffix *-ity* attaches to an adjective to create a noun (as in *insane–insanity*). The form *rebirmity* is illegal because *re-birm* has to be a verb and therefore can't take the suffix *-ity*, whereas *birm-ity* has to be a noun and therefore can't occur with the prefix *re-*. In experiments with these sorts of stimuli, it was found that processing times were significantly longer for the illegal nonsense words than for the morphologically legal words. These results suggest that knowledge of the attachment restrictions of affixes does indeed form part of the word-processing system and that violation of these restrictions creates difficulty for automatic lexical processing, which would of course go unnoticed by the language user but is discernible through psycholinguistic techniques.

FIGURE 13.8
Morphologically legal and illegal affixed nonsense roots

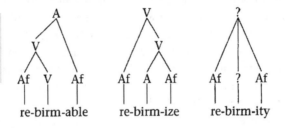

13.2.3 Syntax

Syntax is the system of rules and categories that underlies sentence formation in human language. One of the fundamental insights in the study of syntax is that sentences are unique events. That means that virtually all the sentences that you read in this chapter are sentences that you have never encountered before. They are typically made up of familiar words, but the particular combination of words and the manner in which they are arranged are unique to each sentence. The question that we will consider in this section is, How are these syntactic structures created during sentence processing?

The syntax module

One very simple possibility for how sentences are processed is that production and comprehension employ the system of rules that are used by syntacticians to describe sentence structure. This possibility suggests that speakers use the Merge operation to create deep structure representations and employ Move operations to derive the surface structure characteristics of a sentence. Many psycholinguistic experiments have examined this possibility by testing, for example, whether sentences that have undergone many Move operations take longer to process than sentences with fewer such operations. The results of these experiments show that the number of Move operations that a sentence has undergone does not predict processing time.

Researchers concluded that there is at least some difference between the rules that native speakers use to produce and comprehend sentences and the rules that linguists use to characterize the linguistic knowledge of native speakers. It was therefore necessary to postulate a special module for sentence processing, called the **syntactic parser**, and another module for grammatical knowledge.

The parser is understood to be a system that makes use of grammatical knowledge but that also contains special procedures and principles that guide the order in which elements of a sentence are processed and the manner in which syntactic structure is built up. Because our parsing ability is based on our grammatical knowledge of our language, it is usually the case that there is a close correspondence between sentence parsing and grammatical structure. However, because the parsing module has its own set of principles, sentences that are grammatically complex are not necessarily difficult to parse, while some sentences with relatively simple syntactic structure can create substantial parsing problems.

It should be noted that in discussing how processing takes place, the term **module** has a special meaning. It refers to a mechanism of processing that is relatively autonomous from other processing mechanisms. The idea of processing modules has been very important and controversial in many domains of human information processing. To get a sense of how processing may involve the coordination of separate modules, consider what occurs when you watch a movie. The movie director, in order to obtain a variety of effects, relies on processing modularity. The director knows that in watching an adventure film, your stomach will take a dip when the airplane on the screen goes into a dive or when the canoe goes over the falls. He or she knows that you cannot stop this from happening even though you are aware that you are sitting in a chair that is not moving. Similarly, you will be frightened by the sudden appearance of a monster, even though you know that you are really in no danger. All these effects result from processing modularity. The bottom-up information that comes from processing modules cannot be turned off by the top-down information that you are seated in a stationary and safe environment.

A variety of psycholinguistic studies have investigated whether this same sort of modularity is present in syntactic processing. In other words, they look at whether syntactic parsing operates in an automatic and obligatory manner that is relatively independent of the activity of other processing systems. Two sources of evidence have been very important in the exploration of modularity in sentence processing. These are garden path sentences and sentence ambiguity.

Garden path sentences

Some sentences are extraordinarily difficult to understand even though they are not very complex syntactically. These sentences are called **garden path sentences** because they lead the syntactic parser down the garden path to the wrong analysis. Perhaps the most famous garden path sentence is the one given in (9).

(9) The horse raced past the barn fell.

This sentence is perfectly grammatical but almost impossible to understand. The reason for this is that as we read the sentence, we build up a syntactic structure in which *the horse* is the subject of the sentence and *raced past the barn* is the VP. When we get to the word *fell*, we are surprised because the sentence we have built up has no room for an extra VP (see figure 13.9a). The correct interpretation for the sentence requires that *fell* be the head of the main VP and

a.

b.

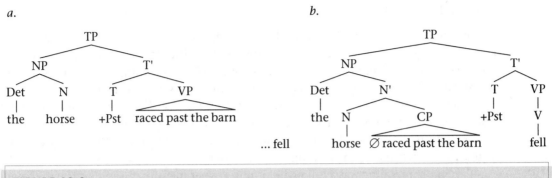

> **FIGURE 13.9**
> A garden path sentence. The garden path effect is shown in *a*. The correct interpretation is represented in *b*.

that *raced past the barn* be a clause (a reduced version of 'which was raced past the barn') that attaches to the NP *the horse* (see figure 13.9b). The sentence thus has an interpretation parallel to that of the unambiguous sentence *The statue taken from the gallery shattered.*

The ways in which native speakers misunderstand garden path sentences reveals how the parser might work. It seems that we construct syntactic representations from the beginning of the sentences to the end and that our sentence parsers are organized so that we make a number of assumptions about how a sentence will proceed. This can be seen by considering the garden path sentence in (10).

(10) Since Jay always walks a mile seems like a short distance to him.

This sentence is not as difficult to process as the sentence in (9), but you probably noticed yourself having to backtrack after an initial mis-analysis. Your parser is inclined to build a single VP out of the string *walks a mile*, when in fact *walks* and *a mile* belong to different clauses. This tendency has been extensively studied by psycholinguists. The backtracking that you might have noticed in your own reading shows up in eye-movement studies in which participants have been found to show more regressive saccades and longer fixation times for these sentences than for sentences that do not require backtracking.

It has been claimed that the garden path effect results from two principles of parsing: **minimal attachment** and **late closure**. The principle of minimal attachment states that, all other things being equal, we do not build more syntactic structure (like the extra embedded phrase in figure 13.9b) than is absolutely necessary. The principle of late closure states that we prefer to attach new words to the clause currently being processed as we proceed through a sentence from beginning to end. The result of late closure can be discerned in sentence (10), where we are inclined to add the NP *a mile* to the VP headed by *walks* rather than beginning a new clause.

Now, there is one last point to be made concerning what garden path sentences can tell us about how people process sentences. Try reading the sentence in (10) again. You might find that although you now know the correct analysis for the sentence, you misread it the second time just as you did the first time. This suggests that the parsing system is in fact a module that operates automatically and independently.

Sentence ambiguity

Another important clue to how syntactic processing is accomplished comes from the study of ambiguity. Consider the sentence in (11).

(11) They all rose.

The last word in (11) is ambiguous. The word *rose* can be related to either *stand* or *flower*. However, the sentence context leads us clearly to favour the *stand* version of the word. Does the sentence context therefore inhibit activation of the other meaning of *rose*? This question was investigated in a lexical decision experiment in which the sentence in (11) served as the prime. After seeing the sentence, participants were presented with either the word *flower* or *stand*. The researchers found that the sentence facilitated lexical decision response times to both words. That is, both meanings for the word *rose* were activated, even though the sentence clearly presented a bias in favour of one reading over the other.

Even more revealing was a follow-up priming experiment that was identical to the one just described except that there was a pause of several hundred milliseconds between the prime and the target. When the pause was present, the priming effect disappeared for the meaning that was unrelated to the sentence context (i.e., *flower*). This suggests that in fact sentence processing proceeds in two stages. In the first stage, all possible representations and structures are computed. In the second stage, one of these structures is selected and all others are abandoned.

Of course, all this happens very quickly and subconsciously, so that we as native speakers of a language are never aware that for a sentence such as (12), we compute two possible interpretations.

(12) The tuna can hit the boat.

In reading this sentence, you ended up imagining either

 a. tuna meat that is packed in a small round can, *or*
 b. a large fish swimming toward a boat

The point of the psycholinguistic experiments just described is this: no matter which interpretation you arrived at (*a* or *b*), you probably considered both of them, chose one, discarded the other, and forgot about the whole thing in less than a second.

13.3 Putting it all together: psycholinguistic modelling

Up to this point, our discussion of psycholinguistic research has been restricted to examining characteristics of phonetic, phonological, morphological, and syntactic processing and the relation between the concepts used in theoretical linguistics and in psycholinguistics. It is important to note, however, that psycholinguistic research seeks to discover not only which types of representations play a role in language processing but also how these representations and processes fit together to make activities such as speaking, listening, reading, and writing possible.

Psycholinguistic researchers often present their ideas about how language is 'done' in terms of models. A psycholinguistic model incorporates the results of experiments into a proposal about how processing takes place.

13.3.1 Approaches to psycholinguistic modelling

Researchers who develop and propose psycholinguistic models often use a visual representation of processing components and how they interact. Traditionally, the most common visual representation has been a box-and-arrow diagram such as the one shown in figure 13.10. This type of model can be described as a **serial processing model** because it depicts processing events occurring one after another. Models of this sort have been useful in developing initial accounts of language processing under artificially simplified circumstances.

The model shown in figure 13.10 says that when processing a sentence such as *They all rose*, we first perform phonological analysis. This is followed by lexical access, in which all words with matching phonological representations are accessed (including the two words *rose* in the example above). Information from lexical access feeds the syntactic parsing module, and information from both the lexical access module and the parsing module are fed to the representation pruning module (the module that discards multiple representations). Finally, the model states that an interpretation becomes conscious only in the final stage of analysis and that there is only one-way information flow to the end point of conscious interpretation (in other words, the conscious mind cannot peek back at how things are going).

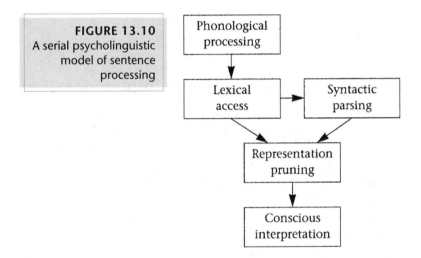

FIGURE 13.10
A serial psycholinguistic model of sentence processing

You will note that in creating this model, we have taken two shortcuts. First, we have created a novel name ('pruning') to describe an operation that has been deduced from the results of psycholinguistic experimentation. Second, our model uses the box notation as a shorthand for a constellation of processes. Thus, it is understood that as the model becomes more elaborated, each one of the boxes in figure 13.10 might need to be expanded into a box and arrow chart of its own in order to account for the details of a particular subprocess.

As you inspect the model in figure 13.10, you should find that it is really very inadequate. It is missing much important detail, it seems to characterize only one aspect of sentence processing, and it avoids any mention of how meaning is accessed and how sentence interpretation actually takes place. To be a model of any real value, it would have to be much more elaborate and would need to take into consideration the processes that occur in parallel with each other, as well as the ones that occur serially. For example, although figure 13.10 shows lexical access occurring before syntactic parsing, it is very unlikely that, in everyday sentence processing, a language user would recognize all the words of a sentence first and only afterward start to analyze the syntactic structure of the sentence. Rather, we would expect that both activities would be going on at the same time.

This kind of simultaneous activity can be captured by modifying the visual representation of a model to display parallel activities. An example of such a representation is the **parallel processing model** shown in figure 13.11. Here, information does not flow in a sequential manner. Rather, all modules operate simultaneously and share information with each other. The model in figure 13.11 claims, therefore, that when we hear a sentence, we begin phonological, lexical, and syntactic processes at the same time. As each type of processing proceeds, it informs the others.

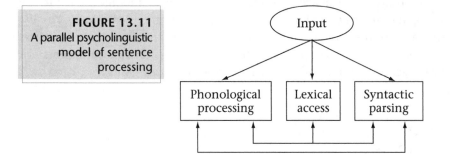

FIGURE 13.11
A parallel psycholinguistic model of sentence processing

From visual representation to computational implementation

The parallel processing model shown in figure 13.11 captures more of the complexity of language processing than does the serial processing model in figure 13.10. Yet it is still highly simplified. A more adequate model would need many more boxes, including sub-boxes, and many more connections among them. Such additions would improve the model because for processing models to be useful, they need to be as detailed and comprehensive as possible, to take a great deal of experimentation into account, and, perhaps most importantly, to show how linguistic and non-linguistic operations (e.g., operations related to memory and recall) work together in the processing of language.

This increase in complexity, however, brings its own set of challenges. As models become more complex, representing them visually can be difficult. It also becomes difficult for the research community to agree on what exactly is predicted by a highly complex box-and-arrow model. To address such problems, developers of psycholinguistic models have increasingly sought to implement their models as computer programs. For example, the Dual Route Model of Reading, which was developed by Max Coltheart in the 1980s as a box-and-arrow model, was later turned into the computer program published in 2001 as the Dual Route Cascaded Model. Presenting a model as a computer program has substantial advantages. It allows researchers who propose a model to be explicit about the processes and representations that may be contained within the model and about exactly how elements of the model interact with one another during language processing. This explicitness enables the model developer to articulate predictions about how the model would perform under particular circumstances and then to test those predictions against observed human behaviour under comparable circumstances.

Which model is right?

Almost certainly, none of the current psycholinguistic models of language processing is correct. All models represent a researcher's claim about the most current best hypothesis.

Because psycholinguistics is a very young field, we can expect that any 'current best hypothesis' will be very far from the truth (if there is one). Perhaps this is why psycholinguistic models are so important. They give us the vocabulary with which to ask important questions about mental processing.

13.3.2 Big questions, emerging perspectives, and the next steps

The alternative approaches to psycholinguistic modelling that we have discussed above capture important questions: Is it reasonable to postulate mental representations that correspond to linguistic categories such as phonemes, words, and phrases, or are mental representations merely the state of a neural network with no symbolic categories? Does the mind settle into a best way to perform a task, or are all processes horse races between alternative ways to solve a problem? Do mental operations proceed in a step-by-step manner?

These are all big issues. The more we investigate the details, the more we realize that language processing offers our best clues to the secrets of human cognition and the more we appreciate how well guarded those secrets are. In the past quarter-century of psycholinguistic research, we have learned a great deal about language representation and processing. In the first part of this chapter, we concentrated on the research techniques that have made these advances possible. In this final section of the chapter, we focus on the still unresolved major issues.

Although we do not yet know which models are right or which hybrids will be most effective in our evolving understanding of human cognition, the research we have reviewed in this chapter points to a view of language processing that is characterized by massive storage of language forms and by extensive connections among these forms. Language processing also seems to involve automatic and obligatory computational procedures that break down complex language structures into their phonological, morphological, and syntactic constituents during language comprehension and build them up during production.

We are thus able to conclude that the language system is, paradoxically, fast and automatic but not necessarily efficient. The reason for this is probably that the language-processing system is designed to exploit all the linguistic resources of the human brain—its massive storage ability, its apparently unlimited capacity for associations among representations, and its ability to carry out complex computations within modular subsystems. So, whereas theoretical characterizations of language structure strive, quite appropriately, for elegance and simplicity, the language-processing system might strive for exactly the opposite—extensive redundancy.

One reason why language processing might have evolved to be highly redundant is that it must, very often, occur under non-optimal conditions. We need to be able to understand language when two or more people are speaking at the same time, when we are in a noisy environment, or when we are rushed. A language system that can 'do' language in many different ways, depending on the individual and on the circumstances, is likely to be the one that is most effective. The exact manner in which different and perhaps redundant methods of 'doing language' might co-exist in a single human brain has been the subject of a great deal of recent research and debate among psycholinguists and constitutes the next big research challenge in the field. By taking up this challenge, psycholinguistics is able to aid in deepening our understanding of human cognition. It is also able to aid in the design of new technologies that may help persons who experience language-processing difficulties as a result of accident or disease.

Summing up

Psycholinguistics is the study of language processing. The field is defined both by a subject matter and a particular methodology. Psycholinguists study how people perform the functions of language comprehension and production. They seek to discover the nature of the mental representations that serve these functions and the nature of the cognitive operations and computations that are employed when we understand and produce language.

Because language processing involves computations and representations that cannot be observed and measured directly, psycholinguists have devised special experimental techniques to investigate language processing. Some of these techniques, such as **lexical decision** and **priming**, measure a participant's response time and response accuracy to linguistic stimuli. Other techniques measure eye movement while participants are reading silently, and yet others measure electrical activity in the brain during language processing.

Language processing involves many processing modules, each of which is specialized for a particular language-processing task and that interacts with other modules in restricted ways. Thus, language processing involves a constant interplay between **bottom-up** and **top-down processing**. We process phonetic features, phonemes, and words all at the same time. We construct syllable representations, morphological representations, and syntactic representations in a spontaneous and obligatory manner. As conscious beings, we are aware of the results of our processing but not of the processing itself.

In general, psycholinguistic studies have revealed that many of the concepts employed in the analysis of sound structure, word structure, and sentence structure also play a role in language processing. However, an account of language processing also requires that we understand how these linguistic concepts interact with other aspects of human processing to enable language production and comprehension.

Psycholinguists typically present their views of how language production and comprehension are achieved in terms of processing models. These models are at the heart of research in psycholinguistics and allow researchers to express the significance of particular research findings, to predict the outcomes of future experiments, and to debate the fundamental characteristics of human cognition.

Recommended reading

Carroll, David. 2007. *Psychology of Language*. Belmont, CA: Wadsworth.
Gaskell, Gareth M., ed. 2007. *Oxford Handbook of Psycholinguistics*. Oxford: Oxford University Press.
Menn, Lise. 2010. *Psycholinguistics: Introduction and Applications*. San Diego, CA: Plural.
Sedivy, Julie. 2019. *Language in Mind: An Introduction to Psycholinguistics*. 2nd ed. New York: Oxford University Press.

Exercises

1. How do psycholinguistic investigations of language differ from theoretical linguistic investigations?

2. Consider the following slips of the tongue. What does each reveal about the process of language production?
   a) They *laked* across the *swim*.
   b) The spy was *gound* and *bagged*.
   c) I will *zee* you in the *bark*.

3. Imagine that you read that a psycholinguist has reported an experiment in which a priming effect was found for morphological roots on suffixed past tense forms in a lexical decision task.
   a) State the dependent variable in the experiment (i.e., the thing that is observed and measured).
   b) Give an example of a prime stimulus.
   c) Give an example of a target stimulus.

4. Complete the following sentences by filling in the blanks. In each case, what type of top-down processing and bottom-up processing guided your decision?
   a) The children __ running in the park.
   b) All __ movies I like have happy endings.
   c) He tends to see everything as __ and white.

5. Recall that according to the cohort model, a word is recognized from beginning to end, one phoneme at a time. According to the cohort model, how many phonemes of each of the following words would have to be processed before a hearer would be sure which word had been spoken?
   a) hippopotamus
   b) splat
   c) computerize

6. Write the sentences in examples (9) and (10) of this chapter on separate index cards. Take a few other cards and write a normal sentence on each of them. Now, have some friends try to read aloud the sentences on the cards. Do they show evidence that the sentences are more difficult to process?

7. Imagine yourself as a psycholinguist trying to devise experiments to investigate how people do language. What experiments would you make up to address the following questions? Be as specific as possible about how you would interpret the question and about what you would do to try to find an answer through psycholinguistic experimentation.
   a) Are semantically abstract words easier to process than semantically concrete ones?
   b) Are simple clauses more difficult to understand than conjoined clauses?
   c) Do people read words from beginning to end?
   d) Do people with different levels of education process language in fundamentally different ways?
   e) Does the way you parse a sentence depend on what language you speak?

To learn more about the topics discussed in this chapter, visit the Companion Website for *Contemporary Linguistic Analysis*.

Brain and language

The biology of mind bridges the sciences—concerned
with the natural world—and the humanities—
concerned with the meaning of human experience.

ERIK R. KANDEL, NOBEL BANQUET SPEECH, 2000

IN THIS chapter we will be concerned with the branch of neuroscience that has as its goal the understanding of how language is represented and processed in the brain. This field of study is called **neurolinguistics**. Although the study of the relationship between brain and language is still in its infancy, much has already been learned about which parts of the brain are involved in various aspects of language production and comprehension. The field of neurolinguistics has also done much to deepen the way we think about the nature of linguistic competence.

The chapter begins with a brief survey of brain structure and the methods that are currently available to study the brain. This is followed by a discussion of the different types of language disturbance that result from brain damage and a discussion of how phonology, morphology, syntax, and semantics may be represented in the brain. The chapter concludes by reviewing the current answers to the important neurolinguistic question, Where is language?

14.1 The human brain

Contained within your skull is about 1400 grams of pinkish-white matter. It may be the most complex 1400 grams in the galaxy. For most of human history, however, the role of the brain as the centre of mental life remained completely unknown. Even the Greek philosopher Aristotle believed that the brain's primary function was to cool the blood.

We now know much more about the structure and functioning of the brain. But in many ways we are still quite like Aristotle, finding it hard to believe that this wrinkled mass of nerve cells could be the stuff that dreams, fears, personality, and knowledge are made of. Nevertheless, it is, and the task of **cognitive neuroscience** is to understand how the breadth and depth of human experience is coded in brain matter.

The brain is composed of nerve cells, or **neurons**, that are the basic information-processing units of the nervous system. The human brain contains about 10 billion neurons that are organized into networks of almost unimaginable complexity. This complexity results from the fact that each neuron can be directly linked with up to ten thousand other neurons. But the brain is not simply a mass of interconnected neurons. It is composed of structures that seem to play specific roles in the integrated functioning of the brain. The following sections provide a brief overview of these structures.

14.1.1 The cerebral cortex

The brain encompasses all the neurological structures above the spinal cord and appears to have evolved from the bottom up. The lower brain structures are shared by almost all animals. These structures are responsible for the maintenance of functions such as respiration, heart rate, and muscle coordination that are essential to the survival of all animals. As we move farther away from the spinal cord, however, we begin to find structures that have developed differently in different species. At the highest level of the brain, the **cerebral cortex**, the differences are most pronounced. Reptiles and amphibians have no cortex at all, and the progression from lower to higher mammals is marked by dramatic increases in the proportion of cortex to total amount of brain tissue. The human brain has the greatest proportion of cortex to brain mass of all animals.

In humans, the cortex (from Latin 'bark of a tree') is the grey outer covering of the wrinkled mass, the **cerebrum**, that sits like a cap over the rest of the brain. The wrinkled appearance results from the cortex being folded in upon itself. This folding allows a great amount of cortical matter to be compressed into the limited space provided by the human skull (in much the same way as the folding of a handkerchief allows it to fit into a jacket pocket). It has been estimated that up to 65 percent of the cortex is hidden within its folds.

It is the human cortex that accounts for our distinctness in the animal world, and it is within the human cortex that the secrets of language representation and processing are to be found. The remainder of our discussion of brain structure, therefore, will focus on the features of the cerebral cortex.

14.1.2 The cerebral hemispheres

The most important orientation points in mapping the cortex are the folds on its surface. These folds have two parts: **sulci** (pronounced /sʌlsaj/; singular: **sulcus**), which are areas where the cortex is folded in, and **gyri** (pronounced /dʒajraj/; singular: **gyrus**), which are areas where the cortex is folded out toward the surface.

Figure 14.1 shows a human brain as seen from above, illustrating the many sulci and gyri of the cortex. A very prominent feature is the deep sulcus (in this case called a **fissure** because of its size) that extends from the front of the brain to the back. This fissure, which is known as the **longitudinal fissure**, separates the left and right **cerebral hemispheres**. In many ways, the cerebral hemispheres can be considered to be separate brains; they are in fact often referred to as the left brain and the right brain. There are two main reasons for this.

First, the hemispheres are almost completely anatomically separate. The main connection between them is a bundle of nerve fibres known as the **corpus callosum**, whose primary function is to allow the two hemispheres to communicate with one another.

Second, the cerebral hemispheres show considerable functional distinctness. In terms of muscle movement and sensation, each hemisphere is responsible for half the body—oddly enough, the opposite half. Thus the left hemisphere controls the right side of the body and the right hemisphere controls the left side of the body. These **contralateral** (contra = opposite; lateral = side) responsibilities of the cerebral hemispheres account for the fact that people who suffer damage to one hemisphere of the brain (e.g., as a result of a stroke or accident) will exhibit paralysis on the opposite side of the body.

FIGURE 14.1
The cerebral hemispheres seen from above. Note the many sulci and gyri of the cortex and the prominence of the longitudinal fissure that separates the left and right hemispheres.

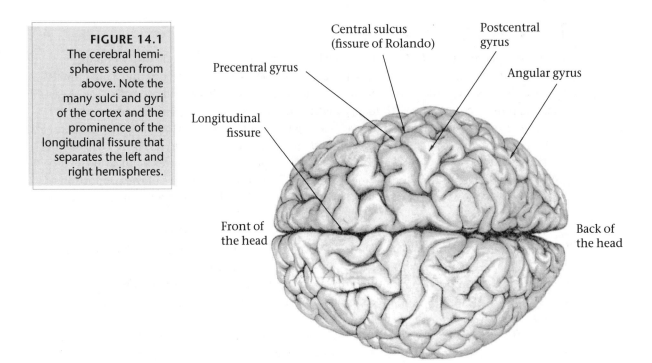

Central sulcus (fissure of Rolando)

Postcentral gyrus

Precentral gyrus

Angular gyrus

Longitudinal fissure

Front of the head

Back of the head

The hemispheres also show functional distinctness with respect to higher cognitive functions. In general, the left hemisphere seems to excel in analytic tasks such as arithmetic, whereas the right hemisphere excels in tasks that require an overall appreciation of complex patterns such as the recognition of familiar faces and melodies. This relatively unilateral control of cognitive functions by either the left or right side of the brain is referred to as **lateralization**.

Despite the fact that the hemispheres show such specialization, we should be cautious about making sweeping generalizations about left brain versus right brain abilities or strategies. In all probability, complex mental activities involve the coordinated functioning of both hemispheres. The representation of language in the brain provides a useful example of this.

Most right-handed individuals have language represented in the left cerebral hemisphere and are therefore said to be left lateralized for language. But not every aspect of language is represented in the left hemisphere of right-handers. Adults who have had their left cerebral hemispheres surgically removed (a procedure sometimes required to treat seizures) lose most, but not all, of their linguistic competence. They typically lose the ability to speak and process complex syntactic patterns but retain some language comprehension ability. Clearly, it must be the right hemisphere that is responsible for whatever language-processing ability remains.

It has also been reported that right-handed patients who suffer damage to the right cerebral hemisphere exhibit difficulty in understanding jokes and metaphors in everyday conversation. These patients are able to provide only a literal or concrete interpretation of figurative sentences such as *He was wearing a loud tie*. They frequently misunderstand people because they cannot use loudness and intonation as cues to whether a speaker is angry, excited, or merely joking. Thus, the right hemisphere has a distinct role to play in normal language use.

Finally, consideration of language representation in the brains of left-handers makes matters even more complex. Contrary to what might be expected, few left-handers have a mirror image representation for language (that is, language localization in the right hemisphere).

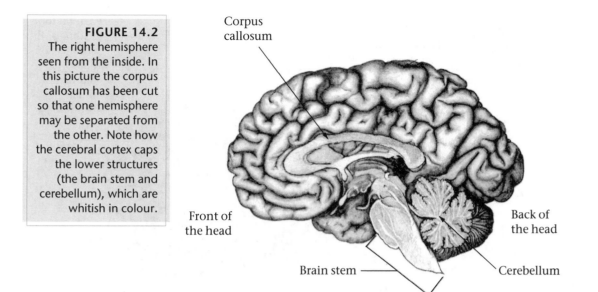

FIGURE 14.2
The right hemisphere seen from the inside. In this picture the corpus callosum has been cut so that one hemisphere may be separated from the other. Note how the cerebral cortex caps the lower structures (the brain stem and cerebellum), which are whitish in colour.

Corpus callosum

Front of the head

Back of the head

Brain stem

Cerebellum

Rather, they tend to show significant language representation in both hemispheres. Thus, left-handers are generally less lateralized for language.

To sum up, although the left and right hemispheres have different abilities and different responsibilities, complex skills such as language do not always fall neatly into one hemisphere or the other. Research into why this is the case constitutes an important part of neuroscience. This research promises to reveal much about the cerebral hemispheres and about the individual representations and processes that constitute language.

14.1.3 The lobes of the cortex

We have seen that the cerebral hemispheres make distinct contributions to the overall functioning of the brain. In addition, each hemisphere contains substructures that appear to have distinct responsibilities. The substructures of the cortex in each hemisphere are called **lobes**. The lobes of the cerebrum can be located with reference to prominent sulci, fissures (deep sulci), and gyri, which are useful as orientation points in much the same way that rivers and mountain ranges are useful in finding particular locations on a map. As can be seen in figure 14.3, the **central sulcus** (also called the fissure of Rolando) extends from the top of the cortex to another groove known as the **lateral fissure** (also called the Sylvian fissure). These two features are important in the delineation of the cerebral lobes. The **frontal lobe** lies in front of the central sulcus and the **parietal lobe** lies behind it. The **temporal lobe** is the area beneath the lateral fissure. The fourth lobe, the **occipital lobe**, is not clearly marked by an infolding of the cortex, but can be identified as the area to the rear of the **angular gyrus** (which has been found to play an important role in reading).

Figure 14.3 shows the left hemisphere of the brain. It indicates the location of each lobe and its specialized functions. (Some of the functions listed, such as those related to movement and the senses, are located in both hemispheres.) Assuming that this is the brain of a right-hander, it is also possible to identify those areas of the cortex that have a particular role to play in language processing, as we will see.

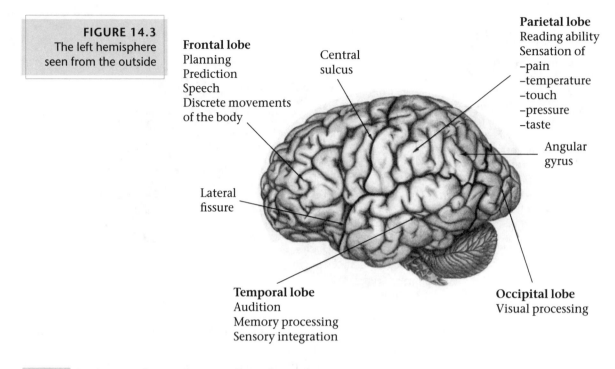

FIGURE 14.3
The left hemisphere seen from the outside

Frontal lobe
Planning
Prediction
Speech
Discrete movements
of the body

Central
sulcus

Parietal lobe
Reading ability
Sensation of
–pain
–temperature
–touch
–pressure
–taste

Angular
gyrus

Lateral
fissure

Temporal lobe
Audition
Memory processing
Sensory integration

Occipital lobe
Visual processing

14.2 Investigating the brain

Imagine that you could open the top of a living human being's skull and observe the brain while the individual is engaged in activities such as reading, writing, watching a hockey game, or having a heated argument. What would you see? The answer is—nothing! To the outside observer, the working brain shows no evidence of its activity. This is clearly a problem for the field of neurolinguistics, which requires the use of special investigative techniques to uncover the secrets of where and how language is processed in the brain. In addition, these special techniques must meet the ethical requirements of research on human subjects. While other neuroscientists are able to do much of their research using non-human animal subjects, this option is not available to neurolinguists.

Imposing as they may be, the problems of investigating the processing of language in the brain are not insurmountable. Recent decades have seen a number of technological advances that have greatly facilitated the investigation of the question, What is going on in the brain when people are engaged in language behaviour? In the following sections, we discuss some of the techniques of neurolinguistic investigation.

14.2.1 Autopsy studies

Until recently, the only way to study the brain was through **autopsy studies**. This technique was most often carried out with patients who were admitted to hospitals displaying a neurological disorder. Careful observations were made of a patient's behaviour, and subsequent to his or her death, the brain was examined to determine which areas were damaged. By comparing the area of brain damage and the type of disorder the patient had displayed while alive, neurologists could develop theories about the role of the damaged brain part(s) in normal brain functioning.

Language Matters **Paul Broca**

When Paul Broca conducted his first studies of aphasia in 1861, he was thirty-seven years old. He was already known for being a bold thinker and a strong supporter of Charles Darwin's new and controversial theory of evolution. Darwin had published his landmark book, *On the Origin of Species*, two years earlier. In that same year, 1859, Broca had founded the Anthropological Society of Paris. Broca's work on aphasia lasted less than ten years. By the 1870s, his interests had turned to other things. He founded the scientific journal *Revue d'anthropologie* in 1872 and was elected to the French Senate in 1879. He also advanced the treatment of brain aneurysms. Ironically and tragically, it was a brain aneurysm that caused his death in 1880 at the age of fifty-six. His scientific contributions, however, continue to have an impact almost 150 years later.

A famous example of this type of analysis comes from the work of Paul Broca, a nineteenth-century French neurologist. In 1860, Broca observed a patient who had been hospitalized for more than twenty years in Paris. For most of his hospitalization, the patient was almost completely unable to speak but appeared to understand everything that was said to him. Toward the end of his life (he died at age fifty-seven), he also developed a paralysis of the right arm and leg. Immediately after the patient's death (as a result of an unrelated infection), Broca examined the brain. It showed severe damage (called a **lesion**) in the lower rear area of the left frontal lobe. Broca concluded that because the patient was unable to speak, this part of the frontal lobe must normally be responsible for speech production. Since that time, many other autopsy studies have supported Broca's conclusions. This portion of the left frontal lobe is now called **Broca's area** (see figure 14.4, which shows this and other language-processing areas of the left hemisphere). As will be discussed in section 14.3.1, the impairment of the ability to speak as a result of brain damage is called **Broca's aphasia**.

FIGURE 14.4
Areas in the left hemisphere responsible for language processing. Damage to Broca's area is usually associated with non-fluent speech and difficulty processing complex syntactic patterns. Damage to Wernicke's area (see section 14.3.2) is usually associated with comprehension disturbances. Damage to the area around the angular gyrus results in reading impairment.

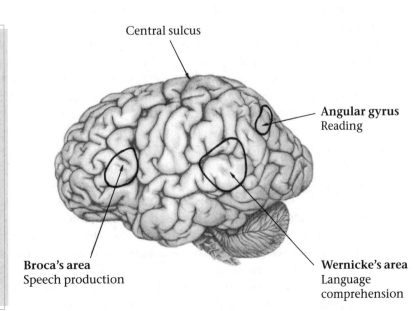

Central sulcus

Angular gyrus
Reading

Broca's area
Speech production

Wernicke's area
Language comprehension

Language Matters **Historic brains reanalyzed with modern imaging techniques**

In 1861, Paul Broca reported on two patients (Leborgne and Lelong) who showed what is now known as Broca's aphasia. The brains of both patients were preserved after their deaths and were reanalyzed in 2007 using high-resolution magnetic resonance imaging techniques by an American-French team led by Nina Dronkers of the University of California. The team reported that in both cases, the damage extended more toward the centre of the brain than Broca had supposed. Of course, because Broca chose not to dissect the brains but rather to leave them intact, he would not have been in a position to know this.

In the concluding paragraph of their article in the journal *Brain*, the authors write:

> Paul Broca began the study of the localization of function that has matured into the fields of neuropsychology, speech-language pathology, neurolinguistics and cognitive neuroscience. We now know that language and cognition are far more complicated than once thought and involve large networks of brain regions and connecting fibres. During Broca's time, though some may have proposed networks to support cognition, scientists could not have imagined the complexity of such systems, nor could Broca have supposed that his discovery would launch such remarkable explorations into the functions of the human brain. Fortunately, Broca had great foresight in preserving these historic brains and in some ways, Leborgne and Lelong can speak to us more eloquently now than they could over 140 years ago.

Source: N.F. Dronkers, O. Plaisant, M.T. Iba-Zizen, and E.A. Cabanis, "Paul Broca's Historic Cases: High Resolution MR Imaging of the Brains of Leborgne and Lelong," *Brain* 130, 5 (2007): 1432–1441.

14.2.2 Images of the living brain

Autopsy analysis has been and continues to be an important tool in the understanding of the brain. But an autopsy can be carried out only after the patient's death. Therefore, whatever information it reveals about the nature and extent of the patient's brain damage can no longer be of any use in his or her treatment.

One of the earliest techniques used to understand how the living brain processes language was pioneered in Canada by the Montréal-based neurosurgeon Wilder Penfield. This technique was developed to map the brain of a person who was about to undergo neurosurgery. Prior to the surgical procedure, a portion of the skull was removed and the surface of the brain was stimulated with electrodes carrying small electrical charges in order to map which areas of the individual's brain were involved in particular functions. This would allow the physicians to better assess how surgery might affect the post-operative abilities of the patient and assist the patient and family in weighing the risk-benefit ratio of the planned intervention. Such preoperative procedures greatly assisted early attempts to produce a functional map of the human cerebral cortex. Interestingly, it was also found that direct electrical stimulation of the brain resulted in temporary loss of neuronal functioning in the area rather than its enhancement.

Since Penfield's pioneering work in the 1950s, the sophistication of pre-operative techniques has increased greatly. It is now possible to insert electrodes deep into the living brain and isolate the function of a very small number of neurons (i.e., fewer than a thousand at a time). But this, of course, remains a very invasive technique that is only carried out on patients whose neurological impairment may require brain surgery. Other techniques that are, comparatively speaking, much less invasive have been devised and refined since Penfield's work.

Computerized axial tomography (also called **CT scanning**) is a technique that uses a narrow beam of X-rays to create brain images that take the form of a series of brain slices. CT scans offered neuroscientists their first opportunity to look inside a living brain. However, like autopsy studies, CT scanning provides a static image of the brain; it is most useful in identifying brain lesions and tumours. In order to study the brain in action, other techniques are required that are sensitive to dynamic activity.

One such dynamic technique is **positron emission tomography** (also called **PET** scanning). This technique capitalizes on one of the brain's many interesting properties—it is extremely hungry for glucose and oxygen. Although the brain accounts for only about 2 percent of total body weight, it consumes about 20 percent of the oxygen the body uses while at rest. This oxygen is, of course, carried to the brain by the blood.

In the PET technique, positron-emitting isotopes, which function as radioactive tracers, are injected into the arteries in combination with glucose. The rate at which the radioactive glucose is used by specific regions of the brain is recorded while the subject is engaged in various sorts of cognitive activities. These recordings are used to produce maps of areas of high brain activity associated with particular cognitive functions. Examples of such PET maps are represented in figure 14.5.

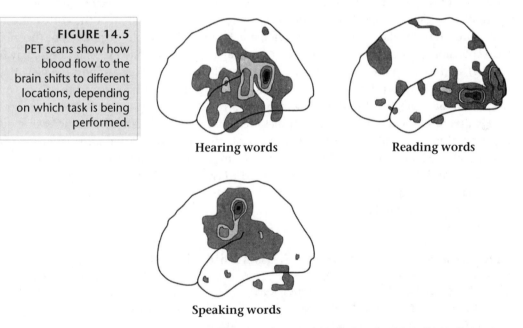

FIGURE 14.5
PET scans show how blood flow to the brain shifts to different locations, depending on which task is being performed.

Hearing words

Reading words

Speaking words

Source: Adapted from Gerald D. Fischbach, "Mind and Brain," *Scientific American* (September 1992). Reprinted by permission of Professor Marcus E. Raichle.

Although PET is much less invasive than electrical stimulation of the brain, which requires prior removal of portions of the skull, it is hardly a technique that most people would volunteer for because of the perceived risks associated with the injection of the radioactive tracer. The two techniques that we will review next also make use of changes in blood flow within the brain in order to associate cognitive function with specific brain regions, but they do so without injections.

At present, **functional magnetic resonance imaging (fMRI)** is the preferred means of gaining information about the functional anatomy of the brain. The technique also monitors increases in blood flow to specific areas of the brain. It does so by making use of the fact that blood is rich in iron. Although iron constitutes only 0.004 percent of the human body, 65 percent of it is found within the hemoglobin of red blood cells. The fMRI technique uses powerful magnetic fields to track this iron, and hence the blood flow within the brain. fMRI installations are currently very expensive and therefore not available at all research centres. Nevertheless, the technique has already yielded dramatic evidence of activity in particular parts of the brain during language-processing tasks.

A final extremely promising technique for the study of how language is processed in the brain is **magnetoencephalography**, or **MEG**. The MEG technique records very subtle changes in the magnetic fields generated within the brain. Although MEG also requires a very expensive apparatus, it has advantages over all the other techniques discussed so far. In contrast to PET, it is non-invasive, and like fMRI, it provides detailed information on which parts of the brain are involved in particular types of language processing (speaking, hearing, reading, or writing). Its key advantage is that it also provides time resolution that is greatly superior to that of fMRI. Using the MEG technique, researchers are able to gain a millisecond-by-millisecond record of how the brain responds to a stimulus event, such as the presentation of a single word. In this way, MEG provides detailed information on both the timing and location of activity in the brain.

Modern brain-imaging techniques such as fMRI and MEG have greatly increased our knowledge of where language processing takes place in the brain. It has been found, for example, that when subjects speak, much blood flows to the left hemisphere of the cortex and to Broca's area in particular. When subjects read, much blood flows to the occipital lobe (because it is responsible for visual processing), to the angular gyrus (which has a special role to play in reading), and to other areas of the left hemisphere. These observations support the view that the left hemisphere is primarily responsible for language in most people and that there are specific language areas within the left hemisphere.

Finally, functional brain imaging studies are playing an important role in increasing our understanding of the differences that might exist between the use of one's first language and that of a second language. Second-language processing has been shown to involve a wider variety of cortical sites. This supports the view that the less automatic nature of language use in a second language requires the involvement of diverse mental processes in addition to those specifically dedicated to language.

Language Matters Phrenology: A Discredited Theory

Franz Joseph Gall was born in 1758 in southwestern Germany. After moving to Vienna, he founded the field of phrenology, which can be considered to have three basic claims:

(1) The mind can be divided into discrete mental 'organs'.
(2) Particular development in any area results in expanded brain size in that location.
(3) This expansion presses on the skull, and produces bumps, which can then be identified and interpreted by the trained phrenologist.

Although it is extremely unlikely that Gall's original mental organs (e.g., combativeness, hope) are correct, the more general idea of mental organs remains a key part of current neuropsychological debate.

We now consider claims (2) and (3) to be discredited. But, interestingly, Gall was reported to be extraordinarily good at assessing the abilities and traits of complete strangers (allegedly using his method of feeling the skull). In his time, Gall gained both fame and notoriety. Forced to leave Vienna, he eventually settled in France, where his work was also discredited within scientific circles.

14.2.3 Learning from hemispheric connections and disconnections

In the techniques that have been described, information about language representation in the brain is gained through an investigation of the brain itself. In this section, we review an alternative approach—one that examines behaviour that can be associated with a particular brain hemisphere.

Dichotic listening studies

Dichotic listening studies have been extremely important in accumulating knowledge about the specialization of the cerebral hemispheres. The technique capitalizes on the property of the brain that we discussed in section 14.1.2—namely, that each hemisphere is primarily wired to the opposite side of the body (including the head). So most of the input to your right ear goes to the left hemisphere of your brain. Now, if the left cerebral hemisphere is indeed specialized for language processing in right-handers, these individuals should process language better through the right ear.

If you are right-handed, you will probably be able to verify this by observing the difference between holding a telephone to your right ear and holding it to your left ear during a conversation. When the phone is held to the right ear, the speech will seem louder and clearer. This phenomenon is known as the **right ear advantage**. In the laboratory technique, stereo earphones are used and different types of stimuli are presented to each ear. In general, the right ear shows an advantage for words, numbers, and Morse code, whereas the left ear shows an advantage for the perception of melodies and environmental sounds such as bird songs.

Split brain studies

If the left hemisphere is wired to the right ear, why is it possible to understand speech presented to the left ear? There are two reasons for this. The first is that the auditory pathways to the brain are not completely crossed—there are also secondary links between each hemisphere and the ear on the same side of the body. The second is that after the right hemisphere receives information from the left ear, that information can be transferred to the left hemisphere via the corpus callosum—the bundle of fibres that connects the two hemispheres.

Evidence concerning the crucial role that the corpus callosum plays in normal brain functioning comes from the study of patients who have had this pathway surgically severed.[1] Studies that have investigated the effects of this surgery on cognition—so-called **split brain experiments**—have provided dramatic illustrations of what happens when the hemispheres cannot communicate with one another.

It appears from the behaviour of split brain patients that although the right hemisphere does show some language understanding, it is mute. In one of the many split brain experiments, a patient is blindfolded and an object, such as a key, is placed in one hand. When the key is held in the right hand, the patient can easily name it, because the right hand is connected to the left hemisphere, which can compute speech output. However, when the key is placed in the left hand, the patient cannot say what it is. The right hemisphere, which receives information from the left hand, knows what is there (as is shown by the person's ability to draw the object with the left hand), but it can neither put this into words nor transfer the information across the severed corpus callosum to the left brain.

Split brain experiments have presented new and important knowledge about the functioning of the brain. In terms of overall investigative methodology, however, they are not quite as exotic as they seem. In fact, the logic of split brain experiments is identical to the logic employed by Broca in 1860. In both cases, the researcher endeavours to learn how the normal brain works by examining which functions are lost as a result of the brain damage. In the case of split brain studies, the damage is surgically induced. In the case of Broca's aphasia, disease caused an 'experiment in nature'. In section 14.3, we return to these experiments in nature and examine what they reveal about language representation in the brain. To view an interview with Dr. Michael Gazzaniga and split brain patient 'Joe', visit the Companion Website.

14.3 Aphasia

The term **aphasia** refers to the loss of language ability as a result of damage to the brain. The most common cause of aphasia is **stroke** (also called a **cerebrovascular accident**). A stroke occurs when the normal flow of blood to the brain is disrupted, preventing neurons from receiving oxygen and nutrients. Aphasia can also be caused by blows to the head, brain infection, brain tumours, and brain hemorrhage. Currently, aphasia affects more than 1 million people in North America. The syndrome is equally common in men and women, and is most likely to occur in persons over the age of fifty.

In general, the amount and type of aphasic disturbance that a patient will exhibit depends on the extent and location of the brain damage. Most individuals who suffer aphasic impairment experience a mixture of deficits in speaking, listening, reading, and writing. However, some other forms of aphasia are much more specific. In these more specific forms, particular skills are lost and others remain intact. The study of these specific aphasias can tell us much about the building blocks of language in the brain. In the next two sections, we discuss the two most widely studied specific aphasias.

14.3.1 Non-fluent aphasia

Non-fluent aphasia (also called **motor aphasia**) results from damage to parts of the brain in front of the central sulcus. Recall that part of the frontal lobe is concerned with motor activity and that the bottom rear portion of the frontal lobe (Broca's area) is responsible for the articulation of speech (see figure 14.4). Not surprisingly, then, non-fluent patients show slow, effortful speech production (hence the term *non-fluent*). The most severe form of non-fluent aphasia is **global aphasia**. In this type of aphasia, the patient is completely mute. Of the less severe forms, Broca's aphasia is the most informative with respect to language in the brain.

Language Matters Brain Size Is Not the Whole Story

Although humans have relatively large brains compared to most other creatures, an even more important factor than size may be the amount of cortex (related to the amount of folding into gyri and sulci) and the proportion of uncommitted cortex—areas not assigned a specific sensory function, such as vision or smell. The amount of uncommitted cortex is related to the degree of flexibility for learning. As shown in the diagram below, humans have a great deal of uncommitted cerebral cortex. Human intelligence is made possible by the richness of associations within that cortex.

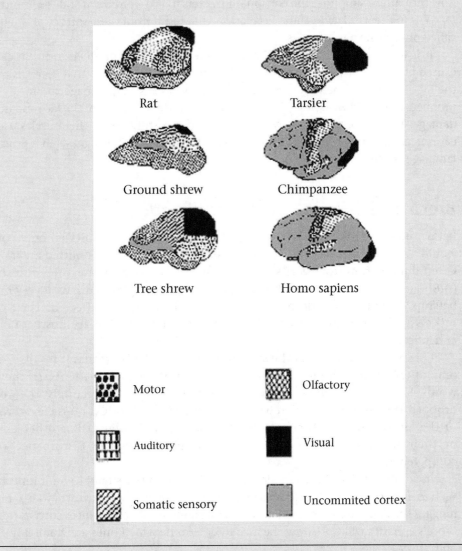

Rat

Tarsier

Ground shrew

Chimpanzee

Tree shrew

Homo sapiens

Motor

Olfactory

Auditory

Visual

Somatic sensory

Uncommited cortex

Source: Adapted from Wilder Penfield, *The Mystery of the Mind* © 1975 Princeton University Press, 2003 renewed PUP. Reprinted by permission of Princeton University Press.

The speech of Broca's aphasics is very halting. Patients have great difficulty in accurately producing the needed sounds to say a word. For example, a patient who wishes to produce the sentence in (1a) would be likely to produce an utterance like the one in (1b).

(1) *a.* It's hard to eat with a spoon.
   b. . . . har eat . . . wit . . . pun

The ellipsis dots (...) between the words in (1b) indicate periods of silence in the production of the utterance. Sentences produced at this slow rate also tend to lack normal sentence intonation. This common characteristic of the speech of Broca's aphasics is called **dysprosody**. Note how the patient simplifies the consonant clusters in the words *hard* and *spoon* and changes the /θ/ to /t/ in the word *with*. The speech errors that result from these sorts of phonemic errors are called **phonemic paraphasias**.

It is tempting to think that the impairment of speech production in Broca's aphasia is caused by the fact that Broca's area is adjacent to the motor strip that controls movement of the facial muscles. The problem with this hypothesis is that damage to Broca's area usually produces only mild weakness of the muscles on the opposite side of the face and no permanent damage. Yet for some reason, even people who can still control the muscles used in speech cannot use language properly after damage to Broca's area. This suggests that Broca's area has a language-specific responsibility.

Broca's aphasia as a syntactic disorder

Returning to the utterance in (1b), note that the patient also omits a number of words that would normally be used in this utterance. The words that are omitted are *it, is, to,* and *a.* Often dubbed **function words**, items of this sort belong to categories and subcategories (pronoun, copula verb, preposition, determiner, and so on) that have a very limited membership. They typically do not carry stress and cannot be inflected. Their omission by Broca's aphasics creates a telegraphic style of speech that consists mostly of nouns, verbs, and adjectives.

One possible account of the speech of Broca's aphasics is that it results from an economy of effort. Speech production is very effortful for these patients, so they use as few words as possible because they are 'paying' by the word. (Interestingly, the words that are dropped are the very items that we tend to omit from short text messages: "I will meet you in the airport lounge" becomes "Meet you airport lounge.") But other characteristics of their linguistic abilities point to a deeper cause—the disturbance of syntactic competence.

In addition to omitting function words, Broca's aphasics tend to omit inflectional affixes such as *-ing, -ed,* and *-en* in words such as *running, chased,* and *broken.* They also show difficulty judging the grammaticality of sentences. For example, given sentences such as the ones in (2), Broca's aphasics will not always be able to determine which ones are grammatical and which ones are not.

(2) *a.* The boy ate it up.
   b. *The boy ate up it.
   c. *Boy ate it up.
   d. The boy ate up the cake.

Finally, a close examination of the comprehension of Broca's aphasics offers further support for the view that there is a syntactic component to the disorder. Consider the following sentences.

(3) *a.* The mouse was chased by the cat.
   b. The dog was chased by the cat.
   c. The cat was chased by the mouse.

Broca's aphasics tend to interpret sentences such as (3a) correctly because knowledge about the behaviour of cats and mice helps them infer the meaning. However, they are unsure about sentences such as (3b), in which knowledge of the world is not a reliable guide to comprehension, and they tend to interpret a sentence such as (3c) as though it means 'The cat chased the mouse'. When we read a sentence like (3c), we recognize it as describing an unlikely event, but our interpretation is driven by the syntax of the sentence (including the presence of the auxiliary verb *be* and the preposition *by*), not by our knowledge of the world. Many Broca's aphasics appear not to have this ability.

These sorts of observations have led many neurolinguists to reconsider the traditional view that Broca's aphasia is simply a production deficit; evidently, it also affects comprehension. The possibility that Broca's aphasia also involves some central disturbance of syntactic competence is intriguing and may lead to a deeper understanding of how syntactic knowledge is represented in the brain. We will return to this question in section 14.4.

A final point about Broca's aphasia is of a less technical nature but is of great importance to the understanding of the syndrome as a whole. Most Broca's aphasics are acutely aware of their language deficit and are typically very frustrated by it. It is as though they have complete understanding of what they should say, but to their constant dismay, they find themselves unable to say it. This plight of Broca's aphasics is consistent with our understanding of the role of the frontal lobe, which is usually the site of lesions in the syndrome.

Broca's area plays an extremely important role in language; however, it does not seem to be involved in the semantic relationships between words and the relationship between units of language and units of thought. The neurological basis of these meaning relationships remains almost entirely unknown. From the analysis of non-fluent aphasia in general and Broca's aphasia in particular, however, we suspect that these semantic relationships are the responsibility of areas of the brain that lie behind the central sulcus—in the temporal and parietal lobes of the brain (see figure 14.3). This suspicion is supported by the type of language deficits associated with damage to the temporal and parietal lobes.

14.3.2 Fluent aphasia

The type of aphasia that results from damage to parts of the left cortex behind the central sulcus is referred to as **fluent aphasia** (or **sensory aphasia**). This type of aphasia stands in sharp contrast to non-fluent aphasia. Fluent aphasics have no difficulty producing language but have a great deal of difficulty selecting, organizing, and monitoring their language production.

The most widely studied type of fluent aphasia is called **Wernicke's aphasia**. The syndrome is named after the German physiologist Carl Wernicke, who, in 1874, published a now famous report of a kind of aphasia that was almost the complete opposite of Broca's aphasia. It was determined from autopsy data that this type of aphasia was associated with a lesion in the temporal lobe just below the most posterior (rear) portion of the lateral fissure. In severe cases, the lesion could also extend upward into the lower portion of the parietal lobe. This area of the brain is now known as **Wernicke's area** (see figure 14.4).

Language Matters: **Carl Wernicke**

Carl Wernicke was born in Prussia and was only twenty-six years old when he published his land-mark study of aphasia. At the time, he was a medical intern and had the opportunity to observe a number of persons with aphasia. Those patients who showed difficulty in language comprehension were of particular interest to him. Wernicke's ideas were very much influenced by his teacher and mentor, the neuroanatomist Theodor Meynert, who also taught Sigmund Freud in Vienna. Meynert's influence motivated Wernicke to link his theory of brain function to networks of specific brain locations. Wernicke went on to become an international authority in neuroanatomy and brain disorders. He completed his *Textbook of Brain Disorders* in 1883 and, together with three other authors, *Atlas of the Brain* in 1903. Wernicke only lived to be one year older than Paul Broca, and like Broca, his death may have been caused by damage to the brain. Wernicke died in 1905 at age fifty-seven as a result of injuries sustained in an accident while riding his bicycle through the forest.

In contrast to Broca's aphasics, Wernicke's aphasics are generally unaware of their deficit. Their speech typically sounds very good: there are no long pauses; sentence intonation is normal; function words are used appropriately; word order is usually correct. The problem is that the patient rarely makes any sense. The following is a conversation between an examiner (E) and a Wernicke's patient (P).

(4) *E:* How are you today, Mrs. A?
   P: Yes.
   E: Have I ever tested you before?
   P: No. I mean I haven't.
   E: Can you tell me what your name is?
   P: No, I don't I . . . right I'm right now here.
   E: What is your address?
   P: I cud /kʌd/ if I can help these this like you know . . . to make it.
      We are seeing for him. That is my father.

The patient in this conversation produces a number of errors, but most of them are different from the kinds of errors made by Broca's aphasics. While the patient is able to produce some well-formed structures (e.g., *no, I don't*), these structures appear intermittently amidst various unrelated fragments. Not only are these constructions unrelated to each other, they are also unrelated to the examiner's questions. It appears that the patient has no understanding of the questions being asked.

This patient displays a significant but not severe form of Wernicke's aphasia. Her speech appears to result from a semi-random selection of words and short phrases. In very severe cases of this syndrome, phonemes are also randomly selected and the result is speech that has the intonational characteristics of English but actually contains very few real words of the language. This is termed **jargon aphasia**.

The type of deficit found in Wernicke's aphasia leads us to a greater understanding and a deeper consideration of the nature of language comprehension. Wernicke's aphasia is primarily a comprehension deficit. But as we have seen, when comprehension breaks down, most of what we call language ability breaks down with it. Patients cannot express themselves because they cannot understand what they have just said and then use that understanding in the planning of what to say next. In a very real sense, these patients have lost contact with themselves (and therefore with the rest of the world). Wernicke's patients cannot have coherent trains of thought—the brain damage does not allow the parts of the train to be connected.[2] To view a video of a stroke survivor with fluent aphasia, visit the Companion Website.

14.3.3 Other types of aphasia

Fluent and non-fluent aphasia demonstrate how language functioning can be affected very differently, depending on which areas of the brain have been affected. However, it's important to acknowledge that persons experiencing aphasia do not always show symptoms that fall neatly into one diagnostic category or another. Moreover, it also important to recognize that various types of aphasia not mentioned in this chapter also exist. One such type, of considerable interest to linguists and non-linguists alike, is **anomia**, in which individuals experience word-finding difficulty (particularly the names of people and objects). In trying to access the word *matches*, for instance, they resort to 'things to make fire with', *tongs* are 'things you pick up with', and so on.

14.4 Acquired dyslexia and dysgraphia

Reading and writing involve a complex array of perceptual and motor skills. In this section, we will consider impairments of reading and writing that are caused by damage to the brain. The impairment of reading ability is called **acquired dyslexia** (or **acquired alexia**). The impairment of writing ability is called **acquired dysgraphia** (or **acquired agraphia**). In both cases, the term *acquired* indicates that the patient possessed normal reading and/or writing ability prior to brain damage and distinguishes the syndromes from developmental dyslexia and developmental dysgraphia, which deal with disturbances of reading and writing development in children.

14.4.1 Reading and writing disturbances in aphasia

Acquired dyslexia and dysgraphia typically accompany the aphasic syndromes that we considered in section 14.3. Most Broca's aphasics show writing disturbances that are comparable to their speaking deficits. In other words, a patient who cannot pronounce the word *spoon* will also not be able to write it correctly. The resulting error in writing (e.g., *poon*) is called a **paragraphia**. In spontaneous writing, Broca's aphasics also tend to omit function words and inflectional affixes. Finally, while the silent reading of Broca's aphasics is very good, their reading aloud shows the same telegraphic style as their spontaneous speech. These observations reinforce the view that the deficit in Broca's aphasia is much more than a speech articulation deficit. It is a production deficit at a very deep level of language planning.

Wernicke's aphasics also show reading and writing deficits that match their deficits in speaking and listening. The writing of Wernicke's aphasics is formally very good. They typically retain good spelling and handwriting. However, like their speaking, what they write makes little sense. Reading comprehension is also severely impaired in Wernicke's aphasia. Patients can see the letters and words but cannot make any sense of them. Again, the conclusion to be drawn is that Wernicke's aphasia, like Broca's aphasia, involves a central disturbance of language competence—the knowledge that underlies language functioning. In such cases of central language disturbance, whatever impairment the patient has in listening and speaking will be matched in reading and writing.

14.4.2 Acquired dyslexia as the dominant language deficit

In addition to the reading and writing deficits that accompany aphasia, there are many cases in which the disruption of reading and writing ability is the dominant symptom. This typically follows damage in and around the angular gyrus of the parietal lobe. An analysis of these types of disabilities has led to some very interesting theories about the nature of reading (at least in English).

Before we proceed to discuss two contrasting types of acquired dyslexia, it might be worthwhile to reflect on the abilities involved in the reading of words. Up to this point in the chapter, you have read over five thousand words. Some of these words (such as the function words) are very familiar to you, and you probably recognized them as wholes. But others, such as *angular gyrus*, are words that you probably read for the first time. How then could you know how to pronounce them? Many theorists believe that readers maintain a set of spelling-to-sound rules that enable them to read new words aloud. These rules are important in the development of reading ability and in the addition of new words to our reading vocabulary.

Phonological dyslexia is a type of acquired dyslexia in which the patient seems to have lost the ability to use spelling-to-sound rules. Phonological dyslexics can only read words that they have seen before. Asked to read a word such as *blug* aloud, they either say nothing or produce a known word that is visually similar to the target (e.g., *blue* or *bug*).

Surface dyslexia is the opposite of phonological dyslexia. Surface dyslexics seem unable to recognize words as wholes. Instead, they must process all words through a set of spelling-to-sound rules. This is shown by the kinds of errors they make. Surface dyslexics do not have difficulty reading words such as *bat* that are regularly spelled. However, they read irregularly-spelled words such as *yacht* by applying regular rules and thus producing /jɑtʃt/. The most interesting aspect of surface dyslexics' reading ability is that they understand what they produce, not what they see. For example, a surface dyslexic would be likely to read the word *worm* as /worm/ (and not /wərm/). When asked what the word means, the patient would answer, "The opposite of *cold*."

Data from acquired dyslexia allow researchers to build models that specify the components of normal reading ability and their relationship to each other. Clearly, this type of analysis plays a very important role in the development of our understanding of language, the mind, and the brain.

14.5 Linguistic theory and aphasia

Looking at aphasia in terms of linguistic theory gives us a new perspective on language in the brain. Linguistic theory has been traditionally concerned with the structure of language, not with how it is used in listening, speech production, reading, and writing. In contrast, the traditional way of looking at aphasia has been in terms of what the patient can and cannot do.

The involvement of theoretical linguists in the study of aphasia has caused a minor revolution in the field. Aphasia researchers have begun to think about the deficit in terms of the loss of semantic features, phonological rules, and perhaps syntactic tree structures. Theoretical linguists have also found that the study of aphasia offers an important area for testing theoretical distinctions such as the one between derivational and inflectional affixes. In this section, we will look at some of the areas in which the marriage of theoretical linguistics and neurolinguistics has been most fruitful. This fruitfulness has usually meant an increase in the sophistication of the questions that are asked about aphasia. It has also meant the discovery of new and often bizarre aphasic phenomena.

14.5.1 Features, morphemes, and meaning

In the area of phonology, we have found that the phonemic paraphasias of Broca's aphasics usually differ from the target phoneme by only one distinctive feature (recall example [1] in section 14.3.1, *with* → /wɪt/, where the distinguishing feature is [continuant]) and can therefore be easily described by phonological rules. Observations such as these lead us to believe that phonological features and rules might be good tools with which to characterize how language is represented and produced.

In the area of morphology, the study of aphasia has offered empirical support for the theoretical distinction between inflection and derivation. As we have discussed, Broca's aphasics show a sensitivity to this distinction in their omission of affixes in speech. Inflectional affixes such as plural *-s* and past tense *-ed* are commonly dropped, but derivational affixes such as *-er*, *-ize*, and *-ment* are usually retained. Perhaps most interesting is the tendency of some aphasics to produce the 'basic' forms of morphemes in reading and repetition. Asked to repeat the word *illegal*, for example, some aphasics will produce *inlegal*, using the most basic form of the negative prefix rather than the allomorph that should occur before a base beginning with /l/. Such errors point to the possibility that the negative prefix has *in-* as its underlying form even in words where it is pronounced as *il-*. This in turn points to an elegant way to represent linguistic competence and provides a possible insight into how language is processed in the brain.

The study of aphasia also has the potential to shed light on the nature of semantic representations. Most of the work in this area has concentrated on the many subvarieties of acquired dyslexia. In a syndrome known as **deep dyslexia**, patients produce reading errors that are semantically related to the word that they are asked to read. Given the word *mother*, for example, a deep dyslexic may read *father*.

The detailed study of semantic deficits associated with brain damage has also led to some very surprising discoveries. Most aphasics and dyslexics find abstract words much more difficult to process than concrete words. But there have been reports of concrete word dyslexia in which the patient shows exactly the opposite problem (having difficulty with concrete words such as *table*). There has even been a report of a patient who shows a selective inability to read words that refer to fruits and vegetables.

14.5.2 Agrammatism

In section 14.3.1, we observed that many theorists now believe that Broca's aphasia involves a syntactic deficit. The syndrome that is characterized by telegraphic speech has been given the name **agrammatism**—to indicate that grammatical ability has been lost. Agrammatism is the aphasic disturbance that has been most studied by linguists. It is characterized by the omission of function words such as *it*, *is*, *to*, and *a*; by the omission of inflectional affixes; and by comprehension deficits in cases where the correct interpretation of a sentence is dependent on syntax alone.

In recent years, many linguists have become involved in the problems of characterizing the agrammatic deficit. These problems have raised both specific questions, such as exactly what a function word is, and general questions, such as whether it is possible to lose syntax. The involvement of linguists along with clinicians has also generated cross-linguistic studies of agrammatism that provide interesting insights into the interaction between characteristics of the syndrome and characteristics of particular languages.

14.5.3 The loss of syntactic competence

Another, much more general, challenge is to define what it means to possess syntactic competence such that we can speak of its loss. This challenge has forced researchers to address the question, What is the essence of syntactic knowledge? Is it the hierarchical arrangement of elements? Is it the representation of abstract entities such as the +Q feature and traces?

Some researchers have suggested that agrammatism involves the loss of the ability to deal with the details of syntactic structure, especially when a Move operation has occurred. They claim that agrammatics rely on word order rather than structure to interpret sentences and that they employ a default strategy that treats the first NP as the agent. This strategy works reasonably well for simple sentences in which the first NP can be assigned the thematic role of agent and the second NP can be assigned the role of undergoer (theme), as in sentence (5a). It results in miscomprehension, however, for sentences such as (5b) and (5c), where the first NP does not have the role of agent.

> **(5)** *a.* The girl kissed the boy.
>   *b.* The girl was kissed.
>   *c.* It was the girl that the boy kissed.

Other researchers have argued that agrammatism does not involve the loss of syntactic competence, but rather an alteration of that competence. They have claimed that agrammatics have full-fledged syntactic structure but can no longer represent the traces that indicate an NP's position in deep structure. As a result, they are unable to recognize that the subject NP in (5b) is the undergoer since they do not realize that it is the complement of the verb in deep structure.

14.5.4 Agrammatism in other languages

Data from other languages has suggested that the original characterization of agrammatism as a syndrome in which function words and inflectional affixes are lost may not reflect the true nature of this phenomenon.

In English, affixes are typically attached to a base that is itself a free form. The past form of the verb *watch*, for example, is created by the addition of *-ed*; the third person singular is created by the addition of *-s*. However, not all languages work this way. In Semitic languages, such as Hebrew, the base is typically a string of three consonants, which is unpronounceable in its uninflected form. Inflected words are produced by inserting vowels into this triconsonantal 'skeleton'. For example, the Hebrew root for the verb *to write* is /ktv/. The masculine third person present form of the verb is /kɔtɛv/ and the masculine third person past form is /katav/. If Hebrew agrammatics simply 'lose' inflectional affixes the way they do in English, they should not be able to produce any verbs. As it turns out, Hebrew agrammatics do produce verbs, but instead of dropping inflectional forms, they choose among them (usually selecting the third person singular form). This sort of evidence has provided a convincing argument against the view that agrammatic language results from a simple economy of effort. Rather, it seems that it is a linguistic deficit that involves the mis-selection of linguistic forms. It is only in languages such as English, where the base is also a free form, that the agrammatism is characterized by affix omission.

14.6 Language in the brain: what's where?

We have seen that, in an important sense, normal language use involves the integrated functioning of the entire cortex. Even right-handers who are strongly left lateralized for language show some language deficit in cases of damage to the right hemisphere. Finally, virtually all forms of aphasia are accompanied by word-finding difficulties. This observation suggests that the storage and retrieval of word forms may be diffusely represented in the brain.

Recent evidence has suggested that lexical knowledge is centred in the temporal lobes. Yet, as was originally discussed by Sigmund Freud in his 1891 book *On Aphasia* (Freud studied aphasia before turning to his better-known work on psychoanalysis), knowledge of a word can be characterized as a rich set of associations. Some of these are actually part of the word—for example, what it looks like, what it sounds like, how it is pronounced, and how it is written. But other aspects are not necessarily linguistic—for example, what the referent of the word feels, or sounds, or smells, or looks like. Given these considerations, it is hardly surprising that the representation of a word in the brain may best be considered to be a network rather than a single entity.

In the past decade, an interesting view of how words are represented in the brain has been put forward using the concept of a **cell assembly**. This concept, first developed by Donald Hebb at McGill University in the 1940s, claims that neurons that are repeatedly activated together come to be associated with each other, creating a cell assembly. Individual words in the brain could each be represented as cell assemblies of this sort and could differ in their brain location in accordance with the nature of the associations that form a particular word's assembly (or network). Figure 14.6 shows a suggestion for how action-related words (e.g., *run, jump*) could differ from object-related words (e.g., *barn, tree*). As shown in this figure, action words are represented more anteriorly and object words are represented more posteriorly. Of course, many, but not all, action words are verbs and many, but not all, object-related words are nouns. Thus, this difference may coincide with a general verb-versus-noun difference in how words are represented in the brain.

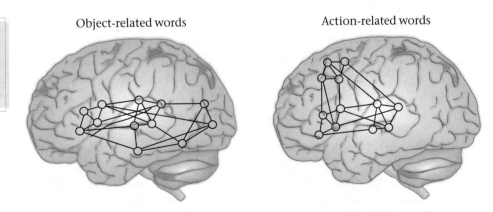

FIGURE 14.6
A view of how words could be represented in the brain

Object-related words   Action-related words

Source: Adapted from the work of F. Pulvermüller. Used by permission of Friedrich Pulvermüller.

There seems to be good evidence that the verb-noun distinction does correspond to differences in brain location. There is less consensus, however, for the reason why. It could be that because verbs are typically associated with actions, they are represented more anteriorly (near the motor strip). Or it could be purely related to their grammatical category. Recently, some scholars have made this latter claim and supported it with evidence from case studies which suggest that patients with anterior lesions are more likely to have difficulty with verbs, whereas patients with posterior lesions are more likely to have difficulty with nouns.

The issue of *why* certain areas of the brain are associated with certain aspects of language is not restricted to the representation of words. We have seen, for example, that Broca's area is particularly involved in syntactic processing. Is this because there is a special place for syntax in the brain? Is it perhaps that syntactic processing represents very complex sequencing, and Broca's area is related to the planning of complex motor sequences in both phonology and syntax? These are questions that are currently under intense debate among neurolinguists.

The nature of the debate can serve to remind us that ultimately, the goal of neurolinguistics is to understand, in neurological terms, what language is. Knowing *where* certain functions are performed in the brain is only the first step. What we really want to understand is how those functions are performed by the brain and why, in the development of our species, particular locations (perhaps because of their cell organization or patterns of neuronal connections) have advantages over others for particular language representations and tasks.

Summing up

This chapter is concerned with how language is represented and processed in the human brain. **Dichotic listening** studies and **split brain** studies have shown that the left hemisphere of the brain carries most of the responsibility for language processing in right-handed individuals. Neuroscientists have also used **autopsy studies, computerized axial tomography, positron emission tomography, functional magnetic resonance imaging**, and **magnetoencephalography** to determine the relationship between particular areas of the left hemisphere and specific language functions. It has been found that **Broca's area** is primarily responsible for speech production, **Wernicke's area** is primarily responsible for language comprehension, and the area surrounding the **angular gyrus** plays an important role in reading. Most of our knowledge concerning language representation in the brain comes from the study of **aphasia**— language disturbance resulting from damage to the brain. Neurolinguists, trained in both linguistics and neuroscience, carefully examine the manner in which linguistic competence is affected by brain damage. Their goal is to increase our understanding of how linguistic knowledge is coded in brain matter and how this knowledge is used in the processes of language comprehension and production.

Notes

1 The callosumectomy is a rare surgical procedure used to treat severe forms of epilepsy. It prevents epileptic seizures from spreading to both hemispheres.

2 It is interesting to note that Wernicke's patients also have difficulty planning and executing many types of sequenced behaviour, such as purchasing groceries, getting home by bus, or washing laundry.

Recommended reading

Gardner, Howard. 1975. *The Shattered Mind*. New York: Knopf.

Ingram, John C. L. 2007. *Neurolinguistics: An Introduction to Spoken Language Processing and Its Disorders*. New York: Cambridge University Press.

Kemmerer, David. 2015. *Cognitive Neuroscience of Language*. New York: Psychology Press.

Stemmer, Brigitte, and Harry A. Whitaker, eds. 1998. *Handbook of Neurolinguistics*. New York: Academic Press.

Stemmer, Brigitte, and Harry A. Whitaker, eds. 2008. *Handbook of the Neuroscience of Language*. New York: Elsevier.

Exercises

1. What distinguishes the human brain from a non-human brain?

2. In what ways can the cerebral hemispheres be considered to be two separate brains?

3. Below is an unlabelled diagram of the left hemisphere. Choose four contrasting colours and colour each lobe of the cortex. Use arrows to point to the central sulcus, the lateral fissure, and the angular gyrus. Finally, use a pencil to indicate areas of lesion that would result in Broca's aphasia, Wernicke's aphasia, and acquired dyslexia. Label these areas.

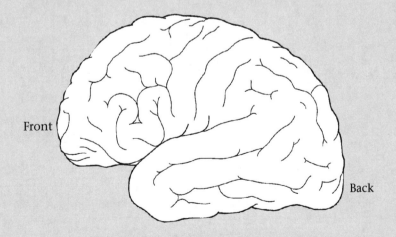

Front

Back

4. What are the relative advantages and disadvantages of the various techniques used to investigate the brain? Consider ethics, cost, intrusiveness, and type of information yielded.

5. What do dichotic listening tests tell us about the specialization of the cerebral hemispheres? Can you think of types of stimuli that would be interesting to present dichotically?

6. Do you think it is possible to learn how the normal brain functions by studying brain-damaged patients? What can the study of aphasia tell us about normal language competence?

7. Contrast the differences in behaviour between fluent and non-fluent aphasics. What could explain these differences?

8. Describe the differences between phonological and surface dyslexia.

9. Many researchers have claimed that agrammatism involves a loss of syntactic knowledge. Imagine a type of aphasia that involves a loss of *phonological* knowledge. How would patients with this type of aphasia behave?

To learn more about the topics discussed in this chapter, visit the Companion Website for *Contemporary Linguistic Analysis*.

Language in social contexts

They talks with grammar.

A NOVA SCOTIAN DESCRIBING OTHER NOVA SCOTIANS

SOCIOLINGUISTICS is the study of the relationship between society and language. Language is central to how we deal with other people, and the way we use language says a lot about us. Details of word choice, syntax, and pronunciation reveal us to be members of a particular **speech community**—a group of people who share social conventions, or **sociolinguistic norms**, about language use.

When I speak English, most people can tell I'm North American (I pronounce *schedule* with a [sk] sound), Canadian (I rhyme *shone* with *gone*, not *bone*), and probably from Québec (I drink *soft drinks* and keep my socks in a *bureau*). And language also tells people with shared norms something about their place in the speech community: I'm probably under eighty (I pronounce *whale* and *wail* the same), but I'm definitely not young (I almost never end sentences with a questionlike rising intonation). When I speak French, most people can tell I'm probably from Québec (I pronounce *tu* with a [ts] sound), from the southwest of the province (by the way I say *garage*), and definitely English (I have English [r] and I say *so* a lot).

Of course, members of my speech community don't have to wait for a sentence about whales, schedules, and beverages to place me. Dozens of features mark my speech. Some are **salient** (noticeable) and recognized within the community as having a particular social meaning; they're also called sociolinguistic **markers**. Other features, such as vowel height or the choice between *used to* and *would*, are 'below the radar' but can be shown by large-scale study to be associated with particular social characteristics; these features are called sociolinguistic **indicators**. A speech community's norms affect both markers and indicators. Because these norms are shared by all members of a speech community, sociolinguists study the language of the community, not the speech (or perceptions of the speech) of a single speaker.

These broad definitions allow us to speak of speech communities of very different sizes. English Montréal is a speech community—its members share norms about what to call soft drinks and whether *marry* and *merry* are pronounced the same (they're not, unlike in most of the rest of Canada). But in a sense, 'all speakers of English' form a (very big) speech community—we share norms about putting adjectives before nouns, for example, and we can usually more or less understand each other. This criterion—**mutual intelligibility**—is what linguists usually use to determine whether people are speaking 'the same language' or not. If people from two different places—say, Birmingham, Alabama, and Birmingham, England—can

> ### Language Matters **One Commercial for Two Languages**
>
> Urdu and Hindi are considered separate languages because they're spoken in different countries—Urdu in Pakistan, Hindi in India. But they're mutually intelligible, so speakers of both languages can understand Bollywood films (in Hindi) on Sunday afternoon television here in Canada. One barrier to communication is that the languages have different writing systems (Arabic for Urdu, Devangari for Hindi). Clever Canadian advertisers get around that problem by using neither system. Instead, words in commercials are often phonetically spelled using the Latin alphabet, which viewers are familiar with from English.

understand each other, then they're speaking the same language, and the systematic differences in their speech reflect different **dialects**, or subsets, of the same language.

In practice, the criterion of mutual intelligibility is sometimes pushed to the side by political considerations. Speakers of Swedish and Norwegian, for example, can understand each other, but Swedish and Norwegian are considered two different languages because they're found in two different countries. (As the linguist Max Weinreich may have once said, "A language is a dialect with an army and a navy.") The Chinese situation is the opposite—Cantonese and Mandarin are *not* mutually intelligible and are therefore two separate languages, but their speakers are encouraged to think of them as 'dialects' because they are spoken in the same country and words of similar meaning in each language are written using the same characters.

Another aspect of the naming issue is that many non-linguists reserve the term *language* for what linguists might call the **standard** variety—the language taught in school, used in formal writing, and often heard from newscasters and other media figures who wish to project authority (or at least competence). All other varieties of the language—those we call **non-standard**—get called 'dialects', as do many full languages spoken by less powerful groups around the world. There are almost always value judgments attached to this practice: the standard is seen as good, pure, clear, and rule-governed—a 'real language'—whereas 'dialects' are perceived as broken, chaotic, limited, or impermanent. Many sociolinguists avoid the naming problem by using the value-neutral term **variety** for any subset of a language: the standard variety, as well as regional, class, or ethnic varieties. Others reclaim the term *dialect* and speak of the standard dialect, as well as **regional dialects**, **sociolects**, or **ethnolects**. They'll often say, "Everybody has a dialect."

Two other naming problems related to dialects need to be cleared up. Non-linguists often call non-standard varieties **slang**. To linguists, 'slang' refers only to *words*—either words new to the language or old words or phrases with new meanings. Slang is usually associated with younger speakers—in fact, a good indicator that a slang term is finished is when middle-aged university professors start using it. Most slang is 'faddish' or short-lived—you don't hear many people saying *groovy* or *the bee's knees* anymore, and *fire* and *fam* will probably sound dated by the time you read this. Some slang terms hang on, however, and become part of the standard language—*mob, freshman*, and *glib* all started out as slang. Unlike slang, a dialect is usually distinct in multiple linguistic domains—lexicon, morphology, syntax, and phonology/phonetics.

A second term sometimes used for dialects is **accent**, which linguists use to refer only to pronunciation. Although dialects usually include accent differences, dialect and accent boundaries don't have to match. For example, many people speak Standard English (in terms of grammar and lexicon), but with an accent reflecting their ethnicity, class, and/or region—think of Martin Luther King, Jr., or CBC personality Rick Mercer. The reverse situation (standard accent, non-standard grammatical features) is much less common. Try imitating Prince William saying, "Ain't no woman like the one I got."

To really study how language and society affect each other, we need to consider the social characteristics of the person speaking—such things as region, gender, or class—as well as the social relationships between participants in a conversation and the treatment of language by societies. Each of these objects of study requires its own methods and approaches.

15.1 Language variation and social distinctions

It's sometimes said that in any society, social distinctions will develop, and where there are social distinctions, we can expect to find them reflected in linguistic distinctions. The branch of linguistics that tries to measure and explain that connection is known as variation theory, or **variationist sociolinguistics**.

A core idea in this approach is **structured variation**. In any language variety, there are many linguistic features that can be produced in more than one way. For example, many varieties of English have more than one way to pronounce the sounds represented by the letter combination '*th*' in *thin, that, brother,* or *path*. In this case, '*th*' is what we call the **variable**—the thing with several possible realizations. Do people say *brother*, or *brudder*, or *bruvver*? Each possible realization (interdental fricative, dental stop, labiodental fricative, etc.) is called a **variant**. Across all the words of the language, the variant that is likely to surface depends on **linguistic factors** like position in the word or voicing. A variable is something like a phoneme, or underlying representation; the variants are like allophones, or surface realizations; and the linguistic factors include what phonologists would call phonetic environments.

But then sociolinguists complicate the analysis, in an attempt to model the complicated situation of language in use. In phonology, rules are usually assumed to apply *every time* a particular environment is found. In other words, they're **categorical**. In sociolinguistic analyses, the 'rules', or **constraints**, are usually **probabilistic**—more or less likely to apply. So '*th*' might be more *likely* to be pronounced as a stop at the beginning of the word, or when voiced, or even with particular lexical items like *this* or *that*, but each linguistic factor explains only part of the variation. At its most complex, sociolinguistic research considers all these factors together, and with the help of computer programs, calculates how much each factor contributes to the likely outcome (see figure 15.1).

In our '*th*' example—and in much variationist work—the focus is on linguistic factors affecting variation. In fact, variationist sociolinguistics is sometimes described as 'too much linguistics and not enough socio'. But the 'socio' component does show up in two ways. First, variationist research is usually conducted among speakers of non-standard varieties; this research has made important contributions to our understanding that non-standard varieties are, like the standard, governed by subtle and complex linguistic rules. In fact, a well-known early paper by William Labov, a pioneer of sociolinguistics, is entitled "The Logic of Nonstandard English." Second, variationist work also concerns itself with **social factors** that influence variation in a structured way. In the case of '*th*', the choice of variant might be affected by the speaker's age, sex, or degree of education.

We assume some variation within individual speakers (**intra-speaker variation**), especially in terms of style shifting, but most of this work looks at how speech varies according

FIGURE 15.1
Method: variation-
ist sociolinguistics

As in other branches of linguistics, the needs of researchers determine how the research proceeds.

1. **Find the speech community.** We may investigate our local community, or we may be interested in a specific community that can contribute to our knowledge of a particular issue (ethnicity, isolation, etc.). We then find **informants** (also known as **consultants**), people from the speech community who are willing to be recorded.

2. **Collect data.** Studying variation usually calls for large amounts of fairly natural language. This can come from existing material (such as letters), but often we use **sociolinguistic interviews**, with questions that encourage informants to forget that someone from a university is recording their every word. Time-tested questions include *Were you ever in a situation where you thought, 'This is it, I'm going to die'?* and *Did you ever get blamed for something you didn't do?* Sometimes, we elicit more formal speech by having informants read written passages or word lists.

3. **Analyze the data you collect.** Some variables, such as vowel height, are **gradient**, with a full range of values possible. These are plotted through acoustic analysis, with separate vowel plots developed for each segment of the community (or even each informant). Others, such as the choice between fricative or stop for *th* or between *going to* and *will* for future marking, are **discrete**, with easily distinguishable separate variants. These are usually coded for variant and a range of social or linguistic factors.

Consider an example from the Ottawa Intensifier Project's work on online subcultures. We looked at intensifiers—the words people use before adjectives to mean *very*. We found nearly ten thousand sentences with adjectives and coded each for the variant, if any (*very, really, way, so, totally,* etc.); location of adjective in the sentence; type of adjective; gender of the informant; and subculture. Each sentence ended up looking something like this:

      ravmc   *That's a really kickass song.*

The codes on the left mean that the variant used was *really,* the adjective occurred in *attributive* position (before a noun) and was a *value* judgment, and the sentence was written by a *male country* fan. When we examined which variants went with which factors, we found strong patterns of variation depending on gender and subculture (e.g., tween girls are definitely leading a change toward the use of *so*). We also found shared linguistic factors, no matter who was using a variant (e.g., people rarely used *so* when the adjective was before a noun, as in *That was a so cool movie*).

to speakers' social characteristics. In other words, researchers are looking at **inter-speaker variation**. In theory, any speaker characteristic could have linguistic consequences; in practice, research has shown that several social factors are particularly important. In the following sections, we look at those factors one by one.

15.2 Time

All spoken languages change. Elsewhere in this book, you've explored the linguistic processes involved in that change. Sociolinguists are interested in the relationship between change over time and the variation found in a community at a single point in time. Think of big changes, like the Great Vowel Shift of earlier English. Presumably, people in England didn't all go to bed one night pronouncing their words one way and wake up the next morning with a completely different vowel system. At some point, either everybody used both the old and the new pronunciation, or some people always used the old way and some always used the new, or some combination of those two.

In other words, change over time results in variation in each time period. Add to that the reasonable assumption that people's basic grammar doesn't change that much during their lifetime, and you get a powerful insight: you can 'see' change happening by looking at the differences between old and young speakers. This idea, called the **apparent time hypothesis**, has opened up whole new areas of research: as one major sociolinguistic article puts it, we can use the present (variation) to explain the past (change). This is particularly true if we use the tools of variation—sound recordings and measurement tools—and probabilities.

Consider *whale* and *wail*. Over a *very* long period of time, English speakers have moved toward pronouncing them the same. What were once two separate phonemes—/w/ and /ʍ/—have **merged**. We can see this change happening by looking at some findings of research by Canadian sociolinguist Jack Chambers. As the graph in figure 15.2 shows, older speakers have lower rates of merger, while younger speakers almost always merge the two sounds.

FIGURE 15.2
Percentage of speakers with [w], not [ʍ], in words like *which* and *whine* in central Canada, by age

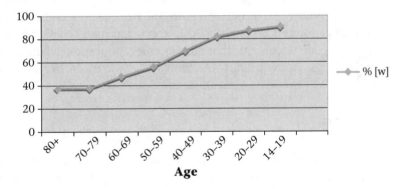

Source: J.K. Chambers,"Patterns of Variation Including Change," in *The Handbook of Language Variation and Change*, ed. J.K. Chambers, Peter Trudgill, and Natalie Schilling-Estes (Oxford: Blackwell, 2002), fig. 14.5, p. 360. © Blackwell Publishing 2002. Reprinted by permission of Blackwell Publishing.

Changes like this are easy to see when they involve an entire segment—two formerly separate sounds merge or an alternative pronunciation dies out or is born. A lot of sound change is subtler than that, especially when we look at vowels. Vowels may shift in the vowel space, sometimes so slightly that the change is only evident through acoustic analysis. Modern technology has let us track some big changes that are happening in North American vowel pronunciations. One dramatic shift, affecting about 40 million speakers in the U.S. Midwest, is known as the Northern Cities Shift (see figure 15.3). Younger speakers in cities like Detroit, Chicago, or Buffalo are involved in this complex vowel shift. Their pronunciation of *hot*, for example, sounds to Canadians like *hat*, while their *Ann* sounds like *Ian*.

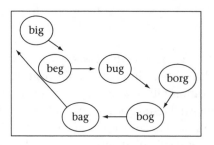

FIGURE 15.3
The vowel movements of the U.S. Northern Cities Shift

Recently, sociolinguists have identified what they call the Canadian Shift, which is almost the opposite of the shift happening in the U.S. Midwest. Young urban Canadians have a lower or 'back-er' pronunciation for some vowels, so that the vowel of *bet* moves toward *bat*, and the vowel of *bat* becomes something like *bought*. Vowels in Canada and in the U.S. Midwest have actually 'moved' far enough that speakers of the two dialects hear the wrong word when they speak to each other. Canadians actually hear *bet* when Americans say *bat*. And American linguists snicker when Canadian linguists talk about the letter *s*. What's interesting about these shifts is that they show the interaction between time and place. The sound shifts show change over time, but they are restricted to pre-existing dialect areas.

The findings of apparent-time studies can sometimes be confirmed by **real-time studies**. In Montréal, speakers who were first interviewed by sociolinguists in the 1970s have been revisited and re-interviewed several times now. For some of their variant linguistic features, apparent-time findings are confirmed; for others, researchers have found some change even in individual speakers, especially if they already used both old and new variants when first interviewed. We can also work farther into the past. Older recordings of speakers of Québec French and African American English (AAE) show that many contemporary features have a long history. Work on documents that provide clues about spoken language shows the same thing. For example, the contemporary AAE term *mother wit*, meaning 'common sense', is found in letters from the 1790s.

15.3 Place

Geographical location is probably the most-studied social factor affecting variation. If it's true that we talk *like* who we talk *with*, it makes good sense that we will share linguistic features with our neighbours. **Dialectology**, the study of regional differences in language, is the oldest major branch of sociolinguistics (see figure 15.4). Early linguistics had a major historical focus, and linguists studied traditional rural dialects because those varieties preserved older speech features and thus held many clues to earlier stages of the language.

15.3.1 The origins of North American English

In Europe, where much early dialect study was done, countries long settled by speakers of the same language have had the time to develop distinct regional varieties. These varieties reflect settlement patterns that are often more than a thousand years old. For example, the major dialect areas of England still largely match the areas settled by different groups—Angles, Saxons, and Jutes—about fifteen hundred years ago. Natural barriers, such as mountain ranges, have helped limit inter-dialect contact, thus allowing dialects to develop along their own distinct paths.

FIGURE 15.4 Method: dialectology	*The goals of dialectology have been to show where particular speech features are found and to discover the boundaries between dialect regions. But dialectology has also tried to find the most traditional speech in each region, based on the assumption that regional dialects are most distinct when they haven't been influenced by their neighbours or by mainstream language. These goals tend to lead to specific methods.*

1. **Find the speakers in a region with the least outside influence.** Traditionally, these were rural older men who had spent their whole lives in the same area, sometimes known as NORMs (non-mobile older rural males).

2. **With each speaker, run through a (very long!) questionnaire of lexical features known to show regional differentiation.** You probably know a few of these already—do you say *running shoes, tennis shoes,* or *sneakers? Hoagies, grinders, subs,* or *hero sandwiches? Soda, pop,* or *soft drink?*

3. **Record each speaker's responses.** In the days before tape recorders, fieldworkers would write these responses down and make notes on pronunciation.

4. **Tabulate the results from lots of questionnaires.** Map out each variant. If you can, draw boundaries between different areas. For example, you might find a boundary between *sneaker* users and *running shoe* users somewhere in Québec or the Maritimes. These boundary lines are called **isoglosses.**

5. **Use your accumulated data to propose dialect areas and boundaries.** If you find a lot of isoglosses in the same place (an **isogloss bundle**), you've probably found a boundary between dialect areas.

Dialect studies in the early and mid-twentieth century collected huge amounts of data, more than could be analyzed with the technology of the time. Dialectologists are still analyzing that earlier material today, using advanced computer modelling.

The same basic combination of factors—origins of the early settlers and limits on intervariety contact—also explains dialect differences in North American English. Newfoundland, England's oldest North American colony, was settled by fishermen from southwestern England (the West Country) and, later, Irish seamen. The New England area of the United States was settled largely by people from East Anglia. Most of the people who settled along the coast farther south came from the south of England, while the later arrivals, who moved into the inland Appalachian area, came mainly from the north of England and northern Ireland. Each group brought the speech patterns of its home area with it. Presumably some mixing took place; perhaps some of the uncommon or distinct features of settler dialects were worn down over time, a process known as **dialect levelling**.

The English of New Zealand, which was formed much more recently and is thus easier to study, sheds some light on how levelling works. Researchers there describe a three-stage process: the original settler generations kept their home dialects, the next generation chose

Language Matters The *r*-ful Truth about American English

A good example of colonial-era variation is '*r*-lessness' (which makes modern British English *far* sound like *fah* to most Canadians). By 1776, this feature was already widespread in the south of England, and this was reflected in North American patterns. New England and the coastal South were settled by people from the south of England who maintained social and economic ties with England, and these areas were *r*-less (and, to some extent, still are). Other North American dialects were (and still are) '*r*-ful'.

somewhat randomly from all the linguistic options available, and the third generation levelled out the diversity in favour of the most frequent variant in most cases. Probably something similar happened in North America, centuries before dialectologists and tape recorders were around to document it.

By the time of the American Revolution (1776–83), three major dialect areas had developed in the eastern United States: a Northern variety in New England and the Hudson Valley, the Midland dialect of Pennsylvania, and the Southern dialect (see figure 15.5). These varieties were already becoming distinct from British English and from each other.

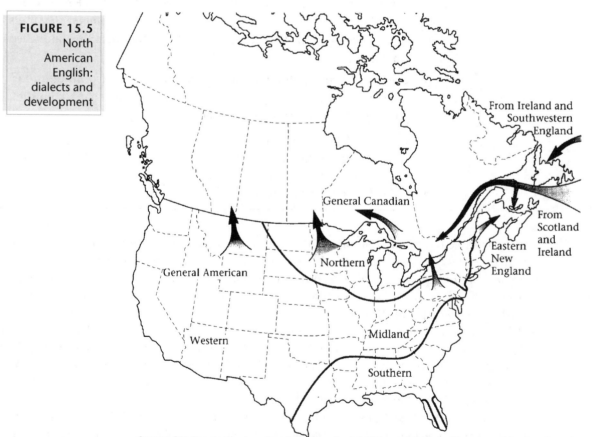

FIGURE 15.5
North American English: dialects and development

Source: C.V. Baeyer, *The Ancestry of Canadian English* (Ottawa: Minister of Supply and Services Canada, 1980). Reproduced with the permission of the Public Service Commission of Canada, 2014.

About 50 000 Americans who remained loyal to Britain moved to the northern colonies after the Revolutionary War, greatly increasing the English-speaking populations of what would later become the provinces of Nova Scotia, Prince Edward Island, New Brunswick, Québec, and Ontario. These Loyalists brought their American dialects with them, in particular the Midland dialect (especially to Ontario), with a strong contribution of New England speech to the Maritimes. A second wave, the 'late Loyalists', arrived in southern Ontario and Québec over the next generation or two. The language mix was further enriched by Scots Gaelic speakers (especially in Cape Breton and the Ottawa Valley), by Irish English and Gaelic speakers (especially in Québec and southern Ontario), and generally by settlers from across the British Isles.

As waves of English-speaking settlers moved westward, they took their dialects with them. The dialect of central Canada spread across the Prairies; the three major American dialects spread west, blurring and merging as they went—dialect maps of North America show a 'fanning out' from the east and a general mixed dialect in the westernmost areas of the United States (see figure 15.5). Even after much migration across the continent and great social change, the dialect distinctions laid down more than three hundred years ago remain strong.

15.3.2 Canadian English

Because much of the linguistic input to Canadian English came from the United States and because Canadians have lived under the cultural and economic influence of their larger neighbour for a long time, it's not surprising that Canadian English in many ways resembles that of parts of the United States. But as with other cultural traits, Canadians measure their linguistic distinctness in terms of how different they are from Americans.

Lexical features

Some Canadian words reflect Canadian legal or political realities, either inherited from Britain (*constable, Crown prosecutor*) or distinct to Canada (*riding* to mean a political district, *acclamation* to mean being elected unopposed). Other words reflect a more immediate reality: we keep our heads warm with a *tuque*, and we fuel ourselves by taking our coffee *double-double*. Unlike Americans, many of us wear *running shoes*, not *tennis shoes* (although some Maritimers, like many Americans, wear *sneakers*). Some of us still wipe away the remains of our double-double with a *serviette*, rather than a *napkin*. We get water from a *tap*, not a *faucet*; we roll up the *blinds*, not the *shades*, and we sit on a . . . *chesterfield*? Perhaps we used to; nowadays, most Canadians, especially younger ones, use the term *couch* or *sofa*. On the whole, however, we are more likely to recognize and use American terms than British ones. Do you call cookies *biscuits* or wear a *jumper* to keep warm? I didn't think so.

Lexical constraints also affect some observed differences in Canadian and American syntax or pronunciation. In most cases, these reflect Canadian retention of British forms. Many Canadians say *She's in hospital* whereas Americans would say *in the hospital*. Most Canadians pronounce *shone* to rhyme with *gone*—in fact, most Canadians are surprised to find out that some Americans rhyme it with *bone*. Canadians all know that the last letter of the alphabet is *zed*, not *zee*. And pronouncing *route* like *rout* is still more American than Canadian. For a few words, Canadians seem split down the middle between British and American pronunciations.

Pronunciation

Only one across-the-board pronunciation feature distinguishes Canadian English from most American dialects, and linguists know it, appropriately enough, as Canadian Raising (even though it's found in many other places). Canadians have different pronunciations for the /aw/ diphthong in *lout* and *loud*. In *lout* (and in all words where the diphthong comes before a voice-less sound), the nucleus of the diphthong is raised (thus 'Raising') from [a] to something like a schwa or [ʌ], the vowel of *cut*. Americans hear the resulting diphthong as [u], thus the stereotype of Canadians saying *oot and aboot* for *out and about*. The same process happens with /aj/—*tight* and *tide* have different diphthongs for most Canadians—but this is less likely to be noticed.

Morphology and syntax

If Canadian English reflects a blend of British and American features, it's hardly a surprise that we can find few specifically Canadian forms when it comes to word or sentence structure. There are very few differences between even British and American English in this respect, at least in the standard varieties. British English speakers are more likely to say *She has just gone* or *She has already gone*, while Americans prefer *She just left* or *She already left*. Britons find *I've done it yesterday* more acceptable than Americans do. One distinctly Canadian form is the use of *be* rather than *have* with the perfect form of a few verbs: *I'm finished my homework* sounds fine to most Canadians but terrible to both British and American speakers, who would say *I've finished my homework*.

Of course, none of the above statements about Americanness or the shortage of distin-guishing features apply to the English of Newfoundland, which reflects its distinct history. And even in mainland Canada, we can find subtle regional differences. Some older speakers of English in the Maritimes have a 'backed' pronunciation of /aj/, so that *light* sounds a bit like *loyt*. Some back the diphthong /aw/, so that *out and about* sounds like *oat and a boat*. And from approximately Sudbury west, you'll often hear long and monophthongal versions of /e/ and /o/—stereotyped in the [goː] and [eː] in Bob and Doug McKenzie's *How's it goin', eh?* Lexical differences can reflect settlement patterns, as when western Canadian restaurants call an all-you-can-eat meal a *smorg* (short for the Swedish-derived *smorgasbord*), and the *Canadian Oxford Dictionary* notes names for schoolyard games that are extremely local, sometimes restricted to a single neighbourhood in Toronto.

15.3.3 Isolation

Speech communities that are isolated in some way seem to preserve older ways of speaking, just as they might also preserve traditional music or farming methods. The isolation involved can be **physical**, isolated from other communities; **linguistic**, isolated from speakers of the same or a similar language; or **social**, isolated by conventions or attitudes. Canadian sociolin-guists are lucky to have all three types of isolated speech communities available to them.

Physical isolation: the case of Newfoundland English

The speech of Newfoundland is distinct from that of the rest of Canada for four reasons, three of them historical and one geographical: it was settled very early, by North American standards; its settlers came largely from two clearly defined areas (southwestern England and southeastern Ireland); most immigration occurred before the mid-1800s; and the island is a long way from other heavily populated areas. This combination of factors creates an almost 'perfect storm' for dialectologists, with Newfoundland English retaining many distinct speech features that have disappeared or diminished elsewhere. In addition, individual communities in Newfoundland were often isolated from each other and were settled by people from only one of the two input populations, making Newfoundland English highly regionally variable within Newfoundland itself.

Several features of the dialect are widely known outside Newfoundland. Many of us have heard mainlanders—comedians, for example—who believe they can sound like a Newfoundlander by adding the word *b'y* 'boy' to the end of every sentence. When the pronunciation of a single word becomes a stereotype of a speech community, linguists call it a **shibboleth**. Many varieties of English have their own shibboleths: Jamaicans say *mon* for *man*. Pittsburghers say *dahntahn* for *downtown*. Canadians say *oot and aboot*.

Many Newfoundlanders do, in fact, use *b'y* as a marker of solidarity in casual speech (in the same way that many Jamaicans, among others, use *man*). And many Newfoundlanders maintain the older southwestern British merger of /aj/ and /oj/, so that *boy* and *bye* are pronounced the same (although the actual pronunciation may vary by region). Other pronunciation features associated with some varieties of traditional Newfoundland English are the stopping of interdentals (*dat* for *that*), word-initial *h*-deletion (*'Olyrood* for *Holyrood*), word-final consonant-cluster deletion (*pos'* for *post*), and raising or tensing of front lax vowels, represented in popular writing by spelling *yes* as *yis*.

Newfoundland English also retains some of the distinct morphology and syntax brought over by the original settlers. Location can be marked with phrase-final prepositions, as in the often quoted *Stay where you're to 'til I comes where you're at*. The plural *-s* suffix is sometimes absent, as in *two pound*, and the verbal *-s* suffix is found with a range of subjects: *I goes, you goes, all the people goes*. This salient feature has surfaced recently on Newfoundland T-shirts (see figure 15.6). Many Newfoundlanders also use the Irish-origin 'after perfect' aspect, saying *I'm after doing it* instead of *I have just done it*.

FIGURE 15.6
The distinct morphology and syntax of the original settlers carries on in contemporary Newfoundland English.

The *Dictionary of Newfoundland English* lists thousands of distinct Newfoundland lexical items. Many are regionally restricted, nearly obsolete, or associated with particular industries. Others describe specifically Newfoundland phenomena: *slob ice* is loose chunks of ice floating on the surface of the water; *toutons* are fried dough chunks; and *scruncheons* are glorious bits of crisp-fried pork fat, used as a garnish.

Linguistic isolation: the case of Québec French

Québec French is so distinct and so filled with interesting variation that it is actually one of the language varieties most studied by sociolinguists. In fact, several major theoretical concepts in sociolinguistics (beyond the scope of an introductory text) have been developed through work on this variety.

Like Newfoundland English, Québec French illustrates how isolated language varieties retain older features of a language. Until 1763, the linguistic history of New France was remarkably similar to that of Newfoundland—early settlement from specific regions of Europe (especially northwestern France) to an area far away, followed by a sudden cessation of immigration. For more than two centuries, French in North America has been isolated, but the isolation has been linguistic rather than physical. The metaphor of an island of French surrounded by a sea of English is often heard, and English influence is sometimes invoked to explain why the French spoken in Québec (and elsewhere in Canada) is different from the European standard variety. Certainly, some English words have been borrowed into Québec French: a restaurant might give you a *bill* (rather than a *facture*) for your order of *bines* ('beans') and *toast* (rather than *feves* or *haricots* and *roties*). On the other hand, Québecers park in a *terrain de stationnement*, whereas in France they use the English loan word *le parking*. And people in both Québec and France look forward to *le weekend*. Other distinct Québec French forms reflect retention of older forms (archaïsmes), such as *flambe* for 'flame' (rather than the European *flamme*) or *doutance* (rather than *doute*) for 'suspicion'. In some cases, words have developed distinct meanings in Québec French: *traversier* means 'ferry' in Québec and 'crossing' in France, *ma blonde* means 'my girlfriend' in Québec and 'my blonde' in France, and *dépanneur* means 'repairman' in France but 'convenience store' in Québec (in both French and English).

Some syntactic features of Canadian French, although sometimes attributed to contact with English, seem to represent either processes that started centuries ago or internally motivated changes. For example, recently unearthed early recordings by folklorists show that the loss of *ne* in casual speech, as when people say *Je sais pas* instead of *Je ne sais pas* for 'I don't know', was widespread even in speakers born as early as 1846. And research on the use of the subjunctive mood in Gatineau seems to show the form strengthening its association with a few verbs and linguistic contexts rather than undergoing across-the-board English-induced decline. Other features of Québec French morphosyntax include the use of *Je vas* (instead of *vais*) for 'I go', *on* 'one' instead of *nous* 'we', and informal *tu* instead of *vous* 'you'. These differences work together to produce a more regular verb-marking system, as is shown in table 15.1.

Around the world, linguistically isolated languages are actually more common than you might think. In the Dominican Republic, the African American community of Samaná has spoken English since 1824, surrounded by Spanish speakers. Western Louisiana preserves Acadian French. Many Mennonites in North America speak an earlier form of German. And in

TABLE 15.1   Present tense verb forms for *go* in standard and spoken Quebéc French

Meaning	Standard (European) French	Spoken Québec French
'I go'	*je vais*	*je vas* (pronounced *va*)
'you (sg) go'	usually *vous allez*	***tu vas***
's/he goes'	*elle/il va*	*elle/il va*
'we go'	*nous allons*	***on va***
'you (pl) go'	*vous allez*	*vous allez*
'they go'	*elles/ils vont*	*elles/ils vont*

Turkey, the descendants of Jews who fled the Spanish Inquisition five centuries ago still speak a form of medieval Spanish. We also see a milder version of linguistic isolation in immigrant neighbourhoods, whose members often find when revisiting their original homelands that language has moved on without them.

Social isolation: the case of African Nova Scotian English

After the American Revolution and again after the War of 1812, groups of African Americans who had fought for the British settled in the Maritime provinces. Some moved on to found Freetown in Sierra Leone. Some integrated into the surrounding white communities. Several communities remained separate, however. The best known of these is Preston, near Dartmouth, which to this day is populated almost entirely by descendants of those original African American settlers. The community remained separated from the surrounding communities by limited road and transportation services and by racial segregation (some Nova Scotia schools remained segregated until 1964).

When older Preston residents were interviewed in the early 1990s, many retained distinct speech features that their ancestors had brought to Canada with them. These included features widespread in African American English (AAE) in the United States, such as copula deletion (*He gonna go*). Even more interesting, they used features of older English not generally found in contemporary American English, black or white, such as verbal-*s* marking (*I goes*). Comparisons of AAE in the socially isolated Preston, in the linguistically isolated Samaná, and in seventy-year-old recordings from the United States showed all three groups using similar forms with similar linguistic constraints, suggesting that the language of these communities was living evidence of earlier AAE.

Less extreme cases of social isolation are often found, and many speech communities prove resistant to change. The sociolinguist Lesley Milroy has proposed the notion of **social networks** to explain why this happens. **Dense** and **multiplex social networks**—where a small group of people interact with each other often and in multiple ways—are much less likely to change. If your neighbours are also your friends, and your co-workers, and your co-worshippers, and your in-laws, the intensity and frequency of these contacts will reinforce your traditional way of speaking. In this model, change is brought into the community by people with looser ties—those who work or go to school or hang out elsewhere.

New conceptions of place and space

Contemporary sociolinguists are developing different ways to think of space. We borrow ideas from cultural geographers to distinguish between physical distance and social perceptions of distance. Some places seem 'closer' because we can easily travel there thanks to transportation routes. For example, a sound change affecting cities in the American Midwest seems to be creeping down Interstate 55 to St. Louis. And some linguistic innovations seem to spread first from big city to big city, 'jumping over' intervening small towns and only later diffusing into the surrounding regions.

In addition, what we think of as space differences often have more to do with who lives where, even though Canadian cities are far less ethnically segregated than their American counterparts. Gottingen Street, Outremont, Regent Park, the Glebe, Gerrard Street, the Downtown East Side . . . if you recognize these place names, your first associations probably have more to do with the ethnicity or socio-economic status of their residents than with their actual physical location. In this way, space reinforces other social distinctions—you speak like who you speak to, and you tend to speak to people like you!

15.4 Contact

The other side of isolation, of course, is linguistic contact—with speakers of other varieties or of other languages. We've already considered the possibility of dialect levelling, where similar dialects that come into contact with each other tend to keep their shared features and get rid of the things that are different (usually by adopting the variant found in the socially or numerically dominant language). A whole range of other phenomena can happen when speakers of different *languages* meet and move toward bilingualism.

15.4.1 Code-switching and borrowing

As we saw in Chapter 12 when discussing the language use of bilingual children, **code-switching** is a common phenomenon when bilinguals get together and use two (or more) languages (or 'codes') to communicate. Not surprisingly, people sometimes decide that only one of their languages is appropriate for a particular situation. An example of this **situational code-switching** would be the use of English in a workplace or to talk about work-related topics and the use of one's native language among friends and family. Some communities are famous for switching back and forth constantly during a single conversation, and the mix that results sometimes gets its own name, usually intended to be derogatory. Spanish-English switching in the United States is often called *Spanglish*, while Canadian French-English switching is *franglais*.

Monolinguals often assume that this kind of switching happens because speakers are not competent in one of their languages—a deficit hypothesis—or because a concept just can't be expressed in one of the languages—a lexical gap explanation. Analysis of recorded multilingual speech doesn't support these ideas, however. Speakers who code-switch most often are usually very fluent in both of their languages, and there are linguistic rules governing where in a sentence a switch can happen. The switching becomes a linguistic resource in many communities, used by speakers to signal a bicultural identity or to evoke attributes associated with one of the languages, such as sophistication or identification with local values. Some neighbour-hoods in northern Toronto boast particularly skilled code-switchers—young people born in Russia, brought up in Israel, and now living in Canada. They're *triple* switchers, moving effort-lessly between Russian, Hebrew, and English.

Often, switches involve long stretches of each language, as in *Sometimes I'll start a sentence in English y termino en Español* [and finish in Spanish]. (Some researchers reserve the term *code-switching* for only this type of switch.) Perhaps more often, a single lan-guage will dominate (sometimes called the **matrix language**), and individual words from another language will be inserted, often being changed to obey the rules of the matrix language. (Some researchers call these **nonce borrowings**, 'one-offs' that don't really involve a change of language.) If particularly useful nonce borrowings happen often enough, eventually they get picked up by monolingual speakers of the matrix lan-guage. Then they're just called **borrowings** (although they're rarely given back). Presumably, borrowings result from other contact situations as well—speakers of one language use terms from another language to describe new things and activities associ-ated with that new language.

English has both borrowed and 'lent' a lot, thanks in part to its distinct history. A thou-sand years ago, it was the language of peasants, borrowing lots of legal and high-society words (*governor, beef*) from French and, later, learned words (*transliterate, oxygen*) from Latin and Greek. Later, it became the language of colonialism and conquest, borrowing words for local phenomena from the languages it encountered (*canyon* from Spanish, *boondocks* from Tagalog). Canadian English has borrowed many words from Indigenous languages, often to describe the animals of North America (*raccoon, chipmunk, moose, skunk*) or tools or clothing (*kayak, anorak, toboggan*), and, obviously, for a lot of place names (*Québec, Toronto, Saskatchewan*, and thousands more, including *Canada* itself). Some words are borrowed directly from North American languages; some via some other language of colonization, especially Spanish (*tomato* from Nahuatl, *hurricane* from Taino). Language borrowing (and contact generally) often happens far from busy scribes, so sometimes the precise language of origin of a borrowing has been lost.

Once a word is truly borrowed, it loses its associations with the original language and is adapted to the pronunciation and morphosyntax of the borrowers. So the Spanish *el legarto* ('the lizard') becomes *alligator*, and when we say *the alligator*, we don't associate it with 'lizard'.

Some types of words are far more likely to be borrowed than others—nouns are especially common, followed by verbs and the occasional adjective or adverb. Much less likely to be bor-rowed are function words—words (like determiners, prepositions, and auxiliary verbs) that belong to categories with limited membership, typically do not carry stress, and cannot be inflected. They occur too often in our first language to be displaced, and we rarely run into a concept that requires a new pronoun or preposition.

Occasionally, grammatical structures are borrowed along with individual words. For example, the Acadian French of the Maritime provinces nonce-borrowed many verbs from English and adapted them to French morphology, as in *J'ai parké* for 'I parked'. Verb + preposi-tion combinations, however, also kept some of their English structure, as in *J'ai hangé around*, 'I hung around'. In communities where both verbs and prepositions are borrowed, even all-French sentences can end up with an Englishlike word order not found elsewhere in French, as in *le gars que j'ai donné la job à*, 'the guy that I gave the job to'.

15.4.2 **Contact languages: mixed languages, lingua francas, pidgins, and creoles**

Occasionally, in heavy switching communities, you will hear sentences where virtually all the content words (nouns, verbs) are borrowed and adapted, while all the function words are from the matrix language. I once heard a co-worker say, "Tu peux pas parker ton truck dans le spot du station wagon du boss" ('You can't park your truck in the spot reserved for the boss's station wagon'). If that sort of process became the norm in a language-contact situation, you might eventually end up with a **mixed language**. Mixed languages are not common, and researchers who work on language contact argue (often fiercely) over whether they really exist and what they tell us about language. One strong candidate for mixed language status is **Michif**, still spoken in and near Manitoba among the Métis, people of mixed Indigenous and European descent. In Michif, most nouns and the words associated with them are derived from French, while most verbs and the words associated with them are derived from Cree (see table 15.2).

TABLE 15.2	French-origin noun morphology and Cree-origin verb morphology in Michif				
PAR LA QUEUE	apoci-pit-ew		kihtwam	LE LOUP	ase-kiwe-pahta-w
by the tail	*inside out-pull-he/him*		*again*	*the wolf*	*back go.home-run-he*
'He pulled him inside out by the tail, and the wolf ran home again.'					

Source: Based on data from Peter Bakker and Maarten Mous, eds., *Mixed Languages: 15 Case Studies of Language Intertwining* (Amsterdam: IFOTT, 1994). © Professor Peter Bakker and Professor Maarten Mous.

Non-linguists sometimes assume that creole languages are mixed languages. However, as we will see shortly, linguists use that label for the outcome of a very different situation of language contact. When people who speak different languages need to interact on a regular basis, they will often come to choose one particular language to communicate between groups. A language used this way is called a **lingua franca**, named after the language used centuries ago in the Mediterranean by traders from different language backgrounds.

Language Matters **Few Words, No Variants, Many Meanings**

In pidgins, words will usually not take different forms to mark grammatical distinctions. Compare the (invented!) sentences below:

Me - **see** - three - **man** - yesiday	One - **man** - **see** - **me** - bai
'I saw three men (yesterday).'	'One man will see me (later).'

Me, see, and *man* would have different forms in the two sentences in English; here, the distinctions of pronoun case, verb tense, and noun plurality are determined by sentence position, numerals, and adverbials (*yesiday* from *yesterday, bai* from *by and by*).

Some contact situations lead to the formation of a **pidgin**, a language stripped down to its essentials. Such a heavily simplified language can convey the basic information needed for many cross-linguistic purposes. Linguistically, pidgin languages consist of a small set of content words and very little grammatical complexity.

Socially, pidgins tend to develop in two different contact situations. Each situation involves one or more groups having limited access to the **lexifier language**, the language that supplies the basic wordstock for the pidgin. Trade is one such situation. Australian Pidgin English and Chinese Pidgin Portuguese are trade pidgins that developed from European lexifier languages. In the Pacific Northwest, North American natives developed the trade pidgin Chinook Jargon. The other common pidgin formation situation is when people from many language backgrounds are brought together to work on large plantations as slaves or indentured workers. Tok Pisin, a language of the South Pacific that is now a full creole (see below), originally developed this way.

If a pidgin operates as a lingua franca, as in trade situations, it may persist in its simplified form for a long time. In plantation situations, though, the children of the original pidgin speakers may learn the pidgin as a first language, and it may become the native language of the new community. When this happens, the pidgin becomes a full-fledged language known as a **creole**. During the process of creolization, the number of lexical items and grammatical rules found in the original pidgin expands greatly. Interestingly, creoles around the world share many grammatical characteristics, despite developing in different situations from different lexifier languages. These characteristics typically include a fixed word order, minimal usage of inflection, derivational affixes with a consistent and transparent meaning, and an absence of tone.

Linguists sometimes disagree about whether a linguistic variety can be classified as a creole. While some argue that Barbadian (Creole) English, or **Bajan**, is not a fully developed creole, it does exhibit a range of creole-like features. A few are shown in table 15.3.

TABLE 15.3   Some features of Barbadian (Creole) English

Linguistic feature	Example
1. Completive *done*	It *done* set there since last year.
2. Present tense *–s* absence	He *send* somebody.
3. Unmarked past tense	Two day before she *pass* away, I *tell* her to start crying now.
4. Copula (*be* verb) absence	*She lucky* that I ain't throw it on her.
5. *Ain't*	It *ain't* concern you.
6. Unmarked possessives	You know some *people* cake, you cut it here, you find a lump.
7. Object forms as subjects	*Them* ain't want to hear you.
8. Subject forms as objects	I ain't mind *she*.

Source: Based on data from Gerard Van Herk's personal fieldwork in Barbados in 1998.

Often, creoles co-exist with a local version of their original lexifier languages. This leads to a range of language varieties between the one least resembling the lexifier (and generally dominant) language, called the **basilect**, and the one most closely resembling the lexifier language, the **acrolect**. Intermediate varieties are called **mesolects**. This range is known as the **creole continuum**. We often assume that the basilect represents something close to the original creole variety—that is, the variety spoken by the first few generations of speakers of that creole—and that mesolects reflecting a wearing away of those deep creole features under the influence of the acrolect—a sort of 'bottom-up' explanation. This scenario is supported by evidence that basilectal features 'drop out' as we move up the continuum, though sometimes they are replaced by a form that *looks* like the standard but continues to *behave* like the original basilectal feature.

15.5 Distinctions within a community: class, ethnicity, and gender

So far, we've looked at social factors that apply to almost everyone in a community. The kinds of change, isolation, and contact we've been discussing affect entire regional groups. Here, we'll look at what language variation tells us about distinctions within regional communities. These distinctions include class, ethnicity, and gender, among others, as well as the interactions between them.

15.5.1 Class

Class, or socio-economic status (SES), is a classic social distinction in studies of industrialized societies and has played a role in sociolinguistic studies from the beginning. We sociolinguists haven't always had an easy time determining just which social class level to assign to the people we interview. Sometimes, we resort to complex weighting scales involving income, amount of education, type of housing, and prestige associated with one's occupation. Over time, we seem to have settled on occupational prestige as the major indicator of class.

A finding across many speech communities has been that certain linguistic variants are more closely associated with the upper classes and that these variants carry the most **prestige**. For example, in most varieties of English, *these things* is a more prestigious utterance than *dem tings*. It involves two higher-prestige forms, one phonological (interdental fricatives rather than dental or alveolar stops), the other syntactic or lexical (demonstrative *these* instead of *them*). Upper classes often adopt prestige norms imported from outside the speech community, as when North Americans adopt British speech features or Quebecers use the French of France as their model.

Classic sociolinguistic studies, such as William Labov's study of New York's Lower East Side, analyzed people's language in situations that encouraged different degrees of attention to speech, from naturalistic interviews to formal word-list reading. They found a strong relationship between class and careful speech styles (those involving a lot of attention to speech). No matter what the task, higher-class speakers used more prestige variants. And no matter what the class, careful style correlated with prestige variants. In other words, as Labov put it, a careful pipefitter spoke like a casual salesman, at least in the use of linguistic variables that had social meaning in his speech community. Generally, people of all classes showed the same rate of increase in the use of prestige forms in careful speech. The exception was members of the second-highest class, who sharply increased their use of prestige forms when paying a great deal of attention to speech—in other words, they overcompensated, or in Labov's terminology, they showed (social) **hypercorrection**. This tendency among the second-highest class has shown up in studies in many different communities; it is generally attributed to **linguistic insecurity** among a social group attempting to move up the class ladder.

Language Matters **Going Up**

The famous **fourth floor study** by William Labov in New York demonstrated that prestige is not an automatic function of a person's income but relates to context and expectations. The researcher asked employees in three different department stores for directions to a department located on the store's fourth floor and tabulated how many of their answers involved pronunciation of the [r] in each word ('*r*-fulness' being the prestige form). Labov found that even though all the employees earned similar (low) wages, those who worked in the higher-prestige stores used more of the higher-prestige variant. Labov hypothesized that store employees 'borrowed' prestige from their customers and that this was reflected in their unconscious language choices.

The concepts of prestige or status seem to transfer across cultures better than the narrower term *class*. In societies where movement between status groups is very difficult, such as in the **caste** system of traditional India, rigid rules have developed (see table 15.4). Members of different castes will often have categorical rules governing word choice. This may sound extreme, but Canadian English has class-related sensitivities too. How many of us can say *You shall do as I say*, or *whilst*, or describe something as *rather thrilling*, without sounding like we're desperately striving for the social heights?

We'll return to issues of class and prestige when we talk about standard languages and prescriptivism in section 15.7.

TABLE 15.4	Caste differences in Bangalore Kannada	
	Brahmin	**Non-Brahmin**
'it is'	ide	ayti
'inside'	-alli	-aga
'sit'	kut-	kunt-

Source: Based on data from Peter Trudgill, *Sociolinguistics: An Introduction to Language and Society* (New York: Penguin, 1974). © Peter Trudgill, 1974, 1983, 1995, 2000.

15.5.2 Ethnicity: the case of African American English

If linguistic distinctions reflect a society's social distinctions, it's no surprise that we find racial or ethnic differences in language. In North America, the ethnic variety (or ethnolect) that has received the most attention by far from sociolinguists is African American English (AAE). This is at least partly to make up for an earlier deficit—AAE was often ignored or marginalized in discussions of North American English until the civil rights movement picked up steam in the 1960s. This shortage of serious study allowed an unearned veneer of respectability to settle over suggestions that the distinct features of AAE resulted from lazy articulation or cultural deprivation or showed that the language was somehow 'incomplete' or a 'restricted code' not suited to abstract thought. When sociolinguists studied urban AAE in New York, Detroit, and Washington, DC, in the late 1960s, they discovered in city after city a linguistic system with remarkably similar structures, governed by similar linguistic constraints, as shown in table 15.5. In this table, you'll see that varieties of English align with each other in complex ways. AAE and NE (Newfoundland English) both express habitual actions with *be*; AAE and Caribbean creoles both use zero copula forms, and *done* in perfect constructions; and almost everybody uses unmarked forms for some past tense verbs (especially *come, run*, and *give*). Even varieties that share forms may have different frequencies of use or different rules for when to use them. It's this complexity that keeps sociolinguists busy sorting out the origins and internal systems of different varieties.

Notice, too, that NE, AAE, and creoles can all use verb forms to express distinctions that Standard English can't (Standard English speakers need to use adverbs like 'usually' or 'just'). In other words, in these respects, these non-standard varieties are *more* complex and precise than the standard language, contrary to common linguistic prejudice.

The 1980s saw a growth of interest in tracing the origins of the distinctive features of AAE. Some researchers argue that contemporary AAE features like copula deletion (e.g., *He bad*) show that AAE was once a creole, or something like it; others argue that the AAE of isolated communities shows features (and linguistic factors affecting them) that more closely resemble the earlier English dialects preserved in places like Newfoundland (e.g., *people goes*). Information from both positions converges, though, in showing that AAE has always been a complete, highly structured language variety; the features of today's AAE have not appeared overnight.

TABLE 15.5 Comparing varieties of English

Function	Standard	Multiple dialects	Newfoundland English	African American English	Caribbean creoles
Recent perfect	I've just eaten.	I **done** ate.	I'm **after** eating.	I **done** ate.	I **done** eat.
Copula	He's coming. He's a fool.	He's coming. He's a fool.	He's coming. He's a fool.	He **coming**. He's a fool.	He **coming**. He's a fool.
Habitual	She always, sometimes, often, usually sings.	She always, sometimes, often, usually sings.	She **bees singing**. She **does be** singing.	She **be singing**. She **steady** singing.	She **does/da** sing. She **does be** singing.
Past	She came. She saw it.	She **come**. She **seen** it.	She **come**. She **seen** it.	She **come**. She **seen** it.	She **come**. She **see** it.

Note: Speakers of a non-standard variety may also use the standard form, to varying degrees. This table represents their least standard uses.

Contemporary AAE continues to provide avenues of research for sociolinguists. For one thing, new grammatical features seem to be developing, including the use of past perfects with simple past meaning (e.g., *had went* for *went*). And research is moving past the previous focus on the grammatical consistency of the variety to look at regional diversity in AAE's sound system. Sociolinguists are also beginning to pay back a variety that has supplied the data for so much study by developing teaching materials that help AAE speakers to bridge the dialect gap in the school system.

Ethnicity and language also intersect in how we talk *about* ethnicity. In particular, the preferred names for ethnic groups, sometimes called **ethnonyms**, change over time, reflecting the status of a group in wider society and the degree of power a group is able to exercise over the naming process. In North America, African slaves and their generations of descendants have been called, roughly in chronological order, *African, coloured, negro, Negro, Black*, and *African American*. The diminishing acceptability in our culture of **ethnic slurs** also reflects changing attitudes toward ethnic naming practices, at least overtly. Terms for ethnic varieties can also change—AAE has also been known at various times as Negro Dialect, Non-standard Negro Vernacular, Black Street Speech, African American Vernacular English, or Ebonics.

15.5.3 Gender

Sociolinguists generally find differences in language use that reflect socially assigned sex roles, or **gender roles**. One frequent finding is that when language variation in a community is stable (no change is occurring), women use more of the standard forms associated with **overt prestige** and switch to prestige forms when paying more attention to their speech. British sociolinguist Peter Trudgill found that men not only use more non-standard forms than women but also claim to use even more of them than they actually do. Trudgill explained this by proposing the idea of **covert prestige**—a sort of linguistic 'street credibility' that men aim for to prove their masculinity.

The second gender difference that often surfaces is that when change *does* occur, women use more of the incoming forms than men. This is especially true with **change from above**, changes that are noticeable in the community and work from the upper classes down. Some sociolinguists suggest that women use overt prestige forms and adopt changes from above because of linguistic insecurity. But these differences may also reflect gender expectations that limit women's ability to demonstrate toughness or the fact that women more often do the jobs that require standard speech, such as teacher or receptionist. And women may lead change simply because of their role as child caregivers. If women adopt a new form, it *becomes* a change because children grow up hearing it from women. If men adopt a new form, nobody listens to them!

Some researchers have also noted gender differences in **discourse**, the way conversations are structured, especially in same-sex conversations. They have observed that women are more likely to use language to build and maintain relationships (a **rapport style**), while men are more likely to use language to communicate factual information (a **report style**). Overall, women do more work to keep conversations going (*M-hm . . . really? Oh my God!*), ask questions to engage others, organize turn-taking, maintain a single topic for longer, and demonstrate sympathy with others by sharing their problems and experiences with them. Men interrupt more often, ask questions to get information, change topics, and avoid disclosing their problems, but they are quick to offer solutions to other people's problems. These differences lead to the facetious observation, "It's pointless to share your problems with a man, because he'll try to fix them." Some researchers see gender differences in language as reflecting women's lack of power in society; some see them as reflecting different cultures of conversation. And other studies suggest that the gender differences in language use are smaller than people expect, but that concepts like 'women's speech' or 'men's speech' still represent symbolic performance targets that speakers consider when deciding how to present themselves linguistically.

Popular culture expresses gender difference by suggesting that men and women are from different (but presumably equal) planets. But in fact we share not only a planet but also a speech community. The saying "You talk like who you talk with"—which helped us explain the linguistic effects of region, class, and ethnicity—breaks down when it comes to gender. Although many of us speak fairly often with people of another gender, gender differences in language persist, which suggests that we might use language to 'perform' gender more often than we use it to perform region or class. Men use male-associated language to 'be a man'— more precisely, to be a stereotypical heterosexual man. For example, men in our culture have deeper voices than women, partly because male vocal folds are longer. But research in Britain has shown that men's voices are even deeper than longer vocal folds would predict and suggests that the rest of the difference is social. In other words, men who buy into their gender role overdo it. The markedness of gender-stereotyped language is easy to see by looking at people who opt out. Some recent Canadian research suggests that people who describe themselves as avoiding traditional sex roles also avoid the poles of traditional male or female pronunciations. Work on the speech of men who are perceived by listeners as gay finds that listeners base their judgments on the use of phonetic features that are also associated with female speech. This also suggests that it is more practical to think of gendered language as a continuum rather than as an either/or phenomenon.

As we saw for ethnicity above, gender and language also intersect when we talk *about* gender . . . or when we assume we're talking about gender. Given the sentence *The nurse wished the professor would stop complaining*, most people will conjure up an image of a female nurse and a male professor because we associate those occupations with those genders. Our language continues to reflect these sexist assumptions: many people speak of *male nurses* (while female nurses are just *nurses*) and of *actors* and *actresses*, where the form for men is the unmarked one. Nowadays, we see a move toward a single inclusive form for both men and women: *actor* for everyone, *chair* rather than *chairman*, and *flight attendant* rather than *stewardess*. Some traditional grammarians still insist on *he* as the pronoun of choice when the sex of the person involved is not specified, as with *someone* or *anyone*: *If anyone wants a good mark, he should study*. Replacing *he* with *he or she* is an inclusive option in formal speech, but in informal speech *they* is much more common and can include people outside the gender binary.

15.5.4 Nuancing social factors

More than fifty years of research shows us that factors like gender and region affect language variation. But ticking off these factors on a sociolinguistic checklist doesn't mean that we've explained a community's language use.

In many situations, completely different aspects of social reality may be reflected in language use. In Ontario, speakers with **restricted use** of French (for example, only in school rather than with friends or family) may lack control of some non-standard, colloquial features. In rural Guyana, language use varies according to whether people work in plantation fields or not. In the fishing community of Martha's Vineyard, young men use traditional pronunciations to distance themselves from the tourist economy, thus showing their **identification** with local values.

Recently, some scholars have adopted the term **community of practice** to explain some language variation—people who come together to engage in some shared activity are likely to develop shared language practices. Penelope Eckert investigated language use in a Detroit-area high school and found that it reflected membership in one of two groups—*jocks* (who identify with the official system of the institution) and *burnouts* (who don't). My own work on online youth subcultures shows that people can adapt their language to reflect participation in groups like hip-hop fans, tweens, and nerds.

A second issue to keep in mind is that all of these social categories *intersect*. It's the combination of social forces that is played out in language use. What it means to be masculine may vary with ethnicity or class; what it means to be working class may vary with gender or ethnicity. Eckert's jocks and burnouts were not identical to middle- and working-class groups, but membership in these groups reinforced students' streaming toward those classes. And being a jock or burnout meant different things for men and women. A gender effect was also clear with online subcultures. For example, male and female hip-hop fans showed strong differences in language use, whereas nerds rejected the most gender-specific variants.

15.6 Social interaction and language

We humans aren't sociolinguistic robots, programmed to speak a certain way because of our region, gender, ethnicity, age, and the like. Instead, we reveal (or perform) our social roles in extended language interaction, or discourse. And society also has rules, or conventions, about how discourse should proceed. Linguists use **discourse analysis** to look at the structure of a conversation and what it reveals about the roles of the participants. Some aspects of discourse, such as conversational maxims, are covered in chapter 6. Here, we look at two methods of analyzing discourse. We also examine the effects of power differences on communication.

15.6.1 Ethnography of communication

Ethnography of communication is a way to analyze discourse by using the same sort of methods that anthropologists might use to study other aspects of a culture, such as religious practices. Within **speech situations** (circumstances involving the use of speech), cultures have developed conventions governing interactions, or **speech events**. Ethnography of communication analysis pulls apart speech events into their component parts. Eight basic components have been identified; the acronym SPEAKING may help you remember them, as illustrated in table 15.6.

Table 15.6 demonstrates how the components of a terrible joke can be identified. In a real conversation, we can expect each component to affect the language that is used and the structure of discourse. You may be familiar with a game popular in improvisational theatre, where actors begin a scene, somebody shouts *Freeze!*, and one of these components is changed—for example, a conversation between two theologians (*participants*) is suddenly performed in the style of a *Game of Thrones* episode (*genre*). We can laugh at the adaptations made by the actors because we share with them an understanding of the often unspoken rules that govern discourse. In other words, we (and they) have **communicative competence**—the ability to use language in a way that is appropriate to the situation or context.

TABLE 15.6   Components of a speech event

Sample speech event: A piece of rope walks into a bar and asks for a drink. The bartender says, "We don't serve pieces of rope." The rope goes outside, ties itself up, and frays its ends. It returns to the bar and asks again. The bartender says, "Aren't you the same piece of rope I just refused to serve?" The rope says, "I'm a frayed knot."

	Component	Explanation	Analysis of sample
S	setting, scene	place, time, social occasion	a bar
P	participants	who was there, including audience	bartender, a piece of rope
E	ends	purpose of event and goals of participants	rope: to get a drink bartender: to refuse
A	act sequences	content of interaction and related forms	request for a drink and refusal, question of rope's identity
K	key	emotional tone, mood	hopeful, later annoyed
I	instrumentalities	mode (spoken, written), type (dialect, style)	spoken, casual speech
N	norms	conventions of interaction	request addressed, refusal acknowledged, question answered
G	genres	category/name of event	conversation (and bad pun)

Instrumentalities—the 'how' of discourse—help show that the language of interaction is more than the sum of its participants and their social characteristics. For most of us, communicative competence includes control of **style**, or how formal our speech is. We use formal style when we are looking for (overt) prestige and when we pay attention to our speech; we use informal style in more relaxed situations and/or when overt prestige is not our goal.

More recent conceptualizations of style focus on how we shift our language use to perform or present aspects of our identities (or perhaps more accurately, influence how we would like to be perceived by our audience). And in constructing those performances, we create a model for others, in terms of how to come across as (for example) masculine, or educated, or casual.

The term **register** also describes a type of speech, but it is more closely associated with a specific speech situation, so we can speak of a *legal register* or *ritual language register*. Sometimes the boundary between register and genre is fuzzy; sociolinguists speak of a *recipe register*, although we can also think of *recipe* as a genre—it's a widely recognized category of event with its own name. Both style and register are associated with particular phonological, lexical, or syntactic properties. The same sentiment is expressed by the formal *I shall never surrender* and the informal *I ain't never quittin'!* And the recipe register is full of imperatives (*Place chicken legs* *in bag containing spiced flour*) and zero object constructions (*Shake vigorously*, where the shaking refers to the chicken, not the reader).

A register associated with a particular occupation or activity often develops its own special vocabulary items, known as **jargon**. Jargon can involve special terms, as when linguists refer to *bilabials* or *mediopassives*, or specialized meanings for existing words, as when we give particular linguistic meanings to the words *register* or *style*. Jargon makes communication more effective for in-group members—rather than constantly saying *those sounds for which we use both lips*, we can use the term *bilabials*. But jargon also excludes non-members and creates barriers to participation, as you may have noticed through the course of reading this book.

15.6.2 Ethnomethodology

Act sequences and norms tell us something about the conventions of conversation. One way to investigate these conventions is through **ethnomethodology**, also called **conversation analysis**. This method lets us search large collections of recorded natural speech to discover patterns in the distribution of utterances. One very common structure is the **adjacency pair**, a sort of minimal act sequence in which a specific type of utterance by one speaker is followed by a specific type by someone else. An obvious example is *question-answer*, but other recurring examples include *compliment-acceptance* and *offer-refusal*. Sometimes the first part permits more than one response: in a store, an offer (*Can I help you?*) can trigger either acceptance (*Yes, I'm looking for a Deuxluxes T-shirt*) or refusal (*No thanks, just browsing*). Sometimes one utterance type can be interpreted as another. For example, in cultures where direct requests are discouraged, an overt compliment (*What a nice hat!*) will be interpreted as a request (*May I have it?*). In other cultures, the same compliment may be interpreted as an attribution of wealth (*You must be rich to afford such a hat*) leading up to a request for money, thus requiring a denial (*This old thing? I've had it forever*).

Conversation analysis also deals with who speaks when. It includes identification of conversational **openings** (*How are you?*) and **closings** (*Well, gotta get back to work*). As well, it studies **turn-taking**. At the end of a conversational 'turn', the speaker may try to determine who should speak next (for example, by asking a question of a particular person) or may 'open the floor' to any participant who has something to contribute. If nobody takes over, the original speaker may continue. Sometimes, the turn-boundary cues are subtler, including the use of intonation or discourse markers (*so . . .* or *but . . .*). Cross-culturally, differences in turn-taking cues may cause confusion. Linguists have identified communities with a **high involvement style**, such as Eastern European Jews in New York or radio talk show callers in Jamaica. Here, turns will often overlap (one speaker will start before another finishes). In other communities, including among the Cree, a longer pause is required to signal the end of a turn. A speaker who hasn't developed communicative competence in these communities might be seen by Jamaicans as unwilling to participate and by Cree people as monopolizing the conversation.

15.6.3 Solidarity and power

Even when participants in a conversation share norms, the conversation may be somewhat unbalanced, depending on the **status** of the speakers. Participants may express closeness or intimacy, and thus shared status (**solidarity**), or they may signal the relative social standing of each participant (the **power** relationship). One clear example of this is found in **forms of address**—what the participants call each other. Participants can express solidarity and shared status through reciprocal naming, as when friends call each other by their first names. When there is a perceived power difference, as with age differences or work relationships, we often see non-reciprocal naming. A teacher or boss, for example, may call students or employees by their first names, while students or employees may use title and last name: *Professor Wharram, Mr. Kadonoff*. If you've worked in factories, you've probably observed a gradient form of address: a fellow worker named Vijay Kumar is *Vijay*, a foreman of the same name is *Mr. Vijay*, while the 'big boss' would be *Mr. Kumar*.

Many languages can express power relationships through a different form of address—the choice of pronoun meaning *you*. Generally, the **T form** is used reciprocally among family and close friends, while the **V form** is used reciprocally among people who have roughly equal status but are not close. (The T and V terminology comes from the French pronouns *tu* and *vous*.) When participants are of unequal status, the powerful employ the T forms to address the less powerful, while the less powerful use V forms to address the powerful. Societies can differ on where to draw the line between people who need T-ing or V-ing; Québec French speakers will use *tu* more readily than European French speakers. This distinction carries so much significance that languages sometimes have a verb meaning 'using the T form': in German, it's *dützen*; in French, it's *tutoyer*. Just last week, a Swiss speaker of French asked me, "Can we tutoyer?"

Language Matters **Solidarity and Childbirth**

The choice of T and V forms can be used to create solidarity. Here's an example from an Ottawa-area French speaker:

> *J'emploi le vous formel avec mes supérieurs ou avec des personnes en position d'autorité. Je l'utilise aussi avec mes clients (je suis infirmière). Le seul moment ou je me permet de déroger à cette règle est quand ma cliente est en train d'accoucher et qu'elle est en période de transition (à partir de 7 ou 8 cm). Une fois l'accouchement terminé et le placenta expulsé, je retourne au vouvoiement.*

> 'I use formal *vous* with my superiors or with people in positions of authority. I also use it with my clients (I'm a nurse). The only time I let myself break this rule is when my client is in labour and she's dilated (from 7 or 8 cm onward). Once childbirth is over and the placenta is expelled, I return to using *vous*.'

In some societies, we find **diglossia**—distinctly different varieties acting as social registers. The high (H) variety is used in formal situations, official proclamations, and the like; the low (L) variety is used among friends. In effect, diglossia involves entire languages or language varieties acting like V and T forms. Examples include Paraguay (Spanish and Guaraní), Morocco (Standard Arabic and Moroccan Arabic, or Darija), Switzerland (Standard German and Schwyzerdütsch), and Javanese, as table 15.7 shows.

Another way in which power imbalances reveal themselves in interaction is through linguistic **accommodation**: speakers modifying their language patterns to make them more like those of the people they're talking to. In a classic study, a Welsh travel agent was wired for sound and recorded through her business day. She adapted her speech to include more local,

TABLE 15.7	Dialect of the Prijajis (Javanese)							
Level	*are*	*you*	*going*	*to eat*	*rice*	*and*	*cassava*	*now*
High	menapa	pandjenengan	baḍé	ḍahar	sekul	kalijan	kaspé	semanika
Low	apa	sampéjan	arep	neda	sega	lan	kaspé	saiki

working-class features when speaking to working-class customers. We often find asymmetrical accommodation, where the less powerful participant in a conversation is forced to accommodate to the more powerful but not vice versa. For example, speakers of Standard English will often claim they can't understand speakers of regional or ethnic dialects, and they expect dialect speakers to do all the accommodating. We can also sometimes find negative accommodation, or divergence—for example, when Welsh speakers develop even stronger Welsh accents when dealing with people from England who are insulting Wales.

15.7 How societies deal with language

So far, we've been taking language as our object of study and looking at how social forces can shape it. But society and language also interact at a strictly social level. In other words, society can treat language in the same way it treats clothing, the arts, or business—as a thing to be debated and regulated. In this section, we look briefly at how societies approach language as a social object.

Most speech communities feature more than one language variety. As we've seen in our discussions of English, sometimes one variety is called the **standard** and is claimed to be more 'correct' than others. Some countries (notably France and Italy) have formal academies responsible for maintaining the purity of language. English has never had a formal academy, but for centuries, our linguistic insecurity has been fed by newspaper columnists, authors of dictionaries and grammars, and other self-proclaimed defenders of the language.

The standard language industry probably had its heyday between about 1750 and 1900, when a growing middle class trying to move up the linguistic ladder provided a ready market for ever-stricter rules about correct language use. This is the time period that gives us such inappropriate analogies with mathematics as *Two negatives make a positive.* (As the linguist Steven Pinker has pointed out, that should mean it's all right to use *three* negatives, as in *I can't never get no satisfaction.*) The demand for **prescriptive** grammars (the ones that tell us how we 'should' use language) remains strong today, judging by the success of books like *Eats, Shoots, and Leaves.* In Québec, a weekly television show tests contestants' knowledge of Standard French.

The standard is difficult, if not impossible, to define objectively. We can agree that some forms, like *ain't*, are probably not part of the standard—at least not anymore. Others, like *There's dozens of ways*, are on the boundary. The standard is slightly easier to pin down on social grounds. It's the language of the upper socio-economic classes and of educated people, the language of literature or printed documents (including this textbook), the variety taught in schools and used by broadcasters; in North American English, it's the accent of the American Midwest and mainland Canada. In effect, the standard is the language of powerful people. By this definition, however, any idea of 'correctness' disappears. We're left with a sociolect.

What's interesting to sociolinguists is the *idea* of a standard: the widely held belief that some ways of speaking are not just different but inherently correct. (Presumably, this is less of an issue for researchers in other disciplines—astronomers don't worry about whether Neptune is 'better' than Mercury.) Because of this belief in the correctness of the standard, language sometimes serves as a barrier to education and employment for speakers of other varieties.

Attitudes toward language have been implicitly involved in much of our discussion so far. The idea of a standard language legitimizes the marginalization of other varieties. People often describe non-standard varieties as lazy, illogical, or sloppy, although they may not feel comfortable saying the same things about the people who speak them. On the whole, though, it's not always easy to determine attitudes toward languages. Researchers in Michigan have encouraged speakers to use maps to rate regional varieties in categories such as 'pleasantness' or 'correctness'. As you might expect, respondents considered Michigan speech to be the most correct. The speech of the U.S. South was seen as extremely incorrect, but pleasant. Language attitudes can also be revealed by deconstructing media images. What accents do you hear from characters who are supposed to be stupid? Criminal? Wise? Pretentious?

Attempts to find objective evidence supporting popular linguistic attitudes and prejudices sometimes result in odd **language myths**. It's easy to be puzzled by the once widespread idea that African American English resulted from its speakers having large lips, or by Korean parents having their children undergo tongue surgery (called a frenulotomy) in the belief that more flexible tongues will lead to accentless English. Other language myths are more widespread, especially the idea that some language varieties have tiny vocabularies or are not capable of expressing complex or abstract ideas. Although these notions may reassure people who wish to dismiss those language varieties, they have no basis in fact.

Language Matters The Matched Guise Test

The **matched guise test**, first developed in Canada, tries to get past people's professed viewpoints to gauge their deeply held language attitudes. In the test, subjects listen to a range of recordings of people speaking and are asked to rate the speakers according to traits like social class, intelligence, and friendliness. What the subjects don't know is that they're actually listening to the same speaker or speakers several times, using different accents or speaking different languages. Because the only thing that differs between recordings is the accent or language, any differences in ratings are taken to reflect differences in attitudes toward the language varieties involved. Early experiments showed that both English and French speakers rated French recordings lower in intelligence. In the years since, matched guise studies have fairly consistently shown a solidarity/prestige split. Standard speakers are seen as more competent, smarter, even taller! Non-standard speakers are seen as warmer and friendlier. Matched guise studies in the United States have shown that human resources personnel are likely to assign lower-status jobs to speakers of African American English, as well as to speakers with Hispanic or Asian accents.

A real-world application of the matched guise test is found in California, where the linguist John Baugh and his associates have spent years collecting information for housing-discrimination cases. They phone landlords and ask about advertised apartments, using identical sentences but adopting African American, Hispanic, or standard American accents. If apartments are available to standard speakers but are either unavailable or more expensive when non-standard speakers call, discrimination is assumed.

Of course, languages do sometimes find themselves at a loss for words. This is particularly true when a language moves into new domains, typically when a community language becomes a language of power. Different language groups have dealt with this in different ways. Some languages borrow words. English borrowed many legal terms from French (*attorney, governor general*). Tok Pisin borrowed them from English (the Tok Pisin term for *public solicitor* is *pablik salisita*). In other situations, governments establish bodies to oversee **language planning**, which often includes coming up with homegrown solutions to lexical gaps. In Québec, the Office québécois de la langue française (OQLF) works to develop French-based terms for new or imported concepts (e.g., for lesser-known foodstuffs imported from other countries). The OQLF is also responsible for other aspects of language planning, including the implementation of government legislation on language.

Language Matters **Language Planning in Tanzania**

The objectives of Tanzania's Institute of Kiswahili Research illustrate the activities of language planning groups that work to expand the role and usefulness of official languages in post-colonial situations:

- To undertake research in various aspects of Kiswahili morphology, syntax, phonology, sociolinguistics and dialectology.
- To undertake research in Kiswahili lexicography and compile general and subject dictionaries.
- To compile terminologies and coin new terms for different academic and/or specialized fields.
- To co-ordinate and provide translation services to government offices, para-statal organizations, industries, institutions and individuals in and outside the country.
- To carry out research in oral and written literature, theatre arts, folklore and the cultures of the Tanzanian and East African societies.
- To co-operate with other institutions in the development of Kiswahili language and provide consultancy services in different aspects of Kiswahili language and literature.
- To publish teaching material on/in Kiswahili for schools, colleges and universities.
- To see to it that Kiswahili acquires a strong foundation for becoming a medium of instruction for primary, secondary, and tertiary levels of education.

Source: Institute of Kiswahili Research, University of Dar es Salaam.

Government language planning often includes the declaration of an **official language** for a particular region or country as a result of legislation. When a language is made an official language, it often affects the political and economic power of the ethnic group that speaks that language. In some cases, official language designations are a response by a majority group to a perceived increase in status or power of a minority group. A good example of this situation is the attempt by 'English-only' groups to have English declared the official language of the United States. Currently, about half of the United States has some sort of law giving English official status. French and English are the official languages of Canada (at the federal level) and of New Brunswick; all other provinces conduct official business in either English or French. Nunavut's official languages are English, French, Inuktitut, and Inuinnaqtun. The Northwest Territories has *eleven* official languages: Chipewyan, Cree, English, French, Gwich'in, Inuinnaqtun, Inuktitut, Inuvialuktun, North Slavey, South Slavey, and Tłįchǫ, although services in all eleven are not available everywhere. According to the 2016 Census, about 9 million Canadians have a mother tongue different from the majority language of their province: 1.1 million French speakers outside Québec, about 0.6 million English speakers in Québec, and

7.3 million speakers of other languages across Canada. In other words, over a quarter of all Canadians are surrounded by a language other than the one they grew up with.

Language planning policies often have their greatest impact in regulating the language of schooling, which in turn places differential barriers on access to education. Proponents of minority-language education or bilingual education argue that teaching subject matter such as science or geography in students' first language levels the playing field by removing the linguistic barrier to learning. Linguistic minority groups have often fought for education in their home languages to help preserve their community's linguistic vitality. These minority-language education programs are sometimes interpreted by majority-language groups as resistance to assimilation, leading to backlash. In California, the Oakland school district's attempt to recognize the legitimacy of AAE in the learning process was harshly criticized. Arizona forbids bilingual education, while Massachusetts and California have recently overturned such bans. In the past, home languages have been banned in schools, with harsh punishments for their use. Welsh was banned in Welsh schools, and Indigenous languages such as Cree and Blackfoot were banned at residential schools in Canada.

In many cases, minority languages are in danger of dying out. Immigrant languages continue to be spoken elsewhere, so their decline here leads to decreased diversity but not to **language death**. The situation is different for Canada's Indigenous languages, some of which now have fewer than one hundred speakers, and for minority languages around the world. Major efforts are being made to support endangered languages through the development of dictionaries, reading materials, and school systems, but the past history of endangered languages is not encouraging. Languages usually come 'back from the brink' only when major political and social will is involved. One such example is Hebrew, which has been built up to become the official language of Israel.

Summing up

Sociolinguistics is the study of language in its social contexts. **Linguistic variation** between **speech communities** reflects social factors such as **region, change over time, isolation**, and **language contact**. Contact situations lead to **bilingualism, code-switching**, and **borrowing**, as well as to such contact-driven language types as **mixed languages, lingua francas, pidgins**, and **creoles**. Within speech communities, language reflects important social distinctions, including **class, ethnicity**, and **gender**, as well as the interactions between these factors and locally relevant norms.

Discourse analysis looks at language in interactions, using such methods as **ethnography of communication** and **ethnomethodology**. Individual speakers adapt their use of **style, register**, and **jargon** to fit each interaction, as well as to reflect **solidarity** and **power** relationships between speakers. Often, the language of a high-status group will become known as the **standard** language; this variety will be described as more 'correct' than other varieties, based largely on **attitudes** toward the variety. Attitudes can restrict the social mobility of non-standard speakers. **Language planning** involves attempts by a society to regulate language use through choice of **official language** and language of education and sometimes even by **banning** languages.

Through analysis of language variation, fifty years of sociolinguistic research confirms that variation is highly patterned and is affected by a range of linguistic and social factors. This patterning helps reveal the social meaning of language and sociolinguistic competence of speakers, who use language to situate themselves with respect to other speakers and the norms of their society.

Recommended reading

Chambers, J.K. 2009. *Sociolinguistic Theory: Linguistic Variation and Its Social Significance*. Rev. ed. Oxford: Blackwell.

Chambers, J.K., Peter Trudgill, and Natalie Schilling-Estes. 2002. *The Handbook of Language Variation and Change*. Oxford: Blackwell.

Lippi-Green, Rosina. 2012. *English with an Accent: Language, Ideology, and Discrimination in the United States*. 2nd ed. London: Routledge.

Mesthrie, Rajend, Joan Swann, Ana Deumert, and William L. Leap. 2009. *Introducing Sociolinguistics*. Amsterdam: John Benjamins.

Meyerhoff, Miriam. 2011. *Introducing Sociolinguistics*. 2nd ed. London: Routledge.

Van Herk, Gerard. 2018. *What Is Sociolinguistics?* 2nd ed. Oxford: Blackwell.

Wolfram, Walt, and Natalie Schilling-Estes. 2006. *American English: Dialects and Variation*. 2nd ed. Oxford: Blackwell.

Exercises

1. What is your word for each of the following? Do you know other words that express these meanings?
   a) an area in front of the door of a house, often covered and usually up a couple of stairs
   b) deliberately missing a class at school
   c) a sweet fizzy beverage
   d) employment insurance
   e) rubber-soled casual shoes sometimes worn to play sports
   f) a small store that sells candy, cigarettes, junk food, phone cards, etc.
   g) marijuana
   h) the police
   i) a sandwich on a long bun, filled with cold cuts, cheese, etc.
   j) spending time with friends doing nothing in particular, perhaps outside on a street corner

2. Imagine a conversation in a cafeteria line in which a young chemistry prof is trying to talk her timid cousin into going on a road trip to the Osheaga Festival with her. Now change two of the components of S-P-E-A-K-I-N-G and consider how the conversation would be different.

3. Which features (if any) of slang or youth language make you cringe the most when you hear older people using them? Which features (if any) would you feel uncomfortable using yourself?

4. Do you remember any conversations in which you used a language feature (maybe a regional name for something) that your listener was completely unfamiliar with? Or features that someone else used that you were unfamiliar with? What were the features? What happened?

5. For the next week, walk around with a Sociolinguistic Angel on your shoulder. By this I mean, be extremely aware of things that people say and the social meanings involved. Do you hear any new terms or phrases? Can you identify language features that are used by some people but not by others? Who? Why?

6. The following words can mean different things in different English-speaking countries. Use the resources available to you (people, books, the Internet) to find an additional meaning for each of these words: that is, different from its meaning in Canadian English.
   a) boot
   b) thong
   c) rasher (of bacon)
   d) draughts
   e) lift
   f) chips
   g) rubber
   h) knock you up
   i) pavement
   j) hoarding (noun)

7. Each of these sentences contains at least one 'odd' feature—something disliked by prescriptive grammarians (now or in the past) or something that sounds wrong to us but used to be required by prescriptivists. Find the feature. How wrong does it sound to you?
   a) A new mall is building next to the highway.
   b) Send an email to Clarisse and myself.
   c) Send an email to Clarisse and I.
   d) You should have went home earlier.
   e) I'm arrived at the airport.
   f) There's hundreds of peasants with torches outside the castle.
   g) Ask your father when he was at the store did he buy the coffee.
   h) I seen five or six moose last summer.
   i) I'm loving the *Glass Boys* album.
   j) This class needs more workers and less complainers.

To learn more about the topics discussed in this chapter, visit the Companion Website for *Contemporary Linguistic Analysis*.

Writing and language

There's nothing like a shovel full of dirt
to encourage literacy.

MARGARET ATWOOD, *THE BLIND ASSASSIN*

SPEAKING AND writing are different in both origin and practice. Our ability to use language is as old as humankind and reflects the biological and cognitive modifications that have occurred during the evolution of our species. **Writing**, the representation of language by graphic signs or symbols, is a comparatively recent cultural development, having occurred within the past five thousand years and only in certain parts of the world. Most of the world's languages have no tradition of writing, and many lack a writing system even today.

A further indication of the contrast between speech and writing comes from the fact that spoken language is acquired without instruction, whereas writing must be taught and learned through deliberate effort. Even in literate societies, there are individuals who cannot read or write. While spoken language comes naturally to human beings, writing does not.

16.1 Types of writing

As different as they are, speech and writing share one major characteristic: just as spoken language shows an arbitrary link between sound and meaning, so written language exhibits an arbitrary link between symbol and sound. A writing system consists of a **script**, which is the set of symbols that it uses, and an **orthography**, which is the set of conventions that determine how the symbols are employed to write the language. All orthographies can be grouped into two basic types, logographic and phonographic, depending on the technique that is used to represent language.

16.1.1 Logographic writing

The term *logographic* (from Greek *logos* 'word') refers to a type of writing in which symbols (called **logograms**) represent morphemes or even entire words. **Logographic writing** is the oldest type of genuine writing. Ancient Mesopotamian cuneiform inscriptions, Egyptian hieroglyphics, and Chinese characters were all highly logographic in their early stages. In fact, all writing systems maintain some logographic writing. To a certain extent, logographic writing can be read independently of its language of origin. We see examples of this even today in our use of numerals (1, 2, 3, etc.) as well as symbols such as &, %, and $, which represent concepts rather than pronunciations.

16.1.2 **Phonographic writing**

In **phonographic writing** (from Greek *phōnē* 'sound'), symbols represent syllables or phonemes. There are two principal types of phonographic writing systems—syllabic and alphabetic.

Syllabic writing

As the name suggests, **syllabic writing** employs signs to represent syllables (a set of syllabic signs is called a **syllabary**). Languages with relatively simple syllabic structures such as CV or CVC (Japanese and Cree, for example) are well suited to this type of writing, since they contain a relatively limited number of syllable types. In Japanese, the word *kakimashita* '(s/he) wrote' can be written with five syllabic signs: かきました. Like logograms, syllabic signs cannot be separated into parts that represent individual sounds.

Alphabetic writing

Alphabetic writing represents consonant and vowel segments. Unlike the International Phonetic Alphabet, which was devised expressly to represent details of pronunciation, ordinary alphabets generally ignore non-phonemic phenomena. Thus, the spelling of the English words *pan* and *nap* represents the phonemes /p/, /n/, and /æ/ but ignores consonant aspiration, vowel nasalization, and other allophonic variation. As we will see in section 16.5.2 of this chapter, some spelling systems also capture certain morphophonemic alternations.

Among alphabetic systems of writing, a distinction can be made between orthographies that assign equal importance to the representation of consonants and vowels (the case in English, for example) and those that focus primarily on the representation of consonants. Among the latter type, scholars often distinguish between **abjads** (pronounced [æbdʒædz]) and **abugidas** (pronounced [abugídəz]). In the abjad system, which is used by languages such as Arabic and Hebrew, vowels are either entirely absent or are optionally expressed with the help of diacritics, as shown in figure 16.1.

FIGURE 16.1 The word 'book' in Arabic (/kita:b/) and Hebrew (/sefer/), with and without vowel diacritics. In both languages, words are read from right to left.

Arabic
كتاب — No vowels
كِتَاب — With diacritics

Hebrew
ספר — No vowels
סֵפֶר — With diacritics

In contrast, in an abugida system, such as the one used for Indic languages, all vowels (other than a default vowel, usually /a/) must be represented. However, instead of having separate vowel symbols, they are marked by diacritics or by modifications to consonants. In figure 16.2, the vowel is not represented at all in /ka/ and is marked by diacritics in /ke/ and /ku/.

FIGURE 16.2
The syllables /ka/, /ke/,
and /ku/ in the
Devanagari writing
system used for Hindi

क के कु

ka ke ku

Writing systems emerged and spread around the earth over a long period of time. Though we can trace the spread of some systems over a wide area, writing may have emerged independently in several different places. The next sections trace the development of some writing systems from their pictorial origins. For a catalogue of the world's many writing systems, see www.omniglot.com.

16.2 The early history of writing

It is surprising that we cannot say with certainty how a comparatively recent cultural phenomenon like writing originated. We do know that writing developed in stages, the earliest of which involved the direct representation of objects. This is sometimes called *pre-writing*.

16.2.1 Pre-writing

Figures and scenes depicted on cave walls and rock faces in the Americas, Africa, and Europe twelve thousand years ago, and perhaps even earlier, may have been forerunners of writing. Some of these drawings may represent a type of pre-literate stage that did not evolve into a full-fledged writing system.

These drawings depict a wide range of human and animal activity and may even have been intended for purposes of linguistic communication. Some illustrations were doubtless a form of religious symbolism to request a successful hunt or other benefits. Perhaps some were for purely aesthetic purposes. Still others, such as those depicting the phases of the moon, may have been part of some form of record keeping. Figure 16.3a shows a pair of elk from a rock wall drawing in Sweden dating from the Old Stone Age (Paleolithic) period, perhaps as far back as 20 000 BC. Figure 16.3b shows an incised eagle bone from Le Placard, France, that dates back

FIGURE 16.3
a. Paleolithic drawing,
Sweden; b. Le Placard
eagle bone

some thirteen to fifteen thousand years. The incisions, which vary subtly, have been analyzed as a record of lunar phases. Pictorial records thus link the origins of writing with the history of representational art.

An even more direct connection links the origin of writing with record keeping. It has been suggested that the idea of writing had its origin in small clay tokens and counters that were used in record keeping and business transactions in the ancient Middle East. These small, fire-baked pieces of clay were apparently used for thousands of years before writing emerged (see figure 16.4).

FIGURE 16.4
Ancient Mesopotamian tokens

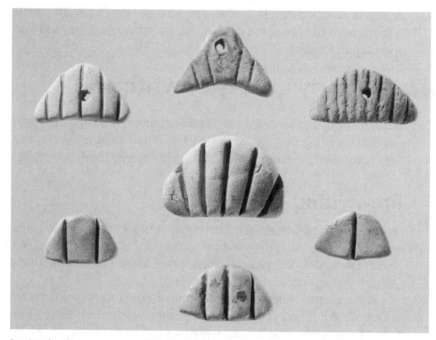

Reprinted with the permission of the Musée du Louvre. Dept. Ant. Orientale.

16.2.2 **Pictograms**

Whatever their purpose, there is no doubt that pictures were among the precursors of the written word. Early writing systems all evolved from pictorial representations called **pictograms** or picture writing. Each pictogram was an image of the object or concept that it represented and, as far as we know, offered no clues to pronunciation. Pictorial representations of this sort have been found among people throughout the ancient and modern world. Figure 16.5 illustrates

FIGURE 16.5
Indigenous pictography: some Dakota records of significant events

Source: Hans Jensen, *Sign, Symbol, and Script: An Account of Man's Efforts to Write*, 3rd ed., trans. George Unwin (London: George Allen and Unwin, 1970), p. 43.

several examples of Indigenous picture writing made by a Dakota named Lonedog; they depict four unrelated events: death as the result of smallpox, the building of a log cabin, the killing of someone with a spear, and the eclipse of the sun.

Pictograms are still used today, often reflecting the function of this form of pre-writing as a memory aid. Many signs indicating roadside services or information in parks are pictographic in nature, as are the standardized set of symbols for Canada's Workplace Hazardous Materials Information System (WHMIS) to identify classes of hazards (see figure 16.6).

FIGURE 16.6
Contemporary pictograms: Workplace Hazardous Materials Information System symbols

Source: © All Rights Reserved. *Do You Know These Vital Signs? The Hazard Symbols of WHMIS.* Health Canada, 2011. Reprinted with permission from the Minister of Health, 2014.

A contemporary and very sophisticated development of pictographic writing, **Blissymbolics** (originally called 'semantography'), was developed by Charles K. Bliss. It makes use of a number of recombineable symbols that represent basic units of meaning, as the example in figure 16.7 illustrates. Though Blissymbolics was intended by its inventor to be a means of international, cross-linguistic communication, its primary use today is to facilitate communication for non-speaking individuals. Blissymbolics Communication International (www.blissymbolics.org) sets the standard for the training and application of Blissymbolics for this specialized purpose.

FIGURE 16.7
Blissymbolics

Person   Forward   Building   Visitor

I would be glad   if   you   want to be   my   guest

As we consider developments that emerge from pictographic representation, it is important to remember that ancient pictograms are not writing in any sense of the word. They do not represent linguistic elements such as segments, syllables, morphemes, or words. They are not written in a sequence that matches the language's word order, and they often provide only limited clues about their intended meaning.

16.3 The evolution of writing

The earliest known logographic writing came from Sumeria, from where it spread to surrounding areas about five thousand years ago. Over time, inherently ambiguous pictograms came to be used to represent abstract notions, as their use was extended to include related concepts. For example, as shown in figure 16.8, the pictogram for 'foot' came to stand for 'go', 'move', and 'go away'; the pictogram for 'star' ended up being used for 'god' as well; the pictogram for 'hand' was employed to signify 'fist', as well as a unit of measurement; and so on.

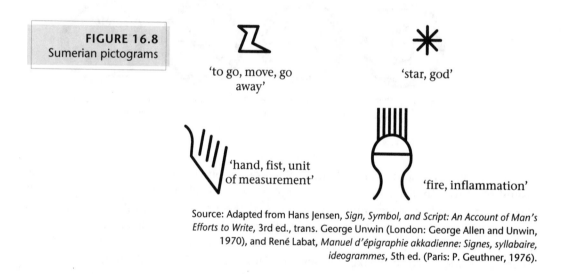

FIGURE 16.8
Sumerian pictograms

'to go, move, go away'

'star, god'

'hand, fist, unit of measurement'

'fire, inflammation'

Source: Adapted from Hans Jensen, *Sign, Symbol, and Script: An Account of Man's Efforts to Write*, 3rd ed., trans. George Unwin (London: George Allen and Unwin, 1970), and René Labat, *Manuel d'épigraphie akkadienne: Signes, syllabaire, ideogrammes*, 5th ed. (Paris: P. Geuthner, 1976).

Sumerian writing also combined signs to express abstract meanings. For example, a head with fire coming out of the top indicated 'anger', as shown in figure 16.9.

FIGURE 16.9
The Sumerian sign for 'anger'

Source: René Labat, *Manuel d'épigraphie akkadienne: Signes, syllabaire, ideogrammes*, 5th ed. (Paris: P. Geuthner, 1976).

Although its evolution was gradual, we can state with some certainty that Sumerian writing represented words (it was logographic rather than just pictographic) because from a fairly early stage, it was written in a consistent linear order that appears to reflect the order of words in speech. We cannot say with certainty at what date pictures began to be read as words, but once this practice took hold, the stage was set for the emergence of phonographic writing.

16.3.1 Rebuses and the emergence of writing

Phonographic writing made its appearance around 3000 BC with the first use of Sumerian symbols to represent sound rather than just meaning. This major development in the history of writing was made possible by the use of the **rebus principle**, which allows a sign to be used for any word with the same pronunciation as the word for which it was originally intended. In the inscription of an economic transaction in figure 16.10, for example, the symbol in the upper left-hand corner, which was originally used to represent the word *gi* 'reed', represents a homophonous word with the meaning 'reimburse'.

FIGURE 16.10
Sumerian rebus inscription (c. 3000 BC)

Source: A.A. Viaman, "Über die protosumerische Schrift," *Acta Antiqua Academiae Scientiarum Hungaricae* 22 (1974): 18, as reproduced in John DeFrancis, *Visible Speech: The Diverse Oneness of Writing Systems* (Honolulu: University of Hawaii Press, 1989), p. 76.

Thanks to the rebus principle, concepts that could not be directly depicted by a pictogram/logogram could be represented in writing. Thus, the sign for the word *ti* 'arrow', ➤━━, was also used for the word *ti* 'life'.

16.3.2 Toward syllabic writing

Once the breakthrough toward phonographic writing had been made, it did not take long (in historical terms) before syllabic writing began to emerge. Within about five hundred to six hundred years, signs that clearly represent not just homophonous words but parts of words—specifically, syllables—had become well established in Sumerian writing. For example, the syllable *kir* was represented by the syllabic signs for *ki* and *ir*, written in sequence. (By allowing the function of the symbols to overlap in this way, they avoided the need for a special sign for *r*.) Figure 16.11 illustrates this with the help of Sumerian cuneiform signs that are discussed in more detail in the following section.

| **FIGURE 16.11** Overlapped Sumerian syllabic signs | ki + ir = kir |

Source: Hans Jensen, *Sign, Symbol and Script: An Account of Man's Efforts to Write,* 3rd ed., trans. George Unwin (London: George Allen and Unwin, 1970), p. 95.

Sumerian writing never developed into a pure syllabary, however. Logographic elements were interspersed with syllabic ones, and many syllabic signs were used to represent syllables with other pronunciations as well.

Cuneiform

Over the centuries, Sumerian writing was simplified and eventually came to be produced with the use of a wedge-shaped stylus that was pressed into soft clay tablets. This form of writing, initiated in the fourth millennium BC, has come to be known as **cuneiform** (from Latin *cuneus* 'wedge'). In time, a change in writing practices led the cuneiform signs to be modified so that they ended up bearing even less resemblance to their pictographic origins than before. Figure 16.12 illustrates this development for two words.

FIGURE 16.12 Changes in cuneiform writing over time

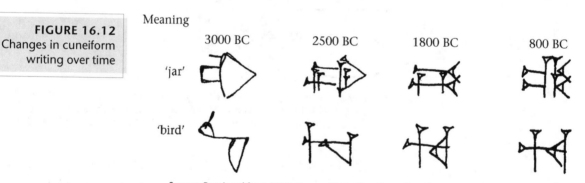

Source: Reprinted from M.W. Green, "Early Cuneiform," in *The Origins of Writing*, edited by Wayne M. Senner (Lincoln: University of Nebraska Press, 1989), p. 45. By permission of the University of Nebraska Press. Copyright 1989 by the University of Nebraska Press.

The cuneiform system was borrowed by the Elamites and Akkadians in the third millennium BC, a little later by the Persians, and in the second millennium BC by the Hittites far to the north in the ancient region of Anatolia (modern Asian Turkey). Cuneiform writing persisted until about the first few centuries of the Christian era in some areas and then disappeared from use, not to be rediscovered until the nineteenth century. It was first deciphered from Old Persian texts, a breakthrough that led to the deciphering of Akkadian, Sumerian, and Hittite, among other languages that employed it. This script was used for thousands of years but was generally replaced by systems of writing employed by the Semitic peoples of the Eastern Mediterranean.

16.3.3 Another Middle Eastern writing system: hieroglyphic

At about the time Sumerian pictography was flourishing, a similar system of pictorial communication was in use in Egypt. The Egyptian signs have become known as **hieroglyphs** (meaning 'sacred inscriptions' in Greek). The earliest texts display about five hundred such symbols. Like Sumerian pictograms, the hieroglyphic signs at first represented objects, but later they became logographic as they began to be associated with words.

Egyptian hieroglyphs developed into a mixed system of logographic writing and phonographic writing. For example, the sign for the heart and trachea was ♀; this represented the word itself: *nfr*. (Only the consonants of words represented by hieroglyphs are known with certainty. The Egyptians did not represent vowels—these can only be partially reconstructed from transcriptions in Greek and other languages that were made much later.) Eventually, this sign came to be disassociated from the word it represented and was used to transcribe other words that consisted of or included the same sounds, such as the word for 'good', which also contained the consonants *nfr*.

Hieroglyphic symbols eventually came to be used to represent individual consonant phonemes by application of what is called the **acrophonic principle** (from Greek *acros* 'extreme'): a consonant was represented by a picture of an object whose pronunciation began with that sound. For example, the hieroglyph for 'horned viper'

is read logographically as *f-t*. Thanks to the acrophonic principle, this sign was also used to represent the phoneme /f/ in spellings such as *fen* 'pleasant'.

As we will see in the next section, the acrophonic principle was crucial to the development of true alphabets. In Egyptian writing, however, it was only part of a system that mixed logographic and phonographic elements.

Figure 16.13 provides some additional examples of hieroglyphs. Hieroglyphs were used with decreasing frequency until Christian times. By the second century AD, Egyptian began to be written with Greek letters, and by the third century AD, hieroglyphs had been replaced by the Greek alphabet.

FIGURE 16.13
Egyptian hieroglyphs
(c. 1500 BC)

zaa-j
son-my

ndtjj-j
saviour-my

Source: Hans Jensen, *Sign, Symbol, and Script: An Account of Man's Efforts to Write*, 3rd ed., trans. George Unwin (London: George Allen and Unwin, 1970), p. 66.

16.3.4 The emergence of alphabets

Alphabetic writing emerged slowly from mixed writing systems over a long period in the Middle East. Building on this tradition of mixed writing, the Semitic peoples of ancient Phoenicia (modern Lebanon) devised an abjad writing system consisting of twenty-two symbols for consonants (but none for vowels) as early as 1000 BC. This system was written horizontally, right to left, as had been common in earlier scripts. It ultimately led to the development of many alphabetic writing systems, including both the Greek and Latin alphabets.

The pictorial (and eventually logographic) origins of the Phoenician alphabet are evident in some of its symbols, which were derived from Egyptian hieroglyphs. Figure 16.14 illustrates the creation of alphabetic symbols from the logograms corresponding to an ox's head, a throwing stick (some say a camel's hump), and a wavy flow of water.

FIGURE 16.14
Pictorial and logographic origins of some signs in the Phoenician alphabet

ʔāleph   gīmel   mēm

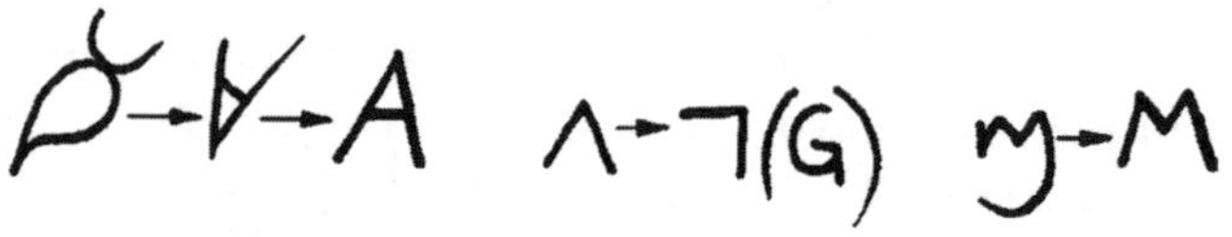

Source: Adapted from Geoffrey Sampson, *Writing Systems: A Linguistic Introduction* (Stanford, CA: Stanford University Press, 1985). Copyright © 1985 Geoffrey Sampson. All rights reserved. Used with the permission of Stanford University Press, www.sup.org.

These symbols eventually came to be used to represent the consonant phonemes of words by application of the acrophonic principle (see section 16.3.3). In this way, *ʔāleph* was used to represent a glottal stop; *gīmel*, the consonant /g/; and *mēm*, the consonant /m/. Some of the symbols of the Phoenician alphabet had developed from Egyptian hieroglyphics, and, as in hieroglyphic writing, vowels were not represented (see figure 16.13).

The Phoenicians were a trading people, and their alphabetic writing spread to adjacent countries and beyond. Eventually, the Greeks acquired and adapted the Phoenician alphabet.

The Greek alphabet

The Greeks developed the Phoenician writing system into the world's first full alphabet, with separate symbols for each consonant and vowel. (Phoenician symbols for consonant sounds not found in Greek were adapted to represent Greek vowels.) Figure 16.15 illustrates the evolution of the Classical Greek and ultimately the Latin (Roman) alphabet from the original Phoenician consonantal signs.

Phoenician *'ālep* represented a glottal stop. Since Greek had no such phoneme, the *'ālep* was employed to represent the vowel /a/ in Greek. Phoenician *hē* (/h/) was used to represent the Greek vowel /e/, and other signs were added to the system by the Greeks, including Φ for /f/, X for /kʰ/ and then /ks/, /ψ/ for /ps/, and /Ω/ for /oː/.

The Phoenician names for the letters (*'ālep, bēt, gīml, dālet*, and so on) were maintained by the Greeks (as *alpha, beta, gamma, delta*, and so on), but the possible pictorial origins were lost,

FIGURE 16.15
Evolution of the Greek and Latin alphabets from Phoenician signs

Phoenician			Greek			Latin	
Name	IPA	Symbol	Name	Early Symbol	Classical Symbol	Early Symbol	Classical Symbol
'ālep	ʔ	𐤀	alpha	Α	A	A	A
bēt	b	𐤁	beta	8	B		B
gīml	g	𐤂	gamma	Γ	Γ		C
dālet	d	𐤃	delta	Δ	Δ	O	D
hē	h	𐤄	epsilon	Ε	E	Ε	E
wāw	w	Υ	digamma	Ϝ		Ϝ	F
							G
zayin	z	I	zeta	I	Z		
ḥēt	ħ	𐤇	eta	𐤇	H	𐤇	H
ṭēt	tˤ	⊗	theta	⊗	θ		
yōd	j	𐤉	iota	ζ	I	I	I
							(J)
kāp	k	𐤊	kappa	Κ	K	Κ	K
lāmed	l	𐤋	lambda	Λ	Λ		L
mēm	m	𐤌	mu	M	M	M	M
nūn	n	𐤍	nu	N	N	N	N
sāmek	s	𐤎					
'ayin	ʕ	o	ŏmicron	O	O	O	O
pē	p	𐤐	pi	Π	Π		P
çādē	sˤ	𐤑	san	M			
qōp	q	Φ	qoppa	Ϙ			Q
reš	r	𐤓	rho	Ρ	P		R
šin	ʃ	W	sigma	Σ	Σ	Σ	S
tāw	t	×	tau	Χ			T
			upsilon		Υ	V	V
			chi		X		X
							Y
			omega		Ω		Z

Source: Based on David Diringer, "Alphabet," *The Encyclopedia Americana*, 1968 edition.

and the names carried no other meaning.[1] The writing system itself gained its name from the first two letters of the series: *alphabet*.

The Roman alphabet

When Greek colonists occupied southern Italy in the eighth and seventh centuries BC, they brought their alphabet with them. It was in turn taken up and modified by the Etruscan inhabitants of central Italy, a non-Latin-speaking people who were a political and cultural power before the rise of Rome. It is believed that the Romans acquired their alphabet through the Etruscans. As the Romans grew in power and influence during the following centuries, first as masters of Italy and later of Europe, the Roman alphabet spread throughout their empire.

Under the Romans, the Greek/Etruscan alphabet was again modified, this time with some symbols influenced by the Etruscans. Innovations included *C* for the phoneme /k/ and *G* for /g/. The oldest inscriptions also retained *K* for /k/ in some words, but it was generally replaced by *C*. Similarly, *Q* was retained before /u/. Roman script (which at the time consisted only of upper case letters) also employed Greek *U* (= V), *X, Y,* and *Z*, and moved *Z* to the end of the alphabet. The symbols Φ, ϴ, ψ and Ω were among those discarded, and *H* was converted back to a consonant symbol.

Some subsequent changes were made in the alphabet as it was adapted by various peoples of the Roman Empire. In English, for example, *W* was created from two juxtaposed *V*s. Spanish employs a tilde over *n* (ñ) to signify a palatal nasal, as in *año* /aɲo/ 'year', and French uses a cedilla under *c* (ç) to indicate the dental fricative /s/, as in the spelling of *français* /frãsɛ/ 'French'.

16.4 Some non-European writing systems

This section focuses on the nature and development of writing systems that originated outside the Middle East. While some of these systems emerged in response to external influences, others seem to have been entirely independent innovations. We will briefly examine the writing systems of China, Japan, and Korea, as well as a script developed for use with Cree in western Canada.

16.4.1 Chinese writing

The Chinese system of writing developed out of pictograms that eventually came to represent morphemes (most of which are also words). The oldest inscriptions are the oracle texts, written on animal bones and tortoise shells and dating back to about 1200 BC. These include many recognizable images, such as ⊙ 'sun' and ☽ 'moon'.

A change toward more **symbolic signs** began at an early date as more abstract notions were symbolized, such as ‿ 'above' and ⌒ 'below'. Symbols were also combined to extend meanings. For example, the sign for 'to tend (animals)' 牧 is composed of 牛 'cow' and 攴 'hand and whip'. 'To follow' 从 is two men in sequence, and so on. In time, the characters became more abstract.

Calligraphy is an ancient and respected art in China, and Chinese writing exists in a number of styles. The script is usually written from left to right along a horizontal axis, although newspapers and older texts are written in vertical columns that are read downwards, beginning on the right side of the page. The units of contemporary Chinese writing are called **characters**. Many monosyllabic words are presented in true logographic fashion by a character consisting of a single symbol. For example, the Mandarin words [ʃǒu] 'hand' and [mǎ] 'horse' are written 手 and 馬, respectively. However, the overwhelming majority of characters (one estimate is 99 percent) consist of two parts.

The main component of a two-part character, called the **phonetic determinative**, provides information about the pronunciation of the corresponding morpheme. Although about four thousand different phonetic determinatives are used in Chinese writing, they represent pronunciation very imperfectly. Tone, which is contrastive in the Chinese family of languages, is not represented at all, and many phonetic determinatives indicate only part of the morpheme's pronunciation. For instance, the determinative in column C of table 16.1 is used for a wide variety of words ending in *ao* without regard for tone or for whether the initial consonant is *j, n, r,* or some other element. Furthermore, because of sound changes over the last centuries, about one-third of all phonetic determinatives provide little or no useful information about current pronunciation. Finally, because Chinese languages have many homophones, even the most informative phonetic determinatives can be used for many different words.

Chinese characters also include a semantic component, called the **radical** or **key**, which provides clues about the morpheme's meaning. There are about two hundred different radicals in contemporary Chinese writing. Table 16.1 provides examples of some of the characters that can be formed by combining phonetic determinatives with radicals. Notice that only the phonetic determinative in column A indicates the precise pronunciation (ignoring tone) of the four characters in which it appears. The other determinatives supply helpful, but incomplete, phonetic information.

The usefulness of the information supplied by the radicals also varies. The characters in row 1 represent morphemes whose meaning is at best indirectly associated with that of the radical ('person'), but the radicals in rows 2, 3, and 4 are much more informative: the characters in row 2 all denote actions involving the hand, while those in row 3 refer to things made of wood and those in row 4 all have something to do with liquids.

Although neither phonetic determinatives alone nor semantic radicals alone suffice to identify the morphemes that they are used to represent, they are more than adequate when used in conjunction with each other. Despite these complexities, Chinese writing provides its users with an effective way to represent the words and morphemes of their language. Moreover, the lack of efficiency is offset by the fact that the same literary script can be understood by speakers of different Chinese languages. Although a speaker of Mandarin and a speaker of Cantonese may pronounce the word for 'fire' differently—/xwǒ/ and /fɔ̌/, respectively—both can read it from the same character (火), since Chinese writing does not represent a word's pronunciation.

TABLE 16.1   Some Chinese characters

	Semantic radical	Phonetic determinatives as pronounced in Mandarin Chinese			
		A 敖 (*áo*)	B 参 (*cān*)	C 尧 (*yáo*)	D 甫 (*fū*)
1	亻 'person'	傲 (*ào*: 'proud')	傪 (*cān*: 'good')	侥 (*jiǎo*: 'lucky')	俌 (*fǔ*: 'help')
2	扌 'hand'	擞 (*ào*: 'shake')	掺 (*shān*: 'seize')	挠 (*náo*: 'scratch')	捕 (*bǔ*: 'catch')
3	木 'wood'	橄 (*áo*: 'barge')	椮 (*shēn*: 'beam')	桡 (*náo*: 'oar')	楠 (*fú*: 'trellis')
4	氵 'water'	潵 (*ào*: 'stream')	渗 (*shèn*: 'leak')	浇 (*jiāo*: 'sprinkle')	浦 (*pǔ*: 'creek')

Source: John DeFrancis, *Visible Speech: The Diverse Oneness of Writing Systems* (Honolulu: University of Hawaii Press, 1989), p. 107. © 1989 John DeFrancis. Reprinted with permission.

In the 1950s and 1960s, the government of the People's Republic of China introduced simplified characters (some with fewer strokes and newly invented) in an attempt to promote literacy. At the same time, a system of writing Mandarin with a modified Latin alphabet, called **pinyin**, has also been introduced. Pinyin is used as a subsidiary system for writing such things as street signs, addresses, and brand names as well as for teaching children how to pronounce characters. It is also sometimes used to input Chinese into electronic devices (computers, cell phones, etc.), which then automatically convert it into characters.

16.4.2 Japanese writing

The writing system of modern Japanese is arguably the most complicated in the world. Its use requires knowledge of three distinct scripts, including a pair of syllabaries—**hiragana** and **katakana**—which were created by modifying Chinese characters. Although Japanese can be written exclusively with either syllabary, normal writing involves the use of Chinese characters (called **kanji** in Japanese) in addition to hiragana and katakana. Kanji symbols are typically used to represent all or part of a word's root while affixes are represented by hiragana symbols. The phrase *the man's car*, for example, can be written as in figure 16.16, with the roots 'man' and 'car' represented by kanji and affixes such as *no* (marking possession) and *de* (marking location) written in hiragana.

FIGURE 16.16 The Japanese phrase meaning 'the man's car' written in a mixture of kanji and hiragana	hito-no 人 の man GEN kanji hiragana	kuruma-de 車 で car LOC kanji hiragana

The katakana syllabary, whose symbols are less rounded than their hiragana counterparts (see figure 16.17), is used to write **onomatopoeic words** as well as words borrowed into Japanese from other languages.

Finally, it should be noted that the Roman alphabet, which the Japanese call *romaji*, is also making inroads. It is not unusual to see all four writing systems used together, especially in advertising.

Learning to read Japanese is a formidable task, in part because of the way the various scripts are intermingled and in part because of complexities in the use of kanji symbols, which can have more than one pronunciation depending on whether they are used to represent a word of Chinese or Japanese origin. For example, Japanese has two morphemes with the meaning 'mountain'—/san/, which is of Chinese origin, and the native Japanese /jama/. Both are written with the kanji character 山.

16.4.3 Korean writing

Korean was once written with Chinese characters, which had been introduced in the first centuries AD. However, Korean suffixes could not be easily represented by Chinese writing. Various devices were used to alleviate this problem, but inadequacies persisted. Finally, King Sejong (1419–52) created an alphabetic script called **hangul** (pronounced [haŋgil]). After some

FIGURE 16.17
Hiragana and katakana syllabaries and their phonetic values. (The conventions for representing voicing, vowel length, and gemination are not indicated here.)

Katakana chart

	A	I	U	E	O
SINGLE VOWEL	ア A	イ I	ウ U	エ E	オ O
K	カ KA	キ KI	ク KU	ケ KE	コ KO
S	サ SA	シ SHI	ス SU	セ SE	ソ SO
T	タ TA	チ CHI	ツ TSU	テ TE	ト TO
N	ナ NA	ニ NI	ヌ NU	ネ NE	ノ NO
H	ハ HA	ヒ HI	フ FU	ヘ HE	ホ HO
M	マ MA	ミ MI	ム MU	メ ME	モ MO
Y	ヤ YA		ユ YU		ヨ YO
R	ラ RA	リ RI	ル RU	レ RE	ロ RO
W	ワ WA				ヲ O
N (in a coda)	ン N				

Hiragana chart

	A	I	U	E	O
SINGLE VOWEL	あ A	い I	う U	え E	お O
K	か KA	き KI	く KU	け KE	こ KO
S	さ SA	し SHI	す SU	せ SE	そ SO
T	た TA	ち CHI	つ TSU	て TE	と TO
N	な NA	に NI	ぬ NU	ね NE	の NO
H	は HA	ひ HI	ふ FU	へ HE	ほ HO
M	ま MA	み MI	む MU	め ME	も MO
Y	や YA		ゆ YU		よ YO
R	ら RA	り RI	る RU	れ RE	ろ RO
W	わ WA				を O
N (in a coda)	ん N				

Source: Adapted from Len Walsh, *Read Japanese Today* (North Clarendon, VT: Tuttle, 2009). Reprinted with permission from Tuttle Publishing, www.tuttlepublishing.com.

modifications over the centuries, it became the standard Korean writing system. An especially interesting feature of hangul is that symbols are grouped together into syllable-sized clusters (see figure 16.18).

Another intriguing feature of hangul is that it typically provides a single spelling for each morpheme, regardless of contextually induced variations in its pronunciation. For instance, the word

FIGURE 16.18
Some hangul symbols

Some hangul symbols:

ㄴ ㄹ ㅁ ㅂ ㅅ ㅏ ㅜ
/n/ /l/ /m/ /p/ /s/ /a/ /u/

Some words written in hangul:

불　　　밥　　　사람
/pul/ 'fire'　/pap/ 'rice'　/salam/ 'person'

for 'rice' has the same spelling (see above), regardless of whether it is pronounced /pap/ (the basic pronunciation) or /pam/, as happens in front of a nasal consonant (e.g., /pam man/ 'rice only').

Like Japanese, Korean also makes use of Chinese characters (called **hanja**), although in a more restricted way. Approximately half the vocabulary of contemporary Korean is of Chinese origin, and many words of this type are written with the help of Chinese characters in newspapers and in scientific articles. However, this practice has been reduced somewhat in recent years in South Korea, and it has been eliminated entirely in North Korea.

16.4.4 Cree writing

The syllabic script of the Cree was the creation of a missionary, James Evans, in the nineteenth century. It was employed for religious literature, and by 1861, the entire Bible had been written in the Cree syllabary. Today, in somewhat modified form, this script is used by Cree speakers across Canada.

Cree morphemes are made up of syllables that combine one of ten initial consonants with one of seven vowels; in some cases, there is also a postvocalic consonant. The Cree writing system provides a separate symbol for each V and CV syllable. As in syllabaries in general, the symbols representing the CV syllables bear no resemblance to those representing syllables consisting of a single vowel; there is no connection, for instance, between the symbols for the syllable /ki/ **ᑭ** and the syllable /i/ **ᐃ**. However, the Cree system is not wholly syllabic since consonants that occur at the end of a syllable must be represented by a separate symbol.

A striking feature of the Cree syllabary is its phonetic symbolism. Vowels are indicated by the direction in which a syllabic symbol faces. Symbols that face 'south' (downward on the printed page) contain /e:/, those facing 'north' (upward) contain /i/ or /i:/, those pointing 'east' (rightward) have /o/ or /o:/, and those looking to the 'west' (leftward) contain /a/ or /a:/. Vowel length is indicated by a superposed dot, as in **ᓯ** = /si:/.

Plains Cree, a variety of Cree spoken in Western Canada, is written with the symbols in figure 16.19 (other dialects use slightly different ones). A macron indicates a long vowel in the transliteration.

FIGURE 16.19
The Cree syllabary

Δ	*i, ī*	▽	*ē*	▷	*o, ō*	◁	*a*	◁̇	*ā*
Λ	*pi, pī*	V	*pē*	>	*po, pō*	<	*pa*	<̇	*pā*
∩	*ti, tī*	U	*tē*	⊃	*to, tō*	C	*ta*	Ċ	*tā*
⌐	*ci, cī*	⌐	*cē*	J	*co, cō*	L	*ca*	L̇	*cā*
P	*ki, kī*	ᖅ	*kē*	d	*ko, kō*	b	*ka*	ḃ	*kā*
Γ	*mi, mī*	⌐	*mē*	⌐	*mo, mō*	L	*ma*	L̇	*mā*
σ	*ni, nī*	ᓄ	*nē*	ᓄ	*no, nō*	ₐ	*na*	ₐ̇	*nā*
ᒉ	*si, sī*	ᔆ	*sē*	ᒉ	*so, sō*	ᔆ	*sa*	ᔆ̇	*sā*
ᕒ	*yi, yī*	ᕽ	*yē*	ᕽ	*yo, yō*	ᕚ	*ya*	ᕚ̇	*yā*

Finals

ᑉ *p* ᐟ *t* - *c* ᒃ *k* ᒻ *m* ᐢ *s* ᐣ *n* • *y* ○ *w* ᑊ *h* × *hk* ᖧ *l* ᖩ *r*

The examples in figure 16.20 illustrate the use of the Cree syllabary.

FIGURE 16.20 Three words in the Cree syllabary	

16.5 English orthography

English employs an alphabetic orthography in which symbols are used to represent individual consonants and vowels. In this section, we will consider the nature and history of English orthography. Section 16.6 examines the relationship between writing and reading.

16.5.1 Irregularities

A frequently expressed complaint about English orthography is that it does not establish a one-to-one relationship between symbols and phonemes. Table 16.2 lists some well-known examples of this.

TABLE 16.2   Some problems with English orthography

Problem	Examples
Some letters do not represent any phonemes in a particular word.	throu<u>gh</u>, si<u>g</u>n, giv<u>e</u>, pa<u>l</u>m
A group of two or more letters can be used to represent a single phoneme.	<u>th</u>ink /θ/, <u>sh</u>ip /ʃ/, philoso<u>ph</u>y /f/
A single letter can represent a group of two or more phonemes.	sa<u>x</u>ophone /ks/, e<u>x</u>ile /gz/
The same letter can represent different phonemes in different words.	*o* in <u>o</u>n /ɑ/, b<u>o</u>ne /ow/, s<u>o</u>n /ʌ/, <u>o</u>ne /wʌ/
The same phoneme can be represented by different letters in different words.	/u/ in r<u>u</u>de, l<u>oo</u>p, s<u>ou</u>p, n<u>ew</u>, s<u>ue</u>, t<u>o</u>, t<u>wo</u>

Historical factors

The relationship between symbol and phoneme in English orthography has not always been so indirect. In fact, the spelling system used throughout England during the Old English period provided a regular set of symbol-phoneme correspondences. The foundation for today's system, it lacked the symbols *j*, *v*, and *w* but made use of four symbols that are not part of our current alphabet (see table 16.3).

TABLE 16.3	Old English symbols not found in Modern English spelling	
Symbol	**Name**	**Segment(s) represented**
æ	ash	[æ]
ð	eth	[θ] and [ð]
þ	thorn	[θ] and [ð] (used interchangeably with *eth*)
ƿ	wynn	[w]

The relationship between symbol and phoneme in English orthography was significantly disturbed in the Middle English period as the phonological pattern of the language began to change. To see an example of this, we need only consider the Great Vowel Shift, which dramatically altered the pronunciation of long vowels—converting /iː/ into /aj/, /eː/ into /i/, /aː/ into /e/, and so on. Because Old English orthography used the same symbol for long and short vowels, complications arose when the pronunciation of the long vowels changed. Thus, the letter *i*, which had formerly been used only to represent the phonetically similar /iː/ and /i/, ended up representing the very dissimilar /aj/ (the descendant of /iː/) and /ɪ/ (the descendant of /i/). The end result can be seen in the spelling of *hide* and *hid*, *write* and *written*, *ride* and *ridden*, *wide* and *width*, and many other words.

Additional complications arose following the invasion of England by French-speaking Normans in the eleventh century. The use of English in official documents declined and regional orthographies developed in the absence of a national standard. To make matters worse, scribes who were trained primarily to write French and Latin made a number of questionable changes to English spelling. Among those that have survived are the use of *ch* rather than *c* for /tʃ/ (*cheese, chin*, etc.), *th* rather than þ (thorn) and ð (eth) for /θ/ and /ð/ (*thin, this*), and *c* rather than *s* for /s/ (*grace, ice, mice*).

Toward the end of the fifteenth century, yet another trend developed—the practice of spelling words in a manner that reflected their etymological origin. Enduring examples of this influence are found in the spelling of the words *debt, doubt, receipt*, and *salmon* (formerly spelled *dette, doute, receite*, and *samon*), all of which were given a 'silent' consonant to make them look more like the Latin words from which they descended.

By the 1500s, English orthography had become increasingly irregular and idiosyncratic, with many different spellings in use for the same word. The word *pity*, for example, could be spelled *pity, pyty, pitie, pytie, pittie*, and *pyttye*. As printing presses came into greater use and books became more widely available, the need to reform and regularize English orthography became apparent. In the late 1500s and early 1600s, a number of individuals (most notably Richard Mulcaster and Edmond Coote) formulated and published spelling rules, which were gradually adopted by printers and other literate speakers of English. While these rules were far from perfect, they at least had the effect of stabilizing English spelling. By the 1700s, English orthography was more or less fixed.

> **Language Matters** **How Do You Spell 'Shakespeare'?**
>
> During William Shakespeare's time (1564–1616), English spelling was still in a state of flux, which may explain why there were so many spellings for his name—Shakespeare, Shakespere, Shakespear, Shakspear, among others. Shakespeare himself wrote his name in different ways and wavered on the spelling of many words in his plays—he used three different spellings for 'more', three for '-ness', and five for 'sheriff', to mention a few examples.

The vast majority of the spelling conventions introduced during this period are still in use today. One of the most famous, proposed by Mulcaster in 1582, involves the use of 'silent' *e* at the end of words to indicate a preceding long (tense) vowel, as in *late and bone*. Even here, though, there are complications and exceptions, as can be seen in the modern spelling of *have*, *done*, and *come*, which contain lax vowels. In these cases, the *e* represents a word-final /ə/ that has since been lost.

16.5.2 Obstacles to reform

Over the years, there have been numerous proposals for the reform of English orthography, including ones put forward by Benjamin Franklin, George Bernard Shaw, and Noah Webster. However, far-reaching reforms are unlikely for a variety of reasons. For one thing, they would require a long and difficult period of transition. As the following tongue-in-cheek suggestion (variously attributed to Mark Twain, M.J. Shields, and W.K. Lessing) shows, reform would not be painless even if it took place over a period of many years.

> *For example, in Year 1 that useless letter 'c' would be dropped to be replased either by 'k' or 's', and likewise 'x' would no longer be part of the alphabet. The only kase in which 'c' would be retained would be the 'ch' formation, which will be dealt with later. Year 2 might reform 'w' spelling, so that 'which' and 'one' would take the same konsonant, wile Year 3 might well abolish 'y' replasing it with 'i' and Iear 4 might fiks the 'g–j' anomali wonse and for all.*
>
> *Jenerally, then, the improvement would kontinue iear bai iear with Iear 5 doing awai with useless double konsonants, and Iears 6–12 or so modifaiing vowlz and the rimeining voist and unvoist konsonants. Bai Iear 15 or sou, it wud fainali be posibl tu meik ius ov thi ridandant leterz 'c', 'y' and 'x'—bai now jast a memori in the maindz of ould doderers—tu replais 'ch', 'sh' and 'th' rispektivli.*
>
> *Fainali, xen, after sam 20 iers ov orxogrephkl riform, we wud hev a lojikl, kohirnt speling in ius xrewawt xe Ingliy spiking werld . . .*

People who knew only the reformed spelling system would have difficulty reading books written in traditional orthography. Those who wished to read any of the millions of books or articles currently in print would therefore have to either learn the traditional spelling system or have the documents that interested them converted into the new orthography.

A second factor militating against serious orthographic reform has to do with the dialectal variation found within English. Because English is spoken in more parts of the world than any other language, it has many different dialects. Any attempt to establish an orthography based on a principle of 'one phoneme, one symbol' would result in serious regional differences in spelling. For instance, speakers of Boston English would write *far* as *fa* since they do not pronounce syllable-final /r/. Speakers of some dialects of Newfoundland English would write both *tin* and *thin* as *tin* and both *den* and *then* as *den* since they have no /t/-/θ/ or /d/-/ð/ distinction.

Moreover, while most Canadians would have identical spellings for *cot* and *caught* (since these words are homophones in their speech), speakers of English in many other parts of the world pronounce them differently and would therefore spell them differently as well.

Other considerations

Even if considerations relating to practicality and dialectal variation did not rule out major reforms to our orthography, there might still be reasons for retaining at least some of the current spelling conventions.

One advantage of the contemporary system is that it often indicates derivational relationships among words. For instance, if the words *music* and *musician* or *sign* and *signature* were spelled phonetically, it would be difficult to perceive the relationship between them since the root is pronounced differently in each case.

(1) music   [mjuzɪk]   musician   [mjuzɪʃ-ən]
     sign   [sajn]   signature   [sɪgn-ɪtʃər]

As illustrated in table 16.4, there are many other such cases where English orthography ignores differences in pronunciation so that a morpheme can have the same or nearly the same spelling in different words.

TABLE 16.4   Examples of a single English spelling for roots with different pronunciations

electri<u>c</u> – electri<u>c</u>ity	[k] and [s] represented as *c*
inser<u>t</u> – inser<u>t</u>ion	[t] and [ʃ] as *t*
righ<u>t</u> – righ<u>t</u>eous	[t] and [tʃ] as *t*
bom<u>b</u> – bom<u>b</u>ard	Ø and [b] as *b*
dam<u>n</u> – dam<u>n</u>ation	Ø and [n] as *n*
impre<u>ss</u> – impre<u>ss</u>ion	[s] and [ʃ] as *ss*
analo<u>g</u>y – analo<u>g</u>ous	[dʒ] and [g] as *g*
re<u>sign</u> – re<u>sign</u>ation	[aj] and [ɪ] as *i*; Ø and [g] as *g*
ch<u>a</u>ste – ch<u>a</u>stity	[ej] and [æ] as *a*
pl<u>ea</u>se – pl<u>ea</u>sant	[i] and [ɛ] as *ea*

Examples such as these show that English orthography often seeks to provide a single spelling for the variants of a morpheme, even though they may have quite different pronunciations. This is sometimes called a 'deep orthography' or a 'morphophonemic orthography'. Once this aim is taken into account, it is possible to see the usefulness of orthographic conventions that allow *c* to stand for both /k/ (*electric*) and /s/ (*electricity*), *t* to represent both /t/ (*insert*) or /ʃ/ (*insertion*), and so on.

Morphological considerations are reflected in English orthography in other ways as well. Consider in this regard the spelling of the following words.

(2) mess   lapse
     crass   dense
     kiss   house
     floss   mouse

Although these words all end in the phoneme /s/, this segment is not represented as a simple *s*. Instead, the *s* is either doubled to *ss* (when preceded by a lax vowel, as in the first column) or followed by an *e* (in all other cases, as exemplified in the second column). This reflects a general rule of English orthography, which reserves word-final *s* mostly for inflectional suffixes (particularly, the plural and the third person singular). Thus, a single word-final *s* is permitted in the word *laps* (the plural of *lap*) but not in *lapse*.

Another example of morphological influence is found in the rule that prohibits a final *ll* in polysyllabic words—*plentiful, excel, repel*, and so on. As the following examples show, this rule is systematically suspended in two morphological patterns: compounds (the first column) and derivations consisting of a prefix and its base (the second column).

(3) baseball   unwell
     spoonbill   resell
     landfill   recall

Yet another morphologically constrained rule of English orthography usually converts postconsonantal *y* in a polysyllabic root to *i* in front of a suffix.

(4) carry   carri-ed
     merry   merri-ly
     marry   marri-age
     candy   candi-es
     beauty   beauti-ful

The existence of conventions and practices such as these demonstrates that English orthography is much more than a system for phonemic transcription. Its intricacies can be understood only through the careful study of the history and structure of the linguistic system that it is used to represent.

Language Matters **Linguists and the Development of Orthographies**

According to estimates in the twenty-first edition of *Ethnologue*, only about 4000 of the world's 7000 languages have a writing system. Linguists are often called upon to develop orthographies and literacy programs for communities that have no writing system. The task requires a sensitivity not only to details of the language's phonology and morphology, but also to practical considerations such as ease of learning, compatibility with keyboards, similarity to other orthographies in the region, the dialect on whose pronunciation the writing system will be based, and the like.

You can find more information about the development of orthographies in these resources:

Cahill, Michael. 2018. "Orthography Design and Implementation for Endangered Languages." In *The Oxford Handbook of Endangered Languages*. Edited by Kenneth L. Rehg and Lyle Campbell, 327–46. Oxford, UK: Oxford University Press.

Cahill, Michael, and Elke Karan. 2008. *Factors in Designing Effective Orthographies for Unwritten Languages*. SIL International. Available at www.sil.org.

Lüpke, Friederike. 2011. "Orthography Development." In *The Cambridge Handbook of Endangered Languages*. Edited by Peter K. Austin, 312–36. Cambridge, UK: Cambridge University Press.

16.6 Writing and reading

The three types of writing described earlier in this chapter each represent different types of linguistic units—morphemes and words in the case of logographic systems, syllables in the case of syllabaries, and consonants and vowels in the case of alphabets. Because of these differences, each orthography places different demands on readers. We know that different parts of the brain are used for reading logographic writing systems compared to phonographic orthographies such as syllabaries and alphabets. Because phonological structure is largely irrelevant to logographic writing, people suffering from phonological deficits caused by damage to the brain typically do not lose the ability to write and read logograms. In contrast, the use of syllabaries and alphabets can be severely disrupted by this type of disorder. Indeed, there are reports of Japanese stroke patients who are unable to use hiragana or katakana (the Japanese syllabaries) but retain mastery of kanji (the logographic writing system).

Further information about the relationship between language and writing systems comes from the study of the congenitally deaf. Because their hearing impairment undermines their access to the phonological units that alphabets represent, they often have significant difficulty learning to read orthographies of this type.

Language Matters Do Spelling Irregularities Hurt Young Readers?

Perhaps. One study reports that children whose language has highly regular symbol-phoneme correspondences (e.g., Greek, Finnish, German, Spanish, and Italian) can read both words and non-words with almost 100 percent accuracy by the middle of grade 1. In contrast, children learning to read English have success rates of around 34 percent, on average. Children whose language falls somewhere in the middle in terms of orthographic regularity (Danish, Portuguese, and French) show mean success rates of around 75 percent.

Source: J.C. Ziegler and U. Goswami, "Becoming Literate in Different Languages: Similar Problems, Different Solutions," *Developmental Science* 9, 5 (2006): 429–53.

The type of linguistic unit represented by an orthography also has an effect on how children with normal hearing learn to read. Each system has its own advantages and disadvantages. Children learning Chinese characters have little difficulty understanding what each symbol represents, but it takes them many years to learn enough symbols to be able to write and read all the items in their vocabulary. (Knowledge of several thousand separate symbols is required just to read a newspaper.) Even educated people typically know only a few thousand characters and must use dictionaries for new or unfamiliar words.

This problem does not arise in syllabic and alphabetic orthographies. Because languages have far fewer syllable types and phonemes than morphemes or words, the entire inventory of symbols can be learned in a year or two and then used productively to write and read new words. This is the major advantage of sound-based orthographies over word-based writing systems.

There is reason to think that children find syllabaries easier to master than alphabets. Children learning syllabaries (such as Japanese hiragana) are reported to have fewer reading problems than children learning alphabetic orthographies. Of course, the difficulties associated with learning an alphabetic orthography can be compounded by irregularities in the system itself. This is at least part of the reason that children learning to read English are more likely to have problems than are children learning to read a language with a more regular system of spelling.

The advantage of syllabaries over alphabets for young readers apparently stems from the fact that children have less difficulty identifying syllables than phonemes. One study revealed that 46 percent of four-year-olds and 90 percent of six-year-olds can segment words into syllables. In contrast, virtually no four-year-olds and only about two-thirds of all six-year-olds can segment words into phoneme-sized units. Since learning to read involves an understanding of the type of unit represented by written symbols, it is not surprising that syllabaries are generally easier for young children to learn.

Language Matters **Processing the Words**

A common source of problems in reading, writing, and spelling is developmental dyslexia, a learning disability of neurological origin that may affect 10 to 15 percent of the population to some degree. Research suggests that dyslexics process certain types of information in different parts of the brain than do non-dyslexics and that they have particular trouble discriminating among the sounds within words. Even a small processing problem can disrupt the relationship between symbols on the page and the corresponding words, creating an unrecognizable jumble of letters.

> Hav ingdys lexiac anmake it hardtodo wellins chool.
> Eaxly trexxmxnt xs impxrtant.

You can find out more about dyslexia from the International Dyslexia Association website at www.interdys.org.

Of course, it must be remembered that syllabaries may have disadvantages of other sorts. While syllabic writing is feasible for languages such as Japanese that have a relatively small number of syllable types, it would be quite impractical in English, where there are dozens of different syllable structures. Ultimately, an orthography must be judged in terms of its success in representing language for the purpose of reading and writing. There is no doubt that an alphabetic orthography is superior to a syllabary for representing the phonological structure of English.

Summing up

The development of writing has been one of humanity's greatest intellectual achievements. From **pictograms** and **logograms**, the graphic representation of language has developed into **syllabic writing** and the **alphabet**. This was achieved by establishing the relationship between graphic symbols and sounds.

Many of the numerous writing systems found throughout the modern world owe their origin directly or indirectly to the Semitic writing systems of the eastern Mediterranean. As the idea of writing spread, new forms of the signs were independently invented and sound-symbol correspondences were altered to accommodate individual languages. Some writing systems that were derived from the Graeco-Phoenician tradition are today scarcely recognizable as such, since so little remains of the original symbols. In cases where the entire system was invented, perhaps only the idea of writing is traceable to the early traditions.

In all cases, the historical line of development is clear. There seems to be no evidence of a culture that has developed an alphabet and then followed this with the development of a logographic script or a syllabary. But this cultural line of development does not imply that earlier forms of writing are inferior to alphabetic writing. In the case of languages such as Japanese or Cree, the syllabic writing system is as well suited to the phonological structure of the language as an alphabetic script would be.

Note

1. Ancient Greek was represented by reversing the direction of writing at the end of each line. If the first line of a text was written right-to-left, the next line continued left-to-right, then right-to-left, and so on. This practice was typical of many old writing systems and is known as **boustrophedon** (Greek for 'as the ox turns'), since it was said to resemble the pattern made by plowing a field.

Recommended reading

Collier, Mark, and Bill Manley. 1998. *How to Read Egyptian Hieroglyphs*. Berkeley: University of California Press.

Cummings, D.W. 1988. *American English Spelling: An Informal Description*. Baltimore, MD: Johns Hopkins University Press.

Daniels, Peter T., and William Bright. 1996. *The World's Writing Systems*. Oxford, UK: Oxford University Press.

DeFrancis, John. 1989. *Visible Speech: The Diverse Oneness of Writing Systems*. Honolulu: University of Hawaii Press.

Gelb, I. 1952. *A Study of Writing*. Chicago: University of Chicago Press.

Gibson, Eleanor J., and Harry Levin. 1975. *The Psychology of Reading*. Cambridge, MA: MIT Press.

Gleitman, Lila R., and Paul Rozin. 1977. "The Structure and Acquisition of Reading I: Relations between Orthographies and the Structures of Language." In *Toward a Psychology of Reading*. Edited by Arthur S. Reber and Don L. Scarborough, 1–53. Hillsdale, NJ: Lawrence Erlbaum.

Jensen, Hans. 1970. *Sign, Symbol and Script: An Account of Man's Efforts to Write*. 3rd ed. Translated by George Unwin. London: George Allen and Unwin.

Sampson, Geoffrey. 1985. *Writing Systems: A Linguistic Introduction*. Stanford, CA: Stanford University Press.

Schmandt-Besserat, Denise. 1989. "Two Precursors of Writing: Plain and Complex Tokens." In *The Origins of Writing*. Edited by Wayne M. Senner, 27–42. Lincoln: University of Nebraska Press.

Senner, Wayne M., ed.. 1989. *The Origins of Writing*. Lincoln: University of Nebraska Press.

Wallace, Rex. 1989. "The Origins and Development of the Latin Alphabet." In *The Origins of Writing*. Edited by Wayne M. Senner, 121–36. Lincoln: University of Nebraska Press.

Exercises

1. Suppose you are the user of a pictographic writing system that can already represent concrete objects in a satisfactory way. Using the pictographic symbols of your system, propose ideographic extensions of these symbols to represent the following meanings.

   a) hunt
   b) cold
   c) fast
   d) white
   e) strength
   f) cook
   g) tired
   h) wet
   i) angry
   j) weakness

2. Construct a syllabary for English that can be used to spell the following words. What problems do you encounter?

foe	law	shoe
slaw	slow	slowly
lee	day	daily
sue	pull	shop
ship	loop	food
lock	shock	unlock
locked	shocked	pulled
shops	locker	shod
float	splint	schlock

3. How does English orthography capture the morphophonemic alternations in the following words? Begin your analysis with a phonemic transcription of the forms.

   a) hymn   hymnal
   b) part   partial
   c) recite   recitation
   d) reduce   reduction
   e) design   designation
   f) critical   criticize   criticism
   g) analog   analogous   analogy

4. After discussing the forms in exercise 3, consider the following forms. Does the spelling system treat all cases of allomorphic variation the same way?

   a) invade   invasion
   b) concede   concession
   c) assume   assumption
   d) profound   profundity

5. Briefly outline the advantages and disadvantages of the three major types of writing that have evolved throughout history.

To learn more about the topics discussed in this chapter, visit the Companion Website for *Contemporary Linguistic Analysis*.

Glossary

Abjad An alphabetic writing system in which vowels are either absent or are optionally expressed with the help of diacritics.

Ablaut A vowel alternation that marks a grammatical contrast (e.g., *mouse/mice*).

Absolute universals Patterns or traits that occur in all languages.

Abugida An alphabetic writing system in which all vowels, except for a default vowel (usually /a/), are represented by diacritics and/or modifications to consonants.

Accent Phonetic qualities of a language variety that identify it to speakers of other varieties as different from their own.

Accommodation The modification of speech patterns to match those of other participants in a discourse.

Acoustic phonetics An approach to phonetics that is concerned with measuring and analyzing the physical properties of sound waves produced when we speak.

Acquired agraphia *See* **Acquired dysgraphia**.

Acquired alexia *See* **Acquired dyslexia**.

Acquired dysgraphia The impairment of writing ability in patients who previously possessed normal writing ability (also called **acquired agraphia**).

Acquired dyslexia The impairment of reading ability in patients who previously possessed normal reading ability (also called **acquired alexia**).

Acrolect The variety of a creole that most closely resembles the lexifier language.

Acronym A word that is formed by taking the initial letters of some or all of the words in a phrase or name and pronouncing them as a word (e.g., *NATO* for *North Atlantic Treaty Organization*).

Acrophonic principle The representation of sounds by pictures of objects whose pronunciation begins with the sound to be represented (e.g., the sound [b] might be represented by a picture of a bird).

Active sentence A sentence in which the NP with the agent role is the subject (e.g., *Helen painted the room*).

Additive bilingualism The situation in which a bilingual child is proficient in two languages because both languages are supported sociopolitically, as well as in the education system and media.

Adjacency pair An ordered pair of utterances spoken by two different participants in a conversation (e.g., *question-answer*).

Adjective (A) A lexical category whose members designate a property or attribute of an entity, can often take comparative and superlative endings in English, and function as the head of an adjective phrase (e.g., *red*, *obese*, *hearty*).

Adstratum influence The mutual influence of two equally dominant languages on each other (e.g., the influence of English and French on each other in Montreal).

Adverb (Adv) A lexical category whose members typically denote a property of the actions, sensations, and states designated by verbs (e.g., *quickly, fearfully*).

Affix A morpheme that does not belong to a lexical category and is always bound (e.g., *-ing, un-*).

Affixation The process that attaches an affix to a base.

Affricates Non-continuant consonants that show a slow release of the closure (e.g., [tʃ, dʒ]).

Affrication A process in which palatalized stops become affricates.

Agent The participant doing the action denoted by the verb. (e.g., *Marilyn* in *Marilyn fed the dolphin*).

Agglutinating languages Languages in which words often include several well-demarcated affixes, each expressing a single piece of grammatical information.

Agrammatism An aphasic disturbance characterized by the omission of function words and inflectional affixes and by syntactic comprehension deficits.

Agreement The result of one category being inflected to mark properties of another (e.g., the verb is marked for the person and/or the number of the subject).

Allomorphs Variants of a morpheme (e.g., [-s], [-z], and [-əz] are allomorphs of the English plural morpheme).

Allophones The sounds that make up a phoneme. Allophones are phonetically similar and are usually in complementary distribution (e.g., voiced and voiceless *l* in English).

Alphabetic writing A type of writing in which symbols represent consonant and (usually) vowel segments.

Alveolar ridge The small ridge that protrudes from just behind the upper front teeth.

Alveopalatal (area) The area just behind the alveolar ridge where the roof of the mouth rises sharply (also called **palatoalveolar**). Sounds made with the tongue touching or near this area are called alveopalatals.

Ambiguous A characteristic of a word, phrase, or sentence that has more than one meaning.

Amelioration The process in which the meaning of a word becomes more favourable (e.g., *pretty* used to mean 'tricky, sly, cunning').

Amerind Hypothesis A controversial hypothesis which claims that the languages of North America can be classified into only three families.

Analogy A source of language change that involves the generalization of a regularity, on the basis of the inference that if elements are alike in some respects, they should be alike in others as well (e.g., *bring* becoming *brung* by analogy with *ring/rung*).

Analytic languages *See* **Isolating languages**.

Angular gyrus An area of the brain that plays an important role in reading and is located just in front of the occipital lobe.

Anomia A relatively mild form of aphasia in which the individual experiences word-finding difficulty (particularly the names of people and objects).

Antecedent The NP to which a pronoun looks for its interpretation. (e.g., *Jeremy* in *Jeremy looked at himself in the mirror*).

Anterior A place feature that characterizes coronal sounds articulated in front of the alveopalatal region.

Antonyms Words or phrases that are opposites with respect to some component of their meaning (e.g., *big* and *small*).

Aphasia A language deficit caused by damage to the brain.

Apocope The deletion of a word-final vowel (e.g., *name* used to be pronounced with a word-final schwa).

Apparent time hypothesis The hypothesis that change over time can be revealed by comparing the speech of older and younger speakers at a single time.

Appendix position A position outside the onset or coda of a syllable for consonants that violate the Sonority and/or Binarity Requirements.

Areal classification An approach to language classification that identifies characteristics shared by languages that are in geographical contact.

Argument The NP to which a thematic role is assigned.

Articulator features Features that indicate the activity of the lips and tongue.

Articulatory phonetics An approach to phonetics that studies the physiological mechanisms of speech production.

Articulatory simplification A process that facilitates acquisition (e.g., by deleting a consonant in a complex cluster or inserting a vowel to break up a cluster).

Arytenoids Two small cartilages in the larynx that are attached to the vocal folds, enabling the vocal folds to be drawn together or apart.

Aspectual properties The properties of the event or situation denoted by verb phrases.

Aspectual verbs Verbs that help indicate that an action is ongoing or complete (e.g., *continue, stop*); such verbs trigger the presuppositions about the temporal properties of the event described by the predicate.

Aspiration The lag in the onset of vocalic voicing, accompanied by the release of air, that is heard after the release of certain stops (e.g., in English, the first sound of *top* is aspirated).

Assimilation The influence of one segment on another, resulting in a sound becoming more like a nearby sound in terms of one or more of its phonetic characteristics (e.g., in English, vowels become nasal if followed by a nasal consonant).

Association line A line linking a symbol that represents a sound segment with a symbol that represents a tone or feature.

Atelic (event) An event that does not have a natural end point.

Attitude Beliefs and feelings that an individual may have about a particular language variety.

Autopsy studies Studies based on a post-mortem examination.

Auxiliary verb Verbs such as *will*, *can*, *may*, *be*, and *have* that must always occur with another verb in complete sentences.

Back A dorsal feature that characterizes sounds articulated behind the palatal region in the oral cavity.

Back (of the tongue) The part of the tongue that is hindmost but still lies in the mouth (versus the throat).

Back (vowel) A vowel that is made with the tongue positioned in the back of the oral cavity (e.g., the vowel sounds in *hoot* and *board*).

Backformation A word formation process that creates a new word by removing a real or supposed affix from another word in the language (e.g., *edit* came from *editor* through the removal of *-or*).

Bajan Barbadian (creole) English.

Base The form to which an affix is added (e.g., *book* is the base for the affix *-s* in *books*, *modernize* is the base for the affix *-ed* in *modernized*).

Basic syllable A syllable that complies with the Sonority Requirement and the Binarity Requirement.

Basilect The variety that shows the greatest number of differences from the lexifier (and usually dominant) language on which a creole is based.

Bilabials Sounds made by using both lips.

Binarity Requirement The requirement that within basic syllables, onsets and codas have no more than two constitutents.

Binary A property of phonological and semantic features that have either plus (+) or minus (−) values.

Binding Theory A theory of pronoun interpretation based on two principles: Principle A states that reflexive pronouns must have a c-commanding antecedent in the same clause; Principle B states that plain pronouns cannot have a c-commanding antecedent in the same clause.

Blade (of the tongue) The area of the tongue just behind the tip.

Blending A process that creates a word from the non–morphemic parts of two already existing items (e.g., *brunch* from *breakfast* and *lunch*).

Blissymbolics A contemporary development of pictographic writing that uses a number of recombineable symbols representing basic units of meaning; primarily used for non-speaking individuals.

Body (of the tongue) The main mass of the tongue.

Borrowing A source of language change that involves adopting aspects of one language into another.

Bottom-up processing A type of processing in which the activation of higher mental representations (e.g., words) occurs through the activation of simpler constituent representations (e.g., phonemes).

Bound morpheme A morpheme that must be attached to another element (e.g., the past tense marker *-ed*).

Bound variable A pronoun whose referent co-varies with the individuals in the set denoted by a quantified antecedent (as in *Everyone lost his way*). A bound variable interpretation is possible only if the antecedent c-commands the pronoun.

Boustrophedon The practice of reversing the direction of writing at the end of each line, which is found in some old writing systems.

Breathy voice *See* **Murmur**.

Broca's aphasia A non-fluent aphasia characterized by very halting speech, numerous phonemic errors, grammatical deficits, and a lack of intonation.

Broca's area The area in the lower rear portion of the left frontal lobe that plays an important role in language production.

C-command A syntactic notion that is involved in pronoun interpretation and is formulated as 'NP$_i$ c-commands NP$_j$ if and only if the first category above NP$_i$ contains NP$_j$'.

Canadian Raising The phonological phenomenon of using the allophones [ʌj] and [ʌw] before a voiceless stop in words such as *right* and *out*.

Canonical Sentence Strategy A processing strategy that leads children to expect the first NP in a sentence to bear the agent role and the second NP to bear the theme role.

Caregiver speech The type of speech that is typically addressed to young language learners (also called **motherese**).

Case A morphological category that encodes information about an element's grammatical role (subject, direct object, and so on) (e.g., the contrast between *he* and *him*).

Caste A hereditary social group that is prohibited from having contact with members of other groups.

Categorical (rules) Rules that apply every time a particular environment is encountered.

Cell assembly A collection of neurons that are repeatedly activated together.

Central sulcus The sulcus that extends from the top of the cerebral cortex to the lateral fissure (also called the fissure of Rolando).

Cerebral cortex The outermost layer of the cerebrum, composed mainly of neurons and capillaries.

Cerebral hemispheres The left and right halves of the cerebrum separated by the longitudinal fissure.

Cerebrovascular accident *See* **Stroke**.

Cerebrum The grey wrinkled mass that sits like a cap over the rest of the brain and is the seat of cognitive functioning.

Change from above Changes that begin in the speech of members of the upper social classes and spread to the lower classes.

Character The extra layer of meaning of a pronoun that functions as an 'instruction' about how to find its referent.

Characters The units of contemporary Chinese orthography, many of which consist of two parts, a phonetic determinative and a semantic radical.

Class A classic social distinction in studies of industrial societies (also called socio-economic status).

Class 1 affixes A group of affixes in English that often trigger changes in the consonant or vowel segments of the base and may affect the assignment of stress.

Class 2 affixes A group of affixes that tend to be phonologically neutral in English, having no effect on the segmental makeup of the base or on stress assignment.

Clipping A word formation process that shortens a polysyllabic word by deleting one or more syllables (e.g., *prof* from *professor*).

Clitic A morpheme that is like a word in terms of its meaning and function but is unable to stand alone as an independent form for phonological reasons (e.g., *'m* in *I'm*).

Closed syllable A syllable with a coda (e.g., both syllables in *camping*).

Closing A discourse unit conventionally used to end a conversation.

Coarticulation One sound influencing the articulation of another in a sequence of phonetic segments (e.g., in the sequence [pl], the tongue tip will start to move toward the alveolar ridge before the lips separate; more than one articulator is active).

Coda (C) The constituent of a syllable that immediately follows the nucleus.

Code-switching The use of words or phrases from two languages in one sentence or stretch of discourse.

Cognates Words of different languages that have descended from a common source, as shown by systematic phonetic correspondences (e.g., English *father* and German *Vater*).

Cognitive neuroscience The scientific study of the brain.

Cohort model A proposal about spoken word recognition based on the idea that word recognition proceeds by isolating a target word from a cohort of words that share initial segments.

Coinage *See* **Word manufacture**.

Common ground All the information that the participants in a conversation (knowingly) share.

Communicative competence A speaker's knowledge of the linguistic and social rules or principles for language production and perception.

Community of practice A group of individuals who come together for a shared purpose (and hence develop shared language practices).

Comparative method The reconstruction of properties of a parent language through comparison of its descendant languages.

Complement The element or elements for which a head is subcategorized and which provide(s) information about entities and locations implied by the meaning of the head (e.g., *the book* in *bought the book*).

Complement clause A sentence-like construction that is embedded within a larger structure (e.g., *that his car had been totalled* in *Jerry told Mary that his car had been totalled*).

Complementary distribution The situation in which two or more sounds occur in non-overlapping, mutually exclusive environments.

Complementizer (C) A functional category that takes a TP complement, forming a CP (complementizer phrase) (e.g., *whether* in *I wonder whether Lorna has left*).

Complex (word) A word that contains two or more morphemes (e.g., *theorize, unemployment*).

Compounding The combination of lexical categories (N, V, A, or P) to form a larger word (e.g., *fire + engine*).

Computerized axial tomography A technique for observing the living brain that uses a narrow beam of X-rays to create brain images that take the form of a series of brain slices (also called **CT scanning**).

Conjunction A functional category that joins two or more categories of the same type, forming a coordinate structure (e.g., *and* in *a man and his dog*).

Consonant deletion A phonetic process that deletes a consonant (e.g., the deletion of [θ] in *fifths*).

Consonant weakening A process that weakens a consonant, usually between vowels, according to the scale of consonantal strength.

Consonantal A major class feature that characterizes sounds produced with a major obstruction in the vocal tract.

Consonantal strength The articulatory property of a consonant that enables us to place it on a scale from weak to strong.

Consonants Sounds that are produced with a narrow or complete closure in the vocal tract.

Constituent One or more words that make up a syntactic unit (e.g., *the apple* in *the apple fell onto the floor*). (*See also* **Coordination test**, **Substitution test**, and **Movement test**.)

Constraints Conditions that determine the property of a linguistic form.

Constricted glottis (CG) A laryngeal feature that characterizes sounds made with the glottis closed (in English, only [ʔ]).

Consultant See **Informant**.

Context The situation, including time and place, in which an utterance occurs and which affects the meaning that is expressed.

Context-dependent adjectives Adjectives whose interpretation depends on the discourse context.

Contextual standard of comparison The baseline that is used to assess the degree to which a particular property is manifest (the standard for saying that someone is tall is thus different from the standard for saying that a tree is tall).

Continuant A manner feature that characterizes sounds made with free or nearly free airflow through the oral cavity: vowels, fricatives, glides, and liquids.

Continuants Sounds that are produced with a continuous airflow through the mouth.

Contour tones Moving pitches on a single segment that signal meaning differences.

Contradiction A relationship between sentences wherein the truth of one sentence requires the falsity of another sentence (e.g., *Raymond is married* contradicts *Raymond is a bachelor*).

Contradiction test A test used to see whether one sentence entails another: if we join sentence *p* with the negation of sentence *q* and the result is contradictory, then we know that *p* entails *q*.

Contralateral The control of the right side of the body by the left side of the brain and vice versa.

Contrastive segments Segments that can distinguish between words (e.g., [s] and [z] in the words *sip* and *zip*).

Conversation analysis *See* **Ethnomethodology**.

Conversational implicature An inference derived by a listener in a conversation when the speaker appears to flout one of the maxims of the Cooperative Principle.

Conversion A word formation process that assigns an already existing word to a new syntactic category (also called **zero derivation**) (e.g., *nurse* [V] from *nurse* [N]).

Cooperative Principle A principle that interlocutors assume will be followed in a conversation and that can be stated as follows: Make your contribution to the conversation as required by the goal of the conversation.

Coordinate structure A pattern built around a conjunction such as *and*, *or*, or *but* (e.g., *Mary and the white horse*).

Coordination The grouping together of two or more categories with the help of a conjunction such as *and* or *but*.

Coordination test A test used to determine if a group of words is a constituent by joining it to another group of words with a conjunction such as *and* or *or*.

Co-referential The relation between a noun and a pronoun when they refer to the same entity.

CORONAL A place feature that characterizes sounds made with the tongue tip or blade raised (e.g., [t d s θ]).

Corpus callosum The bundle of nerve fibres that serves as the main connection between the cerebral hemispheres, allowing the two hemispheres to communicate with one another.

Covert prestige Prestige that is not part of a society's widely expressed and approved belief system.

Creativity The characteristic of human language that allows novelty and innovation in response to new thoughts, experiences, and situations.

Creole A variety that arises as the native language of the children of members of a pidgin speech community.

Creole continuum The gradient differences among basilects, acrolects, and mesolects.

Cricoid cartilage The ring-shaped cartilage in the larynx on which the thyroid cartilage rests.

Critical period A particular time frame during which children have to be exposed to language if the acquisition process is to be fully successful.

Cross-linguistic influence The influence of one language on another during bilingual acquisition, resulting in a morphosyntactic or phonological rule being transferred from one language to the other.

Cross-sectional research Research that investigates and compares children (or groups of children) of distinct ages.

CT scanning *See* **Computerized axial tomography**.

Cuneiform Writing that was initiated in the fourth millennium BC in Sumeria and was produced by pressing a wedge-shaped stylus into soft clay tablets.

D-structure *See* **Deep structure**.

Deaffrication A type of segmental simplification that turns affricates into fricatives by eliminating the stop portion of the affricate (e.g., [dʒ] becoming [ʒ]).

Deep dyslexia A type of acquired dyslexia in which the patient produces a word that is semantically related to the word he or she is asked to read (e.g., producing *father* when asked to read *mother*).

Deep structure The structure formed by the Merge operation in accordance with the X' schema and subcategorization properties of the heads (also called **D-Structure**).

Degemination The weakening of a geminate consonant to a non-geminate consonant (e.g., [tt] becoming [t]).

Degree word (Deg) A functional category that serves as the specifier of a preposition or an adjective (e.g., *quite* in *quite tired*, *very* in *very near the house*).

Delayed release (DR) A manner feature that characterizes all and only affricate consonants.

Deletion A process that removes a segment from certain phonetic contexts (e.g., the pronunciation of *fifths* as [fifs]).

Denasalization A common substitution process in child language acquisition that involves the replacement of a nasal stop by a non-nasal counterpart (e.g., *come* is pronounced [kʌb]).

Dentals Sounds made with the tongue placed against or near the teeth.

Dependent variable In an experiment, the behaviour or event that is measured.

Derivation (morphology) An affixational process that forms a word with a meaning and/or category distinct from that of its base.

Derivation (phonology) The application of phonological rules to underlying representations.

Descriptive A characteristic of linguistic research that seeks to describe human linguistic ability and knowledge, not to prescribe one system in preference to another. (*See also* **Prescriptive**.)

Determiner (Det) A functional category that serves as the specifier of a noun (e.g., *a*, *the*, *these*).

Devoicing Voicing assimilation in which a sound becomes voiceless because of a nearby voiceless sound (e.g., the *l* in *place* is devoiced because of the voiceless stop preceding it).

Diacritic A mark added to a phonetic symbol to alter its value in some way (e.g., a circle under a symbol to indicate voicelessness).

Dialect A language variety that is systematically different from another variety of the same language and spoken by a socially identifiable subgroup of some larger speech community.

Dialect levelling In a region with many dialects, the process by which certain features are lost and a more homogeneous dialect emerges.

Dialectology The study of regional differences in language.

Diaphragm The large sheet of muscle that separates the chest cavity from the abdomen and helps to maintain the air pressure necessary for speech production.

Diary study A type of naturalistic investigation in which a researcher (often a parent) keeps daily notes on a child's linguistic progress.

Dichotic listening A technique in which stimuli (either linguistic or non-linguistic) are presented through headphones to the left and right ears to determine the lateralization of various cognitive functions.

Diglossia The situation in which multiple varieties are spoken by one speech community but with sharply distinct domains of use.

Diphthong A vowel that shows a noticeable change in quality during its production (e.g., the vowel sounds in *house* and *ride*).

Diphthongization A process in which a monophthong becomes a diphthong (e.g., [iː] became [aj] during the Great English Vowel Shift).

Direct negative evidence Language instruction involving correction or focus on form.

Direct object The NP complement of a verb (e.g., *a fish* in *Judy caught a fish*).

Discourse Any social interaction or expression involving language.

Discourse analysis The analysis of how utterances are structured in discourse.

Discrete variable A variable whose variants are distinctly separate, with no in-between variants possible (e.g., the choice of *gonna* or *will* to express the future).

Dissimilation A process whereby one segment becomes less like another segment in its environment (e.g., *anma* 'soul' in Latin became *alma* in Spanish).

Distinctive feature A feature that is able to signal a difference in meaning by changing its plus or minus value (e.g., the feature [voice] in the words *peer* and *beer*).

Distribution The set of elements with which an item can co-occur.

Dominant language The language in which a bilingual child is more proficient.

DORSAL A place feature that characterizes sounds made with the body of the tongue (e.g., [k], [j], [u]).

Dorsum (of the tongue) The body and back of the tongue.

Downdrift The maintenance of a distinction among the pitch registers of an utterance even as the overall pitch of the utterance falls.

Durative (event) An event that develops over (at least some) time.

Dynamic (event) An event that is not static.

Dysprosody The lack of sentence intonation; a common characteristic of the speech of Broca's aphasics.

Early bilinguals Individuals who learned two languages in childhood.

Enclitic A clitic that attaches to the end of a word.

Endocentric compound A compound whose head (the rightmost component in English) identifies the general class to which the meaning of the entire word belongs (e.g., *dump truck* is a type of truck). (*See also* **Exocentric compound**.)

Entailment A relation between sentences in which the truth of one sentence necessarily implies the truth of another (e.g., *Gary is Bernice's husband* entails the truth of *Bernice is married*).

Environment The phonetic context in which a sound occurs.

Epenthesis A process that inserts a segment into a particular environment (e.g., the insertion of a schwa in the pronunciation of *athlete* as [æθəlɪt]).

Eponym A word created from a name (e.g., *watt*, after the Scottish engineer James Watt).

Ergative The case associated with the subject of a transitive verb in some languages.

Ethnic slur A socially stigmatized name for an ethnic group.

Ethnolect A language variety associated with a particular ethnic group.

Ethnomethodology A type of discourse analysis that focuses on the structural relationship between utterances in conversations.

Ethnonym The name used for a particular ethnic group.

Euphemisms Words or phrases used in place of taboo items.

Event-related potentials (ERPs) A measurement of electrical activity in the brain that is correlated with the presentation of particular stimulus events.

Evidentiality A system of morphological contrasts indicating the type of evidence for the truth of a statement.

Exclusive A contrast in some languages that indicates that the addressee is to be excluded in the interpretation of the first person plural morpheme. (*See also* **Inclusive**.)

Existence presupposition The presupposition that an entity to which a speaker refers exists.

Exocentric compound A compound whose meaning does not follow from the meaning of its parts (e.g., *redneck*, since its referent is not a type of neck). (*See also* **Endocentric compound**.)

Experimental approach An approach to investigating language in which researchers make use of specially designed tasks to elicit linguistic activity relevant to a particular phenomenon.

Experimental paradigm A method of investigation that involves a particular way of presenting stimuli and a particular way of measuring responses.

Extension The set of entities to which a word or expression refers (also called its **denotation** or **referents**).

Factive predicates Verbs or adjectives that take a sentential complement that is presupposed to be true (e.g., *know, be glad*).

Feature (phonetic) The smallest unit of analysis of phonological structure, combinations of which make up segments (e.g., [nasal], [continuant]).

Feminine A noun class category in languages that assign nouns to different genders (e.g., in German, *Sprache*, meaning 'language', is treated as feminine and therefore occurs with the determiner *die* 'the'.)

Field technique A method of study that does not involve manipulation and control of factors in a laboratory, but rather involves observing phenomena as they occur.

Fissure A relatively deep sulcus of the cerebral cortex.

Fixed stress languages Languages in which the position of stress in a word is predictable.

Flap A sound commonly identified with *r* in some languages and produced when the tongue tip strikes the alveolar ridge as it passes across it (e.g., in North American English, the medial consonant in *bitter* and *bidder*).

Flapping A phonetic process in which a dental or alveolar stop changes to a flap in the environment of other continuants.

Fluency The ability to produce speech automatically and without noticeable hesitation.

Fluent aphasia The aphasia that occurs due to damage to parts of the left cerebral cortex behind the central sulcus, resulting in fluent speech but great difficulty in selecting, organizing, and monitoring language production (also called **sensory aphasia**).

Folk etymology Reanalysis of a word that is based on an incorrect historical analysis (e.g., *hamburger* being reanalyzed into two morphemes, *ham* and *burger*).

Forms of address How an individual is addressed (e.g., *Professor, Bob*, etc.).

Fossilized A property of an interlanguage grammar that has reached a plateau and has ceased to change.

Fourth floor study The study by William Labov that relied on eliciting the phrase 'the fourth floor' in department stores frequented by shoppers of different socio-economic statuses. Labov hypothesized that store employees 'borrowed' prestige from their customers and that this was reflected in their unconscious language choices.

Free form An element that does not have to occur in a fixed position with respect to neighbouring elements and may even be able to appear in isolation.

Free morpheme A morpheme that can be a word by itself (e.g., *fear*).

Free stress languages Languages in which the position of stress in a word is not predictable and must be learned on a case-by-case basis.

Free variation A situation in which a word has more than one pronunciation. As a result, different sounds occur in exactly the same environment without creating a difference in meaning (e.g., *either* can be pronounced [iðɚ] or [ajðɚ]).

Frequency effect The common experimental finding that words that occur more commonly in a language are processed more quickly and more accurately.

Frication The weakening of a stop to a fricative (e.g., [d] becoming [ð]).

Fricatives Non-sonorant consonants produced with a continuous airflow through the mouth, accompanied by a continuous audible noise (e.g., [f], [ʃ]).

Front (vowel) A vowel that is made with the tongue positioned in the front of the oral cavity (e.g., the vowel sounds in *seal* and *bat*).

Frontal lobe The lobe of the brain that lies in front of the central sulcus and in which Broca's area is located.

Fronting A common process in child language acquisition that involves the moving forward of a sound's place of articulation (e.g., *cheese* pronounced as [tsiz]).

Full reduplication A morphological process that duplicates the entire word (e.g., in Turkish, *çabuk* 'quickly'—*çabuk çabuk* 'very quickly').

Function words Words such as determiners and conjunctions that typically do not carry stress, cannot be inflected, and are lacking in the speech of Broca's aphasics, resulting in telegraphic speech.

Functional category A word-level syntactic category whose members are harder to define and paraphrase than those of lexical categories (e.g., auxiliary verbs, conjunctions, determiners, and degree words) (also called **non-lexical category**).

Functional magnetic resonance imaging (fMRI) A brain imaging technique that yields information on areas of high brain activity during the performance of cognitive tasks.

Fusion The process by which words develop into affixes over time.

Fusional languages Languages in which words typically consist of several morphemes; each affix typically expresses several bits of grammatical information simultaneously (e.g., Russian) (also called **inflectional languages**).

Garden path sentence A sentence that is difficult to process and interpret because the manner in which the words are arranged encourages an incorrect interpretation.

Gender roles Roles or occupations traditionally performed by only one sex.

Generative grammar A system that explicitly builds syntactic structure.

Genetic classification The categorization of languages according to the ancestor languages from which they developed.

Genetic relationships Relationships among languages that have descended from a common ancestor.

Genetically related languages Languages that have descended from a common parent (e.g., German and Italian both descended from Proto-Indo-European).

Glides Sounds that are produced with an articulation like that of a vowel but move quickly to another articulation (e.g., [j], [w]).

Gliding A common substitution process in child language acquisition that involves the replacement of a liquid by a glide (e.g., *play* is pronounced [pwej]).

Global aphasia The most severe form of nonfluent aphasia, in which the patient is completely mute.

Glottals Sounds produced by using the vocal folds as the primary articulators (e.g., [h], [ʔ]).

Glottis The space between the vocal folds.

Gradient A variable with continuous values.

Grammar The mental system of rules and categories that allows humans to form and interpret the words and sentences of their language.

Grammatical The status of a sentence that speakers judge to be a possible sentence of their language.

Grammaticalization The encoding of a concept as an affix or a non-lexical category (e.g., past tense in English expressed by the suffix *-ed*).

Great English Vowel Shift A set of related sound changes involving long vowels that took place in English from the fifteenth to eighteenth centuries.

Grimm's Law A set of consonant shifts that took place between Proto-Indo-European and Proto-Germanic.

Gyrus An area where the cerebral cortex is folded out (plural: *gyri*).

Habitual interpretation The interpretation of a sentence when an activity or an accomplishment predicate occurs in the present tense in English: that is, the event occurs regularly (e.g., *Shandra takes the bus to work*).

Hangul The alphabetic script used to represent Korean, the symbols of which are grouped into syllable-sized clusters.

Hanja The Korean word for the Chinese characters used in Korean writing.

Head (of a phrase) The element around which a phrasal category is built (e.g., V, N, A, P).

Head (of a compound) The morpheme that determines the category of the entire word (e.g., *bird* in *blackbird*).

Heavy syllable A syllable that has a rhyme consisting of a vowel plus at least one other element (a glide or a consonant).

Heritage language A minority language spoken in a community or region with a majority language.

Hieroglyphs The signs used in an Egyptian pictorial writing system, which later developed into a mixed writing system.

High A dorsal feature that characterizes sounds produced with the tongue body raised.

High involvement style A style of turn-taking in a conversation where speaker turns overlap.

High (vowel) A vowel that is made with the tongue raised in the mouth.

Hiragana The Japanese syllabary that is used (typically to represent affixes) in conjunction with katakana and kanji to write Japanese.

Historical linguistics The linguistic discipline that is concerned with the description and explanation of language change.

Holophrases Utterances produced by children in which one word expresses the type of meaning that would be associated with an entire sentence in adult speech (e.g., *up* used to mean 'Pick me up').

Homographs Words with different meanings but the same written form (e.g., *bank* [financial institution], *bank* [the land alongside a river]).

Homonyms Words that have different meanings but either sound the same or have the same written form.

Homophones Words that have different meanings but sound the same (e.g., *bear, bare*).

Host The element to which clitics are attached.

Hypercorrection The overuse of a variant as a result of its prestige value.

Identification The use of particular linguistic variants to indicate solidarity with a particular community.

Illocutionary competence The ability to convey a particular meaning via a variety of linguistic forms.

Immigrant languages The non-official languages spoken by the newcomers who have been arriving in waves since the initial periods of French and English colonization.

Immersion program An education program in which all or almost all the academic content (e.g., science or math) is taught through the students' L2, with the goal of building greater proficiency in that language.

Impaired Representation Hypothesis The hypothesis that second language learners' grammars are lacking certain grammatical features.

Implicational universal A universal of language that specifies that the presence of one trait implies the presence of another (but not vice versa).

Inclusive A contrast in some languages which indicates that the addressee is to be included in the interpretation of the first person plural morpheme. (*See also* **Exclusive**.)

Indexical adverbs Adverbs whose interpretation depends on the time and place they are uttered (e.g., *now*).

Indexical pronouns Pronouns that have a character.

Indicator A linguistic variable that is generally not noticeable to the listener but can be shown by large-scale study to be associated with particular social characteristics.

Indigenous languages The non-official languages spoken by the Indigenous peoples in Canada: First Nations, Métis, and Inuit.

Indirect negative evidence Evidence from the non-occurrence of particular forms that those forms are in fact ungrammatical.

Infix An affix that occurs within another morpheme.

Inflection The modification of a word's form to indicate the grammatical subclass to which it belongs (e.g., the *-s* in *books* marks the plural subclass).

Inflectional languages *See* **Fusional languages**.

Informant A native speaker of a language or variety who provides data to the linguist (also called a **consultant**).

Initialism An abbreviation created by pronouncing a series of letters (e.g., PEI or USA) as letters rather than as a word. (*See also* **Acronym**.)

Instantaneous (event) An event that happens instantaneously rather than developing over a period of at least some time.

Instrumental motivation The desire to achieve proficiency in a new language for utilitarian reasons, such as job promotion.

Integrative motivation The desire to achieve proficiency in a new language in order to participate in the social life of the language community.

Intercostals The muscles between the ribs that help to maintain the air pressure necessary for speech production.

Interdentals Sounds made with the tongue placed between the teeth (e.g., [θ], [ð]).

Interlanguage The dynamic grammatical system that an L2 learner is using at a particular period in his or her acquisition of a second language.

Internal change A process that substitutes one non-morphemic segment for another to mark a grammatical contrast (e.g., *foot/feet*, *run/ran*).

International Phonetic Alphabet (IPA) The universal system for transcribing the sounds of speech, which has been developing since 1888.

Inter-speaker variation Variation that occurs across individuals (e.g., some speakers have the voiceless labiovelar glide [ʍ] and some do not).

Intonation Pitch movement in spoken utterances that is not related to differences in word meaning.

Intransitive verb A verb that does not take a direct object (e.g., *sleep*).

Intra-speaker variation Variation that occurs within the speech of an individual (e.g., sometimes a speaker will say *often* with the /t/ and sometimes without).

Inversion A transformation that moves the element in the T position to the C position; formulated as 'Move T to C'.

Isogloss A line drawn on a dialect map to indicate that two regions differ for a particular linguistic feature.

Isogloss bundle Several isoglosses clustered along the same point on a map.

Isolate A language with no known relatives (e.g., Basque).

Isolating languages Languages whose words typically consist of only one morpheme (also called **analytic languages**) (e.g., Mandarin).

Jargon The vocabulary associated with a specific register.

Jargon aphasia A symptom of severe cases of Wernicke's aphasia in which speech contains very few real words of the language.

Kanji The Japanese word for the Chinese characters used to write Japanese.

Katakana The Japanese syllabary that is used (typically to represent loan words and onomatopoeic words) in conjunction with hiragana and kanji to write Japanese.

Key *See* **Radical**.

LABIAL A place feature that characterizes sounds articulated with one or both lips (e.g., [f], [b], [w]).

Labials Sounds made with closure or near closure of the lips (e.g., the initial sounds of *bit* and *pot*).

Labiodentals Sounds involving the lower lip and upper teeth (e.g., the initial sounds of *freedom* and *vintage*).

Labiovelars Sounds made with the tongue raised near the velum and the lips rounded at the same time (e.g., the initial sound of *wound*).

Language contact A source of language change that involves the speakers of one language frequently interacting with the speakers of another language.

Language death The situation in which there are no more speakers of a particular language.

Language myth Unsubstantiated beliefs about a language variety.

Language planning Official policy with the goal of increasing or limiting the domain of use of a particular language or languages.

Laryngeal features Features that represent voicing states.

Larynx The box-like structure located in the throat through which air passes during speech production, commonly known as the voicebox.

Late bilinguals Individuals who began to learn an L2 in adolescence or adulthood.

Late closure A proposed parsing principle which claims that in sentence comprehension, humans tend to attach incoming material into the phrase or clause currently being parsed.

Lateral fissure The fissure that separates the temporal lobe from the frontal and parietal lobes (also called the Sylvian fissure).

Lateralization The relatively unilateral control of cognitive functions by either the left or the right side of the brain (e.g., language is lateralized in the left hemisphere in most people).

Laterals Sounds made with the sides of the tongue lowered (e.g., varieties of *l*).

Lax (vowel) A vowel that is made with a placement of the tongue that results in relatively less vocal tract constriction (e.g., the vowel sounds in *hit* and *but*).

Length The auditory property of a sound that enables us to place it on a scale that ranges from short to long.

Lesion An abnormality in the tissue of an organ (such as the brain), usually caused by disease or trauma.

Lexical ambiguity Ambiguity at the level of the word.

Lexical category A word-level category whose members have substantial meaning. The most studied categories of this type are noun (N), verb (V), adjective (A), and preposition (P).

Lexical decision An experimental paradigm in which a person sees or hears a stimulus and must judge as quickly as possible whether that stimulus is a word of his or her language.

Lexical diffusion Linguistic change that first manifests itself in a few words and then gradually spreads through the vocabulary of the language.

Lexicon A speaker's mental dictionary, which contains information about the syntactic properties, meaning, and phonological representation of a language's words.

Lexifier language The source of most of the lexical items for a language that arises through language contact.

Light syllable A syllable consisting of just a vowel or a syllabic consonant.

Lingua franca A language used for the primary purpose of communicating across speech communities whose members speak different languages; often the second language of all speakers involved.

Linguistic competence Speakers' knowledge of their language, which allows them to produce and understand an unlimited number of utterances, including many that are novel.

Linguistic factor A linguistic property that may be correlated with structured variation (e.g., at the beginning of a word, before a vowel, etc.).

Linguistic insecurity A feeling that one's own variety is inadequate compared to the standard, often resulting in attempts to change one's speech.

Linguistic isolation A situation in which a speech community is isolated from other speakers of the same language (e.g., Quebec French is surrounded by English in North America).

Linguistic typology An approach to language classification that classifies languages according to their structural characteristics without regard for genetic relationships.

Linguistic universals Structural characteristics that occur across the languages of the world.

Linguistics The discipline that studies how language works.

Liquids The class of /l/ and /r/ sounds.

Lobes Substructures of the cerebral hemispheres that appear to have distinct responsibilities (e.g., frontal lobe, temporal lobe).

Logical complementarity The relation between words that holds just in case the meanings of word *a* and word *b* do not overlap and together exhaust the set of relevant possibilities (e.g., *animate* and *inanimate* are logically complementary).

Logical contradiction The relation between sentences *p* and *q* that holds just in case they have opposite truth values: *p* is true and *q* is false, or *p* is false and *q* is true.

Logical contrariety The relation between sentences *p* and *q* just in case *p* and *q* cannot both be true: if *p* is true, then *q* must be false.

Logical entailment The relation between sentences that holds just in case the truth of one sentence requires the truth of another. Given two sentences *p* and *q*, *p* logically entails *q* if the truth of *p* requires the truth of *q*.

Logical equivalence (sentences) The relation between sentences *p* and *q* that holds just in case *p* entails *q* and *q* entails *p*.

Logical equivalence (words) The relation between words that holds just in case word *a* and word *b* have the same meaning (e.g., *single* is equivalent to *unmarried*).

Logical incompatibility The relation between words that holds just in case the meanings of word *a* and word *b* do not overlap but do not exhaust the set of relevant possibilities (e.g., *dog* and *cat* are logically incompatible).

Logical subordination The relation between words that holds just in case word *a* is subordinate to word *b* in the sense that word *a* denotes a subset of the set denoted by word *b* (e.g., the word *beagle* is subordinate to the word *dog*).

Logogram A written symbol representing a morpheme or word.

Logographic writing A type of writing in which symbols represent morphemes or even entire words.

Longitudinal fissure The fissure that extends from the front of the brain to the back and separates the left and right cerebral hemispheres.

Longitudinal studies Studies that examine language development over an extended period of time.

Loudness The auditory property of a sound that enables us to place it on a scale that ranges from soft to loud.

Low A dorsal feature that characterizes vowels made with the tongue body distinctly lowered from a central position in the oral cavity.

Low (vowel) A vowel that is made with the tongue quite flat in the mouth.

Macrofamilies *See* **Phyla**.

Magnetoencephalography (MEG) A technique for studying how language is processed that records subtle changes in the magnetic fields generated within the brain.

Major class features Features that represent the classes consonant, obstruent, nasal, liquid, glide, and vowel.

Majority language A language that is widely spoken in a community, region, or nation; has high status; and is used as a language of government institutions and schools.

Majority rules strategy A secondary strategy used to reconstruct proto-forms which stipulates that the segment found in the majority of cognates should be assumed to be part of the proto-form. (*See also* **Phonetic plausibility strategy**.)

Manner features Features that represent manner of articulation.

Manners of articulation The various configurations produced by positioning the lips, tongue, velum, and glottis in different ways (e.g., nasal, fricative, liquid).

Marked traits Those characteristics of language that are considered to be more complex and/or universally less common in languages.

Markedness Differential Hypothesis The hypothesis that L2 elements that are different and more marked than the L1 elements will cause difficulty in learning.

Marker A linguistic variable that is noticeable to the listener.

Masculine A noun class category in languages that assign nouns to different genders (e.g., in German, *Wagen*, meaning 'car', is treated as masculine and therefore occurs with the determiner *der* 'the').

Matrix clause The larger clause in which a complement clause occurs.

Matrix language The dominant language in a code-switching exchange.

Maxim of Manner One of the four maxims associated with the Cooperative Principle, stated as follows: Make your contribution as clear as possible. Avoid obscurity and ambiguity, be brief, and be orderly.

Maxim of Quality One of the four maxims associated with the Cooperative Principle, stated as follows: Do not say what you think is false and do not say what you lack evidence for.

Maxim of Quantity One of the four maxims associated with the Cooperative Principle, stated as follows: Say as much as is required by the goal of the conversation. Do not say too much and do not say too little.

Maxim of Relevance One of the four maxims associated with the Cooperative Principle, stated as follows: Be relevant to the goal of the conversation.

Meaning The message or content that a sign conveys.

Merge A syntactic operation that combines elements to create phrases and sentences.

Merger A change in a phonological system in which two or more phonemes collapse into one, thereby reducing the number of phonemes in that language.

Mesolect A variety with characteristics that place it at a mid point along the continuum between the acrolect and the basilect in a creole speech community.

Metalinguistic awareness The ability to access and manipulate explicit knowledge of linguistic structures and to intentionally separate linguistic structures from their meanings.

Metaphor The understanding of one concept in terms of another (e.g., 'argument' understood in terms of 'war': *She annihilated him in the debate*).

Metathesis A process that reorders a sequence of segments (e.g., in child language, pronouncing *ask* as [æks]).

Michif The mixed language of the Métis people.

Mid (vowel) A vowel that is made with the tongue neither raised nor lowered (e.g., the vowel sounds in *set* and *Coke*).

Minimal attachment A proposed parsing principle which claims that in sentence comprehension, we do not create more syntactic structure than is absolutely necessary.

Minimal pair Two words with distinct meanings that differ by only one segment in the same position (e.g., *bit* and *pit*).

Minority language A language that is less widely spoken, has lower status, and might be used in a limited way or not all in government institutions and schools.

Missing Surface Inflection Hypothesis The hypothesis that even though second language learners may omit inflection at times, they are nonetheless sensitive to the relevant grammatical contrasts.

Mixed language A language with many features from two different source languages (e.g., Michif).

Modifier An optional element that describes a property of a head (e.g., *blue* in *that blue car*).

Morpheme The smallest unit of language that carries information about meaning or function (e.g., *books* consists of the two morphemes *book* and *-s*).

Morphology The component of the grammar that is concerned with the structure of words.

Morphophonemics The study of how morphological factors affect pronunciation (also called **morphophonology**).

Morphophonology *See* **Morphophonemics**.

Motherese *See* **Caregiver speech**.

Motor aphasia *See* **Non-fluent aphasia**.

Move A syntactic operation that transports an element to a new position within syntactic structure (also called **Transformation**).

Movement test A test used to determine if a group of words is a constituent by moving it as a single unit to a different position within the sentence.

Multillingualism At the societal level, a community, region, or nation where more than two languages are spoken and might be used in government, the legal system, and schools. A multilingual individual is someone who has proficiency in more than two languages.

Multiplex social network A social network in which the individuals interact with each other in multiple ways.

Murmur The glottal state that produces voiced sounds with the vocal folds relaxed enough to allow sufficient air to escape to produce a simultaneous whispery effect (also called **breathy voice**).

Mutual intelligibility The situation in which speakers of two different varieties are able to understand one another's speech; often used by linguists to determine whether two varieties are separate languages or dialects of one language.

Narrow scope A quantified NP1 is said to have narrow scope with respect to another quantified NP2 or negation if the interpretation of NP1 depends on the interpretation of NP2 or negation.

Nasal A manner feature that characterizes any sound made with the velum lowered.

Nasal (sounds) Sounds produced by lowering the velum, allowing air to pass through the nasal passages.

Nasalization The nasalizing effect that a nasal consonant can have on adjacent vowels.

Native speaker One who has acquired a language as a child in a natural setting.

Natural class A class of sounds that share a feature or features (e.g., voiced stops).

Naturalistic approach An approach to investigating child language in which researchers observe and record children's spontaneous verbal behaviour.

Naturalness A criterion that guides language reconstruction by determining whether changes are natural.

Near-minimal pair Two words that contain differences other than the one involving the key contrast; the extra differences must not involve sounds right next to the contrast (e.g., in English, [mɪʃən]–[vɪʒən] *mission–vision*).

Negative evidence Information, obtained through instruction or observation, that particular forms are ungrammatical.

Neurolinguistics The study of how language is represented and processed in the brain.

Neurons The basic information-processing units of the nervous system, also called nerve cells.

Neuter A noun class category in languages that assign nouns to different genders (e.g., in German, *Boot*, meaning 'boat', is treated as neuter and therefore occurs with the determiner *das* 'the').

Neutralization The loss of a contrast between two phonemes in a particular environment.

Nonce borrowing A word from one language that is used occasionally in another language by bilinguals but does not become established in that language.

Non-concatenative morphology A morphological pattern in which words are not built in a linear, additive way by adding prefixes and/or suffixes (e.g., the systems of infixing found in Tagalog and Arabic).

Non-fluent aphasia Aphasia that results from damage to parts of the brain in front of the central sulcus and is characterized by slow, effortful speech production (also called **motor aphasia**).

Non-lexical category *See* **Functional category**.

Non-standard variety A variety of language containing forms that are generally viewed pejoratively in the community and that are generally considered 'incorrect' by prescriptive grammarians.

Non-terminal (intonation) contour Rising or level intonation at the end of an utterance, often signalling that the utterance is incomplete.

Noun (N) A lexical category that typically names entities, can usually be inflected for number and possession (in English), and functions as the head of a noun phrase (e.g., *key*, *Bob*, *perception*).

Nucleus (N) The element around which a syllable is built. Nuclei are usually vowels or diphthongs, but some languages allow certain sonorant consonants to function in this way as well.

Number The morphological category that expresses contrasts involving countable quantities (e.g., in English, the two-way distinction between singular and plural).

Obstruent Any non-sonorant consonant: fricatives, affricates, oral stops.

Obviative A verb form used in some languages to indicate that the referent of the subject is not the entity previously chosen as the focus of the conversation. (*See also* **Proximate**.)

Occipital lobe The area of the brain at the back of the cerebral hemispheres, just behind the angular gyrus, in which the visual cortex is located.

Official language In the Canadian context, French and English are the official languages of the federal government and the legal system. All other languages are non-official languages.

Old information The presuppositions that the participants in a conversation (knowingly) share.

Onomatopoeic words Words that sound like the thing that they name (e.g., *plop*, *hiss*).

Onset (O) The constituent of a syllable that immediately precedes the nucleus.

Open syllable A syllable that has no coda.

Opening A discourse unit conventionally used to begin a conversation.

Oral sounds Sounds produced with the velum raised and the airflow through the nasal passage cut off.

Orthography A set of conventions that determine how the symbols of a script are used to write the language.

Overextension A developmental phenomenon in which the meaning of the child's word is more general or inclusive than that of the corresponding adult form (e.g., *daddy* used to refer to any adult male).

Overgeneralization A developmental phenomenon that results from the overly broad application of a rule (e.g., *falled* instead of *fell*) (also called **overregularization**).

Overregularization *See* **Overgeneralization**.

Overt prestige Linguistic variables that are associated with prestige (e.g., the use of a word like *salubrious*).

Palatalization The effect that front vowels and the palatal glide [j] typically have on velar, alveolar, and dental stops, making their place of articulation more palatal (e.g., the first sound of *keep* is palatalized).

Palatals Sounds produced with the tongue on or near the palate (e.g., [j]).

Palate The highest part of the roof of the mouth.

Palatoalveolar *See* **Alveopalatal (area)**.

Paragraphia A writing error associated with a linguistic deficit.

Parallel processing model A proposal based on the idea that phonological, lexical, and syntactic processes are carried out simultaneously.

Parameter The set of alternatives for a particular phenomenon made available by Universal Grammar to individual languages.

Parameter setting The determination of which option permitted by a particular parameter is appropriate for the language being learned.

Parietal lobe The lobe of the brain that lies behind the central sulcus and above the temporal lobe.

Parsing The processing of linguistic input with a view to assigning it a syntactic structure.

Part of speech See **Syntactic category**.

Partial reduplication A morphological process that duplicates part of the base to which it applies (e.g., in Tagalog, *takbuh* 'run' and *tatakbuh* 'will run').

Partial suppletion A morphological process that marks a grammatical contrast by replacing part of a morpheme (e.g., *think/thought*).

Passive sentence A sentence in which the NP bearing the theme role is encoded as subject (e.g., *The report was prepared by the committee members*).

Patient The participant undergoing and being affected by the action denoted by the verb.

Pejoration The process by which the meaning of a word becomes less favourable (e.g., *wench* used to mean simply 'girl').

Performance Actual language use in particular situations.

Person A morphological category that typically distinguishes among the first person (the speaker), the second person (the addressee), and the third person (anyone else) (e.g., in English, the difference between *I, you,* and *she/he/it*).

PET scanning *See* **Positron emission tomography**.

Pharyngeals Sounds made through the modification of airflow in the pharynx by retracting the tongue or constricting the pharynx.

Pharynx The area of the throat between the uvula and the larynx.

Phone Any sound used in human language (also called a **speech sound**).

Phoneme A class of phonetically similar sounds that do not contrast with each other.

Phonemic paraphasias Speech errors that result from phonemic substitutions and omissions (e.g., *spoon* may be pronounced as *poon*).

Phonetic determinative The part of a Chinese character that provides information about the pronunciation of the corresponding morpheme.

Phonetic plausibility strategy The primary strategy used to reconstruct proto-forms, which requires any sound changes posited to be phonetically plausible. (*See also* **Majority rules strategy**.)

Phonetic representation A representation of speech sounds that includes phonetic details that are not contrastive.

Phonetic sound change A sound change that results in a new allophone of an already existing phoneme.

Phonetically conditioned sound change Sound change that begins as subtle alterations in the sound pattern of a language in particular phonetic environments.

Phonetics The study of how speech sounds are articulated and perceived.

Phonographic writing A type of writing in which symbols represent syllables or segments.

Phonological change A sound change that results in the addition, elimination, or rearrangement of phonemes (e.g., splits, mergers).

Phonological dyslexia A type of acquired dyslexia in which the patient seems to have lost the ability to use spelling-to-sound rules and can only read words that he or she has seen before.

Phonological representation *See* **Underlying representation**.

Phonological rules Rules that derive phonetic representations from underlying representations, accounting for alternations among allophones.

Phonology The component of the grammar that is concerned with the system of contrasts and patterns involving speech sounds.

Phonotactics The set of constraints on how sequences of segments pattern.

Phrase A unit of syntactic structure consisting of an obligatory head and an optional specifier and/or complements.

Phyla The groups into which purportedly related language stocks are placed (also called **macrofamilies**).

Physical isolation A situation in which speech communities are geographically isolated from other speech communities (e.g., island communities).

Pictograms Pictorial representations of objects or events.

Pidgin A variety that emerges when speakers of different languages are brought together in a stable situation requiring intergroup communication; it has no native speakers and generally is considered to have a reduced grammatical system relative to a non-pidgin.

Pinyin The system of writing Mandarin with a modified Latin alphabet, used for such things as street signs and brand names.

Pitch The auditory property of a sound that enables us to place it on a scale that ranges from low to high.

Places of articulation The points at which the airstream can be modified to produce different sounds (also called **points of articulation**).

Plain pronoun A pronoun whose interpretation may be, but does not have to be, determined by an antecedent in the same sentence (e.g., *he, her*).

Points of articulation *See* **Places of articulation**.

Polysemy The situation in which a word has two or more related meanings (e.g., <u>set</u> *the table, a chess* <u>set</u>).

Polysynthetic languages Languages in which single words can consist of long strings of lexical categories and affixes, often expressing the meaning of an entire sentence in English (e.g., Inuktitut).

Positive evidence Well-formed utterances in the input to language learners.

Positron emission tomography A brain imaging technique that uses radioactive isotopes to measure changes in brain metabolism associated with particular cognitive and behavioural tasks (also called **PET scanning**).

Postposition A member of the P category that occurs after its complement. (*See also* **Preposition [P]**.)

Power The relative social standing of conversation participants that can affect characteristics such as forms of address.

Predicate A verb phrase.

Prefix An affix that is attached to the front of its base (e.g., *re-* in *replay*).

Preposition (P) A lexical category that functions as the head of a prepositional phrase and occurs before its complement (e.g., *into, with, for*). (*See also* **Postposition**.)

Prescriptive A characteristic of certain approaches to grammar in that they seek to prescribe one

system in preference to another. (*See also* **Descriptive**.)

Prestige The social value attached to a linguistic variant considered to be the one used by the group holding the highest esteem in the community; frequently also believed to be the grammatically 'correct' form.

Presupposition An entailment relation between sentence *p* and sentence *q* that survives even when sentence *p* is negated (e.g., *Corinne fired Yusuf* is presupposed by *Corinne regrets firing Yusuf* because the truth of the first sentence is retained even when the second sentence is negated, as in *Corinne didn't regret firing Yusuf*).

Primary stress The most prominent stress of a word.

Prime In a priming experiment, the stimulus that is expected to affect a subject's response accuracy and latency to a subsequent stimulus (called the target).

Priming A situation in which the presentation of a stimulus has a positive effect on the ease with which a subsequent related stimulus is processed.

Priming effect In a priming experiment, the extent to which a priming stimulus facilitates the processing of a target stimulus.

Principle A The principle that constrains the interpretation of reflexive pronouns and is formulated as 'A reflexive pronoun must have a c-commanding antecedent in the same clause'.

Principle B The principle that constrains the interpretation of pronominals and is formulated as 'A pronominal must not have a c-commanding antecedent in the same clause'.

Probabilistic rules Rules or constraints that are not absolute (e.g., [r] is usually deleted after vowels).

Process An operation that modifies a representation (phonological, morphological, or syntactic).

Proclitic A clitic that attaches to the beginning of a word.

Productivity The relative freedom with which affixes can combine with bases of the appropriate category.

Progressive assimilation Assimilation in which a sound influences a following segment (e.g., liquid-glide devoicing in English).

Pronoun A word whose interpretation can be determined by another element (an antecedent) (e.g., *him, she, themselves, herself*).

Prosodic properties *See* **Suprasegmental properties**.

Proto-forms Forms of a proto-language, written with a preceding asterisk to indicate their hypothetical character.

Proto-Indo-European (PIE) The proto-language from which evolved most of the languages of Europe, Persia (Iran), and the northern part of India.

Proto-language A language reconstructed through the methods of historical linguistics.

Proximate A verb form used in some languages to indicate that the subject of the verb has been chosen as the focus of the conversation and any further use of which (without an overt subject) indicates a reference to that focused entity. (*See also* **Obviative**.)

Psycholinguistics The experimental study of the mental processes and representations involved in language comprehension and production.

Quantifier A type of determiner that indicates quantity (e.g., *all, every, some*).

Radical The part of a Chinese character that provides clues about the morpheme's meaning (also called a **key**).

Rapport style A discourse style designed to build and maintain relationships.

Real-time studies Studies that investigate a language over a period of time.

Reanalysis A source of language change that involves an attempt to attribute an internal structure to a word that formerly was not broken down into component morphemes (e.g., *ham + burger*).

Rebus principle In writing, the use of a sign for any word with the same pronunciation as the word for which it was originally intended.

Recast A repetition of a child's utterance that includes adjustments to its form and/or content.

Recursion The application of an operation to its own input to create a more complex structure.

Reduced A dorsal feature that characterizes only schwa.

Reduced vowel *See* **Schwa**.

Reduplication A morphological process that duplicates all or part of the base to which it applies. (*See also* **Partial reduplication** and **Full reduplication**.)

Reflexive pronoun A pronoun that must have a c-commanding antecedent in the same clause (e.g., *himself, herself*).

Regional dialect A dialect spoken in a specific geographical region.

Register A set of linguistic structures that is associated with a particular speech situation; it may carry an association with a particular style.

Register tones Level tones that signal meaning differences.

Regressive assimilation Assimilation in which a sound influences a preceding segment (e.g., nasalization in English).

Regressive saccades Eye movements in which the eyes dart backward to a section of text that has been previously read.

Relative clause A CP that serves as modifier of a noun.

Relative pronouns Words such as *who* and *which* in English that appear at the beginning of a relative clause and help link it to the noun to its left.

Report style A discourse style designed to communicate factual information.

Response accuracy The correctness of a subject's responses to particular stimuli provided in an experiment.

Response latency The amount of time taken by a subject in an experiment to respond to a stimulus.

Restricted use Social situations in which the use of a particular language is restricted to certain environments (e.g., school).

Retroflex Sounds made by curling the tongue tip back into the mouth, as is done in producing the English *r*.

Rhotacism A type of weakening that typically involves the change of [z] to [r].

Rhyme (R) The nucleus and the coda of a syllable (e.g., [uts] in the word *boots*).

Right ear advantage The phenomenon in which people with language lateralized in the left hemisphere hear speech louder and clearer with the right ear.

Root (of a word) The morpheme in a word that carries the major component of the word's meaning and belongs to a lexical category (e.g., *collect* in the word *collections*).

Root (of the tongue) The part of the tongue that is contained in the upper part of the throat.

Round A place feature that characterizes sounds made by protruding the lips (e.g., [u], [w]).

Rounded (sounds) Sounds made with the lips protruding (e.g., [u], [w]).

S-structure *See* **Surface structure**.

Saccades The quick and uneven movement of the eyes during reading.

Salient features Linguistic variables that are easily perceived by a speech community.

Sandhi Phonemic alternations that occur specifically at morpheme boundaries.

Scalar adjectives Adjectives, such as *courage*, that are associated with a scale of degrees (more courageous, less courageous, as courageous).

Schwa The lax vowel that is characterized by briefer duration than any of the other vowels (also called a **reduced vowel**) (e.g., the underlined vowels in *Canada*, *suppose*).

Scope A relation of interpretive dependence between two quantifier NPs or between a quantifier NP and negation.

Script The set of symbols that are used in a writing system.

Second language acquisition (SLA) The acquisition of proficiency in a language that is not one's first language.

Secondary stress The second most prominent stress in a word.

Segments Individual speech sounds.

Semantically opaque compound A compound for which the meanings of the parts do not obviously accord with the meaning of the whole word (e.g., *grapefruit*).

Semantically transparent compound A compound whose morphological constituents contribute to the meaning of the whole word in a clear manner (e.g., *suntan*).

Semantic broadening The process in which the meaning of a word becomes more inclusive than its earlier form (e.g., *barn* used to mean 'a place to store barley').

Semantic narrowing The process in which the meaning of a word becomes less inclusive than its earlier form (e.g., *meat* used to mean 'any type of food').

Semantic shift The process in which a word loses its former meaning, taking on a new, often related, meaning (e.g., *immoral* used to mean 'not customary').

Semantics The component of the grammar that is concerned with the meaning of words and sentences.

Sensory aphasia *See* **Fluent aphasia**.

Sequential bilinguals Early bilinguals who begin to learn their L2 between the age of two to three years and adolescence.

Serial processing model A psycholinguistic theory built around the claim that language processing proceeds in a step by step manner.

Shibboleth A word whose pronunciation has become a stereotype for a speech community.

Shift A change in a phonological system in which a series of phonemes is systematically modified so that their organization with respect to each other is altered (e.g., the Great English Vowel Shift).

Sibilants *See* **Stridents**.

Simple vowels Vowels that do not show a noticeable change in quality during their production (e.g., the vowel sounds of *cab* and *get*).

Simple (word) A word that consists of a single morpheme (e.g., *horse*).

Simultaneous bilinguals Early bilinguals who begin to learn their L1 and L2 before two to three years of age.

Situational code-switching Switching between languages for clearly identifiable reasons such as reporting the speech of another or when the topic of conversation switches from personal to business affairs.

Slang Informal or faddish usages of language.

Social factor Non-linguistic factors that are correlated with linguistic variation (e.g., [r] is dropped more often by working-class speakers).

Social isolation A situation in which a speech community is socially isolated from other speech communities (e.g., the case of African Nova Scotian English).

Social network The connections among members of a speech community.

Societal bilingualism Communities, regions, or nations where two languages are spoken by many residents and where two languages might be used in government institutions, the legal system, and schools.

Sociolect A variety of language associated with a particular social group.

Sociolinguistic competence The subcomponent of communicative competence that characterizes the knowledge and skills necessary for second language learners to use language appropriately in a specific situation.

Sociolinguistic interview An interview designed to elicit the most natural speech possible from the consultant.

Sociolinguistic norms Conventions for use of language structures in particular social situations.

Sociolinguistics The study of the relationship between language structures as they are used in discourse and the social roles and/or situations associated with them.

Solidarity The degree of intimacy or similarity that one group or individual may feel for another.

Sonorant A major class feature that characterizes all and only the 'singables': vowels, glides, liquids, and nasals.

Sonority Requirement The requirement that sonority within a basic syllable rises before the nucleus and declines after the nucleus.

Sound shift The systematic modification of a series of phonemes (e.g., Grimm's Law).

Specifier An element that helps to make more precise the meaning of the head of the phrase and that occurs immediately beneath XP (e.g., *the* in *the book*).

Speech community Any group of people who share a set of conventions for language use.

Speech event An identifiable type of discourse associated with a particular speech situation.

Speech situation Any circumstance that may involve the use of speech.

Speech sound *See* **Phone.**

Spelling pronunciation A source of language change whereby a new pronunciation arises that reflects more closely the spelling of the word (e.g., *often* pronounced as [aftən] rather than [afən]).

Split A situation in which allophones of the same phoneme come to contrast with each other due to the loss of the conditioning environment, resulting in one or more new phonemes.

Split brain experiments Studies that investigate the effects of surgically severing the corpus callosum.

Spoonerisms A type of speech error, named after Reverend William A. Spooner, in which words or sounds are rearranged with often humorous results.

Spread glottis ([SG]) A laryngeal feature that distinguishes unaspirated from aspirated sounds.

Standard variety The variety of language spoken by the most powerful group in a community and generally held to be 'correct' by prescriptive grammarians.

Static (event) An event that is durative and uniform (with no natural beginning and end).

Stative predicates Predicates that describe a state.

Status The social position of a person in relation to others.

Stem The base to which an inflectional affix is added (e.g., *modification* is the stem for *-s* in the word *modifications*).

Stocks The groups into which purportedly related language families are placed.

Stopping A common substitution process in child language acquisition that involves the replacement of a fricative by a corresponding stop (e.g., *zebra* is pronounced [dibrə]).

Stops Sounds made with a complete and momentary closure of airflow through the vocal tract (e.g., the initial sounds of *pleasure* and *grab*).

Stress A property usually found on vowels that are perceived as relatively more prominent due to the combined effects of pitch, loudness, and length.

Strident A place feature that characterizes the 'noisy' fricatives and affricates (in English, [s z ʃ ʒ tʃ dʒ]) (also called **sibilants**).

Stroke A hemorrhage in the brain or the blockage or rupture of an artery causing brain damage (also called a **cerebrovascular accident**).

Structural ambiguity A property of phrases or sentences whose component words can be combined in more than one way (e.g., *fast cars and motorcycles*).

Structured variation Language variation that is correlated with other factors (e.g., age, sex, or socio-economic status).

Style The level of formality associated with a linguistic structure or set of structures classified along a continuum from most informal to most formal.

Subcategorization The classification of words in terms of their complement options (e.g., the verb *devour* is subcategorized for a complement NP).

Subinterval property A property of an event whose subparts all involve the same type of activity as the whole event. (If it true that that Max swam for an hour, then it is true that each sub-part of that event also involved swimming.)

Subject The NP occurring immediately under TP (e.g., *Irene* in *Irene is a tailor*).

Subset Principle A learning principle stating that the initial or default setting of a parameter will correspond to the most restrictive option (i.e., the option that permits the fewest patterns).

Substitution A type of auditorily based change involving the replacement of one segment with another similar segment (e.g., in the history of English, [f] replaced [x] in some words).

Substitution test A test used to determine if a group of words is a constituent by replacing them with a single word or simple phrase like *do so*.

Substratum influence The influence of a politically or culturally non-dominant language on a dominant language in the area (e.g., the borrowing of words into English from Aboriginal languages).

Subtractive bilingualism The situation in which the minority or heritage language of a bilingual child is not supported socio-politically or in the education system and media, resulting in decreased proficiency in that language.

Suffix An affix that is attached to the end of its base (e.g., *-ly* in *quickly*).

Sulcus An area where the cerebral cortex is folded in (plural: *sulci*).

Superstratum influence The influence of a politically or culturally dominant language on another language in the area (e.g., the effects of Norman French on English during the Middle English period).

Suppletion A morphological process that marks a grammatical contrast by replacing a morpheme with an entirely different morpheme (e.g., *be/was*).

Suprasegmental properties Those properties of sounds that form part of their makeup no matter what their place or manner of articulation: pitch, loudness, and length (also called **prosodic properties**).

Surface dyslexia A type of acquired dyslexia in which the patient seems unable to recognize words as wholes but must process all words through a set of spelling-to-sound rules (e.g., *yacht* would be pronounced /jatʃt/).

Surface structure The structure that results from the application of whatever transformations are appropriate for the sentence in question.

Syllabary A set of syllabic signs used for representing a language.

Syllabic (feature) A major class feature that characterizes vowels.

Syllabic liquids Liquids that function as syllabic nuclei (e.g., the *l* in *bottle*).

Syllabic nasals Nasals that function as syllabic nuclei (e.g., the *n* in *button*).

Syllabic writing A type of writing in which each symbol represents a syllable.

Syllable A unit of linguistic structure that consists of a syllabic element and any segments that are associated with it. (*See also* **Onset, Nucleus, Coda**.)

Symbolic sign A sign that bears an arbitrary relationship to its referent (e.g., a stop sign, non-onomatopoeic words).

Syncope The deletion of a word-internal vowel (e.g., the deletion of the schwa in *police*).

Synonyms Words or expressions that have the same meanings in some or all contexts (e.g., *buy* and *purchase*).

Syntactic category The category into which an element is placed depending on the type of meaning that it expresses, the type of affixes it takes, and the type of structure in which it occurs (includes both lexical and functional categories) (also called a **part of speech**).

Syntactic parser The theoretical construct that accounts for the human ability to assign grammatical categories and hierarchical structure to elements in a stream of language input.

Syntax The component of the grammar that is concerned with the form of grammatical sentences.

Systematic phonetic correspondences Sound correspondences between two or more related languages that are consistent throughout the vocabularies of those languages.

T form A form of address used for people who are close friends—from the French word *tu*.

Target In a priming experiment, the stimulus to which a subject must respond and for which response accuracy and latency are measured.

Target language The language that a second language learner is learning.

Telegraphic speech Speech lacking bound morphemes and non-lexical categories.

Telegraphic stage The stage in child language acquisition in which children's utterances are generally longer than two words but lack bound morphemes and most non-lexical categories.

Telic (event) An event that has a natural end point.

Temporal lobe The lobe of the brain that lies beneath the lateral fissure and in which Wernicke's area is located.

Tense (feature) A dorsal feature that captures the tense-lax distinction among vowels.

Tense (verb) A grammatical category that provides information about the time of an event's occurrence (e.g., past, present, or future).

Tense (vowel) A vowel that is made with the placement of the tongue that results in relatively more vocal tract constriction (e.g., the vowels in *seen* and *go*).

Terminal (intonation) contour Falling intonation at the end of an utterance, signalling that the utterance is complete.

Textual competence The subcomponent of communicative competence that characterizes the knowledge and skills necessary for second language learners to produce and comprehend well-formed texts beyond the sentence level.

Thematic grid A representation of information about the thematic roles associated with particular verbs, usually listed within angled brackets.

Thematic role The relations of the NPs in a sentence with respect to the verb.

Theme The thematic role of the entity directly affected by the action designated by the verb (e.g., *the ball* in *Tom caught the ball*).

Theta Criterion A criterion of grammaticality involving thematic roles and arguments and consisting of two parts: *a.* each thematic role is assigned to exactly one argument; *b.* each argument is assigned exactly one thematic role.

Thyroid cartilage The cartilage that forms the main portion of the larynx, spreading outward like the head of a plow.

Tip (of the tongue) The narrow area at the front of the tongue.

Tone Pitch movement in spoken utterances that is related to differences in word meaning.

Tone language A language in which differences in word meaning are signalled by differences in pitch.

Top-down processing A type of processing using a set of expectations to guide phonetic processing and word recognition.

Trace The empty element, marked by the symbol *t*, that is left in syntactic structure after a word or phrase has been moved.

Trachea The tube below the larynx through which air travels when it leaves the lungs; commonly known as the windpipe.

Transfer The process by which the first language (L1) influences the interlanguage grammar.

Transformation *See* **Move.**

Transitive verb A verb that takes an NP complement (a direct object) (e.g., *hit* in *hit the ball*).

Tree structure A diagram depicting the internal organization of a linguistic unit such as a word, phrase, or sentence.

Turn-taking The changeover between speakers' turns in a conversation.

Typological plausibility A criterion that guides language reconstruction by referring to universals or existing properties of language.

Umlaut The fronting of a vowel in the root under the influence of a front vowel in a suffix.

Underextension A developmental phenomenon in which a child uses a lexical item to denote only a subset of the items that it denotes in adult speech (e.g., *car* used to refer only to the family car).

Underlying representation *See* **Phonological representation**.

Uniqueness presupposition The presupposition that an entity to which a speaker refers is unique.

Universal Grammar (UG) The innate system of categories, operations, and principles that are shared by all languages.

Universal tendencies Patterns or traits that occur in all or most languages.

Unmarked traits Those characteristics of language that are considered to be less complex and/or universally more common in languages.

Uvula The small fleshy flap of tissue that hangs down from the velum.

Uvulars Sounds made with the tongue near or touching the uvula.

V form A form of address used for people who are not close friends—from the French word *vous*.

Vagueness A word is vague if the corresponding concept has fuzzy boundaries (e.g., *big, smart*).

Variable A set of forms, any of which may be used to express the same function or meaning and the use of which cannot be expressed by a categorical rule (e.g., the *th* in *brother*, which can be pronounced in various ways).

Variant One of a set of several possible forms that can be used to express the same function or meaning (e.g., each of the possible pronunciations of the variable *th* in *brother* is a variant).

Variationist sociolinguistics The branch of linguistics that seeks to explain the connection between social distinctions and linguistic variation.

Variety A cover term used to refer to language used by a particular speech community; it merely implies that some set of sociolinguistic norms is present.

Velars Sounds made with the tongue touching or near the velum (e.g., [ŋ], [k]).

Velum The soft area toward the rear of the roof of the mouth.

Verb (V) A lexical category that typically designates actions, sensations, and states, can usually be inflected for tense, and functions as the head of a verb phrase (e.g., *see, feel, remain*).

Verb raising A Move operation that moves a verb to the T position.

Vocal cords *See* **Vocal folds**.

Vocal folds A set of muscles inside the larynx that may be positioned in various ways to produce different glottal states (also called **vocal cords**).

Vocal tract The oral cavity, nasal cavity, and pharynx.

Voice A laryngeal feature that distinguishes between voiced and voiceless sounds.

Voiced The glottal state in which the vocal folds are brought close together, but not tightly closed, causing air passing through them to vibrate (e.g., [æ], [z], [m] are voiced).

Voiceless The glottal state in which the vocal folds are pulled apart, allowing air to pass directly through the glottis (e.g., [t], [s], [f] are voiceless).

Voicing A historical process in which a voiceless sound becomes voiced.

Voicing assimilation Assimilation in which one segment becomes more like a nearby segment in terms of voicing (e.g., liquid devoicing in English).

Vowel reduction A process that reduces a full vowel, typically unstressed, to a schwa.

Vowels Sounds that are produced with little obstruction in the vocal tract and that are generally voiced.

Weakening (phonetic) A process that weakens a segment according to a particular scale of strength.

Wernicke's aphasia The aphasia that results in fluent but nonsensical speech, sometimes characterized by jargon aphasia.

Wernicke's area The area in the rear of the temporal lobe and the lower portion of the parietal lobe that plays an important role in language comprehension.

***Wh* Movement** A transformation that moves a *wh* phrase to the beginning of the sentence, formulated as 'Move a *wh* phrase to the specifier position under CP'.

***Wh* question** A question that contains a *wh*-word (e.g., *Who did you see?*).

Whisper The glottal state in which the vocal folds are adjusted so that the front portions are pulled close together, while the back portions are apart.

Wide scope A quantified NP1 is said to have wide scope with respect to another quantified NP2 or negation if the interpretation of NP1 does not depend on the interpretation of NP2 or negation.

Word-based morphology Morphology in which most complex words are formed from a base that can itself be a word.

Word manufacture The creation of a word from scratch, (also called **coinage**) (e.g., *Kodak*).

Words The smallest free forms found in language.

Writing The representation of language by graphic signs or symbols.

X' Schema The blueprint for the internal structure of phrases.

***Yes-no* question** A question for which the expected response is 'yes' or 'no'.

Zero derivation *See* **Conversion**.

Sources

Chapter 1

p. 2: The description of the density of the nerves that control the vocal cords is based on John Colapinto, "Giving Voice," *The New Yorker*, March 4, 2014, pp. 48–57. pp. 3–4: The discussion of word creation is based in part on information in Eve Clark and Herb Clark, "When Nouns Surface as Verbs," *Language* 55 (1979): 767–811. p. 6: The information about Warlpiri is based on Kenneth Hale, "Person Marking in Walbiri," in *A Festschrift for Morris Halle*, edited by Stephen R. Anderson and Paul Kiparsky (New York: Holt, Rinehart and Winston, 1973). p. 7: The block quotation in section 1.3.2 is from Steven Pinker, *The Language Instinct: How the Human Mind Creates Language* (New York: Morrow, 1994), p. 370. p. 9: Information on word order preferences in human language is based on Matthew Dryer, "Order of Subject, Object and Verb," in *The World Atlas of Language Structures Online,* edited by Matthew S. Dryer and Martin Haspelmath (Leipzig: Max Planck Institute for Evolutionary Anthropology, 2013) (available online at wals.info). p. 10: The 1857 speech quoted on the status of Canadian English is from Rev. A.C. Geikie, "Canadian English," *The Canadian Journal* 2 (September 1857): 344–55, as cited in Mark Orkin, *Speaking Canadian English* (Toronto: General, 1970).

The exercises for this chapter were prepared by Joyce Hildebrand.

Chapter 2

p. 14: The epigraph from Wallace Stevens's "The Plot against the Giant" was first published in *Harmonium* in 1923. Rights are held by Random House. p. 14: The estimate of 600 consonants and 200 vowels is from a talk by Peter Ladefoged given at the University of Hawaii, April 27, 1999. pp. 18–20: The information on glottal states is based in part on Jimmy G. Harris, "States of the Glottis for Voiceless Plosives," in *Proceedings of the 14th International Congress of Phonetic Sciences*, vol. 3, edited by John J. Ohala, Yoko Hasegawa, Manjari Ohala, Daniel Granville, and Ashlee C. Bailey, 2041–44 (San Francisco: Linguistics Department, University of California, 1999). p. 41: Sarcee data are based on information in E.-D. Cook, "Vowels and Tones in Sarcee," *Language* 47 (1971): 164–79. p. 42: Bini data are adapted from P. Ladefoged, *A Course in Phonetics*, 4th ed. (Toronto: Harcourt, 2001). p. 48: Gaelic data are courtesy of James Galbraith (personal communication).

Chapter 3

pp. 66–77: The discussion of syllable structure draws on the ideas put forward by G.N. Clements in "The Role of the Sonority Cycle in Core Syllabification," in *Papers in Laboratory Phonology I: Between the Grammar and the Physics of Speech,* edited by J. Kingston and M. Beckman, 283–333 (London: Cambridge University Press, 1990). p. 93: Data for exercise 1 are based on information in Inuktitut: B. Harnum (personal communication). Data for exercise 2 are based on information in Mokilese: S. Harrison, *Mokilese Reference Grammar* (Honolulu: University of Hawaii Press, 1976). Data for exercise 3 are based on information in Gascon: R.C. Kelly, *A Descriptive Analysis of Gascon* (Amsterdam: Mouton, 1978). p. 94: Data for exercise 6 are based on information in Cree: Y. Carifelle and M. Pepper (personal communication). p. 96: Data for exercise 13 are based on information in Canadian French: D.C. Walker, *The Pronunciation of Canadian French* (Ottawa: University of Ottawa Press, 1984), and A. Teasdale (personal communication). p. 97: Data for exercise 14 are based on information in English fast speech: G. Zhang, *Phonological Representation and Analyses of Fast Speech Phenomena in English* (Master's thesis, Memorial University of Newfoundland, 1994).

Chapter 4

p. 100: The estimate that the average high school student knows 60 000 "basic" words comes from Steven Pinker, *The Language Instinct: How the Mind Creates Language* (New York: Morrow, 1994), 150. pp. 105–6: The Arabic examples in section 4.1.2 are from Andrew Spencer, *Morphological Theory* (Cambridge, MA: Blackwell, 1991), 17. p. 106: The tier-based analysis of Arabic word structure is based on work by John McCarthy, including his article "A Prosodic Theory of Nonconcatenative Morphology," *Linguistic Inquiry* 12 (1981): 373–418. p. 110: The facts concerning the requirement that -*ant* combines with a base of Latin origin are noted in Francis Katamba, *Morphology* (London: Macmillan, 1993), 71. p. 114: The discussion of the difference between regular and irregular inflection is based on information from Steven Pinker, "Rules of Language," *Science* (August 1991): 530–35. p. 115: The definition of *stem* is based on Stephen R. Anderson, "Morphological Theory," in *Linguistics: The Cambridge Survey*, vol. 1, edited by Frederick J. Newmeyer (New York: Cambridge University Press, 1988), 163. p. 121: The examples of tense marking in Mono-Bili are based on information in Kenneth S. Olson, "The Phonology and Morphology of Mono" (PhD diss., University of Chicago, 2001). p. 122–23: The examples of conversion come largely from the discussion in John T. Jensen, *Morphology: Word Structure in Generative Grammar* (Amsterdam: John Benjamins, 1990) and in Laurie Bauer, *English Word-Formation* (New York: Cambridge University Press, 1983), 229–31. p. 124: The examples of Malay blends come from Michael Dobrovolsky, "Malay Blends—CV or Syllable Templates," unpublished manuscript, University of Calgary. p. 126: The data on Slavey onomatopoeia are from Mary Pepper, "Slavey Expressive Terms," *Kansas Working Papers in Linguistics* 10 (1985): 85–100. pp. 127–28: The examples used in the section on morphophonemics are from the discussion of this subject written by Michael Dobrovolsky for the third edition of this book. p. 131–2: The Kwakum data in exercise 4 are based on information in Malcolm Guthrie, *The Bantu Languages of Western Equatorial Africa* (Oxford: Oxford University Press, 1953). p. 132: The Zapotec data and romanization in exercise 6 are based on information in *Grammática de la lengua zapoteca* by an anonymous author (Mexico: Oficina Tip. de la Secretaría de Formento), 8. p. 136: The Samoan data in exercise 19 are based on information in A. Koutsoudas, *Writing Transformational Grammars* (New York: McGraw-Hill, 1966). p. 136: The Chamorro data in exercise 20 are based on information in Donald M. Topping, *Chamorro Reference Grammar*, with the assistance of Bernadita C. Dungca (Honolulu: University of Hawaii Press, 1973).

Exercises whose authorship is not otherwise noted were prepared by Joyce Hildebrand.

Chapter 5

p. 171–2: The Welsh data is based on information in Richard Sproat, "Welsh Syntax and VSO Structure," *Natural Language and Linguistic Theory* 3 (1985): 173–216.

The exercises for this chapter were prepared by Joyce Hildebrand.

Chapter 7

p. 214–6: Section 7.1.2 was written by William O'Grady. Numerical data is based on information in Lyle Campbell and Eve Okura, "New Knowledge Produced by ELCat," in *Cataloguing the World's Endangered Languages,* edited by Lyle Campbell and Anna Belew (Abingdon: Routledge, 2018); *Ethnologue: Languages of the World* (www.ethnologue.com); David Harmon and Jonathon Loh, "The Index of Linguistic Diversity: A New Quantitative Measure of Trends in the Status of the World's Languages," *Language Documentation and Conservation* 4 (2010): 97–151; and UNESCO's policy statement "Language Vitality and Endangerment," document submitted to the International Expert Meeting on UNESCO Programme Safeguarding of Endangered Languages, Paris, March 10-12, 2003. p. 216: The 2007 study noted in the second paragraph is Darcy Hallett, Michael J. Chandler, and Christopher E. Lalonde, "Aboriginal Language Knowledge and Youth Suicide," *Cognitive Development* 22 (2007): 392–99. p. 226: The Inuktitut example is from Marianne Mithun, *The Languages of Native North America* (Cambridge, UK: Cambridge University Press, 1999), 43. p. 227: Estimates of word order patterns are based on data in Matthew S. Dryer, "Order of Subject, Object and Verb," in *The World Atlas of Language Structures Online,* edited by Matthew S. Dryer and Martin Haspelmath (Leipzig: Max Planck Institute for Evolutionary Anthropology, 2013). Available online at wals.info. p. 227–8: The OVS and OSV examples are from Desmond C. Derbyshire and Geoffrey K. Pullum, "Object-Initial Languages," *International Journal of American Linguistics* 47, 3 (1981): 192–214. p. 231: The discussion of consonant systems in section 7.2.4 is based on data in Björn Lindblom and Ian Maddieson, "Phonetic Universals in Consonant Systems," in *Language, Speech and Mind: Studies in Honor of Victoria Fromkin,* edited by L. Hyman and C. Li (New York: Routledge and Kegan Paul, 1988), 62–78. p. 233: Section 7.3: Information about membership in language families is based on data in *The World's Major Languages,* edited by Bernard Comrie (Oxford: Oxford University Press, 1990); Joseph H. Greenberg, *The Languages of Africa* (Bloomington, IN: Indiana University Press, 1963); Merritt Ruhlen, *A Guide to the Languages of the World* (Stanford, CA: Stanford University, Language Universals Project, 1976); and C.F. Voegelin and F.M. Voegelin, *Classification and Index of the World's Languages* (New York: Elsevier, 1976).

Chapter 8

p. 248: The catalogue of sound changes based on articulatory factors is adapted from catalogues proposed by Theo Vennemann in "Linguistic Typologies in Historical Linguistics," Società di linguistica italiana 23 (1985): 87–91, and in Theo Vennemann, *Preference Laws for Syllable Structure and the Explanation of Sound Change* (Amsterdam: Mouton de Gruyter, 1988). p. 257: The data on vowel laxing in Canadian French is based on information in Douglas C. Walker, *The Pronunciation of Canadian French* (Ottawa: University of Ottawa Press, 1984). p. 266: The data on word order in Old and Middle English in table 8.33 is based on information in Joseph Williams, *Origins of the English Language: A Social and Linguistic History* (New York: Free Press, 1975). pp. 270–1: The examples of English loan words in Gwich'in are based on information in *Dene* 1, 1 (1985), published by the Dene Language Terminology Committee, Yellowknife, Northwest Territories. p. 276: Figure 8.10, depicting lexical diffusion of the stress change in English nouns derived from verbs, is taken from Jean Aitchison, *Language Change: Progress or Decay?* (New York: Universe Books, 1985). Aitchison's remarks are, in turn, based on M. Chen and W. Wang, "Sound Change: Actuation and Implementation," *Language* 51 (1975): 255–81. p. 277: The data on the realization of [s] as [h] in Spanish were provided by the late Herbert Izzo of the University of Calgary. p. 281: Some of the Romance cognates in table 8.56 are based on Robert A. Hall, Jr., *Proto-Romance Phonology* (New York: Elsevier, 1976). p. 285: The quotation from Jones is taken from *The Quarterly Review* vol. 119 (London: John Murray, 1866), 399–400. p. 286: The quotation from Rask is taken from Holger Pedersen, *The Discovery of Language: Linguistic Science in the Nineteenth Century* (Bloomington: Indiana University Press, 1959). p. 294: Exercise 2 is based on data provided by Dr. George Patterson, whose generosity we hereby acknowledge. p. 294: The data for exercises 3 and 4 are from F. Columbus, *Introductory Workbook in Historical Phonology* (Cambridge, MA: Slavica, 1974). p. 297: The data in exercise 14 are drawn from W. Cowan and J. Rakusan, *Source Book for Linguistics* (Philadelphia: John Benjamins, 1987).

Chapter 9

p. 299: The discussion of the genetic relationships among Indigenous languages is based on information found in the following works: John Wesley Powell, "Indian Linguistic Families of America North of Mexico," in the Seventh Annual Report, Bureau of American Ethnology (1891); Edward Sapir, "Central and North American Languages," in *Encyclopedia Britannica*, 14th ed., 5:138–41 (1929); C.F. and F.M. Voegelin, *Map of North American Indian Languages* (Washington, DC: American Ethnology Society, 1966); Michael Foster, "Canada's Indigenous Languages: Past and Present," *Language and Society* 7 (1982): 3–16; *Handbook of North American Indians*, vol. 17: *Languages*, edited by Ives Goddard (Washington, DC: Smithsonian Institution, 1996); and Lyle Campbell, *American Indian Languages: The Historical Linguistics of Native America* (Oxford: Oxford University Press, 1997). pp. 300–5: The estimates of speaker populations reported here are based primarily on the following sources: Statistics Canada's 2016 census; Michael Foster, "Canada's Indigenous Languages: Past and Present," *Language and Society* 7 (1982): 3–16; D.M. Kinkade, "The Decline of Native Languages in Canada," in *Endangered Languages*, edited by R.H. Robins and E.M. Uhlenbeck, 157–76 (New York: Berg, 1991); E.-D. Cook, "Aboriginal Languages: A History," in *Language in Canada*, edited by J. Edwards, 125–43 (New York: Cambridge University Press, 1998); B.F. Grimes, *Ethnologue*, 14th ed. (SIL International, 2000); Michael Krauss, "The Indigenous Languages of the North: A Report on Their Present State," in *Northern Minority Languages: Problems of Survival*, edited by H. Shoji and J. Junhunen, 1–34 (Osaka, Japan: Senri Ethnological Studies 44, National Museum of Ethnology, 1997); Marianne Mithun, *The Languages of Native North America* (Cambridge, UK: Cambridge University Press, 2001); the Yukon Native Language Centre at the Yukon College in Whitehorse; the Alaska Native Language Center; and numerous expert consultations. p. 303: The Dakota classification is based on information found in D. Parks and R. DeMallie, "Sioux, Assiniboine, and Stoney Dialects: A Classification," *Anthropological Linguistics* 34 (1992): 233–55. p. 305: The discussion of Michif is based on information found in P. Bakker, *A Language of Our Own: The Genesis of Michif, the Mixed Cree-French Language of the Canadian Métis* (Toronto: Oxford University Press, 1997). pp. 306–7: Overall Indigenous population estimates are from Statistics Canada's 2016 census and based on information found in Thornton Russell, "Population History of North American Indians," in *A Population History of North America*, edited by Michael R. Haines and Richard H. Steckel, 9–50 (New York: Cambridge University Press, 2000). p. 308: The data on Cree are based on information in H.C. Wolfart, "Sketch of Cree, an Algonquian

Language," in *Handbook of North American Indians*, vol. 17: *Languages*, edited by Ives Goddard, 390–439 (Washington, DC: Smithsonian Institution, 1996), and in C.H. Wolfart and J. Carroll, *Meet Cree: A Guide to the Cree Language*, 2nd rev. ed. (Edmonton: University of Alberta Press, 1981). p. 309–10: The data on Dënesųłiné vowels is based on information in F.K. Li, "Chipewyan," in *Linguistic Structures of Native America*, by H. Hoijer et al. (Viking Fund Publications in Anthropology, No. 6, 1946), and in E.-D. Cook, "Chipewyan Vowels," *International Journal of American Linguistics* 49 (1983): 413–27. p. 312: Mohawk data are based on information in M.C. Baker, *The Polysynthesis Parameter* (New York: Oxford University Press, 1996). Organizations such as the Saskatchewan Indian Cultural Centre, the Yinka Dene Language Institute (especially Bill Poser), and Aboriginal Languages of Manitoba (especially Carol Beaulieu) provided helpful information.

Chapter 10

p. 320: The cross-linguistic data on babbling are based on information in John L. Locke, *Phonological Acquisition and Change* (San Diego: Academic Press, 1983) and in Bénédicte de Boysson-Bardies and Marilyn May Vihman, "Adaptation to Language: Evidence from Babbling and First Words in Four Languages" *Language* 67, 2 (1991): 297–319. pp. 320–1: The data on developmental order for speech sounds are based on information in Chapter 8 of David Ingram, *First Language Acquisition: Method, Description and Explanation* (New York: Cambridge University Press, 1989). pp. 320–3: The data in the discussion of early phonetic processes are based on information in David Ingram, *Phonological Disability in Children* (London: Edward Arnold, 1976); C.H. Echols, "A Role for Stress in Early Speech Segmentation," in *Signal to Syntax*, edited by J.L. Morgan and K. Demuth, 151–70 (Mahwah, NJ: Erlbaum, 1996); and Margaret Kehoe and Carol Stoel-Gammon, "The Acquisition of Prosodic Structure: An Investigation of Current Accounts of Children's Prosodic Development" *Language* 73, 1 (1997): 113–44. p. 324: The sample vocabulary in Table 10.8 is based on information in David Ingram, *First Language Acquisition: Method, Description and Explanation* (New York: Cambridge University Press, 1989), 149. p. 325: Estimates of word types in children's early vocabulary are based on information in Katherine Nelson, *Structure and Strategy in Learning to Talk*, vol. 38, no. 149 of *Monographs of the Society for Research in Child Development* (Hoboken, NJ: Wiley, 1973). p. 325: The description of strategies for learning word meaning are based on the proposals outlined in Ellen M. Markman, *Categorization and Naming in Children: Problems of Induction* (Cambridge, MA: MIT Press, 1989). p. 326: The description of the *dax* experiment on proper and common nouns is based on N. Katz, E. Baker, and J. MacNamara, "What's in a Name? A Study of How Children Learn Common and Proper Nouns," *Child Development* 45 (1974): 469–73. p. 326: The description of the *tiv* experiment is based on information in Susan Carey, "The Child as Word Learner" in *Linguistic Theory and Psychological Reality*, edited by M. Halle, J. Bresnan, and G.A. Miller, 264–93 (Cambridge, MA: MIT Press, 1978). p. 326: The Social Strategy is based on a proposal in Michael Tomasello, "The Social-Pragmatic Theory of Word Learning" *Pragmatics* 10, 4 (2000): 401–13. p. 328: The report of overextension in Allen's speech is based on the discussion in Eve V. Clark *The Lexicon in Acquisition* (New York: Cambridge University Press, 1993), 92. p. 328: The description of the experimental study on overextension is based on information in Jean R. Thomson and Robin Chapman, "Who Is 'Daddy' Revisited: The Status of Two-Year-Olds' Overextended Words in Use and Comprehension" *Journal of Child Language* 4, 3 (1977): 359–75.

pp. 328–9: The experiment on *pour* and *fill* can be found in J. Gropen, S. Pinker, M. Hollander, and R. Goldberg, "Syntax and Semantics in the Acquisition of Locative Verbs," *Journal of Child Language* 18, 1 (1991): 115–51. pp. 329–30: The description of the experiment on dimensional terms is based on information in Peter L. Harris, Jeremy E. Morris, and Mark Meerum Terwogt, "The Early Acquisition of Spatial Adjectives: A Cross-linguistic Study," *Journal of Child Language* 13, 2 (1986): 335–52. pp. 330–1: The remarks on inflectional overgeneralization are based in part on information in Gary F. Marcus, Steven Pinker, Michael Ullman, Michelle Hollander, T. John Rosen, and Fei Xu, *Overregularization in Language Acquisition*, vol. 57, no. 4 of *Monographs of the Society for Research in Child Development* (Hoboken, NJ: Wiley, 1992). p. 331: The description of overgeneralizations is based on data in Michael Maratsos, "More Overregularizations After All: New Data and Discussion on Marcus, Pinker, Ullman, Hollander, Rosen and Xu," *Journal of Child Language* 27, 1 (2000): 183–212. p. 331: The results of the *wug* test are based on information in Jean Berko, "The Child's Learning of English Morphology," *Word* 14, 2–3 (1958): 150–77. p. 332–3: The description of developmental order for English bound morphemes and function words is based on information in Roger Brown, *A First Language: The Early Stages* (Cambridge, MA: Harvard University Press, 1973) and in D.I. Slobin, "Universal and Particular in the Acquisition of Language," in *Language Acquisition: The State of the Art*, edited by E. Wanner and L.R. Gleitman, 128–72 (New York: Cambridge University Press, 1982). p. 333: The description of the development of derivational affixes and compounding in English is based on information in Eve V. Clark, *The Lexicon in Acquisition* (New York: Cambridge University Press), and in Eve V. Clark and Barbara F. Hecht, "Learning to Coin Agent and Instrument Nouns," *Cognition* 12, 1 (1982): 1–24. p. 333: Sample word order errors within compounds are based on information in Eve V. Clark, Barbara F. Hecht, and Randa C. Mulford, "Coining Complex Compounds in English: Affixes and Word Order in Acquisition," *Linguistics* 24, 1 (1986): 7–29. p. 334: The data on mastery of the prohibition against inflection within compounds are based on information in Peter Gordon, "Level-Ordering in Lexical Development," *Cognition* 21, 2 (1985): 73–93. p. 336: The data on four-year-olds' preference for SVO word order with nonsense verbs is based on information in Nameera Akhtar, "Acquiring Basic Word Order: Evidence for Data-Driven Learning of Syntactic Structure," *Journal of Child Language* 26, 2 (1999): 339–56, and in Julie Franck, Séverine Millotte, and Romy Lassotta, "Early Word Order Representations: New Arguments against Old Contradictions," *Language Acquisition* 18, 2 (2011): 121–35. p. 336: The description of the difference between *is V-ing* and *can V-ing* is based on information in Lynn Santelmann and Peter W. Jusczyk, "Sensitivity to Discontinuous Dependencies in Language Learners," *Cognition* 69 (1998): 105–34. p. 338: The data on the auxiliary copying error in question structures are based on information in Mineharu Nakayama, "Performance Factors in Subject-Auxiliary Inversion," *Journal of Child Language* 14, 1 (1987): 113–25. p. 338–9: The data on the development of question structures are based on information in Edward S. Klima and Ursula Bellugi's classic article, "Syntactic Regularities in the Speech of Children," in *Psycholinguistic Papers: The Proceedings of the 1966 Edinburgh Conference*, edited by J. Lyons and R. Wales, 183–207 (Edinburgh: Edinburgh University Press, 1966). p. 338–9: The description of the developmental order for *wh* words is based on information in Lois Bloom, Susan Merkin, and Janet Wootten, "*Wh* Questions: Linguistic Factors That Contribute to the Sequence of Acquisition," *Child Development* 53, 4 (1982): 1084–92. p. 339: The description of the acquisition of passive structures is based on information in Elizabeth Ann Turner and Ragnar Rommetveit, "The Acquisition of Sentence Voice and Reversibility," *Child Development* 38, 3 (1967): 649–60. p. 340–1: The data on children's use of *me* and *myself* are based on information in Paul Bloom, Andrew Barss, Janet Nicol, and Laura Conway, "Children's Knowledge of Binding and Coreference: Evidence from Spontaneous Speech," *Language* 70, 1 (1994): 53–71. p. 341–2: The data on the effects of exposure to language are based on information in Betty Hart and Todd Risley, *Meaningful Differences in the Everyday Experience of Young American Children* (Baltimore: Paul H. Brookes, 1995). p. 343: The description of the relationship between *yes-no* questions in maternal speech and the development of auxiliaries is based on information in E. Newport, H. Gleitman, and L. Gleitman, "Mother, I'd Rather Do It Myself: Some Effects and Noneffects of Maternal Speech Style," in *Talking to Children: Language Input and Acquisition,* edited by C. Snow and C. Ferguson, 109–49 (New York: Cambridge University Press, 1977). pp. 343–4: The examples of mothers' reactions to children's ungrammatical and grammatical utterances are based on information in Kathy Hirsh-Pasek, Rebecca Treiman, and Maita Schneiderman, "Brown and Hanlon Revisited: Mothers' Sensitivity to Ungrammatical Forms," *Journal of Child Language* 11, 1 (1984): 81–88. p. 344: The "other one spoon" example is based on information on p. 161 of M. Braine, "The Acquisition of Language in Infant and Child," in *The Learning of Language,* edited by C.E. Reed (New York: Appleton-Century-Crofts, 1971). p. 344: The description of the recast experiment involving nonsense verbs is based on information in Matthew Saxton, "The Contrast Theory of Negative Evidence," *Journal of Child Language* 24, 1 (1997): 139–61. p. 345: The description of Rick's case is based on information in S. Curtiss, "Abnormal Language Acquisition and the Modularity of Language," in *Linguistic Theory: Extensions and Implications,* vol. 2 of *Linguistics: The Cambridge Survey,* edited by F.J. Newmeyer, 96–116 (New York: Cambridge University Press, 1988). p. 345: The examples of sentences produced by speakers who have problems with inflection is based on information on Steven Pinker, *The Language Instinct: How the Mind Creates Language* (New York: Morrow), 49. p. 347–8: The description of Genie's case is based on information in S. Curtiss, "Abnormal Language Acquisition and the Modularity of Language," in *Linguistic Theory: Extensions and Implications,* vol. 2 of *Linguistics: The Cambridge Survey,* edited by F.J. Newmeyer, 96–116 (New York: Cambridge University Press, 1988). p. 348: The description of Chelsea's case is based on information in S. Curtiss, "The Independence and Task-Specificity of Language," in *Interaction in Human Development,* edited by Marc H. Bornstein and Jerome S. Bruner, 105–37 (Hillsdale, NJ: Erlbaum, 1989).

Exercises for this chapter were prepared by Joyce Hildebrand.

Chapter 11

p. 356: The model of communicative competence is an adaptation of Lyle F. Bachman, *Fundamental Considerations in Language Testing* (Oxford, UK: Oxford University Press, 1990). p. 360: The discussion of the Markedness Differential Hypothesis is based on information found in Fred R. Eckman. "Markedness and the Contrastive Analysis Hypothesis," *Language Learning* 27 (1977): 315–30. p. 362: The discussion of L2 acquisition of [r] is based on information found in C. Brown, "The Interrelation between Speech Perception and Phonological Acquisition from Infant to Adult," in *Second Language Acquisition and Linguistic Theory,* edited by John Archibald, 4–63 (Oxford: Blackwell, 2000), and J. Larson-Hall, "Predicting Perceptual Success with Segments: A Test of Japanese Speakers of Russian," *Second Language Research* 20, 1 (2004): 33–76. p. 362–3: The data from Arabic syllabification are based on information found in Ellen Broselow, "Prosodic Phonology and the Acquisition of a Second Language," in *Linguistic Theory in Second Language Acquisition,* edited by Suzanne Flynn and Wayne O'Neil, 295–308

(Dordrecht: Kluwer, 1988). p. 363: The data on epenthesis versus deletion strategies come from Chilin Wong, "The Acquisition of English Word-Final Obstruents by Chinese Speakers" (PhD diss., State University of New York at Stony Brook, 1995). p. 363: The discussion of illusory vowels in second language perception is based on information found in E. Dupoux, K. Kakehi, Y. Hirose, C. Pallier, and J. Mehler, "Epenthetic Vowels in Japanese: A Perceptual Illusion?" *Journal of Experimental Psychology: Human Perception and Performance* 25, 6 (1999): 1568–78. p. 364: The stress data are based on information found in John Archibald, *Language Learnability and L2 Phonology* (Dordrecht: Kluwer, 1993). p. 364–5: The null subject analysis is based on information found in Lydia White, *Universal Grammar and Second Language Acquisition* (Amsterdam: John Benjamins, 1989). p. 365–6: The Verb Movement discussion is based on information found in Lydia White, "Adverb Placement in Second Language Acquisition: Some Effects of Positive and Negative Evidence in the Classroom," *Second Language Research* 7 (1991): 133–61. p. 368: The L2 morphology data is based on information found in H. Zobl and J. Liceras, "Functional Categories and Acquisition Order," *Language Learning* 44, 1 (1994): 159–80. p. 371–2: The discussion of Patty is taken from D. Lardiere, "Mapping Features to Forms in Second Language Acquisition," in *Second Language Acquisition and Linguistic Theory*, edited by John Archibald, 102–29 (Oxford, UK: Blackwell, 2000). p. 373: The ultimate attainment results for syntax are based on information found in Lydia White and Fred Genesee, "How Native Is Near-Native? The Issue of Ultimate Attainment in Adult Second Language Acquisition," *Second Language Research* 12 (1996): 238–65. p. 373: The discussion of ultimate attainment in phonology is based on information found in Theo Bongarts, Susan Mennen, and Frans van der Slik, "Authenticity of Pronunciation in Naturalistic Second Language Acquisition: The Case of Very Advanced Late Learners of Dutch as a Second Language," *Studia Linguistica* 54, 2 (2000): 298–308. p. 374: The French gender information is based on information found in Susanne Carroll, "Second-Language Acquisition and the Computational Paradigm," *Language Learning* 39, 4 (1989): 535–94. p. 375: The instrumental/integrative distinction is based on information found in R. Gardner, J.B. Day, and P.D. MacIntyre, "Integrative Motivation, Induced Anxiety and Language Learning in a Controlled Environment," *Studies in Second Language Acquisition* 14, 2 (2000): 197–214. p. 377: The discussion of the L2 Status Factor Model is based on information found in Camilla Bardel, and Ylva Falk, "The Role of the Second Language in Third Language Acquisition: The Case of Germanic Syntax," *Second Language Research* 23 (2007): 459–84. p. 377–8: The discussion of the Typological Primacy Model is based on information found in J. Rothman, "Linguistic and Cognitive Motivation for the Typological Primacy Model of Third Language (L3) Transfer: Considering the Role of Timing of Acquisition and Proficiency in the Previous Languages," *Bilingualism: Language and Cognition* 18, 2 (2015): 179–90. p. 378: The discussion of the Linguistic Proximity Model is based on information found in M. Westergaard, N. Mirofanova, R. Mykhaylyk, and Y. Rodina, "Crosslinguistic Influence in the Acquisition of a Third Language: The Linguistic Proximity Model," *International Journal of Bilingualism* 21, 6 (2017): 666–82. p. 378: Some of the discussion of section 11.5 is based on Dick Allwright and Kathleen M. Bailey, *Focus on the Language Classroom: An Introduction to Classroom Research for Language Teachers* (Cambridge, UK: Cambridge University Press, 1991). p. 379: The evidence from 'focus on form' is based on information presented by Patsy M. Lightbown and Nina Spada, "Focus-on-Form and Corrective Feedback in Communicative Language Teaching: Effects on Second Language Learning," *Studies in Second Language Acquisition* 12, 4 (1990): 429–48, as well as in Catherine Doughty, "Cognitive Underpinnings of Focus on Form," in *Cognition and Second Language Instruction,* edited by Peter Robinson, 206–57, Cambridge Applied

Linguistics Series (Cambridge, UK: Cambridge University Press, 2001). p. 380: The discussion of pronunciation instruction is based on information found in Murray J. Munro, "Foreign Accent and Speech Intelligibility," in *Phonology and Second Language Acquisition,* edited by Jette G. Hansen Edwards and Mary L. Zampini, 193–218 (Amsterdam: John Benjamins, 2008).

Chapter 12

p. 385: The epigraph quotation is from François Grosjean, "Interview on Bilingualism," www.francoisgrosjean.ch. p. 386, section 12.1: Data on speakers of French, English, Indigenous, and immigrant languages in Canada is based on the following reports and infographics from the 2016 Canadian census: Statistics Canada, *English, French and Official Language Minorities in Canada,* catalogue no. 98-200-X2016011, 2017; Statistics Canada, *Linguistic Diversity and Multilingualism in Canadian Homes,* catalogue no. 98-200-X2016010, 2017; Statistics Canada, *French-English Bilingualism Reaches New Heights,* catalogue no. 98-200-X20116009, 2017; Statistics Canada, *Immigrant Languages in Canada* (infographic), catalogue no. 11-627-M, 2017; Statistics Canada, *Aboriginal Languages in Canada* (infographic), catalogue no 11-627-M, 2017. Retrieved from www.statcan.gc.ca. p. 386, section 12.1: Discussion of laws pertaining to languages in Canada is based on information from the Official Languages Act, the Charter of Rights and Freedoms, and the Multiculturalism Act. All are available at laws-lois.justice.gc.ca. pp. 387–9, section 12.2: Discussion is based on information in Johanne Paradis, Fred Genesee, and Martha B. Crago, *Dual Language Development and Disorders: A Handbook on Bilingualism and Second Language Learning,* 2nd ed. (Baltimore, MD: Brookes, 2011). pp. 390, section 12.3.1: Discussion and data are based on information in Johanne Paradis, Martha B. Crago, and Fred Genesee, "Domain-Specific Versus Domain-General Theories of the Deficit in SLI: Object Pronoun Acquisition by French-English Bilingual Children," *Language Acquisition* 13 (2005/2006): 33–62; Johanne Paradis, Antoine Tremblay, and Martha Crago, "French-English Bilingual Children's Sensitivity to Child-Level and Language-Level Input Factors in Morphosyntactic Acquisition," in *Input and Experience in Bilingual Development,* edited by Theres Grüter and Johanne Paradis, 161–80 (Amsterdam: John Benjamins, 2014). p. 390–1, section 12.3.2: Discussion is based on information from Johanne Paradis, Fred Genesee, and Martha B. Crago, *Dual Language Development and Disorders: A Handbook on Bilingualism and Second Language Learning,* 2nd ed. (Baltimore, MD: Brookes, 2011). pp. 392, section 12.3.3: Discussion is based on information in Theres Grüter and Johanne Paradis (eds.), *Input and Experience in Bilingual Development* (Amsterdam: John Benjamins, 2014), and in Johanne Paradis, Fred Genesee, and Martha B. Crago, *Dual Language Development and Disorders: A Handbook on Bilingualism and Second Language Learning,* 2nd ed. (Baltimore, MD: Brookes, 2011). pp. 392–5: Discussion and data are based on/adapted from Virginia Yip and Stephen Matthews, *The Bilingual Child: Early Development and Language Contact* (Cambridge, UK: Cambridge University Press, 2007); Elena Nicoladis, "Crosslinguistic Transfer in Adjective-Noun Strings by Preschool Bilingual Children," *Bilingualism: Language and Cognition* 9 (2006): 15–32; Johanne Paradis, "Cross-Linguistic Influence and Code-Switching," in *Bilingual Language Development and Disorders in Spanish-English Speakers,* 2nd ed., edited by Brian A. Goldstein, 73–91 (Baltimore: Brookes, 2012). p. 395: Discussion of congruence and examples in (7) are based on information in Jeff MacSwan, "Code Switching and Grammatical Theory," in *The Handbook of Bilingualism,* edited by Tej K. Bhatia and William C. Ritchie, 283–311 (Oxford, UK: Blackwell). pp. 396–8, section 12.5: Discussion is based on information in Sylvia Montrul, *The Acquisition of Heritage Languages* (Cambridge,

UK: Cambridge University Press, 2016), and in Victoria A. Murphy, *Second Language Learning in The Early School Years: Trends and Contexts* (Oxford: Oxford University Press, 2014). p. 396: Data on immigrant languages spoken and maintained across generations is based on information in Statistics Canada, *Passing on the Ancestral Language: Canadian Social Trends*, catalogue No. 11-008, 2006, www.statcan.gc.ca. pp. 398–9, section 12.6: Discussion is based on information in Ellen Bialystok, "Cognitive Effects of Bilingualism: How Linguistic Experience Leads to Cognitive Change," *International Journal of Bilingual Education and Bilingualism* 10 (2007): 201–23; Ellen Bialystok, *Bilingualism in Development: Language, Literacy and Cognition* (New York: Cambridge University Press, 2001); Elena Nicoladis, "Bilingual Speakers' Cognitive Development in Childhood," in *Bilingualism across the Lifespan: Factors Moderating Language Proficiency*, edited by Elena Nicoladis and Simona Montanari (Washington, DC, and Berlin: American Psychological Association and De Gruyter, 2016). p. 399–401, section 12.7: Discussion is based on information from Joseph Dicks and Fred Genesee, "Bilingual Education in Canada," in *Encyclopedia of Language and Education*, vol. 5: *Bilingual and Multilingual Education*, edited by Ofelia García, Angel Lin, and Stephen May, 453–67 (Heidelberg: Springer, 2017); Victoria A. Murphy, *Second Language Learning in the Early School Years: Trends and Contexts* (Oxford, UK: Oxford University Press, 2014); Patricia A. Duff, and Duanduan Li, "Indigenous, Minority, and Heritage Language Education in Canada: Policies, Contexts, and Issues," *Canadian Modern Language Review/La Revue canadienne des langues vivantes* 66, 1 (2009): 1–8. p. 400–1, section 12.7.2: Description of programs at Edmonton public schools is based on information from the Edmonton Public Schools website (www.epsb.ca). p. 401, section 12.7.2: Description of the Kativik school board is based on information from the Kativik Ilisarniliriniq website (www.kativik.qc.ca). p. 401, section 12.7: Data on speakers of Indigenous languages is based on information in Statistics Canada, *Aboriginal Languages in Canada* (infographic), 2016 Census, catalogue no 11-627-M, 2017, and in Statistics Canada, *The Aboriginal Languages of First Nations People, Métis, and Inuit*, 2016 Census, catalogue no. 98-200-X2016022, 2017. p. 403: Exercise 3 is based on information in Elena Nicoladis, "What's the Difference between 'Toilet Paper' and 'Paper Toilet'? French–English Bilingual Children's Crosslinguistic Transfer in Compound Nouns," *Journal of Child Language* 29 (2002): 843–63, and in Elena Nicoladis, "Cross-Linguistic Transfer in Deverbal Compounds of Preschool Bilingual Children," *Bilingualism: Language and Cognition* 6 (2003): 17–31. p. 404: Exercise 8 is based on information in Ellen Bialystok, "Cognitive Effects of Bilingualism: How Linguistic Experience Leads to Cognitive Change," *International Journal of Bilingual Education and Bilingualism* 10 (2007): 201–23.

Chapter 13

p. 406. The 'slip of the tongue' material is based on information found in Victoria Fromkin and Nan Bernstein Ratner, "Speech Production," in *Psycholinguistics*, 2nd ed., edited by Jean Berko Gleason and Nan Bernstein Ratner, 309–39 (Belmont, CA: Thomas Wadsworth, 1998). p. 412. The discussion of eye-movement data in psycholinguistics is based on information found in K. Rayner and S.C. Sereno, "Eye Movements in Reading: Psycholinguistic Studies," in *Handbook of Psycholinguistics*, edited by Morton Ann Gernsbacher, 57–81 (New York: Academic Press, 1994), as well as on information found in Keith Rayner, Alexander Pollatsek, Jane Ashby, and Charles Clifton, Jr., *The Psychology of Reading*, 2nd ed. (New York: Psychology Press, 2012). p. 413. The material on event-related potentials is based on information found in Marta Kutas,

Cyma K. Van Petten, and Robert Kluender, "Psycholinguistics Electrified II (1994–2005)," in *Handbook of Psycholinguistics*, 2nd ed., edited by Matthew J. Traxler and Morton A. Gernsbacher, 659–724 (Oxford, UK: Elsevier, 2006). p. 418. The discussion of the syllable-processing experiment is based on information in Juan Segui, Ulrich Hans Frauenfelder, and Jacques Mehler, "Phoneme Monitoring, Syllable Monitoring, and Lexical Access," *British Journal of Psychology* 72, 4 (1981): 471–77, which is discussed in Jennifer S. Pardo and Robert E. Remez, "The Perception of Speech," in *Handbook of Psycholinguistics*, 2nd ed., edited by Matthew J. Traxler and Morton A. Gernsbacher, 201–48 (Oxford, UK: Elsevier, 2006). p. 418. The discussion of word-blending studies is based on information found in Rebecca Treiman, "The Structure of Spoken Syllables: Evidence from Novel Word Games," *Cognition 15* (1983): 49–74, and in G.E. Wiebe and B.L. Derwing, "A Forced-Choice Word-Blending Task for Testing Intra-syllabic Break Points in English, Korean, and Taiwanese," in *The Twenty-First LACUS Forum 1994*, edited by M.J. Powell, 142–51 (Chapel Hill, NC: LACUS, 1994). p. 419. The discussion of morphological activation is based on information found in M. Lehtonen, P.J. Monahan, and D. Poeppel, "Evidence for Early Morphological Decomposition: Combining Masked Priming with Magnetoencephalography," *Journal of Cognitive Neuroscience* 23 (2011): 3366–79; G. Libben and S. Weber, "Semantic Transparency, Compounding, and the Nature of Independent Variables," in *Morphology and Meaning*, edited by Franz Rainer, Wolfgang U. Dressler, Francesco Gardani, and Hans Christian Luschützky, 205–22 (Amsterdam: Benjamins, 2014); and G. Libben, "The Nature of Compounds: A Psychocentric Perspective," *Cognitive Neuropsychology* 31 (2014): 8–25. p. 419. The discussion of morphological priming experiments is based on information found in William Marslen-Wilson, Lorraine Komisarjevsky Tyler, Rachelle Waksler, and Lianne Older, "Morphology and Meaning in the English Mental Lexicon," *Psychological Review* 101 (1994): 3–33. p. 420. The discussion of experiments on selectional restrictions is based on information found in Gary Libben, "Are Morphological Structures Computed during Word Recognition?" *Journal of Psycholinguistic Research* 22 (1993): 535–44, and in Gary Libben, "Computing Hierarchical Morphological Structure: A Case Study," *Journal of Neurolinguistics* 8 (1994): 49–55. p. 422. The section on the processing of garden path sentences is based on information found in Lynn Frazier, "Sentence Processing: A Tutorial Review," in *Attention and Performance 12: The Psychology of Reading*, edited by M. Coltheart (London: Lawrence Erlbaum, 1987), pp. 559–86. This sentence type is also discussed in David Caplan, *Language: Structure Processing and Disorders* (Cambridge, MA: MIT Press, 1994). p. 423. The discussion of sentence ambiguity is based on information found in Michael K. Tanenhaus, Greg N. Carlson, and Mark S. Seidenberg, "Do Listeners Compute Linguistic Representations?" in *Natural Language Parsing*, edited by David R. Dowty, Lauri Karttunen, and Arnold M. Zwicky, 359–408 (New York: Cambridge University Press, 1985).

Chapter 14

p. 438. The discussion of the MEG technique is based on information found in the chapter by Andrew C. Papanicolaou, Panagiotis G. Simos, and Luis F.H. Basile, "Applications of Magnetoencephalography to Neurolinguistic Research," in *Handbook of Neurolinguistics*, edited by Brigitte Stemmer and Harry A Whitaker, 143–58 (Oxford, UK: Elsevier, 1998). p. 440. The discussion of aphasia is based on information found in David Caplan, *Language: Structure, Processing and Disorders* (Cambridge, MA: MIT Press, 1996). p. 445. The material on acquired dyslexia is based on information in M. Coltheart, J. Patterson, and J.C. Marshall, eds., *Deep Dyslexia* (London: Routledge and Kegan Paul, 1980); K.E. Patterson, J.C. Marshall, and M. Coltheart, eds., *Surface Dyslexia* (Hillsdale, NJ: Lawrence Erlbaum, 1986); and Y. Zotterman, *Dyslexia: Neuronal, Cognitive, and Linguistic Aspects* (Oxford: Pergamon Press, 1982). p. 447. Some of the discussion of agrammatism is based on information found in M.-L. Kean, ed., *Agrammatism* (New York: Academic Press, 1985), and in Yosef Grodzinsky, *Theoretical Perspectives on Language Deficits* (Cambridge, MA: MIT Press, 1990).

Chapter 15

p. 457: Information on the pronunciation of *wh* words is based on information found in J.K. Chambers, Peter Trudgill, and Natalie Schilling-Estes, eds., *The Handbook of Language Variation and Change* (Oxford: Blackwell, 2002). p. 458: Some information on American English dialects is based on information found in Walt Wolfram and Natalie Schilling-Estes, *American English* (Oxford: Blackwell, 1998). p. 461: Some Canadian lexical items are from the *Canadian Oxford Dictionary*, 2nd ed., edited by Katherine Barber (Don Mills, ON: Oxford, 2004). p. 462: Much of the North American pronunciation information is based on information found in the extremely detailed *Atlas of North American English* by William Labov, Sharon Ash, and Charles Boberg (New York: Mouton de Gruyter, 2006). p. 462: The discussion of Newfoundland English draws on information found in the *Dictionary of Newfoundland English*, edited by G.M. Story, W.J. Kirwing, and J.D.A. Widdowson (Toronto: University of Toronto Press, 1990). p. 465: Information on isolated African American communities is based on information found in Shana Poplack and Sali Tagliamonte, *African American English in the Diaspora* (Oxford: Blackwell, 2001). p. 465: Discussion of social networks information is based on information found in Lesley Milroy, *Language and Social Networks* (Oxford: Blackwell, 1987). p. 469: The Barbadian English discussion is based on information found in Gerard Van Herk, "Barbadian Lects: Beyond Meso," in *Contact Englishes of the Eastern Caribbean*, edited by Michael Aceto and Jeffrey P. Williams (Amsterdam: John Benjamins, 2003). p. 470: The discussion of social class—including the *r*-lessness studies reported here—is based on information found in William Labov, *Sociolinguistic Patterns* (Philadelphia: University of Pennsylvania Press, 1972). p. 471: The discussion of caste is based on information found in Peter Trudgill, *Sociolinguistics: An Introduction to Language and Society* (Toronto: Penguin, 2000). p. 473: The discussion of gendered interaction style information is based on information found in Deborah Tannen, *You Just Don't Understand: Women and Men in Conversation* (New York: William Morrow, 1990). p. 475: The Martha's Vineyard discussion is based on information found in one of the very first sociolinguistic studies, reported in William Labov, "The Social Motivation of a Sound Change," in *Word* 19 (1963): 273–309. p. 475: The discussion of ethnography of communication is based on information found in John Gumperz and Dell Hymes, *Directions in Sociolinguistics: The Ethnography of Communication* (New York: Holt, Rinehart and Winston, 1972). p. 478: The discussion of T and V pronouns is based on information first detailed in Roger Brown and Albert Gilman, "The Pronouns of Power and Solidarity," in *Style in Language*, edited by T. Sebeok (Cambridge, MA: MIT Press, 1960). p. 478: The discussion of diglossia is based on information found in Charles A. Ferguson, "Diglossia," in *Word* 15 (1959): 325–40. p. 478: The discussion of accommodation in Wales is based on information found in Nik Coupland, "Accommodation at Work: Some Phonological Data and Their Implications," *International Journal of the Sociology of Language* 46 (1984): 49–70. p. 481: The discussion of Canadians' mother tongues is based on information found in Statistics Canada, "Language Highlight Tables, 2016 Census," 2017, www12.statcan.gc.ca.

Chapter 16

p. 488: The idea that writing may have originated in record keeping with clay tokens is based on information in Denise Schmandt-Besserat, "Two Precursors of Writing: Plain and Complex Tokens," in *The Origins of Writing*, edited by W.M. Senner, 27–42 (Lincoln: University of Nebraska Press, 1989). pp. 500–1: The description of the Cree syllabary is based on information in D.H. Pentland, *Nēhiyawasinahikēwin: A Standard Orthography for the Cree Language*, rev. ed. (Calgary: Department of Linguistics, University of Calgary, 1978). pp. 502–4: The discussion of the history of English spelling is based on information in D.G. Scragg, *A History of English Spelling* (New York: Barnes and Noble, 1974), and in D.W. Cummings, *American English Spelling: An Informal Description* (Baltimore: Johns Hopkins University Press, 1988). p. 506: The discussion of children's ability to segment words into syllables and phonemes is based on information in E. Gibson and H. Levin, *The Psychology of Reading* (Cambridge, MA: MIT Press, 1975), 119–23.

Language Index

The letter *f* following a page number denotes a figure.
The letter *t* following a page number denotes a table.

Subject Index

The letter *f* following a page number denotes a figure.
The letter *t* following a page number denotes a table.

areal classification, 217
argument, 191–192
articulator feature, 81–83,
    84*t*, 85*t*
articulatory phonetics, 14
articulatory simplification,
    246
articulatory-based change,
    248–256
arytenoids, 18
aspectual properties,
    192–196
aspectual verb, 200–201
aspiration, 29–30, 75–76,
    86
assimilation, 48–49, 249–250,
    324
association lines, 41
atelic vs. telic, 192
attitudes, 4, 479–480, 482
auditory-based change,
    256–257
Austro-Asiatic family, 239
Austronesian family, 239
autopsy study, 434–436
auxiliary verb, 140–141,
    148

B

babbling, 319–320
[±back], 81, 82–83, 84*t*, 85*t*
back (of the tongue), 22
back vowel, 36–37
backformation, 124–125,
    268
Baltic family, 237
bar-pressing experiments,
    411–412
base, 104–105
The Basic Level Assumption,
    326–327
basilects, 470
benefactive, 191
bilabial, 24
bilingual education, 400–401,
    482
bilingualism, 385–404
    acquisition by monolinguals
        vs. bilinguals, 392

additive, 396
bilinguals, types of, 387–389
    in Canada, 386–387
    code-switching, 393–395
    cognitive consequences of,
        398–399
    cross-language interactions
        in early, 392–395
    cross-linguistic influence,
        392–393
    early bilingual acquisition,
        389–392
    estimating language input,
        391
    heritage L1 vs. majority L2,
        397*f*
    heritage language education,
        400–401
    heritage language and,
        396–398
    immersion program,
        399–401
    individual, 385
    language dominance and,
        390–391, 392
    rate of language acquisition,
        392
    societal, 385
    subtractive, 396
bilingual
    balanced, 390
    early, 387, 389*f*
    language acquisition vs.
        monolinguals, 392
    late, 387, 389*f*
    referent-to-word mapping,
        399*f*
    sequential, 387, 389*f*
    simultaneous, 387, 389*f*,
        390, 392
Binarity Requirement,
    71–72
binary feature, 79–82
Binding Theory, 206
bird song, 373
blade (of the tongue), 22
blending, 124, 268
blend, 125
Blissymbolics, 489

blueprint (X' Schema), 144
body (of the tongue), 22
borrowed prestige, 471
borrowing. *See also* loan words,
    247, 256, 270–273, 274,
    467, 481
bottom-up processing, 416
bound morpheme, 102
bound variable, 208
brain activity, 413–415
brain and language. *See*
    neurolinguistics
brain imaging, 436–438
brain size, 441
breathy voice, 19
broadening, semantic, 274
Broca's aphasia, 435, 440,
    442–444, 445, 447
Broca's area, 435, 450

C

Canada, official languages in,
    386, 481
Canada's Workplace Hazardous
    Materials Information
    System (WHMIS), 489
Canadian Charter of Rights and
    Freedoms, 386
Canadian English, 461–462
Canadian Multiculturalism
    Act, 386
Canadian Raising, 61, 355,
    461
Canadian Shift, 458
caregiver role, 473
caregiver speech, 342–343
case inflection, 118–119,
    261–262, 265–266
caste system, 471
categorical rule, 455
causes of language change,
    246–248
c-command, 206–207, 346
cell assembly, 449
Celtic family, 236
central sulcus, 432*f*, 433, 434*f*,
    435*f*
cerebellum, 433*f*
cerebral cortex, 431, 436